Principles of Database
Query Processing
for Advanced Applications

Principles of Database Query Processing for Advanced Applications

Clement T. Yu
University of Illinois, Chicago

Weiyi Meng
SUNY Binghamton

Morgan Kaufmann Publishers, Inc.
San Francisco, California

Senior Editor Diane D. Cerra
Production Manager Yonie Overton
Production Editor Cheri Palmer
Editorial Assistant Antonia Richmond
Cover Design Ross Carron Design
Cover Photograph Keiji Watanabe/PHOTONICA
Text Design (based on a series design) Stuart Silberman
Composition Ed Sznyter, Babel Press
Copyeditor Publication Services
Proofreader Jennifer McClain
Indexer Ty Koontz
Printer Courier Corporation

Morgan Kaufmann Publishers, Inc.
Editorial and Sales Office
340 Pine Street, Sixth Floor
San Francisco, CA 94104-3205
USA
Telephone 415 / 392-2665
Facsimile 415 / 982-2665
E-mail mkp@mkp.com
WWW http://www.mkp.com
Order toll free 800 / 745-7323

Library of Congress Cataloging-in-Publication Data

Yu, C. T. (Clement T.)
    Principles of database query processing for advanced applications
    / Clement T. Yu, Weiyi Meng.
         p. cm
    Includes bibliographical references and index.
    ISBN 1-55860-434-0
    1. Database management. 2. Database searching. I. Meng, Weiyi.
    II. Title.
QA76.9.D3Y82 1997
005.74′1–dc21

97-38044
CIP

With love to
Teresa, my wife
Victor and Christine, my children
Ching-Hang and Chen-Chun, my parents
Bill, Alex and Greg, my brothers
C.Y.

To my father, Jihe Meng
mother, Jinxiang Guo
wife, Xia Chen
and children, Connie and Melissa
for their love and support
W.M.

Contents

Preface

During the last four decades, database technology has experienced very rapid growth. Today, centralized relational database systems can no longer satisfy the ever-growing demand of database support from diversified applications. In response to the demand, researchers and practitioners in the database community have continuously put forward new ideas for developing new systems and enhancing existing ones. Some of these new systems, such as object-oriented database systems and text retrieval systems, have already entered the commercial market; others have been prototyped, and many of them are still in the research stage.

Database systems can be classified in different ways. For example, they are classified by the underlying data model used. Based on this method, we have relational database systems, object-oriented database systems, etc. Another classification method is based on the type of data stored. Some databases store only well-structured and precise data, such as records. Most traditional database systems belong to this category. Some databases can handle well-structured but imprecise data. Fuzzy databases and probabilistic databases are such systems. Yet some databases are designed for less-structured data. For example, text retrieval systems are for text documents, whereas multimedia database systems may also handle images and audio data. A third classification method is based on the storage locations of the data in the database and the number of processors that can be used to process database queries. For example, most database systems manage data stored at a central site using a single processor. Parallel database systems utilize multiple processors to speed up query processing. Distributed database systems manage data that are stored at geographically distributed locations. Distributed multidatabase systems can provide uniform access to data stored in other usually autonomous and heterogeneous database systems. Table 1 summarizes different types of classifications.

Query processing and optimization have always been one of the most critical components of database technology. This component deals with efficient and effective processing of user queries against a database. In other words, the goal of query processing and optimization is to find user-desired data from an often very large database efficiently and with an acceptable

TABLE 1   **Different Ways to Classify Database Systems**

Classification Method	Classification Criterion
Data Model	Relational
	Object-Oriented
	. . .
Data Type	Well structured and precise
	Well structured but imprecise
	Less structured
Data Distribution and Number of Processors	Centralized
	Parallel
	Distributed
	Multidatabase

accuracy. When the database system is a one-site relational database system, both efficiency and accuracy of retrieval can be relatively easily guaranteed by the current technology. When all data in a database are stored at a single site, user queries can always be processed without the need of transferring data from one site to another site. As a result, efficient processing of user queries can be more easily achieved. Another factor contributing to the efficiency is that relational database systems manage only simple data, such as numbers and character strings organized in well-structured record format. Such types of data can be easily compared and retrieved. The high accuracy of retrieval in relational database systems is also the direct consequence of having well-structured simple data. When data in a database are stored in geographically distributed locations connected via computer networks or when data in a database are not well structured, it becomes much harder to achieve efficiency and accuracy. For example, text and images are not well structured in comparison with records in a relational database. They are much more difficult to retrieve precisely. Note that most data in the real world are not well structured.

The main theme of this book is to provide basic techniques for achieving efficient and accurate retrieval of data from different types of database systems for advanced applications. In the single site situation, we discuss techniques for retrieving information from object-oriented database systems, from fuzzy relational database systems, from text database systems, and from image database systems. In distributed environments, we address retrieval from relational database systems containing data residing in multiple sites and from heterogeneous database systems containing data stored in different types of autonomous database systems. We also present techniques for retrieving data from parallel database systems. Internet users have already been experiencing data of different types stored in numerous sites. With the widespread use of the Internet, it is expected that the number of users as well as the number of sites containing potentially useful information will both undergo rapid growth. There is no lack of information. The difficulty is to be able to identify the useful information precisely, without the help of a human expert. This book is an attempt to address retrieval of information from an environment beyond a centralized relational database system.

Despite the importance of query processing and optimization in different types of database systems, a book dedicated to this topic that is not in the form of a simple collection of papers written by numerous authors with different styles has not been published. Technical papers are usually written in a way that can be understood only by experts working in the same area. As such they are not suitable for nonexperts who want to learn the state-of-the-art techniques in this important area with moderate efforts. This book represents the first effort in this regard and is written with these people in mind.

Overview of the Book

The first chapter provides a review of query processing and optimization techniques in centralized relational database systems. Many basic concepts introduced in this chapter are used in later chapters. Chapter 2 discusses the processing of object-oriented database queries. The processing of path expressions and the use of indexes are the focus of this chapter. Chapter 3 discusses query processing in distributed relational database systems. The discussion is centered on techniques that move subqueries/data across different sites to improve efficiency of execution. Chapter 4 investigates techniques for processing queries in a heterogeneous multidatabase system. The problem is essentially how to access data across different types of systems that are managed independently. Chapter 5 presents parallel processing techniques of relational queries in a multiprocessor environment. Basic concepts of fuzzy relational database systems and basic ideas for processing fuzzy queries are presented in Chapter 6. Query processing techniques in deductive database systems are discussed in Chapter 7. One common feature among the above seven chapters is that they typically manage only well-structured data. As such, the query processing techniques presented in these chapters are closely related. In fact, many are extended from the corresponding techniques in relational database systems.

Chapter 8 presents several well-known index structures for multidimensional objects. These structures can apply to well-structured data such as tuples of relations, and less-structured data, such as features of images. The last three chapters of the book focus on less-structured data. In particular, Chapter 9 discusses techniques for retrieving text documents in a text database, and Chapter 10 discusses techniques for organizing text documents into clusters for browsing, more effective retrieval, and other applications. These two chapters are closely related. Chapter 11 discusses some emerging techniques for retrieving image data and video data. Techniques from fuzzy databases and deductive databases are employed in retrieving images and videos. Although exact match is standard in retrieving well-structured data, similarity-based retrieval is essential for text and images. Many techniques that are useful in text retrieval are also applicable in image retrieval.

Use of the Book

This book can be used as a textbook for the second course in databases for computer science and information science students and professionals. It can be used for a two-quarter/two-semester course (supplemented by current conference papers), with one quarter/semester concentrating on well-structured data and the other on less-structured data. An alternative is to use the book for a single quarter/semester, covering some materials on well-structured data and some materials on less-structured data. It can also be used as a reference book for computer science graduate students (as well as undergraduate students to some extent) and professionals. Individual chapters of the book can be used as supplemental materials for both introductory and advanced database courses. Most chapters are written in such a way that they are self-contained, provided that the reader has some basic knowledge about query processing in relational database systems (i.e., the materials in Chapter 1). To achieve this, many chapters have one or more sections that introduce the reader to the concerned systems before query processing techniques are discussed. Bibliographic notes are provided at the end of each chapter for readers who would like to explore certain issues in more detail.

Acknowledgments

During the course of writing the book, the following people have provided valuable input to the book proposal or to a draft version of the book. Many of them spent much time carefully reading some or all chapters of the book. Their suggestions have greatly helped to improve the quality of the book. We are deeply indebted to their efforts and suggestions.

Abraham Bookstein at University of Chicago
Forbes Burkowski at University of Waterloo
Ed Fox at Virginia Tech
Goetz Grafe at Microsoft
Jim Gray at Microsoft
Lawrence Henschen at Northwestern University
Yannis Ioannidis at University of Wisconsin, Madison
Don Kraft at Louisiana State University
Kui-Lam Kwok at Queen's College, Flushing
Jorge Lobo at University of Illinois at Chicago
Mike Pong at Tandem Computers, Inc.
Peter Scheuermann at Northwestern University
Don Slutz at Microsoft
Gottfried Vossen at Universitaet Muenster, Germany
Yiming Yang at Carnegie Mellon University

A number of our students, Ma'n Altaher, Alp Aslandogan, Yuhsi Chang, Rongquen Chen, King-Lup Liu, Joseph Raj, and Danny Tran, as well as some students in Clement's EECS580 (Query Processing in Database Systems) and EECS582 (Information Retrieval) classes, also read parts of the book and provided valuable comments.

Clement is also grateful to his former Ph.D. supervisor, the late G. Salton, for bringing Clement into his information retrieval group.

Clement would also like to thank his daughter, Christine, for formatting and editing parts of the manuscript.

We are also grateful to the editor of the book, Diane Cerra, for her help concerning the preparation of the book.

1

Introduction to Relational Query Processing

In 1970, Codd's classic paper, "A Relational Model for Large Shared Data Banks," laid the foundation for relational database systems. Since then, many commercial relational database systems, such as Oracle, DB2, and Sybase, have been built. In fact, relational database systems have dominated the database market for years. The remarkable success of relational database technology can be attributed to such factors as having a solid mathematical foundation and employing an easy-to-use query language, i.e., SQL (*Structured Query Language*). SQL is a *declarative* (or *nonprocedural*) language in the sense that users need only specify *what* data they want from the database, not *how* to get the data. Furthermore, relational databases employ sophisticated query processing and optimization techniques so that user queries can be processed efficiently.

In this chapter, we provide an introduction to the processing and optimization techniques of relational queries in a centralized uniprocessor environment. Many of the terminologies introduced in this chapter are essential for the understanding of other chapters of the book. In Section 1.1, a brief review of the relational data model will be provided. An overview of problems in query processing and optimization will be given in Section 1.2. Indexing techniques commonly used in relational database systems will briefly be described in Section 1.3. The evaluation of several relational operations, including selection, projection, and join, and the analysis of the evaluation cost will be presented in Section 1.4. Approaches for determining the order of processing multiple operations will be discussed in Section 1.5.

1.1 The Relational Data Model

In this section, we briefly review the relational data model, basic relational operators, and the relational query language SQL.

1.1.1 Data Model

In a relational database, data are organized into table format. Each table (or relation) consists of a set of *attributes* describing the table. Each attribute corresponds to one column of the table. Each attribute is associated with a *domain* indicating the set of values the attribute can take. Each row of a table is called a *tuple*, and it is usually used to describe one real-world entity and/or a relationship among several entities. For any tuple and any attribute of a relation, it is required that the value of the tuple under the attribute be atomic (e.g., no composite value or set value is allowed). For each relation, there exists an attribute or a combination of attributes such that no two tuples in the relation can have the same values under the attribute or the combination of attributes. Such an attribute or combination of attributes is called a *superkey* of the relation. Namely, each tuple of a relation can be uniquely identified by its values under a superkey. If every attribute in a superkey is needed for it to uniquely identify each tuple, then the superkey is called a *key*. In other words, every key has the property that if any attribute is removed from it, then the remaining attribute(s) can no longer uniquely identify each tuple. Clearly, any superkey consisting of a single attribute is also a key. Each relation must have at least one key. But a relation may have multiple keys. In this case, one of them will be designated as the *primary key*, and each of the remaining keys will be called a *candidate key*. Note that key and superkey are concepts associated with a relation, not just the *current instance* (i.e., the current set of tuples) of the relation. In other words, a key (superkey) of a relation must remain to be a key (superkey) even when the instance of the relation changes through insertions and deletions of tuples.

Example 1.1 Two relations, *Employee* and *Department*, are shown in Figure 1.1. The first relation has six attributes, and *SSN* (Social Security Number) is a superkey as well as a key of the relation. {SSN, Name} is a superkey of *Employee*. However, {SSN, Name} is not a key of *Employee* because if *Name* is removed from the set, the remaining attribute, SSN, can still uniquely identify each employee. Each tuple in *Employee* represents an employee entity. In addition, it also represents a relationship, *works_in*, between an employee and a department. For example, the first tuple describes an employee as SSN = 123456789, Name = John, Age = 34, Birthdate = 5/18/1963, and Salary = 30000, and it also describes the relationship that John works in the Sales department.

The second relation has three attributes, and *Name* is a superkey as well as a key of this relation. If each department has a different phone number, then attribute *Phone* also will be a key of *Department*. In this case, if we designate *Name* as the primary key, then *Phone* will be a candidate key. Each tuple in *Department* represents a department entity but no relationship. ■

SSN	Name	Age	Birthdate	Salary	Dept
123456789	John	34	5/18/1963	30k	Sales
234567891	Ketty	27	9/21/1970	25k	Service
345678912	Wang	39	2/24/1958	32k	Sales

Employee

Name	Budget	Phone
Sales	200k	4567890
Service	100k	5678900
Advertising	100k	6789123

Department

FIGURE 1.1   Two Sample Relations

If the value of an attribute of a tuple in a relation is *not available* or *not defined*, then a *null value*, denoted as *null*, is used to occupy its position. For example, when the budget of a department has not been decided, it can be left as null. The *entity integrity constraint* of the relational database requires that no attribute in the primary key may take *null* values.

Dependencies may exist among the values under different attributes. For example, for any two employees, if they have the same birthdate, then they will have the same age. In other words, birthdate of an employee determines the age of the employee. Let $\{A_1, \ldots, A_n\}$ be the set of attributes of relation R. Let X and Y be two subsets of $\{A_1, \ldots, A_n\}$. X is said to *functionally determine* Y (or Y is *functionally dependent on* X) if for any two tuples $t1$ and $t2$ in any instance of R, and if they have the same X-value (i.e., $t1[X] = t2[X]$, where $t1[Z]$ represents a subtuple of $t1$ obtained by retaining only values under attributes in Z), then they also have the same Y-value (i.e., $t1[Y] = t2[Y]$). Equivalently, "X functionally determines Y" can be defined as "for each X-value, there is a unique Y-value." Based on this definition, it can be seen that if X is a superkey of R, then X functionally determines any subset of attributes of R. Functional dependency is an extremely important concept in relational database design.

Attributes of different relations (or even the same relation) may be closely related. For example, the *Dept* attribute of *Employee* and the *Name* attribute of *Department* are closely related since they both take department names as their values. Since an employee can be either without a department temporarily or work in an existing department, it makes sense to require that the *Dept* attribute takes only values currently under the *Name* attribute of *Department* or null values. If this requirement is enforced, we say that the attribute *Dept* of relation *Employee* references the attribute *Name* of relation *Department*, or that the *referential integrity constraint* between the two relations is satisfied. In general, if a set of attributes *FK* of relation $R1$ references the primary key of another relation $R2$ (note that $R1$ and $R2$ need not be different), then *FK* is called a *foreign key* of $R1$. For our example, attribute *Dept* is a foreign key of *Employee*.

1.1.2 Relational Algebra

Relational algebra is a collection of operations that are used to manipulate relations. Each operation takes one or two relations as the input and produces a new relation as the output. The basic relational algebra operations and their notations are described below. In the following discussion, R, $R1$, and $R2$ denote relations.

Selection (σ). $\sigma_C(R)$ is used to find all tuples of R that satisfy the selection conditions specified in C. A simple selection condition can be "A op v" or "A op B," where A and B are attributes of R, op is an operator in $\{=, \neq, <, \leq, >, \geq\}$, and v is a value in the domain of A. For example, if $Asset$ and $Debt$ are two attributes of relation $People$, then "$Debt >$ $Asset$" can be used to find those people who are in financial difficulty. A complicated condition can be constructed from simple conditions through logical operators in $\{and,$ $or, not\}$. As an example, for the relation $Employee$ in Figure 1.1, the query to find all employees who are older than 30 and who earn no more than 30k can be expressed as $\sigma_{Age>30 \text{ and } Salary \leq 30k}(Employee)$.

Projection (π). $\pi_{AL}(R)$ is used to return, for each tuple in R, the values under attributes listed in AL. In other words, the columns of R that are not specified in AL are removed. It is required that all attributes in AL are from R. The query to find the names and salaries of all employees can be written as $\pi_{Name,Salary}(Employee)$. When attributes that are not in AL are removed, the resulted (sub)tuples may have duplicates. For example, for the *Department* table in Figure 1.1, there will be two tuples with 100k in $\pi_{Budget}(Department)$ if duplicate tuples are kept. Duplication is automatically removed by the projection operator.

Cartesian Product ($\times$). $R1 \times R2$ returns a new relation that contains all tuples that can be obtained by concatenating every tuple in $R1$ with every tuple in $R2$. Cartesian product provides a means to relate tuples from different relations. Cartesian product is a very expensive operation because it performs exhaustive tuple pair concatenation and it generates a very large result.

Union ($\cup$). $R1 \cup R2$ returns all tuples that belong to either $R1$ or $R2$. The union operator requires *union compatibility* of its two operands. Two relations are union compatible if they have the same number of attributes and each pair of corresponding attributes has the same domain.

Set Difference ($-$). $R1 - R2$ returns all tuples that belong to $R1$ but not $R2$. This operator also requires the union compatibility of its two operands.

Set Intersection ($\cap$). $R1 \cap R2$ returns all tuples that belong to both $R1$ and $R2$. This operator also requires the union compatibility of its two operands.

Join ($\bowtie_C$). $R1 \bowtie_C R2$ returns all tuples in $R1 \times R2$ that satisfy the join condition C, which consists of one or more *basic join conditions* connected by logical operators. Each basic join condition is of the form "$R1.A$ op $R2.B$"; that is, each join condition compares attribute values of tuples from different relations. In comparison with Cartesian product, join is a more efficient alternative to relate tuples from different relations since it puts a

SSN	Name	Age	Birthdate	Salary	Dept	Department.Name	Budget	Phone
123456789	John	34	5/18/1963	30k	Sales	Sales	200k	4567890
234567891	Ketty	27	9/21/1970	25k	Service	Service	100k	5678900
345678912	Wang	39	2/24/1958	32k	Sales	Sales	200k	4567890

FIGURE 1.2 Employee $\bowtie_{Employee.Dept\ =\ Department.Name}$ **Department**

restriction on tuples in the output; i.e., a tuple in $R1$ concatenates a tuple in $R2$ only if the two tuples satisfy the join condition C.

If the operator in every basic join condition of a join is the equal operator, the join is called an *equijoin*. Otherwise, it is called a θ-*join*. Most joins are equijoins between a foreign key of a relation and the referenced primary key in another relation. Most relations are related through the key/foreign-key relationships between them. For example, to relate the employees with their corresponding departments (see Figure 1.1), the following equijoin is used: Employee $\bowtie_{Employee.Dept\ =\ Department.Name}$ Department. A relation generated by an equijoin has columns that have identical contents. For example, the above equijoin will generate a relation with two columns, Employee.Dept and Department.Name, that have identical values for each tuple in the relation (see Figure 1.2). Such redundant columns are automatically removed by the *natural join*. The natural join between $R1$ and $R2$, usually denoted as $R1 \bowtie R2$ without any join condition explicitly specified, evaluates an equality condition between every pair of identically named attributes from $R1$ and $R2$ and keeps only one of every pair of these identically named attributes. If the Dept attribute in Employee and the Name attribute in Department are both renamed as Dept-Name, then the above equijoin with only one column of department name in the result can be replaced by the natural join: Employee $\bowtie$ Department.

Division (÷). This operator requires the relation that is to be divided (the dividend) contain all attributes of the relation that divides (the divisor). Suppose $R1$ has attributes $(A_1, \ldots, A_n, B_1, \ldots, B_m)$ and $R2$ has attributes $(B_1, \ldots, B_m)$. Let $T = \pi_{A_1, \ldots, A_n}(R1)$. Then $R1 \div R2$ returns each such tuple of T whose concatenation with every tuple of $R2$ is in $R1$. Intuitively, $R1 \div R2$ finds all the tuples of $R1$ that relate with every tuple in $R2$. For example, if $R1$ is Participate(SSN, Proj#), representing which employee is participating in which project, and $R2$ is Project(Proj#), representing a set of projects, then $R1 \div R2$ returns the SSNs of those employees who participate in every project.

Note that not every one of the above relational algebra operators is independent. Some operators can be expressed in terms of other operators. It can be shown that set intersection, various types of joins and division can be expressed in terms of the other five operators. For example, the natural join between $R1(A, B, C)$ and $R2(B, C, D)$ can be expressed in terms of selection, projection, and Cartesian product as follows:

$$R1 \bowtie R2 = \pi_{A,R1.B,R1.C,D}(\sigma_{R1.B\ =\ R2.B\ \text{and}\ R1.C=R2.C}(R1 \times R2))$$

1.1.3 SQL

SQL is the standard language for relational databases. SQL has many components dealing with different aspects of managing data in the database, such as the definition and manipulation of data, interfacing with host programming languages (embedded SQL), definition of constraints, and support for transactions. In this chapter, we are interested mainly in SQL as language for manipulating data. As a query language, SQL is mostly nonprocedural. In contrast, relational algebra is a procedural language.

A basic SQL query consists of three clauses: the select-clause, which specifies the target (output) attributes to be returned; the from-clause, which specifies the relations involved in the query; and the where-clause, which specifies the conditions to be satisfied by the result of the query. Using the relations in Figure 1.1, a query to find the name of each employee in the Sales department together with the department telephone number can be written in SQL as follows:

```
select Employee.Name, Department.Phone
from Employee, Department
where Employee.Dept = 'Sales' and Employee.Dept = Department.Name
```

Approximately, the select-clause corresponds to the *projection* operator, the from-clause corresponds to one or more Cartesian products, and the where-clause corresponds to the *selection* operator in relational algebra. The difference between the select-clause and the *projection* operator is that the former does not remove duplicate tuples and the latter does. To remove duplicate tuples in the result, *select distinct* instead of *select* should be used. There are two reasons for giving the users the choice of whether to keep or remove duplicate tuples. First, duplicate tuples sometimes provide additional information to the user. For example, suppose only Employee.Name is in the select-clause of the above query. If a name appears twice in the result, then we know there are two employees who have the same name. This information is lost if duplicate tuples are removed. Second, removing duplicate tuples incurs a much higher cost than keeping them because the former typically requires sorting the tuples. If *select* is replaced by *select distinct* in the above query, then it is equivalent to the following relational algebra expression: $\pi_{Employee.Name,Department.Phone}(\sigma_{Employee.Dept='Sales'}$ and $_{Employee.Dept=Department.Name}$ $(Employee \times Department))$. Note that though the above SQL query is equivalent to the above relational algebra expression, that fact does not necessarily imply that the SQL query should be evaluated based on this relational algebra expression. Query optimization techniques that exploit this to improve efficiency will be discussed in Sections 1.4 and 1.5.

A complicated SQL query may contain (1) aggregate functions (i.e., min, max, avg, sum, and count); (2) up to three additional clauses (i.e., the *group by* clause, which groups tuples of the input relations based on the values of specified attribute(s) for computing aggregate values for each group; the *having* clause, which specifies conditions on aggregate values; and the *order by* clause, which sorts the output based on the values of specified attribute(s)); (3) nested subqueries (*correlated*, in which an inner query references some attribute in the outer query, or *uncorrelated*, in which no inner query references any attribute in an outer query); and (4) subqueries that are connected by set operators such as union, intersection, and set difference.

It can be shown that any query that can be expressed by relational algebra can also be expressed by SQL. Therefore, SQL is as powerful as relational algebra. Strictly speaking, SQL is more powerful than relational algebra because it can do many things, such as computing aggregates for different groups of tuples, that relational algebra cannot do.

1.2 An Overview of Query Processing and Optimization

When a user query (in SQL) is received, the query processor first checks whether the query has the correct syntax and whether the relations and attributes it references are in the database. Next, if the query is acceptable, then an *execution plan* for the query is generated. An execution plan defines a sequence of steps for query evaluation. Typically, each step in the plan corresponds to one relational operation plus the method to be used for the evaluation of the operation. Usually, for a given relational operation, there are a number of methods that can be used to evaluate it. For example, the join operation can be evaluated by *nested loop, sort merge,* and other join methods (see Section 1.4.3).

Example 1.2 Consider the following SQL query:

```
select *
from R, S, T
where R.A > a and R.B = S.B and S.C = T.C
```

where R, S, and T are relations; A, B, and C are attributes, and a is a constant. This query involves two joins and a selection. A possible execution plan for this query consists of the following three steps:

1. Perform selection $\sigma_{A>a}(R)$ based on a sequential scan of the tuples of R. Let $R1$ denote the result of $\sigma_{A>a}(R)$.

2. Perform join $R1 \bowtie_{R1.B=S.B} S$ using the sort merge join algorithm. Let $R2$ denote the result of the join.

3. Perform join $R2 \bowtie_{R2.C=T.C} T$ using the nested loop join algorithm. ■

For a given query, there may be different execution plans that can produce the same result. For instance, an alternative execution plan to the one given in Example 1.2 is to modify the second and third steps as follows. (2) Perform join $S \bowtie_{S.C=T.C} T$ using the nested loop join algorithm. Let $R3$ denote the result. (3) Perform join $R1 \bowtie_{R1.B=R3.B} R3$ using the sort merge join algorithm. Different execution plans that can always produce the same result are said to be *equivalent*. However, different equivalent plans are usually evaluated with very different costs. The goal of query optimization is to find an execution plan, among all possible equivalent plans, that can be evaluated with the minimum cost. Such a plan is called an *optimal* plan.

In a centralized database system, the cost of evaluating a query is the sum of two components, the I/O cost and the CPU cost. The I/O cost is caused by the transfer of data between main memory and secondary storage (typically, magnetic disk) because in most applications the data is too voluminous to be held entirely in memory. The CPU cost is incurred when tuples in memory are joined or checked against conditions. For most database operations, the

I/O cost is the dominant cost. To reduce I/O cost, special data structures, such as B^+ trees, are utilized. Discussion on these data structures will be given in Section 1.3. For a single processor environment, minimizing the total cost implies the minimization of the *response time* (i.e., the real time needed to complete the query).

In general, the number of equivalent execution plans for a given query is determined by two factors, namely, the number of operations in the query and the number of methods that can be used to evaluate each operation. For example, if there are m operations in a query and each operation can be evaluated in k different ways, then there can be as many as $(m!) \cdot k^m$ different execution plans. The set of all equivalent execution plans is the *search space* for query optimization. Due to the very large number of possible execution plans, the problem of finding an optimal execution plan for a general query becomes a very difficult problem. On the one hand, we would like to find an optimal plan so that we can minimize the query execution cost. On the other hand, if a query is to be used only once, we do not want to spend too much time in searching for an optimal plan because ultimately the time needed to process such a query will be the sum of the time used to find a plan and the time needed to execute the plan. In practice, some queries are submitted to a system many times. For such queries, spending great effort to find an optimal or nearly optimal execution plan is worthwhile because the large initial investment can be amortized over the efficient, repeated executions of the query. Thus we need to strike a balance between the time used to find an optimal plan and the time needed to execute the plan. Some ideas for achieving the balance are summarized below.

1. For some special types of queries for which an optimal execution plan can be found in a reasonable amount of time, it is worthwhile to find the optimal plan. Some well-known special queries are the *chain query*, in which the referenced relations are arranged in a straight line such that only adjacent relations have joins between them; the *star query*, in which a *central relation* joins with other relations and these are the only joins; and the *tree query*, which has a tree-shaped (i.e., has no cycle) *join graph*, where the join graph of a join query contains relations as vertices and joins between relations as edges. A *dynamic programming*–based algorithm for processing chain queries will be discussed in Chapter 3.

2. For general queries, either heuristics are used to obtain a reasonable but not necessarily optimal plan or a reduced search space is used so that an optimal plan based on the reduced space can be found. Neither solution guarantees the finding of a real optimal execution plan. The *algebra-based optimization* technique uses a set of heuristic rules to guide the transformation from one execution plan to another execution plan. One such rule is to process selections as early as possible, and another rule is to replace Cartesian products with selections by joins whenever possible. In most cases, these rules lead to better execution plans. However, in some cases, they produce worse execution plans. Discussion about the algebra-based optimization technique will be provided in Section 1.5. Most database systems (including, for example, IBM's DB2) employ the *cost estimation–based optimization* technique. The basic idea of this technique is to, for each query, estimate the cost of every possible execution plan and choose the execution plan with the lowest estimated cost. Due to the large number of possible execution plans, some systems attempt only to find an optimal execution plan for each query based on a reduced search space. For example, in System R, only execution plans corresponding

to *left deep join trees* are considered. One of the characteristics of such a join tree is that at least one of the input relations to each join, except for the first join, is an intermediate result. More discussion on different types of join trees can be found in Chapter 5. Discussion on cost estimation–based query optimization technique will be provided in Sections 1.4 and 1.5.

1.3 Fast Access Paths

Special data structures are frequently used in database systems for speeding up searches and for reducing I/O costs. These data structures play a very important role in query optimization. It is safe to say that they are an indispensable part of query optimization techniques. In this section, we describe two of these data structures, namely B^+ tree and hashing. But first we describe a typical storage hierarchy for database applications as it is important for the understanding of I/O cost.

1.3.1 Storage Hierarchy

A typical storage hierarchy for database applications consists of two levels. At the first level is main memory (or primary storage), which is storage media that can be operated on directly by the CPU. At the second level is secondary storage (typically, magnetic disk or disk pack). Data stored on secondary storage cannot be directly processed by the CPU; it must be brought to main memory first. The characteristics of the two storages can be summarized below.[1]

Characteristics of main memory:

- fast access to data (0.01 μs per instruction for a processor of 100 mips)

- small storage capacity (typically a few dozen megabytes)

- volatile; i.e., contents will be lost upon power failure

- expensive (about $10 per megabyte)

Characteristics of secondary storage:

- slow access to data (about 17 ms per disk block)

- large storage capacity (on the order of gigabytes)

- nonvolatile

- cheap (about $200 per gigabyte)

---

[1] Note that the numbers quoted in the characteristics of main memory and secondary storage may become obsolete quickly as technology advances quickly.

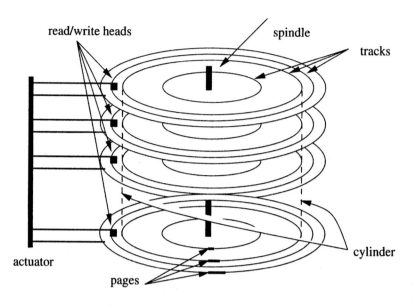

FIGURE 1.3   A Typical Disk Pack

Although the costs for both main memory and secondary storage have been falling sharply and the trend is likely to continue, the cost ratio between them has been reasonably steady, with main memory costing a few dozens of times more than secondary storage for the same capacity. Even though main memory has become more and more affordable, using it to store all data in a database is still too expensive for most applications as database systems are being used in more and more large applications.

A typical disk pack consists of a number of disks sharing the same spindle. Each disk has two surfaces. Each surface typically has a few hundred information-storing circles and each such circle is called a *track*. The set of tracks with the same diameter on all disk surfaces is called a *cylinder*. Each track is typically partitioned into many *pages* (*sectors* or *blocks*). The structure of a typical disk pack is illustrated in Figure 1.3. The size of a page is typically 2 KB or 4 KB. The page is the smallest unit for transferring data between main memory and secondary storage. In summary, disk-based secondary storage is typically organized into pages, tracks, and cylinders. Each page can be addressed through a triplet (cylinder#, track#, page#).

The cost of transferring one page of data between main memory and disk is the sum of three components. The first component is the *seek time*, which is the time needed to position the read/write head of the disk drive on the correct track. The second component is the *rotational delay* (or *latency*), which is the time needed for the beginning of the page to rotate under the read/write head. The third component is the *block transfer time*, which is the actual time needed to transfer the data in the page. The block transfer time can be defined as rotation time · (page size/track size), where rotation time is the time needed for the spindle to perform a full rotation. The seek time heavily depends on the relative positions of the read/write head and the desired page on the disk. If the read/write head is currently on the outermost track and the desired page is on the innermost track, then the seek time will be long. On the other hand, if they happen to be on the same track when the transfer is needed, then the seek time will be zero. The expected seek time is the time for traversing half of the tracks on the surface and is around 10 ms. The rotational delay depends on the relative position of the read/write head and the beginning of the desired page. In the worst case, a full rotation is needed, and in the best case no rotation is needed. On the average, half a rotation is expected. The expected rotational delay takes about 6 ms. The time needed to actually transfer one page of data is only about 1 ms. Clearly, most of the time in transferring one page of data is spent on moving the read/write head to the right place, and the actual transferring is very small. Therefore, if we need to transfer two pages of data and the second page is next to the first page on the same track, then after the data in the first page is transferred, the data in the second page can be transferred without additional seek time and rotational delay. In this case, the first page is expected to take 17 ms to be transferred, and the second page takes only 1 ms. A page I/O is *sequential* if transferring the data incurs neither seek time nor rotational delay; otherwise, the page I/O is *random*. A typical random page I/O requires the repositioning of the read/write head. For our example, transferring the data of the first page incurs a random page I/O, and transferring the data of the second page incurs a sequential page I/O. Since a sequential page I/O is much cheaper than a random page I/O, it is important to organize data on disk in such a way that the number of random page I/Os can be reduced.

Although the two-level storage architecture described above is expected to remain typical for most database applications in the foreseeable future, the following architectures are likely to be used in more and more applications.

One-level architecture. In this architecture, all data in the database are kept in main memory. Such a database system is known as a *main memory database system*. Due to the sharp decrease of main memory cost and the availability of nonvolatile (battery backup) main memory, a main memory database is an attractive choice for applications that require fast data access.

Three-level architecture. In recent years, the amounts of data involved in several high-profile applications are so large that secondary storage is no longer capable of accommodating them. For example, EOS/DIS (earth observation system/data information system) will eventually contain as many as 10 petabytes (i.e., 1 million gigabytes) of data. Massive databases are also emerging in the areas of environmental study, medical research, telecommunications networks, digital information services, space exploration, etc. In this case, another level of storage—*tertiary storage*—is needed. Optical disks and/or tape drives can be used as the storage media for tertiary storage; tertiary storage is much slower than secondary storage, much larger in capacity, and nonvolatile.

Another type of storage media, namely, *cache*, is now widely used in database systems. Cache permits substantially faster access than main memory. However, it is also much more expensive. As a result, the capacity of cache is usually small.

1.3.2 B$^+$ Tree

B$^+$ tree is an index structure widely used in database systems. A node in the tree is either an *internal node* or a *leaf node*. An internal node has one or more children whereas a leaf

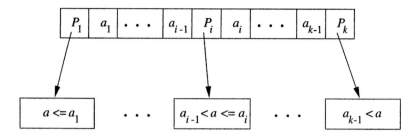

FIGURE 1.4 An Internal Node

node has no children. Each node is stored as a page. B$^+$ tree is a *balanced tree* in the sense that all leaf nodes in the tree are the same distance away from the root node. Suppose the index is based on the values of attribute A of relation R; i.e., A is the *search key* of the index. The internal nodes of a B$^+$ tree have the format $(P_1, a_1, P_2, a_2, \ldots, a_{k-1}, P_k)$, where a_i's are values in attribute A satisfying $a_1 < a_2 < \cdots < a_{k-1}$, and P_i's are *tree pointers*, pointing to nodes at the next lower level of the tree. Every value of A in the node pointed to by P_1 is less than or equal to a_1, every value of A in the node pointed to by P_k is greater than a_{k-1}, and every value of A in the node pointed to by P_i is greater than a_{i-1} and less than or equal to a_i, $1 < i \leq k - 1$. An internal node is illustrated in Figure 1.4. It is required that every nonroot internal node is at least half full. Let M be the maximum number of pointers that can be placed in a node (M can be computed from the size of a page, the size of an A-value, and the size of a pointer). Then, $\lceil \frac{M}{2} \rceil \leq k \leq M$. The leaf nodes of the tree have the format $(a_1, P_1; a_2, P_2; \ldots; a_m, P_m; P)$, where a_i's are A-values satisfying $a_1 < a_2 < \cdots < a_m$ and P is a *leaf node pointer*, pointing to the next leaf node. These leaf nodes form a linked list. Leaf nodes are ordered in ascending/nondescending values; that is, if node i precedes node j in the linked list, then all A-values in node i are less than (or equal to, see case 2(b) below) all A-values in node j. The leaf node pointers in leaf nodes provide a way to access the tuples in an ordered manner and are useful for evaluating *range conditions* (e.g., $b \leq A < c$). The pointers P_i in the leaf nodes are described as follows:

1. If the tuples of R are stored in ascending (or descending) A-values, then the B$^+$ tree index is called a *clustered index* (or a *primary index*). In practice, the search key of a clustered index is usually the primary key of a relation. In this case, depending on the implementation, each P_i is either a *tuple pointer* pointing to the tuple whose A-value is a_i or a *page pointer* pointing to a page of R that contains the tuple whose A-value is a_i. When A is not a key, P_i's are usually implemented as page pointers.

   Note that there can be at most one clustered index on each relation because the tuples of a relation can be stored in only one way at any given time. For example, if we have a clustered index on attribute A and a clustered index on attribute B, then the tuples of R would have to be stored in ascending A-values as well as in ascending B-values. This is usually impossible.

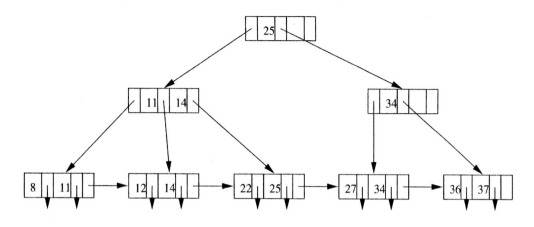

FIGURE 1.5 An Example B⁺ Tree

2. If the tuples of R are not stored in ascending (or descending) A-values, then the B⁺ tree index is called a *nonclustered index* (or a *secondary index*). Usually, the following two cases are distinguished.

(a) A is a key. In this case, each P_i is a *tuple pointer*, pointing to the tuple whose A-value is a_i.

(b) A is not a key. In this case, several implementations for the pointers are possible. The most common method is to let each P_i be a pointer to a page N that contains tuple pointers to tuple(s) whose A-value is a_i. Notice that in this case, an additional indirection is needed since page N does not directly contain tuple(s) whose A-value is a_i. More specifically, from pointer P_i, page N is fetched first. Since N does not contain tuples of R, the pointers in N have to be followed to obtain desired tuples. An implementation that can avoid this additional indirection is by repeating each A-value as many times in leaf nodes as there are tuples containing the A-value. With this implementation, each P_i will be a *tuple pointer* to a tuple whose A-value is a_i, and the condition $a_1 < a_2 < \cdots < a_m$ for each leaf node must be modified to $a_1 \leq a_2 \leq \cdots \leq a_m$. Alternatively, we can factor out the repeating A-values by associating with each A-value a number of tuple pointers. For example, suppose four tuples in R have the same A-value, say a', and the four tuple pointers to the four tuples are P_1, P_2, P_3, and P_4, respectively. If the A-value is repeated, then "$a', P_1; a', P_2; a', P_3; a', P_4;$" will be in a leaf node. If the A-value is factored out, then "$a', (P_1, P_2, P_3, P_4);$" will be in a leaf node.

It is also required that each leaf node remain at least half full (i.e., has at least $\lceil \frac{N}{2} \rceil$ pointers if N is the maximum number of pointers that can be placed in a leaf node). Figure 1.5 illustrates a B⁺ tree with the maximum number of pointers in each node (internal or leaf) being three.

The algorithm for searching a tuple (or tuples) with A-value equal to a is described below. Let T denote the pointer pointing to the root node of the B⁺ tree.

Search(a, T)

1. If T is an internal node, then compare a with the A-values in T to determine the tree pointer to follow and the next node to search. Specifically, if $a \leq a_1$, then call Search(a, P_1); if $a_{i-1} < a \leq a_i$, $1 < i \leq k - 1$, then call Search(a, P_i); if $a > a_{k-1}$, then call Search(a, P_k). The comparison stops as soon as the tree pointer is determined. A binary search is often utilized to speed up the search of the right P_i.

2. If T is a leaf node, compare a with the A-values in T. If no A-value in T is equal to a, report *not found*. If a_i in T is equal to a, follow pointer P_i to fetch the tuple(s).

The above algorithm can be modified easily for searching all tuples whose A-values are in a specified range, say $[a, b]$. This is described as follows. The first step of the above algorithm is used to find a leaf node N for a. Next, the smallest value in N that is greater than or equal to a is determined. If this value is greater than b, then return *not found* and exit. If it is less than or equal to b, then the corresponding pointer is used to fetch the tuple(s). In this case, the successive A-values in N are compared with b, and if they are less than or equal to b, then their corresponding pointers are used to fetch the tuples. If the largest A-value in N is less than b, then the search continues to the node next to N using the leaf node pointer in N. The process stops either when an A-value greater than b is encountered or all A-values have been considered.

The performance of the search algorithm is closely related with the height of the B^+ tree. In theory, if n is the number of distinct A-values in R, then the height of the B^+ tree is approximately $\log_F n$, where F is the average *fanout* of the tree (i.e., F is the average number of children of an internal node). In practice, since F is usually large, a B^+ tree of 3 to 4 levels can easily accommodate a very large relation. For example, consider a relation with 1 million distinct A-values (i.e., R has at least 1 million tuples). Suppose each page has 2k bytes and each (A-value, pointer) pair has 15 bytes. Suppose each page stores 100 such pairs (25% of the space is left to accommodate future insertions). Then 10,000 leaf nodes are needed. With $F = 100$, the next upper level needs 100 nodes, and 1 node is sufficient for the next upper level (i.e., the root level). For this particular example, a 3-level B^+ tree is sufficient. Therefore, in practice, a small number is often used to indicate the height of a B^+ tree.

Although searching in a B^+ tree is straightforward, inserting into and deleting from a B^+ tree are much more complicated. The complication for insertion comes from the fact that inserting a new value into a leaf node, say N, may cause the node to overflow (i.e., no space left in the node to accommodate the new value and the pointer). The overflow causes N to be split into two nodes. As a result, an additional pointer and an A-value need to be added in the parent node of N. The additional pointer and A-value may cause the parent node of N to overflow and split. In the worst case, the effect may propagate all the way to the root node. When the root node is split, the height of the tree will be increased by one. Similarly, deleting a value from a leaf node may cause it to underflow (i.e., the node becomes less than half full) and the underflow causes the merge of this node with one of its sibling nodes. Such a merge may then cause its parent node to underflow. Again, in the worst case, the effect may cascade all the way to the root node. If the root node has only two child nodes, then the merge of its two child nodes will result in the deletion of the root node (the merged child node of the old root becomes the new root of the tree) and a decrease in the height of the tree by one.

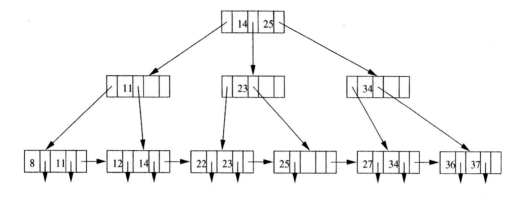

FIGURE 1.6 The B⁺ Tree after 23 is inserted

Example 1.3 Consider the B⁺ tree in Figure 1.5. Suppose we need to insert a tuple with A-value equal to 23 into the relation R. This will cause the insertion of the entry (23, P) into the B⁺ tree, where P is the address of the new tuple. Using the search procedure described in the search algorithm, the leaf node containing A-values 22 and 25 is identified to be the node into which (23, P) should be inserted. The insertion causes the node to overflow since the maximum number of pointers allowable is three. As a result, the node is split into two nodes, N1 with 22 and 23, and N2 with 25. The split results in the need to add a pointer and a value (23, the largest value in N1) to the parent node. This causes the parent node to be split into two nodes as shown in Figure 1.6. This split causes the addition of a pointer and the value 14 to the root node (14 is the largest value in the leftmost subtree). This did not cause a split of the root node since in this case the root node still has room to accommodate the new pointer and the new value. ∎

1.3.3 Hashing

Hashing is another frequently used method for providing fast access to desired tuples in a relation. The idea is to build a *hash table* that contains an *index entry* for each tuple in the relation and to use a *hash function h( )* to quickly identify each entry in the hash table. The hash table consists of many *buckets*. Usually, the number of *buckets* to be used is allocated in advance based on the number of tuples in the relation. Each bucket corresponds to one or more disk pages. Suppose A is the attribute of a relation that is to be used to provide fast access. The contents of each bucket is a number of index entries of the form (a, P), where a is the A-value of some tuple and P is a *tuple pointer*, pointing to the tuple on disk. A hash function h( ) is used to map each value of A in the relation to a number, known as the *bucket number*. Buckets are usually numbered from 0 to $n - 1$, where n is the number of buckets used. The hash function is designed in such a way that it maps any valid value of A to an integer between 0 and $n - 1$. For example, if A takes nonnegative integers, then $h(x) = x$ mod n—which returns the remainder of x divided by n—is such a function. Let t be a tuple and a be the A-value of t. If $h(a) = k, 0 \leq k \leq n - 1$, then entry (a, P) is placed in the kth bucket of the hash table.

After an entry is created and placed in an appropriate bucket for every tuple of the relation, the build of the hash table is complete. It is possible that too many A-values are mapped to the same bucket and it cannot hold all the entries. This is known as *bucket overflow*. A carefully chosen hash function can relieve the problem by distributing A-values into buckets reasonably evenly. However, choosing a good hash function alone may not avoid the problem entirely. A common solution to the bucket overflow problem is to place overflow entries into *overflow buckets* and link these overflow buckets to regular buckets.

Example 1.4 Consider the stored Employee relation in Figure 1.7. Suppose we are interested in building a hash table for the relation based on attribute Name. Suppose five buckets are allocated initially and each bucket can hold three index entries and an overflow pointer. Consider the hash function $h(X) = \text{seq}(X) \bmod 5$, where for a given name X, the function $\text{seq}(X)$ returns the serial number of the first letter in X in the English alphabet. For example, since the first letter of Bob is B and B is the second letter in the alphabet, $\text{seq}(\text{Bob}) = 2$. It is easy to see that $h(\text{Bob}) = 2$. Therefore, an index entry, namely (Bob, P), is placed in the bucket with number 2, where P is a pointer to the tuple with Name = 'Bob'. The complete hash table for the Employee relation is shown in Figure 1.7. Note that an overflow bucket is linked to the bucket with bucket number 2 as the entry involving Beth can no longer be held in the latter bucket.   ■

To find the tuple(s) that satisfy the condition "$A = a$", the same hash function used to build the hash table is used to map a to a bucket, say B. Note that it is possible for different A-values to be mapped to the same bucket. Therefore, the entries in B as well as in all overflow buckets linked to B must be searched to find those whose A-values are equal to a. For each correct entry found, the page that contains the corresponding tuple can be directly read in.

Hashing is considered to be the fastest method for finding tuples with a given A-value. However, hashing does have several drawbacks. First, bucket overflow may occur. Although overflow buckets can be used to solve the problem, each overflow bucket in a linked list implies an additional page I/O. This slows down the access. Second, hashing is effective only when equality conditions are involved. For example, hashing is not very useful if the search condition is "$A > a$". Although hash functions that preserve the order of tuples exist, these functions are usually poor in distributing A-values evenly. Third, since the space of the hash table is allocated in advance, the hash table may become underutilized if too many tuples are deleted from the relation or overflow frequently if too many tuples are inserted into the relation. *Dynamic hashing* and *extendible hashing* techniques can be used to overcome this problem.

1.4 Single Operation Processing

As mentioned in Section 1.2, an execution plan consists of a sequence of operations and a strategy for evaluating each operation. In this section, we discuss techniques for evaluating several relational operations—selection, projection, and join. We also provide cost analysis for each strategy.

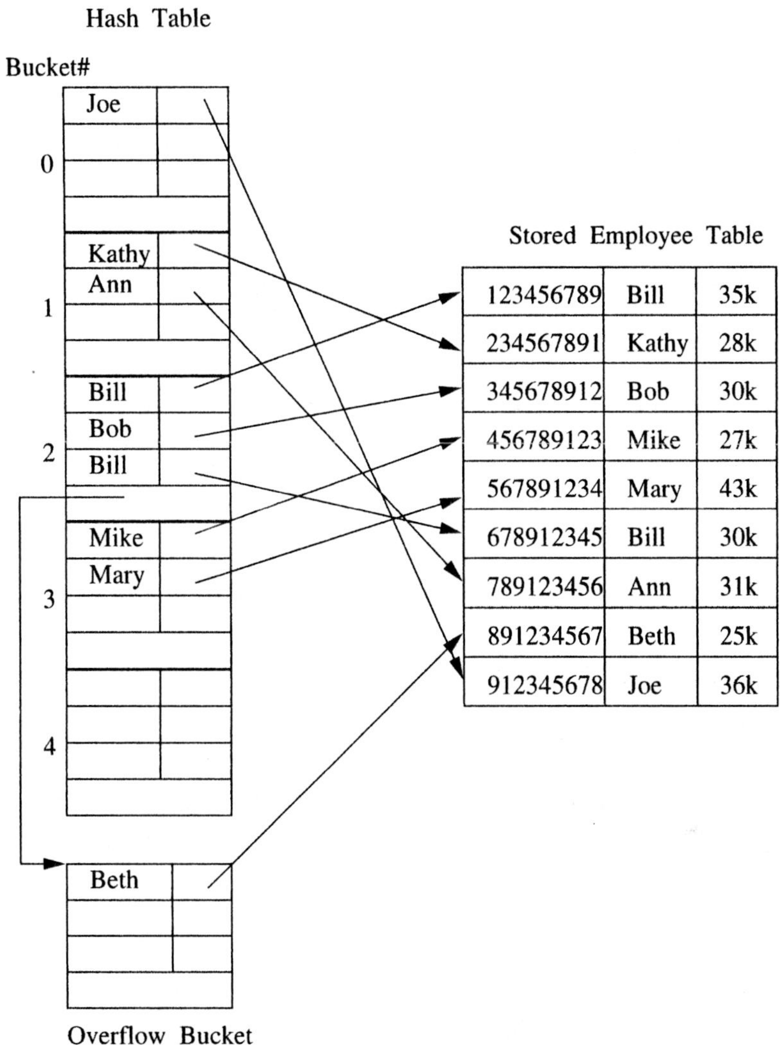

Hash Table

Bucket#

Stored Employee Table

FIGURE 1.7   Illustrating a Hash Table

Let R and S be two relations under consideration. Let n and m be the numbers of tuples in R and S, respectively. Let N and M be the sizes of R and S in pages, respectively. We consider two types of costs in our analysis, namely, I/O cost and CPU cost. The total cost of evaluating an operation or an execution plan is a weighted sum of the I/O cost and the CPU cost. I/O cost is usually the dominating cost. For CPU cost, the number of comparisons needed and/or the number of tuples searched is used. Two methods have been used in the literature for estimating I/O cost. The first method uses the total number of pages that are read or written. This method has the drawback of not differentiating random page I/Os and sequential page I/Os. The second method uses the number of I/O operations initiated. One I/O operation may read/write many pages. This method may be inaccurate because two I/O operations could have very different costs. For example, an I/O operation that reads/writes 5 pages incurs a much smaller cost than that incurred by an I/O operation that reads/writes 500 pages. In a multiuser environment, it is usually difficult to know the actual number of I/O operations. For example, consider X pages of data that are stored in consecutive storage space. The X pages may be read in by one I/O operation when it is the only I/O request and the buffer is large enough to hold them. However, the same X pages may be read in using several I/O operations when there are concurrent I/O requests. This example can also be used to illustrate that, in a multiuser environment, it is difficult to know the actual number of random page I/Os. For example, if the above X pages can be read in by one I/O operation, then only one random page I/O is incurred. However, if several I/O operations are needed, then several random page I/Os are incurred. Thus, both methods may lead to inaccuracy. Our analysis will be based on the first method unless using the second method has a significant impact on the processing strategy, and in that case, both methods will be used.

A simplification we use in the analysis of the I/O cost is to ignore the cost of outputting the result of an evaluation. This is because the goal of analyzing the cost is to find out the most efficient strategy. Since the size of the result is the same regardless of the strategy used, ignoring the cost of outputting does not affect the finding of the most efficient strategy.

1.4.1 Evaluating Selection

Suppose the selection under consideration is $\sigma_{A\ op\ a}(R)$, where A is a single attribute, a is a constant, op is one of $=, \neq, <, \leq, >, \geq$. If op is $\neq$, then most tuples of R are likely to satisfy the condition. In this case, sequentially scanning the entire relation is likely to be a better way to evaluate the condition than using any index structure. The following discussion assumes that op is not $\neq$.

The cost of evaluating a selection is closely related with the number of tuples in R that satisfy the condition.

Definition 1.1 *The* selectivity *of "A op a" on R, denoted as $S_{A\ op\ a}(R)$, is the percentage of the tuples of R that satisfy "A op a".*

Clearly, $0 \leq S_{A\ op\ a}(R) \leq 1$. The selectivity factor for any condition can be estimated based on some known statistics about the relation and some assumptions about the data distribution of the A-values in R. In addition to the number of tuples n in R, these statistics include dist(A), the number of distinct values of A in R; min(A), the smallest value of A in R; and max(A), the largest value of A in R. A frequently used assumption is that the values of A satisfy the *uniform distribution* between min(A) and max(A). Based on the above statistics and the uniform distribution assumption, $S_{A\ op\ a}(R)$ can be estimated easily. For example, $S_{A=a}(R)$ can be estimated to be $\frac{1}{\text{dist}(A)}$ and $S_{A>a}(R)$ can be estimated to be $\frac{\max(A)-a}{\max(A)-\min(A)}$. Since the actual values of A could deviate substantially from the uniform distribution assumption, selectivities estimated based on this assumption may be poor. To alleviate this problem, most commercial systems maintain detailed statistics about the values of each attribute. These statistics are typically in the form of a *histogram*. The basic idea is to partition the values of A into disjoint subsets and store summary statistics for each subset such that the true distribution of the values of A can be better approximated.

Let k be the number of tuples in R that satisfy the condition "A op a". Then k is estimated to be $n \cdot S_{A\ op\ a}(R)$. The cost of evaluating $\sigma_{A\ op\ a}(R)$ can be analyzed as follows:

Case 1. Fast access path is not available or not used.

> *Subcase 1.1.* Tuples are stored in sorted A-values. In this case, binary search can be used. The CPU cost is $O(\log n + k)$ and the I/O cost is $O(\log N + \lceil \frac{k}{n} \cdot N \rceil)$, where N is the number of pages needed to hold the tuples of R and $\lceil \frac{k}{n} \cdot N \rceil$ is the number of pages needed to hold the k tuples satisfying the selection condition.

> *Subcase 1.2.* Tuples are not stored in sorted A-values. In this case, a sequential scan of all tuples is needed. The CPU cost is $O(n)$ and the I/O cost is $O(N)$.

Case 2. Fast access path is used.

> *Subcase 2.1.* Tuples are stored in sorted A-values. This is the case when the fast access path is a clustered index. Since all qualified tuples are stored together and it takes a constant number of steps (as pointed out earlier, a B$^+$ tree is usually no more than 3 or 4 levels high) to find the first qualified tuple using the fast access path, the CPU cost is $O(k)$ and the I/O cost is $O(\lceil \frac{k}{n} \cdot N \rceil)$.

> *Subcase 2.2.* Tuples are not stored in sorted A-values. This is the case when the fast access path is a nonclustered index. Since each qualified tuple can be obtained in a constant number of comparisons using the index, the CPU cost is $O(k)$. Similarly, since each qualified tuple can be obtained by fetching a constant number of pages, the I/O cost is bounded by $O(k)$. At the same time, we never need to read in more than N pages. Therefore, the I/O cost is bounded by $O(\min\{k, N\})$.

> The number of pages containing the k qualified tuples can be more accurately estimated. A classic problem is as follows. There are n balls with N different colors such that the number of balls with each color is the same. If k balls are randomly selected from the n balls, then the expected number of colors that the k balls have is given by the following formula:

$$N \times \left[1 - \prod_{r=1}^{k} \left(\frac{n((N-1)/N) - r + 1}{n - r + 1} \right) \right] \qquad (1.1)$$

> The correspondences between the *colors-of-balls* problem and the problem of estimating the number of pages containing the k qualified tuples are as follows: the n tuples in R correspond to the n balls, the N pages of R correspond to the N colors, and the k qualified tuples correspond to the k randomly selected balls. Therefore, Formula (1.1) also computes the number of expected pages containing the k qualified tuples.

1.4.2 Evaluating Projection

Suppose the projection under consideration is $\pi_{A_1,\ldots,A_t}(R)$, where $A_1, \ldots, A_t$ are attributes of relation R. Two cases may occur.

Case 1. Duplicate rows are not removed. In SQL, duplicate rows are removed only when *select distinct* is used. In this case, the projection can be evaluated by scanning each tuple once. Therefore, the CPU cost is $O(n)$ and the I/O cost is $O(N)$.

Case 2. Duplicate rows are removed. This is usually accomplished in three steps. First, the relation is scanned and a projection that keeps duplicate rows is performed. Second, the result of the first step is sorted. After the sort, duplicate rows must appear in adjacent locations. Third, the sorted result is scanned for duplication removal. The CPU cost is dominated by the sorting and the cost is $O(n \log n)$. The I/O cost is dominated by the first two steps. The I/O cost for the first step is $O(N)$. The second step typically requires an *external sort* as the memory may not be able to accommodate all the data to be sorted. Let W be the size of the result of the first step ($W = n \cdot (\sum_{i=1}^{t} \text{length}(A_i))/\text{PageSize}$). Then the I/O cost for the second step is $O(W \cdot \log W)$.

1.4.3 Evaluating Join

Among the three most frequently used relational operations (i.e., selection, projection, and join), join is the most expensive operation. Consequently, it has been studied extensively. In this subsection we describe several well-known algorithms for evaluating the join operation. Only equijoin will be considered. Suppose the join under consideration is $R \bowtie_{R.A=S.B} S$. Recall that n and m are the numbers of tuples in R and S, respectively, and N and M are the sizes of R and S in pages, respectively. Without loss of generality, we assume that S is the smaller of the two relations (i.e., $M \leq N$).

Nested Loop

This algorithm compares every tuple of R with every tuple of S directly for finding the matching tuples, which is illustrated below.

```
for each tuple x in R
        for each tuple y in S
                if x[A] = y[B] then return (x, y)
```

In the above implementation, R is used in the outer loop and is therefore called the *outer relation*; S is used in the inner loop and is the *inner relation*. An alternative is to use S as the outer relation and R as the inner relation. As we will see shortly, the choice of which relation to use as the outer/inner relation is significant for optimizing the I/O cost if the optimization criterion is to minimize the number of I/O pages. However, it has little impact on the CPU cost. In fact, the CPU cost for this algorithm is always $O(n \cdot m)$.

To estimate the I/O cost, the above algorithm needs modification to be page based. Let K be the size (in pages) of the available memory buffer for the join. Clearly, $K \geq 3$ is required since the buffer needs to hold at least one page for each of the two relations and one page for accumulating the result. In the following analysis, K is used to denote only the buffer pages available for the two join relations (i.e., output buffer page(s) are excluded from K).

We consider a special case first. In this case $K = 2$. When R is the outer relation and S is the inner relation, we have the following modified algorithm:

for each page P of R
　　for each page Q of S
　　　　for each tuple x in P
　　　　　　for each tuple y in Q
　　　　　　　　if $x[A] = y[B]$ then return (x, y)

This algorithm scans the inner relation once for each page in the outer relation. An improvement can be made by alternating the scanning order of the inner relation. That is, if the inner relation is scanned from the first page to the last page for the current iteration, then it will be scanned from the last page to the first page for the next iteration. As a result, the last page of S, which has just been compared against the current page of R, becomes the first page of S to be compared against the next page of R. In this way, this page of S is not reread into main memory, saving one I/O page. This technique is known as *rocking scan*. With the improved algorithm, the I/O cost is $N + M + (N - 1) \cdot (M - 1) = N \cdot M + 1$ as relation R will be scanned once; for the first page of R, the entire S is scanned once; for each of the $N - 1$ remaining pages of R, $M - 1$ pages of S are read in via rocking scan. For this special case it can be seen that if S is the outer relation and R is the inner relation, the I/O cost will still be $N \cdot M + 1$.

We now consider the general case when K is any positive integer greater than or equal to 2. Without loss of generality, we assume $K < N + M$ since otherwise both R and S can be held in the buffer in their entirety and the I/O cost will be $M + N$. Suppose R uses $K1$ buffer pages and S uses $K2$ buffer pages, where $K1$ and $K2$ are two positive integers satisfying $K1 + K2 = K$, $K1 \leq N$ and $K2 \leq M$. When R is the outer relation and S is the inner relation, the following algorithm is obtained:

for each $K1$ pages P of R
　　for each $K2$ pages Q of S
　　　　for each tuple x in P
　　　　　　for each tuple y in Q
　　　　　　　　if $x[A] = y[B]$ then return (x, y)

Since R will be read only once, for the first $K1$ pages of R, the entire S needs to be read, and for each subsequent $K1$ pages of R (there are $(\lceil \frac{N}{K1} \rceil - 1)$ such $K1$ pages of R), only $M - K2$ pages of S need to be read (rocking scan is used); the I/O cost is

$$N + M + \left(\left\lceil \frac{N}{K1} \right\rceil - 1 \right) \cdot (M - K2) \tag{1.2}$$

It can be shown that Expression (1.2) reaches the minimum when $K1 = \min\{N, K - 1\}$. Namely, the outer relation should use as many buffer pages as needed (need no more than N buffer pages). Using similar analysis as above, it can be shown that when S is the outer relation, the I/O cost is

$$M + N + \left(\left\lceil \frac{M}{K2} \right\rceil - 1 \right) \cdot (N - K1) \tag{1.3}$$

and this expression reaches the minimum when $K2 = \min\{M, K - 1\}$. It can further be shown that when the ceiling is ignored, the minimum reached by Expression (1.2) is greater than or equal to the minimum reached by Expression (1.3). For example, consider the case when

$N = 20$, $M = 10$, and $K = 15$. In this case, Expression (1.2) reaches the minimum when $K1 = 14$ and the cost is approximately (with the ceiling ignored) 34, and Expression (1.3) reaches the minimum when $K2 = 10$ and the cost is 30. Note that when the ceiling is kept, the result is not always true. For example, when $N = 20$, $M = 10$, and $K = 5$, the minimum reached by Expression (1.2) is 66, whereas the minimum reached by Expression (1.3) is 68. But the minimum reached by Expression (1.2) is much more likely to be greater than the minimum reached by Expression (1.3).

The above analysis is based on the number of I/O pages being the I/O cost metric. The optimization can be summarized as follows. If the optimization criterion is to minimize the number of I/O pages, then use the smaller relation as the outer relation and let the outer relation use as many buffer pages as needed (i.e., $\min\{M, K - 1\}$).

However, if the optimization criterion is to minimize the number of I/O operations initiated, then a different buffer allocation strategy should be used. This is discussed below. Note that each I/O operation can read in $K1$ pages of R or $K2$ pages of S. Therefore, R can be read in with $\lceil \frac{N}{K1} \rceil$ I/O operations. Similarly, S can be read in with $\lceil \frac{M}{K2} \rceil$ I/O operations. When R is used as the outer relation, R needs to be read in once; for the first $K1$ pages of R, S needs to be scanned once; for each of the $(\lceil \frac{N}{K1} \rceil - 1) K1$ pages of R, one I/O operation can be saved when reading in S due to the rocking scan scheme. Therefore, when R is used as the outer relation, the number of I/O operations needed is

$$\left\lceil \frac{N}{K1} \right\rceil + \left\lceil \frac{M}{K2} \right\rceil + \left(\left\lceil \frac{N}{K1} \right\rceil - 1 \right) \cdot \left(\left\lceil \frac{M}{K2} \right\rceil - 1 \right) = \left\lceil \frac{N}{K1} \right\rceil \cdot \left\lceil \frac{M}{K2} \right\rceil + 1 \qquad (1.4)$$

It can be shown that when the ceilings are ignored, the above expression reaches the minimum when $K1 = K2 = K/2$. In other words, to minimize the number of I/O operations, R and S should use the same number of buffer pages. From Expression (1.4), it is easy to see that if the optimization criterion is to minimize the number of I/O operations, it does not matter which of R and S is used as the outer relation.

Example 1.5 When $N = 20$, $M = 10$, and $K = 6$, the number of I/O pages is minimized at 49 when S is used as the outer relation and allocated with five buffer pages. However, with such a buffer allocation, the number of I/O operations needed is 41. When both R and S are allocated with three buffer pages, the number of I/O operations is 29. Interestingly, when R is allocated with four buffer pages and S is allocated with two buffer pages, the number of I/O operations is minimized at 26. The reason that the number of I/O operations is not minimized when R and S are allocated with the same number of buffer pages is due to the effect of the ceilings in Expression (1.4). ∎

Sort Merge

This join algorithm consists of the following two steps:

1. Sort the two relations in ascending order of their respective joining attributes, i.e., sort R on A and sort S on B if they are not already sorted.

2. Perform a merge join. We first consider the case when the values under at least one joining attribute are distinct. This is a frequently encountered case since most joins are

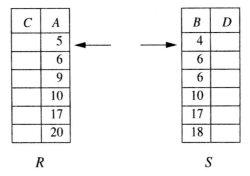

R S

FIGURE 1.8 Illustrating Sort Merge

between attributes that have the key/foreign-key relationships and the values under the attribute corresponding to the key are distinct. Without loss of generality, we assume that A is a key of R. Initially, two pointers are used to point to the two tuples of the two relations that have the smallest values of the two joining attributes (see Figure 1.8). If the two values are the same, then first concatenate the two corresponding tuples to produce a result and then move the pointer pointing to a tuple of S one position lower, to the next tuple of S. If the two values are different, then the pointer pointing to the tuple with the smaller value is moved down one position, to the next tuple. This process is repeated until all values under the two attributes are exhausted.

We now consider the case when both attributes have repeating values. In this case, modification must be made to the above procedure to ensure that all equal values under the two attributes are exhaustively matched. This is described as follows. Suppose the pointer to tuples of R points to a tuple $a1$ and the pointer to tuples of S points to a tuple $b1$. If the two tuples have the same value, say x, under A and B, advance both pointers until each pointer points to a tuple whose value under the joining attribute is different from x. Let the corresponding tuples be $a2$ from R and $b2$ from S, respectively. Then a Cartesian product between the set of tuples from $a1$ to $a2$ (excluding $a2$) and the set of tuples from $b1$ to $b2$ (excluding $b2$) is taken.

The cost of this algorithm depends heavily on whether one or both relations have already been sorted on the joining attribute and on how many repeating values appear under both joining attributes. In the best-case scenario, both relations are sorted and there are no repeating values under at least one joining attribute. In this case, only step 2 is needed and one scan of each relation is sufficient to perform the merge join. Therefore, in this case, the CPU cost is $O(n + m)$ and the I/O cost is $O(N + M)$. In the worst-case scenario, none of the two relations is sorted and nearly all values under the two joining attributes are the same. In this case, both relations need to be sorted and almost a full Cartesian product between the two relations is needed. Therefore, the CPU cost is $O(n \log n + m \log m + n \cdot m)$ and the I/O cost is $O(N \log N + M \log M + C(R, S))$, where $C(R, S)$ is the cost of performing the Cartesian product between R and S. When the cost of outputting the result is not included, $C(R, S)$ is the same as the I/O cost for performing a join between R and S using the nested loop algorithm. The most frequently encountered scenario is when one relation is already sorted and there are no repeating values under at least one joining attribute. This is the case when the join is between two attributes that have the key/foreign-key relationship and the relation with key has a clustered index on the key. In this case, the cost (both CPU cost and I/O cost) is the sum of the cost of sorting the relation with the foreign key and the cost of scanning each relation once to merge them.

Hash Join

The basic hash join algorithm consists of the following two steps:

1. Build a hash table for the smaller relation S based on the joining attribute. This process is similar to the hashing process described in Section 1.3. However, in this case, rather than putting the pointers to tuples in the buckets, the tuples themselves are placed in the buckets.

2. Use the larger relation R to probe the hash table to perform the join. The probe process is described below.

```
for each tuple x in R
        {hash on the joining attribute using the same hash function used in step 1
            to find a bucket in the hash table;
        if the bucket is nonempty
            for every tuple y in the found bucket
                if x[A] = y[B] then return (x, y)
    }
```

Using the same hash function in both steps is essential for hash join as it guarantees that tuples with the same joining attribute values from the two relations will be mapped to the same bucket. However, tuples mapped to the same bucket may have different values on the joining attribute. Therefore, comparing with every entry in the found bucket is needed.

The tuples of the smaller relation are gone through once for building the hash table. For each tuple t of the large relation, every tuple in the bucket to which t is mapped needs to be examined for entries matching with t. Therefore, the CPU cost is $O(m + n \cdot b)$, where b is the average number of tuples per bucket. If the hash table can be held in memory, then each relation need be read in only once. Therefore, the I/O cost of the algorithm in this case is $O(N + M)$.

One potential problem of hash join is that the hash table is too large to fit into the available memory buffer. Building the hash table for the smaller relation helps relieve the problem but may not avoid it entirely. The following variation of hash join, called *hybrid hash join*, is a very effective hash join method for dealing with the hash table overflow problem. This join method can be described as follows. First, the smaller relation S is partitioned into disjoint fragments $S_1, S_2, \ldots, S_F$ using some partitioning method (see Chapter 5 for several partitioning methods). The number of fragments F is determined in such a way as to ensure that the hash table for each fragment can fit into main memory. Clearly, if the hash table for S can fit into the available memory, then no partition is necessary. The tuples of one of the fragments, say S_1, will be used to build a hash table, say T_1, immediately while other fragments will be written to secondary storage. Next, the larger relation R is also partitioned into F fragments, say $R_1, R_2, \ldots, R_F$, based on the same partitioning scheme used to partition S. For each fragment of S, say S_i, there is a corresponding fragment of R, say R_i. It is required that only tuples from the corresponding fragment pairs can possibly match. The tuples of R_1, which corresponds to S_1, will be used immediately to probe the hash table T_1 to evaluate the join between S_1 and R_1 while other fragments of R will be written to secondary storage. After the join between S_1 and R_1 is carried out, hash table T_1 becomes useless and the memory occupied by it can be released. The next fragment of S, namely S_2, is then read in the memory to build a hash table T_2. After T_2 is built, R_2 is read in to probe T_2. This process is repeated until all corresponding fragments of S and R are joined. Cost analysis for hybrid hash join is left as an exercise. More discussions on hybrid hash join will be provided in Chapter 5 in the context of performing joins in parallel.

Comparison of the Join Algorithms

1. Hash join is a very efficient join algorithm when it is applicable. However, hash join is only applicable to equijoin.

2. Sort merge join performs better than nested loop when both operand relations are large. This is especially true if one or both relations are already sorted on the joining attributes. When both input relations are already sorted, sort merge join is as good as hash join. Further, sort merge join is less sensitive to the size of the memory buffer available for performing the join than are other algorithms.

   When a secondary index exists on one or both joining attributes of the two relations, a variation of the sort merge join exists. The case when both joining attributes have a secondary index can be described as follows. Note that the values of each joining attribute are sorted in the leaf nodes of the corresponding index. Therefore, a merge can be performed based on the sorted values of the two joining attributes. When a match is found between the two values currently under consideration, the corresponding pointers in the leaf nodes are used to fetch the tuples for join. Although this variation of sort merge join can save the cost of sorting the two joining attributes, it may incur two or more page I/Os for each matching value(s) of the joining attributes. This variation can be very effective if the relations are large but the join result is small (i.e., very few values of the joining attributes match) since only matched values incur additional I/O cost.

3. Nested loop join performs well when one relation is large and one relation is small. A special case is when the smaller relation can be entirely held in main memory. In this case, both relations need to be read in only once.

   When nested loop join is combined with the index on the joining attribute of the inner relation, excellent performance can yield. With an index on the joining attribute of the inner relation, for each tuple in the outer relation, the index can be utilized to find the matching tuples in the inner relation quickly. This combination is most effective when one joining relation is very large and the other is very small, and the larger relation has an index on the joining attribute. For example, when S has 100 tuples and R has 1 million tuples, the number of pages read is limited by a few hundreds if the said combination is used. This is because in this case, each of the 100 tuples in S can be processed, i.e., joined with the tuples of R, with a few I/O pages using the index. Clearly, no other algorithm can deliver a performance as good as this.

1.5 Determining the Execution Order of Operations

A typical database query consists of a number of operations. The order of operations has significant impact on the cost of evaluating the query. In this section, we discuss techniques and problems in determining optimal execution order.

There are primarily two approaches for determining the execution order of operations: the algebra-based approach and the cost estimation–based approach. Both use a set of rules that can transform one execution plan (represented as a relational algebra expression) to other, equivalent execution plans. We first describe the transformation rules, in Section 1.5.1. We then discuss the two approaches in Sections 1.5.2 and 1.5.3, respectively.

1.5.1 Transformation Rules

There are numerous rules that can transform one relational algebra expression to other, equivalent expressions. Two expressions are equivalent if they always produce the same result. In this subsection, we present only a few of these transformation rules.

Let R, S, and T be three relations.

Transformation Rule 1. Cascade of selections: Let $C1$ and $C2$ be two selection conditions on R. Then

$$\sigma_{C1 \text{ and } C2}(R) = \sigma_{C1}(\sigma_{C2}(R)) = \sigma_{C2}(\sigma_{C1}(R))$$

Transformation Rule 2. Commuting selection with join: If condition C involves attributes of only R, then

$$\sigma_C(R \bowtie S) = (\sigma_C(R)) \bowtie S$$

From rules (1) and (2), the following rule can be deduced: If condition $C1$ involves attributes of only R and condition $C2$ involves attributes of only S, then

$$\sigma_{C1 \text{ and } C2}(R \bowtie S) = (\sigma_{C1}(R)) \bowtie (\sigma_{C2}(S))$$

Note that this rule, as well as the next two rules, apply to Cartesian product. That is, if $\bowtie$ is replaced by $\times$, these rules are still true.

Transformation Rule 3. Commuting projection with join: Assume $AL = \{A_1, \ldots, A_n, B_1, \ldots, B_m\}$, where A's are attributes from R and B's are attributes from S.

(a) If the join condition C involves attributes in only AL, then

$$\pi_{AL}(R \bowtie_C S) = (\pi_{A_1, \ldots, A_n}(R)) \bowtie_C (\pi_{B_1, \ldots, B_m}(S))$$

(b) If, in addition to attributes in AL, C also involves attributes $A'_1, \ldots, A'_u$ from R and attributes $B'_1, \ldots, B'_v$ from S, then

$$\pi_{AL}(R \bowtie_C S) = \pi_{AL}((\pi_{A_1, \ldots, A_n, A'_1, \ldots, A'_u}(R)) \bowtie_C (\pi_{B_1, \ldots, B_m, B'_1, \ldots, B'_v}(S)))$$

Transformation Rule 4. Associativity of θ-join and natural join:

$$R \bowtie_{C1} (S \bowtie_{C2} T) = (R \bowtie_{C1} S) \bowtie_{C2} T \qquad R \bowtie (S \bowtie T) = (R \bowtie S) \bowtie T$$

The reason for listing the rules for θ-join and natural join separately is that mixing them in the same rule yields an incorrect rule. Note that the following rule is incorrect:

$$R \bowtie_C (S \bowtie T) = (R \bowtie_C S) \bowtie T$$

As an example, suppose R has attributes (A, B), S has attributes (D, E), T has attributes (A, E), and the join condition C is "$R.A = S.D$". In this case, the natural join on the left-hand side of the above rule will evaluate only "$S.E = T.E$", whereas the natural join on the right-hand side of the above rule will evaluate "$S.E = T.E$" and "$R.A = T.A$".

Transformation Rule 5. Replacing $\times$ by $\bowtie$ and σ: If C is a selection condition of the form "$R.A$ op $S.B$" or the conjunction of the form, then

$$\sigma_C(R \times S) = R \bowtie_C S$$

1.5.2 Algebra-Based Optimization

The basic idea of the algebra-based optimization approach is to first represent each relational query as a relational algebra expression and then transform it to an equivalent but more efficient relational algebra expression. The transformation is guided by heuristic optimization rules. The following four rules are commonly used:

Optimization Rule 1. Perform selections as early as possible. The rationale behind this rule is that selections can often substantially reduce the sizes of relations. As a result, if they are performed early, later operations such as joins can be evaluated more efficiently with reduced input. This rule can be achieved using the Transformation Rules 1 and 2 ($\bowtie$ may be replaced by $\times$) presented in the last subsection. Specifically, Transformation Rule 1 is to separate two (or multiple) selections into individual selections, which can then be distributed over joins or Cartesian products using Transformation Rule 2.

Optimization Rule 2. Replace Cartesian products by joins whenever possible. A Cartesian product between two relations is typically much more expensive than a join between the two relations. This is because the former performs exhaustive tuple pair concatenation and can generate a very large result. This rule can be achieved using Transformation Rule 5.

Optimization Rule 3. If there are several joins, perform the most *restrictive* joins first. A join is more restrictive than another join if it yields a smaller result. A determination needs to be made on which join is most restrictive based on selectivities and other statistical information. Algebraically, the transformation can be achieved using Transformation Rule 4.

Optimization Rule 4. Project out useless attributes early. If an attribute of a relation is not needed for future operations, then it should be removed so that smaller input relations can be used by future operations. This can be achieved using Transformation Rule 3.

The above heuristic optimization rules can be illustrated graphically using the concept of *query tree*, which is essentially a tree representation of a relational algebra expression. In a query tree, each input relation is represented as a leaf node and each operation is represented as an internal node. The tree has bottom-up execution semantics; that is, an operation can be evaluated only if all its descendant operations have been evaluated.

Example 1.6 Consider the following SQL query involving three relations Student(SSN, Name, Age, GPA, Address), Course(Course#, Title, Credit), and Take(SSN, Course#, Grade):

```
select Name
from Student, Take, Course
where GPA > 3.5 and Title = 'Database System'
     and Student.SSN = Take.SSN and Take.Course# = Course.Course#
```

This query can be directly transformed to the following unoptimized relational algebra expression:

$$\pi_{Name}(\sigma_{GPA>3.5 \text{ and } Title='Database System' \text{ and } Student.SSN=Take.SSN \text{ and }}$$
$$\text{}_{Take.Course\#=Course.Course\#}(Student \times Take \times Course))$$

Figure 1.9(a) shows the query tree of the above relational algebra expression. First, Optimization Rule 1 is followed to push the selection conditions as far as possible down the tree. The four conditions are pushed down separately. For instance, the condition "Student.SSN = Take.SSN" is pushed over (commuted with) the first Cartesian product since it involves only attributes in the left child branch of this Cartesian product. The result of this step is shown in Figure 1.9(b). Next, Optimization Rule 2 is followed and the two Cartesian products together with the selection conditions immediately above them are replaced by two joins. Incidentally, natural joins can be used since for each join the joining attribute is the only common attribute between the child branches. Figure 1.9(c) shows the result of this step. There are two joins in the tree. Optimization Rule 3 says that the more restrictive join should be performed first. Clearly, the join "Take.Course# = Course.Course#" is more restrictive than the join "Student.SSN = Take.SSN" since the number of students satisfying the condition "GPA > 3.5" is likely to be much greater than the number of courses satisfying the condition "Title = 'Database System' ". Therefore, the join "Take.Course# = Course.Course#" should be performed first. The new query tree after the change is shown in Figure 1.9(d). Finally, we apply Optimization Rule 4 and see whether any useless attributes can be projected out early. Consider the attributes from Course. After the selection, only Course# is needed for a later join. Therefore, other attributes can be projected out. Other relations can be considered similarly. Figure 1.9(e) shows the final tree generated by the heuristic optimization rules.

In Figure 1.9(e), selections are performed before projections. But in practice, projections and selections on the same relation can usually be performed using the same scan of the relation. The actual execution plan generated from Figure 1.9(e) could have the following steps:

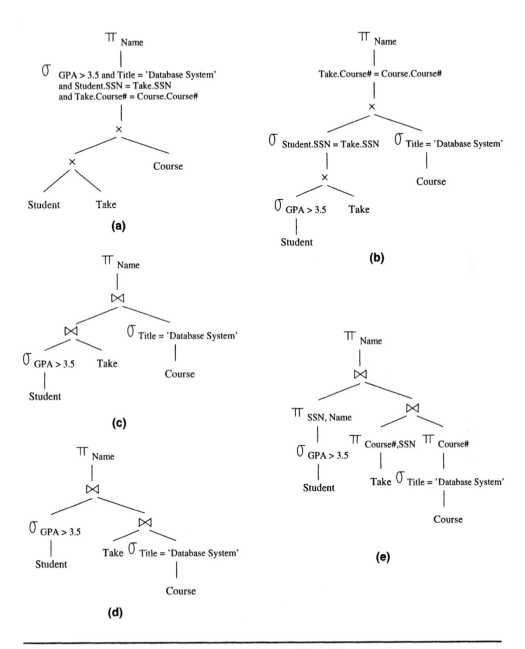

FIGURE 1.9 Illustrating the Heuristic Optimization Rules

1. Perform $\pi_{Course\#}(\sigma_{Title='Database\ System'}(Course))$. Let $T1$ denote the result.

2. Perform $\pi_{SSN,Course\#}(Take)$. Let $T2$ denote the result.

3. Perform $T1 \bowtie T2$. Let $T3$ denote the result.

4. Perform $\pi_{SSN,Name}(\sigma_{GPA>3.5}(Student))$. Let $T4$ denote the result.

5. Perform $\pi_{Name}(T3 \bowtie T4)$.

Note that the first two steps can in fact be carried out in any order because neither is dependent on the other. Similarly, step 3 and step 4 can be evaluated in reverse order. ∎

Although the algebra-based heuristic optimization approach can work reasonably well for simple queries in most cases, it may sometimes result in very bad execution plans. This is illustrated by the following example.

Example 1.7 Consider two relations *Student* and *Faculty*. Suppose a clustered index exists on attribute SSN of both relations. The following are two possible execution plans for the query "Identify those faculty members who are also students with GPA higher than 2":

Plan A. $\sigma_{GPA>2}(Student \bowtie_{Student.SSN=Faculty.SSN} Faculty)$

Plan B. $(\sigma_{GPA>2}(Student)) \bowtie_{Student.SSN=Faculty.SSN} Faculty$

Plan B will be chosen by the above heuristic optimization method (Optimization Rule 1: Perform selections as early as possible). However, Plan A is likely to be much better than Plan B if there is no index on GPA of *Student*. This is because (1) $\sigma_{GPA>2}(Student)$ is an expensive operation (relation *Student* is large and there is no index on GPA) with little benefit (i.e., the relation cannot be reduced much as a vast majority of students have a GPA higher than 2) and because (2) the join can be carried out efficiently by nested loop join using the index on SSN of Student with the much smaller Faculty relation as the outer relation (note that performing the selection first cannot improve the efficiency of the join). As the result of the join is likely to be very small, the selection will be very cheap to perform after the join as in Plan A. ∎

1.5.3 Cost Estimation-Based Optimization

The basic idea of this approach can be described as follows. For each query, enumerate all possible execution plans. For each execution plan, estimate the cost of the execution plan. Finally, choose the execution plan with the lowest estimated cost.

Clearly, if the cost of every execution plan can be estimated accurately, then an optimal plan can eventually be found. This is the main appeal of this approach. Two difficulties with this approach are as follows:

1. There may be too many possible execution plans to enumerate. In general, the number of possible execution plans is an exponential function of the number of relations referenced in a query.

2. It may be difficult to estimate the cost of each execution plan accurately. In Section 1.4, we illustrated how to estimate the cost (CPU cost and I/O cost) for several operations. In a more complex execution plan, the result of an operation, say Op1, may be used as input to another operation, say Op2. To estimate the cost of Op2, it is necessary to estimate the size of the result of Op1. For example, to estimate the cost of $(R \bowtie S) \bowtie T$, we need the following. (a) Estimate the cost of $(R \bowtie S)$. Let W denote the result of $(R \bowtie S)$. (b) Estimate the size of W. (c) Estimate the cost of $(W \bowtie T)$. The estimated total cost is the sum of the estimated costs obtained in steps (a) and (c). The most difficult part in accurately estimating the cost of an execution plan is to accurately estimate the sizes of intermediate results.

A common approach for dealing with the first difficulty is to enumerate only a subset of all possible execution plans such as considering only left deep tree plans. An example left deep tree plan for joining five relations R_1, R_2, R_3, R_4, and R_5 is $((((R_1 \bowtie R_2) \bowtie R_3) \bowtie R_4) \bowtie R_5)$. It is so named because its query tree goes left deep. Some of the issues will be revisited in more detail in later chapters of the book. More discussions also can be found from the references listed at the end of the chapter.

For the rest of this section, we briefly discuss techniques for estimating the result size of the three operations—selection, projection, and join.

Selection $\sigma_C(R)$. Let $S_C(R)$ denote the selectivity of the condition C on the relation R. Then the number of tuples in $\sigma_C(R)$ is estimated to be $n \cdot S_C(R)$, where n is the number of tuples in R, and the size of $\sigma_C(R)$ in pages is estimated to be $N \cdot S_C(R)$, where N is the size of R in pages.

Clearly, the key to ensure that the above estimation is accurate is to have an accurate estimation of the selectivity. When the condition C is a *simple condition* of the form "A *op* a", the selectivity depends largely on the distribution of the values of A in R. A common assumption is that the distribution is uniform. In this case, selectivities can be derived straightforwardly. If the actual distribution deviates from the assumed distribution severely, then the estimation will not be accurate. Sometimes, the selectivity can also be derived from the characteristics of the attribute A. For example, if A is a key, then $S_{A=a}(R)$ can be estimated as $1/n$. When C is a conjunction or disjunction of several simple conditions, then the selectivity also depends on the dependencies among the involved attributes. For example, if the condition is "A *op* a and B *op* b" and the two attributes A and B are independent, then the selectivity can be estimated as $S_{A \ op \ a}(R) \cdot S_{B \ op \ b}(R)$.

Projection $\pi_{A_1,...,A_t}(R)$. We consider the case when duplicates are removed. In general, it is extremely difficult to estimate the result size of a projection. Several special cases exist in which the estimation can be done reasonably accurately.

Case 1. $\{A_1, \ldots, A_t\}$ forms a superkey. In this case, no duplicate is possible. Therefore, the number of tuples in $\pi_{A_1,...,A_t}(R)$ is still n and the size of $\pi_{A_1,...,A_t}(R)$ in pages is

$$\frac{n \cdot \left(\sum_{i=1}^{t} \text{length}(A_i)\right)}{PageSize}$$

where $\text{length}(A_i)$ denotes the number of bytes of the values of A_i.

Case 2. $t = 1$; i.e., the result contains only one attribute. In this case, the number of tuples in the result is the number of distinct A-values in R and the size of the result in pages is

$$\frac{\text{dist}(A_1) \cdot \text{length}(A_1)}{PageSize}$$

Case 3. One of the attributes, say A_j, $1 \leq j \leq t$, *functionally determines* other attributes. In this case, the number of tuples in the result is $\text{dist}(A_j)$ and the size of the result in pages is

$$\frac{\text{dist}(A_j) \cdot \left(\sum_{i=1}^{t} \text{length}(A_i)\right)}{PageSize}$$

Case 4. All A_i's are independent. In this case, the number of tuples in the result can be estimated easily. For example, when $t = 2$, the number is

$$n \cdot \left(\frac{\text{dist}(A_1)}{n} + \frac{\text{dist}(A_2)}{n} - \frac{\text{dist}(A_1)}{n} \cdot \frac{\text{dist}(A_2)}{n}\right)$$

$$= \text{dist}(A_1) + \text{dist}(A_2) - \frac{\text{dist}(A_1) \cdot \text{dist}(A_2)}{n}$$

After the number of tuples is estimated, the size also can be estimated easily since each tuple in the result has length $\sum_{i=1}^{t} \text{length}(A_i)$.

Join $R \bowtie_{R.A \ op \ S.B} S$. We consider the case when op is $=$. If A and B are arbitrary attributes of R and S, then estimating the number of tuples in the result of the join is very difficult. Fortunately, most joins in practice are between a foreign key and the referenced key. For this most frequently encountered case, the estimation can be reasonably made. Suppose A is the primary key of R, and B is a foreign key of S that references A. Then the number of tuples in the result of the join is m—the number of tuples of S if there is no null value under B. This is because every tuple of S will join with exactly one tuple of R. In this case, the size of the result in pages is

$$\frac{m \cdot (\text{length}(R) + \text{length}(S))}{PageSize}$$

When null values exist in B, those tuples in S that have null values under B cannot join with tuples in R. As a result, the number of tuples in the result of the join will be less than m. In this case, m can be used as an approximation for the number of tuples in the result. One complication is that often R and S are not the *base relations*; i.e., R and S could be intermediate results with selections having been performed. In this case, it can no longer be guaranteed that every tuple of S with a non-null B-value will match some tuple of R although it is still true that every tuple of S can join with at most one tuple of R. In this case, the number of tuples in the result can be estimated to be $m' \cdot r$, where m' is number of tuples in S after the selection and r is the ratio of the number of tuples in R after the selection over that in R before the selection.

How to accurately estimate the sizes of intermediate results has been studied extensively in the literature. The methods proposed can be roughly classified into three categories, and they are (1) *sampling methods*, which estimate the sizes based on the information collected from a small fraction of instances from the relations; (2) *histogram methods*, which use prestored detailed information about the relations to estimate the sizes; and (3) *parametric methods*, which use analytical and/or statistical techniques for size estimation. Parametric methods typically make assumptions about the distribution of data values (e.g., uniform distribution) and about the correlation between the values of different attributes (e.g., independent). These assumptions may be inaccurate, affecting the effectiveness of this type of method. Nevertheless, parametric methods are widely used in commercial database systems. Histogram methods need to store and maintain detailed statistics about the data in the database. Even though maintaining these statistics incurs additional overhead in terms of both space and computation, it is practically manageable. Histogram methods are also widely used in commercial database systems. Sampling methods do not require any assumptions about data distribution nor the storage of any detailed statistics in advance. Sampling is performed based on the current data instances. Sampling methods have been shown to be quite accurate in estimation. However, the cost of this type of method is substantially higher than that of the other two methods. Details of these methods can be found from the references provided at the end of the chapter.

Exercises

1.1 Given the following two relations R and S:

A	B	C	D
a1	b1	c1	d1
a2	b2	c2	d2
a3	b3	c2	d3
a1	b1	c2	d3

R

C	D	E	F
c1	d1	e1	f1
c2	d3	e1	f2
c4	d5	e3	f3

S

compute **(a)** $\pi_{A,B}(\sigma_{B=b1}(R))$; **(b)** $R \times S$; **(c)** $R \bowtie_{R.C=S.C} S$; **(d)** $R \bowtie S$; **(e)** $R \div \pi_{C,D}(\sigma_{E=e1}(S))$.

1.2 Let R and S be two relations. Express each of the following relational algebra expressions in terms of the other relational algebra operators introduced in Section 1.1.2.

(a) $R \cap S$. In this case, R and S are assumed to be union compatible.

(b) $R \bowtie_C S$, where C is a join condition.

(c) $R \div S$. In this case, R is assumed to contain all attributes of S.

1.3 Express relational algebra operators *selection*, *projection*, and different variations of *join* in SQL format.

1.4 Suppose the maximum number of pointers allowed for each node in a B$^+$ tree is three. Draw a new B$^+$ tree resulted from the insertion of 26, 31, and 35 into the B$^+$ tree in Figure 1.6.

1.5 Design a new hash function for Example 1.4 such that the index entries can be distributed more evenly in the hash table; i.e., every bucket contains some entry and no overflow bucket is needed.

1.6 Let A be an attribute of relation R. Assume that the values of A in R satisfy the uniform distribution. Suppose dist(A), min(A), and max(A) are the number of distinct values, the minimum value, and the maximum value of A in R. Derive the selectivity for each of the following predicate conditions: **(a)** $A < a$; **(b)** $A \leq a$; **(c)** $a \leq A \leq b$, where a and b are constants in the domain of A.

1.7 Show that Expression (1.2) reaches the minimum when $K1 = \min\{N, K - 1\}$.

1.8 Show that when the ceiling is ignored, the minimum reached by Expression (1.2) is greater than or equal to the minimum reached by Expression (1.3).

1.9 Show that when the ceilings are ignored, Expression (1.4) reaches the minimum when $K1 = K2 = K/2$.

1.10 Let R and S be two relations with sizes 100 pages and 20 pages, respectively. Suppose a memory buffer of 10 pages is available for performing join $R \bowtie S$ (output buffer page(s) are excluded). Suppose nested loop join algorithm will be used to evaluate the join.

    (a) What is the buffer allocation for each relation in order to minimize the number of I/O pages? With this buffer allocation, what is the number of I/O pages and what is the number of I/O operations?

    (b) What is the buffer allocation for each relation in order to minimize the number of I/O operations? With this buffer allocation, what is the number of I/O pages and what is the number of I/O operations?

1.11 When the second step of the sort merge join algorithm, namely merge join, is performed, only tuples from the two operand relations that are in the memory buffer can be directly compared. Suppose the available memory buffer is K pages and the sizes of the two relations are M and N pages ($M \leq N$), respectively. Discuss how to allocate the memory buffer to the two relations in order to minimize the number of I/O operations initiated.

1.12 Consider join $R \bowtie S$. Suppose the available memory buffer is K pages and the sizes of the two relations are M and N pages ($M \leq N$), respectively. Show that if $K \geq \sqrt{N}$ and we ignore the buffer requirement for outputting join result, then two scans of each relation are sufficient to process the join using the sort merge join algorithm. (Hint: The first scan is used to read each relation and generate sorted runs on disk. The second scan of each relation is used to perform the merge join. See Reference [327].)

1.13 The hybrid hash join requires relations to be partitioned into multiple fragments so that the hash table for each fragment of the smaller relation, say S, can fit into the memory buffer. Suppose the size of the available memory buffer is K, the size of

S is M, and the size of the larger relation is N, all in pages. Suppose further that the partitioning method used can generate fragments of the same size except for the fragment whose tuples are to be used to build a hash table immediately. Suppose the size of the hash table for a fragment of size X is $c \cdot X$, where c is a small constant. Determine the minimum number of fragments that must be partitioned from S in order for the hash table for each fragment of S to fit into the memory buffer. (Hint: If F fragments are to be generated, then $F - 1$ buffer pages are needed for outputting the $F - 1$ fragments that are to be written to secondary storage. As a result, the fragment whose tuples will be used immediately to build a hash table cannot use all the memory buffer.)

1.14 Suppose the notations in Exercise 1.13 are used. Analyze the I/O cost for hybrid hash join.

1.15 Consider the following three relations:

Supplier(Supp#, Name, City, Specialty)
Project(Proj#, Name, City, Budget)
Order(Supp#, Proj#, Part_name, Quantity, Cost)

Apply the heuristic optimization rules discussed in Section 1.5.2 to find an efficient execution plan for the following SQL query. It is assumed that there are many more suppliers in New York City than there are projects with budgets over $10 million. Draw the corresponding query tree after each rule is applied.

```
select Supplier.Name, Project.Name
from Supplier, Order, Project
where Supplier.City = 'New York City' and Project.Budget > 10000000
    and Supplier.Supp# = Order.Supp# and Order.Proj# = Project.Proj#
```

1.16 Suppose three different methods can be used to process each join. How many execution plans exist for $R_1 \bowtie R_2 \bowtie R_3 \bowtie R_4 \bowtie R_5$?

1.17 Let $R(A, B, C)$, $S(C, D, E)$, and $T(E, F, G)$ be three relations such that attribute C of R is a foreign key referencing the primary key C of S and attribute E of S is a foreign key referencing the primary key E of T. Assume that there are no null values in these relations. Suppose R has 200 tuples, S has 500 tuples, and T has 100 tuples. Estimate the number of tuples in the result of $R \bowtie S \bowtie T$.

1.18 Consider join $R \bowtie_A S$. Assume that the values of A in both R and S satisfy uniform distribution, and the two attributes, $R.A$ and $S.A$, are independent. Estimate the number of tuples in the result of the join. (Hint: Given the number of distinct values of each of the two relations on A, estimate the probability that a value in attribute A is common to both relations.)

Bibliographic Notes

Processing and optimization of relational queries is one of the most researched areas in relational database systems. Most database textbooks have one or more chapters dealing with indexing and query optimization techniques [93, 114, 211, 282, 367, 369]. An early survey on query optimization techniques can be found in [193]. A recent survey on query processing can be found in [144].

A study on managing multilevel storage can be found in [347]. B^+ tree is discussed in [23, 84, 210]. Hashing is extensively discussed in [210]. Extensible hashing is discussed in [116, 236], and dynamic hashing is discussed in [223].

Optimization of relational algebra expressions is discussed in [159, 267, 338]. More detailed presentation and discussion on the transformation rules of relational algebra expressions and the algebra-based optimization technique can be found in [367]. Reference [381] discusses a query optimization strategy for the INGRES system. Cost estimation–based optimization is discussed in [12, 45, 324]. Nested loop join is first discussed in [288, 289]. Combining nested loop with index on the joining attribute of the inner relation is from [149]. Extending the nested loop join to page based is discussed in [200]. Rocking scan is also from that paper. That allocating equal buffer pages to both operand relations minimizes the number of I/O operations is from [158]. Sort merge join is first discussed in [37]. Discussion on hybrid hash join can be found in [105]. Join processing with large memories is discussed in [327]. A recent survey on join processing techniques can be found in [268]. Optimization of SPJ queries (i.e., queries involving only selection, projection, and join) is discussed in [394]. The optimization of conjunctive queries is discussed in [62]. Transformation of nested queries to unnested queries is discussed in [201].

There are many studies on estimating the selectivities and the sizes of intermediate results. Sampling techniques can be found in [131, 157, 172, 171, 234, 235]. Various histogram methods are discussed in [76, 185, 186, 273, 292, 295]. Discussions on parametric methods can be found in [75, 76, 250, 269, 324].

Query Processing in Object-Oriented Database Systems

Object-oriented database (OODB) systems, hailed by many as next-generation database systems, have become a reality. During the past several years, a number of commercial OODB systems, such as O_2 and ObjectStore, have entered the market. The object-oriented data model is more expressive than the relational data model, and as a result, it has a greater potential to be used in more applications. However, being more expressive alone is not sufficient to make OODB technology succeed in the market. To be successful, OODB systems must also perform well. One of the key factors for achieving good performance is the development of a good query processor. As a matter of fact, many attribute the success of the relational database technology to the sophisticated query processors of relational database systems. In this chapter, we discuss techniques for processing OODB queries.

An OODB system is a database developed from object-oriented concepts, which originated with object-oriented programming languages, such as SmallTalk. It is different from a relational database system because it incorporates all core object-oriented concepts, such as *object-identity*, *encapsulation*, and *inheritance*, whereas a relational database system does not. It differs from an object-oriented programming language because it has all key features of a database system, such as *persistent data, transaction management, concurrency control*, and *ad hoc query language*, whereas an object-oriented programming language does not have these features.

Before we can discuss OODB query optimization, we need to have a reasonable understanding of the basic concepts in the object-oriented data model and OODB query language.

Note that unlike the relational data model and query language, which follow ANSI and ISO standards, there are no such standards for the object-oriented data model and query language. Nevertheless, several industry consortia, notably the Object Database Management Group (ODMG) and the Object Management Group (OMG), have proposed standards for the object-oriented data model and query language. Although these standards are not officially endorsed by ANSI or ISO, they give us a good idea of what a basic object-oriented data model and an OODB query language would look like. In the first two sections of this chapter, we introduce the key concepts and constructs of the object-oriented data model and query language based primarily on the standards proposed by ODMG (i.e., ODMG-93). However, our presentation will be informal, so that jargon and lengthy definitions are avoided.

2.1 Object-Oriented Data Model

An object can be simple, such as an integer, a real number, a character string, or a Boolean value—or complex, such as an airplane, a person, or an organization. Complex objects are constructed from simpler objects using constructors such as *tuple, set, bag* (a multiset, or a set that permits duplicate elements), *list* (in which the order of elements is significant), and *array*. Each complex object in the database has a system-generated and system-wide unique *object-identifier* (OID). And each object has a structural aspect and a behavioral aspect. The structural aspect describes the organization of the object's data. It contains a set of *attributes*, and each attribute has a domain type that specifies the kind of values the attribute takes. The behavioral aspect of an object describes how its data can be acted upon. The behavior of an object is defined by a set of *methods*. Each method has a *signature*, which specifies the name of the method, the arguments and their types, and the result type of the method, and a *body*, which contains the implementation code of the method. Strictly speaking, the values of an object can be accessed only through the use of methods defined upon the object. This is known as *encapsulation*. However, in practice, due to performance and other considerations, such a restriction is often compromised. A common practice is to allow the values of an object to be retrieved without using methods, especially when the retrieval is done in an interactive mode. Modification of the values of objects, on the other hand, is allowed only through the use of methods.

To avoid the tedium of defining each and every individual object, objects with the same *characteristics* (i.e., attributes, relationships, and methods—we will define *relationships* shortly) are grouped into a *class* and are defined collectively. The following is an example of a class definition:

```
class Employees
type tuple (SSN: string,
            Name: string,
            Title: string,
            Address: tuple (Streetno: integer,
                            Street: string,
                            City: string,
                            State: string,
                            Zipcode: integer),
```

```
            Age: integer,
            Salary: real,
            Hobby: set(string),
            Project: Projects)
method increase_salary(amount: real),
       number_of_hobbies(): integer
```

In the above example, the class *Employees* has eight attributes organized into tuple format. Among the eight, the attribute *Address* in turn has five attributes of its own, which are also organized into tuple format. Attribute *Hobby* is a set attribute, indicating that an employee may have a number of hobbies. Attribute *Project* will be discussed in the next paragraph. This class also has two methods, and their signatures are defined within the class definition. The name of the first method is *increase_salary*; it has one argument, *amount*, with type *real*. Each method has an implicit (hidden) parameter, usually called *self*, with type being the class in which the method is defined. This parameter refers to the object for which the method is invoked. The first method allows a user to increase the salary of employee objects, and the second method can count the number of hobbies of any employee. The bodies of the methods are not shown here.

Relationships may exist between the objects of different classes. For example, employees may participate in projects and projects may be participated in by employees. To represent the relationship between employee objects of class *Employees* and project objects of class *Projects*, a pair of matching declarations will be used in the definitions of the two classes. For example, to declare the one-to-many relationship between project objects and employee objects (i.e., each employee may participate in at most one project but each project may be participated in by a set of employees), an attribute *Project* with the class *Projects* as its type is defined in class *Employees* (see the definition of *Employees* above) and an attribute *Participants* with type *set(Employees)* is defined in class *Projects*. One-to-one and many-to-many relationships are also supported by the ODMG-93 model. However, *n*-ary relationships when $n > 2$ are not supported by the ODMG-93 model. Physically, for each employee, the OID of the project participated in by the employee will be the value of attribute *Project*, and for each project, the set of the OIDs of the employees who participate in the project will be the value of *Participants*. In other words, these OIDs establish the relationships between employee objects and project objects. In addition, OIDs allow the traversal from objects of one class to objects of another class. As such, attributes *Project* and *Participants* are called *traversal paths*. Conceptually, a class definition can be treated as a user-defined type. Therefore, a traversal path can be considered as a special kind of attribute whose domain types are class definitions and whose values are OIDs. In fact, traversal paths are better known as *complex attributes* in the literature; we adopt this term in this book. In addition to one-to-one, one-to-many, and many-to-many relationships, numerous other semantic relationships, such as the *part-of* relationship, can be represented by complex attributes. Through complex attributes, links are established to connect objects of different classes. The hierarchy created by these links is known as the *composition hierarchy*.[1]

---

[1] Strictly speaking, it is a general graph rather than a hierarchy.

The set of all instances (or objects) of a class is called the *extent* of the class. Strictly speaking, the name of a class should not be used to represent the extent of the class since the extent of a class is not always maintained by the database application. However, for simplicity of presentation, we will use the name of a class to denote its extent when no confusion is possible.

Classes are organized into a *class hierarchy*. Saying class C2 is a subclass of class C1, or equivalently, saying class C1 is a superclass of class C2, has two meanings: (1) the set of characteristics (i.e., attributes, including complex attributes, and methods) of C1 is a subset of the set of characteristics of C2, and (2) the set of objects in C2 is a subset of the objects in C1. Semantically, a subclass is a specialization of its superclass. As such, a subclass must have all the characteristics its superclass has. But a subclass may have additional characteristics. Further, because of the specialization, each object in a subclass must also be an object in its superclass. For example, since an employee is a special type of person, each employee must be a person and have all properties that a person has. Hence, we can define class *Employees* as a subclass of class *Person*. An important advantage of the class hierarchy is providing a framework for subclasses to reuse the attribute and method definitions as well as the implementations of the methods of the superclasses. This is achieved through the *inheritance* mechanism—each subclass inherits all the characteristics defined for its superclass. Because of the inheritance, attributes and methods that have already been defined on a superclass need not be defined when a subclass is created. For example, to define a subclass *Managers* for class *Employees*, only attributes and methods that are needed for *Managers* but not for *Employees* have to be defined.

```
class Managers inherit Employees
type tuple (Office: string,
            Budget: real)
method change_budget(amount: real)
```

In the above definition, the key word *inherit* is used to establish the relationship that *Managers* is a subclass of *Employees*. As a result of this definition, *Managers* has a total of ten attributes, of which eight are inherited from *Employees*, and three methods, of which two are inherited from *Employees*. A subclass may override the definition of a characteristic inherited from its superclass by redefining the characteristic. For example, suppose that the method *increase_salary( )* in *Employees* is implemented as "salary = salary + amount": that is, when the method is applied to an employee, the salary of the employee will be increased by the specified amount. Suppose we want managers' salaries to be increased in a different way, say double the specified amount. Namely, we want a new implementation (i.e., "salary = salary + 2 · amount") of the method for manager objects. To achieve this, we can redefine the method by simply adding "increase_salary(amount: real)" as a method in the definition of class *Managers* and by associating a new implementation body with the new definition of the method. In this way, the same method *increase_salary( )* has two different implementations associated with it. When the method is applied to an object, the system decides which implementation to invoke based on the type (*Employees* or *Managers*) of the object. The ability to apply a single method, with different implementations, to objects of different types is called *polymorphism*. By allowing polymorphism, the name of a method can be chosen based on its functionality rather than on which objects it can operate. For example, if polymorphism is not supported, then we may have to use *increase_salary_for_employee*( ) for employee objects and *increase_salary_for_manager*( ) for manager objects. The advantages for using polymorphism include (1) the names of the methods will be easier to remember and (2) the code of application programs can be simplified, because the need for checking when a method should be used can be reduced. For example, let O be a set of heterogeneous objects containing both employee objects and manager objects, and suppose we want to increase the salary for every object in O. With polymorphism, this can easily be programmed as "for each o in O, o.increase_salary(amount)". Without polymorphism, an *if-statement* would have to be used to detect different types of objects, so that the correct method can be applied, requiring more effort from the programmer. The price we pay for having polymorphism is that the system will not always be able to decide which implementation of a method should be used before seeing an object. In other words, the existence of polymorphism dictates that the binding between the signature and a body of a method referenced in a query can be determined not at compile time but rather at run time. This is called *late-binding*.

Every class has at least one superclass. If a class does not have a user-defined superclass, then it is treated as a subclass of a system-defined class *Object*. A class may have multiple subclasses. A class can also have multiple superclasses. If a class has multiple superclasses, then it will inherit characteristics from multiple classes. This is called *multiple inheritance*. One problem associated with multiple inheritance is the *inheritance conflict*, which arises when a subclass inherits a characteristic with the same name but different definitions (e.g., different domain types for attribute names and different signatures for methods) or the same name and the same definition but different semantics, from two or more superclasses. The standard method for resolving inheritance conflict is to inherit all conflicting characteristics accompanied with proper *renaming*. For example, consider a class *Teaching_Assistants* that has two superclasses *Employees* and *Graduate_Students*. Suppose both *Employees* and *Graduate_Students* have attribute *Performance_Ranking* with domain type *string*. The attribute has the same name and same definition but different semantics in the two classes. In class *Graduate_Students*, it is used to measure the academic performance of a graduate student. In class *Employees*, it is used to measure the work performance of an employee. It is possible that an outstanding student is only an average teaching assistant when considered as an employee. For this example, one could use the following two statements in the definition of *Teaching_Assistants* to allow inheriting both *Performance_Ranking*s:

Performance_Ranking from class Graduate_Students as Graduate_Student_Ranking,
Performance_Ranking from class Employees as Employee_Ranking

As a result, each teaching_assistant object will have two rankings, one for academic performance and the other for work performance.

A general object-oriented database (OODB) schema can be best described as a *class composition hierarchy* since it typically contains both the class hierarchy and the composition hierarchy. An OODB schema can often be represented graphically for easy understanding. An OODB schema for a simplified university database is shown in Figure 2.1. In the figure, a thin arrow from a complex attribute to a class indicates that the class is used as the domain type of the attribute, and a thick arrow from class C2 to class C1 indicates that C2 is a subclass of C1. All set attributes are marked by *. For example, the star (*) on attribute *Course* indicates that it is a set attribute of *Student*. Methods are not shown in the figure.

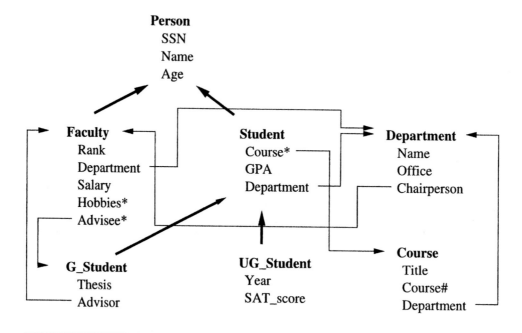

FIGURE 2.1   **An Example OODB Schema**

Sample instances of five classes in Figure 2.1, namely *Student, G_Student, UG_Student, Department*, and *Faculty*, are shown in Figure 2.2. These instances will be used throughout this chapter for illustration. Note that if a class C has subclasses, then only objects that belong to C—but not one of its subclasses—are stored in C.

2.2 OQL: An Object-Oriented Query Language

Most object-oriented database systems provide a declarative database query language. Although object-oriented databases can often be accessed through code written in an object-oriented programming language such as C++, the use of a query language is considered very important for writing interactive ad hoc queries and for simplifying the C++ code of application programs. Because of the success and popularity of SQL relational query language, most proposed object-oriented database query languages have adopted a syntax similar to that of SQL. *OQL* is an OODB query language proposed in ODMG-93. The latest version of OQL, as in ODMG-93 (Release 1.2), is a superset of SQL92. Although OQL is not limited to select-from-where three-clause syntax, most nontrivial OQL queries have the above three clauses. We will limit ourselves to this type of query only. The *select*-clause specifies the attributes whose values are to be retrieved as well as the structure into which the retrieved values are to be organized. The *from*-clause specifies the classes from which data are to be retrieved or used to evaluate the conditions of the query. The *where*-clause specifies the conditions that must be satisfied by the retrieved result. For example, the following is an OQL query that can be used

OID	SSN	Name	Age	Course	GPA	Department
s1	123456789	John	34	{c1, c3, c4}	3.2	d1
s2	234567891	Ketty	27	{c2, c3, c5}	2.8	d1
s3	345678912	Wang	19	{c3, c6}	3.5	d2

Student

OID	SSN	Name	Age	Course	GPA	Department	Thesis	Advisor
g1	456789123	Young	24	{c11, c15}	3.5	d1	Title1	f1
g2	567891234	Wang	32	{c17}	3.8	d2	Title2	f2
g3	678912345	Mary	27	{c12, c15}	3.5	d1	Title3	f1

G_Student

OID	SSN	Name	Age	Course	GPA	Department	Year	SAT_score
u1	789123456	Julie	19	{c1, c5, c9}	3.5	d2	2	1268
u2	891234567	Bob	20	{c4, c7, c8}	3.2	d1	2	1198

UG_Student

OID	Name	Office	Chairperson
d1	Biology	B-110	f1
d2	Mathematics	N-210	f3

Department

OID	SSN	Name	Age	Rank	Department	Salary	Advisee
f1	912345678	Kent	45	Professor	d1	63k	{g1,g3}
f2	112345678	Maria	39	Assoc. Prof.	d2	45k	{g2}
f3	123456781	Lisa	47	Professor	d2	65k	{ }

Faculty

FIGURE 2.2 **Instances of Five Classes**

to find the names of all undergraduate students whose GPA is higher than 3.5. All the queries in this section are based on the OODB schema in Figure 2.1 unless the otherwise is explicitly stated.

```
select s.Name
from UG_Student s
where s.GPA > 3.5
```

where *s* is a *class instance variable* of *UG_Student*, similar to a *relation tuple variable* in a relational query. The result of the query is a *bag* of names. To remove duplicate names, *select distinct* can be used to replace *select*. By doing so, the result of the query becomes a *set* of names. The above OODB query is very much like a relational query. But in general, an OODB query can differ substantially from a typical relational query because of the differences between the relational data model and the object-oriented data model. In the following, we will use examples to illustrate some of the major query constructs that can appear in an OODB query but not in a relational query.

2.2.1 Path Expressions

The domain type of an attribute of a class can be another class. This provides a means to traverse from the objects of one class to the objects of another class via the composition links. In OODB query language, dot notation (.) is used to specify such traversals. For example, the following query can be used to find the names of all undergraduate students who major in a department chaired by Tom:

```
select s.Name
from UG_Student s
where s.Department.Chairperson.Name = 'Tom'
```

For a given undergraduate student object *s*, the construct *s.Department* identifies the department object *d* in which *s* majors. The construct *s.Department.Chairperson* then allows *s* to traverse first to *d* and then to the chairperson object *c* of *d* through *d*. Finally, *s.Department. Chairperson.Name* identifies the name of *c*. Constructs such as *s.Department.Chairperson. Name* are known as *path expressions*. A typical path expression starts with the name of a class (or a variable referencing the class) followed by a sequence of complex attributes connected by a dot and ends with either a complex attribute or a regular attribute. If the left of a dot is a class (or a variable referencing the class), then the right of the dot is an attribute of the class. If the left of a dot is an attribute, then it must be a complex attribute whose domain class contains the attribute on the right of the dot. Since each object has an OID, we can imagine there is a system-defined OID attribute for each class. Then a path expression can be considered as an abbreviated notation for expressing a sequence of joins. For example, the where-clause in the above query is equivalent to "s.Department = Department.OID and Department.Chairperson = Faculty.OID and Faculty.Name = 'Tom'", where "s.Department = Department.OID" is a join between the class *UG_Student* and the class *Department* and "Department.Chairperson = Faculty.OID" is a join between the class *Department* and the class *Faculty*. The joins hidden in a path expression are *implicit joins*. Explicit joins are also permitted in OQL query language.

2.2.2 Set Attributes and Quantifiers

Predicates in an OODB query can be formed using set attributes and membership operator *in*. For example, the following query can be used to find the name of each faculty member who likes to play golf:

```
select f.Name
from Faculty f
where 'golf' in f.Hobbies
```

The above query can also be expressed using the existential quantifier *some* as follows:

```
select f.Name
from Faculty f
where f.some Hobbies = 'golf'
```

The universal quantifier *all* can be applied to set attributes to form predicates.[2] It is possible that one or more attributes on a path expression are set attributes. A path expression containing no set attribute is called *single-valued*. Otherwise, it is called *set-valued*. Quantifiers can also be in set-valued path expressions. For example, finding the names of all undergraduate students who take at least one course offered by the computer science department can be expressed as follows:

```
select s.Name
from UG_Student s
where s.some Course.Department.Name = 'computer science'
```

Similarly, the query to find the names of all undergraduate students such that all courses they take are offered by the computer science department can be obtained by replacing *some* by *all* in the above query. A path expression may have more than one quantifier with an arbitrary combination of *all* and *some*. For instance, the query to find the names of all faculty members who have at least one student such that all courses they take are offered by the computer science department can be expressed as follows:

```
select f.Name
from Faculty f
where f.some Advisee.all Course.Department.Name = 'computer science'
```

2.2.3　Reference Variables

We can bind a variable to the objects of a class through a path expression. For example, the following query can be used to find the names of those graduate students who are older than their advisors:

```
select s.Name
from G_Student s, s.Advisor f
where s.Age > f.Age
```

In this query, f is a variable that references the faculty objects through graduate student objects. Note that "s.Advisor f" is different from "Faculty f". For each student s, the former stands for the faculty who is the advisor of s, and the latter can be any faculty in the class. Variables that specify a path expression that ends with a complex attribute, like f as defined in "s.Advisor f", are called *reference variables*. Reference variables can be considered as a shorthand for the path expressions themselves. For example, the above query is equivalent to the following query:

---

[2]In OQL, *exists* and *forall* are used for the existential and universal quantifiers, respectively. The syntax for their usage differs from that for *some* and *all* as presented in this book. *some* and *all* as well as their usage as presented in this book are from the ORION system of MCC. We find ORION's syntax to be easier to understand.

```
Select s.Name
From G_Student s
Where s.Age > s.Advisor.Age
```

2.2.4 Part of a Class Hierarchy

Let C be a superclass of C_1, C_2, . . . , C_n. Since the extent of C is a superset of the extent of every C_i, $i = 1, \ldots, n$, retrieving C retrieves all objects in the class hierarchy rooted at C.[3] There may be times when we only want to retrieve objects from some but not all classes in the hierarchy rooted at C. For example, consider the class hierarchy rooted at *Student* in Figure 2.1. We may want to find the names of all nongraduate students. We may also be interested in finding the names of all students who are neither graduate nor undergraduate (e.g., students in a nondegree program). Such type of queries can be formed with the help of set operators: *union*, *difference*, and *except*. For example, the above two queries can be written as follows:

```
select s.Name
from (Student except G_Student) s
```

```
select s.Name
from (Student except (G_Student union UG_Student)) s
```

2.2.5 Reference Methods

Two types of methods can be used in an OODB query. The first type is *derived-attribute method*, which can be used to compute a value for each object in the class on which the method is applicable. For example, suppose in the OODB schema in Figure 2.1, the class *Person* has an attribute *Birthdate* rather than *Age*. If this is the case, then a method that computes the age of a person from the current date and the birthdate of the person can be defined on the class *Person*. In a query, a derived-attribute method can be used just like any attribute. The second type is *predicate method*, which returns a Boolean value for each object in the class. For example, suppose we have a method "large( ): boolean" on class *Department*, which returns true if the department is large in size, say it has more than 30 faculty members or more than 300 students, and false if the department is not large. Then the following query can be written to find the names of chairpersons of large departments.

```
select f.Name
from Department d, d.Chairperson f
where d.large( )
```

2.2.6 Structured Output

Just as the object-oriented data model allows the use of object constructors such as set, list, and tuple to construct complex objects from simple objects, OQL query language allows us

---

[3]In some OODB systems, say ORION, C* is used to represent all objects in the class hierarchy rooted at C and a plain C represents only those objects in C but not in its subclasses.

to construct complex values in the result of a query by using the same set of constructors in the select-clause. For example, the following query constructs a set of tuples with one of its attributes, CS_courses, being a complex set attribute.

```
select tuple(SSN: s.SSN, Name: s.Name,
             CS_courses: select c
                         from s.Course c
                         where c.Department.Name = 'computer science')
from UG_Student s
where s.GPA > 3
```

2.3 OODB Query Processing and Optimization

Note that OQL is a superset of SQL. Therefore, if we regard classes as relations and objects as tuples (of course, there are many significant differences between these concepts), then many OQL queries are identical to their SQL counterparts. Even path expressions, when quantifiers are absent, can be expressed in terms of simple joins. As such, it is natural that many techniques and concepts developed for processing relational queries can be reused to process OODB queries. These techniques and concepts include but are not limited to join processing, making use of fast access paths to speed up processing, and developing algebra and equivalence transformation rules to create alternative query execution plans. However, most techniques for processing relational queries need to be extended, and some new techniques need to be developed for processing and optimizing OODB queries since there are many fundamental differences between the relational and object-oriented data models, and between the relational and OODB query languages. The following summarizes some of these major differences that make query processing and optimization in OODB systems more difficult.

Different data types.   Relational query languages involve only one data type, namely, relation. Both the input and the output of relational queries are relations. In contrast, OODB query languages may involve different data types, i.e., set, bag, tuple, list, and array. Some of these types are ordered types (i.e., list and array). The input type and the output type of an OODB query may well be different. One of the consequences of this situation is the difficulty in designing an *object algebra*. Because of the difficulty, there is still no agreement on the set of algebra operators despite a large number of proposals involving object algebra. Most proposed object algebras are *many-sorted* in the sense that there is one *sort* (i.e., one set of algebra operators) for each of the data types. As a result, both the object algebra and the equivalence transformation rules are much more complicated than their relational counterparts.

Complex objects.   An object may have references to other objects. References are implemented using OIDs. Since the use of OIDs is so fundamental in OODB systems, many proposed object algebras have special operators for objects and OIDs. Traversings from object to object are expressed as path expressions in OODB queries. Path expressions are considered as a key feature in OODB queries, and the processing and optimization of them have received extensive investigations.

Class hierarchy. Class hierarchy also brings new problems to the processing of OODB queries. A query may access objects in some or all classes in a class hierarchy rooted at a class. One problem caused by this is how to create indexes that can accommodate different access requirements. Another problem is that intermediate results with heterogeneous object collections may result from accessing the class hierarchy and when a method is applied to such a heterogeneous collection, it is possible that we cannot determine which implementation of the method to use at compile time (i.e., late-binding is needed). This implies the need for run-time optimization in addition to compile-time optimization.

Methods. In addition to the aforementioned problem that can be caused by methods, another is the difficulty in estimating the cost of executing a method because they are usually written in high-level programming languages and the codes are usually hidden (or encapsulated) from the query optimizer.

Despite the above differences between relational query processing and OODB query processing, methodologies for processing relational queries can be adopted for processing OODB queries. There are basically two such methodologies, *algebra-based optimization* and *cost estimation–based optimization*. There are overlapping components between the two methodologies. Algebra-based optimization consists of primarily two steps. In the first step, the input query is expressed in an algebraic expression, which is then transformed into a semantically equivalent but more efficient expression using equivalence transformation rules. The transformation is guided by optimization rules, which by their heuristic nature are unlikely to produce a truly optimal expression. Of course, the algebra used here is an *object algebra*, and the transformation rules are also based on that object algebra. In the second step, physical characteristics of the database such as the existence of fast access paths and database statistics are taken into consideration to generate a concrete and efficient execution plan for the algebraic expression obtained in the first step. The advantages of this methodology include its extensibility and its relative easiness to implement. The main drawback is as follows. Since the search space for optimization in the second step is limited by the algebraic expression generated in the first step, there is a good possibility that the resulting execution plan is not close to an optimal plan. The cost estimation–based optimization methodology tries to combine the above two steps as follows. The equivalence transformation rules are used to systematically transform the initial algebraic expression to all reasonable (e.g., without Cartesian products) and equivalent expressions, and for each such expression, the cost of its best execution plan is estimated using the physical characteristics of the database. Eventually, the execution plan with the lowest estimated cost is selected for actual execution. The cost estimation–based approach is usually more effective than the algebra-based approach.

The rest of this section is organized as follows. In Section 2.3.1, an object algebra and some transformation rules will be introduced. In Section 2.3.2, we present techniques for processing path expressions. A technique for processing queries involving methods will be discussed in Section 2.3.3.

2.3.1 Object Algebra and Algebraic Transformation

Despite the progress on OODB systems and many proposals of object algebra, a standard object algebra is yet to emerge. At the present, the situation is quite chaotic. Different proposals are often based on different philosophies and have different sets of algebraic operators. Some proposed object algebras are very similar to the relational algebra, whereas others are substantially different. The expressive powers of the proposed object algebras may also be different. Nevertheless, common features can be found since most proposed object algebras are modified and extended from relational algebra. As mentioned earlier, many proposed object algebras are many-sorted with one sort for each basic data type. The basic data types are from the underlying object-oriented data model, and they are the set, bag, tuple, list, and array. A number of proposals treat OIDs as a special basic data type and define a set of algebra operators (i.e., one sort) for OIDs. The object algebra presented in this subsection is derived from several proposed object algebras.

Algebra Operators

The operators of algebra are divided into six sorts: *object operators*, *tuple operators*, *set operators*, *bag operators*, *list operators*, and *array operators*.

Object operators. Note that each object can be represented as a triplet (oid, class_name, value), where oid is the OID of the object and class_name is the name of the class the object belongs to.[4] The value of a user-defined object is usually a tuple. For example, a course object in class Course (see Figure 2.1) can be represented as (c1, Course, (Database Systems, CS532, d1)), where (Database Systems, CS532, d1) is the value of the object with OID c1 and d1 is the OID of the department object that offers the course "Database Systems."

Following are three object operators:

- projection to OID: $\pi_O(\ )$. This operator takes an object and returns the OID of the object.

- projection to value: $\pi_V(\ )$. This operator takes an object and returns the value of the object.

- dereference operator: $\pi_D(\ )$. This operator takes an OID and returns the object having the OID.

Tuple operators. There are four tuple operators.

- tuple constructor: tuple($a_1 : v_1, \ldots, a_n : v_n$). This operator takes a number of attribute and value pairs (i.e., (a_i, v_i)'s) and returns a tuple.

- tuple projection: $\pi_{(Attrs)}(\ )$. This operator takes a tuple and returns a subtuple using the attribute names specified in *Attrs*. The difference between this operator and the relational projection is that the former takes one tuple at a time and the latter takes a set of tuples at a time.

---

[4]If the object belongs to multiple classes in the class hierarchy, then the class at the lowest level is used.

- attribute extractor: $\pi_{Attr}(\ )$. This operator takes a tuple and returns the value of the specified attribute. Note that the value of an attribute could be structured such as a set and a list.

- tuple concatenator: tuple_cat( ). This operator takes two tuples and concatenates them into a new tuple. This operator can be used to simulate Cartesian product.

Set operators. There are six set operators.

- set constructor: set( ) or { }. This operator constructs a set out of some elements.

- set union: set_union.

- set difference: set_diff.

- set selection: $\sigma^s_{\lambda s.f}(\ )$. This operator takes a set (usually, a set of objects) and returns a set (of objects) such that each element in the result set satisfies the condition specified in formula f. For example, if $A = \{2, 6, 4, 9\}$, then $\sigma^s_{\lambda s.s > 5}(A) = \{6, 9\}$. The λ-notation "λs" is used to define a variable enumerating each element in the given set. When the given set is a class, s is like a class instance variable.

- set flatten: set_flat( ). This operator takes a set of sets and returns a set obtained by taking the union of the nested sets. For example, set_flat($\{\{1, 2, 3\}, \{2, 3, 4\}, \{4, 5\}\}$) = $\{1, 2, 3, 4, 5\}$.

- set application: set_apply$_{\lambda s.e}(\ )$. This operator takes a set and applies the algebraic expression e to each element in the set. For example, let $A = \{\{1, 2, 3\}, \{2, 3, 4\}, \{4, 5\}\}$ be a set of sets. Then set_apply$_{\lambda s.A\ set\_diff\ \{3\}}(A) = \{\{1, 2\}, \{2, 4\}, \{4, 5\}\}$. The set_apply operator and the tuple projection operator (or attribute extractor) are normally used together to simulate projection on a set of tuples. For example, the query "find the names and ages of all students" can be expressed as set_apply$_{\lambda s.\pi_{(Name,Age)}(\pi_V(s))}(Student)$. The meaning of this expression is as follows. The set_apply operator takes a set of student objects as input and applies the algebra expression in the subscript to each student object. For each student object, its value (a tuple) is projected out, which is then used as input for a tuple projection to obtain the needed data.

Bag operators. There are seven bag operators and six of them have their corresponding set operators except that the bag operators permit duplicates. The seven bag operators are

- bag constructor: bag( ).

- bag union: bag_union.

- bag difference: bag_diff.

- bag selection: $\sigma^b_{\lambda s.f}(\ )$.

- bag flatten: bag_flat( ).

- bag application: bag_apply$_{\lambda s.e}(\ )$.

- set converter: bagtoset( ). This operator converts a bag to a set by removing the duplicates in the bag.

List operators. There are seven list operators, and their semantics are obvious.

- list constructor: list( ).
- first element: first( ).
- last element: last( ).
- list concatenation: list_cat( ).
- list selection: $\sigma^l_{\lambda s.f}($).
- list flatten: list_flat( ).
- list application: list_apply$_{\lambda s.e}($).

Array operators. There are five array operators.

- array constructor: array( ).
- element extractor: $\pi_i($). This operator returns the ith element of the given array.
- array projection: $\pi_{i,j}($), where $j > i$. This operator returns a subarray containing the elements between and including the ith and the jth elements of the given array.
- array concatenation: array_cat( ).
- array application: array_apply$_{\lambda s.e}($).

We described a total number of 32 operators for object algebra. For the rest of this subsection, we will focus our discussion on the first three sets of operators, namely, object operators, tuple operators, and set operators. Consequently, we can simplify set_union, set_diff, $\sigma^s_{\lambda s.f}($), set_flat( ), and set_apply$_e($) to union, diff, $\sigma_{\lambda s.f}($), flat( ), and apply$_e($), respectively. We now use examples based on the OODB schema in Figure 2.1 and the instances in Figure 2.2 to illustrate the use of these operators.

Example 2.1 Find the names of all undergraduate students whose GPA is higher than 3.3.

$$apply_{\lambda t.\pi_{Name}(\pi_V(t))}(\sigma_{\lambda s.\pi_{GPA}(\pi_V(s))>3.3}(UG\_Student))$$

This algebraic expression can be explained as follows. The selection takes a set of objects in class *UG_Student* and projects each object to its value (a tuple) from which the GPA value is obtained and compared with 3.3. The result is a set of undergraduate student objects whose GPA is higher than 3.3. Based on the instances in Figure 2.2, the result of the selection is {u1}. This set of objects is then taken as input to the *apply* operator to produce a set of names. This is carried out by first projecting each object to its value and then, from the tuple, projecting on the name attribute to obtain its value. This produces {Julie}. Note that, in general, the result of the above expression could be a bag. To ensure the result is a set, bag operator bagtoset( ) should be applied. ■

Example 2.2 Find the names of all undergraduate students who major in a department chaired by Kent.

$$apply_{\lambda s.\pi_{Name}(\pi_V(s))}(\sigma_{\lambda t.\pi_{Name}(\pi_V(\pi_D(\pi_{Chairperson}(\pi_V(\pi_D(\pi_{Department}(\pi_V(t))))))))='Kent'}(UG\_Student))$$

This example shows how to use object algebra to express the traversal of the path expression *UG_Student.Department.Chairperson.Name*. The selection takes a set of undergraduate student objects as input, and for each such object, its value is obtained by a projection; and from this value (a tuple), the OID of the department that the student majors in is obtained by $\pi_{Department}$. From this OID, the department object is then obtained by applying the dereference operator π_D. From this object, its value (a department tuple) is obtained next. From the department tuple, the OID of the chairperson object is obtained by $\pi_{Chairperson}$. From this OID, the faculty member object who is the chairperson is obtained by another π_D. From the value of the chairperson, the name of the chairperson is obtained and compared with Kent. Eventually, the result of the selection is a set of undergraduate student objects who major in a department chaired by Kent. The reader can verify that the final result of the query is {Bob}. Based on the object algebra, traversing a path expression is a sequence of obtaining the OID of the referenced object and dereferencing. The steps for obtaining the names of these students are identical to those in Example 2.1.　　∎

Example 2.3 Find the name and thesis of every graduate student who is older than his or her advisor. Using OQL, this query can be written as follows:

```
select tuple(s.Name, s.Thesis)
from G_Student s
where s.Age > s.Advisor.Age
```

An algebraic expression of this query can be written as

$$apply_{\lambda t.\,\pi_{(Name,Thesis)}(\pi_V(t))}\left(\sigma_{\lambda s.(\pi_{Age}(\pi_V(s))>\pi_{Age}(\pi_V(\pi_D(\pi_{Advisor}(\pi_V(s))))))}\right)(G\_Student))$$

This expression can be similarly explained as the expressions for previous examples. This example illustrates how to express an explicit join in object algebra. Notice the use of the parentheses in $\pi_{(Name,Thesis)}$ for obtaining the result in tuple format.　　∎

Example 2.4 Find the names of all nongraduate students. An OQL query for this request can be found in Section 2.2. The following is an algebraic expression for this query:

$$apply_{\lambda t.\,\pi_{Name}(\pi_V(t))}(apply_{\lambda u.\,\pi_D(u)}(apply_{\lambda s.\,\pi_O(s)}(Student)\;\text{diff}\;apply_{\lambda g.\,\pi_O(g)}(G\_Student)))$$

$apply_{\lambda s.\,\pi_O(s)}(Student)$ returns the set of OIDs for all students, including undergraduate students and graduate students (the set is {s1, s2, s3, g1, g2, g3, u1, u2} based on the instances in Figure 2.2), and $apply_{\lambda g.\,\pi_O(g)}(G\_Student)$ returns the set of OIDs for all graduate students (i.e., {g1, g2, g3}). The set of OIDs for all nongraduate students can then be obtained by performing a set difference between the above two sets (the result is {s1, s2, s3, u1, u2}). We then dereference each such OID to obtain all nongraduate student objects. Next the value of each of these objects is obtained by π_V. Finally, the name is extracted from each such value. The final result is {John, Ketty, Wang, Julie, Bob}.　　∎

Example 2.5 Find all name pairs of graduate and undergraduate students such that they have the same age. This query involves an arbitrary join, and the result contains data from two classes. We use the tuple concatenation operator followed by a selection to simulate the join as follows:

$$Temp = apply_{\lambda s.\,\lambda t.\,tuple\_cat(\pi_V(s)(G\_Student),\,\pi_V(t)(UG\_Student))}$$

where *Temp* saves the result of the join. The final result of the query can be obtained from this algebra expression:

$$apply_{\lambda v. \pi_{(G\_Student.Name, UG\_Student.Name)}(v)}(\sigma_{\lambda u.(\pi_{G\_Student.Age}(u) = \pi_{UG\_Student.Age}(u))}(Temp)) \quad \blacksquare$$

From the above examples, we can see that it is much harder to use an object algebra than OQL to form OODB queries. There are at least two obvious reasons for this. The first is that the object algebra is *procedural*; that is, it needs to convey both what data are desired as well as how to obtain them. In contrast, OQL as a declarative query language is *nonprocedural*; namely, an OQL query only needs to specify what data are wanted without mentioning how to get them. It is for the same reason that relational algebra is more difficult to use than SQL. The second reason is that object algebra is even more difficult to use than its relational counterpart because the former is many-sorted and the latter is one-sorted. Queries written in a many-sorted algebra need to handle and coordinate intermediate results of different types.

Algebraic Transformation

Usually, a given query can be written in different but equivalent object algebraic expressions. Different expressions may be evaluated with drastically different costs. Therefore, it is desirable in theory to generate all possible equivalent expressions for a given query so that the most efficient execution plan can eventually be found. However, in practice, because of the very large number of all possible equivalent expressions, usually only a subset of these expressions is generated, with expressions that are obviously not good not being generated. To generate different equivalent expressions, a set of equivalence-preserving transformation rules is needed. We now present a number of such rules. As we mentioned earlier, there is no standard object algebra at present. Therefore, it can be expected that the standard set of transformation rules does not exist either. All we hope to accomplish here is to present a number of transformation rules to illustrate the idea that equivalence-preserving transformation is possible based on object algebra.

In the following presentation of the transformation rules, S, $S1$, $S2$, and $S3$ are used to represent a set of elements. Again, we concentrate on the rules involving only object operators, tuple operators, and set operators.

Commutativity of selection. Multiple selections may be evaluated in any order.

$$\sigma_{\lambda t.g}(\sigma_{\lambda s.f}(S)) = \sigma_{\lambda s.f}(\sigma_{\lambda t.g}(S))$$

Cascade of selection. A set of selections in conjunctive form can be replaced by a sequence of selections and vice versa.

$$\sigma_{\lambda s.(f \wedge g \wedge \cdots \wedge h)}(S) = \sigma_{\lambda s.f}(\sigma_{\lambda t.g}(\cdots (\sigma_{\lambda u.h}(S)) \cdots))$$

Distributivity of selection and apply over union and diff. When *op* is either *union* or *diff*, we have

$$\sigma_{\lambda s.f}(S1 \ op \ S2) = \sigma_{\lambda s.f}(S1) \ op \ S2 \quad \text{if } f \text{ involves only data in } S1.$$

A more general rule is as follows:

$$\sigma_{\lambda s.(f \wedge g \wedge h)}(S1 \ op \ S2) = \sigma_{\lambda u.h}(\sigma_{\lambda s.f}(S1) \ op \ \sigma_{\lambda t.g}(S2)) \quad \text{if } f \text{ involves only data in } S1,$$
$$g \text{ involves only data in } S2, \text{ and } h \text{ involves data in both } S1 \text{ and } S2.$$

In object algebra, projection over a set of tuples is normally carried out through the use of *apply* and tuple projection (or attribute extraction). Therefore, the following rule implies the distribution of projection over *union* and *diff*:

$$apply_{\lambda s.e}(S1 \ op \ S2) = apply_{\lambda s.e}(S1) \ op \ apply_{\lambda s.e}(S2)$$

Commuting apply and selection. If the selection condition involves only attributes to be returned by the *apply* operator, then we have

$$apply_{\lambda s.e}(\sigma_{\lambda t.f}(S)) = \sigma_{\lambda t.f}(apply_{\lambda s.e}(S))$$

Clearly, commuting selection and projection constitutes a special case of this rule.

Commuting flatten and apply. Suppose S is the extent of a class and CSA is a complex set attribute of the class. Then we have the following rule:

$$flat(apply_{\lambda s.(apply_{\lambda t.e}(\pi_{CSA}(\pi_V(s))))}(S)) = apply_{\lambda t.e}(flat(apply_{\lambda s.\pi_{CSA}(\pi_V(s))}(S))) \qquad (2.1)$$

The expression on the left-hand side applies the expression e before the set of sets (obtained by π_{CSA}) is flattened into a set, whereas the expression on the right-hand side does so after the flatten operator is applied. We use an example to illustrate how to understand this rule and how to apply this rule to obtain more efficient execution plans. Consider the OODB schema in Figure 2.1. Suppose we want to find the titles of all courses that are currently taken by students. In OQL, this query can be written as follows:

```
select s.Course.Title from Student s
```

The result is a set of sets of titles, since each student may take a set of courses. The following is a possible algebraic expression for this query:

$$flat(apply_{\lambda s.(apply_{\lambda t.\pi_{Title}(\pi_V(\pi_D(t)))}(\pi_{Course}(\pi_V(s))))}(Student)) \qquad (2.2)$$

Note that the outer *apply* is applied first in this expression since variable s is used by the innermost projection. For each student object, its value is first obtained by a projection (π_V); from this value, a set of course OIDs is obtained next. This set of OIDs is then immediately taken as input by the inner *apply* operator before a power set is formed. The inner *apply* converts each set of course OIDs to a set of course titles by first obtaining an object from each OID (i.e., dereferencing), then obtaining the course tuple from the object by a projection to value, and finally obtaining the title of the course. Therefore, the final result of the outer *apply* is a set of title sets, which is then made flat by the *flatten* operator.

According to Transformation Rule (2.1), Expression (2.2) is equivalent to the following expression (note that for this particular example, the expression e in (2.1) is $\pi_{Title}(\pi_V(\pi_D(t)))$.

$$apply_{\lambda t.\pi_{Title}(\pi_V(\pi_D(t)))}(flat(apply_{\lambda s.\pi_{Course}(\pi_V(s))}(Student))) \qquad (2.3)$$

In this expression, the inner *apply* takes a set of student objects as input. For each student object, its value is first obtained by a projection to value, and the value is then used to obtain a course value. Since *Course* is a complex set attribute of *Student*, each course value is a set of course OIDs. Therefore, the result of the inner *apply* is a set of OID sets. The *flatten* operator is applied to convert the power set to a flat set of OIDs. This set of OIDs is then taken as input by the outer *apply*. For each of these OIDs, it is first dereferenced to obtain the object, then projected to its value, from which the title value is finally obtained by another projection. Intuitively, Expression (2.3) is likely to be more efficient than Expression (2.2), especially when each course is taken by many students. The reason is that Expression (2.2) needs to perform a dereference, a projection to value, and a projection to title for each course occurrence in each student (i.e., if a course is taken by 10 students, then the three operations will be performed 10 times for the course), whereas Expression (2.3) needs to perform the above three operations only once for each course.

Associativity of union.

    (S1 union S2) union S3 = S1 union (S2 union S3)

Inheritance rules for selection and apply. Recall that if *S2* is a subclass of *S1*, then the extent of *S2* is a subset of the extent of *S1*. Based on this, we have

$$\sigma_{\lambda s.f}(S1) \; union \; \sigma_{\lambda s.f}(S2) = \sigma_{\lambda s.f}(S1)$$
$$apply_{\lambda s.e}(S1) \; union \; apply_{\lambda s.e}(S2) = apply_{\lambda s.e}(S1)$$

For each of the above two rules, the expression on the right-hand side is clearly more efficient than that on the left-hand side.

Many of the algebraic transformation rules for object algebra are similar to the corresponding rules for relational algebra. This implies that some of the heuristics for optimizing relational algebra queries, such as distributing selections and projections over binary operators, can also be used for optimizing object algebra queries. Nevertheless, there are rules unique to object algebra, such as the inheritance rules and the rule that commutes *flatten* and *apply*. Therefore, new optimization heuristics for object algebra queries are possible. For example, applying the inheritance rules whenever possible (they remove unnecessary operations on the subclass and the union operation) and performing *flatten* early are likely to be good optimization heuristics for object algebra queries.

In the cost estimation–based optimization, these transformation rules can be used to derive various execution plans for the same query. The cost of each of these execution plans can then be estimated using basic cost formulas for the operators in object algebra. Thus, the plan with the lowest estimated cost can be identified.

2.3.2 Path Expression Optimization

Path expression is a simple yet powerful mechanism for specifying navigation or traversal along composition hierarchies in an OODB schema. Path expressions appear most often in the where-clause of OODB queries, although they can appear also in the select- and from-clauses.

The optimization of path expressions has received a lot of attention because path expressions are a fundamental construct for specifying OODB queries. In fact, many old prototype OODB systems allow only one class (i.e., the target class) to be queried directly, and most such queries have conditions that are only in conjunctive form and are along path expressions starting with the target class.

Although it is possible to use object algebra to help generate different execution plans to process path expressions, we choose to state the problem and solutions at an intuitive level in this subsection. To focus on the essentials, we assume that path expressions appear only in the where-clause of OODB queries, and they are in conjunctive form. Explicit joins are assumed not to appear in the where-clause. For now, we also assume that all path expressions are *single-valued*; that is, there is no set attribute in the path expression. A brief discussion on the processing of *set-valued* path expressions (i.e., they contain at least one complex set attribute) will be provided at the end of this subsection.

We use the following as a running example in our discussion on the optimization of path expressions.

Example 2.6 Find all graduate students who major in a department chaired by Tom and whose advisor is a full professor younger than 40. This query can be expressed in OQL as follows:

```
select s
from G_Student s
where s.Department.Chairperson.Name = 'Tom'
      and s.Advisor.Rank = 'full professor'
      and s.Advisor.Age < 40
```

This query has conditions along three path expressions in conjunctive form. The first path expression involves three classes, *G_Student*, *Department*, and *Faculty*, and the second and third path expressions involve the same two classes, *G_Student* and *Faculty*.   ■

OODB queries can be represented graphically for easier discussion. For the type of OODB queries we consider in this subsection, we have the following definition for OODB query graphs.

Definition 2.1 *For a given OODB query, we define its query graph as an annotated directed graph: OG(OV, OE), where OV is a set of vertices and OE is a set of directed edges. Each vertex v in OV corresponds to a class instance variable of some class referenced in the query. Each vertex is associated with two types of annotations,* predicate annotation *and* target annotation. *The former contains all selection predicates on the corresponding class instance variable, and the latter contains target attributes of the corresponding class instance variable. A directed edge e from vertex v_1 to vertex v_2 with annotation Attr indicates that Attr is a complex attribute of the class corresponding to v_1 and the domain class of Attr corresponds to v_2.*

Note that there can be several class instance variables for the same class. In Example 2.6, for each graduate student, the faculty instance used in the first path expression to evaluate

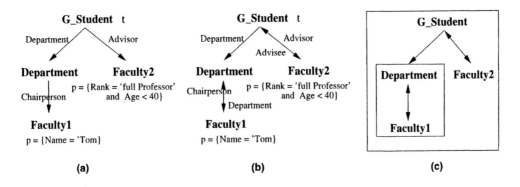

FIGURE 2.3 **A Query Graph and Block Examples**

the first condition is independent of the faculty instance used in the second path expression to evaluate the second condition. Therefore, different class instance variables should be used for the first two involvements of class *Faculty* in the query. On the other hand, for the same graduate student, the two faculty instances used in the second and the third path expressions to evaluate the corresponding conditions must be the same since each graduate student has only one advisor. In other words, the same class instance variable should be used for the last two involvements of class *Faculty* in the query. Formally, it can be shown that when only single-valued path expressions are considered, two involvements of the same class in two path expressions should be mapped to the same class instance variable if and only if the two subpaths from the beginning of the path expressions to the places the involvements occur are identical. The mapping of multiple involvements of each class to the same class instance variable whenever possible achieves the factorization of common subpath expressions, which is an important technique for avoiding redundant computation of path expressions. It can be further shown that for the type of OODB queries we consider (i.e., path expressions are in conjunctive form and there is no explicit join), the query graphs will always be trees.

The tree for the query in Example 2.6 is shown in Figure 2.3(a). The little *t* beside G_Student indicates that it is a target class. Predicate annotations are denoted by p = { }. *Faculty1* and *Faculty2* are used to represent the two class instance variables of class *Faculty*. Since the two involvements of the class *Faculty* in the second and the third path expressions are mapped to the same variable *Faculty2*, the two conditions along the two path expressions are combined into one. Directed edges indicate the existence of predefined traversal paths (i.e., complex attributes). A query tree can be augmented by adding predefined inverse traversal paths of existing traversal paths. For example, for the traversal path *Advisor* from *G_Student* to *Faculty2*, there is an inverse traversal path *Advisee* from *Faculty2* to *G_Student* (see Figure 2.1). Inverse traversal paths allow the query optimizer to consider alternative query execution plans. Figure 2.3(b) shows the *augmented query tree* for the query tree in Figure 2.3(a). In Figure 2.3(b), a double-arrowed edge is a simplification notation for two directed edges in opposite directions. In later discussions, the phrase *query tree* means "augmented query tree."

In general, a query tree consisting of *n* vertices roughly corresponds to a relational query that joins *n* relations. Therefore, we potentially have a huge number of ways (orders) to evaluate a query tree with n vertices. Clearly, heuristic methods are needed to guide the process of selecting a good execution strategy. In this subsection, we present a block-based heuristic-driven query optimization method. This method consists of two steps. In the first step, the query graph is transformed into a tree with nested *blocks*, where each block is a subtree rooted at some internal vertex in the original tree. In the second step, subqueries that correspond to blocks are evaluated in an *inside-out* manner; that is, the subqueries that are in the innermost blocks are evaluated first, followed by the subqueries next to the innermost blocks, and so on. When a block is evaluated, the root of the corresponding subtree is reduced; that is, the set of instances of the class corresponding to the root of the subtree that satisfy the conditions imposed on the subtree are returned as an intermediate result. Conceptually, after a block is evaluated, it is reduced to a single vertex corresponding to the root of the subtree. Figure 2.3(c) shows a possible transformed tree with two nested blocks. The inner block contains two vertices. When the inner block is evaluated, department objects chaired by Tom will be the result. After the inner block is evaluated, the outer block can be effectively considered as a block with three vertices.

The following definition is useful for further discussion.

Definition 2.2 *For a given query tree, a* block configuration *is a set of nested blocks satisfying the following conditions:*

1. *Every vertex of the tree is in at least one block.*

2. *Each block contains at least two vertices.*

3. *For any two blocks b1 and b2, exactly one of the following is true:*
   - *Every vertex in b1 is also in b2 (i.e., b1 is nested in b2).*
   - *Every vertex in b2 is also in b1 (i.e., b2 is nested in b1).*
   - *There is no overlap between b1 and b2.*

For the query tree in Figure 2.3(b), there are only two valid block configurations. One is shown in Figure 2.3(c), and the other has only one block containing all four vertices.

The basic rationale behind the block-based technique is simple: when a problem is too complex, divide it into multiple simpler problems and solve them separately. This technique is especially useful in a multiprocessor (including distributed database) environment since subqueries in nonoverlapping blocks can be processed in parallel.

Two important issues need to be addressed here. The first is how to choose a block configuration. For an arbitrary query tree, there may be a large number of valid block configurations. The second issue is how to evaluate each block in a given block configuration. Shortly, we will see that each block can be evaluated in a number of ways. An optimal execution plan is a combined choice of a block configuration and the execution strategy for the block. Since the number of such combinations can be large, a heuristic method should guide the choice. We will discuss first the choice of a block configuration and then the evaluation of each block.

Choosing a Block Configuration

The query optimizer of the ORION system has a simple way of choosing a block configuration: form a block for every subtree rooted at an internal vertex of the query tree. Such a block configuration has the following properties: (1) the number of blocks is the same as the number of internal vertices of the query tree; and (2) when the blocks are evaluated inside out, each block, at evaluation time, has exactly two levels of vertices, i.e., the root of the subtree in the block and its child vertices. This is true because after a block is evaluated, it is reduced to a single vertex.

Clearly, for a given query tree, there is a unique block configuration based on this method, and such a configuration may not lead to a final optimal execution plan. We now present a heuristic-based method for achieving a better block configuration. This heuristic uses the following two additional pieces of information.

Indexes on path expressions. Different types of indexes can be built along path expressions. For example, one such index is the *nested index*. Consider the path expression $C.A_1.A_2 \ldots A_{n-1}.A_n$. A nested index on attribute A_n of class C_{n-1} (C_{n-1} is the domain class of complex attribute A_{n-1}) for class C along the path expression is a set of pairs (v, O), where v is a value in the domain of attribute A_n and O is a set of OIDs of objects in class C such that each object in C with an OID in O can traverse to some object in C_{n-1} whose A_n-value is v. Such an index allows us to quickly find out, for a given v, those objects in C that can traverse to v. For this nested index, we call C the *indexed class* and C_{n-1} the *indexing class*. Consider the path expression *G_Student.Department.Chairperson.Name*. If there is a nested index on the *Name* attribute of class *Faculty* (note that *Faculty* is the domain class of *Chairperson*) for the fast access of graduate students, then we can quickly identify those graduate students majoring in departments chaired by Tom without going through the objects of *Faculty* and *Department*. For this example, *G_Student* is the indexed class and *Faculty* is the indexing class. The heuristic for selecting a good block configuration assumes the knowledge of the existence of all indexes along path expressions. More detailed discussions on various types of indexes along path expressions will be provided in Section 2.4.3.

Clusters. A cluster is a group of objects stored together. Objects in an OODB system may be stored in many different ways. For example, all objects in an OODB are stored in a single file or the objects of each class are stored in a separate file. These are the two most frequently used default organizations of objects. However, OODB systems usually allow alternative object organizations. For example, if graduate students and their advisors are frequently retrieved together, then storing each faculty together with his or her advisees may reduce the I/O cost during the retrieval. In other words, the objects of the two classes *G_Student* and *Faculty* are organized as a cluster. The heuristic also assumes the knowledge of the existence of all clusters.

The following heuristic rules can be used together with the method used in ORION for choosing a block configuration.

Rule 1 *The classes in a (sub)path expression between the indexed class and the indexing class of a nested index should be kept in the same block. The only exception is when the indexing class is the root of a block.*

Several remarks about this rule are in order. First, the motivation behind this rule can be explained as follows. Recall that when a block is evaluated, the class corresponding to

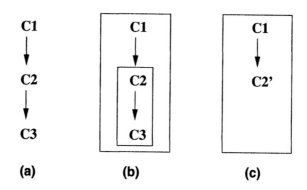

FIGURE 2.4 **Illustrating the Exception in Rule 1**

the root of the subtree of the block is reduced (i.e., the objects of the class corresponding to the root that satisfy the conditions imposed on the subtree are obtained). If the indexed class and the indexing class are in separate blocks, then the corresponding index cannot be used to process the query. For example, consider the nested index along the path expression *G_Student.Department.Chairperson.Name* with *faculty* as the indexing class and *G_Student* as the indexed class. To make use of the index to reduce *G_Student*, *G_Student* and *faculty* must be in the same block. Second, this rule becomes more effective as the number of classes between the indexed class and the indexing class increases provided there are no predicate conditions on the classes between the indexed class and the indexing class, because this implies that more classes can be bypassed. Third, the reason to allow the stated exception is illustrated as follows.

Example 2.7 Suppose along a path expression there are two nested indexes, one with C1 and C2 as the indexed and the indexing classes, respectively, and the other with C2 and C3 as the indexed and the indexing classes, respectively. Suppose C1 is an ancestor of C2 and C2 is an ancestor of C3 in the query tree (see Figure 2.4(a)). By Rule 1, C2 and C3 with all classes between them should be in the same block. Suppose we create a block for the subtree rooted at C2 so that we can use the index between C2 and C3 when we evaluate this block. In this case, C1 and C2 are not in the same block (see the inner block in Figure 2.4(b)). However, C2, the indexing class for the indexed class C1, is the root of the block. Note that after this block is evaluated, it will be reduced to a single vertex corresponding to the reduced C2 (denoted by C2′, see Figure 2.4(c)). Now if the next block we create is for the subtree rooted at C1, then C1 and C2′ will be in the same block (see Figure 2.4(c)) and the index between C1 and C2 can be readily used to evaluate this block. In summary, if C2 is the root of a block, then the index between C1 and C2 can still be used.   ■

It is possible for several indexes to conflict with each other in the sense that no block configuration satisfying Rule 1 exists for these indexes. This is illustrated by the following example.

Example 2.8 Consider the query tree in Figure 2.5(a) (annotations on vertices and edges

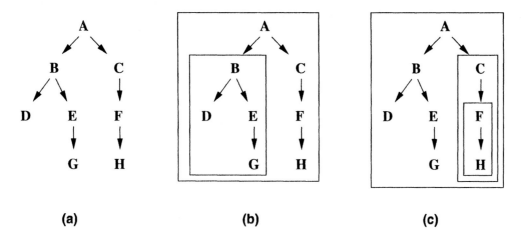

FIGURE 2.5 Illustrating Conflicting Indexes

are omitted). Suppose there are two nested indexes, one with A and D as the indexed and indexing classes, respectively, and the other with B and G as the indexed and indexing classes, respectively. When Rule 1 is applied to the two indexes, two blocks as shown in Figure 2.5(b) will be created. However, the inner block makes the first index not applicable since this block will reduce B and after B is reduced, D will disappear. A sensible way to resolve this conflict is not to form the smaller block. In this way, Rule 1 can be satisfied and both indexes may be used. ∎

In general, if a nested block violates Rule 1 as a result of conflicting indexes, then the block should not be formed.

Rule 2 *In the absence of appropriate indexes, i.e., when Rule 1 is not applicable, vertices corresponding to classes whose objects are stored in the same cluster should be kept in the same block.*

The reason for using Rule 2 is to take advantage of the clusters. The above discussion can be summarized into the following algorithm for selecting a good block configuration.

Select-Block-Configuration

1. Create a block for the entire tree.

2. Define a partial order "≤" among all indexes based on the indexed classes such that "index $I1 \leq$ index $I2$" if the indexed class of $I1$ is an ancestor of that of $I2$ in the query tree.

3. For each index I in the partial order obtained in step 2, if there is no block for the subtree rooted at the indexed class of I and creating such a block does not violate Rule 1, then create it—otherwise, do not.

4. For each cluster C, let $C(H)$ be the class in C that is closest to the root of the entire tree. If there is no block for the subtree rooted at $C(H)$ and creating such a block does not violate Rule 1, then create it—otherwise, do not.

5. For each internal vertex V in the query tree, if there is no block for the subtree rooted at V and creating such a block does not violate Rule 1 and Rule 2, then create it—otherwise, do not.

Clearly, because of step 5, when there is no index or cluster, the block configuration generated by this algorithm is the same as that by the ORION method.

Example 2.9 Consider the query tree in Figure 2.5(a). Suppose there are two nested indexes as described in Example 2.8. Suppose there are also two clusters; one covers E and G, and the other covers C and F. According to the algorithm, after the block for the entire tree is created, the index with A as the indexed class should be considered first as it is ahead of the other index in the partial order. Since there is already a block for the subtree rooted at A, the index with B as the indexed class is considered next. As discussed in Example 2.8, creating a block for the subtree rooted at B will violate Rule 1. Therefore, no block is created for this index. Now consider the cluster that covers E and G. Since creating a block for the subtree rooted at E will violate Rule 1 (for the index with B as the indexed class), no block is created for this cluster. For the cluster covering C and F, a block for the subtree rooted at C is created. In the last step of the algorithm, the block for the subtree rooted at F is created. The final block configuration is shown in Figure 2.5(c).   ∎

Evaluation of a Block

We assume that when a block is to be evaluated, all blocks nested in it have been reduced to their root vertices. In other words, when a block is to be evaluated, no nested block is present. If the tree in a block has only one leaf vertex, then it is called a *chain block*. If it has multiple leaf vertices, it is called a *tree block*. The following three methods are used to evaluate a block.

Forward Traversal

This method starts the evaluation at the root vertex of the block and proceeds in a top-down fashion. Since the goal is to reduce the root vertex, this method consists of two phases: *top-down* phase and *bottom-up* phase. We consider chain blocks first.

Top-down phase. In this phase, there is a sequence of steps and each such step consists of a projection on the complex attribute on the edge between the current vertex and its child vertex (the result is a set of OIDs of the objects in the class corresponding to the child vertex), a removal of duplicates, and an evaluation of these objects using the conditions associated with the child vertex. The top-down process continues until the leaf vertex is encountered and the set of OIDs of the qualified objects of the corresponding class is obtained. For example, consider the chain block consisting of *Department* and *Faculty1* in Figure 2.3(c). To evaluate this block, we first perform a projection on the *Chairperson* attribute of the *Department* class to obtain the faculty members who are chairpersons. In this particular case, no removal of duplicates is needed since each department has only one chairperson. Next, the condition "Name = 'Tom'" is used to find those chairpersons named Tom.

Bottom-up phase. In this phase, the set of the OIDs for the qualified objects in the leaf vertex obtained in the top-down phase is used to filter objects in the class corresponding to the parent vertex. This process continues until the root vertex is encountered. To ensure that only the correct objects of the root class are obtained, this phase needs to be carried out with caution. In general, if only the leaf vertex is associated with conditions, then the correctness can be guaranteed. Otherwise, if a nonleaf vertex is also associated with conditions, then these conditions need to be reevaluated to ensure the correctness. The efficiency of this phase can be improved considerably if there are appropriate indexes and/or inverse traversal paths. For example, owing to the traversal path *Department* in class *Faculty*, the departments chaired by Tom can be obtained quickly.

An alternative to the above technique is to combine the two phases. This can be achieved by always carrying the OIDs of the objects in the root class during the top-down phase. For example, for the same block considered above, OID pairs (department_OID, faculty_OID) instead of only the faculty OIDs will be sent to the child vertex for further evaluation. As a result, the bottom-up phase can be entirely avoided. The price paid is that a large intermediate result is used as input for each step in the top-down process. Intuitively, if there are conditions associated with nonleaf vertices of the tree and/or there is a lack of inverse traversal paths/indexes, then the alternative approach should be used. Otherwise, the two-phase approach should be considered.

We now consider the evaluation of a tree block. A tree block can be considered as the union of a number of subtrees, each corresponding to a chain block. If a subtree is not a chain, then the evaluation can be recursively applied to each vertex with more than one child. The two-phase approach described above for chain blocks can be applied to each of the subtrees to reduce the root class. As an example, consider the outer block in Figure 2.3(c) after the inner block has been evaluated. Let Dept' denote the node corresponding to the reduced *Department* class. For this tree block, we can first apply the above two-phase approach to the subtree G_Student–Dept' to reduce G_Student. Let G_Student' be the reduced class for G_Student. We can then apply the above two-phase approach again to the subtree G_Student'–Faculty2 to further reduce G_Student. Alternatively, we can consider the subtree G_Student–Faculty2 first before considering the other subtree.

In general, if the root vertex of the block has n children, then there are $n!$ different orders to apply the two-phase approach to the subtrees. The following heuristic method can be used to find an order with good performance. For $i = 1, \ldots, n$, let C_i be the cost of applying the two-phase approach to the ith subtree independently and r_i be the *reduction rate* of the ith subtree to the root vertex. If applying the two-phase approach to the ith subtree, the number of objects in the root class is reduced by 40%, then we say that the reduction rate of the ith tree is 0.4. The reduction rate of a subtree can be considered as the benefit of applying the two-phase approach to the ith subtree. Intuitively, it is desirable to apply the two-phase approach to the subtrees with lower costs and higher reduction rates early because reduced root class may reduce the cost of evaluating subsequent subtrees. The following proposition can be proven.

Proposition 2.1 *If the cost of applying the two-phase approach to a subtree is proportional to the number of objects in the root class, then the optimal order for applying the two-phase approach to the subtrees is the descending order of $\{R_i/C_i\}$.*

The assumption used in Proposition 2.1 does not hold in general. Therefore, applying the two-phase approach to the subtrees in the descending order of $\{R_i/C_i\}$ is only a heuristic approach.

The aforementioned alternative approach to the two-phase approach can also be applied to each subtree. When the alternative approach is used, Proposition 2.1 can also be used to determine the order in which different subtrees should be considered. In a distributed or multi-processor environment, subtrees may be processed at different sites or by different processors in parallel to reduce the response time of the query.

Reverse Traversal

This method starts the evaluation with the leaf vertices of the tree and proceeds toward the root in a bottom-up manner. First, the set of OIDs of the objects satisfying the conditions associated with the corresponding vertex in each leaf vertex is obtained. Next, this set of OIDs are matched with the values of the corresponding complex attribute of the parent class to find the corresponding objects in the parent vertex. This step essentially performs a semi-join. This process continues until the root vertex is encountered. If a vertex in the tree has two or more children, then these subtrees can be considered in certain order. However, the order is not as important as in the case of forward traversal because the evaluation of a subtree is largely independent of the order.

Reverse traversal can be effective if the classes corresponding to the leaf vertices have only a small number of objects satisfying the associated conditions and/or there are appropriate inverse traversal paths and/or indexes. Most existing OODB systems do not automatically create inverse traversal paths, and indexes need to be created explicitly.

Mixed Traversal

In this case, some subtrees are evaluated using the forward traversal, and others are evaluated using the reverse traversal. This method has the potential to overcome the disadvantages and keep the advantages of the above two methods. For example, for the block containing G_Student, Dept' (i.e., the reduced Department), and Faculty2 (see Figure 2.3(c)), a good strategy is to use the reverse traversal to evaluate the subtree G_Student–Faculty first, taking advantage of the inverse traversal path *Advisee*. After G_Student is reduced to G_Student', the forward traversal is then used to evaluate the remaining subtree, taking advantage of the forward traversal path *Department*.

There are two ways to implement a traversal (forward or reverse) between two classes. One is instance-to-instance traversal and the other is set-oriented join. Join is a logical operation and can be implemented in many ways such as nested loop and sort merge. Nested loop can be considered as a special case of instance-to-instance traversal since the latter includes traversal across more than two classes. For example, for the block containing G_Student, Dept' (i.e., the reduced Department), and Faculty2, the instance-to-instance forward traversal could traverse from each graduate student object to both a department object and a faculty object at the same time to qualify the student object. The combination of different traversal methods (forward, reverse, and mixed) and different ways to implement each traversal method has the potential of creating a large number of possible evaluation plans for each block. The way a block is created provides some clues for the choice of an evaluation plan. For example, if the block is created based on a cluster (see Rule 2), then instance-to-instance traversal should be used. Whether it should be forward traversal or reverse traversal depends on the way the cluster is specified. For instance, suppose a cluster contains Department and Faculty1 (see Figure 2.3(c)). If the cluster is specified as Department(Faculty)—that is, faculty objects associated with each department are stored together with the department object—then forward traversal should be used. On the other hand, if the cluster is specified as Faculty(Department)—that is, the department object associated with each faculty is stored together with the faculty object—then reverse traversal should be used. If a block is created based on an index (see Rule 1) such that the indexed class and the indexing class are not adjacent, then again, instance-to-instance traversal is preferred over join. When join is chosen to implement the traversals between classes in a block, then the problem of finding an evaluation plan for the block is very similar to the problem of finding an optimal execution plan for joins among a number of relations. Since a single path expression is likely to be mapped to chain blocks, the optimization of chain queries becomes especially important. The optimization of chain queries in a distributed relational database is discussed in Chapter 3.

We now provide a brief discussion on the optimization of *set-valued* path expressions. Two quantifiers could be used for set attributes along a path expression, one is the existential quantifier *some* and the other is the universal quantifier *all*. The join operator is known to carry the existence semantics. Specifically, an instance of an operand satisfies a join if it matches with some instance in the other operand. Because of this, the techniques discussed above will remain applicable in the presence of the existential quantifier in some path expression with a minor modification to handle the set attribute. When a projection is performed on a complex set attribute, the result is a set of sets with OIDs as elements. An example of this is $\pi_{Course}(Student)$ since each student takes a set of courses. The set of sets needs to be flattened into a set before relevant join or instance-to-instance traversal is launched.

Operations involving the universal quantifier cannot be easily converted to joins. As a result, instance-to-instance traversal is usually employed. As a matter of fact, using instance-to-instance traversal can be advantageous for both quantifiers. Suppose class *Course* has a complex set attribute *Students* indicating who take which courses. Consider the predicate "Course.*some* Students.Age < 20". This can be a predicate for the query "find all courses taken by at least one student younger than 20." For a given course, when (forward) instance-to-instance traversal is used, the students taking the course can be examined one by one and as soon as one student is found to be younger than 20, the traversal can stop (i.e., other students taking the course need not be examined) and the course can be declared qualified. In other words, not all students taking the course need to be examined. In contrast, when join is used, all students taking the course will be examined. Similar observation can be made for the universal quantifier when an object is to be disqualified. For example, suppose the *some* in the above predicate is replaced by *all*. In this case, for a given course, as soon as one of the students taking the course is found to be 20 or older, the remaining students need not be examined.

One problem associated with this version of instance-to-instance traversal is that a lot of redundant work may be performed by traversing to and examining the same objects as well as their descendants. For example, a student may take several courses, and the student may be retrieved and examined for the evaluation of different courses. Although this problem also exists for nonset attributes, it becomes more serious with set attributes. One solution is to cache the results of previous traversals for later use. For example, suppose a course satisfies the above predicate because its *Students*-value contains an OID, say o1, such that o1 is the OID of a student younger than 20. If this information is saved in the cache, then when we encounter another course whose *Students*-value also contains o1, we will know that this course also satisfies the predicate without traversing to the object with o1 and examining the conditions. This technique is especially effective if the path to be traversed is long.

2.3.3 Method Materialization

The behaviors of objects are defined by a set of methods. A method may be expressed as a query, or defined in terms of other methods, or implemented in a high-level, general-purpose programming language, such as C++ and SmallTalk. Although the use of methods is important in defining the behavioral aspects of objects, it has the following two negative effects from the perspective of query processing and optimization.

1. It is expensive to invoke a method as it causes the execution of a program. If a query needs to invoke a method for each object in a large set of objects, it may take a very long time to process the query.

2. Due to the encapsulation of the object-oriented data model, the implementation—i.e., the code, of each method—is hidden. As such, it is very difficult to estimate the cost of invoking a method in a query. Since method access is often part of an OODB query, without a reasonable estimate on the cost of using a method, the execution plan produced by a cost estimation–based query optimizer may be far from the optimal plan.

Method materialization is a technique that can be used to alleviate these two problems. The basic idea is to compute the results of frequently accessed methods *in advance* and store the results for later use. Only *derived-attribute method* and *predicate method*, which compute a value when invoked, are appropriate for materialization. These two types of methods behave like a function and can be called *function methods*. Clearly, if the results of every method referenced in a query are readily accessible, the query can be processed in much less time. Also, it is usually much easier to estimate the cost of accessing the result of a method than that of invoking the method. Therefore, if the results of every method referenced in a query have been precomputed, it will be much easier for the query optimizer to generate a good execution plan for the query.

Let $m(a_1 : t_1, \ldots, a_k : t_k) : t_r$ be the signature of a function method defined for class C, where a_i's are arguments, t_i's are their types, and t_r is the result type of the method. The method has a hidden argument that accepts the OIDs of the objects in C. The materialized result of the method can be stored as a table with the following format:

C-OID	a_1	a_2	$\cdots$	a_k	m

where C-OID is an attribute for OIDs of the objects in C. The first $k + 1$ columns correspond to the arguments of the method and the last column corresponds to the result of the method for each argument value combination. We call a method together with an argument value combination a *method instance*.

Example 2.10 Suppose a method *standing( ): string* is defined for the G_Student class (see Figure 2.1). This method has no explicit argument except the hidden argument. For graduates whose GPA is between 3.8 and 4, the method returns excellent; for those whose GPA is between 3.4 and 3.8 (excluding 3.8), the method returns good; for those whose GPA is between 3 and 3.4 (excluding 3.4), the method returns fair; and for those whose GPA is below 3, the method returns poor. Three method instances exist based on the instances of the class (see Figure 2.2) and they are *standing(g1)*, *standing(g2)*, and *standing(g3)*. When this method is materialized based on the given instances of the class, the result as shown in the following table will be obtained.

G_Student-OID	standing
g1	good
g2	excellent
g3	good

∎

Although method materialization allows more efficient processing of retrieval queries, it incurs higher cost for update queries. An update operation may cause the precomputed result to become inconsistent with the updated data. For instance, if the GPA of graduate student Mary is changed from 3.5 to 3.2 (see Figure 2.2), then the standing of this student, whose OID is g3, must be changed to "fair" in the materialized result (see Example 2.10) to maintain the consistency between the database and the materialized method. An important issue in method materialization is to efficiently handle this inconsistency problem. In the following, we briefly discuss how to maintain materialized methods when the OODB is modified.

Insert. When a new object is created for a class, new entries need to be inserted into the materialized results of those methods that are defined based on the objects of the class. For example, when a new graduate student is added to class G_Student, a new tuple recording the student's standing must be inserted into the materialized result, i.e., the table in Example 2.10, of the method *standing( )*.

Delete. When an existing object o is deleted, all materialized entries that use o need to be removed. Identifying the entries that use o can be inefficient because for a given object o, most OODB systems maintain only information on what objects o references but not on what objects reference o. To improve efficiency, a *reverse reference table* of the following format should be maintained:

OID	method	argument_value_combination

A tuple (o1, m1, a1) in the above table indicates that an object with OID o1 is accessed when method m1 with argument value combination a1 is materialized (i.e., when method instance m1(a1) is materialized). This table can be used as follows: when an object with OID o1 is deleted, all tuples in the table with OID = o1 are identified first; for each such tuple, say (o1, m1, a1), the result of m1(a1) is removed from the materialized result for m1. Clearly, (o1, m1, a1) itself should also be deleted from the reverse reference table.

Update. When an existing object o with OID o1 is modified, all materialized results that use the modified o need to be recomputed (i.e., rematerialized). In accordance with the above discussion for delete, we can use the reverse reference table to find out the method instances that need to be recomputed. The recomputation of a method instance can be either carried out immediately, when such a method instance is identified, or delayed until the result of the method instance is needed to evaluate a query. The latter approach is called *lazy rematerialization*. A flag bit is needed to indicate whether the result of a method instance is valid (i.e., no rematerialization is needed).

We have the following remarks about method materialization:

1. If several methods for the same class have the same set of arguments, then the materialized results of these methods can be stored in the same table. For example, for two methods m1 and m2 on class C as defined by $m1(a_1 : t_1, \ldots, a_k : t_k) : t_r$ and $m2(a_1 : t_1, \ldots, a_k : t_k) : t_s$, the combined result table will have the following format:

C-OID	a_1	a_2	$\cdots$	a_k	m1	m2

This approach has two advantages over the approach that stores the results separately. First, less storage space is needed because only one copy of each argument value combination is stored. Second, if these methods are referenced in the same query, then only one table needs to be searched to evaluate these methods, resulting in a lower processing cost.

2. If a method has one or more arguments that do not take OIDs, then materializing the method needs special caution because the domains of these arguments may have an infinite number of values. As an example, suppose the following method is defined for a class *Investor*:

accumulation(retirement_age: integer, annual_return: real): real

For any specified retirement age of an investor and an annual return on the investment, this method computes the total accumulation for the investor at retirement, based on the current age and the current accumulation of the investor. Since an infinite number of combinations for retirement_age and annual_return exist for each investor, it is clearly not feasible to precompute the result for each such combination. In this case, we should employ *restricted method materialization*, which restricts the values that can be taken by each non-OID argument. For example, restrictions "$55 \leq$ retirement_age ≤ 70" and "annual_return in $\{7, 7.5, 8, 8.5, 9, 9.5, 10, 10.5, 11, 11.5, 12\}$" can be used. Note that if a method referenced in a query uses a combination of argument values that cannot be derived from the restriction set, then the method needs to be invoked to compute the result on the fly.

3. The size of the result table of a materialized method could be very large. Indexes can be created to speed up accesses to the table.

4. Several techniques exist to reduce the maintenance cost of materialized methods. Please see Reference [197] for details.

2.4 Indexes in OODB Systems

Building and using indexes is an important technique for speeding up the processing of selection predicates as well as joins. Indexes contribute significantly to the efficient processing of database queries. In a relational database system, indexes are built for the tuples of a relation based on the values of some attribute(s) of the relation. In an object-oriented database system, both the OODB schema and the query language involve more complicated structures. More specifically, a typical OODB schema has *class hierarchy* and *composition hierarchy*. Owing to the class hierarchy, an OODB query may reference a class itself (i.e., only instances in the class but not its subclasses), the class subhierarchy rooted at a class, or a subset of the classes in the class subhierarchy rooted at a class. Due to the composition hierarchy, an OODB query may have path expressions. To support the efficient processing of these queries, new and more sophisticated index structures have been developed over the years.

In addition to the indexes for the instances of a class based on the attribute values of the same class (similar to the indexes in relational systems), three new categories of indexes have been developed for OODB systems. The first category is for class hierarchies rooted at individual classes. Within this category, several index structures have been investigated. Examples of index structures in this category are the *class hierarchy index* and *H-tree index*. The second category contains indexes built along path expressions for speeding up their evaluations. *Nested index, path index*, and *multiindex* are among the indexes studied in this category. The third category contains those index structures for both class hierarchies and composition hierarchies. One such index is known as *nested inherited index*. Several indexes in the first two categories will be discussed in this section. In Section 2.4.1, we describe the class hierarchy index. In Section 2.4.2, we discuss the H-tree index. Nested index, path index, and multiindex are presented in Section 2.4.3. The nested inherited index will not be discussed here, but a reference to it can be found in the Bibliographic Notes of this chapter.

2.4.1 Class Hierarchy Index

Let C be a class. To make the presentation easier, we also use C to represent the set of instances in C as well as instances in all subclasses in the class hierarchy rooted at C as we did in Section 2.1 (i.e., C is also used to denote the *extent* of C). In addition, we use C^s to represent the set of instances only in C itself (i.e., no instance from the subclasses of C). A class hierarchy index on attribute A of C for the class hierarchy rooted at C is an index structure that can efficiently fetch, for any given value a in the domain of A, the OIDs of those instances in C whose A-value is a. This is in contrast with the *single class index* on attribute A for class C, which returns only the OIDs of those matching instances in C^s for each given a of A. Note

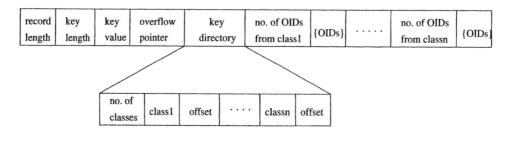

FIGURE 2.6 **The Structure of an Index Record**

that A can be either a primitive attribute with numerics and character strings as values or a complex attribute with OIDs as values.

One important point to keep in mind when building a class hierarchy index for C is that we also want to use the index to support queries that access individual classes in the class hierarchy rooted at C. As a result, if there is a class hierarchy index on attribute A for class C, then no single class indexes on A for classes in the class hierarchy rooted at C need to be built. This is to avoid duplicate indexes for better space utilization and more efficient index maintenance.

Suppose the index structure is a B$^+$ tree-like structure. The format of the internal nodes of this structure is the same as a B$^+$ tree. Specifically, each internal node is of the format $(P_1, K_1, P_2, K_2, \ldots, P_{n-1}, K_{n-1}, P_n)$, where each K_i is a value in the domain of the indexing attribute and each P_i is a tree pointer (i.e., a physical address) to a child node in the tree; the K_i's satisfy $K_1 < K_2 < \cdots < K_{n-1}$; the key values of the indexing attribute in the subtree pointed to by P_1 are less than or equal to K_1; the key values in the subtree pointed to by P_n are greater than K_{n-1}; and the key values in the subtree pointed to by P_i, $1 < i < n - 1$, are greater than K_{i-1} and less than or equal to K_i. To support different types of accesses to the class hierarchy (e.g., single class, the entire hierarchy, or a portion of the hierarchy), the leaf nodes of the tree have a quite different format. Each leaf node contains a number of *index records* and a *leaf node pointer* pointing to the next leaf node in the tree. The leaf node pointers facilitate sequential access to the indexed objects based on the key values. They are also useful for processing range queries involving the index. There is an *index record* for each distinct key value in the database. In the index record for key value v, instead of lumping all OIDs of the matching objects for v from different classes into a single set, these OIDs are partitioned into groups based on the classes. That is, two OIDs are in the same group if and only if their corresponding instances are from the same class (here the class means the class itself with subclasses excluded). The structure of an index record is depicted in Figure 2.6. Record length is the length of the index record in bytes. The key directory provides a quick way to locate the set of OIDs associated with each class in the class hierarchy. In the key directory *class1*, ... , *classn* are the OIDs of these classes (note that classes themselves are objects of a system-defined class). When an index record is too large to be held in a page, an overflow page will be used and the overflow pointer is used to point to such a page. Clearly, by partitioning the OIDs into groups, the index structure becomes quite flexible to accommodate different types of queries against the classes in the hierarchy.

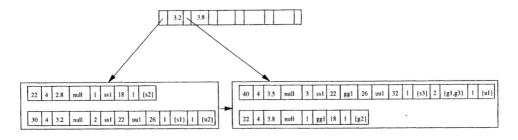

FIGURE 2.7 A Class Hierarchy Index

Example 2.11 Consider the OODB schema in Figure 2.1. Suppose we want to build an index on the GPA attribute for the class hierarchy rooted at the class *Student*. For the sake of illustration, we assume that each OID and integer occupies two bytes and each GPA value and pointer occupies four bytes. We also assume that each internal node can hold five key values and six pointers and each leaf node can hold two index records. Based on the instances given, a two-level tree can be constructed as shown in Figure 2.7. In this figure, ss1, gg1, and uu1 represent the OIDs of the three classes, respectively. The index record for GPA = 2.8 is the first record of the left leaf node in Figure 2.7. This record is 22 bytes long; the key value 2.8 occupies 4 bytes; there is no overflow pointer; only one class contains instances with GPA = 2.8 and the OID of the class is ss1; the index information about class ss1 starts with the 18th bytes in the record; there is one instance in the class having GPA = 2.8 and the instance has an OID s2. Other index records can be understood similarly. The pointer between the two leaf nodes is the *leaf node pointer*. ■

The use of a class hierarchy index for search is similar to that of a B⁺ tree. The search starts from the root of the tree and proceeds to a leaf node in exactly the same manner as a B⁺ tree is searched. When a leaf node is located, the key value of each index record in the leaf node is compared with the search key. If a match is found, then the index record is examined further for desired OIDs. For example, if the entire class hierarchy for which the class hierarchy index is built is referenced by the query, then all OIDs in the index record are returned; if only one class in the class hierarchy is referenced, then the key directory of the index record is consulted to quickly locate the OIDs associated with the class.

Intuitively, if only one class in a class hierarchy involves a predicate, then a corresponding single class index is better than the class hierarchy index. On the other hand, if all classes in the class hierarchy are involved, then the class hierarchy index is better than a set of single class indexes. Initial experimental results indicate that if at least two classes in a class hierarchy are involved, then the class hierarchy index is more efficient than single class indexes. Initial experimental results also show that there is no apparent winner or loser between a class hierarchy index and the set of single class indexes for the classes in the hierarchy when their sizes are compared.

2.4.2 H-Tree Index

H-tree is an index structure alternative to the class hierarchy index for supporting queries that access one or more classes in a class hierarchy. The basic idea of the H-tree is to first build an H-tree for each class, and then, through special links, connect these H-trees based on the subclass/superclass relationships among these classes to create a larger H-tree to support queries accessing multiple classes in a class hierarchy. An H-tree has two advantages over the corresponding class hierarchy index. First, queries that access only one class can be supported almost as well as a single class index. Second, H-tree supports the subclass/superclass relationship more naturally.

An H-tree for a single class is very much like a B^+ tree except for the following differences:

1. A leaf node of an H-tree is like a leaf node of a single class index, which in turn is similar to the leaf node of a class hierarchy index except that there is no *key directory* and there is only one (number of OIDs, a set of OIDs) pair.

2. An internal node of an H-tree for class C is the same as the internal node of a class hierarchy index except it may have special *linking cells* pointing to the nodes of the H-trees for the subclasses of C. Each linking cell is a triplet (cn, L, r), where cn is the name of the subclass such that a node of the subclass's H-tree is pointed to, L denotes a pointer pointing to node n of the subclass's H-tree, and r denotes the *range* of node n. The range of a node defines the index key values that are allowed by the node and its descendant nodes. Linking cells are placed at the end of each internal node.

Let $C1$ be a superclass of $C2$. Let H($C1$) and H($C2$) be the H-trees for $C1$ and $C2$, respectively. The following rules are followed when linking H($C2$) nested under H($C1$).

1. To have a linking cell in node $n1$ of H($C1$) pointing to a node $n2$ of H($C2$), it is required that the range of $n2$ is within the range of $n1$.

2. There exists exactly one path to reach each leaf node in H($C2$) from the nodes in H($C1$). This rule ensures that every leaf node in H($C2$) is reachable and that no redundant paths exist.

3. If all child nodes of node $n2$ in H($C2$) are referenced in node $n1$ in H($C1$), then only $n2$ should be linked to $n1$. This is to reduce the number of linking cells in $n1$.

4. If node $n2$ in H($C2$) can be linked to node $n1$ in H($C1$), then $n2$ should not be linked to the parent of $n1$. This rule requires that every link should be as specific as possible. This makes the access to the H-tree more efficient.

The actual linking procedure can be outlined as follows. Let N and n be the root nodes of H($C1$) and H($C2$), respectively. We start with the idea of linking n in N. But, before we actually place a linking cell in N for n, we first check if n can be linked in a child node $N1$ of N. If yes, then N is replaced by $N1$ and the procedure continues in a recursive manner. If no, we check if the child nodes of n can be linked in the child nodes of N. This is carried out by replacing n by each child node of n in the above procedure, again in a recursive manner. In the end, a descendant node $n1$ of n is linked in N only if $n1$ cannot be linked in any of the nonleaf descendant nodes of N.

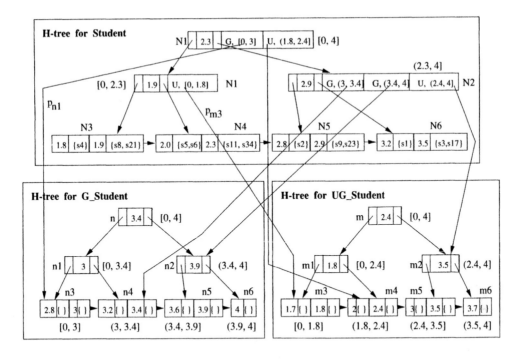

FIGURE 2.8 An H-Tree

Example 2.12 Figure 2.8 shows an H-tree for the class hierarchy rooted at *Student*. The index is on the GPA attribute. The H-trees for individual classes are in the large rectangles. For simplicity, for the H-tree for *Student*, only the index key values and the corresponding OIDs are shown, and for the other classes, only the index key values are shown. Note that the H-trees for *Student*, *G_Student*, and *UG_Student* are based on larger extents than those shown in Figure 2.2. The range of each node is also shown in the figure. Links across different large rectangles denote the pointers of *linking cells*, and the numeric pairs indicate the ranges of the corresponding nodes pointed. In a linking cell, *U* and *G* indicate that the pointed node is a node in the H-tree for class *UG_Student* and *G_Student*, respectively. Suppose the valid range for GPA is [0, 4].

Consider the process of linking the root node *n* of the H-tree for *G_Student* in the root node *N* of the H-tree for *Student*. First, none of the ranges of the child nodes of *N* contains the range of *n*. Therefore, we next try to link each child node of *n* in *N*. Consider *n1* first. Again, since none of the ranges of the child nodes of *N* contains the range of *n1*, the child nodes of *n1* need to be considered first. Since *n3* cannot be linked in any of *N*'s child nodes, it is linked in *N* with the linking cell (*G*, p_{n1}, [0, 3]). Since the range of *n4* is within the range of *N2*, *n2* is linked in *N2* with the linking cell (*G*, p_{n1}, [3, 3.4]). Now consider *n2*, the other child node of *n*. In this case, since all child nodes of *n2* can be linked in *N2*, by the third rule above, *n2* is linked in *N2*. Similarly, the nodes of the H-tree for *UG_Student* can be linked in the nodes of the H-tree for *Student*. Readers are encouraged to verify that all rules described above are satisfied by the links in Figure 2.8. ∎

Given an H-tree for a class hierarchy, we can start the search from the root of any H-tree for individual classes. If only the instances in C^s of a class C are of interest, then the corresponding H-tree is searched without following any links across different H-trees. If all instances, including those in the subclasses, of C are of interest, then the H-tree for C is searched and all links across different H-trees whose corresponding ranges intersect with the search key value(s) are followed. By using the class name in each linking cell, we can also restrict the search to a subset of the classes rooted at C.

Example 2.13 Suppose we are interested in all students, including graduate and undergraduate students, whose GPA is 1.8. We start the search from the root node of the H-tree for *Student*. From the root node, we find out that the pointer on the left of 2.3 needs to be followed and no link pointers to other H-tree nodes need to be followed since none of the ranges in the two linking cells covers 1.8. Therefore, we follow the pointer on the left of 2.3 to node $N1$. In $N1$, we find out that the pointer on the left of 1.9 should be followed. Since the range of the linking cell in $n1$ covers 1.8, the corresponding link pointer p_{m3} should also be followed. Suppose we first follow the pointer on the left of 1.9 to leaf node $N3$. In $N3$, student OID s4 is found to satisfy the search condition. We then follow p_{m3} to node $m3$. Suppose u1 and u5 are the OIDs of the undergraduate students that satisfy the search condition. The result of the search is the set $\{s4, u1, u5\}$.

Note that in the search, the H-tree for *G_Student* is not searched (not even the root), and the H-tree for *UG_Student* is only partially searched (again, the root is not searched). Clearly, it is more efficient than searching the three H-trees for individual classes independently. ∎

For a class hierarchy having three or more levels, special attention needs to be paid when searching an internal node of an H-tree for a class that is neither the root nor a leaf of the class hierarchy. Specifically, when such a node is searched, its ancestor nodes should also be searched to see if they contain useful links to other nodes. As an example, suppose *Student* has a superclass *Trainee* and in the H-tree for *Trainee*, an internal node has a linking cell with range (1.9, 2.3] and a pointer pointing to the node $N1$. To find all trainees, including student trainees, whose GPA is below 2.2, node $N1$ will be reached from the above internal node in the H-tree for *Trainee*. In this case, the parent node of $N1$, namely N, also needs to be searched since it has linking cells whose ranges, [0, 3] and (1.8, 2.4], intersect with the range of the search condition.

Initial experimental results indicate that H-tree index performs better than class hierarchy index for retrieval queries, especially when only a small number of classes in a class hierarchy are referenced by a query. There is no sufficient study on whether H-tree index or class hierarchy index performs better for update queries.

2.4.3   Indexes along Path Expressions

We have seen many example queries with predicate conditions along path expressions in the previous sections. We now investigate how to create appropriate indexes to support the efficient evaluation of this type of condition.

A typical path expression has the following format: $C_0.A_1.A_2 \ldots A_n$, where C_0 is a class name (or a class instance variable name), A_i is a complex attribute of C_{i-1} and its domain class is C_i, $1 \leq i < n$, and A_n is either a primitive attribute or a complex attribute with domain class C_n. For simplicity, only path expressions ending with a primitive attribute will be used to illustrate the ideas here although the same indexing technique can be readily applied to path expressions ending with a complex attribute. We first define several needed terms.

Definition 2.3 *Given a path expression $P = C_0.A_1.A_2 \ldots A_n$, an instantiation (or instance) of P is a sequence of n OIDs followed by a simple value: $OID_0.OID_1 \ldots OID_{n-1}.v$, where OID_0 is the OID of an object in C_0, OID_i, $1 \leq i < n$, is the value of the attribute A_i of the object with OID_{i-1}, and v is the value of attribute A_n of the object with OID_{n-1}.*

Example 2.14 Consider the OODB schema in Figure 2.1 and the instances of the classes in Figure 2.2. The following are the instances for path G_Student.Department.Chairperson.Name: g1.d1.f1.Kent, g2.d2.f3.Lisa, g3.d1.f1.Kent. ∎

Definition 2.4 *Given a path expression $P = C_0.A_1.A_2 \ldots A_n$, a partial instantiation of P is a sequence of k, $1 \leq k < n$, OIDs followed by a simple value: $OID_{n-k}.OID_{n-k+1} \ldots OID_{n-1}.v$, where OID_{n-k} is the OID of an object in C_{n-k}, OID_i, $n - k + 1 \leq i < n$, is the value of the attribute A_i of the object with OID_{i-1}, and v is the value of the attribute A_n of the object with OID_{n-1}.*

Based on this definition, any subpath instance resulting from a path instance by removing one or more leading OIDs (i.e., any leading subsequence of OIDs) is a partial instantiation. Some of the partial instantiations of the path expression G_Student.Department.Chairperson. Name are d1.f1.Kent, f1.Kent, and f3.Lisa. Note, however, that a partial instantiation of a path expression is not necessarily a subpath instance of some instance of the path expression. For example, for the above path expression, if a department (with OID d3) chaired by Tom (a faculty with OID f4; d3 and f4 are not shown in Figure 2.2) has no graduate student, then d3.f4.Tom is a partial instantiation but not a subpath instance of any of the three instances of the path expression. For a given path expression, a (partial) instantiation is *redundant* if it is a subpath instance of any longer (partial or nonpartial) path instance. For example, d1.f1.Kent is a redundant partial instantiation, whereas d3.f4.Tom is not. Also, no nonpartial instance is redundant. Redundant partial instantiations are not very useful since they do not carry any new information.

The following types of indexes along path expressions can be defined:

Nested index. For a given path expression $C_0.A_1.A_2 \ldots A_n$, a nested index is a set of pairs (v, O), where v is a value in the domain of attribute A_n and O is a set of OIDs of objects in C_0 such that v and each OID in O appear in the same path instance. In other words, a nested index of a path expression associates each distinct ending value of the path instances of the path expression with the set of corresponding starting values (OIDs). For example, for the given database instance, the nested index for G_Student.Department. Chairperson.Name is {(Kent, {g1,g3}), (Lisa, {g2})}.

Path index. For a given path expression $C_0.A_1.A_2 \ldots A_n$, a path index is a set of pairs (v, P), where v is a value in the domain of attribute A_n and P is a set of nonredundant path instances (partial or nonpartial) of the path expression with the ending value truncated.

As an example, with d3 and f4 added to the current database instance, the path index for G_Student.Department.Chairperson.Name is {(Kent, {g1.d1.f1, g3.d1.f1}), (Lisa, {g2.d2.f3}), (Tom, {d3.f4})}.

For each distinct ending value of the path instances of the path expression, by keeping track of all the corresponding nonredundant path instances (rather than just the OIDs of the objects from one class), a path index can be used to evaluate various types of queries along the path expression. These queries include those with different target classes and with conditions on several classes in the path expression as far as one of the conditions is on the indexing attribute (i.e., A_n). For example, the path index for G_Student.Department.Chairperson.Name can be used to find all graduate students together with their departments with any specified department name and chair name.

Multiindex. For a given path expression $C_0.A_1.A_2 \ldots A_n$, a multiindex is a set of nested indexes on the following n subpath expression: $C_i.A_{i+1}$, $0 \leq i \leq n - 1$, where C_i is the domain class of the complex attribute A_i, $1 \leq i \leq n - 1$. For example, with the current database instance (without d3 and f4), the multiindex for G_Student.Department. Chairperson.Name consists of three nested indexes. The nested index for G_Student. Department is {(d1, {g1,g3}), (d2, {g2})}, the nested index for Department.Chairperson is {(f1, {d1}), (f3, {d2})}, and the nested index for Faculty.Name is {(Kent, {f1}), (Lisa, {f3}), (Maria, {f2})}. Note that except for the last nested index, the other two indexes are on complex attributes and the index key values are OIDs.

In principle, a path expression may be split into subpath expressions of different lengths, and we can have a nested index for each such subpath expression. Multiindex is a special case of this general method when all subpath expressions have length two except the last subpath, which has length one. A multiindex on a path expression is quite flexible, in supporting the evaluation of various types of queries along the path expression.

All three types of indexes discussed above can be organized into B^+ tree-like structures with internal node and leaf node very much like the ones described for class hierarchy index (note that when a class C is referenced possibly as a domain class of a complex attribute in a path expression, either extent C or C^s could be specified) with the following two obvious differences. (1) For a nested index of length greater than one, the OIDs indexed are for objects from a class different from the class containing the index key attribute. (2) For a path index, path instances (partial or nonpartial) replace indexed OIDs.

We now briefly compare the three index structures along path expressions based on the initial experimental results reported in the literature (see the Bibliographic Notes). First, we consider the storage requirement of these index structures. The nested index always has the lowest requirement for storage space. Among the path index and the multiindex, the former usually requires more space than the latter except when there is no or very little sharing of references among objects. This is because the same OID may appear in many path instances, causing the OID to be stored many times. Second, we consider the performance of these index structures for supporting retrieval queries. The nested index usually has the best performance since it is created to process only one type of query (target class is the starting class, and the condition is on the indexing attribute). The path index in general performs much better than the multiindex because the latter needs to access several indexes. The path index performs worse than the nested index because the former has a large size. Third, we consider the cost of these index structures for supporting update queries. When the database is updated, all involved indexes need to be updated accordingly. A main reason for introducing the multiindex is its advantage in supporting update queries over the other two index structures. It is very expensive to update a nested index because when an OID in a path instance is modified to a new OID (note that the path instance is not stored by the nested index), forward traversal and reverse traversal to find the starting and ending values of those path instances containing the old and new OIDs are needed for the update. Updating a path index requires forward traversal to find the corresponding ending values. The corresponding starting values can be found from the ending values using the path index. In contrast, updates to a multiindex can be carried out locally without traversing the path expression. Overall, in most mixes of different kinds of queries (retrieval, update, insert, and delete), path index performs most consistently and performs better than the other two index structures.

Exercises

2.1 Discuss the differences between the concept of OID in an OODB and the concept of primary key in a relational database.

2.2 Discuss the relationship between *polymorphism* and *late-binding*.

2.3 Based on the OODB schema in Figure 2.1, express the following queries in OQL.

(a) Find the names of all faculty members who are younger than 35 and work in the computer science department.

(b) Find the titles of all courses that are offered by a department chaired by someone who likes to play golf.

(c) Rewrite query (b) using a different OQL construct.

(d) Find the names of all graduate students whose GPA is higher than 3.5 and who only take courses offered by the computer science department.

(e) Find the names of all nongraduate students who take both Database Systems and Information Retrieval.

(f) Find the SSN, name, and the advisees' names of each faculty member in the computer science department.

2.4 Based on the OODB schema in Figure 2.1, express the following queries in object algebra discussed in this chapter.

(a) Find the names of all faculty members who are younger than 35.

(b) Find the titles of all courses that are offered by a department chaired by Kent.

(c) Find the names of all nongraduate students whose GPA is higher than 3.3.

(d) Find the SSNs and advisees' names of faculty members in the computer science department.

2.5 Prove the following two transformation rules.

(a) Commuting apply and selection: If the selection condition involves only attributes to be returned by the *apply* operator, then

$$apply_{\lambda s.e}(\sigma_{\lambda t.f}(S)) = \sigma_{\lambda t.f}(apply_{\lambda s.e}(S))$$

(b) Commuting flatten and apply: Suppose S is the extent of a class and CSA is a complex set attribute of the class. Then

$$flat(apply_{\lambda s.(apply_{\lambda t.e}(\pi_{CSA}(\pi_V(s))))}(S)) = apply_{\lambda t.e}(flat(apply_{\lambda s.\pi_{CSA}(\pi_V(s))}(S)))$$

2.6 Suppose the following change has been made to the OODB schema in Figure 2.1: a complex attribute *Instructor* with domain class *Faculty* is added to class *Course*. Show the query tree and augmented query tree of the following OQL query:

```
select c.Title
from Course c
where c.Department.Chairperson.Rank = 'full professor'
      and c.Department.Name = 'computer science'
      and c.Instructor.Department.Name = 'mathematics'
```

2.7 Show that when only single-valued path expressions are considered, two involvements of the same class in two path expressions should be mapped to the same class instance variable if and only if the two subpaths from the beginning of the path expressions to the places the involvements occur are identical.

2.8 Consider the two path expressions in the where-clause of the following query:

```
select f.Name
from Faculty f
where f.some Advisee.GPA = 4.0 and f.some Advisee.Age > 35
```

(a) Discuss whether the two occurrences of *Advisee* can be mapped to the same class instance variable.

(b) Replace the two occurrences of *some* by *all*. Discuss whether the two occurrences of *Advisee* can be mapped to the same class instance variable.

(c) Replace the first occurrence of *some* by *all*. Discuss whether the two occurrences of *Advisee* can be mapped to the same class instance variable.

2.9 Consider the query tree in Figure 2.5(a). Suppose there are three nested indexes, the first with A and B as the indexed and indexing classes, respectively; the second with B and E as the indexed and indexing classes, respectively; and the third with C and H as the indexed and indexing classes, respectively. Suppose there are also two clusters: one covers E and G and the other covers F and H. Apply the algorithm Select-Block-Configuration to the query tree.

2.10 Prove Proposition 2.1.

2.11 Provide efficient strategies for evaluating the blocks obtained in Exercise 2.9.

2.12 Propose a new table format for materialized methods such that *lazy rematerialization* can be supported. Based on the new format and the reverse reference table,

 (a) design an algorithm for *lazy rematerialization*.

 (b) design an algorithm for *immediate rematerialization*.

2.13 Outline an algorithm for insertion to a class hierarchy index.

2.14 Consider Figure 2.2. Suppose the following objects have been added to the student class (only OIDs and ages are shown since other attribute values are not important for this exercise): (s4, 25), (s5, 18), (s6, 19), (s7, 27), (s8, 20), (s9, 22), (s10, 18), (s11, 21), (s12, 20), (s13, 22); the following objects have been added to the graduate student class: (g4, 24), (g5, 26), (g6, 26), (g7, 28), (g8, 31), (g9, 25), (g10, 27), (g11, 32); and the following objects have been added to the undergraduate student class: (u3, 22), (u4, 18), (u5, 19), (u6, 25), (u7, 29), (u8, 25), (u9, 21), (u10, 29), (u11, 22), (u12, 26). Build an H-tree on the Age attribute for the class hierarchy rooted at the student class. Only index key values and OIDs need to be shown for leaf nodes. Assume that the valid range for age is [16, 40]. Also assume that each leaf node can accommodate only two different key values and each internal node can accommodate only one key value (there is no limitation on the number of pointers and linking cells).

2.15 Outline an algorithm for deletion from an H-tree.

2.16 Suppose we have a nested index on path expression $C_0.A_1.A_2 \ldots A_n$. Outline an algorithm for maintaining the nested index for the following update operation: $o_i[A_{i+1}]$ is updated from o_{i+1} to o'_{i+1}, $1 \leq i \leq n - 1$, where o_i is an object in the domain class of A_i, and o_{i+1} and o'_{i+1} are objects in the domain class of A_{i+1}.

Bibliographic Notes

The book by Kemper and Moerkotte [199] covers many basic OODB concepts. It also surveys several existing OODB systems.

 The book edited by Freytag, Maier, and Vossen [124] is an excellent source for different techniques and issues concerning the processing and optimization of OODB queries. The article by Ozsu and Blakeley [285] also has good reviews of OODB query processing techniques. Many techniques for developing the ORION system are summarized in [202]. A collection of the major articles on the O_2 system can be found in [15]. The kind of object algebra presented in this chapter is adopted primarily from [100], but some ideas and notations from the EX-CESS algebra [373] are used. Other proposals of object algebras include the algebra for the ENCORE OODBS [329], association-algebra [352], and the algebra in [350]. A method for algebra-based optimization of object-oriented queries is reported in [26].

 Processing of path expressions is studied extensively in the literature. The materials on this subject presented in this chapter are developed from the basic ideas in [80, 81, 194]. In particular, the idea of block (called *cluster* in [194]) and the three traversal methods are presented in [194] and are used in the ORION system. The two rules for creating blocks are derived from [80, 81]. The idea of treating instance-to-instance traversal and join differently is also from [81]. A technique based on extended dynamic programming for optimizing chain queries can be found in [354]. An interesting technique using the *materialize operator* for processing path expressions is presented in [36].

A cost-based optimization method for object-oriented recursive queries is discussed in [220].

There are relatively few studies on the techniques for optimizing queries involving methods. The material on method materialization in this chapter is primarily from [197]. Several techniques for reducing the cost of maintaining materialized methods are also discussed in this paper. A revelation technique that seeks to reveal the operations in a method by breaking the encapsulation on the method is discussed in [253] and some technical reports by the authors.

Indexes are widely used in OODB systems to improve the speed of processing OODB queries. Class hierarchy index is reported in [204], and it is employed in the ORION system. H-tree index is investigated in [244]. Two other index structures for class hierarchies can be found in [303, 342]. The three index organizations along path expressions are studied and compared in [32]. Among them, multiindex is first proposed in [254] and is used in the GemStone system. Nested inherited index is presented in [31]. Using a join index hierarchy to speed up traversals is reported in [387].

Clustering techniques in object-oriented databases are discussed in [28, 71, 344, 363]. A comparison of several clustering strategies is reported in [364].

Query Processing in Distributed Relational Database Systems

In a centralized database system, the database management system (DBMS) and all the data managed by the DBMS are at the same site. However, there are many applications that cannot be supported well by a centralized database system. For example, consider a large bank with many branches. If a centralized database system is used and all data in the bank are stored at one site, say S_1, then it will be very inefficient to process database requests originating from a different site, say S_2, because such a request needs to be shipped from S_2 to S_1, and after the request is processed at S_1, the result needs to be transferred back to S_2. This is not acceptable if different sites are in a wide area network and a large number of requests are nonlocal. In addition to the setback on performance, another potential problem of this setup is that the system may be vulnerable. For example, if the computer at S_1 is down, then the entire system is unusable. An alternative solution is to store data in each branch locally and employ a separate DBMS at each site. In other words, a set of independent centralized database systems, each managing data at its own site, is used. With this arrangement, all local requests can be processed very efficiently without data transfer. This setup also results in a high degree of reliability and availability. For example, the unavailability of the system due to failure at one branch does not affect the use of the systems at other branches. Unfortunately, this solution also has a serious problem: requests that reference data stored in more than one site, such as "find those customers who have accounts in more than one branch," cannot be processed. Another alternative solution is to use a single DBMS to manage data stored at different sites. Clearly, the DBMS must be powerful enough to process requests that access data at one site or across multiple sites. This is the *distributed database system* approach. There may be different ways to define a distributed database system. The following is one possible definition.

Definition 3.1 *A distributed database system consists of a collection of logically interrelated databases distributed at multiple sites connected by a computer network such that each site has autonomous processing capability and each site participates in the execution of requests that require accessing data across multiple sites.*

Many problems regarding centralized database systems, such as database design, query processing, and concurrency control, are much more difficult in distributed database systems because data and processing capabilities are distributed at multiple sites. In this chapter, we concentrate on the techniques for processing and optimizing queries in distributed database systems. In Section 3.1, several important concepts that are essential for understanding the techniques for distributed query processing and optimization will be introduced. Since join is the most expensive operation for most relational queries, the distributed processing and optimization of queries involving joins will be discussed in great detail. Several algorithms for joins will be discussed in Section 3.2. The algorithms in this section assume that data communication cost is not dominant. They try to make use of parallel processing in different sites so as to minimize response time. A dynamic-programming-based technique for processing a special subset of distributed queries—*chain queries*—will be presented in Section 3.3. In Section 3.4, we describe several interesting semi-join-based algorithms. They are mostly intended to minimize communication cost. An example in which these algorithms are particularly useful is the case in which the use of computers is free but users are charged for data communication costs. In some situations, after the execution of a semi-join, one operand can be eliminated and an attribute can be eliminated from the second operand (this will be discussed in Section 3.4). In such situations, a very substantial amount of data can be discarded, resulting in a significant reduction in both data communication costs and local processing costs. Section 3.5 illustrates that both joins and semi-joins can be utilized in a strategy to optimize the processing of a query.

3.1 Distributed Database Concepts

3.1.1 Computer Networks

A computer network is a collection of computers that are capable of exchanging information. Computer networks come in different topologies. Figure 3.1 depicts several different network topologies. In a meshed network, every two nodes (sites) are directly connected. However, in a star network or an irregular network, it is possible that two nodes are connected indirectly through other nodes.

Depending on the distances between the nodes, some networks are wide area networks (WANs), in which the distances between some sites are large, and others are local area networks (LANs), in which the distances between all sites are relatively small. As an example, a network connecting computers within a college campus is usually a local area network, whereas a network connecting computers in different cities or states is a wide area network.

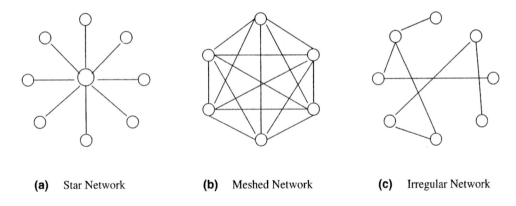

(a) Star Network **(b)** Meshed Network **(c)** Irregular Network

F i G U R E 3 . 1 Various Computer Networks

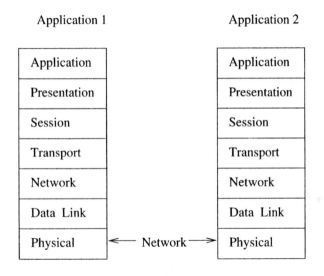

F I G U R E 3 . 2 Communication in the ISO/OSI Environment

To transmit data between two nodes in a network, the corresponding communication channel needs to be set up properly. For example, based on the ISO/OSI (International Standards Organization/Open System Interconnection) architecture, we need to go through seven layers of protocols in order for the communication channel to be ready for actual data transmission. Specifically, an application goes through the seven layers in the order *application, presentation, session, transport, network, data link,* and *physical,* before transmitting the data via the communication network to a different site. When the data arrive at the receiving site, the seven layers are traversed in reverse order before another application processes the data (see Figure 3.2). These layers facilitate two applications in communication by hiding details from these applications. For example, the data link layer handles error control, and the network layer handles the establishment, maintenance, and termination of connections. In practice, usually the first three layers, namely the physical, data link, and network, are utilized.

In this chapter, we assume that the cost (or time) of shipping X amount of data from one site to another site in the network is modeled as $c_0 + c_1 \cdot X$, where c_0 is the cost for setting up the communication channel and c_1 is the cost of transferring one unit of data (i.e., the transmission rate). In general, the data transmission rate between two nodes in a network depends on many factors, such as the distance between the two nodes, whether the two nodes are directly or indirectly connected, and the transmission medium (e.g., cable or satellite). This variation can be accommodated by using different sets of c_0's and c_1's for different communication channels. As a further simplification, we assume that any two nodes in the network can communicate with each other as if they were directly connected. The fact that they are indirectly connected may be modeled by attaching a larger c_0 to the communication channel.

3.1.2 Distributed Database Design

The process of designing a distributed relational database is very similar to that of designing a centralized relational database. The only difference is after the (global) conceptual schema is obtained, a new phase for *data distribution* is added for the distributed database system. For example, for the relation *Customer* of a distributed bank database, we want to decide in the data distribution phase where to store the data in the relation. One possible strategy is to store all customer data at a single site. Another is to store the data at different sites according to which branch the customer maintains an account at. In the latter case, the relation *Customer* is broken into multiple fragments.

In general, distribution of data is carried out in two phases:

Phase 1: Fragmentation. This phase determines how each relation is to be fragmented. A relation may be fragmented horizontally or vertically or both. If a relation is fragmented horizontally, each fragment is a subset of tuples of the relation and the relation can be reconstructed by unioning its fragments. If a relation is fragmented vertically, each fragment is a projection of the relation on a subset of its attributes and the relation can be reconstructed by joining its fragments. Clearly, fragmentation should be carried out carefully in order to ensure that the relation can be reconstructed correctly. Since horizontal fragments are more common, we will restrict our attention to horizontal fragments in this chapter.

Phase 2: Allocation. This phase determines how to place (allocate) each fragment in the network. This includes the determination of the number of copies of each fragment and the locations of these copies. A fragment is replicated if it has multiple copies. While a higher degree of replication can improve performance for retrieval queries, it incurs higher cost for update queries.

In this chapter, we assume that the initial distribution of data has already been determined before query processing and optimization starts. For issues concerning good techniques for the distribution of data, see the Bibliographic Notes at the end of the chapter.

	S_1	S_2	S_3	S_4
$R1$	$R1$		$R1$	
$R2$	F_{21}	F_{22}		F_{24}

FIGURE 3.3 Whole and Fragmented Relations

Example 3.1 In Figure 3.3, relation $R1$ exists as a whole relation with replications in sites S_1 and S_3, and relation $R2$ is the union of three fragments F_{21}, F_{22}, and F_{24}, in sites S_1, S_2, and S_4, respectively. ∎

The following notation is used above and will be used throughout this chapter: Each fragment has two subscripts. The first subscript denotes the relation number, and the second subscript denotes the site number.

In practice, fragments are naturally formed. For example, a company may have many branches in different locations. Each branch has a set of employees. Thus, the employee relation is naturally partitioned into as many fragments as the number of branches, with each fragment stored in a computer at the same location as the corresponding branch. In many situations, fragments of the same relation are disjoint and will be assumed to be disjoint in this chapter. The information describing which relation or fragment is in which site is stored in a directory. It can be in the form of a table. For example, a table with the fields (name, fragment/relation, location, replication) can store the information, where *name* is the name of the relation, *fragment/relation* indicates whether the stored item is a relation or a fragment, *location* gives the site where the item is stored, and *replication* indicates whether the item is replicated in multiple sites. If a relation has *i* fragments, then there will be *i* tuples in this table, the location of each fragment being given in one of the *i* tuples. Similarly, if a relation is replicated *j* times, there will be *j* tuples, with each tuple giving the location of a copy of the relation. In principle, the table can be distributed with different sets of tuples in different sites, or it can be replicated in all sites. We shall assume full replication in all sites so that when a query is submitted to any site, a query processing strategy can be planned at that site without requiring information from other sites. We note that the table given here is a simplification, because information about the processing powers of computers in different sites, physical access paths at local sites, and so on, which is essential for planning good processing strategies, is not included.

3.1.3 Issues in Query Optimization

In a centralized database system, the goal of query optimization is to find an execution strategy for each user query such that the *total cost* is the minimum. Typically, the total cost is a weighted sum of the CPU cost and the I/O cost incurred when processing the query. Since most centralized database systems run on a single computer with a single processor, minimizing the total cost implies the minimization of the *response time* (i.e., the real time needed to complete the query).

In a distributed database system, two different goals for query optimization are often considered. One is to minimize the total cost just as in a centralized database system except that the total cost also includes the communication cost for transmitting data across the network, in addition to the CPU and I/O costs. An alternative optimization criterion is to minimize the response time for each query. This is meaningful in a distributed database system because such a system consists of multiple computers that can process the query in parallel. It is possible to optimize a query using both criteria, with one as the primary goal and the other as a secondary goal. For example, we may first find an execution plan that minimizes the total cost and then modify the plan to minimize the response time with the condition that the total cost is not to be increased. The *tree-balancing algorithm* discussed in Chapter 4 is an example of such an approach. In this chapter, most of our discussions assume that minimizing the response time is the goal for query optimization.

Before we leave this section, we should point out that distributed database systems provide many transparencies, such as *network transparency, fragmentation transparency*, and *replication transparency*, to simplify the use of the systems. From a user's point of view, these transparencies effectively mean that a distributed database system can be used (i.e., queried) just like a centralized database system.

3.2 Distributed Processing of Joins

Selection, projection, and join are the three most frequently used operations. The execution of the first two operations is fairly straightforward. Consider executing the selection operation on a relation R. If R is a whole relation, then simply execute the selection at the site containing R and ship the result back to the user site. If R is fragmented in several sites, then for each site containing a fragment of R, execute the selection operation. The results of the different selection operations are then unioned to yield the answer. For the projection operation, the same process as selection is applicable. The only difference is that tuples obtained after the projection operation may contain duplicates that may need to be removed.

The join operation is not only frequently used but also expensive. As a result, many algorithms have been developed for the efficient processing of the join operation in a distributed database system. In this section, we focus on the processing of the join operation and present several join processing algorithms.

3.2.1 Utilizing Placement Dependency Information

Consider the join of two relations $R1$ and $R2$ on attribute A. Suppose both are fragmented relations with the initial distribution as shown in Figure 3.4.

Consider the following strategy for processing the above query: Take the joins of the fragments within the same site, and then take the union of the join results. That is, perform $(F_{11} \bowtie F_{21}) \cup (F_{12} \bowtie F_{22})$.

It would be nice if $R1 \bowtie R2$ could be obtained in this manner, because the join operations involving the fragments can be executed in parallel and without data transfer. Furthermore, indexes available at local sites can be utilized. Unfortunately, this strategy may yield an in-

	S_1	S_2
$R1$	F_{11}	F_{12}
$R2$	F_{21}	F_{22}

FIGURE 3.4 Two Fragmented Relations

correct result. As an example, if a tuple s in F_{11} and a tuple t in F_{22} both contain value "a" for attribute A, then s will concatenate with t in the join of $R1$ and $R2$. However, they will not participate in the join of the fragments, because the tuples are in different sites and no data transfer takes place for joining the fragments in this strategy. Even though it is not always correct, in many practical situations the strategy will obtain the correct result. For example, let $R1$ be the *Employee* relation with attributes (SSN, Name, Title, Sex, Dept#), and let $R2$ be a relation containing the dependents of the employees. Suppose the attributes of $R2$ are (SSN, SSND, Dname, Age), where SSN and SSND are the social security numbers of employees and their dependents, respectively. Let the join be on the social security number of the employees. We further assume that the tuples of the dependents of an employee always stay with the tuple of the employee. Thus, if an employee works in one branch and his or her tuple appears in fragment F_{1i}, then the tuple of each dependent of the employee would appear in F_{2i}. As a result, $R1 \bowtie R2 = (F_{11} \bowtie F_{21}) \cup (F_{12} \bowtie F_{22})$. This concept is formalized as follows:

Definition 3.2 *Two fragmented relations R_i and R_j have a* placement dependency *on attribute A if $F_{is} \bowtie_A F_{jt} = \emptyset$ for $s \neq t$. In other words, $R_i \bowtie_A R_j = \bigcup (F_{is} \bowtie_A F_{js})$, for each site s containing fragments of both relations.*

As a convenient notation, when two relations are involved in an equijoin in a query, we will label the joining attributes in the two relations to be the same, and the join condition can be expressed as $R_i.A = R_j.A$. Sometimes, a join condition between two relations is not explicitly written but can be inferred. For example, if $R_i.A = R_j.A$ and $R_j.A = R_k.A$, then $R_i.A = R_k.A$ can be inferred. The inference can be made by any transitive closure algorithm (see Chapter 7) or an algorithm for finding connected components (see Chapter 10), where each connected component contains relations having the same joining attribute. We will assume that all such inferences have been made for a given query.

Observation 1. If R_i and R_j have a placement dependency on A, then they have a placement dependency on any set of attributes B containing A. The reason is that if F_{is} and F_{jt}, $s \neq t$, have no common value under attribute A, then they cannot have any common value under the composite attribute B that contains A.

We further observe that if R_i and R_j have a placement dependency on attribute A, and another attribute (or set of attributes) B functionally determines A and A has no null values, then R_i and R_j also will have a placement dependency on B. To see that, suppose the two relations do not have the placement dependency on B. This means that there are two sites s and t, $s \neq t$, such that the fragment of R_i at site s, F_{is}, and the fragment of R_j at site t, F_{jt}, have a same value, say b, under attribute B. By functional dependency and because A has no null values, the tuple of F_{is} and the tuple of F_{jt} having the value b under attribute B must have the same value under attribute A. This directly contradicts the assertion that R_i and R_j have a placement dependency on A. Thus, R_i and R_j must have a placement dependency on B. In other words, attribute B is directly inferred by attribute A to be an attribute on which R_i and R_j have a placement dependency. If attribute C is directly inferred by attribute B to be such an attribute, then it is indirectly inferred by attribute A. We assume that for a given set of placement dependencies and a set of functional dependencies, all placement dependencies, including the deduced ones, can be obtained. A transitive closure algorithm (see Chapter 7) can be utilized to compute a set of attributes, on each of which R_i and R_j have a placement dependency.

Observation 2. If R_i and R_j have a placement dependency on A, and R_j and R_k have a placement dependency on B, then $(R_i \bowtie_A R_j \bowtie_B R_k) = \bigcup (F_{is} \bowtie_A F_{js} \bowtie_B F_{ks})$, where s ranges over all sites that contain a fragment for each of R_i, R_j, and R_k. In other words, all the join operations can be carried out locally and there is no need for data transfer. This can be derived as follows: $(R_i \bowtie_A R_j \bowtie_B R_k) = \bigcup_{s,t}((F_{is} \bowtie_A F_{js}) \bowtie_B F_{kt}) = (\bigcup_s (F_{is} \bowtie_A F_{js} \bowtie_B F_{ks})) \cup (\bigcup_{s,t \neq s}(F_{is} \bowtie_A F_{js} \bowtie_B F_{kt}))$. The last joins on B always yield an empty result, due to the placement dependency condition between R_j and R_k on B.

This observation says that the join operations in the query $R_i \bowtie_A R_j \bowtie_B R_k$ can be processed without data transfer. A slight generalization of this observation is as follows. Suppose a query Q contains a subquery Q' and an additional join $R_j \bowtie_B R_k$, where R_j is a relation referenced in Q' and R_k is outside Q'. Suppose that the join operations in Q' can be processed without data transfer and there is a placement dependency between R_j and R_k on B or a subset of B. Then the join operations in the entire query can be executed without data transfer. An example of this occurs when Q is $R_i \bowtie_A R_j \bowtie_B R_k$ and Q' is $R_i \bowtie_A R_j$, as given above. That a subset of B is sufficient for avoiding data transfer is due to the first part of Observation 1.

Based on these observations, a simple algorithm can be constructed to determine whether the join operations in a query can be executed without data transfer by making use of placement dependency information P.

Placement-Dependency (Q, P, S)

/* Let $R = \{R_1, R_2, \ldots, R_n\}$ be a set of relations referenced by query Q. P is the placement dependency information. Let S be a maximal set of relations whose join operations can be executed without data transfer, i.e., S cannot be enlarged further without causing data transfer. Initially, S is empty. At the termination of the algorithm, if $S = R$, then Q can be executed without data transfer. */

Initialize $S = \emptyset$;
Let $R = \{R_1, R_2, \ldots, R_n\}$;
If a pair of relations R_i and R_j in R can be found such that R_i and R_j have a placement
        dependency on some attribute A and $R_i \bowtie_C R_j$ is in Q, for C containing A,
            then place R_i and R_j in S;
If no such pair of relations can be found,
            then the algorithm terminates with S equal to empty;
While (there is a relation R_k in R but not in S satisfying the following property)

	S_1	S_2
R1	F_{11}	F_{12}
R2	R2	R2

FIGURE 3.5   Configuration before Executing the Joins

insert R_k into S;
If $S = R$, then Q can be processed without data transfer.

The property for R_k to be included in S is that there is a relation in S, say R_j, that has a placement dependency with R_k on some attribute B and $R_j \bowtie_B R_k$ is in Q or can be inferred from Q. Observation 2 permits R_k to be included in S.

Example 3.2 Let a query be $R_1 \bowtie_A R_2 \bowtie_B R_3 \bowtie_C R_4$. Suppose that there is a placement dependency between R_1 and R_2 on attribute A, a placement dependency between R_2 and R_3 on attribute B, and a placement dependency between R_3 and R_4 on attribute C. Initially, S is empty. After the first if-statement is executed, two relations, say R_1 and R_2, will be placed into S. Then R_3 is added to S due to the placement dependency and the join condition between R_2 and R_3 on attribute B. Finally, R_4 is added to S due to the placement dependency and the join condition on attribute C. Thus $S = \{R_1, R_2, R_3, R_4\}$. Since all relations referenced by the query are included in S, the query can be processed without data transfer.   ■

It is obvious that in order for the placement dependency information to be utilized in query processing, it has to be stored in some table. The construction of such a table is left as an exercise.

3.2.2   Fragment and Replicate Algorithm

If the join operations in a query Q cannot be processed without data transfer, then another algorithm needs to be used for the query. One such algorithm is the *Fragment and Replicate* algorithm. In this algorithm, a set of sites is chosen and the fragments of one referenced relation are assigned to the chosen sites while the other relations referenced in the query are replicated in the chosen sites. As an example, in Figure 3.4, suppose the fragments of R1 remain at sites S_1 and S_2. Then R2 can be replicated at S_1 and S_2 by transferring F_{21} from S_1 to S_2 and by transferring F_{22} from S_2 to S_1. When the fragment F_{21} arrives at S_2, it is unioned with F_{22} to obtain a copy of R2. Similarly, another copy of R2 is obtained from the transferred F_{22} and the local fragment F_{21}. This results in the configuration shown in Figure 3.5.

Consider a tuple t in R1. It is either in F_{11} or F_{12}. If it is in F_{11}, then it will be joined with the copy of R2 at site S_1; if it is in F_{12}, then it will be joined with the copy of R2 at site S_2. Since this is true for every tuple of R1, we have $R1 \bowtie R2 = \bigcup_i (F_{1i} \bowtie R2)$, where the union is over each site S_i having a fragment of R1. In each site S_i, a join takes place between F_{1i} and R2. These joins can be executed in parallel. Since F_{1i} is part of R1 and is therefore smaller than R1, the Fragment and Replicate algorithm is usually more efficient, in terms of response time, than a method in which all relations are transferred to one site and then the join is taken at that site. This strategy is applicable to queries involving two or more relations. When more than two relations are involved, only one relation will be left fragmented at the chosen sites while the other relations will be replicated. Conceptually, the replicated relations can be joined first to form a relation T with copies at the sites containing the fragments of the fragmented relation, and then at each of these sites, the copy of T can be joined with the corresponding fragment. Since this is equivalent to the two-relation situation, a correct result will be guaranteed.

Suppose a relation is to be left fragmented and the fragments of that relation are to be processed at their local sites. Our goal is to determine what relation is to be left fragmented so that the time to process the given query is minimized. Consider the example in Figure 3.4. We have two strategies: either $R1$ or $R2$ is left fragmented. For each strategy, the expected response time, i.e., the time to complete processing the query is computed. Then the strategy having the smallest expected response time is chosen. Suppose we leave $R1$ fragmented. The cost (time) spent at site S_1 is due to data transfer of F_{22} to site S_1, the union of F_{22} to F_{21} to form a copy of $R2$ at site S_1, and the time to execute the join between F_{11} and $R2$ at site S_1. The data transfer time for F_{22} can be assumed to be $c_0 + c_1 \cdot |F_{22}|$, where c_0 is the cost for setting up the communication channel, c_1 is the data transfer cost per unit (packet), and $|F_{22}|$ is the size of fragment F_{22}. The cost of performing the union of the two fragments can be assumed to be proportional to the sum of the sizes of the fragments, i.e., $|R2|$. The join operation is the more expensive operation. Its cost depends on the sizes of the fragments/relations in the join operation, the algorithm employed at the local site, and whether fast access paths or indexes are available. It should be noted that when a relation/fragment is transferred to another site, indexes that were built for the fragment/relation in the original site are likely to be useless in the destination site, since addresses referenced in the indexes are not preserved in the transfer to the destination. Estimation of the join cost (see Chapter 1) should take into consideration the effect of data transfer, which affects local processing costs. The sum of these costs gives an estimate of the total amount of time spent at S_1. Let the time be called *finish time* and be denoted by FT(Q, S_1, $R1$), where the relation to be left fragmented is denoted by the third parameter. Similarly, the time to process the subquery at site S_2 can be estimated and denoted by FT(Q, S_2, $R1$). Thus, the response time to the entire query when relation $R1$ is left fragmented can be given by max{FT(Q, S_1, $R1$), FT(Q, S_2, $R1$)}, since the operations at different sites can be executed in parallel. Similarly, the response time of the query when relation $R2$ is left fragmented is max{FT(Q, S_1, $R2$), FT(Q, S_2, $R2$)}. The relation to be left fragmented is the one that yields the smallest estimated response time. In this computation, we ignore the cost to transfer the result back to the site where the user wants the answer, and the cost to assemble the partial results to form the answer. These costs are assumed to be not very significant or unlikely to differ much when another strategy is used. If more than two sites are involved, the estimated finish time spent at each of these sites is obtained and the response time is the maximum of the finish times at these sites. Again, choose the relation to be left fragmented to be the one with the least expected response time. This applies to queries referencing two or more relations.

Example 3.3 Suppose a query is to join relations $R1$ and $R2$ with the data distributed as shown in Figure 3.4. Suppose the sizes of the fragments are as follows: $|F_{11}| = 50$, $|F_{12}| = 50$, $|F_{21}| = 100$, and $|F_{22}| = 200$. Suppose the data communication cost is given by C(X) = X (i.e.,

	S_1	S_2	$\cdots$	S_k	S_{k+1}	S_{k+2}
R1	F_{11}	F_{12}	$\cdots$	F_{1k}		
R2					R2	R2

FIGURE 3.6   Assigning Fragments to Processing Sites

$c_0 = 0$ and $c_1 = 1$); the local join processing cost at each site is given by $J(X_1, X_2) = 5 \cdot (X_1 + X_2)$, and the union cost at each site is $U(X_1, X_2) = 2 \cdot (X_1 + X_2)$. When relation $R1$ is left fragmented, the finish time at site S_1, FT$(Q, S_1, R1)$, is $200 + 2 \cdot (100 + 200) + 5 \cdot (50 + 300) = 2550$ where 200 is the data communication cost to transfer F_{22}, $2 \cdot (100 + 200)$ is the cost for the union of F_{21} and F_{22}, and $5 \cdot (50 + 300)$ is the cost for joining $R2$ with F_{11}. Similarly, FT$(Q, S_2, R1) = 100 + 2 \cdot (100 + 200) + 5 \cdot (50 + 300) = 2450$. Therefore, the response time of the query, when relation $R1$ is left fragmented, is 2550. A similar computation for the case in which relation $R2$ is left fragmented yields FT$(Q, S_1, R2) = 1250$ and FT$(Q, S_2, R2) = 1750$. Thus the response time of the query, when relation $R2$ is left fragmented, is 1750. Since the response time when relation $R1$ is left fragmented is greater than that when relation $R2$ is left fragmented, the latter choice is taken. It should be noted that in practice different sites have different processing speeds and fast access paths or indexes may exist for some relations at some sites but not for others, and this type of information needs to be taken into consideration by the query optimizer in order to obtain a good execution strategy. ∎

A sketch of the Fragment and Replicate algorithm follows.

Fragment-and-Replicate(Q, R, S)

/* Q is the query that references a set of relations R situated in a set of sites S. */

For each relation R_i that is left fragmented,
    For each site S_j containing a fragment of relation R_i,
        compute the estimated finish time of the subquery executing at site S_j,
            FT(Q, S_j, R_i);
        compute the response time if relation R_i is left fragmented, $RR_i = \max_j\{\mathrm{FT}(Q, S_j, R_i)\}$;
The relation to be left fragmented is relation R_k, where $RR_k = \min_i\{RR_i\}$.

The above algorithm assumes that the fragments of the relation that remains to be fragmented are not moved. This may not yield good response time.

Consider the problem of selecting appropriate processing sites and assigning the fragments of the relation that is to remain fragmented to the processing sites in such a way that the response time to the given query is minimized. Suppose there are two relations $R1$ and $R2$, and $R2$ is much larger than $R1$ so that transferring copies of $R2$ to other sites will not yield optimal strategies.

Consider the initial data configuration as shown in Figure 3.6. An optimal strategy is to transfer the fragments of $R1$ to sites S_{k+1} and S_{k+2} such that the finish time at each of the two sites is about the same. In other words, the fragments $\{F_{11}, F_{12}, \ldots, F_{1k}\}$ should be distributed in the two sites in such a way that the difference between the sum of the sizes of the data at one site and that at the other site is a minimum. Unfortunately, this problem is known to be NP-complete, so a brute force solution to choose the best set of sites and to distribute data to those sites to process the fragments of the chosen relation is likely to take exponential time. In the following we present a heuristic solution to this problem.

First, we arbitrarily pick a relation, say R_i, to remain fragmented and use the sites containing the fragments of the relation R_i as the processing sites. One of these sites, say site S_j, has the largest estimated finish time. Next, for each site S_t (including the initial processing sites as well as other sites that do not contain a fragment of R_i), the finish time that would be needed to process the subquery at site S_t if fragment F_{ij} were moved to site S_t from S_j is estimated. If a site S_t exists such that the estimated finish time at site S_t is less than that at site S_j, then pick a site S_{t_0} with the smallest estimated finish time. Since the response time of the query is determined by the maximum finish time at all sites, this strategy of replacing site S_j by site S_{t_0} as a processing site will not increase the response time. (A reduction in response time may not happen, because the finish time at another site can be the same as that at site S_j.) This process is repeated for each different fragment of R_i until no further reduction in finish time due to a change in a single processing site is possible. Then the entire process is repeated for a different relation to remain fragmented. For each relation, we keep track of its least estimated response time by means of the heuristic. The relation with the least estimated response time will be the one to remain fragmented.

As an example of this heuristic solution, consider the configuration given in Figure 3.6. Suppose site S_j, $1 \leq j \leq k$, has the largest estimated finish time. Suppose site S_{k+1} has a smaller estimated finish time if fragment F_{1j} is moved to site S_{k+1}, and site S_{k+2} has a higher estimated finish time than site S_{k+1}. This implies that fragment F_{1j} should be moved to site S_{k+1}. This process is repeated for other fragments of relation $R1$. Since site S_{k+1} already has F_{1j}, the next fragment of $R1$, say F_{1s}, will have a higher finish time if moved to S_{k+1} than if moved to S_{k+2}. As a result, the next fragment of $R1$ is moved to site S_{k+2}. As this process continues, the fragments of $R1$ will be allocated to sites S_{k+1} and S_{k+2}.

3.2.3 Combining Placement Dependencies and Data Replication

It is sometimes possible to combine placement dependency information with data replication information so that the join operations of certain queries can be processed without data transfer. The following example illustrates this idea.

Example 3.4 Consider the data configuration in Figure 3.7. Suppose there is a placement dependency between $R1$ and $R2$ on attribute A and the query is $R1 \bowtie_A R2 \bowtie_B R3$. Then the first join can be answered without data transfer due to the placement dependency information and the second join can be executed without data transfer due to the replication of $R3$. Another way to see that the query can be answered without data transfer is that after the join between $R1$ and $R2$ is performed, a relation, say $R4$, is formed. This relation has two fragments, one given by $F_{11} \bowtie F_{21}$ and the other given by $F_{12} \bowtie F_{22}$. By the Fragment and Replicate algorithm, the joining of the two fragments of $R4$ with the copies of $R3$ will yield the correct answer. ∎

	S_1	S_2
$R1$	F_{11}	F_{12}
$R2$	F_{21}	F_{22}
$R3$	$R3$	$R3$

FIGURE 3.7 Combining Placement Dependencies and Replication

The following definition can be utilized to combine the placement dependency information and the data replication information.

Definition 3.3 *There is a* join dependency *between relation R_i and relation R_j on attribute A if (1) there is a placement dependency between R_i and R_j on A or (2) relation R_i is replicated at the sites containing fragments of R_j or (3) relation R_j is replicated at the sites containing fragments of R_i.*

With this definition, the Placement Dependency algorithm can be generalized to an algorithm to determine whether the joins in a query can be processed without data transfer by using both placement dependency and replication information. The only change to be made is to replace placement dependency in the original algorithm by join dependency in the generalized algorithm. Let the generalized algorithm making use of join dependency information be called the *Join Dependency* algorithm.

It is clear that for some queries, the data distribution will not satisfy join dependency. However, by suitable redistribution or replication of data, join dependency can always be satisfied. For example, we can execute the Join Dependency (Q, J, S) algorithm for the query Q with join dependency information J. If S, a maximal set of relations referenced by Q that satisfies join dependency, is the same as R, the set of relations referenced by Q, then there is no need for data transfer; otherwise, the relations in $R - S$ need to be replicated to the sites containing S.

3.2.4 Hash Partitioning Algorithm

Another algorithm to process a query that does not satisfy join dependency utilizes hashing. As an example, consider the configuration in Figure 3.4. Suppose the join is on attribute A and A takes only integers. We apply the hash function $h(a) = 1$ if a is odd, 0 if a is even. Whenever a hash value of 1 is obtained, the tuple is sent to site S_1; otherwise, it is sent to site S_2. Then the fragment F_{11} is partitioned into subfragments F_{11}^o and F_{11}^e, where o and e stand for odd and even values under attribute A, respectively. Similarly, F_{12} can be partitioned into F_{12}^o and F_{12}^e. F_{11}^e is transferred to site S_2 to be combined with F_{12}^e to form a new fragment F_{12}'. Fragment F_{11}' is obtained by unioning F_{11}^o and F_{12}^o. Similarly, fragments F_{21}' and F_{22}' can be obtained by data transmission and unions. It is clear that $\pi_A(F_{11}')$ and $\pi_A(F_{22}')$ have no values in common, as the former has only odd numbers and the latter has only even numbers. Thus, $F_{11}' \bowtie F_{22}'$ is empty. This implies that there is a placement dependency between $R1$ and $R2$ on attribute A based on the newly formed fragments. Therefore, $R1 \bowtie_A R2$ can be evaluated by

S_1	S_2
$F_{11}^o(A)$	$F_{12}^e(A)$
$F_{21}^o(A) \cup F_{21}^o(B)$	$F_{22}^e(A) \cup F_{22}^e(B)$
$F_{31}^o(B)$	$F_{32}^o(B)$

FIGURE 3.8   Illustrating Tuple Duplication

$(F_{11}' \bowtie_A F_{21}') \cup (F_{12}' \bowtie_A F_{22}')$. If the domain of attribute A is not the set of integers, the last bit of its binary representation can be used to determine the site. Alternatively, a hash function mapping to the range [0, 1] can be devised so that a hash value in [0, 0.5] implies that the tuple goes to site S_1 and a hash value in (0.5, 1] implies that the tuple goes to site S_2.

Consider the join of three relations $R1$, $R2$, and $R3$. Suppose the relations are in two sites. There are two cases: the joins are on the same attribute A or they are on different attributes.

Case 1. $R1 \bowtie_A R2 \bowtie_A R3$

In this situation, the hash function given earlier can be applied to the fragments of the three relations, and placement dependencies among $R1$, $R2$, and $R3$ on attribute A will be satisfied using the newly formed fragments. As a result, after hashing and data transmission, the resulting fragments in the two sites are joined on attribute A in parallel and their results are unioned to give the final answer.

Case 2. $R1 \bowtie_A R2 \bowtie_B R3$

If we apply the same hash function on attribute A and the same (or even a different) hash function on attribute B, then the desired placement dependencies may not be achieved for the following reason. Tuples of $R1$ with odd values under A will be in site S_1; tuples of $R3$ with odd values under B will be in site S_1. However, some tuples of $R2$ may have odd values under A and even values under B. Each of these tuples is mapped by the two hash functions to two different sites. One solution is to permit these tuples to be duplicated at both sites. For example, in Figure 3.8, a tuple of $R2$ having an odd value under A and an even value under B belongs to both $F_{21}^o(A)$ and $F_{22}^e(B)$ and is replicated in both sites S_1 and S_2, where $F_{21}^o(A)$ represents those tuples of $R2$ having odd values under A and $F_{22}^e(B)$ represents those tuples of $R2$ having even values under B; F_{ij} represents the fragment of relation R_i that should reside at site S_j before the actual joins are taken. In general, a relation may have multiple attributes participating in joins with other relations. If a tuple of the relation is mapped by the hash functions associated with the joining attributes to several sites, then it should be replicated at those sites.

Another solution is to execute one join at a time. In other words, the join between $R1$ and $R2$ on A can be carried out using the hashing method to yield a relation, say $R4$. Then the join between $R4$ and $R3$ on B can be executed using the same hashing method with possibly a different hash function.

We have the following observations:

1.   If there are i sites, then a hash function such as $h(a) = j + 1$, where $j = a \bmod i$, can be applied, i.e., when "a" is divided by i with remainder j, then the tuple goes to site S_{j+1}.

In this way, a tuple with a given value on the joining attribute is mapped to one of the i sites, as j varies from 0 to $i - 1$.

2. Another way to partition a relation/fragment is based on the ranges of values of some attribute. For example, if the joining attribute A has range [Low, High], then the range can be divided into i disjoint intervals [Low, a_1], $(a_1, b_1]$, ..., $(a_{i-1}, \text{High}]$ such that a tuple in the interval [Low, a_1] goes to site S_1, a tuple in the interval $(a_j, b_j]$ goes to site S_{j+1}, $1 \geq j \geq i - 2$, and a tuple in the interval $(a_{i-1}, \text{High}]$ goes to site S_i. This is known as *range partitioning*. If the distributions of the values of the relations on the joining domain are uniform, then the values $a_1, a_2, \ldots, a_{i-1}$ should be evenly spaced; otherwise, adjustments to the boundary points of the intervals should be made to have approximately an equal number of tuples per interval. More discussion on hash partitioning and range partitioning can be found in Chapter 5.

3. It is worthwhile to study the trade-off between the two methods for Case 2, one in which parts of $R2$ are replicated and the other in which hash joins are performed sequentially. It is likely that the scheme that permits replications of data will have smaller response times because there are fewer sequential operations.

3.2.5 A Comparison of Different Methods

We make the comparison on the basis of a simple example. In this example, the costs of sending and assembling the partial results at the site where the answer is required are ignored. Suppose there are two relations $R1$ and $R2$ of equal size and distributed as given in Figure 3.4. It is assumed that each fragment is of equal size, which is denoted by $R/2$, where R is the size of each relation.

The performance characteristics of the Placement Dependency algorithm are as follows:

■ No data are transferred.

■ Indexes available for joining at local sites can be utilized.

■ The total amount of data to be joined in each site is R, as each fragment has size $R/2$ and there are two fragments at each site.

The performance characteristics of the Fragment and Replicate algorithm are as follows:

■ The total amount of data transfer is R, as all fragments of the replicated relation need to be transferred to other sites.

■ After data transfer, indexes that were available for the transferred relation may need to be reconstructed or may be useless.

■ The total amount of data to be joined in each site is $\frac{3}{2}R$, as each site contains one whole relation and one fragment.

The performance characteristics of the Hash Partitioning algorithm are as follows (assume that data distribution under the joining attribute is uniform):

■ The total amount of data transfer is R, as half of each fragment at each site needs to be transferred to the other site.

■ On the use of indexes, the Hash Partitioning algorithm is even more ineffective than the Fragment and Replicate algorithm, because indexes on both relations are likely to be useless after data transfer.

■ The total amount of data to be joined at each site is the same as that in the case of the Placement Dependency algorithm.

Based on the above information, the Placement Dependency algorithm has the least amount of data transfer (actually none) and the least amount of data to be joined and can utilize indexes. Thus it should give the best performance. It is followed by the Hash Partitioning algorithm and then the Fragment and Replicate algorithm. However, the Placement Dependency algorithm is applicable only when suitable semantic information is given and is applicable. The good performance of the Hash Partitioning algorithm requires a relatively uniform distribution of data values. In the worst case, both relations may end up at one site and load balancing is not achieved. In situations where one of the relations is already replicated at the sites containing the fragments of the other relation, immediate local processing without transfer can be performed. Thus there are situations where the Fragment and Replicate algorithm can outperform the Hash Partitioning algorithm.

3.3 Processing Chain Queries

A chain query is rather common and is of the form

$$R1 \bowtie_{A_1} R2 \bowtie_{A_2} R3 \bowtie_{A_3} \cdots \bowtie_{A_{n-2}} R_{n-1} \bowtie_{A_{n-1}} R_n$$

where nonadjacent relations have no common joining attribute. This implies that $A_i \neq A_j, i \neq j$. To avoid Cartesian products, the relative position of each relation is fixed during chain query optimization. For example, $R2$ and $R3$ should not exchange their positions, because if they do, a Cartesian product between $R1$ and $R3$ will appear.

For the three-relation case, $R1$ can be joined with $R2$ and then with $R3$ (i.e., $(R1 \bowtie_{A_1} R2) \bowtie_{A_2} R3$), or $R2$ can be joined with $R3$ and then with $R1$ (i.e., $R1 \bowtie_{A_1} (R2 \bowtie_{A_2} R3)$). The problem is to determine the order in which the joins are to be taken such that the least cost will be incurred. This is equivalent to placing the parentheses around the relations to determine their order of execution.

If the relations are whole (unfragmented) and the cost to be minimized is the sum of communication costs, then a straightforward application of dynamic programming on the processing of chain queries will yield an optimal result. This approach with adjustments to incorporate both local processing costs and data communication costs will be presented in the following paragraph. If the relations are fragmented and response time composed of both local processing costs and data communication costs is to be minimized, the same approach with some adjustments can be utilized. However, optimality is not guaranteed.

We first obtain the least cost of joining two adjacent relations together. Let the costs for joining relations R_i and R_{i+1} be denoted by $cost_{i,i+1}, 1 \leq i \leq n - 1$. The join between two relations can be performed using different methods, such as hash partitioning join or fragment and replicate join. The least cost of joining two relations, which depends on the method used as well as the physical aspects of the data (such as the locations of the data and the indexes on the data), can be obtained by choosing the strategy that has the overall minimum estimated cost. This cost involves both data communication cost and local processing cost. Let the relation obtained by joining R_i with R_{i+1} be denoted by $R_{i,i+1}$. Then the least cost for joining the three relations R_i, R_{i+1}, and R_{i+2} together is achieved by either joining $R_{i,i+1}$ with R_{i+2} or joining R_i with $R_{i+1,i+2}$. Before the second join is considered, $\text{cost}_{i,i+1}$ and $\text{cost}_{i+1,i+2}$ have been obtained. Thus the least cost for joining three relations together can be expressed from the least cost for joining two relations together plus some additional join costs. This process is repeated for all sets of four adjacent relations, five adjacent relations, and so on, until the least cost for joining the n relations is obtained. A more precise description is given as follows.

Let $\text{cost}_{i,j}$, $i < j$, be the least cost for joining adjacent relations $R_i, R_{i+1}, \ldots, R_j$, resulting in relation $R_{i,j}$. $R_{i,j}$ can be obtained by joining R_i with $R_{i+1,j}$ or joining $R_{i,i+1}$ with $R_{i+2,j}$ to ... or joining $R_{i,j-1}$ with R_j. Since the cost for obtaining $R_{i+1,j}$ is $\text{cost}_{i+1,j}$, one cost for obtaining $R_{i,j}$ is $\text{cost}_{i+1,j} + \text{joinc}(R_i, R_{i+1,j})$, where $\text{joinc}(\ )$ denotes the least cost of joining the two relations. Since the aim is to obtain the least total cost, the minimum of the different costs is taken. Thus we have

$$\text{cost}_{i,j} = \min_{i \le k < j}\{\text{cost}_{i,k} + \text{cost}_{k+1,j} + \text{joinc}(R_{i,k}, R_{k+1,j})\} \tag{3.1}$$

where $\text{cost}_{k,k} = 0$ and $R_{k,k} = R_k$. The goal of chain query optimization is to find an execution plan for computing $R_{1,n}$ with the least cost $\text{cost}_{1,n}$. Since the actual cost in Equation (3.1) cannot be obtained until the query is executed, it needs to be estimated. As noted before, the join cost is based on the sizes of the two operand relations, their physical aspects, and the joining algorithm employed. In addition, the size of the resulting relation, which has an impact on the join cost, needs to be estimated. Another reason for estimating its size is that it may join with another relation in a later join. Based on Equation (3.1), the following bottom-up algorithm for chain query optimization can be derived. In the following algorithm, when $j - i = s$, the minimum costs for joining all $(s + 1)$ relations together are computed.

Chain-Query-Optimization

Compute cost$_{1,n}$

> For $j - i = 1$ to $n - 1$ do
> > {compute $\text{cost}_{i,j}$ based on Equation (3.1);
> > let $K(i, j)$ be the value of k that minimizes the right-hand side of Equation (3.1)—
> > that is, $\text{cost}_{i,j} = \text{cost}_{i,K(i,j)} + \text{cost}_{K(i,j)+1,j} + \text{joinc}(R_{i,K(i,j)}, R_{K(i,j)+1,j})$;
> > }

Generate the execution plan. The optimal execution plan can be generated by tracing back the appropriate $K(i, j)$'s. First, there is a unique $K(1, n)$, and it indicates that the last join operation is $R_{1,K(1,n)} \bowtie_{A_{K(1,n)}} R_{K(1,n)+1,n}$. The minimum cost for obtaining $R_{1,K(1,n)}$ is $\text{cost}_{1,K(1,n)}$. Again, there is a unique $K(1, K(1, n))$, and from it the last join for obtaining $R_{1,K(1,n)}$ can be derived. Similarly, the last join for obtaining $R_{K(1,n)+1,n}$ can be derived. By repeating this line of analysis, the orders among the $n - 1$ joins can be determined.

$$
\begin{array}{c}
\text{cost}_{1,n} \\
\text{cost}_{1,n-1} \quad \text{cost}_{2,n} \\
\cdots \\
\text{cost}_{1,3} \quad \text{cost}_{2,4} \quad \cdots \quad \text{cost}_{n-2,n} \\
\text{cost}_{1,2} \quad \text{cost}_{2,3} \quad \text{cost}_{3,4} \quad \cdots \quad \text{cost}_{n-1,n} \\
\text{cost}_{1,1} \quad \text{cost}_{2,2} \quad \text{cost}_{3,3} \quad \text{cost}_{4,4} \quad \cdots \quad \text{cost}_{n,n}
\end{array}
$$

FIGURE 3.9 **Bottom-Up Computation of $\text{cost}_{1,n}$**

It takes $n - 1$ iterations to compute $\text{cost}_{1,n}$. In the first iteration, all $\text{cost}_{i,j}$'s with $j - i = 1$ are computed. There are $n - 1$ such computations. In the second iteration, all $\text{cost}_{i,j}$'s with $j - i = 2$ are computed, and there are $n - 2$ such computations. In general, in the lth iteration, all $\text{cost}_{i,j}$'s with $j - i = l$ are computed, and there are $n - l$ such computations. Therefore, the total number of $\text{cost}_{i,j}$'s that need to be computed is $\sum_{l=1}^{n-1} l = \frac{1}{2}(n - 1)(n - 2) = O(n^2)$. For any given i and j, $\text{cost}_{i,j}$ can be obtained by computing and comparing $j - i$ expressions. Clearly, $j - i$ is upper-bounded by $n - 1$. Therefore, the total number of computations needed to obtain $\text{cost}_{1,n}$ is $O(n^3)$. The second phase of the algorithm takes only $O(n)$ steps. Thus, the time complexity of the above Chain Query Optimization algorithm is $O(n^3)$. Figure 3.9 illustrates the bottom-up computation of $\text{cost}_{1,n}$. In the figure, $\text{cost}_{i,i} = 0$, $i = 1, \ldots, n$.

Example 3.5 Consider the computation of the join of four relations,

$$R_1 \bowtie_{A_1} R_2 \bowtie_{A_2} R_3 \bowtie_{A_3} R_4$$

Initially, the least costs for joining adjacent relations are estimated. Suppose the estimated join costs are given as follows: $\text{cost}_{1,2} = \text{joinc}(R_1, R_2) = 3$, $\text{cost}_{2,3} = \text{joinc}(R_2, R_3) = 5$, and $\text{cost}_{3,4} = \text{joinc}(R_3, R_4) = 6$. Clearly, $K(1, 2) = 1$, $K(2, 3) = 2$, and $K(3, 4) = 3$. Then the minimum cost for computing $R_1 \bowtie_{A_1} R_2 \bowtie_{A_2} R_3$, $\text{cost}_{1,3}$, is given by

$$\min\{\text{cost}_{1,2} + \text{joinc}(R_{1,2}, R_3), \text{cost}_{2,3} + \text{joinc}(R_1, R_{2,3})\}$$

Suppose $\text{joinc}(R_{1,2}, R_3) = 4$ and $\text{joinc}(R_1, R_{2,3}) = 1$. Then $\text{cost}_{1,3}$ is $\min\{3 + 4, 5 + 1\} = 6$ and $K(1, 3) = 1$. The minimum cost for computing $R_2 \bowtie_{A_2} R_3 \bowtie_{A_3} R_4$, $\text{cost}_{2,4}$, can be similarly estimated. Suppose $\text{joinc}(R_{2,3}, R_4) = 3$ and $\text{joinc}(R_2, R_{3,4}) = 4$. Then $\text{cost}_{2,4}$ is $\min\{5 + 3, 6 + 4\} = 8$ and $K(2, 4) = 3$. Finally, the minimum cost for computing the join of the four relations, $\text{cost}_{1,4}$, is given by

$$\min\{\text{cost}_{1,3} + \text{joinc}(R_{1,3}, R_4), \text{cost}_{1,2} + \text{cost}_{3,4} + \text{joinc}(R_{1,2}, R_{3,4}), \text{cost}_{2,4} + \text{joinc}(R_1, R_{2,4})\}$$

Suppose $\text{joinc}(R_{1,3}, R_4) = 5$, $\text{joinc}(R_{1,2}, R_{3,4}) = 4$, and $\text{joinc}(R_1, R_{2,4}) = 2$. Then $\text{cost}_{1,4} = \min\{6 + 5, 3 + 6 + 4, 8 + 2\} = 10$ and $K(1, 4) = 1$. We now use the $K(i, j)$'s to construct the execution plan whose total cost is 10. From $K(1, 4) = 1$, we know that the last join is $R_1 \bowtie_{A_1} R_{2,4}$. From $K(2, 4) = 3$, we know that $R_{2,4}$ is obtained from $R_{2,3} \bowtie_{A_3} R_4$. Finally, from $K(2, 3) = 2$, we know that $R_{2,3}$ is computed from $R_2 \bowtie_{A_2} R_3$. Therefore, the execution plan that we are looking for is $R_1 \bowtie_{A_1} ((R_2 \bowtie_{A_2} R_3) \bowtie_{A_3} R_4)$. ∎

The following observations can be made:

1. The above algorithm assumes the dynamic programming principle, in which an optimal solution to a problem can be constructed from optimal solutions to different subproblems. The dynamic programming principle may not hold for this problem. For example, consider the problem of joining R_1, R_2, and R_3. Suppose the fragments of R_1 and those of R_2 are in sites S_1 and S_2 and those of R_3 are in sites S_2 and S_3. An optimal solution to join R_1 and R_2 may require the fragments of the resulting relation to be in sites S_1 and S_2. A suboptimal solution to join the two relations may have the fragments in sites S_2 and S_3. However, the resulting relation with fragments at S_2 and S_3 may yield the optimal solution to the join of the three relations when joined with the fragments in R_3. Thus, the dynamic programming principle may not be satisfied exactly. Although some of these problems can be solved (see Section 3.5 for classifying strategies into types), the solutions cause considerable complications and will not be given here. Equation (3.1) also assumes that all operations are carried out sequentially. In other words, total cost rather than response time is minimized. It is possible that some operations can be performed in parallel. For example, while relations R_i and R_{i+1} are joined, relations R_{i+2}, R_{i+3}, ..., R_j can be joined. Thus the algorithm described above should be considered as a heuristic.

2. The above technique may be used in conjunction with the three join algorithms discussed in Section 3.2 (the Placement Dependency algorithm, the Fragment and Replicate algorithm, and the Hash Partitioning algorithm). For example, for each join, we may estimate the cost of applying each of these algorithms and then take the algorithm with the least expected cost.

3.4 Semi-Join

Consider the situation in which communication cost is large relative to local processing cost. Such would be the case if the users own the local computers but have to pay for communication costs. Suppose a function that characterizes communication cost is $C(X) = c_0 + c_1 \cdot X$, where X is the amount of data shipped from one site to another. This function assumes a startup connection cost c_0 and a cost that is linearly proportional to the amount of data transferred. Distance between the sites is assumed to be insignificant. Clearly, data transfer across continents is costlier than transfer across cities. The trend is that the difference in cost is becoming smaller and smaller. If communication cost is the only cost to be minimized, then all data that are clearly unnecessary for answering a given query should be removed by selections and projections before joins are considered.

Example 3.6 Suppose we have two relations $R1$ at site S_1 and $R2$ at site S_2. Consider the query that joins $R1$ and $R2$ on attribute A and requires the result to be at site S_2. A straightforward method is to send relation $R1$ to site S_2 and perform the join at S_2. The cost of this method is $c_0 + c_1 \cdot |R1|$, where $|X|$ is the size of X. In this case, $|R1|$ is the number of tuples of the relation times the number of bytes needed to store each tuple. Assume that the number of tuples of $R1$ is n, the relation has two attributes A and B, and each attribute value takes one unit of space. Then the communication cost using the straightforward method is $c_0 + c_1 \cdot 2 \cdot n$. Now consider the following alternative method. At site S_2, a projection of $R2$ on the joining

R1	
A	B
1	b_1
2	b_2
3	b_3
⋮	⋮
n	b_n

(a)

R2	
A	C
1	c_1
2	c_2
1	c_3
⋮	⋮
2	c_m

(b)

Another R2 with $n \leq m$

A	C
1	c_1
2	c_2
3	c_3
⋮	⋮
m	c_m

(c)

FIGURE 3.10   Illustrating the Semi-Join Method

attribute A is taken. After the duplicates are eliminated, the distinct values of $R2$ under A, $\pi_A(R2)$, are sent to site S_1, where π represents the projection operator. A join is then taken between $\pi_A(R2)$ and $R1$. Finally, the result is sent back to site S_2 for another join to obtain the final result. Unlike the first method, which requires data transfer once and performs one join, the second method transfers data across sites twice and performs two joins. However, the total amount of data transferred by the second method could be less than that transferred by the first method. To see this, consider the data associated with the relations shown in Figure 3.10.

Suppose the numbers of distinct values in $\pi_A(R1)$ and $\pi_A(R2)$ are n and 2, respectively. The communication cost to transfer $\pi_A(R2)$ is $c_0 + c_1 \cdot 2$. The result of joining $R1$ and $\pi_A(R2)$ are the first two tuples of $R1$. The cost to transfer these two tuples back to site S_2 is $c_0 + c_1 \cdot 2 \cdot 2$, since each tuple occupies 2 units. Thus the total communication cost for the second method is $2 \cdot c_0 + 6 \cdot c_1$. Therefore, the second method incurs a lower communication cost when $c_0 + 6 \cdot c_1 < c_1 \cdot 2 \cdot n$. ∎

In the above example, the operation $\pi_A(R2) \bowtie R1$, denoted by $R2 \xrightarrow{A} R1$, is called the *semi-join* from $R2$ to $R1$ on attribute A. The left operand $R2$ is sent to the site containing the right operand $R1$. The direction of movement of data is indicated by the arrow. From this example, the following observations can be made.

1. The result of $R2 \xrightarrow{A} R1$ is guaranteed to be no larger than the original $R1$, since only those tuples of $R1$ that have common values with $\pi_A(R2)$ are retained. In other words, a selection is performed on $R1$, based on the distinct values of $\pi_A(R2)$. Thus, a semi-join operation is a reduction operation, attempting to use the relation on the left of $\longrightarrow$ (in this case $R2$) to reduce the size of the relation on the right of $\longrightarrow$ (in this case $R1$).

2. In Example 3.6, all the data in $R1$ needed to answer the query (in this case, $(1, b_1)$ and $(2, b_2)$) are obtained after executing the semi-join. A data item $((i, b_i), 3 \geq i \geq n$, in this example) is unnecessary if deleting it will not affect the answer to the query. There are no unnecessary data left for the join after the semi-join operation. A natural question to ask is whether semi-joins can always eliminate all unnecessary data from the referenced relations for a given query.

3. In some situations the semi-join method may yield lower communication costs, whereas it may be more expensive in other situations. It is therefore worthwhile to estimate the cost of a method before it is applied. To see that the semi-join method can be more expensive, let the relation $R2$ in Figure 3.10(b) be replaced by the new relation $R2$ in Figure 3.10(c). It is clear that the semi-join $R2 \xrightarrow{A} R1$ does not reduce $R1$, since for $n \leq m$, all values in $\pi_A(R1)$ are contained in $\pi_A(R2)$. Therefore, the method is not effective in this situation. Thus it is of interest to differentiate effective semi-joins (see the definition of a profitable semi-join in the Process General Queries algorithm in Section 3.4.2) from noneffective ones.

4. An efficient way to implement a semi-join $R2 \xrightarrow{A} R1$ is to employ a *Bloom filter* as follows. A bit vector is initialized to be all zeros. Each value in $\pi_A(R2)$ is hashed by a hash function h into a bit in the bit vector; i.e., the bit is set to 1. The bit vector is sent from the site containing $R2$ to the site containing $R1$. In order to determine which tuples of $R1$ may join with $R2$ on attribute A, each value in $\pi_A(R1)$ is hashed by the same hash function h into the bit vector. If it is hashed into a 0 bit, it will definitely not join with $R2$; if it is hashed into a 1 bit, it may join with $R2$. Those tuples of $R1$ whose hashed bits are 1 are sent to the site containing $R2$ to perform $R1 \bowtie_A R2$. Checking whether a tuple in $R1$ may match a tuple in $R2$ on A by means of the filter is efficient because constant time by the use of hashing is sufficient.

We now address the above items 2 and 3 in the next two subsections.

3.4.1 Eliminate All Unnecessary Data for a Query Using Semi-Joins

In this subsection, we characterize two types of queries: (1) queries in which semi-joins can guarantee the elimination of all unnecessary data, and (2) queries in which such a guarantee cannot be made by semi-joins.

Definition 3.4 *A relation R is* fully reduced *with respect to a query Q if all unnecessary data of the relation R for Q have been eliminated.*

For the query $R1 \bowtie_A R2$ in Example 3.6, relation $R1$ is fully reduced after the semi-join $R2 \xrightarrow{A} R1$ is executed. All unnecessary data, $\{(i, b_i), 3 \geq i \geq n\}$, have been eliminated for the case in which $R2$ is given by Figure 3.10(b). In the situation in which $R2$ is given by Figure 3.10(c), after the semi-join is executed, $R1$ is also fully reduced, although no data are eliminated from $R1$. This is due to the fact that all data in $R1$ are necessary. The next example illustrates that semi-joins may not be able to eliminate all unnecessary data from certain queries.

Example 3.7 Consider the query Q1 involving the join of three relations as follows: $R1.A = R2.A$ and $R2.B = R3.B$ and $R3.C = R1.C$. Suppose the contents of the relations are as shown in Figure 3.11.

The answer to the query Q1 is empty, because no combination of tuples from the three relations can satisfy the query qualification. As an example, the combination of tuples $(0, 5)$

R1

A	C
0	5
1	4

R2

A	B
0	2
1	3

R3

B	C
2	4
3	5

FIGURE 3.11   **Three Relations**

from $R1$, $(0, 2)$ from $R2$, and $(2, 4)$ from $R3$ does not satisfy $R3.C = R1.C$. Thus, the fully reduced relations should be $R1 = \emptyset$, $R2 = \emptyset$, and $R3 = \emptyset$. Since none of the six possible semi-joins $R_i \xrightarrow{X} R_j$, where X is A or B or C, $i \neq j$, and $1 \leq i, j \leq 3$, has any effect on R_j, none of the three relations can be fully reduced by semi-joins. ∎

Since semi-joins can be utilized to fully reduce relations for some queries but not for other queries, it is desirable to characterize the type of queries that can be fully reduced by semi-joins. The following definition is introduced to facilitate the characterization.

Definition 3.5 *Given a query* Q, *its join graph* G(V, E) *consists of vertices representing the relations referenced by* Q *and edges representing the join conditions. Each edge* (R_i, R_j) *with label* X *represents the set of attributes* X *that are to be equijoined between* R_i *and* R_j. *It is assumed that attributes have been renamed, if necessary, so that* R_i *and* R_j *have the same attribute* Y *if and only if they are joined on* Y.

In this subsection, we will use the terms *query* and *qualification* interchangeably, because only the qualification condition (not the target) is used to characterize the type of a query with respect to semi-joins.

Example 3.8 The join graph for the query (Q1) in Example 3.7 is as follows:

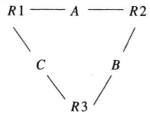

We note that the graph is cyclic—i.e., there are multiple ways to go from one vertex to another vertex. Specifically, $R1$ can go to $R3$ either directly via the edge with label C or via the two edges with the intermediate relation $R2$. ∎

It can be shown that an *inherently cyclic query* (to be defined later) makes the relations of a query not fully reducible. In the following example, the join graph is cyclic but the query is not inherently cyclic.

Example 3.9 Consider the qualification of query Q2: $R1.A = R2.A$ and $R2.A = R3.A$ and $R1.B = R3.B$. The join graph of this query is as follows:

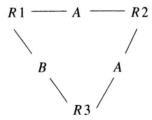

The join graph is cyclic. However, the query is not inherently cyclic because by the following transformation, an equivalent qualification that has an acyclic join graph can be obtained. Note that $R1.A = R2.A$ and $R2.A = R3.A$ imply that $R1.A = R3.A$, due to the transitivity of equality, and $\{R1.A = R2.A, R2.A = R3.A\}$ is equivalent to the set of two equijoins $\{R1.A = R2.A, R1.A = R3.A\}$. (In fact, it is equivalent to any two equijoins of the two pairs of relations from $R1$, $R2$, and $R3$ on attribute A, because the third equijoin is deducible from the chosen two.) By using the latter set of equijoins instead of the given set, together with the given equijoin $R1.B = R3.B$, the following acyclic join graph is obtained:

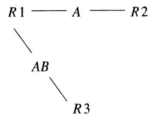

It will be shown later that the three relations can be fully reduced by semi-joins. Motivated by this example, we can define the concept of an *inherently cyclic query*:

Definition 3.6 *A query Q is (inherently) cyclic if the join graph of every query Q' that is equivalent to Q is cyclic. Equivalence of qualification conditions is established by transitivity of equijoins. A query Q is a tree query if the join graph of some query Q' that is equivalent to Q is acyclic.*

As explained above, query Q1 is inherently cyclic, but query Q2 is acyclic. The basic result for cyclic and acyclic queries is stated as follows:

Proposition 3.1 *Relations referenced by acyclic queries can be fully reduced by semi-joins, whereas relations referenced by cyclic queries might not be fully reduced by semi-joins.*

The relations referenced by query Q1 in Example 3.7 are not fully reduced by semi-joins. However, if they were empty relations, they would be fully reduced, as there would be no unnecessary data. Thus, due to some initial condition or after executing some semi-joins, it is possible that the relations referenced in a cyclic query have been fully reduced. Semi-joins cannot guarantee the referenced relations to be fully reduced, but such guarantee is possible for tree queries.

The following is a two-phase algorithm that fully reduces every relation referenced in a tree query. The first phase employs semi-joins from leaves to root to fully reduce the relation at the root, and the second phase employs semi-joins from root to leaves to fully reduce all other relations referenced by the query.

Fully-Reduce (Q)

/* Q is a tree query, and the reduction of the relations referenced in Q is by semi-joins. */

Since query Q is a tree query, its join graph or the join graph of an equivalent query is a tree. Let the tree graph be $G(V, E)$. One of the vertices in V can be chosen to be the root of the tree. With the root determined, its children and therefore their children, and so on, can be identified. Finally, the leaves of the tree having no children are identified.

Phase 1.   /* From the leaves to the root */
Execute semi-joins from leaves to their parents. For each intermediate vertex v, which is neither the root nor a leaf, if the semi-joins executing on it by its children have been completed, then a semi-join from v to its parent can be executed.

At the end of this phase, all semi-joins from vertices to their parents have been executed. The last semi-joins to be executed are those directed to the root from its children. The intention of this phase is to fully reduce the relation at the root.

Phase 2.   /* From the root to the leaves */
Execute semi-joins from the root to its children. For each intermediate vertex v, except the root and the leaves, if a semi-join executing on it by its parent has been completed, then the semi-joins from v to its children can be executed.

In Phase 2, the semi-joins are executed in reverse order in comparison to those in Phase 1. The intention is to fully reduce the relations at vertices other than the root vertex.

Example 3.10 Consider the query $R_1.A = R_2.A$ and $R_1.B = R_3.B$ and $R_3.C = R_4.C$ and $R_3.D = R_5.D$. This query has the tree join graph as shown in Figure 3.12(a). In this example, we apply the Fully Reduce algorithm to fully reduce all relations referenced by the query.

Let the semi-joins $R_4 \xrightarrow{C} R_3$, $R_5 \xrightarrow{D} R_3$, $R_3 \xrightarrow{B} R_1$, and $R_2 \xrightarrow{A} R_1$ be represented by S1, S2, S3, and S4, respectively. When the semi-joins S1 and S2 are executed, the resulting relation R_3' satisfies $R_3.C = R_4.C$ and $R_3.D = R_5.D$. By executing the semi-joins S3 and S4, the resulting relation R_1' satisfies $R_1.A = R_2.A$ and $R_1.B = R_3'.B$. After the constraints satisfied by R_3' are included into the constraints satisfied by R_1', R_1' satisfies $R_1.A = R_2.A$, $R_1.B = R_3.B$, $R_3.C = R_4.C$, and $R_3.D = R_5.D$. As a result, R_1 satisfies the entire query and is therefore fully reduced by the semi-joins executed in Phase 1 of the above algorithm. Note that the order in which semi-joins S1 and S2 are executed is not important. Similarly, the order in which semi-joins S3 and S4 are executed is also not important. In fact, semi-join S4 can be executed before semi-join S1. But semi-joins S1 and S2 should be executed before S3 in order to satisfy

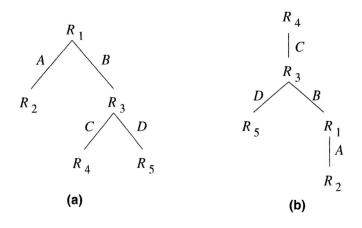

FIGURE 3.12   Different Tree Graphs

the condition that semi-joins from children to their parent, p, are executed before a semi-join from p to its parent is executed.

In Phase 2, let the semi-joins $R_1 \xrightarrow{A} R_2$, $R_1 \xrightarrow{B} R_3$, $R_3 \xrightarrow{C} R_4$, and $R_3 \xrightarrow{D} R_5$ be represented by S5, S6, S7, and S8, respectively. After the semi-join S5 is executed, the relation R_2 will be fully reduced; after the semi-join S6 is executed, the relation R_3 will be fully reduced; after the semi-joins S7 and S8 are executed, the relations R_4 and R_5 will be fully reduced. Thus, after these four semi-joins are executed, all relations will be fully reduced. To see why the relations in Phase 2 are fully reduced, let us use relation R_4 as an example. We can construct a tree with R_4 as the root (see Figure 3.12(b)).

By Phase 1 of the algorithm, if the semi-joins in the order $R_2 \xrightarrow{A} R_1$, $R_1 \xrightarrow{B} R_3$, $R_5 \xrightarrow{D} R_3$, and $R_3 \xrightarrow{C} R_4$ are executed, then the relation R_4 will be fully reduced. These semi-joins are S4, S6, S2, and S7, respectively. First we note that when the two phases of the algorithm with R_1 as root have been completed, these four semi-joins will be completed. They will also be executed in the right order, because for the intermediate vertex R_1 in Figure 3.12(b), semi-join S4 is executed before S6, and for the intermediate vertex R_3, S2 and S6 are executed before S7. Thus, the leave-to-root phase of the algorithm with root R_4 will be completed, with the result that the root relation is fully reduced. The same reasoning applies to all other relations in the tree.   ■

Clearly, it is possible to enumerate all possible queries that are equivalent to a given query and, for each such query, determine whether the join graph is cyclic. Thus the type of query—either a tree query or a cyclic query—can be determined. However, this method is very inefficient. We now give a very simple algorithm for determining the cyclicity of a query.

Determine-Type (Q)

Step 1. For each relation, determine its set of joining attributes, i.e., the set of attributes that participate in joins. For each relation R, let its set of joining attributes be denoted by $J(R)$.

Step 2. While there exist relations R_i and R_j such that $J(R_i)$ is contained in $J(R_j)$,

(a) Remove R_i. /* Since every joining attribute of R_i is in R_j, it is possible to modify the join graph in such a way that there is an edge between R_i and R_j in the modified join graph and any cycle involving R_i in the original join graph becomes a cycle involving R_j but not R_i. Thus, the removal of R_i will not cause any *inherent cycle* to disappear. */

(b) If the removal of R_i causes a joining attribute A to involve a single relation only, say R_k, then remove the joining attribute from $J(R_k)$ (note that a joining attribute should involve at least two relations to be meaningful).

Step 3. If there is no remaining joining attribute, then the query is a tree query; otherwise, the query is a cyclic query.

Example 3.11 Consider the query Q given in Example 3.10. The following can be determined easily: $J(R_1) = \{A, B\}$; $J(R_2) = \{A\}$; $J(R_3) = \{B, C, D\}$; $J(R_4) = \{C\}$; $J(R_5) = \{D\}$. It should be noted that when the join graph of Q changes from one root to another, the sets of joining attributes remain unchanged. In fact, it is easy to verify that the sets of joining attributes of the relations for the two join graphs in Example 3.9 are identical, although one join graph is a tree and the other has a cycle.

Since $J(R_4)$ is contained in $J(R_3)$, relation R_4 is eliminated. The elimination means that even if the join graph of Q has a cycle, R_4 will not be part of the cycle. After R_4 is removed, attribute C appears in one relation only, namely R_3. Therefore, C can be removed. Thus, $J(R_3)$ is modified to be $\{D, B\}$. Since $J(R_5)$ is contained in $J(R_3)$, eliminate relation R_5, as it will not be part of any cycle, if one exists, in the join graph. Again, D appears in a single relation only, namely R_3. Thus, D is eliminated, resulting in $J(R_3) = \{B\}$. Now, $J(R_3)$ is contained in $J(R_1)$, causing the elimination of relation R_3. This leads to the elimination of attribute B, reducing $J(R_1)$ to $\{A\}$. Relation R_1 is eliminated, because its joining attribute set is a subset of that of $J(R_2)$. Finally, A is eliminated from $J(R_2)$, because it occurs in a single relation only. No joining attribute remains, implying that the query is a tree query. ∎

3.4.2 Estimation of Cost

Even a strategy that can fully reduce all relations referenced by a query may not be a good one, because the cost of such a strategy could be higher than that of another strategy that does not fully reduce all relations. It is essential to estimate the cost of executing a strategy. Cost estimation is outlined below.

Definition 3.7 *The selectivity of a relation R_i on attribute A is the probability that a value in the domain of A is in $\pi_A(R_i)$. Specifically, it is given by $|\pi_A(R_i)| / |\text{domain}(A)|$, where $|X|$ is* *the cardinality of the set X. This selectivity will be denoted by* sel($R_i.A$). *It is assumed that the domain is discrete.*

Example 3.12 Suppose A is the attribute Age of an *Employee* relation R of a company. $\pi_A(R)$ gives all distinct ages of employees in the company. If $|\pi_A(R)| = 20$ and $|\text{domain}(A)| = 100$ (assuming nobody has age beyond 100), then sel($R.A$) = 0.2. ∎

Consider a simple semi-join operation $R_i \xrightarrow{A} R_j$. It is desired to estimate the size of $\pi_A(R_j)$ after the semi-join is executed. Assuming that the values in $\pi_A(R_i)$ and $\pi_A(R_j)$ are independently distributed, the probability that a value in domain(A) is a value in both $\pi_A(R_i)$ and $\pi_A(R_j)$ (i.e., in the result of executing the semi-join) is sel($R_i.A$) · sel($R_j.A$). Thus, the expected size of $\pi_A(R_j)$ after the semi-join is executed is $|\text{domain}(A)|$ · sel($R_i.A$) · sel($R_j.A$). In general, consider a sequence of semi-joins $R_{i1} \xrightarrow{A} R_{i2} \xrightarrow{A} R_{i3} \xrightarrow{A} \cdots \xrightarrow{A} R_{ik}$, where the first semi-join from R_{i1} is used to reduce R_{i2}, which is then used to reduce R_{i3}, and so on, until R_{ik} is reduced. If all the relations are distinct, then the expected size of the projection of R_{ik} on attribute A after the sequence of semi-joins is executed is $|\text{domain}(A)| \prod_{t=1}^{k} \text{sel}(R_{it})$. If a relation appears multiple times in the sequence, we use its selectivity only once in the product, because the reductive power of a relation is lost when it is used in the second and subsequent occurrences. For example, for the sequence $R_1 \xrightarrow{A} R_2 \xrightarrow{A} R_1 \xrightarrow{A} R_3$, the second occurrence of R_1 does not cause further reduction of R_3, because the final result should be $\pi_A(R_1) \cap \pi_A(R_2) \cap \pi_A(R_3)$, irrespective of the number of occurrences of R_1 in the semi-join sequence.

The estimation given above is on a single attribute A. In general, there are multiple joining attributes and therefore the estimation method needs to be generalized. Consider the semi-join sequence $R_i \xrightarrow{A} R_j \xrightarrow{B} R_k$, where the first semi-join is on attribute A but the second one is on attribute B. Clearly, R_j has both joining attributes A and B. We want to estimate the size of $\pi_B(R_j)$ after the execution of the first semi-join. The estimation will be based on an analogy of a problem involving *colors of balls*.

Suppose there are n balls with m colors uniformly distributed among the balls. The problem is to find the expected number of colors of r randomly selected balls. Due to the uniform distribution of colors, the number of balls having a given color is n/m. Consider one of these colors, say c. In order to guarantee that the r randomly chosen balls do not have color c, the n/m balls having color c are removed and the r balls are selected from the remaining $s = (n - n/m)$ balls. The number of ways to select r balls from these s balls is $t1 = \binom{s}{r}$; the number of ways to select r balls from the original n balls is $t2 = \binom{n}{r}$. Thus, the probability that the color c is not selected when r balls are randomly chosen is $t1/t2$. This implies that the probability that the color c is selected is $1 - t1/t2$. Since the same reason applies to each of the m colors, the expected number of colors in the r randomly chosen balls is $m \cdot (1 - t1/t2)$.

The correspondence between the colors-of-balls problem and the problem of estimating the size of $\pi_B(R_j)$ after the execution of the semi-join $R_i \xrightarrow{A} R_j$ is as follows:

n balls: the number of distinct values in $\pi_A(R_j)$ before the execution of the first semi-join

m colors: the number of distinct values in $\pi_B(R_j)$ before the execution of the first semi-join

r selected balls: the number of distinct values in $\pi_A(R_j)$ after executing the first semi-join

the expected number of colors: the expected number of distinct values in $\pi_B(R_j)$ after the execution of the first semi-join

There is, however, a slight difference between the two problems. In the colors-of-balls problem, the number of balls to be selected, r, is given and is exact. In the semi-join size estimation problem, the number of distinct values in $\pi_A(R_j)$ after executing the semi-join needs to be estimated. Thus, the correspondence is not perfect.

In summary, a method has been provided to estimate the size of $\pi_C(R_j)$ after executing the semi-join $R_i \xrightarrow{A} R_j$, where C can be A or different from A. The cost of executing the semi-join is $|\pi_A(R_i)|$, assuming that the two relations are in different sites. (This is a simplification achieved by ignoring the connection cost c_0 and assuming the proportionality constant c_1 to be 1.) Otherwise, the cost is 0. This permits us to continue the estimation for the next semi-join from $\pi_C(R'_j)$, where relation R'_j is the relation R_j reduced by the semi-join from relation R_i. The cost of such a semi-join is $|\pi_C(R'_j)|$, assuming that the next relation to be reduced is in a different site. By repeatedly applying this process, the cost of a strategy involving a sequence of semi-joins can be estimated. Based on the estimation, it is possible to give optimal strategies (strategies having least estimated cost) for *simple queries* that have only a single joining attribute.

Assume that the relations are referenced by a simple query that references relations involving a single common joining attribute A. Let the query be $R_1 \bowtie_A R_2 \bowtie_A \cdots \bowtie_A R_n$. Assume that the relations when projected on the common joining attribute A are arranged in nondescending order of their sizes, i.e., $|\pi_A(R_1)| \le |\pi_A(R_2)| \le \cdots \le |\pi_A(R_n)|$. Then, assuming that the answer can be at any site, it can be shown that the optimal strategy to minimize the total communication cost for the query is to send the relations in ascending order of size—i.e., execute the sequence of semi-joins $R_1 \xrightarrow{A} R_2 \xrightarrow{A} \cdots \xrightarrow{A} R_n$. (If the answer must be at a designated site, the optimal strategy needs to be slightly modified. See Exercise 3.14.) This can be verified by contradiction: Suppose the relations are not in nondescending order of size—say R_k immediately precedes R_j and $|\pi_A(R_k)| > |\pi_A(R_j)|$, in the sequence of semi-joins with $k > j$. Then by interchanging R_k and R_j in the sequence, a lower-cost strategy will be obtained. This can be verified by comparing the cost of each semi-join of one strategy with that of the corresponding semi-join of the other strategy. In fact, an optimal strategy to fully reduce relations in a tree query involving multiple joining attributes can be obtained using dynamic programming. Since it is not clear whether the approach can be generalized to cyclic queries and whether an optimal strategy to process a query needs to fully reduce all its relations, we will consider a heuristic algorithm that is suitable for all queries. The first three steps of the algorithm are intended to reduce the sizes of the relations referenced by the query; in the fourth step, the reduced relations are sent to a single site where joins are taken to compute the final result. It is assumed that selections and projections have been taken locally to remove unnecessary data.

Process-General-Queries

Initialization. $SS = \emptyset$; /* SS will be the sequence of semi-joins to be executed. It is initially empty. */

Step 1. For each joining attribute A, enumerate all possible semi-joins. If there are m relations having joining attribute A, then there are $\binom{m}{2}$ pairs of relations, each of the form (R_i, R_j). For each such pair, there are two possible semi-joins, namely, $R_i \xrightarrow{A} R_j$ and $R_j \xrightarrow{A} R_i$.

Step 2. For each semi-join of the form $R_j \xrightarrow{A} R_i$,

(a) Compute its cost. The cost is simply $|\pi_A(R_j)|$.

(b) Compute its benefit. The benefit of the semi-join is defined to be $|R_i| - |R_i'|$, where R_i' is the relation R_i reduced by the semi-join. The cost to transfer the relation before the semi-join is executed is $|R_i|$; that to transfer the same relation after the semi-join is executed is $|R_i'|$. The benefit of the semi-join is the reduction in data communication cost for executing the semi-join. $|R_i'|$ can be estimated to be $|R_i| \cdot \text{sel}(R_j.A)$.

(c) Compute the profit of the semi-join: profit = benefit − cost. A semi-join is *profitable* if its profit is greater than zero. Intuitively, a profitable semi-join is one that should be considered for execution.

Step 3. While there are profitable semi-joins that have not been chosen,

(a) Choose either the semi-join with the least cost and the least profit or the one with the highest profit. Let the chosen semi-join be S: $R_i \xrightarrow{A} R_j$ (see the comments given after the algorithm).

(b) Update the estimates of the cost, benefit, and profit of semi-joins from R_j to other relations. /* Assuming that S is executed, R_j changes in size and therefore it is necessary to do the reestimation. */

Step 4. For each site t that contains one or more of the relations referenced in the query,

(a) Compute weight(t), the weight of site t, defined to be the sum of the estimated sizes of the referenced relations at site t after the semi-joins described in Step 3 are executed.

(b) Send the reduced relations and other referenced but not reduced relations to the site having the largest weight. This site will receive the least amount of data relative to other sites.

The answer of the query is the joins of the relations that are referenced by the query and are now at this site.

Note that it is possible to define the cost of a semi-join as a combination of both local processing cost and communication cost. The same applies to benefit and profit.

In Step 3, two choices are given. The intuitive choice is to first execute the semi-join that yields the largest profit. However, this choice is not consistent with the optimal strategy for evaluating simple queries. For a simple query, the best strategy is to send relations in ascending order of size, but the most profitable semi-join is $R1 \xrightarrow{A} R_n$, where R_n is the largest relation and A is the joining attribute. The second choice, in which the lowest-cost semi-join (among the lowest-cost semi-joins, pick the one with least profit) is selected, is consistent with the optimal strategy for the simple query (the first semi-join to be chosen is $R1 \xrightarrow{A} R2$, where $R2$ is the second smallest relation). In practice, estimation is likely to be inaccurate and small profit need not be translated into actual savings in communications. Thus, both choices are reasonable. The following example illustrates the key weaknesses of the above algorithm.

Example 3.13 Suppose the query under consideration is $\pi_{R3.C}(R1 \bowtie_A R2 \bowtie_B R3)$. Assume that the relations are in different sites. The set of all possible semi-joins is $\{R1 \xrightarrow{A} R2,$ $R2 \xrightarrow{A} R1, R2 \xrightarrow{B} R3, R3 \xrightarrow{B} R2\}$. A possible sequence of semi-joins that can be generated by Step 3 of the above algorithm is

$$R1 \xrightarrow{A} R2 \xrightarrow{B} R3 \xrightarrow{B} R2 \xrightarrow{A} R1$$

The first semi-join uses $R1$ to reduce $R2$, which reduces $R3$, which in turn reduces $R2$. Thus, $R2$ is reduced once by $R1$ and once by $R3$. Finally, $R1$ is reduced by the reduced $R2$. In Step 4 of the algorithm, the three reduced relations are sent to one common site to be joined together to produce the final result. Altogether there are six data transfers, four due to the semi-joins and two due to Step 4. (One of the three reduced relations need not be transferred, as the two other relations will be transferred to its site.)

We now examine the sequence of semi-joins and determine if all of them are necessary. After the execution of the first semi-join, $R1 \xrightarrow{A} R2$, we note that relation $R1$ is no longer needed in answering the query, because the target of the query does not include any attribute from $R1$ and the effect of the semi-join on the qualification of the query is completely incorporated into the reduced $R2$ through the execution of the semi-join. In other words, the reduced $R2$, R'_2, satisfies $R2.A = R1.A$. After the execution of the second semi-join, $R2 \xrightarrow{B} R3$, relation $R2$ is no longer needed for the same reason. The reduced $R3$ satisfies $R3.B = R'_2.B$. Thus, relation $R3$ satisfies $R3.B = R2.B$ and $R2.A = R1.A$; i.e., it satisfies all conditions in the qualification. Thus the answer of the query is obtained by taking the projection of the reduced $R3$ on attribute C. None of the data transfer in Step 4 nor the third and fourth semi-joins are needed.   ■

We now identify the precise situations in which a relation, after executing a semi-join, can be eliminated. When a relation is eliminated, not only subsequent semi-joins from and to that relation are removed but the relation need not participate in the join operation in the assembling site (i.e., Step 4 in the Process General Queries algorithm). This saves both communication cost and local processing cost.

Proposition 3.2 *Consider the semi-join $R_i \xrightarrow{A} R_j$. Relation R_i can be eliminated after executing the semi-join if (1) either the target of the query does not contain any attribute of R_i or, if the target of the query contains an attribute of R_i, the attribute is A and the semi-join passes the required information to R_j (i.e., $R_i.A$ in the target can be replaced by $R_j.A$), and (2) A is the only joining attribute of R_i in the query.*

Note that attribute A in the above proposition can be a composite attribute consisting of several attributes. In that case, if the target of the query contains B, which is a subset of A, $R_i \cdot B$ in the target can be replaced by $R_j \cdot B$.

If condition (2) is satisfied, then the set of joining attributes of R_i, $J(R_i)$, is contained in $J(R_j)$. By the algorithm to determine the type of a query (tree versus cyclic query), R_i can be eliminated. In fact, that algorithm together with checking for condition (1) can be used to eliminate unnecessary relations. This is illustrated by the following example.

Example 3.14 Consider the query in Example 3.13. $J(R1) = \{A\}$ is contained in $J(R2) = \{A, B\}$. Since the target does not contain any attribute of $R1$, relation $R1$ can be eliminated after executing the semi-join $R1 \xrightarrow{A} R2$. After $R1$ is eliminated, A appears in a single relation, namely $R2$. The elimination of attribute A causes $J(R2) = \{B\}$. Now, $J(R2)$ is contained in $J(R3)$. After the execution of the semi-join $R2 \xrightarrow{B} R3$, since the target does not contain attributes of $R2$, both conditions of the proposition are satisfied, permitting the elimination of $R2$. Since the only remaining relation is $R3$, its projection on the target attribute is performed to produce the answer.   ∎

The preceeding example illustrates situations in which semi-joins can be utilized to optimize both local processing costs and data communication costs. More precisely, for a semi-join $R_i \xrightarrow{A} R_j$, if the hypotheses stated in Proposition 3.2 hold and R_i and R_j are the only relations containing attribute A before the execution of the semi-join, then after executing it, relation R_i can be discarded and attribute A can be removed from R_j. The reduction of data to be processed later is very significant.

Based on Proposition 3.2, the algorithm Process General Queries should be modified as follows. During each iteration in Step 3, whenever a semi-join is selected for execution, it should be checked as to whether a relation can be eliminated. No semi-joins involving the eliminated relation need to be considered in subsequent operations. In Step 4, only the remaining relations need to be transferred to a common site for the join operations.

3.5 Combining Semi-Joins with Joins

Suppose two relations $R1$ and $R2$, situated at sites S_1 and S_2, respectively, are to be joined on an attribute A. There are many ways to perform the operation:

1. Send the relation $R1$ from site S_1 to site S_2 and then join the two relations at site S_2.

2. Send the relation $R2$ from site S_2 to site S_1 and then join the two relations at site S_1.

3. Perform a semi-join from $R1$ to $R2$ on A and then send the result back to site S_1 to join with $R1$.

4. Perform a semi-join from $R2$ to $R1$ on A and then send the result back to site S_2 to join with $R2$.

5. Send both relations $R1$ and $R2$ to a common site S_3 that is different from S_1 and S_2 and join the two relations at the common site.

The cost, including both local processing costs and communication costs, of executing each of the above five strategies is estimated. If there is no more operation to be performed— i.e., the query consists of only a single join—then the strategy with the minimum estimated cost is chosen. However, if the join operation is part of a query to be optimized, it is essential to differentiate between types of strategies and to keep the lowest-cost strategy for each type. Two strategies are of the same type if their intermediate results have identical physical aspects. (The physical aspects of the intermediate relations involve their locations, the availability of indexes, and the tuples in ascending or descending order according to a later joining attribute.) Strategy 1 and strategy 2 given above are not of the same type, because the result produced by strategy 2 is in site S_1, and that produced by strategy 1 is in site S_2. Thus, if the result of joining $R1$ and $R2$ is to be joined with another relation $R3$, then if $R3$ is situated at site S_2, strategy 1, unlike strategy 2, will not need to incur additional communication cost in the second join. In other words, a slower strategy of one type for a subquery Q' may be part of an optimal strategy for the entire query Q, whereas a faster strategy of another type for the subquery Q' may not be part of an optimal strategy. It is therefore important to retain a fastest strategy for each type. Strategy 1 and strategy 4 may be considered to be of the same type, as their results are in site S_2. It may be sufficient to keep the strategy with the lower cost. Similarly, strategy 2 and strategy 3 are of the same type, and the one with the lower cost is retained. Strategy 5 is of a different type, as its result is in a different site, so it is retained. Actually, a finer distinction than that based on the location of the result is required for classification of strategies into types. For example, it may be that two strategies produce the same result, say R_r, in the same site, but R_r produced by one strategy is in ascending order of values on some attribute A, and the relation produced by the other strategy is not in any particular order. If R_r is to be joined with another relation on attribute A and if the sort merge method is applied for the join, then in one case, R_r need not be sorted, and in the other case, it needs to be sorted on attribute A before the merge operation. Without getting into the fine details of type classification of strategies, it is sufficient to say that in order to produce an optimal strategy for the entire query, all different types of strategies have to be enumerated and an optimal strategy of each strategy type needs to be kept for each subquery, while other strategies can be pruned. This is an application of the dynamic programming principle.

Exercises

3.1 Suppose a company has a headquarters and n branch offices. Each branch office has data of its own, but a copy of its data is also stored in the headquarters. If a query requests data, then an attempt is made to process it locally. If the query cannot be processed locally, it is sent to the headquarters for processing. Suppose each computer at each branch office and at the headquarters has a probability p of failure, but the network is always available. Find the probability that a query can be answered. There are two cases, one for a query accessing local data and the other for a query accessing data from $n > 1$ sites.

3.2 Create a relation schema to store placement dependency information. The schema should allow placement dependency information to be utilized for efficient query processing. Describe each attribute of the relation.

3.3 There are two airports, one for small planes and the other for larger planes. There are two relations. Relation Plane(Model, Size) gives the size of each model of a plane. Another relation, Airline(Name, Model), describes which airline operates which model of plane. How should the relations be fragmented so that queries of the form π_{Name}(Airline $\bowtie$ Plane) can be answered efficiently using the placement dependency information?

3.4 Determine whether the following query can be answered without data transfer.

$$\pi_{R1.A}(R1 \bowtie_{R1.B=R2.B \text{ and } R1.C=R2.C} R2 \bowtie_D R3 \bowtie_E R4)$$

There is a placement dependency between $R1$ and $R2$ on attribute B and another placement dependency between $R2$ and $R3$ on attribute D. Relation $R4$ is replicated at the sites containing fragments of $R3$.

3.5 Consider the following distribution of relations $R1$, $R2$, and $R3$ in the three sites S_1, S_2, and S_3:

	S_1	S_2	S_3
R1	F_{11}	F_{12}	
R2		F_{22}	F_{23}
R3	R3	R3	

Let the sizes of the relations/fragments be $|F_{11}| = 50$; $|F_{12}| = 60$; $|F_{22}| = 30$; $|F_{23}| = 30$; $|R3| = 70$. Suppose the Fragment and Replicate algorithm is used to process the query $R1 \bowtie R2 \bowtie R3$. Suppose the cost to transfer X amount of data is X and the cost to join three relations of sizes X_1, X_2, and X_3 is $X_1 + X_2 + X_3$. Assume, as a simplification, that the union operation does not incur any cost.

(a) Estimate the response time if relation $R1$ is left fragmented and its fragments are not moved.

(b) Estimate the response time if relation $R2$ is left fragmented and its fragments are not moved.

(c) Determine the relation to leave fragmented so that the response time is minimized.

Two assumptions can be made for making these estimations. (i) If data are shipped from one site to multiple sites, the transmissions are assumed to be carried out in parallel. (ii) An operation cannot start until all data for the operation are available. (In practice, the operations can be pipelined so that as soon as one operation has produced some data, the next operation can act on the produced data.)

3.6 Assume the same distribution of relations/fragments to sites and the same cost functions as given in Exercise 3.5. Suppose the hash partitioning method is used to answer the same query.

(a) Find the response time assuming that the data are hashed uniformly.

(b) Find the response time assuming that when the data of a relation/fragment is hashed to i sites, the site receiving the most data gets 30% more data (than it would if they were evenly distributed) and the remaining data are distributed evenly among the remaining sites.

3.7 Assume the same distribution of relations/fragments to sites as that given in Exercise 3.5. The cost of data transfer is also assumed to be the same as that given in Exercise 3.5. The cost of joining two relations of sizes X_1 and X_2 is assumed to be $X_1 + X_2$, and the resulting relation is assumed to have size $\frac{1}{2}(X_1 + X_2)$. Consider the chain query $R1 \bowtie_A R2 \bowtie_B R3$. Apply dynamic programming to obtain an optimal solution in total cost for this query.

3.8 Suppose relations $R1$ and $R2$ have a placement dependency on attribute A. Provide an efficient processing strategy for the following query.

```
select max(R1.B), min(max(R1.B  group by  A))
from R1, R2
where R1.A = R2.A and R2.C = 'c'
```

The purpose of min(max($R1.B$ group by A)) is to obtain, for each distinct value in $\pi_A(R1)$, the maximum value of $R1.B$; among all these maximum values, the minimum value is taken. (Hint: More information on processing aggregate queries can be found in Reference [66].)

3.9 Suppose relation $R1(A, B, C, D)$ is fragmented in sites S_1 and S_2, and relation $R2(A, E, F, G)$ is fragmented in sites S_2 and S_3. Assume that the Fragment and Replicate algorithm is used to process the query $\pi_{R1.B}(R1 \bowtie_A R2)$.

(a) Identify all different ways in terms of the selection and the projection operations to process this query. (Note that selections and projections may be performed before or after the join. Again, assume that pipelining is not allowed.)

(b) If optimal estimated response time is desired, is it necessary to enumerate the different ways of processing the query and obtain the minimum expected cost? Why or why not?

3.10 Consider the following partitioning strategy for the query $R1 \bowtie R2$, where the two relations are distributed as follows. Initially, relation $R1$ has one copy only and it is situated at site S_1, and relation $R2$ has one copy at site S_1 and another copy at site S_2.

(a) To process this query, relation $R1$ is partitioned into two fragments: F_{11}, which stays at site S_1, and F_{12}, which is shipped to site S_2. F_{11} is then joined with $R2$ at site S_1, while F_{12} is joined with $R2$ at site S_2. If the speeds of the computers in processing information at site S_1 and site S_2 are f_1 and f_2, respectively, describe how $R1$ should be partitioned so that the response time for answering the query can be minimized.

(b) Consider another query, which is the join of three relations $R1$, $R2$, and $R3$. The initial distributions of relations $R1$ and $R2$ are given above. Relation $R3$

is replicated in sites S_2 and S_3. In this case, one relation needs to be partitioned, while other relations may need to be replicated. Determine a strategy that provides an optimal choice of the relation to be partitioned.

3.11 Consider the query $\pi_{I.A,I.B}(A_1 \bowtie A_2 \bowtie \cdots \bowtie A_n \bowtie I \bowtie B_1 \bowtie B_2 \bowtie \cdots \bowtie B_m)$, where A_i is a single-attribute relation with joining attribute A, B_j is a single-attribute relation with joining attribute B, and I is a two-attribute relation with joining attributes A and B. Suppose each relation is in a distinct site.

(a) Apply dynamic programming techniques to obtain an optimal semi-join strategy to fully reduce the I relation.

(b) Generalize the method so that it can be applicable to a *star query*. A star query has a central relation having two or more joining attributes, and each peripheral relation has a common joining attribute with the central relation.

3.12 Consider the algorithm Chain Query Optimization.

(a) In step 1 of the algorithm, the variable "$j - i$" is used. Rewrite this step using standard notation.

(b) Describe how the algorithm can be modified to keep track of sites where the joins are to be executed.

3.13 Consider the query $R1 \bowtie_A (\sigma_{B='b'}(R2))$, where b is a constant. Suppose the values of A in $R1$ have been prehashed to a bit vector before the execution of the query and the bit vector is stored at the site containing $R2$.

(a) Describe how the query may be processed efficiently.

(b) Generalize this approach for processing a star query. (See Exercise 3.11 for the definition of a star query.)

3.14 Consider the simple query $R_1 \bowtie R_2 \bowtie \cdots \bowtie R_n$, where all the relations are single-attribute relations with the same attribute A. Suppose each of the relations is in a distinct site. Assume that data communication cost is the only cost to optimize and that the answer must be produced at the site containing relation R_i, which is one of the referenced relations.

Give a strategy to optimize the total communication cost for the simple query, where the total communication cost is the sum of communication costs. Recall that the transfer of X amount of data from one site to another costs $c_0 + c_1 \cdot X$. (Hint: All sites except the site containing relation R_i are visited once. The site containing relation R_i may be visited twice.)

3.15 Given the query $R1 \bowtie_A R2 \bowtie_B R3$, suppose the semi-joins $R3 \xrightarrow{B} R2$ and $R2 \xrightarrow{A} R1$ are to be executed. Estimate the size of $\pi_A(R1)$, assuming that the selectivities of the relations $R1$ and $R2$ on A are p_{1a} and p_{2a}, respectively, and those of the relations $R2$ and $R3$ on B are p_{2b} and p_{3b}, respectively.

Bibliographic Notes

The basic concepts of distributed database systems can be found in [286]. The Placement Dependency algorithm is from [397]. This type of semantic information is also used in distributed database design [380]. The Fragment and Replicate algorithm is from Distributed INGRES [115]. It is modified to include data communication and local processing cost [398]. Hashing algorithms for joins have been discussed very thoroughly; see, for example, [67, 103, 174, 248]. The Bloom filter employed to implement semi-joins is from [251]. Optimal processing of simple queries involving single attributes is from [166]. Full reduction of relations in tree queries is due to [29]. Determining whether a query is a tree query or a cyclic query is from [403]. The same algorithm can be utilized for other applications [369]. The heuristic algorithm to process general queries is from [30]. Identifying the useless relations in that algorithm is from [397]. The use of dynamic programming for optimizing queries using semi-joins can be found in [72, 396, 404]. Its use in optimizing other distributed queries can be found in [328, 354]. Much more elaborate use of semi-joins, including interleaving semi-joins and joins and generalized semi-joins, can be found in [69, 195, 309, 320]. System R* [242, 323] from IBM essentially enumerates all possible strategies while pruning the nonoptimal ones by dynamic programming. Strategies containing Cartesian products are also discarded. Both semi-joins and joins are utilized. The SDD-1 algorithm [30] makes use of the original semi-join algorithm. Mermaid [360], which has been used in several projects, makes use of the placement dependency information, the Fragment and Replicate algorithm, and the enhanced semi-join algorithm. It is actually a front end for different centralized relational systems. Other query optimization issues in distributed databases are discussed in [137, 215].

4

Query Processing in Multidatabase Systems

Due to historical reasons and the fact that different applications can be better supported by different types of database systems, various types of database systems are currently in use today. They range from legacy hierarchical and network database systems, such as IMS and DMS II, to more recent relational database systems, such as Oracle, Sybase, and DB2, to object-oriented database systems, such as O_2 and ObjectStore, and to systems that manage unstructured data such as information retrieval systems and multimedia systems. It is not unusual to see that different types of database systems are employed by different departments of a large organization. Often, information is duplicated to various degrees in these systems. Although each system is primarily developed to satisfy the needs of data management at its own department, the data it manages can also be useful to other departments in the organization. In addition, a global and integrated view of the data stored in these individual systems could be essential for the management at the organization level to make important decisions.

However, the following two characteristics of the database systems in this environment make it very difficult, if not impossible, for data in these database systems to be accessed in an integrated fashion:

Autonomy. Each database system has full autonomy, meaning that the manager of each database system has complete control over the system. Several types of autonomy can be identified: (1) *design autonomy* allows the manager to decide what data should be stored in the database and how data should be modeled and organized; (2) *communica-*

tion autonomy allows the manager to decide what kind of services should be provided to other database systems; and (3) *execution autonomy* allows the manager to decide how requests to the database should be carried out, e.g., what query processing and concurrency control algorithms should be used.

Heterogeneity. Different database systems may have heterogeneity in many aspects. They may operate in different platforms, such as PC with Windows and Workstation with Unix. They may use different data models and query languages (e.g., relational model with SQL and hierarchical model with DL/1). Even with the same data model, they may model identical data differently (e.g., structural heterogeneity). They may also have semantic heterogeneities such as homonyms, synonyms, and scale conflicts. It can also happen that a common property of the same real-world entity has different values in different database systems (data inconsistency).

A number of approaches are available to overcome the difficulties in integrated retrieval caused by the autonomy and heterogeneity of local database systems. One approach, known as *data conversion*, converts and migrates all data stored in one database system, say system 1, to another database system, say system 2. After all data in different local systems are converted, stored, and integrated in a single system, integrated retrieval is a trivial task. The main drawback of this approach can be described as follows: On the one hand, if system 1 is retained, then the data originally in the system will have multiple copies (maybe in different formats). For this reason, it will be difficult to maintain the consistency of the data. Furthermore, multiple copies demand more storage spaces. On the other hand, if system 1 is discarded, then application programs written based on system 1 will have to be rewritten. Often, the cost involved is too high for this approach to be feasible. Another approach is to create *gateways* between database system pairs. With a gateway between system 1 and system 2, a query of system 1 can access the data in system 2 after it is first translated into a query in system 2. Although this approach provides a way for a user to access different individual database systems using a single query language, it is difficult to support queries that need to access data stored in multiple database systems. With this approach, if a user wants to access data from two or more database systems, he or she needs to send a query to each of these systems and combine the results by himself or herself. Another serious problem with this approach is that the number of gateways that need to be created increases rapidly as the number of systems involved increases.

This chapter presents another solution to this problem, namely, the *multidatabase system* approach. This approach has gained a lot of attention in recent years, and a number of prototype systems have been constructed. The phrase *multidatabase system* has different meanings for different people. In this chapter, the expression will also refer to tightly coupled federated database systems in which one or more global schemas are constructed from the schemas of the participating local databases (i.e., component databases) in such a way that uniform and integrated access to data stored in all component databases can be supported. Each global schema is constructed based on a particular data model. For example, a global schema based on the relational model may be constructed for users who are familiar with relational database systems, and a global schema based on an object-oriented data model may be created for object-oriented database (OODB) users. For a given global schema, a multidatabase system consists of its component database systems and a *front-end system* that supports a single

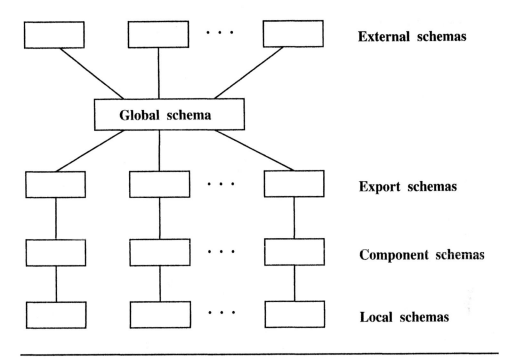

FIGURE 4.1 **Multidatabase System Architecture**

common data model and a single global query language on top of these component systems. The main tasks of the front-end system include the management of the global schema and the processing of the global queries. The main advantage of this approach in comparison with other approaches is that a single query can be issued to access data from multiple databases in an integrated way without affecting any existing application program written on the basis of any component system. As in the gateway approach, the user does not have to use multiple query languages to access data across multiple database systems.

In Section 4.1, a pedagogical reference architecture of a multidatabase system is introduced. Based on this architecture, we outline how a global schema can be constructed and the steps that need to be taken to process a global query. In Section 4.2, some issues involving the construction of a global schema that are relevant to query processing are addressed. In Section 4.3, a number of techniques that can be used for global query optimization are introduced. In Section 4.4, translations between relational queries and object-oriented queries are discussed.

4.1 Multidatabase System Architecture

The reference architecture of a multidatabase system has five levels as depicted in Figure 4.1. Although not every level is needed in any particular application, the architecture serves very well for pedagogical purposes. The five types of schemas in the architecture are discussed below:

Local schema. Each local schema is the conceptual schema of a component database, logically describing all data in the database. Different local schemas may be in different data models.

Component schema. Each component schema is an equivalent transformation of a local schema. All component schemas are required to be in the same data model that the global schema is in. For example, if we want the global schema to be in the relational model, then all component schemas will be in the relational model. This requires that each schema not in the relational model be transformed into a relational schema. If a local schema is already in the same data model as the global schema, then no schema transformation is needed. In this case, the local schema and its component schema are identical.

Export schema. As noted earlier, a distinctive property of multidatabase systems is the autonomy of the component database systems. One consequence of this autonomy is that each component database system can decide what data to share with the users of the global schema and how to share the data. For example, a component database system managing an employee relation may decide that the information on employees' performance evaluations may not be revealed and the salary information may only be viewed but not modified. The view representing the sharable portion of a component schema is called an *export schema* and can be created from the component schema using operations such as selection (to leave out the instances not to be shared), projection (to project out information not to be shared), and possibly others. The process of constructing an export schema is the same as the process of constructing an external schema in a single database environment.

Global schema. After all export schemas become available, they are integrated into the global schema. Note that all export schemas are already in the same data model as the global schema. If there are more than two export schemas to be integrated, then two alternative methodologies could be used. One is to integrate all export schemas at the same time, and the other is to integrate two schemas at a time. The problem of integrating a large number of schemas at the same time is usually too difficult. As a result, most people tend to use the binary method, that is, integrate two schemas at a time.

External schema. An external schema describes only a portion of the data described in the global schema. There are two main reasons to create an external schema. First, it is a security mechanism. By limiting a user to a given external schema, data not described in the external schema are hidden from the user. Second, it is a mechanism to create customized schemas for different user groups. Customized schemas can often increase the productivity of the users. Note that it is possible for an external schema to be in a data model different from that of the global schema. Since the presence of external schemas presents little new challenge for query processing, their presence will largely be ignored in our discussion.

A slightly different version of the five-level architecture can be obtained by exchanging the positions of component schemas and export schemas. In other words, we could generate export schemas first using native data model constructs and then transform each export schema to a component schema. This alternative architecture is likely to involve less work in constructing the global schema. This is because the export schemas in this architecture are likely to be smaller than their corresponding local schemas. As a result, schema transformations may be carried out less expensively.

Schema integration is one of the most researched areas in multidatabase systems. Since query processing is the focus of this chapter, we can only briefly mention most issues in schema integration here. In Section 4.2, issues in schema integration having important impact on query processing will be dealt with in greater depth.

The problem of schema integration consists of several subproblems. The first subproblem is that we need to identify semantically related entity types (relations, classes, etc.) because these are the ones that need to be integrated. This is a very difficult problem because the same concept may be denoted differently in different schemas and different concepts may be represented the same or similarly in different schemas. In addition, the semantics of an entity type in a schema is also related with its context (i.e., how it is related with other entity types) and its usage. It is generally believed that the process of identifying semantically related entity types cannot be fully automated and some human interaction is inevitable. After two entity types are determined to be semantically related, the next subproblem is to identify and resolve many possible conflicts between the two entity types. These conflicts include scale conflict, missing attribute conflict, domain type conflict, and structural conflicts. Most of these conflicts can be resolved easily after they are identified. After the conflicts are resolved, the two entity types can now be integrated. Therefore, the third subproblem is how to integrate the two entity types. Depending on the semantic relationship between the two entity types and the global data model, different integration operators could be used to integrate them, including *union*, *outerunion*, *outerjoin*, and *generalization*.

The global schema of a multidatabase system presents an integrated view of the *sharable* data from multiple component databases. As a result, a global query language pertinent to a global schema can be used to issue queries, called *global queries*, to retrieve data stored in these component database systems. For example, if the global schema is relational, then SQL can be used. The focus of this chapter is the presentation of the techniques that can be used to process such global queries. When a global query is submitted, it is first decomposed into two types of queries by the *query decomposer*. One type is the query against individual export schemas. Queries of this type will be called *export schema subqueries* or simply *subqueries* when there is no confusion. Another type is the query that combines the results returned by subqueries to form the answer. Queries of this type will be called *assembling queries*. When there is only one subquery, no assembling query is needed. An assembling query may be processed by the front end of the multidatabase system or by a local system designated by the front-end system.

Query decomposition is usually accomplished in two steps. The first step is called *query modification*. In this step, the global query using global relation and attribute names is modified to queries using only names in export schemas. Modified queries, though using only names in export schemas, may still reference data from more than one database. Therefore, in the second step, known as *query decomposition* itself, these queries are decomposed into subqueries or assembling queries such that each subquery needs data from only one database. Note that data transmission may be used to aid the decomposition. For example, consider the situation in which a query resulting from query modification is nested as follows:

select $R1.A$ from $R1$ where $R1.B$ in (select $R2.B$ from $R2$)

where $R1$ is from database $D1$ and $R2$ is from database $D2$. In this case, the query may be decomposed into two subqueries, one for database $D2$ (select $R2.B$ into X from $R2$) and one for database $D1$ (select $R1.A$ from $R1$ where $R1.B$ in X). The result X of the first subquery may need to be shipped to the database $D1$ to make all data needed by the second subquery available. Since questions such as how much data should be shipped and what local processing should be performed before data transmission are related to the overall performance of the system, query decomposition is usually tightly coupled with global query optimization. Query decomposition and global query optimization will be discussed in Section 4.3.

After decomposition, each subquery is a query against an export schema. If the export schema is different from the corresponding component schema, then the subquery needs to be modified by incorporating the operations that are used to derive the export schema from the component schema. The modification process is the same as that used to modify a query against an external schema to a query against the conceptual schema in a single-database environment. The modified subquery is still in the global query language. (Note that the modified subqueries obtained in this step are different from the modified queries produced by the modification of a global query.) If the global query language is different from the query language of a component database system, then the modified subquery must be translated to a local subquery by a *query translator*. For example, if the global query language is an OODB query language and a subquery is for a relational system using SQL, then this subquery needs to be translated to an SQL query. In order to translate different subqueries to different local database systems, different query translators are needed. Translations between relational queries and OODB queries will be discussed in Section 4.4.

Results returned from local databases that are not in the desired format need to be converted into the right format by various *data converters*. Finally, converted data are assembled into the final result.

Figure 4.2 illustrates the major steps of query processing in a multidatabase system. In the figure, $SQ_1, \ldots, SQ_n$ are subqueries and $AQ_1, \ldots, AQ_k$ are assembling queries generated by query decomposition; $MSQ_1, \ldots, MSQ_n$ are modified subqueries; $TQ_1, \ldots, TQ_n$ are target queries translated from corresponding source subqueries; and $LR1, \ldots, LR_n$ are results returned from local queries. In general, multiple subqueries may be generated for each local database.

4.2 Schema Integration Operators and Data Inconsistencies

In this section, we introduce some of the most useful operators for schema integration. We also discuss the concept of data inconsistency. The integration operators used and the way data inconsistencies are resolved have important impacts on how global queries are processed. For the rest of this chapter, we assume that the relational data model is used as the global model.

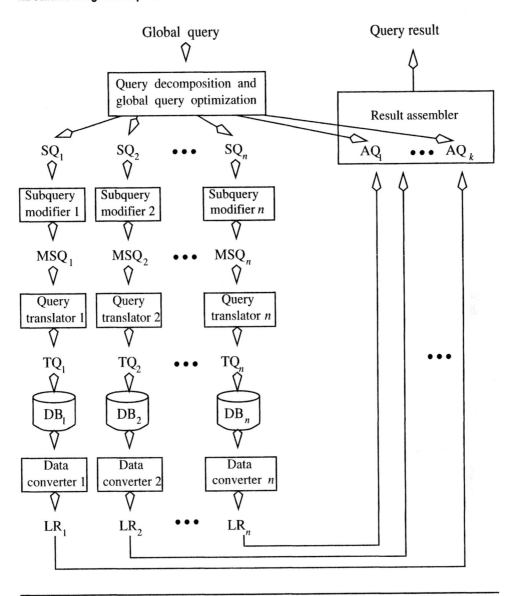

FIGURE 4.2 Major Steps of Query Processing

A real-world object usually has a very large number of properties. For example, a person can have social security number, name, nickname, age, sex, birthdate, height, weight, race, occupation, position, etc. However, not all properties of a real-world object are relevant in any particular database application related to the object. In fact, only a very small fraction of the properties are needed. For example, a person as an employee may have nothing to do with the weight and the eye color of the person. The following definition is useful for differentiating real-world objects with a particular representation of them.

Definition 4.1 *Given a relation R, the* type *of R, denoted by* type(R), *is the set of attributes defined for R and their corresponding domains; the* extension *of R, denoted by* extension(R), *is the set of tuples contained in R; the* world *of R, denoted by* world(R), *is the set of real-world objects described by R.*

Clearly, extension(R) represents one possible concrete representation of the real-world objects in world(R) using the properties in type(R). Often different component databases have information about a common set of real-world objects, but they are represented differently in different component databases. In other words, it is possible to have two semantically related relations $R1$ and $R2$ from different component databases such that world($R1$) $\cap$ world($R2$) $\neq \emptyset$ and type($R1$) $\neq$ type($R2$). It is critically important that those real-world objects in world($R1$) $\cap$ world($R2$) can be identified. If $R1$ and $R2$ have the same attribute that can uniquely identify a real-world object, such as the social security number (SSN) attribute for two employee relations Emp_1 and Emp_2, then the identification is straightforward. Without such a common identifying attribute, the identification can only be done semiautomatically by using the values of other common attributes. For simplicity of discussion, we assume that a common identifying attribute ID exists between $R1$ and $R2$ such that two tuples t_1 in $R1$ and t_2 in $R2$ represent the same real-world object if and only if t_1.ID = t_2.ID.

4.2.1 Integration Operators

The following are some of the most popular operators for integrating two semantically related relations $R1$ and $R2$.

Union ($\cup$). To use this operator, it is required that type($R1$) and type($R2$) are *compatible*. Two types are compatible if for each attribute in one type, there is a unique corresponding attribute in the other type such that the two attributes have compatible domains, and vice versa. Identical domains are always compatible. Examples of nonidentical but compatible domains are integers and real numbers, and character strings of different lengths. For the sake of simplicity, we assume that when union is used to integrate $R1$ and $R2$, type($R1$) = type($R2$). Let R be the relation integrated from $R1$ and $R2$. Then we have type(R) = type($R1$), extension(R) = extension($R1$) $\cup$ extension($R2$), and world(R) = world($R1$) $\cup$ world($R2$).

Outerunion (OU). Outerunion is similar to union except that the former does not require that $R1$ and $R2$ have compatible types. When an outerunion is used to integrate $R1$ and $R2$ into R, each tuple in R comes from either a tuple in $R1$ or a tuple in $R2$ (but not both). In addition, tuples of R that come from $R1$ will have null values for those attributes that appear only in $R2$ but not in $R1$. Similarly, tuples of R that come from $R2$ will have null values for those attributes that appear only in $R1$ but not in $R2$. Therefore, we have type(R) = type($R1$) $\cup$ type($R2$), extension(R) = extension($R1$) $\cup$ extension($R2$) with proper null values added, and world(R) = world($R1$) $\cup$ world($R2$). Clearly, union is a special case of outerunion. As an example, Figure 4.3(c) illustrates the result of

SSN	Name	Age	Salary
123456789	John	34	30k
234567891	Ketty	27	25k
345678912	Wang	39	32k

(a) Relation $R1$

SSN	Name	Salary	Phone
234567891	Ketty	25k	1234567
345678912	Wang	32k	2345678
456789123	Mary	34k	3456789

(b) Relation $R2$

SSN	Name	Age	Salary	Phone
123456789	John	34	30k	null
234567891	Ketty	27	25k	null
345678912	Wang	39	32k	null
234567891	Ketty	null	25k	1234567
345678912	Wang	null	32k	2345678
456789123	Mary	null	34k	3456789

(c) $R1$ OU $R2$

SSN	Name	Age	Salary	Phone
234567891	Ketty	27	25k	1234567
345678912	Wang	39	32k	2345678

(d) $R1 \bowtie R2$

SSN	Name	Age	Salary	Phone
123456789	John	34	30k	null
234567891	Ketty	27	25k	1234567
345678912	Wang	39	32k	2345678
456789123	Mary	null	34k	3456789

(e) $R1$ OJ $R2$

SSN	Name	Salary
123456789	John	30k
234567891	Ketty	25k
345678912	Wang	32k
456789123	Mary	34k

(f) $R1$ Ge $R2$

FIGURE 4.3   Illustrating Integration Operators

$R1$ OU $R2$, where $R1$ and $R2$ are depicted in Figure 4.3(a) and (b), respectively. When outerunion is used, it is possible that several tuples in the integrated relation correspond to the same real-world object. In Figure 4.3(c), the second and fourth tuples are for the same person. Similarly, the third and fifth tuples are also for the same person. To avoid this problem, we use outerunion only when world($R1$) $\cap$ world($R2$) $= \emptyset$. When world($R1$) $\cap$ world($R2$) $\neq \emptyset$, the *outerjoin* operator, to be discussed next, should be used.

Outerjoin (OJ).   Unlike a regular join, which only keeps matched tuples in $R1$ and $R2$, an outerjoin also keeps unmatched (or tangling) tuples. Let $R = R1$ OJ $R2$. Then we have type(R) = type($R1$) $\cup$ type($R2$), extension(R) = ($R1 \bowtie R2$) OU ($R1 - \pi_{\text{Attr}(R1)}(R1 \bowtie$

$R2$)) OU ($R2 - \pi_{Attr(R2)}(R1 \bowtie R2)$), and world($R$) = world($R1$) ∪ world($R2$), where $\bowtie$ is the join operator, π is the projection operator, and Attr($R1$) denotes the set of attributes of $R1$. In the above expression defining extension(R), the first component (i.e., the join) contains those matched tuples, the second component contains the unmatched tuples from $R1$, and the third component contains the unmatched tuples from $R2$. For the purpose of schema integration, the join condition is restricted to $R1.ID = R2.ID$ and only one copy of each pair of common attributes is kept. With the equality condition, R contains all information in both $R1$ and $R2$. Figure 4.3(d) and (e) depicts the results of $R1 \bowtie R2$ (without keeping duplicate information) and $R1$ OJ $R2$, respectively.

Generalization (Ge). The generalization of two relations is a new relation that keeps all tuples in the two relations but retains only values under the common attributes. In other words, if $R = R1$ Ge $R2$, then type(R) = type($R1$) ∩ type($R2$), extension(R) = $\pi_{Attr(R)}(R1)$ ∪ $\pi_{Attr(R)}(R2)$, and world(R) = world($R1$) ∪ world($R2$). Since R does not contain all information in $R1$ and $R2$, both $R1$ and $R2$ need to be kept in the integrated schema to avoid information loss. Figure 4.3(f) depicts the result of $R1$ Ge $R2$.

4.2.2 Data Inconsistency and Resolution Function

When a real-world object is represented by instances in different databases, *data inconsistency* may occur. For example, the same person may be represented in one database as (SSN= 234567891, Name=Ketty, Age=27, Salary=25k) and in another database as (SSN=234567891, Name=Ketty, Age=26). In this example, a data inconsistency occurs on Age because different age values are recorded for the same person in the two databases. Apparently, one of the above two age values for Ketty is incorrect. Independent management of component database systems is the main reason for data inconsistency to occur. Usually, the schema integrator at the front end cannot modify the involved values in component databases to resolve the inconsistency because the integrator may not be authorized to do so (recall that component systems are managed autonomously) or the integrator cannot be certain which values are incorrect. As a result, data inconsistency is often handled at the front end, as will be discussed shortly. To retain the ability to identify instances from different databases representing the same real-world object, we assume that data inconsistency does not occur on the ID attribute.

Sometimes, an *apparent inconsistency* does not necessarily mean that one of the involved values must be incorrect. For example, suppose a salary value of 30k is recorded for Ketty in the second database in the above example. Note that in the first database, Ketty's salary is recorded to be 25k. This *apparent inconsistency* may have different explanations. It is possible that the apparent inconsistency is a real inconsistency in the sense the two values should be the same but they are not. However, it is also possible that it is not a real inconsistency. For instance, it is possible that Ketty has two different salaries in the two databases because she has two different part-time jobs. In this case, both salary values for Ketty are correct and they should both be used to define the salary value for Ketty in the integrated schema. To push the discussion one step further, it is easy to see that if Ketty has two salaries from two jobs, then these two salaries should be used to define the salary value for Ketty in the integrated schema regardless of whether the two salaries are equal. In other words, even if no apparent inconsistency exists between the two values under the same attribute for the same real-world object in two databases, the two values may still both be needed to obtain the integrated value for the object under the attribute in the integrated schema.

To summarize the above discussions, when two values, different or identical, exist for the same attribute of a real-world object in two databases, the following three cases exist:

1. There is no data inconsistency, and only one of the two values is needed to define the value of the object for the same attribute in the integrated schema. This would be the case, for example, if Ketty has only one job and the two salary values in the two databases are the same.

2. There is a data inconsistency, but both values are needed to define the value of the object for the same attribute in the integrated schema. This would be the case if Ketty has only one job but the two salary values in the two databases are different.

3. There is no data inconsistency, and both values are needed to define the value of the object for the same attribute in the integrated schema. This would be the case, for example, if Ketty has two jobs, regardless of whether the pays are the same.

Different methods may be used to define the value of the object under an attribute in the integrated schema from the two corresponding values in the component databases. Whether a particular method should be employed depends on the specific situation and the choice of the integrator. As an example, if the two local values are two age values and the larger age value is deemed to be correct, then the function max can be used to define the global value. As another example, if the two local values are two salary values from a person's two jobs, then the integrator may either choose to define the person's salary in the integrated schema to be the sum of his or her two salaries (the function sum can be used to achieve this) or choose to present both salaries to the global users so that the global users will know that this person has two salaries. In general, for cases 2 and 3 above, the global value in the integrated schema can be defined by a *definition function*. Since cases 2 and 3 can be handled uniformly through the use of definition functions, for the convenience of presentation, when an attribute is involved in either case 2 or case 3, we say that there is a data inconsistency on the attribute and we call the corresponding definition function a *resolution function*.

When relations $R1$ and $R2$ are integrated to another relation R, for each attribute A of R and for each real-world object o in world(R) (= world($R1$) $\cup$ world($R2$)), the A-value of o needs to be defined in terms of the A-values of the tuples in $R1$ and $R2$ that correspond to the same real-world object o. If attribute A appears in both $R1$ and $R2$ and there is no data inconsistency on A, then $R.A = R1.A$ for objects in world($R1$), and $R.A = R2.A$ for objects in world($R2$). If there is a data inconsistency on A, then a resolution function can be used to determine the A-value for each tuple in R. The following is the general format of a resolution function:

$$R.A = \begin{cases} R1.A, & \text{for objects in world}(R1) - \text{world}(R2) \\ R2.A, & \text{for objects in world}(R2) - \text{world}(R1) \\ f(R1.A, R2.A), & \text{for objects in world}(R1) \cap \text{world}(R2) \end{cases}$$

where f is a function computing the value of $R.A$ from the values of $R1.A$ and $R2.A$ for each tuple of R. The function f is often an aggregate function such as max, min, sum, and avg, but it can also be other functions. For example, it may be choose1, meaning that it simply takes values from its first argument. In other words, choose1$(R1.A, R2.A) = R1.A$. This reflects the integrator's belief that the values of $R1.A$ are more reliable than those of $R2.A$. If this is the choice, the above resolution function can be simplified to the following:

$$R.A = \begin{cases} R1.A, & \text{for objects in world}(R1) \\ R2.A, & \text{for objects in world}(R2) - \text{world}(R1) \end{cases}$$

Similarly, f can be choose2 if the values of $R2.A$ are more reliable than those of $R1.A$, or choose_all if the inconsistency is unresolvable and the integrator decides to simply present all values to the users. When choose_all is used for $R.A$, then a separate relation containing attributes ID and A needs to be created since the relational data model does not allow multivalued attributes.

The case in which there is no data inconsistency on A can also be represented in the above format by letting f be choose_any. In this case, the resolution function can be simplified to the following:

$$R.A = \begin{cases} R1.A, & \text{for objects in world}(R1) \\ R2.A, & \text{for objects in world}(R2) \end{cases}$$

When outerjoin is used for the integration, it is possible that A appears only in $R1$. In this case, the following resolution function can be used:

$$R.A = \begin{cases} R1.A, & \text{for objects in world}(R1) \\ \text{Null}, & \text{for objects in world}(R2) - \text{world}(R1) \end{cases}$$

When A appears only in $R2$, a resolution function can be similarly defined.

Note that when a resolution function is used for an attribute, it is used for the attribute values in all tuples. For example, if the function max is used for the age attribute, then for every real-world object o in world$(R1) \cap$ world$(R2)$, its age value in the integrated schema will be computed by taking the maximum of the two corresponding age values from the component databases. Therefore, if the inconsistency is *irregular* (e.g., for some objects in world$(R1) \cap$ world$(R2)$, the larger age value is correct, whereas for some other objects, the smaller age value is correct), then the above resolution approach will not work unless the set of objects in world$(R1) \cap$ world$(R2)$ is appropriately partitioned first and a separate resolution function is used for each such partition.

Now let us get back to the integration operators outerjoin and generalization described in Section 4.2.1. They were defined with the implicit assumption that there is no data inconsistency on any of the attributes. In the presence of data inconsistency, the integration using the two integration operators can be conceptually carried out in two steps. In the first step, an outerjoin (or a generalization) on the ID attribute is performed. If there is data inconsistency on attribute A, then both values of $R1.A$ and $R2.A$ for each tuple will be kept. In the second step, one resolution function is used for each pair of inconsistent attributes, e.g., $R1.A$ and $R2.A$, to resolve the inconsistency. Therefore, the integrated relation R can be expressed as $f_n f_{n-1} \ldots f_1(\text{OJ}(R1, R2))$ if outerjoin is used or $f_n f_{n-1} \ldots f_1(\text{Ge}(R1, R2))$ if generalization is used, where the f_i's are resolution functions and each f_i is used for one pair of inconsistent attributes. Note that R is not materialized at the time of the schema integration. In other words, the above two steps are carried out only when R is queried by a global query.

SSN	Name	Age	Salary	Position
123456789	John	34	30k	Engineer
234567891	Ketty	27	25k	Engineer
345678912	Wang	39	32k	Manager

(a) Relation $R1$

SSN	Name	Age	Salary	Phone
234567891	Ketty	25	20k	1234567
345678912	Wang	38	22k	2345678
456789123	Mary	42	34k	3456789

(b) Relation $R2$

SSN	Name	Age	Salary	Position	Phone
123456789	John	34	30k	Engineer	null
234567891	Ketty	27	45k	Engineer	1234567
345678912	Wang	39	54k	Manager	2345678
456789123	Mary	42	34k	null	3456789

(c) $R = \text{max\_Age sum\_Salary}(R1 \text{ OJ } R2)$

FIGURE 4.4   Integration with Data Inconsistency

Example 4.1 Let $R1$ and $R2$ be two relations from two export schemas (see Figure 4.4(a) and (b)). Data inconsistency occurs on attribute Age and attribute Salary. Suppose outerjoin is used as the integration operator, max is used to resolve the inconsistency on Age, and sum is used to resolve the inconsistency on Salary. Then the integrated result is as shown in Figure 4.4(c) when it is materialized. ∎

When R is integrated from $R1$ and $R2$ using an outerjoin or a generalization, the following information is collected; their uses will be discussed later:

Attr-Only($R1$): the set of attributes appearing only in $R1$. Attr-Only($R2$) can be defined similarly.

Attr-C-N-I: Common attributes of $R1$ and $R2$ that have No data Inconsistency

Attr-C-I-F($R1$): the set of attributes of $R1$ that are Common to both $R1$ and $R2$, with data Inconsistency; for objects in world($R1$) ∩ world($R2$), their values from $R1$ are used (i.e., $R1$'s values are Favored). Attr-C-I-F($R2$) can be defined similarly.

Attr-Agg: the set of common attributes of $R1$ and $R2$ such that for objects in world($R1$) ∩ world($R2$), their values are computed from the corresponding values from both $R1$ and $R2$ by certain (Aggregate) functions

Note that Attr($R1$) = Attr-Only($R1$) $\cup$ Attr-C-N-I $\cup$ Attr-C-I-F($R1$) $\cup$ Attr-C-I-F($R2$) $\cup$ Attr-Agg. If R is integrated using an outerjoin, then Attr(R) = Attr-Only($R1$)$\cup$Attr-Only($R2$)$\cup$ Attr-C-N-I $\cup$ Attr-C-I-F($R1$) $\cup$ Attr-C-I-F($R2$) $\cup$ Attr-Agg. If R is integrated using a generalization, then Attr(R) = Attr-C-N-I $\cup$ Attr-C-I-F($R1$) $\cup$ Attr-C-I-F($R2$) $\cup$ Attr-Agg. For the $R1$ in Figure 4.4(a), we have Attr-Only($R1$) = {Position}, Attr-C-N-I = {SSN, Name}, Attr-C-I-F($R1$) = $\emptyset$, Attr-Agg = {Age, Salary} and Attr-C-I-F($R2$) = $\emptyset$.

Integration Graph

Recall that we have employed the binary approach for schema integration, that is, we integrate two schemas at a time. Therefore, if there are n export schemas, the global schema can be obtained after $n-1$ consecutive binary integrations. Consequently, a particular global relation may be obtained from many relations in the export schemas through multiple integration steps. This process can be graphically represented by an *integration tree*. A directed edge from node R to node S in an integration tree indicates that the relation R is directly used for the formation of the relation S. It is possible that two integration trees corresponding to two global relations have common descendant nodes. Therefore, the integration trees of global relations in the global schema form a directed acyclic *integration graph*. Each node in the integration graph corresponds to a relation.

4.3   Global Query Optimization

In order to investigate query processing and optimization in a multidatabase environment, it is necessary to have a good understanding about the environment the global query optimizer is in and the constraints under which the query optimization is to be carried out. Recall that a multidatabase system consists of a front-end system together with a number of autonomous component database systems. The global query optimizer is a piece of software within the front-end system. A multidatabase system is inherently distributed because different local database systems are likely to be located at different sites. To ease the presentation, we assume that each component database system is at one site. In addition to the local database system, each site is assumed to have its own CPU and I/O resources that can be used from outside the database system. In other words, each site has processing capabilities beyond those within the database system. We assume that these capabilities from all sites can be used and coordinated by the front-end system of the multidatabase system. Conceptually, we can assume that the front end is duplicated at each site and that each site is capable of accepting global queries and carrying out the query optimization process. The front ends at different sites form a distributed computing environment. In summary, there are two levels of processing capabilities in a multidatabase environment: one at the database level within each component database system, and the other at the front-end level.

The autonomy and heterogeneity of component database systems have the following important implications for global query optimization in a multidatabase system. More subtle implications will be pointed out later in this chapter. These implications make the query optimization problem in a multidatabase system quite different and much more challenging than that in a traditional distributed relational database system.

1. The global query optimizer sees only the export schemas; how each export schema is obtained from its corresponding local schema is completely hidden. The only way for the front end to interact with a component database system is to use the export schema to issue queries to the local database. This weakens the ability to coordinate actions at the local database level. For example, the front-end system will not be able to ask a local database system to keep an intermediate result in the memory for further processing.

2. The global schema in a multidatabase system involves more complicated integration operators, such as outerjoins and generalizations. In contrast, the global schema in a traditional distributed relational database system can usually be expressed in terms of the local schemas through unions and joins. In addition, data inconsistency caused by independent operation of component systems may occur in a multidatabase system. The combined use of complicated integration operators and resolution functions substantially increases the complexity of query optimization in a multidatabase system.

3. Important information about local relations and local query cost functions that are needed to select good global query execution plans may not be provided or may be only partially provided to the global query optimizer by local database systems. Such information may include the cardinalities of relations, the availability of fast access paths, the access method, and the buffer size used for a local query. The lack of such information is an important difference between a traditional database system and a multidatabase system because these types of information are always assumed available and are critically important for the global query optimizer in a traditional database system. Without the information, costs of different execution plans cannot be accurately estimated, and as a result, cost-based query optimization techniques cannot be directly applied. One unique problem in query optimization in multidatabase systems is to find approximate cost formulas for local subqueries.

In this section, we discuss several approaches for the processing and optimization of global queries in a multidatabase system. These approaches are outlined below:

Query modification and decomposition. This approach has two steps. In the first step—the query modification step—the global query using global names is modified into queries using only names in export schemas. Query modification may result in multiple queries, and some of them may still reference data from more than one database. These queries are then decomposed into single-database subqueries and possibly also assembling queries in the second step.

The advantages of the decomposition approach include the following: (1) It can reduce the number of times each local relation is accessed because it may be possible to combine some accesses to the same local relation resulting from the decomposition of different modified queries. As a result of this, the number of times each local database system is invoked may be reduced. (2) Some joins involving local relations in the same database can be processed locally, taking advantage of whatever local fast access paths that are available. The main disadvantage is that it may generate a rather large number of subqueries and therefore substantial effort may be needed to combine them and to assemble partial results into the final answer. This approach will be discussed in Section 4.3.1.

Single-query approach. This approach treats each modified query after the query modification step as an independent query and tries to optimize it independently.

Compared with the decomposition approach, the number of queries in this approach is more manageable. Other advantages of this approach are that (1) joins involving local relations in the same database can be processed locally, and (2) it is easy to assemble partial results into the final answer (a union will do). The main disadvantage is that multiple accesses to the same relation may occur if the relation appears in more than one modified query. This approach will be discussed in Section 4.3.2.

Materialization approach. In this approach, each referenced global relation is first materialized (i.e., the tuples of each referenced global relation that satisfy the query conditions on the global relation are computed). After the materialization, the processing capabilities at the front-end level are used to further optimize the query using query processing techniques in distributed relational databases (see Chapter 3).

This approach employs optimization in the materialization phase as well as in the join phase after all global relations are materialized. It guarantees that each local relation is accessed only once if it is used in the integration of only one referenced global relation. The main disadvantage is that joins between different global relations, even if they correspond to local relations from the same database, must be processed at the front end. This approach will be presented in Section 4.3.3.

In Section 4.3.4, a query sampling method for estimating cost formulas for local subqueries will be introduced to deal with the unavailability of some important information of local database systems.

4.3.1   Query Modification and Decomposition

As mentioned above, this approach consists of two steps. The first step is query modification and the second step is query decomposition.

Query Modification

This step modifies the global query using global names to queries using only names in export schemas. More specifically, each global relation referenced in the global query will be modified to relations in the export schemas in a number of steps in the reverse direction to that in which the global relation is integrated from those export schema relations. Since the binary integration method is used, each step involves only two schemas (export schemas or intermediate schemas integrated from export schemas). Since the modification process can be repeated for each step, we present only one step.

The mapping of a global name to a name in an export schema depends on the real-world objects under consideration. For example, suppose attribute Position of relation R in Figure 4.4(c) is referenced in the global query and the resolution function for R.Position is

$$R.\text{Position} = \begin{cases} R1.\text{Position}, & \text{for objects in world}(R1) \\ \text{Null}, & \text{for objects in world}(R2) - \text{world}(R1) \end{cases}$$

Then for objects in world($R1$), R.Position should be mapped to $R1$.Position, and for objects in world($R2$) − world($R1$), R.Position should be mapped to null (i.e., no mapping).

Definition 4.2 *For a given attribute A of a global relation R and the resolution function on A, the classification of R on A, denoted as* Cl($R.A$), *is the set of subsets of* world(R) *used in the resolution function on A.*

Based on the above resolution function for R.Position, the classification of R on Position Cl(R.Position) is {world($R1$), world($R2$) − world($R1$)}. Similarly, we have Cl(R.Salary) = {world($R1$) − world($R2$), world($R2$) − world($R1$), world($R1$) ∩ world($R2$)}. Note that the subsets in a classification need not be disjoint. For example, the two subsets in Cl(R.SSN), namely world($R1$) and world($R2$), may overlap. As a special case, if R corresponds to a single export relation $R1$—i.e., it is not integrated—then for any attribute A of R, Cl($R.A$) = {world($R1$)}.

When multiple attributes of a relation R are referenced in a global query, more than one classification of R may be obtained based on these attributes. A classification C_1 is said to be *finer* than classification C_2 if each subset in C_1 is either in C_2 or is a subset of a subset in C_2, but the reverse is not true. For example, Cl(R.Salary) is finer than Cl(R.Position). It is of interest to find the *finest* classification of R so that all mappings for R can be carried out using the same classification. It is possible that no classification among the classifications obtained based on individual attributes is the finest. In this case, we can construct a classification that is at least as fine as any existing classification. For example, from Cl(R.Position) = {world($R1$), world($R2$)−world($R1$)} and Cl(R.Phone) = {world($R2$), world($R1$)−world($R2$)}, the desired classification is {world($R1$) − world($R2$), world($R2$) − world($R1$), world($R1$) ∩ world($R2$)}. For each global relation integrated from two export relations, the finest classification contains at most three subsets.

After the finest classification for each referenced global relation is obtained, combinations that contain one subset from each classification can be obtained. For each such combination, the global query will be mapped to a query using only names in export schemas. As a result, a single global query may be mapped to a number of queries by the query modification algorithm.

Query-Modification (GQ)

/* GQ is the global query under consideration. */

1. For each attribute A of every global relation R referenced in GQ, compute Cl($R.A$).

2. For each global relation referenced in GQ, identify the finest classification among all the classifications obtained in step 1 (different tuple variables of the same relation can be treated as different relations in this step).

If no classification among the classifications obtained in step 1 is the finest, construct a classification for R such that it is at least as fine as any classification obtained in step 1.

3. If more than one global relation is referenced in GQ, identify all possible combinations that contain one subset from each (finest) classification of each referenced global relation. Let $R_1, R_2, \ldots, R_n$ be all the global relations referenced in GQ, and let $C_1, C_2, \ldots, C_n$ be the corresponding finest classifications obtained for these relations, respectively.

The set of all subset combinations is $C = \{(S_1, S_2, \ldots, S_n) \mid$ where $S_i \in C_i$ is a subset, $i = 1, \ldots, n\}$.

4. Obtain a query for each combination in C. The query corresponding to a given combination can be obtained from the global query by replacing each global attribute by the corresponding export schema attribute or a function of some export schema attributes as defined in the resolution function. If the corresponding export schema attribute is absent and is a target attribute, then it is removed. But if it involves a predicate, then the corresponding query is discarded because such a predicate cannot be evaluated.

In addition, if world($R1$) − world($R2$) is in the combination, then "and $R1$.ID not in (select $R2$.ID from $R2$)" is added to the where-clause of the query. This is needed to ensure that only objects in world($R1$) − world($R2$) are considered.

Similarly, if world($R2$) − world($R1$) is in the combination, then "and $R2$.ID not in (select $R1$.ID from $R1$)" is added to the where-clause of the query.

If world($R1$) ∩ world($R2$) is in the combination, then "$R1$.ID = $R2$.ID" is added to the where-clause of the query to ensure that only real-world objects in world($R1$) ∩ world($R2$) are considered by the query.

When there is no data inconsistency and R is integrated from $R1$ and $R2$, then R will always be classified into two subsets, namely world($R1$) and world($R2$). In this case, the above algorithm can be substantially simplified. We leave the details to the reader as an exercise.

Example 4.2 Consider the following global query:

```
select R.SSN, R.Name, D.Manager
from R, D
where R.Salary < 40k and R.Position = 'Engineer'
        and R.Dept_name = D.Dept_name and D.Manager = 'Smith'
```

where R is as defined by Figure 4.4(c) except that a Dept_name attribute is added that appears in both $R1$ and $R2$ with no data inconsistency, and global relation D(Dept_name, Location, Manager) is integrated from $D1$(Dept_name, Location) and $D2$(Dept_name, Manager).

The finest classification for R is the one based on the attribute Salary, namely {world($R1$) − world($R2$), world($R2$) − world($R1$), world($R1$) ∩ world($R2$)}, and the finest classification for D is {world($D1$) − world($D2$), world($D2$)} because Manager appears in $D2$ but not in $D1$ and there is no data inconsistency on Dept_Name. As a result, six different combinations of subsets can be obtained, as follows:

1. world($R1$) − world($R2$), world($D1$) − world($D2$)

2. world($R1$) − world($R2$), world($D2$)

3. world($R2$) − world($R1$), world($D1$) − world($D2$)

4. world($R2$) − world($R1$), world($D2$)

5. world($R1$) ∩ world($R2$), world($D1$) − world($D2$)

6. world($R1$) ∩ world($R2$), world($D2$)

A query will be obtained for each of the above combinations from query modification. Since "$D1$.Manager = 'Smith' " will always be evaluated to false, the three queries for combinations 1, 3, and 5 are discarded. Similarly, the query for combination 4 can also be discarded due to the condition on attribute Position. The remaining modified queries are as follows:

The query for combination 2:

```
select R1.SSN, R1.Name, D2.Manager
from R1, D2
where R1.Salary < 40k and R1.Position = 'Engineer'
    and R1.Dept_name = D2.Dept_name and D2.Manager = 'Smith'
    and R1.SSN not in (select R2.SSN from R2)
```

The query for combination 6:

```
select R1.SSN, R1.Name, D2.Manager
from R1, R2, D2
where sum(R1.Salary, R2.Salary) < 40k and R1.Position = 'Engineer'
    and D2.Manager = 'Smith' and R1.Dept_name = D2.Dept_name
    and R1.SSN = R2.SSN
```
∎

There is relatively little opportunity for query optimization during query modification. Other than identifying those queries that can be discarded, some flexibility also exists on the choice of the database from which the values of tuples in world($R1$) ∩ world($R2$) under certain attributes should come. For example, for the query for combination 6 above, $R1$.SSN and $R1$.Name in the select-clause and $R1$.Dept_name in the where-clause can be replaced by $R2$.SSN, $R2$.Name, and $R2$.Dept_name, respectively, because there is no data inconsistency on these attributes. Different choices may incur different costs. In the above example, if $D2$ and $R2$ are from the same component database, then replacing $R1$.Dept_name by $R2$.Dept_name makes the join on Dept_name processable in the component database system. The following simple rules can be used to guide the choice: if a choice can make the query a single-database query, then choose it; otherwise, if a choice can make a join locally processable, choose it.

Finally, an assembling query is needed to union the results returned by the queries obtained from the query modification.

Query Decomposition

After query modification, some resulting queries may still reference data from more than one database. None of these queries can be directly evaluated by a single-database system. The query decomposition approach decomposes each modified nonsingle-database query MQ into a set of single-database queries. An assembling query (AQ) that combines the results returned by single-database queries to form the result for each MQ will be generated at the same time. During the decomposition process, two types of predicates in MQ are identified. The first type involves attribute(s) from a single database, and the second type involves attributes from more than one database. Predicates of the first type will be placed in appropriate single-database queries obtained from MQ so that they can be evaluated by the corresponding component database systems. Predicates of the second type will be placed in the assembling query so that they can be evaluated by the front end. In order for the front end to evaluate these predicates, values under the attributes in these predicates need to be returned to the front end from component database systems. This is achieved by adding these attributes in the select-clauses of appropriate single-database queries. Functions for resolving data inconsistencies can be handled similarly as predicates of the second type. The decomposition of MQ is described by the following algorithm.

Query-Decomposition (MQ)

1. Determine the set of databases involved. This can be achieved by determining which attribute in MQ is from which database. The needed information should have been recorded at the time when the corresponding export schemas are integrated.

2. Form a tentative single-database query, SDQ, for each involved database as follows. The select-clause of the tentative SDQ for database $D1$ contains all attributes in all select-clauses of the MQ that are from $D1$ (the MQ may have multiple select-clauses if it is nested), its from-clause contains all relation names in all from-clauses of the MQ that are from $D1$, and its where-clause contains those predicates of the MQ that involve only attributes from $D1$.

3. If in the where-clause of the MQ, an attribute A_1 from database $D1$ is involved in a *comparison* with an attribute A_2 from another database $D2$, then the attribute A_1 needs to be placed in the select-clause of the query for $D1$ if it is not already in the select-clause. Here, the comparison between A_1 and A_2 will have one of the two forms: (a) A_1 *op* A_2, where *op* is an arithmetic comparator, and (b) A_1 *setop* (select $A_2 \ldots$), where *setop* can be either *in* or *not in*.

4. Remove functions used for resolving data inconsistency in the where-clause of the MQ. (An example of such a function is sum($R1$.Salary, $R2$.Salary). Other frequently used functions are avg( ), max( ), and min( ).) If attribute A_1 from database $D1$ is an argument of such a function, then A_1 is placed in the select-clause of the query for $D1$ if it is not already in.

5. Form assembling queries (AQ). Normally, there will be one AQ for each MQ.
    Suppose an MQ is decomposed into n single-database queries and n temporary relations X_i, $i = 1, \ldots, n$, are returned as the results. The AQ for the MQ can be obtained as follows: (a) Its from-clause contains all X_i's. (b) Its select-clause contains attributes in the select-clause of the MQ with the appropriate replacement of qualifying relation names; i.e., the attributes in the assembling query are qualified by X_i's. (c) Its where-clause is the same as the where-clause of the MQ, with two exceptions: (i) X_i's are used to qualify corresponding attribute names, and (ii) all predicates involving attributes from one database are removed (since they were performed when single-database queries were evaluated).

Example 4.3 Let us continue Example 4.2 and decompose the two modified queries. The modified query for combination 2 is decomposed into the following two single-database queries and one assembling query:

```
select R1.SSN, R1.Name, R1.Dept_name into X1
from R1
where R1.Salary < 40k and R1.Position = 'Engineer'

select R2.SSN, D2.Manager, D2.Dept_name into X2
from R2, D2
where D2.Manager = 'Smith'

select X1.SSN, X1.Name, X2.Manager
from X1, X2
where X1.Dept_name = X2.Dept_name and X1.SSN not in (select X2.SSN from X2)
```

The modified query for combination 6 is decomposed into the following two single-database queries and one assembling query:

```
select R1.SSN, R1.Name, R1.Salary, R1.Dept_name into Y1
from R1
where R1.Position = 'Engineer'

select R2.SSN, R2.Salary, D2.Manager, D2.Dept_name into Y2
from R2, D2
where D2.Manager = 'Smith'

select Y1.SSN, Y1.Name, Y2.Manager
from Y1, Y2
where sum(Y1.Salary, Y2.Salary) < 40k and Y1.Dept_name = Y2.Dept_name
      and Y1.SSN = Y2.SSN
```
∎

After algorithm Query-Decomposition is applied to all modified nonsingle-database queries, multiple queries may be generated for each component database system. Even if the set of queries for the same component database system is sent to the database system as a batch, these queries will be processed one by one independently because current query optimizers are designed for optimizing one query at a time and not a set of queries at a time. Consequently, the global query optimizer, not the query optimizer at the component database system, is responsible for the optimization of the set of queries. The problem of optimizing a set of queries at a time is known as *multiple query optimization*. The basic idea is to identify common or related predicates so that they can be grouped and evaluated once. For instance, the two queries for database 2 (it contains $R2$ and $D2$) in Example 4.3 can be combined into one since the two queries have the same from-clause and the same where-clause, and the set of target attributes in the select-clause of the first query is a subset of that of the second query.

4.3.2 Single-Query Approach

As mentioned previously, this approach treats each modified query generated from the modification of the global query as an independent query and tries to process it independently. In such a modified query, each referenced relation corresponds to a relation in some export schema. For simplicity of discussion, in this subsection we assume that each export schema relation corresponds to one local relation.

Processing a Single Join

We first consider a simple query involving a single join: $R1 \bowtie_A R2$, where $R1$ and $R2$ are relations from two export schemas and A is the join attribute. Let $D1$ and $D2$ be the component database systems containing $R1$ and $R2$, respectively. Suppose the join result is to be produced at $D2$. We would like to use this simple query to illustrate the impact of the autonomy of component database systems in a multidatabase system on join processing strategy. The following could be implied by the autonomy of a component database system. They are very relevant to our discussion in this subsection.

Implication 1.   A component system may choose to permit or not to permit the front end to create temporary relations in the component system.

Implication 2.   After a join is submitted to a component system, how the join is to be evaluated is completely up to the component system, and the front end has no control over what join algorithm should be used. In addition, the result of the join will be returned to the front end only after the evaluation of the join is complete. In other words, the front-end system has no means to ask the component system to return any partial result.

Implication 3.   A component system handles each request from the front end independently. In other words, the front-end system has no means to ask the component system to coordinate the evaluation of different requests.

With the above implications in mind, we now discuss how to process the join $R1 \bowtie_A R2$. First, a number of join methods can be used. Suppose we can choose among the following four join methods: nested loop join, semi-join, sort merge join, and hash join. Second, the join can be performed either in component database systems or at the front end (using the processing capabilities at the front-end level). Therefore, eight combinations are possible:

1. *Nested loop join in component systems:* This can be carried out as follows: (i) Retrieve $R1$ from $D1$ and send it to the site containing $R2$. (ii) Create a temporary relation for $R1$ in $D2$. (iii) Perform the join in $D2$. Note that there is no guarantee that the nested loop join method will be used in step (iii). The first two steps provide us the picture on what the front end should do if the nested loop join is to be used.

   Also note that step (ii) is possible only if the front end is permitted to create temporary relations in $D2$. If such permission is not given, then the second and third steps need to be modified as follows: (ii) For each tuple t in $R1$, form a selection query $\sigma_{A=t[A]}(R2)$ and submit it to $D2$, where $t[A]$ denotes the A-value of t. The returned tuples from $R2$ are concatenated with t to complete the join of t with $R2$. (iii) Union the results in (ii) to obtain the final result. It has been shown experimentally that because this approach requires repeated invocations to $D2$ and each such invocation incurs additional cost, unless $R1$ is very small, this approach is unlikely to outperform other join methods.

2. *Nested loop join at the front end:* This can be carried out as follows: (i) Retrieve $R1$ and $R2$ from their respective component databases. (ii) Send $R1$ to the site containing $R2$. (iii) Perform the nested loop join at the front end. The advantage is that each local database system is invoked only once. The disadvantage is that by performing the join

at the front end, fast access paths available at component database systems cannot be made use of.

3. *Semi-join in component systems:* This can be carried out as follows: (i) Retrieve $X = \pi_A(R2)$ from $D2$. (ii) Send X to the site containing $R1$ and form a query $\sigma_{A \ in \ X}(R1)$ and submit it to $D1$. Let the result be Y. (iii) Send Y to the site containing $R2$ and create a temporary table for Y in $D2$. (iv) Perform the join between $R2$ and Y. Compared with a traditional distributed database system, semi-join in a multidatabase system is less attractive because, first, it is more likely that $R2$ needs to be read in twice from the secondary storage, once in step (i) and the second time in step (iv), and second, a temporary relation for Y needs to be explicitly created. The reason it is more likely that $R2$ needs to be read in again in step (iv) is explained as follows: Due to the autonomy of $D2$, the front end can interact with $D2$ only through issuing queries to $D2$. When query $\pi_A(R2)$ is issued to $D2$ in step (i), $D2$ does not know that $R2$ needs to be accessed again in the near future and the front end has no means to inform $D2$ of this. As a result, $D2$ makes no special effort to keep $R2$ in the memory after $\pi_A(R2)$ is processed. Consequently, the likelihood that $R2$ needs to be read in again in step (iv) is higher than in a traditional distributed database system, in which the fact that $R2$ will be used again is known to the system. Also note that if the temporary relation for Y cannot be created in $D2$, then this method will not work.

4. *Semi-join at the front end:* This can be carried out as follows: (i) Retrieve $R2$ to the front end and perform $X = \pi_A(R2)$. (ii) Send X to the site containing $R1$ and form a query $\sigma_{A \ in \ X}(R1)$ and submit it to $D1$. Let the result be Y. (iii) Send Y to the site containing $R2$. (iv) Perform the join between $R2$ and Y at the front end. Since $R2$ is kept in the front end and the join between $R2$ and Y is performed in the front end, the two problems encountered when performing semi-join in component systems are avoided. The drawback of this method is that the join in step (iv) cannot make use of any fast access paths available during its evaluation.

5. *Sort merge join in component systems:* This can be carried out as follows: (i) Retrieve $R1$ with the result sorted on A (using the *order by* clause in SQL) from $D1$. (ii) Send $R1$ to the site containing $R2$ and create a temporary relation for $R1$ in $D2$. (iii) Perform the join. Two remarks are in order here. First, this method will not work if $D2$ does not permit the front end to create a temporary relation in $D2$. Second, there is no guarantee that the sort merge join method will be used in step (iii), although the possibility is increased because of the sorted status of $R1$ on the join attribute A.

6. *Sort merge join at the front end:* This can be carried out as follows: (i) Retrieve $R1$ and $R2$ with the results sorted on A from their respective component database systems. (ii) Send $R1$ to the site containing $R2$. (iii) Perform the merge phase of the join. Since sort merge join typically does not involve fast access paths, whether it is performed at a component database system or at the front end makes little difference.[1] In other words, the sort merge join method is more robust with regard to environment.

---

[1]In Chapter 1, we mentioned a variation of the sort merge join that utilizes the secondary index on one or both joining attributes of $R1$ and $R2$. However, the application of this variation is usually very limited.

7. *Hash join in component systems:* This can be carried out as follows: (i) Build a hash table based on the values of A for R2. (ii) Send R1 to the site containing R2 and create a temporary relation for R1 in D2. (iii) Perform the join by using the A-values of R1 to probe the hash table. Similar remarks made for performing sort merge join in component systems can also be made here.

8. *Hash join at the front end:* This can be carried out as follows: (i) Retrieve R2 to the front end and create a hash table based on the values of A. (ii) Retrieve R1 and send it to the site containing R2. (iii) Perform the join by using the A-values of R1 to probe the hash table. Again, since hash join does not involve fast access paths, whether it is performed at a local database system or the front end makes little difference.

The above discussions can be summarized as follows:

1. To perform joins in component systems, the front end often needs permission to create temporary relations in component systems. This strategy may not be always workable.

2. Semi-join is not as effective in a multidatabase system as in a traditional distributed relational database system if it is to be performed in component systems.

3. Although performing join at the front end can overcome the problems in the above two items, this strategy may not be able to fully utilize fast access paths available in component systems during the evaluation.

4. Sort merge join and hash join are as effective when used at the front end as when used in component systems because they typically do not use fast access paths.

In a traditional distributed relational database system or a multiprocessor environment, if a query involves multiple joins, then pipelined parallelism (see Chapter 5) can often be employed to reduce the response time of the query. For example, if we have $R1 \bowtie R2 \bowtie R3$, then partial results generated from one join, say $R1 \bowtie R2$, can be used to start the second join. Unfortunately, in a multidatabase system, pipelined parallelism might not be applied effectively because an autonomous component system might not return any partial result of an operation. For instance, if $R1 \bowtie R2$ is performed in a component system, we cannot expect the component system to return any partial result to feed to the second join.

Tree Balancing to Reduce Response Time

Some modified queries may involve a number of joins in addition to selections and projections. Therefore it is important to find techniques to optimize these types of queries. In the following, a technique is introduced that can be used in a multidatabase system to optimize both the total cost and the response time. It is assumed that sort merge join is used for all joins, although hash join could be used instead. In our earlier discussion, we already explained why nested loop join and semi-join are not suited in a multidatabase system. Although this technique may also be applicable to traditional distributed relational database systems, it is first developed specifically for multidatabase systems.

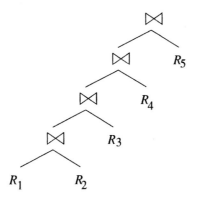

FIGURE 4.5 **A Left Deep Join Tree of Five Relations**

This technique consists of following two steps:

1. A traditional cost-based optimization algorithm is used to find a left deep execution join plan that is optimal among all possible left deep execution join plans with respect to the total cost. Such an algorithm exists in System R.

2. The left deep join tree generated in the first step is transformed into a bushy join tree to allow concurrent execution of different joins. (In contrast with a left deep tree, where all right child nodes are leaf nodes and all left child nodes except the lowest one are internal nodes, in a bushy tree, both child nodes of an internal node could be internal.) As a result, the response time can be reduced.

The name of the left deep execution join plan comes from the fact that the plan can be expressed as a left deep join tree (see Figure 4.5 for an example). The joins are carried out in a bottom-up manner. Although left deep execution may be reasonable for minimizing the total cost, it is often bad for minimizing the response time when sort merge join is used to implement the joins. The reason is that, in this case, the joins in the left deep execution plan can only be done sequentially, one at a time, and one can only start after the previous one has completed. For example, when sort merge join is used, both input arguments must be entirely present and have been sorted before the merge can start.

Clearly, a given left deep tree may be transformed to different bushy trees with drastically different costs in step 2. Since there are a very large number of equivalent join trees to a given left deep tree, it is not cost effective to examine all possible equivalent join trees. Therefore, heuristic algorithms need to be developed to efficiently find a bushy join tree with good performance.

Step 1 has been studied in traditional distributed relational database systems (e.g., System R* employs such an approach) and will not be discussed here. We will only focus on step 2 here. However, we would like to point out that in order to apply the technique of finding the optimal left deep join tree in distributed relational database systems to a multidatabase environment, cost formulas for basic operations such as selections and joins must be available to the global query optimizer. Unfortunately, due to the autonomy of component database

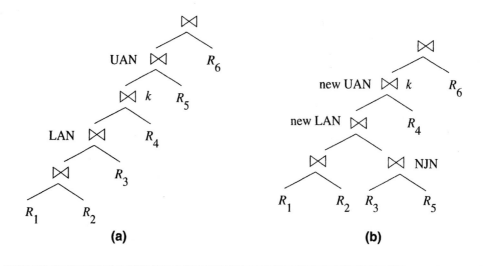

FIGURE 4.6 A Basic Transformation

systems, such cost formulas are unlikely to be available in a multidatabase environment. As a result, special techniques must be used to estimate these cost formulas. We will delay the discussion of this issue until Section 4.3.4. For now we assume that all needed cost formulas are available.

The input to the tree transformation algorithm is the left deep join tree optimized with respect to the total cost. The goal is to reduce the response time of the execution plan while not increasing the total cost through tree balancing. In fact, the total cost could also be reduced because the bushy trees were not in the search space when the optimal left deep join tree was produced.

Basic Transformation

A basic transformation takes as input a tree segment as identified by an *upper anchor node* (UAN) and a *lower anchor node* (LAN), where the LAN is a *left descendant* of the UAN (see Figure 4.6(a)). Node X qualifies as a left descendant of node Y if X is the left child of Y or a left descendant of the left child of Y. The basic transformation transforms the input tree segment into a new tree segment by the following steps: (1) If the UAN has a parent, then connect the left child of the UAN with the parent of UAN; otherwise, the left child of the UAN becomes the root. In both cases, the UAN is removed and its left child becomes the new UAN. (2) Create a new join node (NJN) as the right child of the LAN such that the join predicate on the NJN is the same as that on the old UAN and the two child nodes of the NJN are the right children of the old LAN and UAN. Let ST_L and ST_U denote the subtrees rooted at the right children of the old LAN and UAN, respectively. Then the subtree with the higher response time becomes the left child of the NJN and the subtree with the lower response time becomes the right child of the NJN. If the two subtrees have the same response time, then it does not matter which one becomes the left or right child of the NJN. A basic transformation is illustrated in Figure 4.6. Before the basic transformation, there are five sequential joins.

After the basic transformation, there are only four sequential joins. As a result, the response time of the query can be reduced.

A basic transformation is *valid* if the result of evaluating the transformed query tree is the same as the result of evaluating the original query tree. Due to the associativity and commutativity of the join operator, the validity of a basic transformation can be achieved if all join predicates are preserved and each join node in the transformed query tree has sufficient input data. Each join is associated with a predicate in the original query. If each such join predicate is associated with some join in the transformed query and no new join predicate is created, then all predicates are preserved. A join node has sufficient input data if all relations referenced in the corresponding join predicate are available for the join, i.e., all referenced relations are descendant of the join node. It is easy to see that a basic transformation preserves all join predicates and does not cause insufficient input data to any join node except for possibly the NJN. To ensure that the NJN also has sufficient input data, the UAN and the LAN need to be chosen carefully. More specifically, if "$R.A \theta S.B$" is the join predicate on the old UAN, where θ is an operator, and relation S is in the right subtree of the old UAN, then relation R must be in the right subtree of the old LAN in order for the NJN to have sufficient input data.

A basic transformation is *order preserving* if the sorted status of each direct input relation of every join node is preserved in the transformed query tree. Order preservation is desirable for two reasons. First, it ensures that the sorted status of the result of the query will not change as a result of a basic transformation. Second, it will be more efficient to estimate the cost and response time of the execution plan corresponding to the transformed query tree. Each node in a query tree is associated with a total cost and a response time indicating the cost and time estimated for performing the operations in the subtree rooted at the node. The total cost and response time associated with the root of the query tree are the total cost and response time of the execution plan corresponding to the query tree. With an order-preserving basic transformation, only the costs and response times associated with node NJN and with nodes between the new UAN and LAN need to be estimated. The costs and response times associated with the descendant nodes of the NJN and with the nodes in the left subtree of the LAN can be reused without change, and the costs and response times associated with the ancestor nodes of the new UAN can be easily derived. For example, consider the parent X of the new UAN. Suppose r_l and r_r are the response times associated with the new UAN (i.e., the left child of X) and with the right child of X, respectively. Then the new response time associated with X in the new query tree will be $\max\{r_l, r_r\} + c_X$, where c_X is the cost of performing the join at X. Note that r_r and c_X are the same as in the old join tree.

It is possible that a basic transformation is not order preserving. For example, the order of the result of the NJN may be different from that of the LAN's original right child node. This problem can be overcome by explicitly adding proper sort nodes. Only valid and order-preserving basic transformations will be considered by the tree-balancing algorithms.

A basic transformation is cost-improving if the transformed join tree has a reduced response time and the same or lower total cost in comparison with the original join tree. Cost estimation is needed to determine whether a basic transformation is cost-improving.

For a given UAN, the LAN can only be selected from the left descendants of the UAN in such a way that the resulting NJN has sufficient input data. The search space of the LAN can be reduced further by using some heuristics such as choosing the LAN as the left descendant node that is close to the UAN and satisfies certain conditions, such as that the resulting NJN is more or less balanced (i.e., its two children have similar response times). Based on this, we assume that the following two functions exist: *find-LAN*(U), which returns the LAN L for a given UAN U, and *transform*(U, L), which performs a basic transformation on the input tree segment identified by U and L. With these assumptions, the remaining problem is the selection of UANs. Three algorithms will be discussed below: a top-down approach, a bottom-up approach, and a hybrid approach.

The Top-Down Approach

The algorithm TDT(Root), standing for top-down traversal, selects UANs by traversing the join tree from the root node to leaf nodes. Once a LAN is found by find-LAN( ), procedure transform( ) is called to perform a basic transformation. The algorithm is recursive.

TDT(Root)

Let the first UAN be the root. There are three cases:

1. If the left child of the UAN is a leaf node, then stop since there is nothing left to balance.

2. If the response time of the right child subtree of the UAN is about the same as or greater than that of the left child subtree of the UAN, then recursively call TDT(LeftChild) and TDT(RightChild), where LeftChild and RightChild are the left child node and the right child node of the UAN, respectively. Note that it is possible that a node is more or less balanced but its child nodes are unbalanced.

3. If the response time of the right child subtree of the UAN is smaller than that of the left child subtree of the UAN, then let L = find-LAN(Root) and perform transform(Root, L). Let NUAN be the new UAN after the basic transformation. Call TDT(NUAN) to continue to balance the tree.

With a left deep join tree, most of the processing time will be spent on the left subtree. Step 3 of the algorithm transfers some work to the right subtree. This helps to reduce the response time.

This algorithm is illustrated in Figure 4.7. Each circle in Figure 4.7 highlights the current UAN and LAN. In this example, it is assumed that the response time of a subtree is proportional to the number of joins in the subtree. It can be shown that the number of basic transformations that can be performed by the top-down approach is bounded by $\frac{1}{2}(n-1)(n-2)$. The top-down approach can be used to reduce the response time, but there is no guarantee that the resulting join tree is optimal with respect to the response time. Intuitively, the main problem of this approach is that it tries to balance a node (the UAN) before its child nodes are balanced. Note that it is possible for a balanced node to become unbalanced after its child nodes are balanced.

The Bottom-Up Approach

In contrast to the top-down approach, the bottom-up approach tries to select UANs by traversing the join tree from the bottom up. Therefore, when a node is to be balanced, its child nodes have been balanced. The algorithm starts with the grandparent node of the leftmost

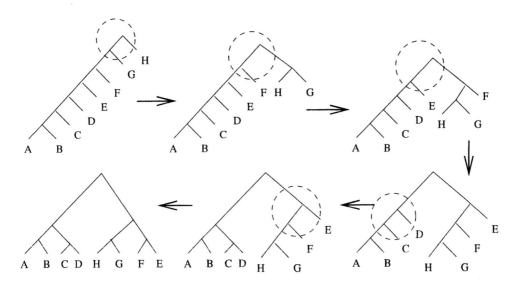

FIGURE 4.7 Illustrating Algorithm TDT

leaf node. That is, the grandparent node of the leftmost leaf node is the first UAN. If there is no valid, order-preserving, and cost-improving basic transformation (i.e., find-LAN(UAN) returns null), then the parent node of the current UAN will become the new UAN immediately. If a non-null LAN is returned, then a basic transformation will be performed, and again, the parent node of the current UAN will become the new UAN afterward. Since the new NJN may be unbalanced, the bottom-up process will also be applied to the subtree rooted at the NJN. This process continues until the root node is reached.

This algorithm is illustrated in Figure 4.8. Again it is assumed that the response time of a subtree is proportional to the number of joins in the subtree. In addition, it can be shown that the number of basic transformations that can be performed by the bottom-up approach is bounded by $\frac{1}{2}(n - 1)(n - 2)$. There is no guarantee that the resulting join tree is optimal with respect to the response time since it is possible that a tree is not balanced while its subtrees are balanced.

The Hybrid Approach

The hybrid approach is designed to combine the strengths and overcome the weaknesses of the above two approaches. The basic idea of this algorithm can be described as follows. Two sequences of transformations are considered in parallel: one proceeds top down from the root while the other proceeds bottom up from the grandparent of the leftmost leaf node. In other words, two UANs, $N1$ and $N2$, will be maintained all the time, where $N1$ and $N2$ are for the bottom-up and top-down sequences, respectively. The root is the initial $N2$, and the grandparent of the leftmost leaf node is the initial $N1$. At any given time, at most one of the two UANs is active. The active UAN is chosen according to the following rules: (1) $N1$ is chosen if the response time of its left child subtree is smaller than that of $N2$'s right child subtree,

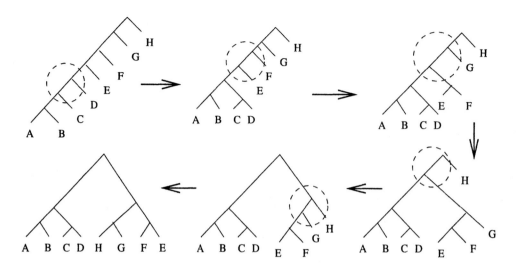

FIGURE 4.8 Illustrating the Bottom-Up Approach

and $N2$ is chosen otherwise. (2) If the two response times are about the same, then choose the UAN with an unbalanced child subtree. After each basic transformation, the algorithm is recursively applied to the left child subtree of $N1$ or the right child subtree of $N2$, depending on which of $N1$ and $N2$ is the active UAN. The algorithm stops when $N1$ meets $N2$. The idea behind the two rules is to maintain similar response times for the two subtrees (i.e., the left child subtree of $N1$ and the right child subtree of $N2$). For example, when the response time of the left child subtree of $N1$ is smaller than that of the right child subtree of $N2$, a basic transformation based on $N1$ will increase the response time of the left child subtree of the new $N1$ (which is the parent of the old $N1$). Similarly, when the response time of the right child subtree of $N2$ is smaller than that of the left child subtree of $N1$, a basic transformation based on $N2$ will increase the response time of the right child subtree of the new $N2$. By keeping the left child subtree of $N1$ and the right child subtree of $N2$ more or less balanced, the root node of the new tree will also be more or less balanced when $N1$ meets $N2$ (note that when $N1$ meets $N2$, they will become the root of the new tree).

Unfortunately, the hybrid approach also does not guarantee the optimality of the transformed join trees. Nevertheless, it is likely to be better than both the top-down approach and the bottom-up approach for most join trees because it avoids extreme cases that may be produced by the other two approaches.

4.3.3 Materialization Approach

The idea of this approach is that a global query can be processed by first materializing only those portions of the global relations referenced by the global query and then applying existing algorithms developed for traditional distributed relational database systems (see Chapter 3 for more details) to process the distributed query. Using such a method, efficient materialization of referenced global relations is critically important in query optimization. We first concentrate on the efficient materialization of referenced global relations without considering at which site each materialized global relation should be placed. Near the end of this subsection, we take the sites into consideration.

A global query may reference several global relations. The materialization process will be applied to each referenced global relation. Let R be a referenced global relation under consideration. By mapping back through export schemas and component schemas, the set of local relations that are used to form R can be identified. To simplify the presentation here, let us assume that the component schemas and the local schemas are the same. The case that they are different involves query translation and will be addressed in the next section. With this assumption, R can be thought of as being obtained through two sets of operations. The first set includes operations that are similar to standard relational algebra operators, such as join, selection, and projection. These operators are used to obtain export schemas from component schemas. The second set includes integration operators, such as outerjoin and generalization, which are used to obtain the global schema from the export schemas.

Conceptually, a query-independent bottom-up process can be used to materialize R. This process can be carried out by first identifying all local relations in local schemas that are used to integrate R and then evaluating the relational operators and integration operators in a bottom-up manner. The component database systems have control over how relational operators are processed, and the global query optimizer in the front end can decide how to process the integration operators. However, such a query-independent materialization approach is not efficient because the conditions imposed on R in the global query are not made use of during the materialization process. Two types of conditions may be imposed on R. Type 1 includes selections and projections on R. Type 2 includes joins between R and other global relations referenced in the same global query.

In this section, we introduce a query-dependent materialization approach that tries to make maximum use of these conditions to improve the efficiency. This approach can be summarized as the following two-phase process:

1. In the first phase, query conditions imposed on R are pushed over integration operators and relational operators and down to the related local relations to reduce the amount of data retrieved. This is done in a recursive manner. If $R1$ is used to form R, then conditions on R related to $R1$ will be pushed down on $R1$. If $R1$ is not yet a local relation, then conditions on $R1$ will be pushed down on relations from which $R1$ is formed. This process continues until only local relations remain. We will describe only one step of this process for each operator, because the same process can be repeated for each step.

2. In the second phase, desired data from each involved local relation are retrieved and then combined by the corresponding binary operators to materialize R in a bottom-up fashion.[2]

The second phase is in spirit the same as the bottom-up process described in the above query-independent materialization. However, the second phase in the two-phase process is

---

[2]As will be shown later in this section, some of these binary operators could be replaced by more efficient operators, and some could even be eliminated.

likely to be much more efficient because some binary operators can be modified to more efficient operators (e.g., an outerjoin may be modified to a regular join) during the first phase, and each operator can expect operand relations of reduced sizes due to the use of query conditions.

Note that the tasks in each of the above two phases are carried out at different places in the system. For example, in terms of the global query optimizer, the pushdown of conditions stops when export schema relations are encountered. After that, component systems will take over and continue the process until local relations are encountered. Since the problem of pushing conditions over standard relational algebra operators such as selections, projections, and joins is well understood, in this section we only present the pushdown of conditions over the integration operators, namely, outerjoin and generalization.

To simplify our discussion, we assume that global queries are conjunctive nonnested queries. In addition, different relation tuple variables will be treated as different relations. For a given global query, we define the *desired data* of a relation as the portion of the relation that must to be retrieved in order to correctly evaluate the global query. The goal of the first phase is to identify the desired data of each local relation related to global relations referenced in the global query through the pushdown of conditions imposed on the global relations. An attribute of a global relation R is a *predicate attribute* if it involves a predicate (selection or join) in the global query. We need the following notation for our discussion:

T   is the set of attributes in R that need to be materialized for further processing. T consists of (1) the target attributes of the global query that belong to R; and (2) those attributes in R involved in some join between R and another global relation S, where $S \neq R$.

AA   is the set of referenced predicate attributes in Attr-Agg of R.

AC   is the set of predicate conditions on attributes in AA (if R is not integrated from a generalization or an outerjoin, then both AA and AC are empty).

PC   is the set of predicate conditions involving only attributes in Attr(R) − Attr-Agg.

PA   is the set of predicate attributes of R.

ID   is the common key attribute of $R1$ and $R2$ if R is integrated from $R1$ and $R2$ by an outerjoin or a generalization.

There are two types of join conditions. Type 1 involves only attributes of R. This type of join is treated like a selection and is put into PC. Type 2 involves attributes of R and another global relation, say S. This case is handled as follows: (1) the join attribute, say A, of R will be materialized for R; (2) the fact that A is involved with a predicate is used to improve the efficiency of materializing R (i.e., $A \in$ PA; also see Proposition 4.1 below); and (3) the join itself is delayed and eventually processed at the front end after both R and S are materialized.

Example 4.4 Consider the global query in Example 4.2. We assume that SSN and Dept_name are the ID attributes for R and D, respectively.

For R, we have T = {SSN, Name, Dept_name}, PA = {Salary, Position, Dept_name}, AA = {Salary}, PC = {Position = 'Engineer'}, AC = {Salary < 40k}, ID = SSN. The reason the join predicate "R.Dept_name = D.Dept_name" is not in PC is because it is a type 2 join. This join will be processed at the front end after the two global relations are materialized.   ∎

With the above notation, the *desired data* of R can be expressed as $\pi_T(\sigma_{\text{PC and AC}}(R))$, where π denotes projection and σ denotes selection.

In general, a selection on an attribute in Attr-Agg cannot be pushed over a generalization or an outerjoin except in a few cases. To simplify our presentation, we first discuss the pushdown of conditions on attributes that are not in Attr-Agg.

Distribution of Conditions Not on Attributes in Attr-Agg

We now describe how conditions on R can be pushed down on the relations from which R is directly obtained for outerjoin and generalization.

Outerjoin

$R = f_n \ldots f_1(\text{OJ}(R1, R2))$. For a query referencing R, the outerjoin may be simplified if part of R is sufficient in answering the query. As a special case, if all needed data of R by a particular query are available from $R1$ (or $R2$) alone, then the needed data of R can be obtained from $R1$ (or $R2$). The following proposition provides a necessary and sufficient condition to determine when $R1$ is not needed in processing the query.

Proposition 4.1 *Let $R = f_n \ldots f_1(\text{OJ}(R1, R2))$. For a noncontradictory query referencing R, let PA be the set of predicate attributes of R. $R1$ will not be needed in answering the query if and only if one of the following two conditions is true:*

1. *No attribute of $R1$ is referenced in the query.*

2. *Of attributes of $R1$, only those in (Attr-C-N-I $\cup$ Attr-C-I-F($R2$)) are referenced in the query. In this case, we have Attr-Only($R2$) $\cap$ PA $\neq \emptyset$.*

It is obvious that $R1$ will not be needed if no attribute of $R1$ is referenced. Attr($R1$) can be considered as consisting of two subsets of attributes: subset 1 includes Attr-Only($R1$), Attr-C-I-F($R1$), and Attr-Agg, and subset 2 includes Attr-C-N-I and Attr-C-I-F($R2$). If an attribute in subset 1 is referenced by a query, then $R1$ must be used. However, if only attributes in subset 2 are referenced, then $R1$ is not necessarily needed. The objects of world($R1$) can be partitioned into world($R1$) $-$ world($R2$) and world($R1$) $\cap$ world($R2$). In Figure 4.9, the black-edged area represents the part of R that is related to $R1$. Attr-Only($R2$) $\cap$ PA $\neq \emptyset$ means that any object from world($R1$) $-$ world($R2$) will definitely not satisfy the predicate condition. Furthermore, Attr-Only($R1$), Attr-C-I-F($R1$), and Attr-Agg are not referenced in the query. Therefore, for $R1$, only the values under Attr-C-N-I and Attr-C-I-F($R2$) of the objects in world($R1$) $\cap$ world($R2$) may be needed (see the shaded area in Figure 4.9). Since these values can also be obtained from $R2$, it can be concluded that $R1$ is not needed in answering the query.

If $R1$ is not needed in answering a particular query, then R can be materialized without evaluating the outerjoin. More specifically, the desired data of R, i.e., $\pi_T(\sigma_{\text{PC and AC}}(R))$, can now be expressed as $\pi_{T'}(\sigma_{\text{PC}'}(R2))$, where T' and PC' are the same as T and PC except that $R1$ is replaced by $R2$ (e.g., $R1.A$ by $R2.A$). AC is removed since in this case it must be empty. Consequently, the expensive outerjoin operation as well as the resolution process can be entirely avoided. Proposition 4.1 is also applicable in query modification (see Section 4.3.1).

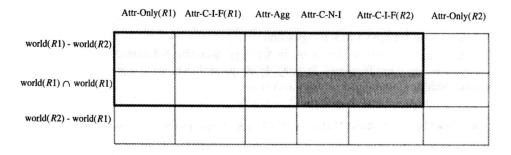

	Attr-Only($R1$)	Attr-C-I-F($R1$)	Attr-Agg	Attr-C-N-I	Attr-C-I-F($R2$)	Attr-Only($R2$)
world($R1$) − world($R2$)						
world($R1$) ∩ world($R1$)						
world($R2$) − world($R1$)						

FIGURE 4.9   **Illustrating Proposition 4.1**

Specifically, if R is integrated from $R1$ and $R2$ by an outerjoin and $R1$ satisfies the conditions in Proposition 4.1, then R in a global query can be modified to $R2$.

Example 4.5 Consider the global schema containing the relations R and D in Example 4.2. We again assume that SSN and Dept_name are the ID attributes for R and D, respectively. Consider the following global query:

```
select R.Name, D.Manager
from R, D
where R.Phone like '%23%' and R.Dept_name = Dept.Dept_name
```

For R, PA = {Phone, Dept_name} and {Name, Phone, Dept_name} is the set of attributes referenced. Of the attributes $R1$, only Name and Dept_name are referenced, and they are in Attr-C-N-I ∪ Attr-C-I-F($R2$) = {SSN, Dept_name, Name}. Furthermore, we have Attr-Only($R2$) ∩ PA = {Phone} ≠ ∅. Therefore, $R1$ is not needed in answering the above query. ∎

Even when both $R1$ and $R2$ are needed in answering a query, the outerjoin may still be reduced to a join or a one-sided outerjoin (i.e., left outerjoin, LOJ, or right outerjoin, ROJ). More specifically, if no object in (world($R1$) − world($R2$)) ∪ (world($R2$) − world($R1$)) is needed in answering a query, then the outerjoin can be reduced to a join; and if no object in world($R2$)−world($R1$) is needed, then the outerjoin can be reduced to a left outerjoin; and if no object in world($R1$) − world($R2$) is needed, then the outerjoin can be reduced to a right outerjoin. It is easy to see that if Attr-Only($R2$) ∩ PA ≠ ∅, then no object in world($R1$) − world($R2$) is needed in answering the query. Similarly, if Attr-Only($R1$) ∩ PA ≠ ∅, then no object in world($R2$) − world($R1$) is needed in answering the query.

Based on the above discussions, the following rules for distributing conditions over an outerjoin to materialize the desired data of R ($= f_n \ldots f_1(\text{OJ}(R1, R2))$) can be derived.

1. If $R1$ is not needed in answering the query, then by Proposition 4.1 the desired data of R can be materialized by performing $\pi_{T \cap R2}(\sigma_{PC_{R2}}(R2))$, where PC_{R2} is the subset of predicates in PC that involve only attributes in $R2$. In the following cases, we assume that both $R1$ and $R2$ are needed in answering the query.

2. If PA∩Attr-Only($R1$) ≠ ∅ and PA∩Attr-Only($R2$) ≠ ∅, then only objects in world($R1$)∩ world($R2$) are needed. In this case, the outerjoin can be reduced to a natural join that inherits all the resolution functions attached to the outerjoin. When the query conditions (selections and projections) are being distributed over the join, the following adjustments need to be made: (a) ID values from both $R1$ and $R2$ must be retrieved; (b) values of attributes AA must be retrieved; (c) for objects in world($R1$)∩world($R2$), no attribute of R_i in Attr(R_i) ∩ Attr-C-I-F(R_j) is needed, $i \neq j$; and (d) for attributes in Attr-C-N-I, their values from either $R1$ or $R2$ can be used. Therefore, we have the following:

$$\pi_T(\sigma_{PC \text{ and } AC}(f_n \ldots f_1(OJ(R1, R2)))$$
$$= \pi_T(\sigma_{AC}(g_m \ldots g_1((\pi_{(T\cup\{ID\}\cup AA)\cap R1^*}(\sigma_{PC_{R1^*}}(R1))))$$
$$\bowtie_{R1.ID=R2.ID} (\pi_{(T\cup\{ID\}\cup AA)\cap R2^{**}}(\sigma_{PC_{R2^{**}}}(R2))))))$$

where $R_i^* = (Attr(R_i) - Attr\text{-}C\text{-}I\text{-}F(R_j)) \cup \{ID\}$ and $R_i^{**} = (Attr(R_i) - (Attr\text{-}C\text{-}I\text{-}F(R_j) \cup Attr\text{-}C\text{-}N\text{-}I)) \cup \{ID\}$, $i, j = 1, 2$ and $i \neq j$. An alternative solution is to replace $R1^*$ by $R1^{**}$ and $R2^{**}$ by $R2^*$. $\{g_m \ldots g_1\}$ is a subset of $\{f_n \ldots f_1\}$ for those attributes in T∪AC. When the join is performed, if a resolution function is defined on an attribute, then all values under the attribute from both $R1$ and $R2$ will be kept. After the join is done, resolution functions are applied to resolve the inconsistencies.

3. If PA∩Attr-Only($R1$) ≠ ∅ and PA∩Attr-Only($R2$) = ∅, then the outerjoin can be reduced to a left outerjoin. In this case, the following distribution rule can be used:

$$\pi_T(\sigma_{PC \text{ and } AC}(f_n \ldots f_1(OJ(R1, R2))))$$
$$= \pi_T(\sigma_{AC}(g_m \ldots g_1(LOJ(\pi_{(T\cup\{ID\}\cup AA)\cap R1}(\sigma_{PC_{R1}}(R1)),$$
$$\pi_{(T\cup\{ID\}\cup AA)\cap R2^{**}}(\sigma_{PC_{R2^{**}}}(R2))))))$$

4. If PA∩Attr-Only($R1$) = ∅ and PA∩Attr-Only($R2$) ≠ ∅, then the outerjoin can be reduced to a right outerjoin. In this case, the following distribution rule can be used:

$$\pi_T(\sigma_{PC \text{ and } AC}(f_n \ldots f_1(OJ(R1, R2))))$$
$$= \pi_T(\sigma_{AC}(g_m \ldots g_1(ROJ(\pi_{(T\cup\{ID\}\cup AA)\cap R1^{**}}(\sigma_{PC_{R1^{**}}}(R1)),$$
$$\pi_{(T\cup\{ID\}\cup AA)\cap R2}(\sigma_{PC_{R2}}(R2))))))$$

5. If PA ∩ Attr-Only($R1$) = ∅ and PA ∩ Attr-Only($R2$) = ∅, then the outerjoin cannot be reduced. In this case, the following distribution rule can be used:

$$\pi_T(\sigma_{PC \text{ and } AC}(f_n \ldots f_1(OJ(R1, R2))))$$
$$= \pi_T(\sigma_{AC}(g_m \ldots g_1(OJ(\pi_{(T\cup\{ID\}\cup AA)\cap R1}(\sigma_{PC_{R1}}(R1)),$$
$$\pi_{(T\cup\{ID\}\cup AA)\cap R2}(\sigma_{PC_{R2}}(R2))))))$$

Let us continue Example 4.4. Since PA ∩ Attr-Only($R1$) = {Position} ≠ ∅ and PA ∩ Attr-Only($R2$) = ∅, the outerjoin between $R1$ and $R2$ can be reduced to a left outerjoin. Therefore, the desired data of R can be materialized by performing

$$\pi_{SSN,Name,Dept\_name}(\sigma_{Salary<40k}$$
$$(sum\_Salary(LOJ(\pi_{Name,Dept\_name,SSN,Salary}(\sigma_{Position='Engineer'}(R1)),$$
$$\pi_{SSN,Salary}(R2)))))$$

Generalization

$R = f_n \ldots f_1(\text{Ge}(R1, R2))$. In this case, R contains only those attributes that are common to both $R1$ and $R2$. In other words, there is no attribute in R that belongs only to $R1$ or $R2$. Therefore $\text{Ge}(R1, R2)$ can be considered as a special case of $\text{OJ}(R1, R2)$ with $\text{Attr}(R) = $ Attr-C-N-I $\cup$ Attr-C-I-F$(R1)$ $\cup$ Attr-C-I-F$(R2)$ $\cup$ Attr-Agg. As a result, both $R1$ and $R2$ will be needed in answering any query referencing R.

When $R = f_n \ldots f_1(\text{Ge}(R1, R2))$, in addition to the attributes in T, attribute ID in both $R1$ and $R2$ must be retrieved in order for the generalization operator to determine the attribute values for objects in world$(R1) \cap$ world$(R2)$. Also, values of attributes in AA need to be retrieved from $R1$ and $R2$ to form the AA values for R in order to evaluate the conditions in AC. Therefore

$$\pi_T(\sigma_{\text{PC and AC}}(R)) = \pi_T(\sigma_{\text{AC}}(g_m \ldots g_1(\text{Ge}(\pi_{\text{T}\cup\{\text{ID}\}\cup\text{AA}}(\sigma_{\text{PC}}(R1)), \pi_{\text{T}\cup\{\text{ID}\}\cup\text{AA}}(\sigma_{\text{PC}}(R2))))))$$

Distribution of Conditions on Attributes in Attr-Agg

Now we study the problem of pushing down selections on attributes in Attr-Agg over an outerjoin or a generalization. We first consider the distribution of selections over generalizations and then consider the distribution of selections over outerjoins.

Distribution over Generalizations

We first consider the case in which data inconsistency occurs on one attribute only. Let $R = f_A(\text{Ge}(R1, R2))$, where A is an attribute of R in Attr-Agg, and $f_A = f(R1.A, R2.A)$ is the function used to construct the values of A for objects in world$(R1) \cap$ world$(R2)$.

In general, a selection on A cannot be distributed over the generalization. For example, when $f = \text{sum}$, we have

$$\sigma_{A<c}(\text{sum}_A(\text{Ge}(R1, R2))) \neq \text{sum}_A(\text{Ge}(\sigma_{A<c}(R1), \sigma_{A<c}(R2)))$$

where c is a constant. This is clear since "sum$(R1.A, R2.A) < c$" on the left side is not equivalent to "$R1.A < c$ AND $R2.A < c$". More interestingly, even when "$f(R1.A, R2.A)$ op c" is equivalent to "$R1.A$ op c AND $R2.A$ op c," the condition on A may still not be distributed over the generalization. For example, the expression "max$(R1.A, R2.A) < c$" is equivalent to "$R1.A < c$ AND $R2.A < c$". However, we still have the following inequality:

$$\sigma_{A<c}(\text{max}_A(\text{Ge}(R1, R2))) \neq \text{max}_A(\text{Ge}(\sigma_{A<c}(R1), \sigma_{A<c}(R2))) \qquad (4.1)$$

The reason is as follows. Let $t1 \in R1$ and $t2 \in R2$ such that $t1.\text{ID} = t2.\text{ID}$. That is, $t1$ and $t2$ correspond to the same real-world object t in world$(R1) \cap$ world$(R2)$. Let $t1.A > c$ and $t2.A < c$. Clearly, t will not be in the result of the expression on the left side of the above inequality. However, for the expression on the right side, $t1$ will not be returned from $R1$ whereas $t2$ will be returned from $R2$. As a result, by the time the generalization is performed, $t2$ will be incorrectly considered a real-world object in world$(R2) -$ world$(R1)$ because $t2$ no longer has its matching tuple $t1$. Consequently, t will be in the result of the expression on the right side.

Nevertheless, in several cases, some of the conditions on A can be distributed over the generalization, as shown by the following rules:

Rule 1. If op is $>$ or $\geq$, then

$$\sigma_{A\ op\ c}(\max_A(\text{Ge}(R1, R2))) = \max_A(\text{Ge}(\sigma_{A\ op\ c}(R1), \sigma_{A\ op\ c}(R2))).$$

Rule 2. $\sigma_{A=c}(\max_A(\text{Ge}(R1, R2))) = \sigma_{A=c}(\max_A(\text{Ge}(\sigma_{A\geq c}(R1), \sigma_{A\geq c}(R2)))).$

Rule 3. If op is $<$ or $\leq$, then

$$\sigma_{A\ op\ c}(\min_A(\text{Ge}(R1, R2))) = \min_A(\text{Ge}(\sigma_{A\ op\ c}(R1), \sigma_{A\ op\ c}(R2))).$$

Rule 4. $\sigma_{A=c}(\min_A(\text{Ge}(R1, R2))) = \sigma_{A=c}(\min_A(\text{Ge}(\sigma_{A\leq c}(R1), \sigma_{A\leq c}(R2)))).$

For Rule 1 and Rule 3, the condition can be distributed over the resolution functions and the generalization operator to $R1$ and $R2$. However, for Rule 2 and Rule 4, the condition pushed on $R1$ and $R2$ is much less restrictive than the original condition. As a result, the original condition is kept to guarantee the correctness.

When A is not the only attribute that has inconsistency, the above rules may no longer be true. In other words, if in addition to A, there is another attribute, say B, that also has data inconsistency, then the above rules may no longer hold. For example, consider Rule 1 with op being $>$. Let $t1 \in R1$ and $t2 \in R2$ such that $t1.\text{ID} = t2.\text{ID}$, and suppose $\text{sum}(R1.B, R2.B)$ is to resolve the inconsistency on B. If $t1.A \leq c$ and $t2.A > c$, then the B-value computed by the expression on the right-hand side will be $t2.B$ instead of the correct $t1.B + t2.B$. This example illustrates a very important fact: when Ge is used, whether selection conditions on one attribute can be pushed down or not is dependent on whether other attributes have data inconsistency.

We now investigate another solution to the distribution problem. Assume that $R1$-tuples and $R2$-tuples that correspond to the real-world objects in $\text{world}(R1) \cap \text{world}(R2)$ are identified in advance. This can be achieved by exchanging the ID values of $R1$ and $R2$ explicitly.

Let $R1\text{-}O$ be the tuples of $R1$ that correspond to the real-world objects in $\text{world}(R1) - \text{world}(R2)$. Then $R1\text{-}C = R1 - R1\text{-}O$ contains the tuples of $R1$ that correspond to the real-world objects in $\text{world}(R1) \cap \text{world}(R2)$. Similarly, $R2\text{-}O$ and $R2\text{-}C$ can be defined. Let CA be the set of common attributes between $R1$ and $R2$. With these definitions, $\text{Ge}(R1, R2)$ can be written as

$$\text{Ge}(R1, R2) = \pi_{CA}(R1\text{-}O) \cup \pi_{CA}(R2\text{-}O) \cup \text{J}(\pi_{CA}(R1\text{-}C), \pi_{CA}(R2\text{-}C))$$

where J is an equijoin on attribute ID with only one copy of any common attribute retained. To simplify the notation, let $R1O = \pi_{CA}(R1\text{-}O)$, $R2O = \pi_{CA}(R2\text{-}O)$, $R1C = \pi_{CA}(R1\text{-}C)$, and $R2C = \pi_{CA}(R2\text{-}C)$. Now the above definition can be rewritten as

$$\text{Ge}(R1, R2) = R1O \cup R2O \cup \text{J}(R1C, R2C)$$

Note that $\text{J}(R1C, R2C) = \text{Ge}(R1C, R2C)$. However, when some tuples from $R1C$ and $R2C$ are not returned by selections, they are no longer the same. More specifically, if $t1 \in R1C$ and $t2 \in R2C$ such that $t1.\text{ID} = t2.\text{ID}$, then after $t1$ is deleted from $R1C$, $t2$ will not appear in the result of $\text{J}(R1C, R2C)$ but will appear in the result of $\text{Ge}(R1C, R2C)$. This difference between Ge and J has two significant impacts on the distribution rules. The first impact is that some conditions that cannot be pushed over Ge can now be pushed over J, as we will see shortly. The second impact, which we will also discuss shortly, is that when J is used, the distribution of a selection condition on one attribute is independent of whether other attributes have data inconsistency.

Since any resolution function $f(R1.A, R2.A)$ applies to only tuples in $R1C$ and $R2C$, any condition on A of R can always be pushed down on A of $R1O$ and A of $R2O$, regardless of whether there are other inconsistent attributes. Therefore, we have

$$\sigma_{A\ op\ c}(f_A(Ge(R1, R2))) = \sigma_{A\ op\ c}(R1O) \cup \sigma_{A\ op\ c}(R2O) \cup \sigma_{A\ op\ c}(f_A(J(R1C, R2C)))$$

We now study how a condition on A of R can be pushed over J on A of $R1C$ and A of $R2C$. First, it is not difficult to verify the following equation:

$$\sigma_{A<c}(\max_A(J(R1C, R2C))) = \max_A(J(\sigma_{A<c}(R1C), \sigma_{A<c}(R2C))) \qquad (4.2)$$

The difference between Inequality (4.1) and Equation (4.2) is due to the difference between J and Ge.

It is still not always possible to distribute conditions over J to $R1C$ and $R2C$. For example, we have the following inequality,

$$\sigma_{A>c}(sum_A(J(R1C, R2C))) \neq sum_A(J(\sigma_{A>c}(R1C), \sigma_{A>c}(R2C)))$$

But for many combinations of resolution functions and comparator operators, some conditions can be distributed over J. More specifically, we have the following distribution rules.

Rule 5. If op is $<$ or $\leq$, then

$$\sigma_{A\ op\ c}(\max_A(J(R1C, R2C))) = \max_A(J(\sigma_{A\ op\ c}(R1C), \sigma_{A\ op\ c}(R2C)))$$

Rule 6. $\sigma_{A=c}(\max_A(J(R1C, R2C))) = \sigma_{A=c}(\max_A(J(\sigma_{A\leq c}(R1C), \sigma_{A\leq c}(R2C)))$

Rule 7. If op is $>$ or $\geq$, then

$$\sigma_{A\ op\ c}(\min_A(J(R1C, R2C))) = \min_A(J(\sigma_{A\ op\ c}(R1C), \sigma_{A\ op\ c}(R2C)))$$

Rule 8. $\sigma_{A=c}(\min_A(J(R1C, R2C))) = \sigma_{A=c}(\min_A(J(\sigma_{A\geq c}(R1C), \sigma_{A\geq c}(R2C)))$

Rule 9. If op is $<$ or $\leq$, then

$$\sigma_{A\ op\ c}(sum_A(J(R1C, R2C))) = \sigma_{A\ op\ c}(sum_A(J(\sigma_{A\ op\ c}(R1C), \sigma_{A\ op\ c}(R2C))))$$

Rule 10. $\sigma_{A=c}(sum_A(J(R1C, R2C))) = \sigma_{A=c}(sum_A(J(\sigma_{A\leq c}(R1C), \sigma_{A\leq c}(R2C)))$

Rule 11. If op is $<$ or $\leq$, then

$$\sigma_{A\ op\ c}(avg_A(J(R1C, R2C))) = \sigma_{A\ op\ c}(avg_A(J(\sigma_{A\ op\ c}(R1C), \sigma_{A\ op\ c}(R2C))))$$

Rule 12. $\sigma_{A=c}(avg_A(J(R1C, R2C))) = \sigma_{A=c}(avg_A(J(\sigma_{A\leq c}(R1C), \sigma_{A\leq c}(R2C)))$

For the remaining combinations of resolution functions and comparator operators, the conditions cannot be pushed over J unless additional information is available. We use Rule 5 as an example to explain why the above rules are correct. Suppose op is $<$. Let t be a tuple in the global relation R. Suppose t is formed from $t1$ of $R1$ and $t2$ of $R2$, that is, $t[A] = \max(t1[A], t2[A])$. (a) If $\max(t1[A], t2[A]) < c$, then tuple t will be retrieved by the expression on the left-hand side. Meanwhile, $\max(t1[A], t2[A]) < c$ implies that $t1[A] < c$ and $t2[A] < c$. Therefore, $t1$ will be returned from $\sigma_{A<c}(R1C)$ and $t2$ will be returned from $\sigma_{A<c}(R2C)$. Consequently, t will also be retrieved by the expression on the right-hand side. (b) If $\max(t1[A], t2[A]) \geq c$, then tuple t will not be retrieved by the expression on the left-hand side. $\max(t1[A], t2[A]) \geq c$ implies that at least one of $t1$ and $t2$ will not survive the local selections in the expression of the right-hand side. Since t is formed by joining $t1$ and $t2$, therefore, if one of $t1$ and $t2$ is not available for the join, t will not be formed. Hence t will also not be retrieved by the expression on the right-hand side.

The above rules also have the following property: they remain correct even when more than one attribute has inconsistency between $R1$ and $R2$. Intuitively, the reason is as follows. Let t be a real-world object integrated from $t1$ in world($R1C$) and $t2$ in world($R2C$). Clearly, t can survive J if and only if both $t1$ and $t2$ are returned from their corresponding local relations. If $t1$ and $t2$ are both returned, then other resolution functions can be applied since both arguments are available. Therefore, in this case, there will be no effect on the application of other resolution functions on $t1$ and $t2$. On the other hand, if one of $t1$ and $t2$ is not returned, then t will not survive J. As a result, there is no need to apply other resolution functions to $t1$ and $t2$. Since the distribution of conditions on A in Rules 5 through 12 has no real effect on the application of other resolution functions on other inconsistent attributes, the correctness of these rules is independent of the existence of inconsistencies on other attributes between $R1$ and $R2$.

In summary, if there is only one attribute that has data inconsistency between $R1$ and $R2$, then Rules 1–4 should be applied whenever possible. Otherwise, Rules 5–12 should be applied whenever possible.

Distribution over Outerjoins

The main difference between Ge($R1$, $R2$) and OJ($R1$, $R2$) is that every attribute in the former belongs to both $R1$ and $R2$ but not every attribute in the latter belongs to both $R1$ and $R2$. In other words, OJ($R1$, $R2$) may contain attributes that belong to only $R1$ or only $R2$. This difference is enough to make some distribution rules for Ge not applicable for OJ. For example, if Ge is replaced by OJ in the above Rule 1, then it will no longer be correct. To see this, let B be an attribute that appears only in $R1$. If $t1 \in R1$ and $t2 \in R2$ such that $t1.\text{ID} = t2.\text{ID}$, $t1.A < c$ and $t2.A > c$, then $t1$ will not be retrieved from $R1$. Consequently, $t1.B$ will not be in the result of the expression on the right-hand side. But $t1.B$ will be in the result of the expression on the left-hand side.

Using similar examples, it is not difficult to show that none of the first four rules (Rules 1 through 4) is applicable to OJ when some attribute in Attr-Only($R1$) $\cup$ Attr-Only($R2$) needs to be retrieved for output or further processing. Of course, if no attribute in Attr-Only($R1$) $\cup$ Attr-Only($R2$) is needed for output or further processing, then the distribution rules for Ge are also applicable to OJ. When a condition cannot be directly distributed over OJ, we partition world($R1$) $\cup$ world($R2$) into three subsets as follows.

$$\text{OJ}(R1, R2) = R1\text{-}O \text{ OU } R2\text{-}O \text{ OU } \text{J}(R1\text{-}C, R2\text{-}C)$$

where OU denotes the outerunion operator. Again, since any resolution function $f(R1.A, R2.A)$ applies to only tuples in $R1$-C and $R2$-C, any condition on $A = f(R1.A, R2.A)$ of R can always be pushed down on A of $R1$-O and A of $R2$-O, regardless of whether there are other inconsistent attributes. Therefore, we have

$$\sigma_{A \; op \; c}(f_n \ldots f_A \ldots f_1(OJ(R1, R2)))$$

$$= \sigma_{A \; op \; c}(R1\text{-}O) \; OU \; \sigma_{A \; op \; c}(R2\text{-}O) \; OU \; \sigma_{A \; op \; c}(f_n \ldots f_A \ldots f_1(J(R1\text{-}C, R2\text{-}C)))$$

Again, the problem of distributing a condition over an OJ can be reduced to the problem of distributing the condition over a J. It can be shown that Rules 5–12 are still valid in this case.

Distributed Optimization

One thing we have not discussed so far in this subsection is at which site each referenced global relation R should be materialized. There are two cases. The first case is that in which all desired data of R are from a single site. This can happen if R originally came from a single database or if R contains data from multiple databases but all desired data of R are from a single database. In this case, R will be materialized at the site that has all the desired data of R. The second case occurs when all the desired data of R are from multiple sites, say $S_1, \ldots, S_k$. In this case, R may be materialized at one of these sites or even another site. The search space for optimization can be very large. More specifically, let $R_i, 1 \leq n$, be the referenced global relations. Suppose R_i may be materialized at k_i sites. Then there will be $\prod_{i=1}^{n} k_i$ ways for the n global relations to be materialized at some site. Let us consider one of these cases. By this time, all selection conditions have been evaluated by component database systems and all materialized global relations are under the control of the front ends at different sites. Therefore, the processing capability at the front-end level should be used to process the remaining part of the global query, which includes mainly joins and projections. Note that the materialized global relations together with the processing capabilities at the front ends form a traditional distributed database system. As such, many algorithms developed for processing and optimizing queries in traditional distributed relational database systems such as those discussed in Chapter 3 can be readily employed here. Since there are $\prod_{i=1}^{n} k_i$ possible cases, estimating the cost of evaluating the query in each case and finding the case with the minimum estimated cost for actual evaluation may not be realistic. To avoid enumerating exponential numbers of cases, heuristic solutions should be used. One heuristic is based on the Fragment and Replicate algorithm discussed in Chapter 3. Applied to our situation here, this algorithm can be stated as follows: (1) Choose one global relation, say R, and partition it based on the local relations from which R is integrated by using the technique described in the first two steps of algorithm Query-Modification in Section 4.3.1. For example, if R is integrated from $R1$ and $R2$ and an attribute in Attr-Agg is referenced in the global query, then R will be partitioned into $\{R1\text{-}O, R2\text{-}O, J(R1\text{-}C, R2\text{-}C)\}$, where $R1\text{-}O$ and $R1\text{-}C$ are the tuples of $R1$ that correspond to the real-world objects in world($R1$) − world($R2$) and in world($R1$) ∩ world($R2$), respectively, $R2\text{-}O$ and $R2\text{-}C$ can be similarly defined, and J is a join on the ID attribute. Let P be the partition obtained for R. (2) Materialize each subset in P at an appropriate site. For example, $R1\text{-}O$ and $R2\text{-}O$ should be materialized at the sites containing $R1$ and $R2$, respectively, and $J(R1\text{-}C, R2\text{-}C)$ may be materialized at a third site. The materialized subsets of R serve as the fragments of a relation in the Fragment and Replicate algorithm. (3) Materialize all other referenced global relations to all the sites where the chosen global relation has a materialized subset. After this step, the global query is partitioned into a number of queries such that each can be processed at one site. The optimizer will estimate the costs of choosing different global relations for partitioning while materializing other relations, and the choice that yields the minimum estimated cost will be used.

4.3.4 Estimating Local Cost Formulas Using Query Sampling

There may be many ways to evaluate a given global query. Different evaluation strategies may result in drastically different costs. To find out an efficient evaluation strategy, we often need to estimate the cost of each strategy and compare them. Since each global query will eventually be decomposed into single-database queries and assembling queries (in the case of the materialization approach, during the second phase of the materialization, the evaluation of binary integration operators corresponds to the evaluation of assembling queries), in order to estimate the cost of each strategy, we need to estimate the cost of evaluating each single-database query and each assembling query. For example, there may be multiple ways to modify a given global query (see the discussion in Section 4.3.1). To determine which modification is the best, we need to know the costs of the single-database queries generated from the queries pertinent to each possible modification. As another example, in the tree-balancing approach, to determine which tree will not result in an increased total cost when reducing the response time, we also need to estimate the costs of evaluating single-database queries at the leaf nodes of each tree. Unfortunately, estimating the costs of single-database queries is no easy task for the global query optimizer. This is because, as mentioned previously, usually not all information needed to make a cost estimation is provided to the global query optimizer by component database systems, due to their autonomy. Such information may include cost formulas for local queries and possibly also information about local relations.

In this subsection, we present one technique for estimating the cost of local queries when not all needed information is available. This technique tries to use sample local queries to estimate cost parameters of local cost formulas. More specifically, all possible queries to each component database are first classified into different classes, a tentative cost formula with unknown coefficients is then put forward for each class, and finally the coefficients are estimated using the costs collected through running the sample queries.

The accuracy of the estimation is closely related to how queries are classified into classes, which in turn is closely related to the amount of information available. The more is known, the more likely the estimation will be more accurate. For example, consider a particular component database system $D1$. Suppose all possible queries for $D1$ can be first classified into selection queries and join queries. If we further know whether an attribute of each relation has no index, a nonclustered index, or a clustered index, then selection queries can be further classified into three classes, one for selections using no index (i.e., sequential scan), one for selections using a nonclustered index, and one for selections using a clustered index. Although in theory there is no guarantee that a selection based on an attribute that has an index will be processed using the index, its use is very likely in practice. Intuitively, the more specific a class becomes, the more accurate the estimation can be made for the class. Similarly, join queries could also be classified into more specific classes if more information is available. Since the query sampling technique can be applied to different classes in different component database systems, we illustrate the technique for one class in one component system only. For more information about other classes, please see Reference [416].

The class to be considered consists of a set of selection queries with nonclustered indexes on involved attributes. Suppose each selection query in the class is of the form $\sigma_C(R)$, where R is a local relation and C is a set of selection conditions in conjunctive form such that none of the attributes involved has a clustered index but at least one of them has an index. Let G be this query class. Since there is no clustered index involved in C, the selection query will not be classified as a query that can use a clustered index. On the other hand, since there is at least one attribute that has an index, it is very likely that this index will be used to evaluate the corresponding condition before other conditions in C are evaluated. Therefore, G is the class of selection queries with indexes but no clustered indexes.

The exact cost formula for queries in G is unknown due to the autonomy of the component system. However, for any relation R, the cost formula for a query on R is approximately proportional to two main quantities: the number of tuples in R and the number of tuples in the result. Let N be the number of tuples in R and S be the selectivity of query conditions C. Then the cost formula can be approximately expressed as

$$\hat{C} = c_0 + c_1 \cdot N + c_2 \cdot S \cdot N \qquad (4.3)$$

where parameters c_0, c_1, and c_2 reflect the initialization cost, the cost of retrieving a tuple from R, and the cost of processing a tuple in the result, respectively. For the purpose of estimating the parameters c_0, c_1, and c_2, Formula (4.3) can be viewed as a *regression equation*. Based on the method of least squares of the linear model in statistics, the parameters (i.e., regression coefficients) can be estimated using the costs collected from the sample queries selected from G.

Let $\{Q_i\}$, $i = 1, \ldots, K$, be a set of sample queries selected from G. Let N_i, S_i, and C_i be the number of tuples in the operand relation of Q_i, the selectivity of the query condition of Q_i, and the cost collected from executing Q_i, respectively. With N_i's and S_i's available, a system of equations can be derived for (4.3):

$$\hat{C}_i = c_0 + c_1 \cdot N_i + c_2 \cdot S_i \cdot N_i, \qquad i = 1, \ldots, K$$

where $\hat{C}_i$ is the estimated cost for $\{Q_i\}$ based on the estimated cost formula after the parameters are found. Standard methods exist in statistics to find the parameters c_0, c_1, and c_2 such that the following sum is the minimum:

$$\sum_{i=1}^{K} (C_i - \hat{C}_i)^2$$

The standard deviation of the error of the estimation is given by

$$e = \sqrt{\frac{\sum_{i=1}^{K} (C_i - \hat{C}_i)^2}{K - 3}}$$

Smaller e indicates a better estimation.

We now discuss how many sample queries should be used and how to select the sample queries. It is a rule of thumb in statistics that if there are n parameters in a regression formula, then the sample size should be at least $10 \cdot (n + 1)$. Therefore, for Formula (4.3), at least 40 sample queries (i.e., $K = 40$) should be used. There are many ways to select a sample from a population (i.e., G). A good sample should be as representative of various queries in G as possible. Let M be the number of attributes in the component database system under consideration that have an index (but not a clustered index). If $M = K$, then a reasonable sample is to have a sample query based on each indexed attribute in the form $\sigma_{A=v}(R_i)$, where v is randomly chosen from the domain of attribute $R_i.A$. If $M > K$, then the sample queries are proportionally allocated to each relation in the database based on the number of attributes in the relation that have the required index. Since the number of sample queries allocated to each relation must be an integer, the sample size could be slightly increased when fractions are rounded to their next larger integer. For example, consider a database that has three relations $R1$, $R2$, and R_3. Suppose $R1$ has two indexed attributes, $R2$ has four indexed attributes, and R_3 has five indexed attributes. If K is originally 5, then one (i.e., $\lceil 2 \cdot 5/11 \rceil$) sample query will be selected for $R1$, two (i.e., $\lceil 4 \cdot 5/11 \rceil$) sample queries will be selected for $R2$, and three (i.e., $\lceil 5 \cdot 5/11 \rceil$) sample queries will be selected for R_3. If $M < K$, then $\lceil K/M \rceil$ sample queries can be used for each indexed attribute.

Preliminary experimental results indicate that the estimated costs for most cases have relative errors below 30%.

4.4 Query Translation

Note that the global query optimizer can only see export schemas from component database systems. Therefore, when a single-database query, say q_0, for component database D is generated by the global query optimizer, it is expressed in the global query language using names in the export schema of D because the global schema and the export schema use the same data model. If the export schema and its corresponding component schema are different, then q_0 needs to be modified so that export schema names in q_0 are replaced by corresponding names in the component schema. The resulting query, denoted by q, is still in the global query language. The modification process is exactly the same as that used to modify a query against a view to a query against base relations in a regular relational database system. This process will not be discussed here. Note that the query processor of D can only process queries written against its local schema and in its own query language. If the component schema and the local schema are in the same data model, and the global query language is the same as the local query language, then q can be processed by the query processor of D directly. If the global query language is different from the local query language, then q must first be translated to a query in the local query language before it can be processed.[3] In general, it is not always possible to translate a query in one query language (the source language) to an equivalent query in another query language (the target language) because different query languages may have different expressiveness. For example, joins on arbitrary attributes in a relational query may not be translated into IMS DL/I commands since IMS DL/I does not support arbitrary joins. As another example, an OODB query referencing a *method* may not be translated into

---

[3]If the component schema and the local schema are in different data models, it must be true that the global query language and the local query language are different.

an SQL relational query. In such cases, the source query may have to be translated into a procedure consisting of a sequence of target queries and other high-level programming language commands. In the first example, a join between relations R and S can be translated into two IMS queries for retrieving the records from the record types corresponding to R and S. The retrieved results are then used to perform the join in the front end. In the second example, a relational query can be used to retrieve the data needed by the method first (such data can be identified using the signature of the method and the mapping from the OODB schema to the relational schema), and the method itself can then be evaluated using the retrieved data in the front end.

In this section, we study the translations between relational queries and object-oriented queries. Studies on query translations for other popular query languages can be found in the literature listed in the Bibliographic Notes of this chapter. The translation from relational queries to object-oriented queries is needed if the global query language is relational and the local query language is object-oriented. Such a translation is also needed if the query language of an external schema is relational and the global query language is object-oriented. The translation from object-oriented queries to relational queries is needed when the global query language is object-oriented while the local query language is relational or when the query language of an external schema is object-oriented while the global query language is relational. It is not our intention to present complete query translators between relational and object-oriented queries, because it is simply beyond the capacity of a chapter section. Instead, we will focus only on the most distinctive constructs of the two query languages. More specifically, we will focus on the translations between *path expressions* in OODB query language and simple predicates (i.e., joins and selections) in SQL. To simplify our discussion, we assume that the OODB queries do not reference *methods*.

In this section, relational queries are assumed to be written in SQL. To facilitate our discussion, the syntax we use for object-oriented queries in this section will be slightly more compact than that used in Chapter 2. The two syntaxes are essentially the same, and queries in one syntax can be translated to queries in another syntax easily. The main difference between the two syntaxes is in path expression. Consider the OODB schema in Figure 4.10. In the syntax used in Chapter 2, the condition "the graduate student's advisor's rank is full professor and the advisor's office is in the engineering building" is expressed in two path expressions, "G_Student.Advisor.Rank = 'Full Professor' and G_Student.Advisor.Office.Building = 'Engineering Building' ". In the more compact syntax, the two path expressions are combined into one, "G_Student.(Advisor: Rank = 'Full Professor').(Office: Building = 'Engineering Building')". In other words, in the more compact representation, simple selections on classes are directly attached to their classes using the colon notation.

We first study the translation from relational queries to object-oriented queries in Section 4.4.1. The reverse translation is presented in Section 4.4.2.

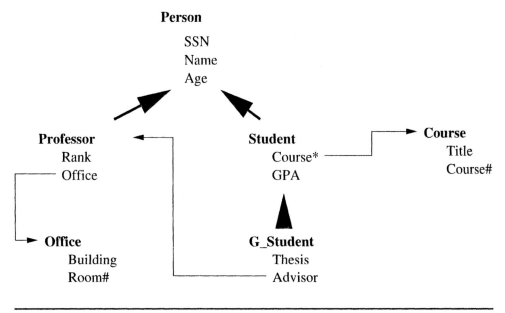

FIGURE 4.10 An OODB Schema

4.4.1 Translation of Relational Queries to OODB Queries

In this subsection,[4] we focus on this scenario: relational queries against a relational component schema RS need to be translated to OODB queries against the object-oriented local schema OS. Note that the RS was transformed from the OS. Clearly, the translation of queries is closely related to the transformation of schemas. Therefore, before we study query translation in this scenario, we need to briefly discuss how an OODB schema is transformed into a relational schema.

Transformation of an OODB Schema to a Relational Schema

In an object-oriented data model, both the structural and the behavioral aspects of real-world objects are modeled. In contrast, only the structural aspect of real-world objects is modeled by the relational data model. In this sense, the object-oriented data model has a more powerful modeling capability than the relational data model. The behavioral aspect (i.e., methods) of an OODB schema may not be directly transformable to constructs in the relational model. Therefore, we consider only the transformation of the structural part of an OODB schema to a relational schema.

Different constructs are used by the object-oriented data model and by the relational data model to model the real world. Table 4.1 lists some of the constructs used by the two data models. Although the is-a relationship is not supported explicitly by the relational data model,

---

[4]Portions of this section were also reported in Meng et al., 1993 [265].

TABLE 4.1   **Modeling of Real-World Concepts**

Real-world concept	Object-oriented data model	Relational data model
entity	object	tuple
entity type	class	relation
identity	OID	key
1-to-m relationship	complex attribute and domain class	key and foreign key
m-to-m relationship	set attribute and domain class	relation
is-a relationship	subclass/superclass	relation with proper foreign key
set attribute	set attribute	relation with proper foreign key

it can be supported implicitly. For example, to support the is-a relationship from entity type E2 to entity type E1, we can use two relations to model E1 and E2, allow relation E2 to have all attributes of relation E1 with possibly other attributes on E2, and define the key of E2 to be also a foreign key referencing the key of E1. Requiring the key of E2 to be a foreign key referencing the key of E1 ensures that every tuple in E2 has a corresponding tuple in E1. Set-valued attributes (or multivalued attributes in general) are supported in object-oriented data models. In the relational data model, each set-valued attribute is modeled by a relation with proper foreign keys.

Based on the above observations, the following rules can be used to transform an OODB schema to a relational schema:

1. Class hierarchy is transformed in a top-down fashion. If $C2$ is a subclass of $C1$, let $C2$ explicitly inherit all attributes of $C1$ by adding all attributes of $C1$ to $C2$.

2. Transform each class to a relation. Let Rel(C) denote the relation transformed from class C. The name of Rel(C) is also C. Rel(C) will be augmented with a special attribute, denoted C-Key, which serves as the primary key for Rel(C) and references the OIDs (object identifiers) of the objects in C. If class $C2$ is a subclass of class $C1$, define the $C2$-Key of Rel($C2$) to be a foreign key referencing $C1$-Key of Rel($C1$).

3. Each non-set primitive attribute of a class C becomes an attribute of the relation Rel(C), and the domain of the class attribute becomes the data type of the corresponding relation attribute.

4. Each non-set complex attribute of a class C, which has domain class $C1$, is renamed to $C1$-Key and stays in Rel(C). Attribute $C1$-Key of relation Rel(C) is a foreign key referencing the key of Rel($C1$).

5. If class C has a primitive set attribute A, then exclude A from relation Rel(C) and create a new relation with name C-A. C-A has two attributes, C-Key and A. The key of C-A consists of the two attributes, and C-Key of C-A is a foreign key referencing the key of C.

6. If class C has a complex set attribute A with domain class $C1$, then exclude A from relation Rel(C) and create a new relation with name C-$C1$. C-$C1$ has two attributes C-Key and $C1$-Key. The key of C-$C1$ consists of the two attributes. C-Key and $C1$-Key of C-$C1$ are foreign keys referencing the key of C and the key of $C1$, respectively.

TABLE 4.2   **Mapping Relation Attributes to Class Attributes**

Relation.Attribute	Class.Attribute
Person.Person-Key	Person
Professor.Professor-Key	Professor
Professor.Office-Key	Professor.Office
Student.Student-Key	Student
G_Student.G_Student-Key	G_Student
G_Student.Professor-Key	G_Student.Advisor
Course.Course-Key	Course
Office.Office-Key	Office
Student-Course.Student-Key	Student
Student-Course.Course-Key	Student.Course
G_Student-Course.G_Student-Key	G_Student
G_Student-Course.Course-Key	G_Student.Course

Example 4.6 Consider the OODB schema in Figure 4.10. Thin arrows indicate the domain classes of complex attributes, and thick arrows indicate the is-a relationships. Attribute Course of class Student is a set attribute with domain class *Course*, as indicated by the * on the right shoulder of the attribute Course. Class Professor and class Student are subclasses of class Person. Class G_Student, which describes graduate students, is a subclass of class Student. Therefore, G_Student also inherits the complex set attribute Course from Student. By using the above schema transformation rules, this OODB schema can be transformed to the following relational schema:

Person: Person-Key, SSN, Name, Age
Professor: Professor-Key, SSN, Name, Age, Rank, Office-Key
Student: Student-Key, SSN, Name, Age, GPA
G_Student: G_Student-Key, SSN, Name, Age, GPA, Thesis, Professor-Key
Course: Course-Key, Course#, Title
Office: Office-Key, Building, Room#
Student-Course: Student-Key, Course-Key
G_Student-Course: G_Student-Key, Course-Key

∎

The names of complex attributes or Key attributes may have been changed during the schema transformation. A table recording the changes must be created. Table 4.2 records the name changes for the transformed relational schema in Example 4.6. Usually when a class name is used by itself in an OODB query, it references the OIDs of its objects. Therefore, it is sufficient to map Person.Person-Key to class Person (see the first row of Table 4.2).

A Relational Query to OODB Query Translation Algorithm

We now present an algorithm for translating relational queries to OODB queries. We make two assumptions to simplify our discussion. First, we assume that the input relational query is unnested since most nested queries can be flattened. Second, we assume that the relational where-clause contains conditions in conjunctive form.

The main difficulty of the translation is the translation of the relational where-clause to the OODB query where-clause. The main objective here is to translate simple relational predicates (selections and joins) to the complex OODB predicates (path expressions along composition hierarchies). The method we present has three steps. In the first step, the query graph of a given relational query is obtained. In the second step, the relational query graph RQG is transformed to its corresponding OODB query graph OQG. Finally, the OODB query is derived from the transformed OQG. One important advantage for using such a formal method is that the translation process can be reversed to translate OODB queries to relational queries, as will be discussed in Section 4.4.2.

Obtaining a Relational Query Graph from a Relational Query

Definition 4.3 *For a given relational query RQ, we define its query graph G(RQ) as an annotated undirected graph: G(RQ) = (RV, RE), where each vertex v in RV represents a relation tuple variable referenced in RQ, and each edge e between vertices v_1 and v_2 in RE represents a join predicate in RQ. Each vertex is associated with two types of annotations: a predicate annotation and a target annotation. The former contains all selection predicates on the corresponding relation tuple variable, and the latter contains target attributes of the corresponding relation tuple variable. Each edge is annotated with a join predicate of the form "R1.A1 op R2.A2," where op is a comparator, and A1 and A2 are the attributes of relation tuple variables R1 and R2, respectively. If op is = and A1 and A2 are the same Key attribute, "R1.A1 op R2.A2" is simplified to A1.*

Note that no RQG can have self-loop since if a join is imposed on a relation, then two tuple variables of the relation will be used. Clearly, the RQG of a relational query contains the same information as the relational query itself. The above definition of the RQG can be extended to accommodate relational queries with nested subqueries. Since we have assumed that the input relational query is unnested, such an extension is not needed here. However, the extension is needed in Section 4.4.2 for the reverse translation because nested relational queries could be translated from OODB queries.

Example 4.7 Consider the following relational query, which is to find the names of all full professors who have an office in the engineering building and who supervise at least one graduate student who takes a course with the title "Database."

```
select  Professor.Name
from    Professor, Office, G_Student, G_Student-Course GC, Course
where   Professor.Rank = 'Full Professor'
        and Professor.Office-Key = Office.Office-Key
        and Office.Building = 'Engineering Building'
        and Professor.Professor-Key = G_Student.Professor-Key
        and G_Student.G_Student-Key = GC.G_Student-Key
        and GC.Course-Key = Course.Course-Key and Course.Title = 'Database'
```

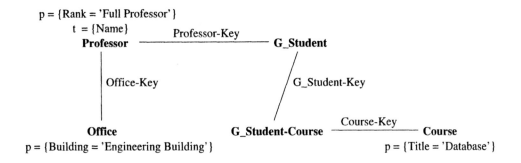

$p = \{Rank = \text{'Full Professor'}\}$
$t = \{Name\}$

FIGURE 4.11   A Relational Query Graph

The query graph of this relational query is given in Figure 4.11, where $p = \{\ \}$ contains predicate annotation and $t = \{\ \}$ contains target annotation.   ■

Syntactically, a relational query can have a join on different Key attributes, such as "Professor.Professor-Key *op* G_Student.G_Student-Key". But, semantically, this type of join predicate makes little sense since these Key attributes will eventually reference OIDs of objects in different classes and OIDs are generated by the OODB system with no meaning associated other than serving as unique identifiers. If *op* is =, then the relational query will have an empty result since different objects have different OIDs. In addition, this type of join predicate can always be handled in a similar way as "$A1$ *op* $A2$" will be handled during the query translation, where $A1$ and $A2$ are non-Key attributes. Therefore, without loss of generality, we assume that joins on different Key attributes will not appear in the where-clause of input relational queries.

Obtaining an OODB Query Graph from a Relational Query Graph

Definition 4.4 *For a given OODB query OQ, we define its query graph as an annotated graph:* $OG(OQ) = OG(OV, OE1, OE2)$, *where OV is a set of vertices, OE1 is a set of directed edges, and OE2 is a set of undirected edges. Each vertex v in OV corresponds to a class instance variable CIV (which corresponds to the concept of a relation tuple variable in relational systems) of some class. A directed edge e from vertex v_1 to vertex v_2 with annotation Attr indicates the need of a traversal from the complex attribute Attr of the class C1 corresponding to v_1 to the domain class of Attr that corresponds to v_2 (i.e., a directed edge represents an implicit join). If Attr corresponds to a set attribute of C1 and is quantified by an all or a some, then the quantifier is included in the annotation on e. An undirected edge in OE2 represents an explicit join between the left-hand side and the right-hand side of a predicate. Each undirected edge is annotated with the explicit join between the corresponding class instance variables. Each v in OV is associated with two types of annotations: predicate annotation and target annotation. The former contains all selection predicates on the corresponding class instance variable, and the latter contains target attributes of the corresponding class instance variable.*

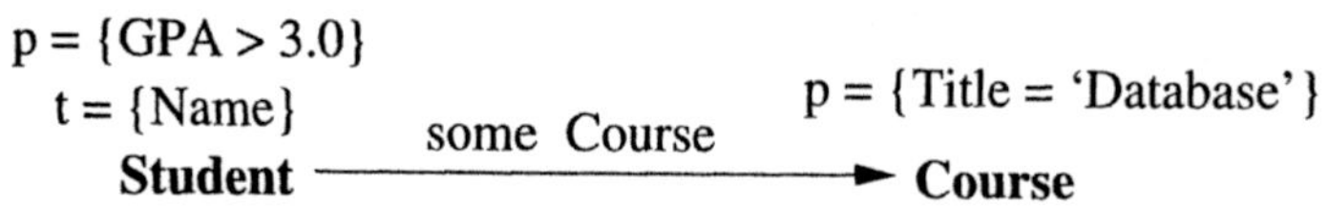

$$p = \{GPA > 3.0\}$$
$$t = \{Name\} \qquad \qquad \qquad p = \{Title = \text{'Database'}\}$$

Student $\xrightarrow{\quad \text{some Course} \quad}$ **Course**

FIGURE 4.12 An OODB Query Graph

Example 4.8 Consider an OODB query against the OODB schema in Figure 4.10: find the names of all students whose GPA is higher than 3 and who take at least one course titled "Database." This query can be expressed as follows:

```
select s.Name
from Student s
where (s: GPA > 3.0).(some Course: Title = 'Database')
```

Figure 4.12 shows the OQG for this OODB query. More discussion on how to obtain an OQG from an OODB query will be discussed in Section 4.4.2. ∎

Let RSchema be the relational schema transformed from an OODB schema OSchema. Let RQ be a relational query using RSchema. We now discuss how to transform an RQG for RQ, $G(RQ) = (RV, RE)$, to an OQG, $OG(OQ) = (OV, OE1, OE2)$. For each relation tuple variable R in RV, it will be transformed to a class instance variable $CIV(R)$ in OV with all annotations copied only if R is transformed from a class (i.e., not from a set attribute of some class). The transformation of an edge depends on the type of the edge. Let ANNO be the annotation on the edge e between vertices v_1 and v_2 in the RQG, where v_1 and v_2 correspond to relation tuple variables $R1$ and $R2$, respectively. The following cases may occur for ANNO:

Case 1. ANNO is $R1$-Key. This means that $R1$ is transformed from a class, say $C1$. $R2$ may be transformed from a class or from a set attribute.

Subcase 1.1. If $R2$ is transformed from a class $C2$, then $C2$ has a complex attribute CA with domain class $C1$. Therefore, the relational join "$R1.ANNO = R2.ANNO$" corresponds to a traversal between the complex attribute CA and its domain class. In this case, transform edge e to a directed edge from $CIV(R2)$ to $CIV(R1)$ with annotation CA in the OQG.

Subcase 1.2. If $R2$ is transformed from a set attribute of class C and C is the same as $C1$, then both $R2$ and $R1$ are transformed from the same class C. In this case, edge e need not be transformed.

Subcase 1.3. If $R2$ is transformed from a set attribute SA of a class C and C is different from $C1$, then the attribute names C-Key and $R1$-Key must be different. Since $R2$ has two different Key attributes, $R2$ must be transformed from a complex set attribute of C. In this case, the semantics of the join "$R1.ANNO = R2.ANNO$" is to impose the constraint "for each instance of $C1$, there is an instance of C that references it". There are two situations. (i) If class C already has a corresponding relation tuple variable, say R, in the RQG, then transform edge e to a directed edge from $CIV(R)$ to $CIV(R1)$

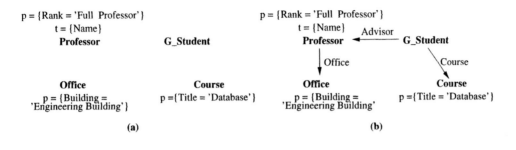

FIGURE 4.13   Illustrating Algorithm RQG to OQG

with annotation SA. (ii) Otherwise, we first create a new class instance variable, say CIV_C, for C and then transform the edge to a directed edge from CIV_C to $CIV(R1)$ with annotation SA.

Case 2.   ANNO is $R2$-Key. This is symmetric to Case 1 and can be handled similarly.

Case 3.   ANNO is R_3-Key and R_3 is a relation tuple variable different from both $R1$ and $R2$. In this case, the join "$R1.ANNO = R2.ANNO$" can be equivalently written as "$R1.ANNO = R_3.ANNO$ and $R_3.ANNO = R2.ANNO$". The above conversion is equivalent to "add a new vertex R_3 to the RQG and then replace the edge $(R1, R2)$ by two edges $(R1, R_3)$ and $(R2, R_3)$ in the RQG". After these changes, Case 3 will be replaced by Case 1 or Case 2 and the transformation techniques discussed above can be applied.

Case 4.   ANNO is of the form "$R1.A1\ op\ R2.A2$," where $A1$ and $A2$ are non-Key attributes. In this case, we transform edge e to an undirected edge between $CIV(R1)$ and $CIV(R2)$ with annotation "$CIV(R1).A1\ op\ CIV(R2).A2$".

Example 4.9   Consider the RQG in Figure 4.11. Figure 4.13(a) shows an intermediate graph after all vertices in the RQG are transformed. The intermediate graph contains only isolated vertices transformed from relation tuple variables that have corresponding classes. The edges of the RQG are transformed next. Let us take the transformation of the edge between relation tuple variables Course and G_Student-Course as an example. The annotation on this edge is Course-Key. G_Student-Course corresponds to a complex set attribute Course of class G_Student that is different from the class Course. Therefore, Subcase 1.3 of Case 1 is encountered. Since class G_Student already has a corresponding relation tuple variable G_Student in the RQG, a directed edge from G_Student to Course with annotation Course is created. Figure 4.13(b) shows the final OODB query graph.   ■

Obtaining an OODB Query from an OODB Query Graph

The third step of the translation is to obtain the OODB query from an OODB query graph. A typical OQG obtained from an RQG may contain directed as well as undirected edges. It may also contain directed cycles. We first explain the semantics of some basic constructs that may appear in a typical OQG. There are four basic constructs, as shown in Figure 4.14 (annotations

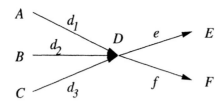

(a) A directed path

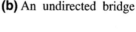

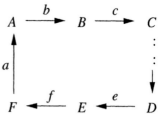

(b) An undirected bridge

(c) A vertex has two or
more incoming edges

(d) A directed cycle

FIGURE 4.14   **Basic Constructs of an OODB Query Graph**

on vertices are not shown). In each of the constructs, uppercase letters represent class instance variables and lowercase letters represent complex attributes. For a given class instance variable, let CC(X) be the corresponding class. Let pa-X represent the predicate annotation on vertex X.

Construct 1. In Figure 4.14(a), the following is assumed: (1) vertex A has no incoming arrow, (2) vertex E has no outgoing arrow, (3) each of the remaining vertices has exactly one incoming arrow and one outgoing arrow, and (4) no vertex appears more than once in the directed path. The semantics of the directed path is that a traversal from class A to class E is needed. Therefore, this construct is translated to the following OODB predicate:

$$(A : \text{pa-}A).(b : \text{pa-}B)\dots(e : \text{pa-}E)$$

At the same time, "CC(A) A" will be added to the from-clause of the OODB query if it is not already in the from-clause. "CC(A) A" defines A as a class instance variable of CC(A).

Construct 2. In Figure 4.14(b), two directed paths are connected by an undirected edge. It is possible that one or both of the directed paths have zero length. Suppose "$E.A1$ *op* $T.A2$" is the annotation on the undirected edge. This construct is translated to an explicit join as follows:

$$(A \mid \text{pa-}A)\dots(e \mid \text{pa-}E).A1 \; op \; (F \mid \text{pa-}F)\dots(t \mid \text{pa-}T).A2$$

At the same time, "CC(A) A" and "CC(F) F" will be added to the from-clause of the OODB query if they are not already in the from-clause.

Construct 3. Consider Figure 4.14(c). Vertex D has at least two incoming edges. At any given time, all edges associated with the same vertex must reference the same instance of the class corresponding to the vertex. For example, d_1, d_2, d_3, e, and f must all reference the same instance of class D at any given time. This can be achieved by introducing a reference variable for one of the incoming paths of the vertex. For the example in Figure 4.14(c), we can specify "(A : pa-A).(d_1 : pa-D) X" in the from-clause and obtain the following OODB predicates:

$$(B : \text{pa-}B).d_2 = X \text{ and } (C : \text{pa-}C).d_3 = X \text{ and } X.(e : \text{pa-}E) \text{ and } X.(f : \text{pa-}F)$$

Note that the first two predicates are explicit joins on complex attributes (d's are complex attributes).

Construct 4. Consider Figure 4.14(d). If we start the evaluation from an instance of the class corresponding to vertex A, then the complex attribute a references the same instance of the class corresponding to vertex A. Therefore, this construct can be translated to the following OODB predicate:

$$(A : \text{pa-}A).(b : \text{pa-}B) \ldots (e : \text{pa-}E).(f : \text{pa-}F).a = A$$

At the same time, "CC(A) A" will be added to the from-clause of the OODB query if it is not already in the from-clause. Note that a different OODB predicate will be obtained if we start from a different vertex. However, all these different predicates are equivalent.

In all of the above translations, if an attribute is a set attribute, then the quantifier *some* will be added. Namely, if b is a set attribute, then it will be replaced by "some b". The reason we add *some* but not *all* is that unnested relational queries cannot express the *all* quantifier.

The full algorithm for constructing an OODB query from an OQG is quite complicated. Here we only present the part of the algorithm that translates a special type of OQG consisting of only directed paths with no cycles and with no vertex associated with more than two edges. The OQGs of most OODB queries are of this type. The OQG in Figure 4.13(b) also is of this type. The complete algorithm for general OQGs can be found in Reference [265].

The algorithm that translates the aforementioned special type of OQG to OODB queries can be described as follows. Recall that a typical OODB predicate is essentially a path expression. Before a predicate is fully formed, a few intermediate results of the predicate may be formed during the process. The partial predicate currently under consideration will be denoted by PartPred.

Repeat until the input OQG becomes empty:

1. First, we choose an *active* vertex in the OQG. The active vertex indicates that the vertex is currently under consideration by the algorithm. The first active vertex can be any vertex that has no incoming arrows. Let V be the newly selected active vertex. If V is associated with a reference variable X, then let PartPred be the X. If V is not associated with any reference variable, then let PartPred = "(V : pa-V)" and put "CC(V) V" in the

from-clause if it is not already in the from-clause.[5] "$(V : \text{pa-}V)$" can be simplified to "V" if V does not have predicate annotation. If V has a target annotation, then for each attribute A in the target annotation, put "$V.A$" into the select-clause.

2. Now one of the following two cases may occur:

Case 1. The active vertex has an outgoing arrow e with annotation ANNO to a vertex $V1$ such that e is the only edge associated with $V1$. This case corresponds to the last vertex of Construct 1. In this case, do (i) form a predicate "PartPred.(ANNO : pa-$V1$)" (or "PartPred.ANNO" if $V1$ does not have predicate annotation); (ii) if $V1$ has a target annotation, then create a new reference variable Y by putting "PartPred′.ANNO Y" in the from-clause, where PartPred′ is the same as PartPred except all conditions of the format "pa-X" are removed, and for each attribute A in the target annotation, put "$Y.A$" into the select-clause; (iii) remove the outgoing arrow as well as any resulted isolated vertex; (iv) inactivate the active vertex and go back to step 1.

Case 2. The active vertex has an outgoing arrow with annotation ANNO to a vertex $V1$ such that $V1$ has exactly one incoming arrow and exactly one outgoing arrow. In this case, $V1$ corresponds to an intermediate vertex in Construct 1. Do (i) let PartPred = "PartPred.(ANNO : pa-$V1$)" (or "PartPred.ANNO" if $V1$ does not have predicate annotation); (ii) if $V1$ has a target annotation, then create a new reference variable Y by putting "PartPred′.ANNO Y" in the from-clause, where PartPred′ is the same as PartPred except all conditions of the format "pa-X" are removed, and for each attribute A in the target annotation, put "$Y.A$" into the select-clause; (iii) remove the outgoing arrow as well as any resulting isolated vertex; (iv) let $V1$ be the active vertex and go back to the beginning of step 2.

3. Connect all predicates generated by "and".

Example 4.10 Consider the OQG in Figure 4.13(b). According to the above algorithm, vertex G_Student is chosen as the first active vertex since it has no incoming arrow. G_Student is not associated with any reference variable at this time. Therefore, "G_Student G_Student1" is put into the from-clause of the query, where G_Student1 represents a class instance variable of class G_Student, and a partial predicate "G_Student1" is created. Vertex G_Student has two outgoing arrows, and either can be followed next. If we follow the directed edge annotated by *Advisor*, then we encounter Case 2. A new partial predicate "G_Student1.(Advisor: Rank = ′Full Professor′)" is now formed. Since vertex Professor has a target annotation, create a new reference variable X by placing "G_Student1.Advisor X" in the from-clause. "X.Name" is then put into the select-clause. After the edge annotated by *Advisor* is removed, vertex Professor becomes the next active vertex. Case 1 is then encountered. As a result, the complete predicate "G_Student1.(Advisor: Rank = ′Full Professor′).(Office: Building = ′Engineering Building′)" is formed. After the edge annotated by *Office* is removed, vertices Professor and Office are isolated and will be removed also. By now, only the edge annotated by *Course* remains, and G_Student will be chosen again next. Case 1 is encountered again, and a new

---

[5]If V and CC(V) are denoted the same, then V should be slightly changed, say by appending an integer to it. An example is given in Example 4.10.

complete predicate is constructed: "G_Student1.(Course: Title = 'Database')". Subsequently, the remaining graph will be removed and the algorithm terminates.

In summary, the following OODB query is translated from the OQG in Figure 4.13(b):

```
select X.Name
from G_Student G_Student1, G_Student.Advisor X
where G_Student1.(Advisor: Rank = 'Full Professor').
            (Office: Building = 'Engineering Building')
      and G_Student1.(Course: Title = 'Database')
```
∎

4.4.2 Translation of OODB Queries to Relational Queries

In this subsection,[6] we consider the translation of OODB queries against an OODB component schema OS into relational queries against the relational local schema RS, where the OS was transformed from the RS. Because query translation is closely related to schema transformation, we need to discuss the latter first.

Transformation of a Relational Schema to an OODB Schema

We assume that the relational schema was transformed from an extended entity relationship (EER) schema because the EER model has become a de facto standard for the logical design of relational databases. To simplify the problem, we assume that the schema transformer has knowledge about how each relation in the relational schema was transformed from the EER schema. Such knowledge could be derived with some help from a knowledged user (see reference [259] for more details). Let $E(R)$ denote the entity type from which relation R was transformed. Here we only present the basic ideas of the transformation. Readers who are interested in more detailed discussions should refer to [259]. The basic ideas of the transformation can be described as follows. (1) Each relation R that is not transformed from a many-to-many relationship is transformed into a class $C(R)$. Each attribute of R becomes an attribute of $C(R)$. (2) For two relations, say $R1$ and $R2$, if $E(R2)$ is a subtype of $E(R1)$, then let $C(R2)$ be a subclass of $C(R1)$ and remove from $C(R2)$ all the attributes that also appear in $C(R1)$. (3) If R is transformed from a many-to-many relationship between entity types $E1(R1)$ and $E2(R2)$, then R is transformed by creating a set attribute in $C(R1)$ and a set attribute in $C(R2)$. (4) If R has a foreign key FK referencing Key($R1$) and this $C(R)$ is not a subclass of $C(R1)$, then change the domain of FK to $C(R1)$. With this transformation, the class hierarchy in the transformed OODB schema is obtained by recovering the subtype/supertype relationships in the EER schema, and the composition hierarchy is obtained by exploring the key/foreign-key relationships in the relational schema.

Example 4.11 Consider a relational schema containing the following relations:

Publishers: *Pub_id*, Pub_name, City, State

---

[6]Portions of this section were also reported in Yu et al., 1995 [407].

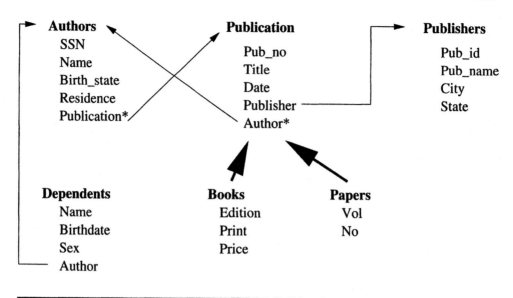

FIGURE 4.15 **The Transformed OODB Schema**

Publication: *Pub_no*, Title, Date, Pub_id
Books: *Pub_no*, Title, Date, Pub_id, Edition, Print, Price
Papers: *Pub_no*, Title, Date, Pub_id, Vol, No
Authors: *SSN*, Name, Birth_state, Residence
Dependents: *Author_SSN, Name*, Birthdate, Sex
Auth-Pub: *SSN, Pub_no*

In the above, the key of each relation is in italics. Clearly, Auth-Pub is transformed from a many-to-many relationship between Authors and Publication. Suppose Publication.Pub_id is a foreign key referencing Publishers.Pub_id, Dependents.Author_SSN and Auth-Pub.SSN are foreign keys referencing Authors.SSN, and Auth-Pub.Pub_no is a foreign key referencing Publication.Pub_no. We assume that Books and Papers were subtypes of Publication in the EER schema before they were transformed to relations. By applying the rules for transforming a relational schema to an OODB schema, we obtain the OODB schema as shown in Figure 4.15.   ∎

An OODB Query to Relational Query Translation Algorithm

In this subsection, we present an algorithm that reverses the three-step translation methodology presented in Section 4.4.1 to translate OODB queries to relational queries. In other words, this algorithm translates a source OODB query to a target relational query by first constructing an OQG from the OODB query, then transforming the OQG to an RQG, and finally obtaining a relational query from the transformed RQG. To do this, we need to extend the definition of RQG (i.e., Definition 4.3 in Section 4.4.1) to accommodate nested queries since some OODB queries can be transformed only to nested relational queries.

Obtaining an OODB Query Graph from an OODB Query

The following rules can be used to construct an OQG from an OODB query:

1. Each OODB path expression of the form $(A1 : \text{Pa-}C(A1)).(A2 : \text{pa-}C(A2)).(A_3 : \ldots)$
   $\ldots$, where $C(A_i)$ is a class instance variable of the domain class of the complex attribute
   A_i, $i = 2, 3, \ldots$, and $A1$ itself is a class instance variable $C(A1)$, is translated as follows:
   (a) Each $C(A_i)$, $i = 1, 2, \ldots$, is translated to a vertex, and the conditions on each $C(A_i)$
   become its predicate annotation. The vertex corresponding to $A1$ will also be labeled
   with "LS" (or "RS") if $A1$ is the starting point of the path expression on the left side
   (or right side) of an OODB predicate. The identification of the "LS" and "RS" will
   facilitate the query translation. (b) A directed edge with annotation A_{i+1} from the vertex
   corresponding to $C(A_i)$ to the vertex corresponding to $C(A_{i+1})$ will be created. If A_i is
   quantified by a *some* (or an *all*), which implies that A_i is a set attribute, then a *some* (or
   an *all*) will also be placed on the directed edge going into A_i.

2. If there are several path expressions in the OODB where-clause, first translate each
   path expression independently according to step 1, and then merge these subgraphs.
   We now describe the merging of two directed paths translated from two path expressions. Let $P1$ and $P2$ be two directed paths translated from path expressions EXP1 and
   EXP2, respectively. Then $P1$ and $P2$ can be merged as follows: (a) Find the longest
   common subexpression EXP between EXP1 and EXP2 with the same starting class instance variable V. Two subexpressions SE1 and SE2 are in common if (i) after selections
   are ignored, they have the same sequence of complex attributes (including possibly *all*)
   from V, and (ii) neither SE1 nor SE2 contains the *some* quantifier. (b) Merge the two
   directed subpaths of $P1$ and $P2$ that correspond to the longest common subexpression
   by keeping one subpath, and if COND_i and COND_j are the predicate annotations on the
   corresponding vertices in the original subpaths, then "COND_i AND COND_j" will be the
   new predicate annotation on the merged vertex. (c) There is no change on the unmerged
   parts of $P1$ and $P2$ except that different names will be used for unmerged vertices that
   correspond to the same class.

3. Consider an OODB predicate that has an explicit join on primitive attributes:

   $$\ldots A1 \; op \ldots A2$$

   Let v_1 and v_2 be the vertices translated from the last instance variables of path expressions on the left and right sides of the operator op, O_1 and O_2, respectively. Then the
   explicit join is translated to an undirected edge between the vertices v_1 and v_2 with the
   annotation "$O_1.A1 \; op \; O_2.A2$".

4. Add target annotations to appropriate nodes in the graph using the select-clause and
   from-clause of the OODB query.

Example 4.12 Suppose we have the query "find the title of each book published in 1991 by
Morgan Kaufmann such that all of its authors live in Chicago and at least one of the authors
was born in the state where the publisher of the book is located" against the OODB schema
in Figure 4.15. The following is the corresponding OODB query:

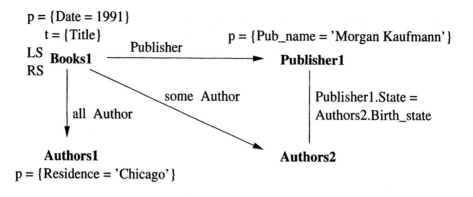

FIGURE 4.16 The OQG Constructed from the OODB Query in Example 4.12

```
select Books1.Title
from Books Books1
where Books1.Date - 1991 and Books1.Publisher.Pub_name - 'Morgan Kaufmann'
      and Books1.all Author.Residence - 'Chicago'
      and Books1.some Author.Birth_state - Books1.Publisher.State
```

Note that the two paths corresponding to the two occurrences of "Books1.Publisher" can be merged whereas the two paths corresponding to "Books1.all Author" and "Books1.some Author" cannot be merged because one of them contains *some*. The OQG of this OODB query is shown in Figure 4.16. The vertex corresponding to Books1 is labeled with both LS and RS since Books1 starts path expressions on both sides of some predicate in the query. ∎

Obtaining a Relational Query Graph from an OODB Query Graph

As we mentioned earlier, we need to extend the definition of RQG to express nested queries for the translation because some OODB queries can be transformed only to nested relational queries. We redefine RQG as follows.

Definition 4.5 *For a given relational query RQ, we define its query graph G(RQ) as an annotated graph: G(RQ) = (RV, RE1, RE2), where RV is a set of vertices representing relation tuple variables referenced in RQ, RE1 is a set of directed edges, and a directed edge e from vertex u to vertex v indicates a nesting operator such as "in," "not in," and " > any," and RE2 is a set of undirected edges representing join predicates. Each vertex is associated with a number that indicates the depth, or the level, of the subquery where the corresponding tuple variable is defined. The outermost query is of depth 0. Each vertex is also associated with two types of annotations, namely, a predicate annotation and a target annotation. Each directed edge is annotated with the nesting operator together with the preceding attribute. Each undirected edge is annotated with a join predicate of the form "R1.A1 op R2.A2", where A1 and A2 are the attributes of relation tuple variables R1 and R2, respectively. If the op is = and A1 and A2 are the same Key attribute, "R1.A1 op R2.A2" is simplified to A1.*

Let OSchema be the OODB schema transformed from a relational schema RSchema. Let OQ be an OODB query against OSchema. We now discuss how to transform the OQG for OQ, OG(OV, OE1, OE2) to an RQG RG(RV, RE1, RE2). The basic ideas of the transformation can be described as follows:

1. Each vertex in OV, v_i, is transformed to a vertex in RV, v_i'. The class instance variable associated with v_i, denoted by O_i, is translated into a relation tuple variable associated with v_i', denoted by $rtv(O_i)$. The annotations on v_i, including LS and RS, are copied on v_i'. Initially, the level number of every vertex in RV is 0.

2. To transform a directed edge e from v_1 to v_2 with annotation ANNO, the following three cases need to be considered.

Case 1. The annotation ANNO on e is a non-set attribute A. Namely, A is a non-set complex attribute of $C(O_1)$ with domain class $C(O_2)$. Let $R(O_1)$ and $R(O_2)$ be the relations corresponding to the classes $C(O_1)$ and $C(O_2)$, respectively. Then e can be translated into the following undirected edge in the RQG:

$$v_1' \underset{\displaystyle \text{PKey}}{\rule{3cm}{0.4pt}} v_2'$$

where v_1' and v_2' are $(rtv(O_1),m)$ and $(rtv(O_2),n)$ respectively, and m and n are the level numbers associated with $rtv(O_1)$ and $rtv(O_2)$, respectively. Set n to m to ensure that $rtv(O_1)$ and $rtv(O_2)$ are eventually defined in the same from-clause in the translated relational query. The above undirected edge in the RQG represents a join, $rtv(O_1).$PKey $= rtv(O_2).$PKey, where PKey is the primary key of the relation $R(O_2)$.

Case 2. The annotation ANNO on e contains the quantifier *some*. Namely, ANNO is a set attribute of $C(O_1)$ with domain class $C(O_2)$. From the schema transformation rules, there is a relation $R(O_{1,2})$ in the original relational schema RSchema that is associated with the two relations $R(O_1)$ and $R(O_2)$ (i.e., $R(O_{1,2})$ corresponds to the many-to-many relationship between $R(O_1)$ and $R(O_2)$). As such, a vertex representing the relation tuple variable $rtv(O_{1,2})$ of the relation $R(O_{1,2})$ needs to be added in the RQG, and the edge e is transformed to the following two undirected edges in the RQG:

$$v_1' \underset{\displaystyle \text{PKey1}}{\rule{2.5cm}{0.4pt}} v_{1,2}' \underset{\displaystyle \text{PKey2}}{\rule{2.5cm}{0.4pt}} v_2'$$

where v_1', $v_{1,2}'$, and v_2' are $(rtv(O_1), l)$, $(rtv(O_{1,2}), m)$, and $(rtv(O_2), n)$, respectively. Both m and n will be set to l. The two undirected edges represent two relational joins, $rtv(O_1).$PKey1 $= rtv(O_{1,2}).$PKey1 and $rtv(O_{1,2}).$PKey2 $= rtv(O_2).$PKey2, where PKey1 and PKey2 are the primary keys of the relations $R(O_1)$ and $R(O_2)$, respectively.

Case 3. The annotation ANNO on e contains the quantifier *all*. That is, ANNO = "all A," where A is a set attribute of $C(O_1)$ with domain class $C(O_2)$. This annotation means that each instance of $C(O_1)$ satisfying the condition imposed on O_1 must have each of its values under the set attribute A satisfy the condition COND imposed on O_2. Let $R(O_{1,2})$ be the relation in the RSchema that corresponds to the set attribute A. A vertex representing the tuple variable $rtv(O_{1,2})$ of $R(O_{1,2})$ needs to be added in the RQG. Furthermore, this edge can be represented by two "not in" nesting operations in the RQG as follows:

$rtv(O_1)$.PKey1 not in
    (select $rtv(O_{1,2})$.PKey1 from $R(O_{1,2})$ $rtv(O_{1,2})$
      where $rtv(O_{1,2})$.PKey2 not in
        (select $rtv(O_2)$.PKey2 from $R(O_2)$ $rtv(O_2)$
        where COND-on-$rtv(O_2)$))

where PKey1 and PKey2 are the primary keys of $R(O_1)$ and $R(O_2)$, respectively. Therefore, edge e is transformed to the following two directed edges in the RQG:

$$v'_1 \xrightarrow{\text{PKey1 not in}} v'_{1,2} \xrightarrow{\text{PKey2 not in}} v'_2$$

where v'_1, $v'_{1,2}$, and v'_2 are $(rtv(O_1), l)$, $(rtv(O_{1,2}), m)$, and $(rtv(O_2), n)$, respectively. We set m to $l+1$ and n to $l+2$ to ensure that $rtv(O_{1,2})$ will be defined in a subquery directly nested under the subquery in which $rtv(O_1)$ is defined and $rtv(O_2)$ will be defined in a subquery directly nested under the subquery in which $rtv(O_{1,2})$ is defined.

3. Each undirected edge between v_1 and v_2 with annotation "$O_1.A1$ *op* $O_2.A2$" is transformed to an undirected edge between v'_1 and v'_2 with annotation "$rtv(O_1).A1$ *op* $rtv(O_2).A2$". There is no change to the level numbers. Each undirected edge in the OQG represents an explicit join in the OODB query, and it is transformed to an undirected edge in the RQG to represent the corresponding relational join.

    In addition, the transformation algorithm always starts with a vertex annotated with "LS". If an OODB predicate has both the left-hand side and the right-hand side (i.e., it corresponds to an explicit join), then the directed path in the OQG corresponding to the left side is transformed first. If v_1 is the last vertex of the path corresponding to the left side and v_2 is the first vertex of the path corresponding to the right side of the same predicate, then the level number of v'_2 will be set to that of v'_1 before the right side is transformed, where v'_1 and v'_2 are transformed from v_1 and v_2, respectively.

Example 4.13 Consider the OQG in Figure 4.16. According to the algorithm described above, the transformation starts with vertex Books1 since it is marked with "LS". Let us take the transformation of the edge from Books1 to Authors1 as an example. The annotation ANNO on the edge is "all Author". This corresponds to Case 3 in Step 2. Author is a set attribute of class Books. The relation associated with Books and Authors in the RSchema is Auth-Pub. Therefore, we add a new relation tuple variable Auth-Pub1 with an initial level number m into the RQG. Then we place a directed edge from the vertex (Books1, 0), which is transformed from Books1 in the OQG, to the new vertex (Auth-Pub1, m) with annotation "Pub_no not in", where Pub_no is the primary key of the relation Authors. We also put a directed edge from (Auth-Pub1, m) to (Authors1, 0), which is transformed from Authors1, with annotation "SSN not in", where SSN is the primary key of the relation Authors. Finally, the level number m of Auth-Pub1 is changed to 1 and the level number of Authors1 is changed to 2. Figure 4.17 shows the transformed RQG. ∎

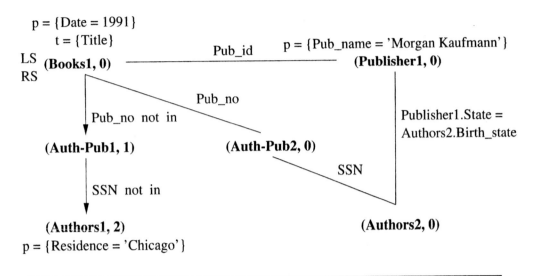

p = {Date = 1991}
t = {Title}

LS (Books1, 0)
RS

Pub_id   p = {Pub_name = 'Morgan Kaufmann'}
                                (Publisher1, 0)

Pub_no

Pub_no not in

(Auth-Pub1, 1)   (Auth-Pub2, 0)

Publisher1.State =
Authors2.Birth_state

SSN

SSN not in

(Authors1, 2)   (Authors2, 0)
p = {Residence = 'Chicago'}

FIGURE 4.17 *The RQG Transformed from the OQG in Figure 4.16*

Obtaining a Relational Query from a Relational Query Graph

The select-clause of the relational query can be formed easily using the target annotations on the vertices of the RQG. The from-clause can be formed during the formation of the select-clause and the where-clause. The most difficult task for obtaining the relational query is to form the where-clause. The following discussion can help us understand the process of forming the where-clause. The transformed RQG has the following properties: Two vertices connected by a directed edge in the RQG always have successive level numbers, but two vertices connected by an undirected edge can have either the same level number (transformed from a direct edge with non-set attribute or set attribute with *some*) or different level numbers (can only be transformed from an undirected edge). If (v_1, n) and $(v_2, n + 1)$ are the two vertices of a directed edge, then the relation tuple variable corresponding to v_2 will be defined in a subquery directly nested within the subquery in which the relation tuple variable corresponding to v_1 is defined. If (v_1, n) and (v_2, m) are the two vertices of an undirected edge, then the transformation depends on whether n and m are the same. The equality $n = m$ implies that the corresponding relation tuple variables should be defined in the same subquery SQ and the join between the two tuple variables should also be put into the SQ. The inequality $n \neq m$ means that the two variables should be defined in different subqueries and the join should be put in the inner subquery. In this case, the transformation of the edge into a join should be delayed until both variables are defined. Recall that during the construction of an OQG from an OODB query, we merged common subexpressions of different predicates into one subpath. Suppose there are two directed paths P_1 and P_2 in the OQG that share a common subpath P. Let P_1 and P_2 be P followed by $P_{1,2}$ and $P_{2,2}$, respectively. Let the last vertex in P be v. $P_{1,2}$ and $P_{2,2}$ are called *branches* of the subpath P. Suppose P, $P_{1,2}$, and $P_{2,2}$ in the OQG are transformed to paths P^*, $P^*_{1,2}$, and $P^*_{2,2}$ in the RQG, respectively. Suppose v in the OQG is transformed to (v', k). After P^* is translated, the translation of $P^*_{1,2}$ and $P^*_{2,2}$ should start in a subquery with the same depth k (i.e., the depth of v'). To ensure this, the vertex (v', k) will be saved in a stack, ON-LINE. In general, the subqueries translated from different branches following a common subpath will be connected by AND. The algorithm for obtaining a relational query from an RQG can be described as follows.

1. /* Form the select clause. */

   For each target annotation of the format $t = \{A_1, A_2, \ldots, A_t\}$ on vertex (rtv, n), first add rtv.A_1, rtv.A_2, $\ldots$, rtv.A_t to the select-clause of the relational query and then add "R(rtv) rtv" to the from-clause of the relational query, where R(rtv) is the relation corresponding to the relation tuple variable rtv.

2. Repeat the following steps to form the where-clause until the input RQG becomes empty:

   Step 1. /* Choose an active vertex. Initially, there is no active vertex. */

   If there is already an active vertex, proceed to Step 2. Otherwise, choose an active vertex as follows. If ON-LINE is not empty, pop out the top vertex from the stack as the active vertex; otherwise, choose any vertex labeled with "LS". Denote the active vertex as $v = $ (rtv, m), where rtv is the relation tuple variable corresponding to the vertex.

   Step 2. /* Process the active vertex. */

   (a) If rtv has not been defined in the from-clause of the subquery SQ currently under construction or any outer subquery under which SQ is nested, add "R(rtv) rtv" into the from-clause of SQ.

   (b) If there are k conditions ANNO(j) on v, $j = 1, \ldots, k$, then (i) add k predicates rtv.ANNO(j), which are connected by AND, into the where-clause of SQ, and (ii) eliminate all the k conditions on v.

   (c) If v adjoins with more than one edge, then push it into the stack ON-LINE.

   (d) If v is associated with any edge, proceed to Step 3; otherwise, if it is an isolated vertex, which indicates the end of the subquery SQ, then append the appropriate number of right parentheses ")" to the where-clause. Let q be the number of right parentheses to be appended. If the stack ON-LINE is empty, then $q = m$; otherwise, $q = m - p$, where p is the level number of the top vertex in the stack ON-LINE. Remove v from the RQG and return to Step 1.

   Step 3. /* Process the edge e associated with the active vertex. */

   Case 1 below discusses the translation of a directed edge from the active vertex v to vertex $v1$. Case 2 translates an undirected edge between v and $v1 = $ (rtv1, n). The undirected edges could have two forms of edge annotations: "A" or "rtv.A op rtv1.$A1$". In the former case, we have $n = m$. In the latter case, the undirected edge is transformed from an explicit join between two path expressions and it is possible that $n \neq m$.

   Case 1. e is a directed edge from v to $v1 = $ (rtv1, n), $n = m + 1$, and its annotation is of the form "A not in". First, add the following new subquery to the where-clause of the current subquery:

   rtv.A not in (select rtv1.A from R(rtv1) rtv1)

Then remove e from the RQG and if v becomes isolated, remove it also. Make $v1$ the next active vertex and return to Step 1.

Case 2. e is an undirected edge between v and $v1$.

Subcase 2.1. $n = m$ and the annotation on the edge is of the form "A". If the relation tuple variable rtv1 has not been defined, then add "$R(rtv1)$ rtv1" in the from-clause of the subquery under consideration. In any case, add "rtv.A = rtv1.A" to the where-clause of the current subquery. Remove e from the RQG, and if v becomes isolated, remove it also. Make $v1$ the next active vertex and return to Step 1.

Subcase 2.2. $n = m$ and the annotation on the edge is of the form "rtv.A *op* rtv1.$A1$". If relation tuple variable rtv1 has been defined, then add the join to the where-clause of the current subquery. Otherwise, delay the transformation of this edge until rtv1 is defined. The next active vertex will be the first vertex of the path corresponding to the path expression on the right-hand side of the OODB predicate (the vertex is marked with "RS" and is connected with v through a path in the RQG). Return to Step 1.

Subcase 2.3. $n < m$. This implies that the relation tuple variable rtv1 has not been defined. In this case, delay the transformation of this edge until rtv1 is defined, as in Subcase 2.2.

Subcase 2.4. $n > m$. This means that $v1$ is the last vertex of the path corresponding to the path expression on the right-hand side of the OODB predicate. Since the algorithm always transforms the path on the left-hand side first (based on Step 1, the first active vertex chosen is always labeled with "LS"), by this time, both rtv and rtv1 have been defined. In this case, we add the join "rtv.A *op* rtv1.$A1$" to the where-clause of the current subquery. Since this case also corresponds to the end of a subquery, we add an appropriate number of right parentheses to the where-clause using the method described in Step 2(d). Now remove e as well as any resulting isolated vertex from the RQG. Return to Step 1 to choose the next active vertex.

Example 4.14 Consider the RQG in Figure 4.17. When the select-clause is formed, the following intermediate result will be obtained:

```
select Books1.Title
from Books Books1
```

The first active vertex will be (Books1, 0) based on Step 1 of the algorithm. After this vertex is processed, a where-clause with condition "Books1.Date = 1991" is added to the query.

Suppose the edge with annotation Pub_id is considered first. Then Subcase 2.1 of Case 2 of Step 3 is encountered. When this step is done, the following intermediate result will be obtained:

```
select Books1.Title
from Books Books1, Publishers Publisher1
where Books1.Date = 1991 and Books1.Pub_id = Publisher1.Pub_id
```

The following is the final translated relational query:

```
select Books1.Title
from Books Books1, Publishers Publisher1,
    Auth-Pub Auth-Pub2, Authors Authors2
where Books1.Date = 1991 and Publisher1.Pub_name = 'Morgan Kaufmann'
    and Books1.Pub_id = Publisher1.Pub_id
    and Books1.Pub_no = Auth-Pub2.Pub_no
    and Auth-Pub2.SSN = Authors2.SSN
    and Publisher2.State = Authors2.Birth_state
    and Books1.Pub_no not in
        (select Auth-Pub1.Pub_no
         from Auth-Pub Auth-Pub1
         where Auth-Pub1.SSN not in
            (select Authors1.SSN
             from Authors Authors1
             where Authors1.Residence = 'Chicago'))                    ■
```

Exercises

4.1 Discuss the differences that may exist between the global schema of a distributed database system and the global schema of a multidatabase system.

4.2 Show that both union and outerunion can be considered as special cases of outerjoin.

4.3 Consider the relations $R1$ and $R2$ in Figure 4.4(a) and (b), respectively. Suppose there is no data inconsistency on SSN and Name, the data inconsistency on Age is to be resolved using max, and the data inconsistency on Salary is to be resolved using sum. Provide a resolution function for each attribute of the relation integrated from $R1$ and $R2$ by an outerjoin.

4.4 List four major differences between a traditional distributed relational database system and a multidatabase system.

4.5 Suppose an organization has an existing relational database system. Now new applications require the use of object-oriented technologies (e.g., OODB schema and query language). Two different methods may be used to accommodate the new applications without affecting existing applications. The first method is to build an OODB interface on top of the relational database system (see Figure 4.18(a)). The second method is to build a relational database interface on top of an OODB system (see Figure 4.18(b)). In both methods, only one database system is employed to manage all data. Discuss the advantages and disadvantages of each method.

4.6 Simplify algorithm Query-Modification(Q) for the case in which there is no data inconsistency, where Q is a global query.

4.7 Suppose we have a global schema with two global relations R and D as in Example 4.2. Apply algorithm Query-Modification for the following global query:

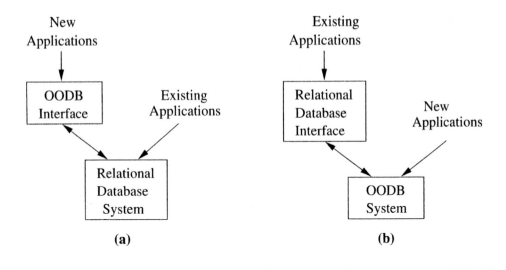

FIGURE 4.18 Two Alternative Methods

```
select R.SSN, R.Name, D.Manager
from R, D
where R.Salary < 40k and R.Position = 'Engineer'
        and R.Phone = '1234567'
        and R.Dept_name = D.Dept_name and D.Location = 'Chicago'
```

4.8 Apply algorithm Query-Decomposition to decompose the modified query in Exercise 4.7.

4.9 Consider a query involving two joins: $R1 \bowtie R2 \bowtie R_3$, where $R1$, $R2$, and R_3 are three relations from three different component databases. Provide a method so that pipelined parallelism can be used to evaluate the query in a multidatabase system. Discuss any drawbacks of your approach.

4.10 Use examples to illustrate that none of the three tree transformation algorithms discussed in Section 4.3.2 (the top-down approach, the bottom-up approach, and the hybrid approach) can guarantee that the resulting join tree is optimal with respect to the response time.

4.11 Prove the following: If there is no data inconsistency on attribute B between two relations $R1$ and $R2$, then the following is true for any relation S:

$$(R1 \ OJ \ R2) \bowtie_B S = (R1 \bowtie_B S) \ OJ \ (R2 \bowtie_B S)$$

where the outerjoin is between the ID attribute of $R1$ and $R2$, and all joins are equijoins on attribute B.

4.12 Show that distribution Rules 6 and 9 given in Section 4.3.3 are correct.

4.13 Assume that $R = J(R1, R2)$, where J is an equijoin on the ID attribute and world($R1$) = world($R2$). Let $R.A = f(R1.A1, R2.A2)$ be the resolution function used to resolve data inconsistency on attribute A; f could be max, min, sum, or avg. Let M_1 and m_1 be the maximum and minimum values, respectively, that can be taken by $A1$, and M_2 and m_2 be the maximum and minimum values, respectively, that can be taken by $A2$. Discuss how to use the new information, namely M_1, M_2, m_1, and m_2, to improve the distribution rules for $\sigma_{A\ op\ c}(J(R1, R2))$, where op is a comparator and c is a constant.

4.14 Consider the following query against the relational schema in Example 4.6: Find the names of all graduate students whose GPA is higher than 3.8, who take a course with course number CS532, and whose advisors are younger than 35.

```
select  G_Student.Name
from    G_Student, Professor, G_Student-Course GC, Course
where   G_Student.GPA > 3.8
        and G_Student.G_Student-Key = GC.G_Student-Key
        and GC.Course-Key = Course.Course-Key
        and Course.Course# = 'CS532'
        and G_Student.Professor-Key = Professor.Professor-Key
        and Professor.Age < 35
```

Translate the above query to an OODB query. Show also the intermediate results (i.e., the relational query graph and the transformed OODB query graph) of the translation.

4.15 Consider the OODB schema in Figure 4.15. Show that the two path expressions Books.*some* Author.Birth_state = 'New York' and Books.*some* Author.Name = 'Tom' are not equivalent to Books.(*some* Author: Birth_state = 'New York' and Name = 'Tom').

Can the equivalence be established if the quantifier *some* in all the above path expressions is replaced by *all*?

4.16 Consider the following query against the OODB schema in Figure 4.15: Find the name of each author who was born in New York state such that all of his or her publications are published by Morgan Kaufmann and some of his or her publications were published before 1995.

```
select  A.Name
from    Authors A
where   A.all Publication.Publisher.Pub_name = 'Morgan Kaufmann'
        A.Birth_state = 'New York' and A.some Publication.Date < 1995
```

Translate the above query to a relational query. Show also the intermediate results (i.e., the OODB query graph and the transformed relational query graph) of the translation.

Bibliographic Notes

Excellent surveys of heterogeneous multidatabase systems can be found in [293, 332]. The five-level multidatabase system architecture in this chapter is from [332]. Two recent books edited by Kim [203] and Bukhres and Elmagarmid [51] also contain chapters that address various aspects of multidatabase systems. Several other works [47, 173, 238] also provide interesting reviews of multidatabase systems.

A review of the query processing techniques in the MULTIBASE system and the Pegasus system can be found in [218] and [110], respectively. A high-level review of issues related to query processing in multidatabase systems can be found in [265]. The materials on query modification and decomposition presented in this chapter are inspired by [95, 260]. Reference [245] makes the observation that semi-join in a multidatabase system is not as attractive as in a traditional distributed database system. The technique of using tree balancing to reduce the response time of multidatabase queries is from [111] and is used in HP's Pegasus system. Efficient materialization of referenced global relations is discussed in [263]. Query processing in the presence of data inconsistency was first investigated in [94], and the result is extended in [263]. The query sampling technique for estimating the cost of local queries in a multidatabase system is proposed in [416]. Another technique for deducing information about cost model parameters is through calibrating the corresponding DBMS [109]. Query processing in multidatabase systems is also discussed in several other papers [65, 245].

Query translation between different query languages has been studied extensively by many researchers. A method for mapping relational queries to CODASYL network database commands is proposed in [308]. An interesting discussion on translating relational algebra to CODASYL commands can be found in [147]. References [79, 224] both mention translating relational queries to hierarchical and network access routines. A formal approach for translating relational queries to generic hierarchical queries is discussed in [264]. Translation between database queries and entity-relationship queries are discussed in several works [55, 56, 168, 182]. Recently, as object-oriented database systems have gained recognition, several works on translation between relational queries and OODB queries have been proposed [196, 265, 287, 298, 407]. The materials on query translation between relational queries and OODB queries used in this chapter are based on the work presented in [265, 407].

Parallel Processing of Relational Queries

As the price of storage devices gets cheaper and cheaper, databases that contain a huge amount of data, on the order of terabytes, have become a reality. For these databases, using the traditional way to store and process queries—i.e., store data in a large storage device associated with a single powerful processor and process the queries based on this hardware architecture—may take a very long time to find the results. This is unacceptable because most users hate to wait very long. Besides, purchasing a computer with a very large storage device and a powerful processor (typically a mainframe) can be very expensive.

An alternative solution is to use a large number of ordinary processors connected by a high-bandwidth network to manage such databases. The data can be stored in many small storage devices, say disk units, attached to or shared by these processors. Each query against such a database can be partitioned into subqueries that can be processed by many processors in parallel. This solution has the potential to substantially reduce the response time for processing queries. In fact, this approach has been employed by many commercial parallel database systems, such as Teradata, Tandem, and VAXclusters with great success. In addition, multiprocessor machines can easily provide more overall power than mainframes with a lower cost.

In this chapter, we present techniques for parallel processing of relational queries in a multiprocessor environment. In Section 5.1, basic concepts that are important for describing query processing techniques in this environment will be introduced. In Section 5.2, we will concentrate on data partitioning techniques, which are fundamental to achieving parallelism. Several

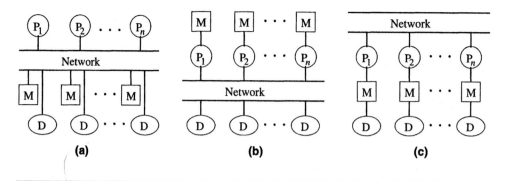

FIGURE 5.1   Three Different Architectures of Parallel Database Systems

parallel sorting algorithms will be presented in Section 5.3. Sorting has many applications for query processing, such as duplicate elimination and (sort merge) join. In Section 5.4, parallel processing of the relational selection and projection operations will be discussed. Techniques for processing joins will be presented in Section 5.5. The processing of general queries will be investigated in Section 5.6.

5.1 Basic Concepts of Parallel Processing

We first describe various multiprocessor architectures in Section 5.1.1, and in Section 5.1.2, basic ideas for achieving parallelism will be presented.

5.1.1 Multiprocessor Architectures

In a parallel database system, there are three major types of resources: processors, main memory modules, and secondary storage (usually disks). Depending on how these resources interact, different architectures of multiprocessor machines can be obtained. The following three architectures are among the best-known architectures of multiprocessor machines developed and implemented in the eighties and nineties.

Shared-memory architecture.   In this architecture, all processors can directly access a common, system-wide memory as well as all disks in the system. This is also known as the *shared-everything architecture*. Figure 5.1(a) depicts the shared-memory architecture. In Figure 5.1, P's represent processors, rectangles with M inside represent memories, and ellipses marked with D represent disk units. In this architecture, synchronization of processors can easily be achieved through the use of the shared memory. This architecture is also suitable for *load balancing* (i.e., different processors have about the same amount of work to do) since every processor has access to any portion of the data (i.e., no data reallocation among different disks is needed). Many query processing algorithms can be simplified based on this architecture. The main problem with this architecture is that a large volume of data needs to be handled by the interconnection network. This is caused by the frequent access to the shared memory and disks by different processors. The network can easily become the bottleneck and slow down the entire system. The problem becomes more severe as the number of processors increases. This, together with the fact that database applications are usually data intensive, results in the poor scalability of this architecture. Example systems that employ this architecture include Berkeley's XPRS and IBM's 3090 system.

Shared-disk architecture. In this architecture, each processor has a private memory that can be directly accessed only by the processor, but all processors can directly access all disks in the system. Figure 5.1(b) depicts the shared-disk architecture. This architecture alleviates the major problem associated with the shared-memory architecture (i.e., network congestion). Therefore, this architecture is more scalable. Unfortunately, it also loses some of the advantages of the shared-memory architecture. DEC's VAXcluster system employs this architecture.

Shared-nothing architecture. In this architecture, each processor is associated with a memory and some disk units, and the processor has exclusive access to its memory and disk units. In other words, no processor can directly access the memory and disk units associated with another processor. In this chapter, we call a processor together with its memory and disk units a *node*. Sometimes, when there is no confusion, we refer to a processor as a node or vice versa. In this architecture, the exchange of information among different nodes is carried out through the network connecting these nodes. Figure 5.1(c) depicts the shared-nothing architecture. By minimizing resource sharing, the shared-nothing architecture tends to minimize the interferences among different processors. As a result, its scalability is much better than the other two architectures. It has been demonstrated that when used to process complex relational queries, this architecture can achieve near-linear *speedup* and *scaleup*. *Linear speedup* means that a system that has *n* times more nodes can reduce the elapsed time by *n* times when the same task is performed. On the other hand, *linear scaleup* means that a system that has *n* times more nodes can perform a task that is *n* times larger in the same elapsed time. Linear speedup and linear scaleup are the two properties that are often used to characterize ideal parallel systems. The main problem of this architecture is how to balance the workload among different nodes, in order to minimize the response time. When data are highly skewed, load balancing becomes a very difficult task. So far, the shared-nothing architecture has had the most success, and many commercial (e.g., Teradata's DBC/1012, Tandem's NonStop SQL, and IBM's DB2 PE) and prototype (e.g., University of Wisconsin's Gamma and Microelectronics and Computer Technology Corporation's (MCC) Bubba) parallel database systems are based on this architecture. It is believed that the shared-nothing architecture has the most potential to be scaled to massively parallel systems, involving thousands of processors.

In this chapter, to simplify our presentation, we assume that each node has a single disk unit and all disk units have the same capacity.

5.1.2 Parallelism for Database Queries

Parallelism may be achieved at different levels for database applications. At the system level, concurrent queries can be processed by different processors in parallel to increase the throughput of the system. This is called *interquery parallelism*. At the next lower level, different operations in the same query may be processed by different processors in parallel. This is called *interoperation parallelism*. For example, one processor may be used to process each of the two selection operations of the same query. At the next lower level, the same operation may be processed by different processors in parallel. For example, a join between two relations can be transformed into a set of joins between the fragments of the two relations. This is called *intraoperation parallelism*. We are mainly interested in the interoperation parallelism and the intraoperation parallelism in this chapter.

The following are the three basic mechanisms for achieving parallelism.

Independent parallelism. Often, a number of operations of the same query can be processed independently in parallel. For example, consider a query involving three joins $R_1 \bowtie R_2 \bowtie R_3 \bowtie R_4$. One strategy to process this query is to evaluate the joins $R_1 \bowtie R_2$ and $R_3 \bowtie R_4$ first and then evaluate the join between the results. Clearly, $R_1 \bowtie R_2$ and $R_3 \bowtie R_4$ can be executed independently in parallel. Independent parallelism is illustrated in Figure 5.2(a). Usually, additional operations need to be executed to obtain the final result. Independent parallelism is one of the mechanisms for achieving interoperation parallelism.

Pipelined parallelism. Consider the scenario that two operations are related in such a way that the output of the first operation is used as the input to the second operation. If we start executing the second operation only after the first operation is completed, then the two operations are executed in sequence but not in parallel. On the other hand, if the first operation can be carried out in such a way that partial results can be produced and immediately channeled to the second operation, then it becomes possible for the first operation to produce the next partial result while the second operation consumes earlier partial results. In this way, both operations can be executed in parallel. Clearly, pipelining can also be applied to three or more operations. Pipelined parallelism is illustrated in Figure 5.2(b), where the partial result produced from evaluating operation i is used to evaluate operation $i + 1$, $1 \le i < n$. It is possible that all operations are being evaluated at the same time. Pipelining is another mechanism for achieving interoperation parallelism.

Partitioned parallelism. Normally, for a given operation, when the size of the input data increases, so does the effort needed to process the operation. When the size of the input data is large, we can partition it into many subsets (fragments or data streams) and employ a different processor to process the operation using one subset as its input. Since all processors process the same operation with smaller inputs in parallel, the operation can be processed in a shorter time. The basic philosophy of partitioned parallelism can be summarized as "divide a large problem into many small problems and conquer all small problems in parallel." This method usually requires that the results produced by participating processors be merged into the final result. In fact, *splitter*, which splits a large task into smaller tasks, and *merger*, which merges partial results into a single result, are

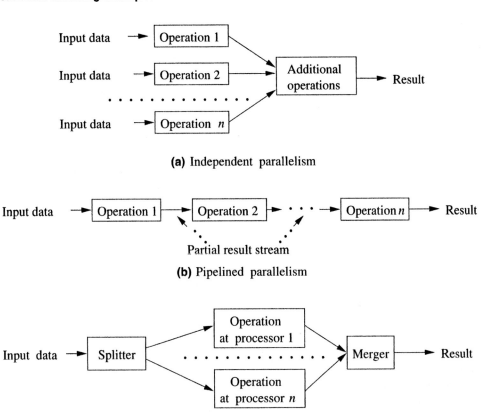

(a) Independent parallelism

(b) Pipelined parallelism

(c) Partitioned parallelism

FIGURE 5.2 Mechanisms for Parallelism

the two most basic operators for achieving partitioned parallelism (see Figure 5.2(c)). Partitioned parallelism is a mechanism for achieving intraoperation parallelism.

The above three parallelisms can often be used together to find a good parallel processing strategy for complex queries. For example, for the query $R_1 \bowtie R_2 \bowtie R_3 \bowtie R_4$ discussed above, the two joins $R_1 \bowtie R_2$ and $R_3 \bowtie R_4$ can be executed independently in parallel, with each join being executed by multiple processors (i.e., partitioned parallelism is employed for each join). At the same time, partial results of the two joins may be channeled to the third join to achieve pipelined parallelism.

5.2 Data Partitioning Techniques

In a parallel database system, there are multiple processors and disk units. For a given query or an operation, if multiple processors and disk units can be used at the same time, then a shorter response time can be expected. An effective way to use multiple processors and disk units is to partition operand relations into multiple subsets or fragments (usually *horizontal fragments*, i.e., fragments that contain subsets of tuples of relations) and distribute them among different nodes. A query or an operation referencing a relation can be mapped to multiple subqueries or suboperations such that each references a fragment of the relation. If the size of each fragment of the relation is much smaller than the relation, then each subquery (or suboperation) can be processed in a much shorter time. Therefore, if all subqueries are processed in parallel, the response time of the original query can be reduced as well.

Since data partitioning is so fundamental to parallel processing, we devote this section to discussing techniques for data partitioning. The basic problem of data partitioning can be stated as follows: for a given relation R and n nodes P_i, $i = 1, \ldots, n$, the relation R is partitioned into n fragments such that (1) all fragments have approximately the same size and (2) they can satisfactorily support expected operations on the relation. The first criterion is to ensure that when the fragments are distributed to n nodes, the data load at all nodes is well balanced. This usually (but not always) implies that the subqueries at these nodes can be processed in roughly the same amount of time. Since the response time is bottlenecked by the node that takes the longest time to process its subquery, trying to make all nodes take the same amount of time is an effective way to reduce the response time. The second criterion is needed because different partitionings may be good for different types of queries. As it will be discussed in the following subsections, some partitioning is good for selections and some is good for joins. In principle, the partition and distribution of a relation could be done either in advance, i.e., before it is referenced, or dynamically, when it is accessed.

5.2.1 Round-Robin Partitioning

Round-robin is the simplest partitioning scheme. Suppose n fragments of relation R are to be generated and distributed to n nodes P_i, $i = 1, \ldots, n$. This technique distributes the kth tuple of R to node $P_{((k-1) \bmod n)+1}$. The main advantage of this scheme is that it always partitions the input relation into fragments of the same size (except that the last round of the distribution may not be able to enumerate all nodes) regardless of any particular value distribution of any attribute. In other words, this method achieves the best possible data load balance. Later, we will see that other partitioning schemes may not have such a nice property. Evenly distributing the tuples of a relation to different nodes means that the CPU and I/O tasks for accessing the relation are also evenly distributed. This is excellent for queries that need all the tuples of the relation. For example, if R is round-robin partitioned, then query *select * from R* can be processed with the least I/O delay.

However, round-robin partitioning is very poor in supporting sophisticated accesses of the relations. For example, if relation R is round-robin partitioned and a query wants only those tuples of R that satisfy a predicate condition P, then all fragments of R need to be accessed because each fragment may contain tuples that satisfy P. This has two possible bad effects. First, those fragments that contain no qualifying tuples will be unnecessarily accessed. Second, since no effort is made to cluster the tuples of the relation, the tuples satisfying P may be scattered—in the worst case, in as many pages and fragments as the number of qualifying tuples, causing substantial I/O overhead. Note that having appropriate indexes for each fragment does not make the two problems disappear. As another example, consider the

456789123	Bob	21	1.5

(b) Fragment for [0.8, 1.6)

SSN	Name	Age	GPA
123456789	John	17	1.9
234567891	Ketty	24	3.4
345678912	Wang	19	3.1
456789123	Bob	21	1.5
567891234	Terry	22	2.4
678912345	Mary	19	2.7
789123456	Susan	25	3.9
891234567	Tom	20	2.2
912345678	Bill	18	2.8

(a) Relation Student

123456789	John	17	1.9
891234567	Tom	20	2.2

(c) Fragment for [1.6, 2.4)

345678912	Wang	19	3.1
567891234	Terry	22	2.4
678912345	Mary	19	2.7
912345678	Bill	18	2.8

(d) Fragment for [2.4, 3.2)

234567891	Ketty	24	3.4
789123456	Susan	25	3.9

(e) Fragment for [3.2, 4)

FIGURE 5.3   Range Partitioning

joining of two relations, R and S, that are partitioned using the round-robin scheme. In this case, every fragment of R must be joined with every fragment of S in order to obtain the correct result. A lot of network traffic may be caused by these joins. As we will see, other data partitioning techniques can overcome most of the above problems.

5.2.2   Range Partitioning

The range partitioning scheme partitions a relation based on the values of a chosen attribute (called the *partitioning attribute*). The general method consists of two steps. In the first step, the domain of the specified attribute is divided into a number of subranges so that each subrange is associated with a node. In the second step, the tuples of the relation are scanned and distributed to different nodes. A tuple t is distributed to the ith node if the value of the specified attribute of t falls into the ith subrange.

Example 5.1 Suppose we have a relation *Student* with an attribute *GPA*. One way to partition this relation into 5 fragments based on *GPA* can be described as follows. We first divide the domain range of *GPA*, say [0, 4], into 5 intervals of the same length $\{[0, 0.8), [0.8, 1.6),$ $[1.6, 2.4), [2.4, 3, 2), [3.2, 4]\}$. We then distribute the tuples of the relation according to their GPA values. Figure 5.3(a) shows the original relation and Figure 5.3(b) shows the result of the partitioning. The fragment corresponding to the interval [0, 0.8) is empty and is not shown. ∎

Range partitioning can overcome most of the problems associated with the round-robin partitioning for processing queries that have conditions on the partitioning attribute (*GPA* in Example 5.1). For example, if a query condition is "GPA = 3.5," then only the disk unit containing the fragment for [3.2, 4) needs to be involved in evaluating the condition. Needless to say, range partitioning is also effective for range conditions, such as $2.5 \leq GPA \leq 3.5$, on the partitioning attribute.

There is, unfortunately, a serious problem with the range partitioning scheme. The problem is that there is no guarantee that all fragments generated by this scheme will have the same size. In fact, the sizes of different fragments could be very different. In Example 5.1, the largest fragment contains four tuples, whereas the smallest fragment contains no tuple. In the worst-case scenario, it is possible that one fragment contains all tuples of the relation. The problem is caused by *data skew*. That is, the values of the partitioning attribute are not evenly distributed along its domain. When severe imbalance among fragments occurs, the effectiveness of the range partitioning scheme can be seriously damaged. This problem is usually handled by analyzing the distribution of the values of the partitioning attribute (e.g., use *sampling*) and using intervals of different lengths to perform the partitioning. For example, the GPA values for students are likely to have normal distribution since most students will have average GPAs and few students are extremely poor or good. Consequently, a better way to partition the domain of GPA is to use larger intervals at the two ends and smaller intervals at the middle.

In most distributed database systems, horizontal fragmentation is carried out based on the range partitioning scheme.

5.2.3 Hash Partitioning

The hash partitioning scheme partitions a relation by applying a hash function to the values of the partitioning attribute of the relation. For a given hash function $h( )$ and a value a in the domain of the partitioning attribute, $h(a)$ returns a value (i.e., a *hash value*). In general, the domain of the hash values is partitioned into n subranges, where n is the number of nodes to be used to store the fragments of the relation, and a tuple is put into the ith fragment if the corresponding hash value falls into the ith subrange. Clearly, based on this partitioning method, tuples that are hashed to the same value will be distributed to the same fragment, and tuples in different fragments share no common hash values.

A special case of the above hash partitioning occurs when each subrange contains a single value. It is this special case that can be used to evaluate joins efficiently. Hash join algorithms will be discussed in Section 5.5.

Example 5.2 Consider the relation *Student* in Figure 5.3(a). Suppose attribute *GPA* is again the partitioning attribute and five nodes numbered 1 to 5 will be used to store the fragments of the partition. If the hash function is $h(x) = (x \cdot 10) \bmod 5 + 1$ and a tuple t with $h(t[GPA]) = i$ is distributed to the fragment for node i, $i = 1, \ldots, 5$, then the result of the partition is as shown in Figure 5.4.   ∎

Hash partitioning can also overcome most of the problems associated with round-robin partitioning. Although hash partitioning may also distribute all tuples to a single or very few fragments, it is known that such an event is much less likely to occur compared with range

SSN	Name	Age	GPA
456789123	Bob	21	1.5

(a) Fragment for node 1

345678912	Wang	19	3.1

(b) Fragment for node 2

678912345	Mary	19	2.7
891234567	Tom	20	2.2

(c) Fragment for node 3

912345678	Bill	18	2.8

(d) Fragment for node 4

123456789	John	17	1.9
567891234	Terry	22	2.4
234567891	Ketty	24	3.4
789123456	Susan	25	3.9

(e) Fragment for node 5

FIGURE 5.4   **Hash Partitioning**

partitioning because a good hash function tends to randomize the values. Obviously, the choice of the hash function is very important to the quality of the partitioning. The topic of selecting a good hash function will not be discussed here. Hash partitioning is also very effective for the parallel processing of joins, as seen in Section 5.5.

Both the round-robin and the range partitioning schemes can be considered as special cases of the hash partitioning scheme. Specifically, round-robin partitioning can be achieved by hashing on the *Identity* attribute (*Identity* attribute stores the sequential numbers of the tuples of a relation and can be supported automatically by many commercial database systems, such as Sybase). With n nodes, the hash function is $h(x) = ((x - 1) \bmod n) + 1$, where x represents a sequential number. As for range partitioning, the corresponding hash function is the *identity function*, which maps each value to itself. As a result, the partitioning of the domain of the hash values is also the partitioning of the domain of the values of the partitioning attribute.

5.2.4 Other Issues Related to Data Partitioning

In this subsection, we briefly discuss several issues that are related to data partitioning.

Number of Fragments

Suppose different fragments will be used by different processors for query processing. This issue concerns this question: when a relation is to be partitioned, how many fragments should it be partitioned into? Intuitively, the answer seems to be the more the better, because typically, when the number of fragments increases, the size of each fragment decreases, and as a result, each fragment can be processed in less time. However, this intuition is not entirely correct. Several studies have revealed that there exists a threshold on the number of fragments for a relation, beyond which the response time of the queries using these fragments may actually increase. There are two explanations for this phenomenon. One is that as the number of fragments increases, so does the effort needed to merge the results from different fragments. The other reason is that when the size of a fragment becomes smaller, the cost of initiating the processes of using the fragments to answer a query may become more significant when compared with the actual processing cost. When the size of a fragment goes below a certain point, little or no savings can be yielded to process the fragment whereas the cost of merging the results keeps going up. Consequently, the response time increases. The exact threshold depends on many factors, such as the cost of merging partial results and the cost of initiating the processes of using a fragment.

Execution Load Balance

In the above several subsections, we have emphasized the issue of *data load balance*; that is, we would like a data partitioning scheme to distribute the tuples of each relation as evenly as possible, even in the presence of *data skew*. However, even if a perfect data load balance can be achieved, it does not guarantee that all processors will always have the same amount of work to perform, for various reasons. First, some portions of a relation may be used more heavily than others. For example, students with extremely low or high GPAs may be accessed more frequently than students with average GPAs because they are likely to be candidates for probation or awards. Second, the sizes of intermediate results produced from the same amount of input data may vary drastically. As an example, consider a query with two joins $R_1 \bowtie R_2 \bowtie R_3$. Suppose each relation R_i has been partitioned into two fragments of the same size, R_{i1} and R_{i2}, $i = 1, 2, 3$. Suppose further that the query is equivalent to the following two subqueries (i.e., the result of the query can be obtained by a simple union of the results of the two subqueries): $Q1 = R_{11} \bowtie R_{21} \bowtie R_{31}$ and $Q2 = R_{12} \bowtie R_{22} \bowtie R_{32}$. Clearly, Q1 and Q2 involve the same amount of data. Suppose Q1 is assigned to processor 1 and Q2 is assigned to processor 2. Thus, both processors will have the same amount of input data. Therefore, data load balance is achieved between the two processors for the two joins. Let T_1 and T_2 be the results of $R_{11} \bowtie R_{21}$ and $R_{12} \bowtie R_{22}$, respectively. The size of T_1 could be very different from that of T_2 as a result of the data skew on the joining attribute in one relation (called *single skew*), or both relations (called *double skew*). Consequently, the execution times of Q1 and Q2 may be very different. In summary, data load balance does not imply execution load balance.

Many strategies have been proposed to achieve execution load balance in the presence of data skew. One such strategy can be sketched as follows. First, generate a large number of initial tasks or subqueries by partitioning each operand relation into many fragments. Typically, the number of initial tasks is larger than the number of processors to be used. Second, sort the tasks in descending order of their expected execution times. Next, allocate the tasks to different processors in a *best-fit* manner. Namely, the next (largest) task is allocated to the processor that is expected to finish first. This step can be carried out either statically, meaning all tasks are allocated before they are processed, or dynamically, meaning that a new task will be allocated to a processor only after the processor has finished the task allocated to it earlier. Another technique for achieving execution load balance is to use the access frequency of each tuple of a relation to partition the relation so that each fragment will be accessed with approximately the same frequency. This approach is used in the Bubba system of MCC.

5.3 Parallel Sorting Algorithms

Sorting the tuples of a relation based on the values of one or more attributes is frequently needed in processing relational queries. For example, in addition to satisfying the explicit *order by* clause in SQL, sorting is also commonly used for *aggregate functions* (e.g., minimum, average, count) whose evaluation requires the grouping of tuples based on the values of certain attribute(s). For instance, students may be grouped based on their age so that the average GPA of students in different age groups can be computed. Grouping is often accomplished through sorting of the values under the relevant attribute(s). Sorting is also often used to facilitate the elimination of duplicates. Some relational operations such as *select distinct* and *union* require duplicate elimination. Some join algorithms (e.g., sort merge join) are also based on sorting. Sorting is an expensive operation. Typically, $O(n \log n)$ is the time complexity of sorting n items in memory and $O(N \log N)$ is the I/O complexity of sorting N pages of data externally (i.e., *external sorting*). Many parallel sorting algorithms have been proposed to take advantage of the multiprocessor environment. In this section, we present some of these algorithms.

Parallel sorting algorithms may be classified based on the number of input streams and the number of output streams. It could be one-to-one, one-to-many, many-to-one, and many-to-many. For example, for a one-to-many algorithm, there is only one input stream; i.e., the input data is from one node, and the result is to be stored at multiple nodes. When the result of a sorting is to be stored at multiple nodes, it is required that (1) the partial result at each node is sorted, and (2) an overall sorted result can be obtained from the partial results by a simple concatenation. Requirement (2) implies that if S_1 and S_2 contain two partial results, then either every item in S_1 is less than or equal to, or greater than or equal to, every item in S_2. A single output stream is useful if the sorting is the last step of processing a query. In this case, the single output stream is also the final result to the query. On the other hand, multiple output streams may be useful as an intermediate result since this may avoid an unnecessary partitioning of the result for the next step of processing. Whether there are single or multiple input streams depends on whether the input data has already been partitioned or not. If the input data has not already been partitioned, then there will be a single input stream; otherwise, there will be multiple input streams.

Another important issue regarding parallel sorting is how many processors to use for a sorting. At one extreme, we can employ a large number of processors so that the data to be sorted can be held entirely in the memories attached to the processors. As a result, the sorting can be carried out entirely in memory with very high parallelism. The problem with this approach is that, in reality, the number of processors available is always limited and there is no guarantee that an arbitrarily large relation can be held in the memories of the processors. Even if that were possible, overpartitioning a relation may cause too much network traffic during sorting because of data exchange among the participating processors. At the other extreme, a single processor may be used to perform the sorting. In this case, no parallelism is achieved, and external sorting is more likely. In practice, a fixed number of processors are used for a given sorting. In this case, whether or not an external sorting is needed depends on the size of the input relation and the total capacity of the memories at the chosen processors.

In the following three subsections, we describe three parallel sorting algorithms. The first algorithm, the *Parallel Binary Merge Sort*, produces the final result at a single processor. The second algorithm, the *Block Bitonic Sort*, produces the final result at multiple processors. The third algorithm, *NOW Sort*, also produces the final result at multiple processors. For the three algorithms, we assume that the relation to be sorted has already been partitioned and distributed to the processors.

5.3.1   Parallel Binary Merge Sort

This algorithm consists of two phases as described below.

Phase 1.   Sort all fragments in parallel at all participating nodes. The sorting of a fragment at a node can be carried out using any appropriate serial sorting algorithm for a single processor environment. For example, if the fragment can be held in the memory, then the *quicksort* algorithm may be used, and if an external sorting is necessary, then the *merge sort* algorithm may be used.

Phase 2.   This phase consists of a number of steps. In the first step, each pair of sorted fragments are merged into a larger sorted fragment. This can be carried out by sending the sorted fragment from one node to another node and by letting the receiving node perform the merge. Clearly, data transfer and merging can all be done in parallel. If there are n initial sorted fragments, then there will be $\lceil \frac{n}{2} \rceil$ larger sorted fragments at the end of this step. This process is repeated until a single fragment is obtained. Note that pipelined parallelism is possible between different steps. To achieve this, the newly produced partial result of merging two earlier sorted results needs to be sent to an unoccupied node to be merged with another stream of newly produced partial result of merging two different earlier sorted results.

Example 5.3   Suppose we have eight initial sorted fragments at eight processors P_i, $i = 1, \ldots, 8$ (see Figure 5.5). The data at P_2, P_4, P_6, and P_8 are sent to P_1, P_3, P_5, and P_7, respectively, to be merged. Suppose the merged data at P_1 and P_3 will be sent to P_2 for further merge. To achieve pipelined parallelism, P_1 and P_3 send their partial results to P_2. For example, P_1 could send $\langle 1, 3 \rangle$ and P_3 could send $\langle 2, 3 \rangle$ to P_2. As a result, while P_1 and P_3 continue to merge the rest of the data at their respective nodes, P_2 can start to merge $\langle 1, 3 \rangle$ and $\langle 2, 3 \rangle$. Similarly, pipelined parallel processing can occur between (P_5, P_7) and P_6, and between (P_2, P_6) and P_4. It is possible that processors P_1, P_3, P_5, P_7, P_2, P_6, and P_4 are all actively participating in the sorting in parallel.   ■

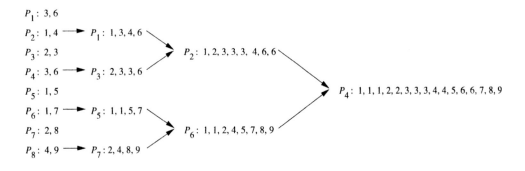

FIGURE 5.5 Parallel Binary Merge Sort

In Phase 1 of the above algorithm, if the size of the fragment at a node is larger than that of the available memory, then multiple passes of the fragment are needed to sort it. In practice, two passes of a fragment are usually sufficient to sort it even when its size is very large. Suppose the size of the fragment to be sorted is F pages and the available memory buffer is K pages. We can show that if $K \geq \sqrt{F/2}$, then the fragment can be sorted with no more than two passes. In the first pass, the fragment is read and sorted into sorted runs on disk. Since on the average the runs are twice the size of the available memory used for generating them (see Reference [210]), each run will be of size at least $2 \cdot \sqrt{F/2}$ pages. This means that at most $F/(2 \cdot \sqrt{F/2}) = \sqrt{F/2}$ sorted runs will be generated. In the second pass, the runs are merged into a single sorted run. Since there are at least $\sqrt{F/2}$ memory pages, one page can be allocated to each of the $\sqrt{F/2}$ runs. As a result, all runs can be merged in one pass. The reader can verify that with a memory buffer of 20 MB (10,000 pages of size 2 KB), a fragment of 400 GB can be sorted in two passes.

The Parallel Binary Merge Sort algorithm can easily be generalized to a parallel N-way merge sort algorithm by sending N fragments to a processor and performing an N-way merge at each such processor. For this to be possible, each node that performs the merge needs a memory buffer of at least $N + 1$ pages, with one page for each of the N fragments and one additional page for buffering the result of the merge. Clearly, when N gets larger, the length of the pipeline will get shorter.

5.3.2 Block Bitonic Sort

This algorithm can be described as follows:

Sort-Split-Ship. At each participating processor, we first sort the fragment. Then each sorted fragment is split into two subfragments of equal size such that every sorting value in the first subfragment (called the *lower subfragment*) is smaller or equal to every sorting value in the second subfragment (called the *higher subfragment*). This is done in parallel at all participating nodes. Finally, each subfragment is shipped to another processor (which could be the same processor). Different variations of the algorithm have different ways of determining the destination processors. Figure 5.6 illustrates

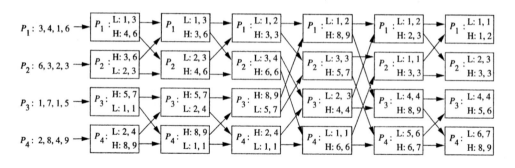

FIGURE 5.6 Block Bitonic Sort

how destinations are determined for four processors based on *Batcher's Bitonic Sorting Network*. In this figure, P_i, $i = 1, \ldots, 4$, are four processors. L and H denote the lower subfragment and the higher subfragment, respectively. A directed edge from the L (or H) of processor P_i to processor P_j indicates that the lower subfragment (or the higher subfragment) produced at P_i is shipped to P_j.

Two-Way Merge Split. When two subfragments are received at a processor, a two-way merge is performed on them to produce a sorted fragment. The fragment is subsequently split into two subfragments (i.e., the lower and higher subfragments), which are then shipped to the corresponding destination processors. This is carried out at all participating processors in parallel. This step is repeated until the sorting completes (i.e., when each processor has a sorted fragment and every sorting value at processor P_i is smaller than or equal to every sorting value at processor P_j, $i < j$). In general, $\frac{1}{2} \log 2n \cdot (\log 2n + 1)$ steps (including the sort-split-ship step) are needed when n processors are used to perform the sorting.

Example 5.4 Figure 5.6 illustrates the sorting of 16 numbers using four processors. Initially, the numbers are partitioned into four fragments that are assigned to four processors. In the first step, the numbers in each fragment are first sorted and then split into the lower subfragment and the higher subfragment. Each subfragment is then shipped to another predetermined processor. For instance, the higher subfragment in P_2 is shipped to P_1 and the lower subfragment remains in P_2. Each processor will have two subfragments after each step. Next, the numbers at each processor are sorted again through a merge and subsequently split into two subfragments. This process continues until the sorting is completed. After six steps (when $n = 4$, $\frac{1}{2} \log 2n \cdot (\log 2n + 1) = 6$), the sixteen numbers are sorted at the four processors.   ■

5.3.3 NOW Sort

NOW Sort is a sorting algorithm developed for a network of workstations. These workstations are connected via a high-speed local area network. Each of them is a powerful high-end workstation with its own disk(s), memory, and cache. Essentially, a NOW can be considered as a parallel system with a shared-nothing architecture. NOW Sort is presently the fastest sorting algorithm. With 64 high-end workstations, each with 64 MB of memory, 512 KB of cache, and two high-speed disks, this algorithm can sort 6 GB of data in under one minute. The data consist of tuples of 100 bytes with a 10-byte key. It is assumed that key values satisfy the uniform distribution.

We first present a simpler version of the NOW Sort algorithm. This version needs to read each tuple from secondary storage into main memory only once. This version can be called the *One-Pass NOW Sort* algorithm. For this algorithm to be applicable, the sum of the sizes of the main memories must be large enough to hold all tuples to be sorted. Initially, the same number of tuples are assumed to be at each workstation. The One-Pass NOW Sort algorithm consists of four steps as outlined and discussed below.

Read. Each processor reads tuples from its local disk into main memory. This is carried out in parallel by all processors.

Distribute. While the tuples are being read into the memory, they are buffered and distributed to appropriate processors (workstations) according to their key values. If P is the number of processors and the processors are numbered from 0 to $P - 1$, then the most significant $\log_2 P$ bits of each key value are used to determine the destination processor of the corresponding tuple. More specifically, if the $\log_2 P$ most significant bits of the key value of a tuple yield a value i, $0 \leq i \leq P - 1$, then the tuple will be shipped to the ith processor. Note that this distribution method guarantees that every key value in the ith processor is less than every key value in the jth processor, $0 \leq i \leq j \leq P - 1$.

When a tuple arrives at a processor, a pair (pk, pt) is formed, where pk is a part of the key value of the tuple and pt is a pointer to the tuple. A 4-byte pk is used. (pk, pt) is then distributed to one of the 2^b local in-memory buckets using the $(\log_2 P + 1)$th to $(\log_2 P + b)$th most significant bits of the key in exactly the same way each key value is used to determine the destination processor of each tuple, for some number b (more discussion about pk and b will be provided after the algorithm). This is repeated for all tuples destined to each processor.

Sort. Each processor employs an in-memory sorting algorithm to sort the local buckets, one bucket at a time.

Write. Up to this point, keys have been sorted based on the most significant $\log_2 P + b + 32$ bits. Additional sorting is needed and this is carried out as follows. At each processor, the pointers in sorted pairs in each bucket, starting with the bucket with the smallest binary string (each string has b bits), are used to fetch the full tuples. Once the tuples are determined, tuples whose key values are identical under the most significant $\log_2 P + b + 32$ bits are further sorted based on the remaining bits. The fully sorted tuples are then written to local disk. Forming tuples from (pk, pt) pairs and performing additional sort can be pipelined with the I/O operations that write sorted tuples to disk.

There are two reasons for distributing these pairs (pk, pt) to buckets in the above distribution step. First, the distribution is carried out based on the most significant b bits (after removing the first $\log_2 P$ bits) of each key value. As a result, the key values can be partially sorted by the distribution process in the sense that every key value whose pk is in one bucket is either less than or greater than every key value whose pk is in another bucket. In other words, the key values are sorted based on the most significant b bits. Second, b is chosen in such a way that the size of each bucket is suitable for the bucket to be sorted in the cache associated with each processor to speed up the sorting of each bucket (see the sort step). The suitable size of each bucket depends on many factors. For example, consider the case when the size of the cache is 512 KB, (pk, pt) occupies 8 bytes, 1 million tuples need to be sorted at each processor, and the in-memory sorting algorithm is an *in-place* algorithm (i.e., no additional space is needed to perform the sorting). In this case, the cache can hold about 512,000/8 = 64,000 pairs. As there are 1 million (pk, pt) pairs, $1,000,000/64,000 \approx 16$ buckets are needed to store them such that each bucket can fit into the cache. As a result, $b = 4$ should be chosen.

The pk in each (pk, pt) is the next most significant 32 bits (after the first $\log_2 P + b$ bits are removed) of each key value. The reason for forming (pk, pt) pairs is to reduce the amount of data to be sorted. In principle, three alternatives exist. The first alternative sorts the tuples on the key directly. In this case, 100 bytes need to be moved around for each tuple. The second alternative is to form pairs (k, pt) first and then sort them on the key, where each k is the key value of a tuple. In this case, full key values are used for the sorting. The amount of data participating in the sorting is substantially smaller than the first alternative. However, this alternative incurs overhead in forming the pairs from tuples before the sorting and in forming tuples from the pairs after the sorting. The third alternative is to form (pk, pt) first and then sort them on pk. In this case, partial key values are used for the sorting. Also, in this case, the amount of data participating in the sorting is the smallest among the three alternatives. In addition to incurring the overhead as in the second alternative, this alternative requires additional sorting on the unsorted portion of the key values. Experiments indicate that the third alternative is the fastest despite the added complexity.

Note that the two distributions in the distribution step—one distributes tuples to appropriate processors and the other distributes (pk, pt) pairs to local in-memory buckets—are CPU intensive. They can be pipelined with the I/O delay (for the first distribution) and with the network delay (for the second distribution). As a result, little additional time overhead is needed. Further, the first distribution effectively sorts the tuples on the first $\log_2 P$ bits of the key values, and the second distribution effectively sorts the tuples on the next b bits of the key values. Consequently, the tuples need to be sorted only on the remaining $80 - \log_2 P - b$ bits of the key values.

For the in-memory sorting algorithm in the sort step, the NOW Sort algorithm employs the *partial-radix sort* with cleanup (see Reference [3]). This algorithm is not an in-place algorithm. It needs an input buffer and an output buffer. As a result, the size of each bucket should be no more than half the size of the cache in order to sort each bucket in the cache quickly. Experiments indicate that this algorithm is about three times faster than the in-place quicksort algorithm.

The above algorithm employs both partitioned parallelism and pipelined parallelism extensively. Each of the four steps can be carried out in parallel by all processors. For each processor, pipelined parallelism exists between the operations within the same step and across multiple steps. For example, the two distributions are pipelined between them and with the I/O in the read step.

The above One-Pass NOW Sort algorithm assumes that the total available memory is large enough to hold all tuples to be sorted. If this assumption does not hold, then this algorithm can be extended to a *two-pass* sorting algorithm. This is achieved by using the one-pass algorithm to generate sorted runs at each node and by adding an additional step, merge, which merges local sorted runs into a single sorted file. The tuples are read in main memory from disk once to generate runs and the second time to merge these runs. During the merge step, a portion of each run is read into the memory to carry out the merge. A large memory buffer should be used for each run so that a large number of pages can be read in during each I/O operation to amortize the seek time and rotational delay.

5.4 Parallel Processing of Selections and Projections

Selections and projections on the same relation are usually performed at the same time (i.e., in the same scan). Therefore, they can be considered as a single *reduction* operation that returns a set of subtuples of those tuples of the relation that satisfy a specified condition.

Suppose we want to perform a reduction on relation R. This can be carried out by first performing the reduction on every node that has a fragment of R and then forwarding the results to a common processor so that the results from all involved processors can be merged to form the final answer. The reduction of a fragment on a single processor is carried out in the same way as it is done in a regular database system. That is, the fragment can either be scanned sequentially or searched using a fast access path if such a path is available and the reduction contains a predicate condition. Reductions on all fragments are carried out in parallel. If no duplicate tuples are possible in the result (e.g., the results contain a key of R) or duplicate tuples are allowed, then the merge can be carried out easily (i.e., just concatenate the results from different processors together). On the other hand, if duplicate tuples are possible but not allowed (e.g., the result contains no key, and *select distinct* is used in the query), then there is a need to eliminate the duplication between the results from different processors. A common method to eliminate duplicate tuples is to first sort the data and then remove the duplicate. In fact, many parallel sorting algorithms can be modified so that duplicate tuples can be eliminated during the sorting. For example, consider the Parallel Binary Merge Sort algorithm discussed in Section 5.3.1. Duplicate tuples can easily be removed when the merge is performed. In the following, we outline a method that can be used to eliminate duplicate tuples without sorting.

Suppose there is no duplicate in the result produced by a single processor. Let P_i, $i = 1, \ldots, n$, be the participating processors. First, the result R_n at processor P_n is sent (broadcast) to all other processors. When processor P_i, $1 \leq i < n$, receives R_n, it uses R_n to remove the duplicates in R_i (R_i is the result at processor P_i). This is done in parallel at all the first $n - 1$ processors. Suppose after this step, R_i is reduced to R_i^1. Additionally, after P_n sends out R_n, it can be released for other purposes since it is no longer needed. Except for the first processor P_1, all other processors do not need to keep R_n once it is used. In the next step, R_{n-1}^1 is sent to the first $n - 2$ processors so that it can be used to remove the duplicates in R_i^1, $1 \leq i < n - 1$. Again, processor P_{n-1} can be released after it sends out R_{n-1}^1, and only processor P_1 needs to keep R_{n-1}^1 after it is used. This process continues until all processors (except the first processor) have the chance to send data to the first processor. Let R_i^k be the result obtained from R_i after processor P_{n-k+1} has sent the data to processor P_i. Then by

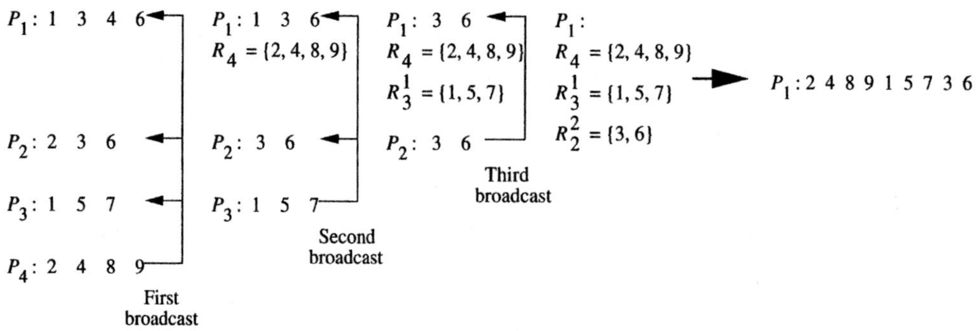

P_1: 1 3 4 6

P_1: 1 3 6
$R_4 = \{2, 4, 8, 9\}$

P_1: 3 6
$R_4 = \{2, 4, 8, 9\}$
$R_3^1 = \{1, 5, 7\}$

P_1:
$R_4 = \{2, 4, 8, 9\}$
$R_3^1 = \{1, 5, 7\}$
$R_2^2 = \{3, 6\}$

P_1: 2 4 8 9 1 5 7 3 6

P_2: 2 3 6

P_2: 3 6

P_2: 3 6

Third
broadcast

P_3: 1 5 7

P_3: 1 5 7

Second
broadcast

P_4: 2 4 8 9

First
broadcast

FIGURE 5.7 Illustrating Broadcast

the time all processors except the first one have been released, processor P_1 has R_n, R_{n-1}^1, ..., R_{n-k}^k, ..., R_1^{n-1} and there are no duplicates among them. Therefore, the final result is the concatenation of these sets. This method achieves parallelism by letting all unreleased processors perform duplicate elimination at the same time. Note that since processor P_i needs to send data to all processors $P_j, j < i$, this method will benefit if the network is a *broadcast network*.

Example 5.5 Consider the initial results as placed on the left in Figure 5.7. After the first broadcast, i.e., the initial result at P_4, R_4, is sent to all other processors, P_4 is released, and R_4 is saved at P_1. The second and third broadcasts can be understood similarly. Note that in the third broadcast, all numbers in the initial result at P_1 are eliminated (i.e., R_1^3 is empty). The final result is a simple union of disjoint sets R_4, R_3^1, and R_2^2.   ∎

5.5 Parallel Processing of Joins

There are three basic methods for processing joins in a traditional centralized relational database system: *nested loop*, *sort merge*, and *hash join*. Most parallel join algorithms are derived from the three basic centralized join algorithms. In this section, we present five parallel join algorithms. Among them, one is derived from the centralized nested loop join algorithm, one from the sort merge algorithm, and three from the hash join algorithm. Join $R \bowtie_A S$ is considered in this section. Without loss of generality, we assume that S is the smaller of the two relations.

5.5.1 Nested Loop Join

In a centralized environment, when neither operand relation has an index on the joining attribute, the optimal way[1] to implement a nested loop join is to use the smaller relation as the

---

[1]The *optimization criterion* used here is the minimization of the number of I/O pages. If a different optimization criterion is used, then the optimal processing strategy may be different. See Chapter 1 for more details.

outer relation (and consequently the larger relation becomes the *inner relation*) and let the outer relation use as many memory buffer pages as possible (i.e., leave one memory page for the inner relation and one page for buffering the result). If one of the operand relations has an index on the joining attribute, then it should be used as the inner relation to make use of the index. In this case, the join value of each tuple in the outer relation can be checked against the index on the inner relation to find the matching tuples in the inner relation. As a result, a scan of the inner relation can be avoided. In the parallel version of this Nested Loop Join algorithm, a similar idea is used.

Suppose the available memory at each processor is of size m pages. The Parallel Nested Loop Join algorithm can be described as follows:

1. Choose the outer relation. Relation R is chosen as the outer relation if one of the following conditions is satisfied:

(a) Both R and S have already been partitioned and distributed to multiple processors, but S has an index on the joining attribute for each fragment and R does not.

(b) R has already been partitioned and distributed to multiple processors but S has not.

For all other cases, S is chosen as the outer relation.

2. Choose processing processors and perform the join. The following cases can be identified:

(a) The chosen inner relation has already been partitioned and distributed to multiple processors, and it has an index on the joining attribute for each fragment. In this case, use the processors in the nodes that contain a fragment of the inner relation as the processing processors for the join. The reason for this choice of the processing processors is that an index can be used only when the data is not relocated.

Now broadcast the outer relation to all processing processors, one page at a time. When a page of the outer relation arrives at a processing node, it is immediately joined with the fragment of the inner relation at the node using the index. In general, more than one page of the outer relation can be broadcast each time as far as enough memory space is left for holding k index pages, one page for the inner relation and one page for buffering the join result, where k is the number of levels of the index tree.

(b) Case (a) is not true. In this case, we have two subcases:

i. The chosen outer relation has already been partitioned and distributed to multiple processors. For this subcase, use the processors in the nodes that contain a fragment of the outer relation as the processing processors for the join. At each processing processor, read in the first $m - 2$ pages of the fragment of the outer relation into the memory. This can be carried out in parallel.

ii. The chosen outer relation has not already been partitioned and distributed. For this subcase, choose n processors as the processing processor for some n

and partition the outer relation into n disjoint fragments and distribute them among the n processing processors. When a fragment arrives at a chosen node, the first $m - 2$ pages (m is the size of the available memory in pages) are kept in the memory and the remaining pages, if there are any, are written to the corresponding disk unit.

For both of the above two subcases, we now broadcast the inner relation to all processing processors, one page at a time. If the inner relation has already been partitioned and distributed, then each node that contains a fragment of the inner relation needs to broadcast its pages to all participating processors, again, one page at a time. When a page of the inner relation arrives at a processing processor, it is immediately joined with the $m - 2$ pages of the outer relation in the memory. The remaining one page of memory is used to buffer the join result. This is carried out in parallel. This process is repeated for each page of the inner relation.

If the fragments of the outer relation are larger than $m - 2$ pages, then each block of $m - 2$ pages of the outer relation needs to be read into the memory and the above process is repeated for each such block.

3. Assemble the result. If the final result is desired at a given node, then all partial results at processing processors are shipped to the given node and assembled.

5.5.2 Sort Merge Join

The Sort Merge Join algorithm in a centralized database system consists of basically two steps: (1) sort both operand relations on the joining attribute and (2) merge join the two relations. A straightforward way to parallelize this algorithm is to apply a parallel sorting algorithm to sort the two relations and then merge them by a single processor. However, this generalization only parallelizes the first step (i.e., sorting) and the merge step has to be done sequentially. The following algorithm parallelizes both sort and merge:

1. Partition and sort. The following actions are performed in this step:

(a) Partition R by using a hash function based on the values of attribute A, and send each fragment to a disk unit associated with a processor. Suppose there are n processors P_i, $i = 1, \ldots, n$, and the ith fragment R_i is sent to P_i.

(b) Sort each fragment of R locally in parallel.

(c) Partition S by the same hash function used for partitioning R based on A and send the ith fragment, S_i, to P_i, $i = 1, \ldots, n$.

(d) Sort each fragment of S locally in parallel.

2. Perform merge join. A merge join is performed at each processor in parallel.

Since the same hash function is used for partitioning both relations, only tuples in the fragments at the same processor may be joined (in other words, after the partitioning, R and S have *placement dependency* on A (see Chapter 3)).

3. Assemble the result. If the final result is desired at a given node, then all partial results at the processing processors are shipped to the given node and assembled.

A	D	E
6	d1	e1
3	d2	e2
2	d3	e3
4	d4	e4
6	d5	e5
1	d6	e6
9	d7	e7
7	d8	e8
3	d9	e9

Relation R

A	B	C
3	b1	c1
5	b2	c2
6	b3	c3
4	b4	c4
4	b5	c5
9	b6	c6
7	b7	c7

Relation S

FIGURE 5.8 Tuples in Relations R and S

Example 5.6 Consider the two relations R and S as shown in Figure 5.8. Suppose two processors are used to process the join using the sort merge algorithm. Suppose that the hash function is $h(x) = x \mod 2$ so that tuples with even A-values will be sent to processor P_1 and tuples with odd A-values will be sent to processor P_2. The intermediate results after the first step of the algorithm are shown in Figure 5.9(a). The results after the local merge joins are performed are shown in Figure 5.9(b). The final result is a simple union of the two partial results in Figure 5.9(b). ∎

Two remarks about the above algorithm:

1. The partition of R and S in the algorithm needs to be carried out carefully. When an arbitrary hash function is used, there will be no guarantee that a sorted final result can be obtained from a simple union of the partial results. For instance, the final result obtained by a simple union of the two partial results in Figure 5.9 is not sorted on the joining attribute A. If it is desired that the final result is sorted on the joining attribute, then it is important to choose a partitioning scheme such that every value of the joining attribute in $R_i(S_i)$ is smaller than every value of the joining attribute in $R_j(S_j)$, $i < j$. As an example, the *range partitioning* method could be used for such a purpose.

2. The above algorithm assumed that R and S are not partitioned already at the beginning of the algorithm. In practice, the following cases may occur for relation R: (a) R is not partitioned already; (b) R is partitioned based on a different attribute (i.e., different from the joining attribute), or it is partitioned based on the joining attribute but the fragments of R do not satisfy the condition that every value of the joining attribute in R_i is smaller than every value of the joining attribute in R_j, $i < j$ (this condition is important to obtain a sorted final result); and (c) R is partitioned based on the joining attribute and the fragments satisfy the above condition. Similar cases may occur for S. Therefore, nine combinations exist. The above algorithm covered the case when both R and S satisfy (a). In the following, we discuss the basic ideas for obtaining a sorted final result through

A	D	E
2	d3	e3
4	d4	e4
6	d1	e1
6	d5	e5

Sorted Fragment R_1

A	B	C
4	b4	c4
4	b5	c5
6	b3	c3

Sorted Fragment S_1

A	D	E
1	d6	e6
3	d2	e2
3	d9	e9
7	d8	e8
9	d7	e7

Sorted Fragment R_2

A	B	C
3	b1	c1
5	b2	c2
7	b7	c7
9	b6	c6

Sorted Fragment S_2

(a) Intermediate results after the first step

A	B	C	D	E
4	b4	c4	d4	e4
4	b5	c5	d4	e4
6	b3	c3	d1	e1
6	b3	c3	d5	e5

$R_1 \bowtie_A S_1$

A	B	C	D	E
3	b1	c1	d2	e2
3	b1	c1	d9	e9
7	b7	c7	d8	e8
9	b6	c6	d7	e7

$R_2 \bowtie_A S_2$

(b) Intermediate results after local joins are performed

FIGURE 5.9   Illustrating the Sort Merge Join Algorithm

a simple union of all partial results. We only consider the case when R satisfies (c) and S satisfies (a) and the case when R satisfies (c) and S satisfies (b). How to handle other cases are left as exercises to the reader.

R satisfies (c) *and S satisfies* (a). In this case, we choose the processors containing the fragments of R as the processing processors. We then partition S and distribute its fragments to the processing processors. Note that the ranges used to partition R must also be used to partition S. The remaining steps are identical to the above algorithm.

R satisfies (c) *and S satisfies* (b). Again, choose the processors containing the fragments of R as the processing processors. In this case, S needs to be repartitioned among the processing processors. The repartitioning of S is carried out as follows. Each fragment S_i is partitioned into k subfragments S_{im}, $m = 1, \ldots, k$, such that the range condition is satisfied, where k is the number of processing processors. Note that the same hash function should be applied to all S_i's. Then all S_{im}'s, with different i's and fixed

bucket #	
0	$\langle 6, s_{13} \rangle$
1	$\langle 4, s_{11} \rangle, \langle 4, s_{12} \rangle$
2	

Hash table for S_1

bucket #	
0	$\langle 3, s_{21} \rangle, \langle 9, s_{24} \rangle$
1	$\langle 7, s_{23} \rangle$
2	$\langle 5, s_{22} \rangle$

Hash table for S_2

FIGURE 5.10 Hash Tables for S_1 and S_2

m, are sent to the mth processing processor where a new fragment of S, $S'_m = \bigcup_i S_{im}$, is obtained. The remaining steps are identical to the above algorithm.

5.5.3 Simple Hash Join

The Simple Hash Join algorithm is a straightforward extension of the hash join algorithm for centralized database systems. The following version of the algorithm assumes that R and S are not partitioned already. If they are already partitioned but the partition is not based on the values of the joining attribute, then they may be repartitioned.

1. Partition the smaller relation S using a hash function h_1 based on the values of A and send the ith fragment S_i to the ith processor P_i.

2. At each processor P_i, create a hash table T_i using a second hash function h_{2i}, again based on the values of A. The hash table consists of many buckets such that tuples whose A-values have the same hash value are placed into the same bucket and tuples whose A-values have different hash values are placed into different buckets. This is done in parallel at all participating processors.

3. Partition relation R using the hash function h_1 based on the values of A and send fragment R_i to processor P_i.

4. At each processor P_i, tuples of R_i are scanned and then hashed using the hash function h_{2i} based on the values of A to probe table T_i for matches with the tuples of S_i. A probe is carried out by first mapping a tuple t_s of R_i to a bucket of T_i and then trying to match t_s with each tuple in the bucket. This step is also carried out in parallel at all participating processors.

Example 5.7 Suppose R and S are as shown in Figure 5.8 and S has been partitioned into S_1 and S_2 as shown in Figure 5.9(a). Suppose hash function $h(x) = x \bmod 3$ is used to create the hash tables for both S_1 at P_1 and S_2 at P_2. Each hash table will have three buckets numbered 0, 1, and 2. A tuple is placed in bucket i if its A-value is hashed to i, $i = 0, 1, 2$. The hash tables for S_1 and S_2 are shown in Figure 5.10. Each bucket contains zero or more entries of the format $\langle a, s_{ij} \rangle$, where s_{ij} denotes the jth tuple in S_i, $i = 1, 2$, and a is the A-value of the tuple. Entries in each bucket may be organized as a linked list. After the hash table at processor P_i is created, tuples in R_i can be used to probe the table. As an example, consider the last tuple in

R_2, $r = (9, d7, e7)$ at P_2. When r is hashed, the bucket with bucket # = 0 ($h(9) = 9 \mod 3 = 0$) in the hash table for S_2 is identified. Tuple r is then compared with every tuple in the bucket. This leads to the joining of r and s_{24}, and the result is $(9, d6, c6, d7, e7)$.   ■

The above description of the Simple Hash Join algorithm assumed that the hash table at each processor can be kept in the memory associated with the processor. In practice, it is quite possible that the memories at some or all processors are not large enough to accommodate the hash tables. When a memory cannot hold the hash table, an *overflow* occurs. Note that when the smaller relation is used to build the hash tables, the likelihood that an overflow occurs is reduced.

Overflow can be handled as follows. Before a hash table is to be built, the size of the hash table is computed based on the statistical information of the corresponding fragment. Usually, the size of the hash table for a relation is slightly larger than that of the relation itself. For simplicity of discussion, in this section, we assume that the size of the hash table for a relation is the same as that of the relation. If the size of the hash table is smaller than that of the available memory, then no overflow will occur and the algorithm described earlier is used. If the size is larger than that of the available memory, choose a range of the hash values so that the hash table for the tuples that will be hashed into the range can be accommodated by the memory. For example, if the estimated size of the hash table is k times that of the available memory, then the range should be at most $1/k$ of the full range of the hash function. The range should be chosen conservatively since few hash functions can distribute tuples evenly among different subranges. When the hash table is being built, tuples whose hash values are in a predetermined range are used to build the hash table and the rest of the tuples are channeled to a temporary relation. When the tuples of R_i are used to perform the join, they are first hashed by the same hash function used for S_i. If the hash value of a tuple is in the predetermined range, it is used to probe the hash table; otherwise, it is channeled to a temporary relation. After all tuples of R_i are considered, the join is done for all tuples that are not in the two temporary relations. Note that tuples in the temporary relations can only be joined with each other. Therefore, the join between the two original fragments has been reduced to one between the two temporary relations that are smaller than their respective original fragments. Now the same process used to join the two fragments can be recursively used to join the two temporary relations. This process continues until no overflow can occur.

5.5.4 GRACE Hash Join

Unlike the Simple Hash Join algorithm, which tries to resolve the hash table overflow problem when it occurs (the approach is called *overflow resolution*), the *GRACE Hash Join algorithm* tries to prevent any hash table overflow from occurring (i.e., *overflow avoidance*). The idea is to first partition R as well as S into fragments and then perform a parallel hash join (e.g., simple hash join) for each pair of corresponding fragments. The number of fragments is chosen to be sufficiently large (or the size of each fragment of S is made sufficiently small) so that when the hash join is performed for each pair of fragments, no hash table overflow can occur. Also, the fragments for each relation are obtained in such a way that only tuples from the corresponding fragment pairs can possibly match. More formally, the GRACE Hash Join consists of two phases. The first phase can be referred to as the *fragment-generating phase*, which partitions each relation into disjoint fragments and saves them on disks. The second phase is called the *fragment-joining phase*, which performs a parallel hash join for each pair of fragments. A detailed description of this algorithm is given below.

1. Fragment-generating phase.

  (a) Partition S into N disjoint fragments using a hash function h_1 based on the values of attribute A. Let these fragments be denoted S_i, $i = 1, \ldots, N$. These fragments may be stored on a single disk or on multiple disks. The number N is chosen to be large enough so that the size of each fragment is smaller than the total capacity of the memories (i.e., the sum of the sizes of all memories) at the participating processors. This is to ensure that all hash tables for each fragment can be held in the memory without causing hash table overflow (see Step 2 below).

  (b) Partition R into N disjoint fragments using the same hash function h_1 based on the values of attribute A, and store each fragment accordingly (where to store these fragments is not important). Let these fragments be denoted by R_i, and R_i is the fragment corresponding to S_i (i.e., their tuples are hashed to values in the same range), $i = 1, \ldots, N$. Because the same hash function is used for the partitioning of both R and S, it is clear that $R_i \bowtie_A S_j = \emptyset$ for $i \neq j$.

2. Fragment-joining phase.

    In this phase, each join $R_i \bowtie_A S_i$ is processed independently as if R_i and S_i are whole relations, $1 \leq i \leq N$. In principle, any of the earlier discussed parallel join algorithms can be used to process the join $R_i \bowtie_A S_i$. In particular, we can apply the Simple Hash Join algorithm to process $R_i \bowtie_A S_i$. This means that another hash function is used to partition S_i into n subfragments such that each subfragment is channeled to one of the n processors. A hash table will be built in the memory at the corresponding processor as the tuples of the subfragment arrive. Because the size of each S_i is smaller than the total memory available and the size of a hash table for a fragment is only slightly larger than the size of the fragment, if the hash function is chosen properly (such that the size of the subfragment channeled to a processor corresponds to the size of the available memory at the processor), each hash table should be accommodated by the corresponding memory. R_i will be partitioned by the same hash function, and its subfragments will be channeled to the corresponding processors. The tuples of the subfragment of R_i channeled to a processor will be used to probe the hash table at the same processor. More detailed description of the Simple Hash Join algorithm is in Section 5.5.3.

Due to data skew, no matter what hash function is used, there is no guarantee that hash table overflow can be completely avoided in the second step of the above algorithm. When an overflow does occur, then the corresponding fragment can be partitioned further to obtain smaller fragments to avoid the overflow or an overflow resolution method such as the one used by the Simple Hash Join algorithm can be used to resolve the overflow. Another way to reduce the chance of encountering hash table overflow is to make the number of fragments, N, in the first phase very large. The side effect is that some fragments may become too small, resulting in too many joins with small input in the fragment-joining phase. Usually, if a hash join between two relations can be carried out without hash table overflow, then breaking the join into two or more joins with smaller input will be less efficient because performing each of the joins with small input needs to initiate many preparation steps and none makes good use of the available memories. The solution is to group the fragments that are too small to obtain more optimally sized fragments for join. This grouping process is known as *partitioning tuning*.

5.5.5 Hybrid Hash Join

In the GRACE Hash Join algorithm, the fragment-generating phase and the fragment-joining phase are completely separate. As a result, each fragment needs to be written to a disk after it is formed and to be read back into memory when it is to be used for joining. The main difference between the Hybrid Hash Join algorithm and the GRACE Hash Join algorithm is that the former tries to merge the two phases to reduce the I/O traffic. Specifically, when relation S is being partitioned in the fragment-generating phase, Hybrid Hash Join distributes the tuples of S that belong to the first fragment to different processors as soon as each such tuple is determined. As these tuples arrive at each processor, they are immediately used to build the hash table. All other fragments are written to disks as in the GRACE Hash Join. When relation R is being partitioned, the tuples belonging to the first fragment also receive the same special treatment. That is, these tuples are directly distributed to different processors without being written to disks first, and as these tuples arrive at a processor, they are used to probe the hash table to perform the actual join. Other fragments of R are written to disks. The Hybrid Hash Join algorithm handles the fragments written on disks the same way as the GRACE Hash Join algorithm.

   This algorithm is called the *Hybrid Hash Join* algorithm because it keeps the good properties of both the Simple Hash Join algorithm and the GRACE Hash Join algorithm. To see this, let us examine two extreme cases. The first case is when the available memory at each participating processor is large enough to hold the hash table even when the fragment-generating phase generates only one fragment. In this case, Hybrid Hash Join completely eliminates the need for writing and reading fragments to/from disks, and consequently, Hybrid Hash Join and Simple Hash Join become identical. The second case is when the memory is very small so that many small fragments need to be generated by both Hybrid Hash Join and GRACE Hash Join. Because of the small memory, the advantage of Hybrid Hash Join over GRACE Hash Join by getting a head start on the first fragment will also be small. In summary, when the memory becomes larger, Hybrid Hash Join becomes closer to Simple Hash Join and farther away from GRACE Hash Join; and when the memory becomes smaller, Hybrid Hash Join becomes closer to GRACE Hash Join and farther away from Simple Hash Join.

5.5.6 Comparison of the Join Algorithms

In this subsesction, an informal comparison between the join algorithms presented in this section is made.

Nested Loop Join.   This algorithm is very sensitive to the number of participating processors. Experimental results show that the performance of this algorithm improves quickly as the number of processors increases. With enough processors, this algorithm may even outperform other join algorithms. This algorithm is also likely to perform well when the two operand relations are very different in size. Moreover, since this algorithm compares each tuple in one relation with every tuple in the other relation, nonequijoin can easily be supported. No other join algorithm can be as robust as the Nested Loop Join algorithm as far as nonequijoin is concerned.

Sort Merge Join.   This algorithm is found to be less sensitive to the number of participating processors. The performance of the algorithm improves relatively slowly as the number of processors increases, compared with other join algorithms. Furthermore, this algorithm's relative performance improves as the sizes of operand relations become larger. Experimental results show that when the number of participating processors is small and the operand relations are large relative to the size of the available memory, the Sort Merge Join algorithm can outperform other join algorithms.

Hash-Based Joins.   Hash-based join algorithms are found to have the best performance in most cases. Among the three hash-based join algorithms, Hybrid Hash Join has an edge over the other two.

The Simple Hash Join algorithm performs very well when there is no hash table overflow or when the hash table at each node can accommodate at least half of its fragment. In the former case, the join can be processed with each tuple being read into the memory exactly once. In the latter case, no more than half of the tuples need to be read into the memory twice, and others are read once. In both cases, Simple Hash Join and Hybrid Hash Join become identical, and they both perform better than GRACE Hash Join, which needs to bring each tuple into the memory twice (assuming no hash table overflow in the fragment-joining phase)—once for each of the two phases. However, when the size of the available memory at a node is much smaller than that of the corresponding fragment, Simple Hash Join will cause repeated hash table overflow. As a result, some tuples need to be written/read to/from disk many times. This is the main drawback of the Simple Hash Join algorithm.

The GRACE Hash Join algorithm tries to overcome the hash table overflow problem by partitioning both operand relations into fragments and processing the join between each pair of fragments independently. When the size of each fragment of the smaller operand relation S is smaller than that of the total memory capacity at participating processors, no tuple needs to be read in the memory more than twice. As a result, this algorithm can outperform Simple Hash Join when the size of the memory is much smaller compared with the size of S. For example, when the size of the memory is one quarter of that of S, using Simple Hash Join, the entire relation will be read once, three quarters of the relation will be read twice, half will be read three times, and one quarter will be read four times. As a result, with respect to S, the volume that is read is 2.5 times of the size of S when Simple Hash Join is used. Similarly, in this case, Simple Hash Join will incur a higher cost for reading R than GRACE Hash Join. However, GRACE Hash Join suffers when the memory is relatively large. For example, when the memory is large enough to avoid overflow without further partitioning (i.e., the *fragment-partitioning phase* produces only one fragment), GRACE Hash Join unnecessarily writes the fragment back to disk, resulting in a higher cost than Simple Hash Join.

The Hybrid Hash Join algorithm is superior to both the Simple Hash Join algorithm and the GRACE Hash Join algorithm. It overcomes the hash table overflow problem of

Simple Hash Join by partitioning each operand relation into fragments just like GRACE Hash Join, and it overcomes the unnecessary I/O problem of GRACE Hash Join by treating the first fragment(s) of the partitions of the two operand relations the same way as Simple Hash Join treats the original relations. Intuitively, Hybrid Hash Join has two main advantages over GRACE Hash Join. The first is that the I/O cost for handling the first fragments of R and S is eliminated in Hybrid Hash Join. This could be significant if the sizes of the first fragments are large. The second advantage is that certain parallelism between the two phases of the algorithm can now be achieved. Note that there is zero parallelism between these two phases in GRACE Hash Join because these two phases are carried out completely sequentially. In contrast, in Hybrid Hash Join, while the hash tables are being built (or probed) for the tuples in the first fragment of R (or S), other fragments can be generated. Experimental results have confirmed these observations.

In summary, for equijoins, Hybrid Hash Join is found to be superior to other join algorithms in most cases.

5.6 Parallel Query Optimization

A single relational query may involve multiple operations. Therefore, parallel query optimization must not only consider intraoperation parallelism as discussed in the previous sections but also pursue interoperation parallelism. In this section, we discuss techniques that can be used to optimize general queries in a multiprocessor environment. Since selections and projections are relatively easier to handle, our focus of discussion will be on the parallel optimization of queries that involve multiple joins (i.e., multiway join queries).

In a centralized or uniprocessor environment, optimizing a multiway join query involves finding an order in which the joins are to be executed and the method (nested loop, sort merge, etc.) to be used to evaluate each join such that the cost is lower than other choices of join order and methods. In a multiprocessor environment, the scheduling and allocation of resources (e.g., processors and memories) are also important in optimizing a query. The general problem of query optimization is known to be NP-hard even for centralized database systems. As such, heuristic solutions are often needed to find good plans for query execution.

Example 5.8 Consider a 4-way join query involving four relations: $R_0 \bowtie R_1 \bowtie R_2 \bowtie R_3$. Owing to the commutativity of joins, many different equivalent queries can be derived from the above query. In fact, there are fifteen equivalent queries for a 4-way join query. The following are the six queries equivalent to the given query when the commutativity rule is not applied.

   (1): $R_0 \bowtie_1 R_1 \bowtie_2 R_2 \bowtie_3 R_3$

   (2): $R_0 \bowtie_1 R_1 \bowtie_3 R_2 \bowtie_2 R_3$

   (3): $R_0 \bowtie_2 R_1 \bowtie_1 R_2 \bowtie_3 R_3$

   (4): $R_0 \bowtie_2 R_1 \bowtie_3 R_2 \bowtie_1 R_3$

   (5): $R_0 \bowtie_3 R_1 \bowtie_1 R_2 \bowtie_2 R_3$

   (6): $R_0 \bowtie_3 R_1 \bowtie_2 R_2 \bowtie_1 R_3$

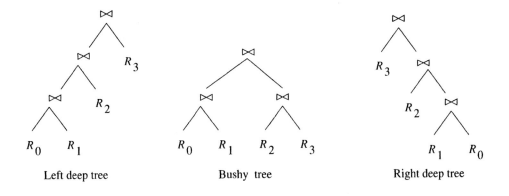

Left deep tree   Bushy tree   Right deep tree

FIGURE 5.11   Different Shapes of Join Trees

where the subscript of each ⋈ indicates the order in which the join is to be evaluated. For instance, for query (2), the leftmost join is to be executed first, followed by the rightmost join and then by the join in the middle. The joins and their evaluation orders can be graphically represented as trees (i.e., *join tree*). The join trees of queries (1), (2), and (6) are shown in Figure 5.11 from left to right. In a left deep tree, all right child nodes are leaf nodes whereas all left child nodes, except the lowest one, are internal nodes. In a right deep tree, all left child nodes are leaf nodes whereas all right child nodes, except the lowest one, are internal nodes. In a bushy tree, both child nodes of an internal node could be internal. Owing to the large number of possible join orders, many query optimizers consider only a subset of them. For example, in System R, only left deep trees are considered for query optimization. Later, we will show that the right deep trees actually have the best potential for exploiting the pipelined parallelism. Bushy trees provide good opportunities for independent parallelism because subtrees in a bushy tree can often be processed independently in parallel.

If there are three methods to carry out each join (say nested loop, sort merge, and hash join), then the total number possible execution plans for this query is $3^3 \cdot 15 = 405$. In general, it has been shown that for an n-way join query with m possible methods for each join, the total number of possible execution plans is

$$m^{n-1} \cdot \binom{2(n-1)}{n-1} \frac{(n-1)!}{2^{n-1}}$$

Resource scheduling and allocation are an added complication to the query optimization problem in a multiprocessor environment. One possible way to allocate the processors for the joins is to use all processors for each join so that the joins are performed one by one. This method tries to exploit more intraoperation parallelism. Another possible way is to partition the processors into clusters so that each cluster of processors are used to process a join. In this way, all joins may be processed at the same time (could be in a pipelined manner) with each join using a fewer number of processors when compared with the first alternative. This alternative exploits both intraoperation and interoperation parallelism. ∎

There are generally two basic strategies to generate an execution plan for a multiway join query in a multiprocessor environment. The first strategy divides the task into two subtasks.

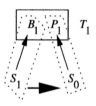

FIGURE 5.12   *Graph Representation of a Hash Join*

The first subtask generates an execution plan without considering resource scheduling and allocation, and the second subtask produces a scheduling and allocation plan for the operations generated by the first subtask. This is known as the *two-phase optimization* strategy. The second strategy combines the two subtasks into one and tries to generate both the execution plan and the allocation plan at the same time. This is known as the *one-phase optimization* strategy. The main advantage of the two-phase optimization strategy is its flexibility and relative simpleness. By separating the two subtasks, the problem becomes easier. Furthermore, since the first subtask can be readily handled by the existing query optimizers developed for uniprocessor systems, only the second subtask is new. The main drawback of this strategy is that there is no guarantee that the final plan is optimal or near optimal. The one-phase optimization strategy is used to overcome this problem.

In Subsection 5.6.1, we present an algorithm that exploits pipelined parallelism for processing multiway join queries when the hash join method is used to evaluate joins. It will be shown that the right deep tree structure is most suitable for this kind of parallelism. This algorithm follows the one-phase optimization strategy. In Subsection 5.6.2, some techniques for scheduling and allocation of processors will be discussed. The two-phase optimization strategy is employed in these techniques. A large number of algorithms for processing multiway join queries have been proposed in the literature. Readers who are interested in more algorithms are referred to the Bibliographic Notes.

5.6.1 Hashing-Based Pipelined Parallelism for Right Deep Trees

With a hashing-based join algorithm, a join between R_0 and R_1 in a uniprocessor environment is carried out in two steps: (1) use the left input relation to build an in-memory hash table and (2) use the right input relation to probe the hash table. We call the first step *build* and the second step *probe*. A *scan* of the corresponding relation is needed for both *build* and *probe*. The hash join of $R_1 \bowtie R_0$ can be graphically represented. Figure 5.12 shows how the join is mapped to a hash join–based implementation. In this figure, S_i represents a scan of R_i, B_1 represents the building of a hash table T_1, and P_1 represents the probing of T_1. Thin arrows are used to indicate the producer/consumer relationships. For example, $S_1 \rightarrow B_1$ means that the tuples of R_1 scanned in by S_1 are used by B_1 to build T_1. Thick arrows between dotted boxes indicate the sequence of actions. For example, the thick arrow in Figure 5.12 indicates

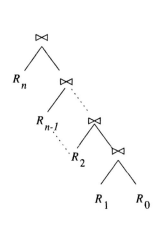

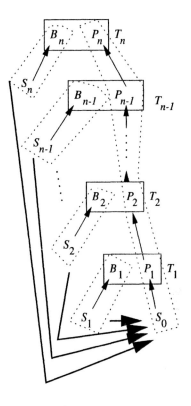

(a) Right deep tree   **(b)** Operator dependency graph

FIGURE 5.13   **Operator Dependency Graph of an *n*-way Join Query**

that the hash table must be completely built before the probe can start. Such a graph is called an *operator dependency graph.*

Now consider the right deep tree for an $(n + 1)$-way join query $R_n \bowtie R_{n-1} \bowtie \cdots \bowtie R_0$ as shown in Figure 5.13(a). The operator dependency graph of the tree is shown in Figure 5.13(b). This figure indicates that all hash tables can be built by different processors in parallel and after all hash tables T_i's are built, the n joins can be carried out in a pipelined manner by n processors, starting from the scanning of R_0, followed by the probing of T_1 using the tuples of R_0 as they arrive, followed by the probing of T_2 using the tuples in the result of the first join, ..., and ending with the probing of T_n using the tuples in the result of the first $n-1$ joins. The length of the pipeline is the same as the number of joins. Clearly, a high degree of parallelism can be achieved with this approach. First, all hash tables can be built in parallel. Second, pipelined parallelism of a long pipeline can also be achieved. Two other advantages associated with this approach are (1) it can largely avoid the difficult problem of estimating the sizes of intermediate results since all hash table buildings and probings are based on the original relations and (2) it can produce the first tuples in the final result very quickly. For

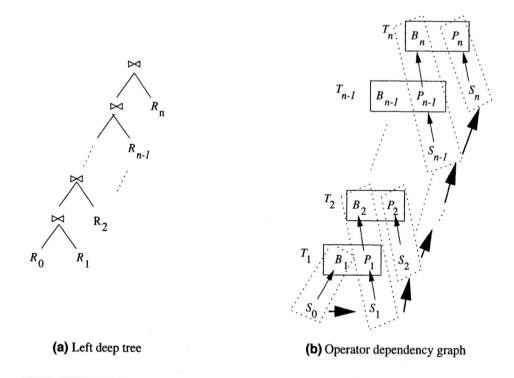

(a) Left deep tree   **(b)** Operator dependency graph

FIGURE 5.14   A Left deep Tree and Its Operator Dependency Graph

example, the first tuple in the final result may be produced as soon as the first tuple scanned in from R_0 is processed. Note that, in principle, each join (i.e., probe) itself can be partitioned into multiple joins among different processors to achieve intraoperation parallelism.

For join query $R_0 \bowtie R_1 \bowtie \cdots \bowtie R_n$, the corresponding left deep tree as well as its operator dependency graph are shown in Figure 5.14(a) and (b), respectively. From this figure, it can be seen that hash tables can only be built one at a time, and the joins can only be carried out in different short pipelines. For example, scan S_1 cannot start before hash table T_1 has been completely built by B_1. When the tuples of R_1 are scanned to probe T_1, the join result can be immediately used to build hash table T_2. However, the length of the pipeline is rather short. Clearly, when compared with the operator dependency graph for a right deep tree, the operator dependency graph for a left deep tree provides much less opportunity for parallelism. Based on similar analysis as above, it can be shown that the degree of pipelined parallelism that can be achieved by the operator dependency graph for a bushy tree is between those for left and right deep trees.

The above discussion for right deep trees assumed that all hash tables can be held in the memory for the duration of processing the query. If some hash table cannot be held in the memory because of limited memory resources, then the performance of this approach will be seriously damaged. One reason for memory shortage is that some processing nodes are forced to hold too many hash tables. For example, this could occur when the number of joining

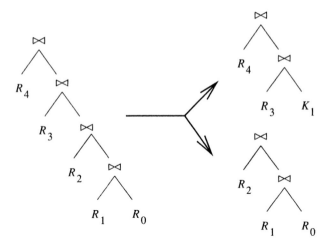

FIGURE 5.15   **Breaking a Right Deep Tree into Two Segments**

relations is greater than the number of processing processors or when some nodes contain fragments of multiple relations. A memory scheduling algorithm called *right deep scheduling* can be used to solve the memory shortage problem. The basic idea of this algorithm is very simple: the number of hash tables that need to be held in the memory at the same time can be reduced if a fewer number of relations are joined. Based on this idea, this algorithm first breaks the right deep join tree into disjoint segments and then processes these segments one at a time in certain sequence. Each of the segments contains a right deep tree. For example, the right deep join tree on the left in Figure 5.15 can be broken into two segments as shown on the right. The lower right deep tree can be evaluated using the approach described above. Let K_1 be the result of evaluating the lower right deep tree. Note that K_1 becomes the rightmost leaf node of the upper right deep tree so it can be used to probe the remaining hash tables.

After the right deep tree in a segment is evaluated, the memory space occupied by the corresponding hash tables can be released and then used to evaluate the right deep tree in the next segment.

The above right deep scheduling algorithm is known as the *Static Right Deep Scheduling* algorithm as it breaks the right deep tree into segments before any segment is processed. In contrast, the *Dynamic Right Deep Scheduling* algorithm breaks the right deep tree into segments dynamically as described below. The hash tables' relations $R_1, \ldots, R_n$ are built in a bottom-up manner. After the hash table for R_i is built, it is checked to see if there is enough memory left for the hash table for R_{i+1}. If the answer is yes, then the hash table for R_{i+1} is built; else, a segment containing $\{R_0, \ldots, R_i\}$ is formed. After this segment is evaluated, the above process is repeated starting with R_{i+1}.

In the above algorithms, the result of evaluating a segment is always used for probing. A more flexible algorithm is to allow the result to be used for building a hash table. As a result, join trees are no longer restricted to right deep trees. A further generalization is to consider join trees that are *segmented right deep trees*, which consist of a number of right

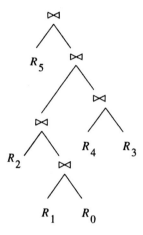

FIGURE 5.16   A Segmented Right Deep Tree

deep segments. Figure 5.16 shows an example of a segmented right deep tree with two right deep tree segments. Note that a right deep tree is a special case of a segmented right deep tree. Allowing a segmented right deep tree improves the search space for better execution strategies. As a result, better performance can be achieved.

5.6.2 Processor Allocation for Multiway Join Queries

As pointed out earlier, the *two-phase optimization* strategy separates the generation of join orders and methods from the allocation of resources. In this subsection, we assume that join orders and methods have been determined by a uniprocessor query optimizer so we can focus on the problem of resource allocation. Clearly, the join order may not be unique if the join tree is a bushy tree (i.e., the order could be *a partial order*). In this subsection, sort merge join is assumed to be the join method for all joins. To further simplify the problem, we assume that each node has the same memory and disk resources and we do not need to concern ourselves with their allocations. This assumption enables us to concentrate on the allocation of processors only.

When allocating processors to joins in a multiway join query, the following two issues must be taken into consideration.

Execution dependency. A join order is depicted by the corresponding join tree. When the sort merge join is used, this means that the processing of a join J cannot be started before the processings of the child joins of J in the join tree are completed. This implies that we should only allocate processors to J after the child joins of J are completed since early allocation can only cause the corresponding processor to be idle.

Number of processors per join. The issue here is how many processors should be allocated to process each join. Although it is generally true that the response time of processing a join can be reduced when we increase the number of processors used to

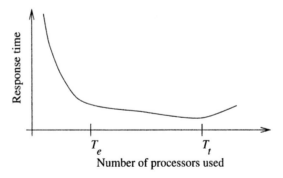

FIGURE 5.17   Illustrating T_e and T_t

process the join, a threshold exists on the number such that when the number of processors exceeds this threshold, the response time will increase rather than decrease. The
reason is briefly discussed in Subsection 5.2.4. In fact, for each join, two thresholds
can be observed, one is for the *minimum response time*, denoted by T_t, and the other is
for the *best execution efficiency*, denoted by T_e. When the number of processors used
to process the join reaches T_t, the minimum response time can be achieved and using
any additional processor has only adverse effect. The *execution efficiency* of using n
processors to evaluate a join is defined as

$$\frac{response\ time\ using\ one\ processor}{n \cdot (response\ time\ using\ n\ processors)}$$

When $n = 1$, the execution efficiency is 1. Clearly, linear speedup will keep the
execution efficiency at 1 and sublinear speedup will cause the execution efficiency to
be less than 1. Therefore, a good execution efficiency can be achieved as long as the
speedup is near linear. T_e indicates the point that using additional processors causes
sharp decline of the execution efficiency (see Figure 5.17).

For a join between two relations R and S, the curve in Figure 5.17 can be approximated by the curve of the following hyperbolic function:

$$RT = \frac{a\,|R| + b\,|S| + c\,|R \bowtie S|}{n} + d \cdot n$$

where RT is the response time when n processors are used and a, b, c, and d are constant
parameters associated with the join method used (e.g., nested loop and sort merge) and
the communication protocol between the processors. T_t and T_e can then be determined
from the curve.

The following are some heuristic algorithms for processor allocation.

Sequential Execution. Joins in the partial order are executed one by one, and all processors (or T_t processors if there are more processors) are used to execute each join.
This algorithm exploits maximum intraoperation parallelism and exploits no interoperation parallelism. *Execution dependency* is easily taken care of by executing the

joins in the partial order. However, this algorithm does not take *execution efficiency* into consideration.

Time-Efficiency Point. For each join whose execution can be started according to the join order, allocate T processors for its execution, where $T = c \cdot T_e + (1 - c) \cdot T_t$ for some parameter c, $0 \leq c \leq 1$. Clearly, T is between T_e and T_t.

When $c = 1$, T becomes T_e. This means that a good execution efficiency can be achieved through this allocation. However, sometimes having a good efficiency may not be good enough for the overall response time. The main reason is that the response time using T_e processors may be substantially longer than that using T_t processors, and it is possible that the execution of a certain join is the bottleneck in the query execution. As an example, consider the scenario in which join J1 is the parent of J2 and J3 in the join tree. Suppose that J1 cannot start before J2 and J3 complete. If J2 has completed and J3 has not, then the execution of J3 becomes the bottleneck. In this case, it makes more sense to complete J4 as soon as possible by allocating more processors to it. When $c = 0$, T becomes T_t. This means that the join can be completed in the shortest time possible. However, sometimes T_t can be substantially larger than T_e and the improvement using more than T_e processors is insignificant. In this case, it may be wise to use some of the processors for other purposes, such as processing the next join that can be started in the order. By properly choosing the parameter c for each join based on the number of processors that are currently available and whether or not the join is likely to be a bottleneck, this algorithm can strike a balance between the minimum response time and the execution efficiency for this join. More formally, this algorithm can be described as follows.

Let N be the number of processors available for the query. For join J, let $T_e(J)$ and $T_t(J)$ be the two thresholds for the minimum response time and the best execution efficiency, respectively, and let $T(J) = c \cdot T_e(J) + (1 - c) \cdot T_t(J)$. This algorithm consists of two procedures, one for processor allocation and the other for processor deallocation. Processor deallocation releases the processors once the execution of a join is completed. There is a producer/consumer relationship between these two procedures: the deallocator (producer) produces (releases) newly available processors, and the allocator (consumer) consumes the processors. Below is the procedure for processor allocation.

For the next join J in the join order that can be processed (i.e., the execution dependency is complied with) until all joins are considered

If T(J) ≤ N, then
    { Allocate T(J) processors for J;
        N = N − T(J); }

This algorithm exploits both intraoperation and interoperation parallelism. The former is achieved by using multiple processors to evaluate each join (i.e., partitioned parallelism), and the latter is accomplished by permitting several independent joins to be performed simultaneously (i.e., independent parallelism). One drawback of this algorithm is that the allocation is done locally for each join without a global picture. As a result, it is possible that the overall response time of the query is large. For example, if the join tree is not balanced, then finishing the shorter and smaller subtree early does not reduce the response time since the bottleneck is on the deeper and larger subtree.

Synchronous Top-Down Allocation. This algorithm assumes that for each internal node in the input join tree, the total cost of evaluating the subtree rooted at the node is known as the *result of the first phase* in the two-phase optimization strategy. The allocation starts with the root node and works its way to the leaf nodes in a top-down fashion. In contrast, both the Sequential Execution and the Time-Efficiency Point algorithms follow a bottom-up strategy since joins at lower levels in the tree are allocated the processors earlier. With the *Synchronous Top-down Allocation* method, no actual evaluation will occur during the allocation phase. The joins are still evaluated in a bottom-up fashion after the allocation phase. In contrast, the first two algorithms can interleave allocation with actual execution.

Let N be the total number of processors available for the query. This algorithm can be described as follows:

1. Allocate $\min\{N, T_t(\text{root})\}$ processors to the join at the root. That is, allocate as many as all processors to the join at the root to make sure that the join can be evaluated with the minimum response time. This is reasonable because by the time this join is to be evaluated, it is the only join left.

   Let J be the join for which processors have just been allocated. Let N_J be the number of processors available when join J is considered. When J is the root, $N_J = N$; that is, all processors are available for the join at the root.

2. If J has only one child join J1, then allocate $\min\{N_J, T_t(J1)\}$ processors to J1. In other words, in this case, use as many as all available processors for J to make sure that J1 can be evaluated with the minimum response time. If J has two child joins J1 and J2, then partition the N_J processors into two clusters that are allocated to the subtrees rooted at J1 and J2, respectively. The number of processors in each cluster is chosen to be proportional to the total cost of the join node to which the cluster is to be assigned. For example, if $N_J = 10$ and the total costs associated with the two join nodes J1 and J2 are 60 and 40, respectively, then 6 processors will be allocated to the subtree rooted at J1 (i.e., make $N_{J1} = 6$) and 4 to the subtree rooted at J2 ($N_{J2} = 4$). Such an allocation policy is intended to balance the times needed to evaluate the two subtrees rooted at J1 and J2, in the hope that the overall response time can be minimized. Note that allocating N_{J1} processors to a subtree rooted at J1 is different from allocating N_{J1} processors to the join J1. The former means that the number of processors available for join J1 is N_{J1}, whereas the latter should be $\min\{N_{J1}, T_t(J1)\}$. Similar comments can be made about J2.

   Replace J by J1 (or J2) and repeat this step until the allocation is done for all joins.

This algorithm also exploits both intraoperation and interoperation parallelism. One potential problem of this algorithm is that the number of processors for a subtree could become too small to achieve meaningful parallel processing. One remedy is to stop further partitioning the processors when the number of processors is getting small, and evaluate the joins at the lower levels sequentially (i.e., apply the Sequential Execution algorithm).

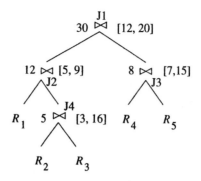

FIGURE 5.18   Illustrating Different Processor Allocation Algorithms

Example 5.9 Consider the initial join tree as shown in Figure 5.18. Each join node is associated with two items. The number on the left of a node indicates the total cost that is needed to evaluate the subtree rooted at the node and the number pair on the right denotes $[T_e, T_t]$ for the join. Suppose 20 processors are available for the query. When the Sequential Execution algorithm is used, the allocation plan is 16 processors for J4 initially, followed by 15 processors for J3; then 9 processors for J2; and finally 20 processors for J1. When the Time-Efficiency Point algorithm is used, one possible allocation plan is 10 processors for J4 and 10 processors for J3 initially; then 9 processors for J2; and finally 20 processors for J1. When the Synchronous Top-Down Allocation algorithm is used, 20 processors will be allocated to J1, followed by 12 processors for the subtree rooted at J2 (9 processors for J2) and 8 processors for J3; finally, 12 processors for J4.   ■

Preliminary experimental results indicate that the Synchronous Top-Down Allocation algorithm is superior to the other two algorithms.

Exercises

5.1   Discuss how each of interquery parallelism, interoperation parallelism, and intraoperation parallelism can improve the throughput of a system.

5.2   Discuss the advantages and disadvantages of the three partitioning algorithms discussed in Section 5.2.

5.3   Suppose we have seven tasks and four processors. Suppose further that the execution times in milliseconds of the seven tasks on a single processor are 10, 8, 7, 5, 4, 3, and 3. Allocate the tasks to the processors using the best-fit method. What is the total elapsed time needed to finish all the tasks? Is there a better way to allocate these tasks?

5.4   Provide a one-input-stream and many-output-stream parallel sorting algorithm. Does your algorithm have partitioned parallelism and/or pipelined parallelism?

5.5 Exchange the input fragment assigned to processor P2 with that assigned to processor P3 in Figure 5.6 and run the Block Bitonic Sort algorithm with the new input.

5.6 Consider the two-pass sorting algorithm discussed in Section 5.3.3. Suppose N workstations are used and each has M MB available memory. Determine the maximum size of the data that can be sorted using the two-pass sorting algorithm. (Hint: Try to manipulate the size of the memory buffer for each run during the merge step and the size of the output buffer.)

5.7 As noted in the second remark following Example 5.6, nine cases can be identified depending on whether one or both operand relations are partitioned and how they are partitioned. Three cases have been discussed in Section 5.5.2. Identify and discuss the remaining six cases.

5.8 Consider a single processor environment. Suppose the smaller operand relation S of join $R \bowtie S$ occupies M pages and the hash table of S occupies $1.4 \cdot M$ pages. Suppose a memory buffer of K pages is available. Determine the number of times a tuple of S could be read in the memory from disk in the worst case if

(a) Simple Hash Join is used;

(b) GRACE Hash Join is used, assuming the hash table of each fragment of S generated in the fragment-generating phase will not exceed K pages;

(c) Hybrid Hash Join is used, assuming the hash table of each fragment of S generated in the fragment-generating phase will not exceed K pages.

5.9 Assume the same notations used in Exercise 5.8. Determine the number of times a tuple of S must be read in the memory from disk in the best case if

(a) Simple Hash Join is used;

(b) GRACE Hash Join is used, assuming the hash table of each fragment of S generated in the fragment-generating phase will not exceed K pages;

(c) Hybrid Hash Join is used, assuming the hash table of each fragment of S generated in the fragment-generating phase will not exceed K pages.

5.10 Assume the same notations used in Exercise 5.8. Show that if $K > \sqrt{1.4 \cdot M}$ and fragments of equal size can be generated, then no hash table overflow can occur when GRACE Hash Join is used.

5.11 Show that for an n-way join query with m possible methods for each join, the total number of possible execution plans is

$$m^{n-1} \cdot \binom{2(n-1)}{n-1} \frac{(n-1)!}{2^{n-1}}$$

5.12 Consider the bushy tree in Figure 5.11. Suppose Hybrid Hash Join is to be used to process the joins. Describe an efficient strategy to process the joins.

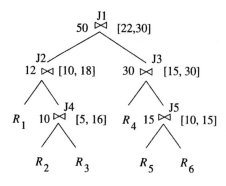

FIGURE 5.19   Join Tree for Exercise 5.13

5.13 Consider the initial join tree as shown in Figure 5.19. Each join node is associated with two items. The number on the left of a node indicates the total cost that is needed to evaluate the subtree rooted at the node and the number pair on the right denotes $[T_e, T_t]$ for the join. Suppose 30 processors are available for the query. Provide the processor allocation plan based on **(a)** the Sequential Execution algorithm; **(b)** the Time-Efficiency Point algorithm; and **(c)** the Synchronous Top-Down Allocation algorithm.

Bibliographic Notes

References [104, 370] are excellent, recent, survey-type articles on parallel database systems. A book containing a number of important papers related to query processing in parallel database systems has been published, with extensive remarks, by H. Lu, B-C. Ooi, and K-L. Tan recently [246].

The three architectures for parallel database systems, namely shared-memory, shared-disk, and shared-nothing architectures, were first carefully analyzed and compared in [346]. The conclusion is that the shared-nothing architecture has many good qualities and it is the only architecture that can scale to a large number of processors. An interesting study of the three architectures based on experiment is reported in [33]. Berkeley's XPRS is reported in [349], and IBM's 3090 system is discussed in [365]. DEC's VAXcluster system is reported in [212]. Teradata's DBC/1012 system is discussed in [96, 97]. Tandem's NonStop SQL is described in [358]. IBM's DB2 PE is reported in [17]. Wisconsin's Gamma prototype system is discussed in [103] and MCC's Bubba in [42, 43, 89].

The three partitioning strategies discussed in this chapter are used in Wisconsin's Gamma system [103]. More complicated partitioning strategies can be found in [89, 140, 176]. Load balancing in the presence of data skew has been the subject of many research activities in recent years [108, 176, 177, 178, 205, 216, 276, 294].

Parallel sorting algorithms have been studied extensively [21, 24, 34, 107, 207, 243, 317]. The first two parallel sorting algorithms presented in this chapter are adopted from [34]. The two algorithms can also be found in a survey paper [35]. A variation of the Block Bitonic

Sort algorithm can be found in [266]. Batcher's Bitonic Sorting Network is presented in [19]. Extending Batcher's Bitonic Sorting Network for block-based sorting is proposed in [20]. Modern sorting algorithms deal with input of very large size (on the order of gigabytes) [280, 9]. NOW Sort algorithms are discussed in [9].

The algorithm for removing duplicates for selection and projection queries without sorting is from [34]. A parallel Nested Loop Join algorithm is presented in [34]. The variation presented in this chapter takes index information into consideration. A more elaborate study of parallel Nested Loop Join algorithms is reported in [106]. Sort Merge Join [38], Simple Hash Join [105], and Hybrid Hash Join [105] are first proposed for centralized systems and are later extended into parallel algorithms [101]. GRACE Hash Join is proposed in [206]. A performance analysis and a study on memory boundaries of these join algorithms in a centralized environment can be found in [327]. The join algorithms are widely used in commercial and prototype parallel database systems. For example, Sort Merge Join is used in Teradata, Tandem, and Gamma; Simple Hash Join is used in Tandem and Gamma; GRACE Hash Join is employed in SDC (Super Database Computer [205]) and Gamma; and Hybrid Hash Join is implemented in Tandem and Gamma. Performance studies of these parallel join algorithms can be found in [46, 102, 321, 371].

Multiway join processing in a multiprocessor environment has been studied extensively [68, 70, 132, 170, 174, 240, 247, 322]. The main source in exploiting pipelined parallelism to process right deep trees used in this chapter is from [322]. More information about employing segmented right deep trees can be found in [68]. Studies that consider bushy trees can be found in [68, 221, 247, 330]. The processor allocation algorithms presented in this chapter are from [70]. More sophisticated resource allocation algorithms that take into consideration the sharing of multiple resources can be found in [170, 135]. Dynamic resource allocation techniques in parallel database systems can be found in [258, 299]. A comparison of several multiway join algorithms is reported in [379].

6

Processing Fuzzy Relational Queries

In standard relational systems, both user queries and data in the database are assumed to be precise. In practice, this assumption may not hold, i.e., there may be imprecisions in data or queries. Consider the population of a city. It is unlikely that the exact number of residents in the city at a given time is known. Even if the population is determined precisely at a given time, it will change due to deaths, births, or migration. Similarly, the weight of a person will change over time. Thus, the occurrences of imprecise data in databases are natural. We believe that many users would prefer to submit imprecise queries than to submit exact queries. For example, a user may want to find all potential friends who are young, without specifying an exact age. In general, the following three types of imprecisions may arise:

1. Queries are imprecise but data in the database are precise.

2. Queries are precise but data in the database are imprecise.

3. Both queries and data are imprecise.

Since cases 1 and 2 are subsumed under case 3, it is sufficient to consider case 3 only.

In Section 6.1, the concept of a fuzzy set and that of a fuzzy term are defined. In Section 6.2, the degree to which a tuple that may contain fuzzy data satisfies a fuzzy query is determined. In Section 6.3, basic techniques in transforming a nested relational query to unnested relational queries are reviewed. The techniques are intended to speed up query processing for standard nested SQL queries. In Section 6.4, these unnesting techniques after

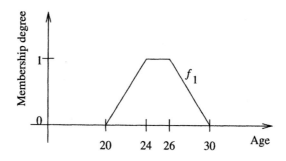

FIGURE 6.1 *Membership Function for Fuzzy Label energetic*

suitable modifications are applied to fuzzy relational queries and databases. In Section 6.5, context-dependent interpretations of fuzzy terms are briefly discussed.

6.1 Fuzzy Set and Fuzzy Term

A classical set S can be represented by a *membership function* f such that if x is an element of S, then $f(x) = 1$; otherwise, $f(x) = 0$. A *fuzzy set* also has a membership function f, but the range of f is the interval [0, 1] instead of just 0 and 1. The membership function can be continuous or discrete. For example, suppose the domain of the attribute Age of persons is [1, 100]. Then the membership function for the fuzzy set that represents the imprecise value *young* can be given as follows. The function is a straight line with $y = 1$ from age = 1 to age = 20, the value of y decreases monotonically after age = 20, it reaches the value 0 when age = 35, and it stays at 0 afterward. If the domain of Age is the discrete set $\{1, 2, \ldots, 100\}$, then the range is $fage(i)$, $1 \leq i \leq 100$, where *fage* is the membership function. Clearly, if the domain contains many discrete values, storing those values and retrieving the appropriate membership value for a given value in the domain can be expensive. In that situation, it may be appropriate to store a continuous function that approximates the discrete values. Clearly, in that situation, the continuous function needs to be efficiently computed.

As indicated previously, imprecisions in data and in queries are natural. Thus, we introduce *fuzzy terms* to indicate imprecision. A fuzzy term is an imprecise value under some attribute. It is either a *fuzzy label* or a *fuzzy number*. For example, under the attribute Age, there could be fuzzy labels such as *energetic* or fuzzy numbers such as *about 30*. Each fuzzy term of an attribute A is characterized precisely by a fuzzy set, which has a membership function. The function has a domain of values, say $D = [L, U]$, in the domain of A. The membership function takes on values in [0, 1]. For example, the attribute Age has domain [1, 100] and the membership function of the fuzzy label *energetic* has domain [20, 30]. (Actually, the domain for *energetic* is [1, 100], but for any value outside [20, 30], the membership function gives 0. In the remaining part of this chapter, with the exception of the last section, the term *domain* refers to the portion that gives nontrivial membership values.) The membership function for *energetic*, f_1, is given by the trapezoid shown in Figure 6.1.

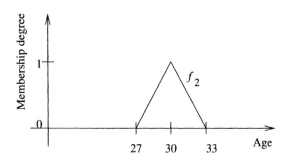

FIGURE 6.2 *Membership Function for Fuzzy Number **about 30***

The interpretation of the membership function f_1 in Figure 6.1 is as follows. The membership of age values between 1 and 19 is zero; i.e., age values in this range are considered not energetic. The membership function f_1 for age values between 20 and 24 is a linear increasing function that has value 0 at age 20 and increases to value 1 at age 24; i.e., age 20 is still considered not energetic, but age 24 is definitely energetic, and ages between 20 and 24 are to some extent energetic. The extent to which they are energetic is determined by the membership function, a higher function value indicating a greater extent of being energetic. From age 24 to age 26, the membership function value is 1, indicating that *energetic* is fully satisfied. Finally, the membership function is a linear decreasing function from age = 26 to age = 30. Similarly, the membership function of the fuzzy number *about 30* has domain [27, 33]. It is the function f_2 as shown in Figure 6.2.

It is possible to add *qualifiers* to fuzzy labels. The result of the addition is another fuzzy term. Usually, the membership function of the new (qualified) fuzzy term can be generated from that of the original fuzzy term. For example, suppose the membership function of the fuzzy label *young* is a straight line with $y = 1$ from $x = 1$ to $x = 20$, followed by a straight line from the point ($x = 20$, $y = 1$) to the point ($x = 35$, $y = 0$). The interpretation is that a person is definitely young from age = 1 to age = 20; after age = 20, the degree of being young goes down monotonically until age = 35 is reached, at which point the person is considered not young; persons with age greater than 35 are definitely not young. Consider adding the qualifier *very* to the fuzzy label *young* to form the new fuzzy label *very young*. A possible membership function, $g(\ )$, for this label is given by $g(x) = (f(x))^2$, where $f(\ )$ is the membership function for *young*. Clearly, $g(x)$ is a straight line with $y = 1$ from $x = 1$ to $x = 20$, as $f(x) = 1$ for x in [1, 20]. For x in (20, 35), $g(x)$ will be smaller than $f(x)$, as $f(x)$ is smaller than 1. This seems to be consistent with intuition, as a person with age in (20, 35) is considered closer to *young* than to *very young*. Similarly, the qualifier *fairly* can also be added to *young* to form the fuzzy label *fairly young*. The membership function of *fairly young* can be given by $h(x) = \sqrt{f(x)}$. It is clear that the resulting function $h(x)$ is a straight line $y = 1$ from $x = 1$ to $x = 20$ and that $h(x)$ is greater than $f(x)$ for x in (20, 35). The interpretation is that a person with age in (20, 35) is considered closer to *fairly young* than to *young*.

Thus, each fuzzy term, whether it is a fuzzy label or a fuzzy number, is represented by a membership function on a domain of values in the domain of the attribute; the fuzzy term appears as one of the values in the attribute. A value that is precise is called a *crisp value*. An attribute that contains only crisp values is a *crisp attribute*. In general, a *fuzzy attribute* may contain both crisp and fuzzy values.

6.2 Satisfaction of a Tuple with Respect to a Query

In standard relational databases, a tuple either satisfies a query or it does not. In fuzzy relational databases, a tuple that may contain a fuzzy term may have a degree of satisfaction with respect to a query that may be fuzzy. The degree of satisfaction ranges from 0 to 1, with 0 indicating complete dissatisfaction and 1 indicating complete satisfaction. Values between 0 and 1 indicate different degrees of satisfaction. Thus, satisfaction of a tuple for traditional relational systems corresponds to the special case in which the degree is either 0 or 1. If the degree is 0, the tuple is not shown to the user; otherwise, the tuple is exhibited. Tuples with degrees greater than 0 may be presented to the user in descending order of degree.

6.2.1 Comparison of Two Attribute Values

Consider the fuzzy relation EMP(Name, Sex, Age, Performance) where the attributes Name and Sex are crisp and the attributes Age and Performance are fuzzy. The attribute Performance permits fuzzy labels such as *excellent*, *very good*, *good*, *marginal*, and *poor*. Consider the following SQL query, which is to find the names of all employees who are energetic.

```
select EMP.Name
from EMP
where EMP.Age = 'energetic'
```

Logically, the value, v, of each tuple under the attribute Age is compared against the fuzzy label *energetic*. If the degree resulting from comparing v with *energetic* is greater than 0, then the tuple will be presented to the user; otherwise, it is discarded. We now determine the degree for the comparison. In general, there are three cases:

1. *Both values to be compared are crisp.* (This case does not hold for this example.) In this case, the degree of satisfaction is greater than 0; in fact it equals 1 if and only if the crisp values are identical.

2. *One value is crisp and the other value is fuzzy.* As discussed earlier, a fuzzy term is represented by the membership function. The crisp value, say c, is represented by a vertical line $x = c$. The intersection point of the membership function and the line $x = c$ is the degree of satisfaction. For example, if the membership function is f_1 (see Figure 6.1) and $x = 24$, then the degree is exactly 1; if the membership function is f_1 and $x = 23$, then the degree is 0.75.

3. *Both values are fuzzy.* The degree of satisfaction between two fuzzy terms v_1 and v_2, which is denoted by $d(v_1, v_2)$, is defined to be the *intersection* of the two membership

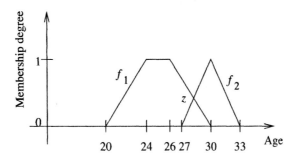

FIGURE 6.3 **Intersection of *energetic* and *about 30***

functions associated with the two fuzzy terms. For example, consider the fuzzy terms *energetic* and *about 30* and their intersection in Figure 6.3. The membership function f_1 in [26, 30] is a linear decreasing function. The membership function of f_2 in [27, 33] is a linear increasing function. Suppose these two linear functions intersect within [27, 30] with value z on the vertical axis (see Figure 6.3). Then the degree $d(energetic, about\ 30)$ $= z$. Clearly, in this case $z > 0$ and therefore the name of the employee having age = 'about 30' is part of the output. If there are multiple intersection points, then the highest intersection value is taken. For example, if the two fuzzy values to be compared are both *energetic*, then there are many intersection points, but the highest value is 1.

The above discussion applies to the equality operator =. It can be extended to the inequality operators, but the extension is not given here. Clearly, the method given above to compute the degree of satisfaction of two fuzzy terms is just one of several ways. Another way is to compute the area of intersection divided by the maximum area of the two membership functions.

6.2.2 Handling Where-Clauses

The where-clause of an SQL statement may contain multiple comparisons connected by AND, OR, and NOT. As an example, the where-clause may consist of EMP.Age = 'energetic' AND EMP.Performance = 'excellent'. For a tuple t of the relation EMP, the evaluation of t.Age with 'energetic' yields a degree d_1 and the evaluation of t.Performance with 'excellent' yields a degree d_2. The degree of the tuple t after the results of the two evaluations are combined is given by $\min\{d_1, d_2\}$.

In general, if the connective AND is specified, the result of combining the degrees is obtained by taking their minimum; if the connective is OR, then the result is obtained by taking the maximum; and if the connective is NOT, then the result is obtained by subtracting the degree from 1. For example, if the degree of t.Age = 'energetic' is d_1, then the result of NOT(t.Age = 'energetic') is $1 - d_1$. Sometimes a tuple t has an initial degree of membership, say d, which indicates the extent to which the tuple belongs to the relation. Suppose the tuple t is evaluated against a fuzzy query and it has a degree of satisfaction d'; then the overall satisfaction of the tuple is $\min\{d, d'\}$.

TABLE 6.1   **Computation of Satisfaction Degree**

	AND	min
Where-clause	OR	max
	NOT	subtract from 1
Tuple has initial degree d and has degree d' from where-clause.		$\min\{d, d'\}$
Select-clause		max

6.2.3 Handling Select-Clauses

We now discuss the output produced by a fuzzy SQL query. As an example, consider the query below:

```
select EMP.sex
from EMP
where EMP.Age = 'energetic'
```

Assume that there are multiple employees of the same sex, say female, satisfying EMP. Age = 'energetic'. Then a tuple (female, df) will be produced, where df is the degree of this tuple. The value df is obtained by taking the maximum of the degrees of all tuples of the form (female, d_i), where d_i is the degree of a tuple t after evaluating t.Age = 'energetic'. Clearly, tuples with degree equal to 0 need not be considered. Similarly, a tuple of the form (male, dm) will be produced, assuming that there is at least one male employee satisfying the age condition with degree greater than 0.

In general, after a set of tuples with degrees greater than 0 is obtained after the evaluation of the where-clause, these tuples are projected on the target attributes as specified in the select-clause of the query. If a set of tuples, say S, having the same projected values on the target attributes produces a single tuple t, then the degree of t in the output is the maximum of the degrees of the tuples in S.

A summary of the different conventions associated with the evaluation and output of a fuzzy query is given in Table 6.1.

We note that the description given above is a logical description of what the output should be. The implementation of a fuzzy relational system could be different from what has been described and yet produce the same answers. For example, instead of comparing each tuple against *energetic* in the above query, the system may have an index on the attribute Age. With the given fuzzy label *energetic*, the lower and upper bounds of the domain for its membership function, namely 20 and 30, respectively, are determined. Then the index is utilized to search for tuples containing fuzzy terms with domains that are either within I = [20, 30] or intersect I. It is necessary to include the latter set of tuples, as they will satisfy the query with degree greater than 0. For example, the fuzzy term *about 31*, which has a membership function similar to that given in Figure 6.2 but with the peak of the function at 31 instead of 30, will overlap [20, 30]. Suppose the domain of each fuzzy term is an interval of length at most L; then it is sufficient to search the index from $20-L$ to $30+L$. Multidimensional structures (see Chapter 8) can also be utilized to facilitate the search.

6.3 Transformation of Nested SQL Queries to Unnested SQL Queries

Nested SQL queries are very common in relational database systems. In this section, we will review some of the basic techniques that transform nested nonfuzzy SQL queries into unnested ones. The latter queries are usually more efficient in execution. In the next section, the transformation from nested fuzzy SQL queries into unnested ones will be discussed. Some of the techniques given in this section will be applicable to fuzzy SQL queries as well.

Nested SQL queries have been classified into different categories. Consider a two-level nested query containing an outer subquery and an inner subquery. Instead of enumerating all the categories and providing techniques for each category, we will concentrate only on the following two representative categories:

J: join between the inner and the outer subqueries

JA: join between the two subqueries together with an aggregation in the predicate connecting the two subqueries

We will make use of the following relational schemas to illustrate the key ideas. Suppose there are two companies C1 and C2 whose employees are in the following two relations:

EMP-C1(Name, Title, Age, Performance, Salary)
EMP-C2(Name, Title, Age, Performance, Salary)

Assume that all data are crisp, i.e., there are no fuzzy data.

The following SQL query, which asks for the name of every employee in company C1 who is 30 years old, has the same title, and makes the same salary as an employee in company C2 who has excellent performance.

```
select EMP-C1.Name
from EMP-C1
where EMP-C1.Age = 30 and EMP-C1.Salary in
      (select EMP-C2.Salary
        from EMP-C2
        where EMP-C1.Title = EMP-C2.Title
            and EMP-C2.Performance = 'excellent')
```

In this nested query, there is a join on the attribute Title between the outer query involving EMP-C1 and the inner query involving EMP-C2. A naive way to evaluate this query is to check each tuple t_1 in relation EMP-C1 for satisfaction of the age condition (equal to 30) and then to check its salary against the output of the inner query. In order to evaluate the inner query, the title of t_1 is obtained and is substituted into the inner query. If there is no index on Title or on Performance for the relation EMP-C2, then each tuple t_2 in the relation EMP-C2 needs to be checked against the title of t_1 and against *excellent* in the attribute Performance. Thus, for each tuple in EMP-C1, all tuples in EMP-C2 are checked. If there are n_1 tuples in the relation EMP-C1 and n_2 tuples in the relation EMP-C2, this naive evaluation will run in time $O(n_1 \cdot n_2)$. This query can be shown to be equivalent to the following query.

```
select EMP-C1.Name
from EMP-C1, EMP-C2
where EMP-C1.Age = 30 and EMP-C1.Title = EMP-C2.Title
      and EMP-C2.Performance = 'excellent'
      and EMP-C1.Salary = EMP-C2.Salary
```

This query is not a nested query, as there is no inner query. The where-clause in the unnested query contains all the predicates that occur in the original nested query, with the exception of the "in" predicate. The "in" predicate is replaced by the equality predicate. This process works for all queries of type J in which the connection between the inner and outer subqueries is the "in" predicate. The transformation from a nested query to an equivalent unnested query is called an *unnest procedure*.

One way to process the unnested query is as follows. The tuples of the relation EMP-C1 are compared against the value 30 specified on attribute Age. Let the resulting relation be denoted by EMP-C1$'$. Similarly, processing of the tuples of EMP-C2 on the attribute Performance results in EMP-C2$'$. The tuples of the relation EMP-C1$'$ are sorted in ascending order according to their salary values. Similarly, the tuples of the relation EMP-C2$'$ are also sorted in ascending order on the same attribute. Then the tuples of the two relations are merged, starting from the first tuple from each relation. The merging process consists of comparing v_1 = t_1.Salary, where t_1 is the current tuple in relation EMP-C1$'$, with $v_2 = t_2$.Salary, where t_2 is the current tuple in relation EMP-C2$'$. If $v_1 = v_2$, then gather all tuples of EMP-C1$'$ having the same value v_1 into a set S_1. These tuples are in adjacent locations, since they are sorted on Salary. Similarly, the tuples of EMP-C2$'$ having the same value v_2 are gathered to form S_2. For each pair of tuples, one from the set S_1 and the other from the set S_2, check if they have the same value on the attribute Title. If they are the same, the name of EMP-C1$'$ is outputted. If $v_1 > v_2$, then examine the tuple after S_2, compare it against t_1, and ignore tuples in S_2 as they will not join with later tuples of v_1; otherwise (i.e., if $v_1 < v_2$), examine the tuple after S_1, compare it against t_2, and ignore tuples in S_1. The process of merging tuples of the two relations continues until one or both relations run out of tuples.

Comparing tuples of EMP-C1 against the value on Age takes $O(n_1)$ time, even in the absence of indexes. Similarly, comparing tuples of EMP-C2 against the value on Performance takes $O(n_2)$ time. Sorting the resulting relations takes time $O(n_1 \log n_1) + O(n_2 \log n_2)$ time, even if the selections do not reduce the relations. The merge of the two relations on Salary takes $O(n_1 + n_2)$ time, assuming that the total size of the Cartesian products of the sets having the same salaries (sets of the form S_1, S_2 given above) is no larger than $O(n_1 + n_2)$. Thus the complexity for the unnested query is $O(n_1 \log n_1 + n_2 \log n_2 + n_1 + n_2)$. (For this specific query, which requires no output from C2, the output is definitely bounded by $O(n_1)$. In order to guard against a large Cartesian product, S_1 and S_2 can be sorted on Title, but this is usually unnecessary in practice.) This complexity is usually much less than the complexity of the naive way to process the nested query.

We now consider the second type of nested queries (JA), in which there is at least one join between the inner and outer subqueries and the connection between the two subqueries involves an aggregate operation. The following two relational schemas will be used for illustration:

EMP(E-name, D-name, Salary)
DEPT(D-name, Revenue, #emp)

D-Name	Revenue	#emp
Toy	100,000	3
Shoe	150,000	2

Relation DEPT

E-name	D-name	Salary
John	Toy	20,000
Mary	Toy	30,000
Peter	Toy	40,000
Joseph	Shoe	90,000
Bill	Shoe	100,000

Relation EMP

FIGURE 6.4   Two Relation Instances

D-name	Total
Toy	90,000
Shoe	190,000

FIGURE 6.5   Relation T-SAL

where E-name and D-name are employee name and department name, respectively, and #emp is the number of positions allocated (but not necessarily filled) to a department. The following SQL query is for finding the name of every department having fewer than 20 allocated positions and having a revenue less than the sum of the salaries of those employees working in that department.

```
select DEPT.D-name
from DEPT
where DEPT.#emp < 20 and DEPT.Revenue <
     (select sum(EMP.Salary)
       from EMP
       where EMP.D-name - DEPT.D-name)
```

Suppose the relations have the tuples given in Figure 6.4. Since the query requires us to compare the revenue of each department with the sum of the salaries of the employees working in that department, we can compute the latter quantity for each department using the aggregate operator sum. This can be obtained by the following SQL query.

```
select D-name, sum(EMP.Salary) into T-SAL(D-name, Total)
from EMP
group by D-name
```

The result of the SQL query is the relation shown in Figure 6.5.

After the relation T-SAL is obtained, a simple equijoin with the Department relation on D-name and an inequality join with the Department relation on Revenue will produce the desired result. This is accomplished by the following SQL query.

D-name	Revenue	#emp
Toy	100,000	3
Shoe	150,000	2
Clothing	0	5

FIGURE 6.6   Relation DEPT

```
select DEPT.D-name
from DEPT, T-SAL
where DEPT.Revenue < T-SAL.Total and DEPT.D-name = T-SAL.D-name
      and DEPT.#emp < 20
```

Thus, the general strategy is to first apply the same aggregate operator (sum) in the above example) that appears in the predicate connecting the inner and outer subqueries after a group-by operation is performed on the attribute on which the join between the two subqueries is specified (D-name in the above example). Then the resulting relation is joined with the relation in the outer query on the group-by attribute. The above method works for all aggregate operators except the aggregate operator count. It may not work for the count operator for the following reason. Suppose a new department, say the clothing department, is created and five positions are allocated for that department, but no employee for that department has been hired. Then, the relation EMP remains unchanged, but the relation DEPT becomes as shown in Figure 6.6.

Consider the following SQL query, which seeks the name of every department having fewer than 20 allocated positions but having more allocated positions than filled positions.

```
select DEPT.D-name
from DEPT
where DEPT.#emp < 20 and DEPT.#emp >
      (select count(EMP.Name)
       from EMP
       where EMP.D-name = DEPT.D-name)
```

Processing of the inner query yields a count of 0 when the department Clothing is considered, since the predicate EMP.D-name = DEPT.D-name is not satisfied. The predicate connecting the inner and outer subqueries, DEPT.#emp > 0, is satisfied, and therefore the department Clothing is in the answer of the query. If the query is unnested, as indicated above, the following SQL queries will be produced.

```
select EMP.D-name, count(EMP.Name) into EMP'(D-name, number)
from EMP
group by EMP.D-name
```

```
select DEPT.D-name
from DEPT, EMP'
where DEPT.#emp < 20 and DEPT.#emp > EMP'.number
      and DEPT.D-name = EMP'.D-name
```

Since no employee has been hired into the clothing department, EMP′ will have no tuple with the value *clothing* under the attribute D-name. As a result, when the second SQL query is executed, the predicate DEPT.D-name = EMP′.D-name will not be satisfied for the clothing department, and therefore department Clothing is not included in the answer. Thus, the unnesting technique is inappropriate for the count operator. The error arises when the join predicate appearing in the inner subquery (EMP.D-name = DEPT.D-name in the above example) is not satisfied for some attribute value that causes the count to be zero, but the predicate connecting the inner and outer subqueries is satisfied (DEPT.#emp > count(EMP.name)). In that situation, the original nested query will produce a non-empty result for that attribute value, but the unnested query will produce null for the same attribute value, because the join predicate is not satisfied. We will defer the solution to this problem to the section on unnesting of fuzzy queries. Again, the main reason for unnesting a nested query is to improve the speed of execution. In a nested query, a naive evaluation is likely to yield a time complexity $O(n_1 \cdot n_2)$, where n_i is the size of one of the two relations, because each tuple of one relation is compared against each tuple of the other relation. After the query is unnested, each of the inner and outer queries is processed against the selection predicates, sorted; then two of them are merged. This takes $O(n_1 \log n_1 + n_2 \log n_2) + O(n_1 + n_2)$.

6.4 Unnesting of Fuzzy Queries

There is a key difference between the answer produced by a fuzzy relational system and that produced by a nonfuzzy relational system. The former system produces tuples with different degrees of satisfaction, whereas the latter system produces tuples with degree of satisfaction equal to 1. When an unnesting technique is applied to a nonfuzzy relational system, it is sufficient to show that both the original query and the unnested query have the same set of tuples as the answer. In the case of fuzzy relational systems, not only must the sets of tuples produced by the nested query and the unnested query be the same, the degrees of satisfaction of the tuples in one set need to be identical to those of the tuples in the other set. We again concentrate only on two types of nested queries, namely type J and type JA. It turns out that the unnesting technique for queries of type J given in Section 6.3 also works for nested fuzzy queries. Thus, it is sufficient to study the unnesting of queries of type JA, which is of the following form.

```
select R1.A
from R1
where pred1 and R1.B op1
    (select Agg(R2.C)
     from R2
     where pred2 and R1.D op2 R2.E)
```

where $pred_1$ and $pred_2$ are selection predicates, op_1 is a comparison operator in $\{=, <, >, \geq, \leq\}$, op_2 is the equality comparison operator =, and Agg is an aggregate operator in $\{count, sum, max, min, avg\}$.

As mentioned in the last section, when the aggregate operator count is encountered, an ordinary unnesting technique may produce an erroneous result in the situation in which $R1.D\ op_2$

$R2.E$ is not satisfied. Thus, two cases will be considered. Case 1 handles all aggregate operators except the count operator. Case 2 handles the count operator only.

Case 1: Agg $\neq$ count. A temporary relation will first be created based on the inner subquery. It is given by the following SQL query.

```
select R2.E, Agg(R2.C) into S(E, AC)
from R2
where pred2
group by R2.E
```

Then the following query will be used to produce the answer, which is the same as that of the original nested query.

```
select R1.A
from  R1, S
where pred1 and R1.B op1 S.AC and R1.D op2 S.E
```

The equivalence of the nested and the unnested queries can be illustrated by the following example.

Example 6.1 Consider the relation schemas given before: DEPT(D-name, Revenue, #emp) and EMP(E-name, D-name, Salary), except that the attribute Revenue is now fuzzy, containing fuzzy terms such as *about 100000*. The following SQL query seeks those departments having fewer than 20 allocated positions and having a revenue equal to (in a fuzzy sense) the sum of the salaries of the employees working in that department.

```
select DEPT.D-name
from DEPT
where DEPT.#emp < 20 and DEPT.Revenue -
    (select sum(EMP.Salary)
     from EMP
     where EMP.D-name - DEPT.D-name)
```

In comparison with the general query form, $R1$ is DEPT, A is D-name, $pred_1$ is DEPT.#emp < 20, B is Revenue, op_1 is =, $R2$ is EMP, $pred_2$ is null, D is D-name, E is D-name, C is Salary, Agg is sum, and op_2 is =. Thus, by applying the technique given above, the following two SQL queries will be generated.

```
select EMP.D-name, sum(EMP.Salary) into S(D-name, Sum-sal)
from EMP
group by EMP.D-name

select DEPT.D-name
from  DEPT, S
where DEPT.#emp < 20 and DEPT.Revenue - S.Sum-sal
    and DEPT.D-name - S.D-name
```

The first query produces the relation given in Figure 6.5. Suppose the relation DEPT is that given in Figure 6.4, except that the values under attribute Revenue are *about 100000* and *about 150000*. When the second SQL query is executed, in the toy department, *about 100000* is compared against 90000, while in the shoe department, *about 150000* is compared against 190000. In each case, a degree of satisfaction is obtained and is associated with the department, if it is greater than zero.   ■

Case 2: Agg = count. In this situation, the first subquery is also generated as in Case 1, but the second subquery is as follows.

```
select R1.A
from R1, S
where pred1 and R1.D = S.E (R1.B op1 S.AC else R1.B op1 0)
```

The above query is actually not strictly an SQL query. Its semantics is such that when the evaluation of "$R1.D = S.E$" yields a positive degree for some tuple of $R1$ and some tuple of S, then "$R1.B\ op_1\ S.AC$" will be evaluated; otherwise (i.e., if $R1.D$ is not equal to S.E for any tuple of $R1$ and any tuple of S), "$R1.B\ op_1\ 0$" is evaluated.

This case can be illustrated by the following example.

Example 6.2 Consider the relation schemas DEPT and EMP given previously, except that DEPT.#emp is now a fuzzy attribute containing fuzzy terms such as *about 2*. Suppose the instance of the relation DEPT in Figure 6.6 is modified so that under the attribute #emp, each number x is replaced by the fuzzy number *about x*. The instance of relation EMP remains unchanged from what is indicated in Figure 6.4. Consider the following SQL query.

```
select DEPT.D-name
from DEPT
where DEPT.Revenue < 180000
     and DEPT.#emp =
     (select count(EMP.Name)
      from EMP
      where EMP.D-name = DEPT.D-name)
```

When the clothing department is encountered, the predicate "EMP.D-name = DEPT.D-name" is not satisfied and therefore a count of zero is produced by the inner subquery. This causes a comparison between *about 5* and 0.

According to the technique given above, two SQL queries will be generated. The first SQL query is the following:

```
select EMP.D-name, count(EMP.E-name) into S(D-name, C-emp)
from EMP
group by EMP.D-name
```

When executed on the relation EMP given in Figure 6.4, this SQL query produces the table shown in Figure 6.7.

The second SQL query is as follows:

D-Name	C-Emp
Toy	3
Shoe	2

FIGURE 6.7   An Instance of S(D-name, C-emp)

E-Name	Title	Age
John	manager	30
Mary	system analyst	27
Peter	senior vice president	45
Francis	senior vice president	55
Denise	senior vice president	40
Richard	programmer	25

FIGURE 6.8   Relation EMP

```
select DEPT.D-name
from DEPT, S
where DEPT.Revenue < 180000 and DEPT.D-name = S.D-name
    (DEPT.#emp = S.C-emp else DEPT.#emp = 0)
```

When the clothing department is encountered, the predicate "DEPT.D-name = S.D-name" is not satisfied, so the predicate "DEPT.#emp = 0" is evaluated. This reduces to comparing *about 5* with 0, which is identical to the situation encountered in the nested query.   ■

6.5 Context-Dependent Interpretations of Fuzzy Terms

In the previous sections, there was precisely one membership function for each fuzzy term. The implication is that each fuzzy term should have one and only one interpretation. This may not be appropriate for some situations. Consider, for example, the query, "Find all young senior vice presidents in a given company." Recall from Section 6.1 that the membership function for *young* is the straight line $y = 1$ from $x = 1$ to $x = 20$ and the straight line from the point $(x = 20, y = 1)$ to the point $(x = 35, y = 0)$. Suppose the relation in Figure 6.8 denotes the information about employees in a company. Using the membership function for *young*, there is no tuple satisfying the query, because each senior vice president is at least 40 years old. However, a more appropriate interpretation of the query is, "First, find all senior vice presidents; second, among the senior vice presidents, identify the young ones." As another example, consider the generic query, "Find all heavy parts that are of type T." In this query, *heavy* is a fuzzy term. If T is a screw, then a screw weighing a few ounces is a heavy part.

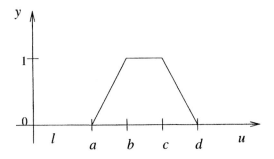

FIGURE 6.9 **A Generic Membership Function**

On the other hand, if T is a hammer, then a hammer needs to weigh at least a few pounds in order to be considered a heavy part. Thus, the fuzzy term *heavy* cannot be represented by a unique membership function. In order to provide a remedy to this problem, we define a generic membership function as shown in Figure 6.9.

In the generic membership function, $[l, u]$ is the domain of the fuzzy term and the trapezoid is defined by the points $(x = a, y = 0)$, $(x = b, y = 1)$, $(x = c, y = 1)$, and $(x = d, y = 0)$. When the fuzzy term is encountered in a fuzzy query, the generic membership function will then be translated into an actual membership function, based on other conditions specified in the query. It is assumed that the other conditions involve either crisp values or fuzzy terms, each having a unique membership function. As an example, consider the query requesting young senior vice presidents. The persons satisfying the condition "senior vice president" are Peter, Francis, and Denise. Their minimum age and their maximum age determine the bounds of the domain of the fuzzy term *young* with respect to the senior vice presidents. That is, if the domain is $[l', u']$, then $l' = 40$ and $u' = 55$. The generic membership function with the list of parameters $[l, a, b, c, d, u]$ is then converted to the actual membership function with the list of parameters $[l', a', b', c', d', u']$ by shifting and scaling as follows. The scaling factor is

$$s = \frac{u' - l'}{u - l}$$

The other parameter values are

$$a' = l' + s(a - l)$$
$$b' = a' + s(b - a)$$
$$c' = b' + s(c - b)$$
$$d' = c' + s(d - c)$$

Example 6.3 Recall that the membership function for *young* is a degenerate trapezoid with the parameters $l = a = b = 1$, $c = 20$, $d = 35$, and $u = 101$, assuming that the oldest person has age 101. Thus the scaling factor is $s = (55 - 40)/100 = 15/100$, and $a' = b' = l' = 40$, $c' = 40 + 15/100 \cdot (20 - 1) = 42.85$, and $d' = 42.85 + 15/100 \cdot (35 - 20) = 45.1$. In this case,

Denise is definitely young, with degree of 1; Peter is only slightly young (the degree is given by the y-intercept of the line between the two points $(x = 42.85, y = 1)$ and $(x = 45.1, y = 0)$ and the line $x = 45$); and Francis is definitely not young, as his degree is 0.) ∎

Exercises

6.1 Suppose there are two fuzzy membership functions. One of them is a trapezoid, and the other is a triangle. Explain why one of them is a generalization of the other.

6.2 What is the degree of satisfaction of one fuzzy number with respect to another fuzzy number that has the same membership functions?

6.3 Find the degrees of satisfaction of one fuzzy label with respect to another fuzzy label. These two fuzzy labels have the following two membership functions. One membership function is a trapezoid with the parameters (a, b, c, d), where $a < b < c < d$. The line joining $(a, 0)$ to $(b, 1)$ is increasing, the line joining $(b, 1)$ to $(c, 1)$ is level, and the line joining $(c, 1)$ to $(d, 0)$ is decreasing. The second membership function is a rectangle with parameters (e, f). There is a vertical line from $(e, 0)$ to $(e, 1)$, a level line between $(e, 1)$ and $(f, 1)$, and a vertical line between $(f, 1)$ and $(f, 0)$. Compute the degrees under the following conditions.

(a) $b < e < c$

(b) $c < e < d$

(c) $d < e < f$

6.4 There are two relations, Person(name, age, occupation) and Friend(name1, name2). Unnest the following query.

```
select name2
from Friend
where Friend.name1 = 'John Smith'
        and Friend.name2 is in (select name
                                from Person
                                where Person.age = 'about 35'
                                and   Person.occupation = 'manager'
```

6.5 Find the answer to the query given in Exercise 6.4. Assume that the two relations are given by the following figure:

name1	name2
John Smith	Peter Smith
John Smith	Mary Thompson
Peter Pan	Francis Wang
Luke Hot	Amy Goldsmith

Relation Friend

name	age	occupation
Peter Smith	35	system analyst
Mary Thompson	36	manager
Peter Pan	38	programmer
John Smith	39	manager
Luke Hot	39	manager
Francis Wang	37	analyst
Amy Goldsmith	34	programmer

Relation Person

Assume that the membership function of *about 35* is an isosceles triangle with the center of the base at (35, 0) and the two vertices of the base at (30, 0) and (40, 0).

6.6 Suppose the relation Friend in Exercise 6.5 is modified to Friend1(name1, name2, number), where *number* is the total number of distinct friends of name1 and name2 (i.e., if A is a friend of both name1 and name2, it is counted once only). Assume that the relation Person is unchanged from Exercise 6.5.

(a) Show step by step how the following query is unnested.

```
select name2
from Friend1
where Friend1.name1 = 'John Smith'
      and Friend1.number > (select Count(name)
                            from Person
                            where Person.age = 35
                                  and Person.occupation = 'manager'
                                  and Friend1.name2 = Person.name)
```

(b) Give a precise condition that a non-null answer is generated.

(c) If the condition Person.age = 35 is changed to Person.age = 'about 35', will this increase or decrease the chance that the query is satisfied?

6.7 Suppose the two relations given in the last two exercises are modified to be Friend(name1, name2, networth) and Person(name, age, occupation, income), where *networth* is the sum of the net worths of name1 and name2 and *income* is the income of *name*. Show step by step how the following query is unnested.

```
select name2
from Friend
where Friend.name1 = 'John Smith'
      and Friend.networth > (select income
                             from Person
                             where Person.age = 'about 35'
                                   and Person.occupation = 'manager'
                                   and Friend.name2 = Person.name)
```

6.8 Does unnesting always yield a more efficient query for execution? If not, provide an example to illustrate your answer.

Bibliographic Notes

Fuzzy set theory was first introduced by Zadeh [408] to capture impreciseness. Since then, numerous techniques have been proposed to handle uncertain or incomplete information. See, for example, [2, 44, 83, 112, 184, 296, 297, 310, 331, 411]. Some early systems have fuzzy queries but precise data in the database [183, 271]. The description of fuzzy terms, their membership functions, and how they are employed to compute the degrees of satisfaction is based on the fuzzy relational system from Omron Corporation [275, 127]. Unnesting of standard relational queries originates from Kim [201]. Improvements of his techniques can be found in [133, 272, 326]. Employing the unnesting techniques and modifying them so that they can be utilized in fuzzy databases is due to [389]. The unnesting techniques that are applicable in standard relational databases can be applied to SQL queries having an arbitrary number of levels of nesting. In this chapter, the techniques are applied to fuzzy SQL queries with two levels only. It is not clear whether they can be generalized to arbitrary fuzzy SQL queries with arbitrary numbers of levels of nesting. Many research issues in fuzzy databases remain to be solved. For example, the interpretation of a fuzzy term may depend on context or the user. This implies that the membership function of the fuzzy term may need to be determined dynamically [414]. This requires an efficient implementation. The determination of whether the domains of two membership functions intersect is similar to that of whether two time intervals intersect. Thus, efficient techniques in temporal databases (see, for example, [340]) may be utilized for fuzzy relational databases.

Query Processing in Deductive Database Systems

A traditional database system, such as a relational database system, is incapable of answering queries that ask for data that are not explicitly stored in the database. For example, if a relational database contains the relation *parent(par, child)*, where parent(c, d) means that c is a parent of d, and there is no relation containing information about who are the ancestors of whom, then the relational database system cannot answer such questions as *Who are the descendants of Jack?* In order to provide the desired capability, rules relating parents with ancestors can be added. The result is a deductive relational database system. This permits the query to be answered, although there may not be an explicitly stored relation for ancestors. Actually, the relation for ancestors can be constructed from the rules, from the stored parent relation, and from possibly the query. Such a relation is called a *derived relation*, versus a stored relation such as the parent.

7.1 Basic Concepts

A deductive database system consists of a database system, such as a relational system, and a set of rules. In this chapter, we assume that the data are stored as relations with each relation having a unique name. Each rule is restricted to the following form.

A predicate :− a conjunction of predicates

where the left-hand side consists of a single predicate that takes on values of true or false and the right-hand side consists of a number of predicates that are "ANDed" together. This rule means that if each of the predicates on the right-hand side is true, then the predicate on the left-hand side is true. A predicate is of the form $p(t_1, t_2, \ldots, t_n)$. It has n arguments, t_i, $1 \leq i \leq n$. Each t_i is a term that can be a constant or a variable that can take on a constant as its value. The name of a predicate can be the name of a relation in the database, the name of a *derived relation*, or the name of a *system predicate* (which is a predicate predefined by the system and is evaluated by the system during query execution).

Suppose p is a relation in the database and t_i takes on the constant c_i, $1 \leq i \leq n$, as its value; then $p(c_1, c_2, \ldots, c_n)$ is true if and only if $(c_1, c_2, \ldots, c_n)$ is a tuple in the relation p. Suppose p is a system predicate such as ">" or "=". Then, it is evaluated to be true or false when the terms take constant values. For example, "> (3, 2)", meaning "3 > 2", is evaluated to be true. Unlike a relation in the database, which contains a finite number of tuples, a system predicate may be infinite, as there are infinitely many pairs (a, b) satisfying "a > b". When the arguments of a system predicate are given constant values, the system evaluates the predicate and produces either a true or a false value.

Suppose $p(t_1, \ldots, t_n)$ is a derived relation, which is neither a relation in the database nor a system predicate. It has to appear as the head (i.e., the left-hand side) of at least one rule. Let r be such a rule. Let the variables appearing in rule r be $\{t_1, t_2, \ldots, t_n, \ldots, t_m\}$, where the first n ($n \leq m$) variables appear on the left-hand side of the rule and the other variables appear only on the right-hand side. Some of the first n variables may also appear on the right-hand side. Suppose these m variables take on the constants $c_1, c_2, \ldots, c_m$. If each predicate on the right-hand side of r is true, then $p(c_1, \ldots, c_n)$ is true. The predicate $p(t_1, \ldots, t_n)$ may appear on the right-hand side of another rule r'. If it has been established in rule r that $p(c_1, \ldots, c_n)$ is true, then it is also true on the right side of r'. Consider as an example the following rule, where parent is the name of a relation in the database and ancestor is the name of a derived relation.

ancestor(X, Y) :− parent(X, Y)   Rule (1)

The rule says that if the predicate parent(X, Y) is true, then the predicate ancestor(X, Y) is also true. In order for the predicate parent(X, Y) to be true, we need to find constants a and b such that when X and Y are replaced by the constants a and b, respectively, (a, b) is a tuple in the parent relation. A true value of parent(a, b) implies a true value of ancestor(a, b).

The predicate on the left-hand side of a rule is called the *rule head*; the right-hand side is the *rule body*, which gives a definition of the rule head predicate. In Rule (1), X and Y are variables that take as values the objects of interest. In this case, X and Y can take on persons identified by their names as values. A *fact* (a tuple in relational database) is a special case of a rule in which there is no precondition (rule body) and there is no variable. For example, the fact parent(a, b) denoting that person a is a parent of person b can be written as a rule: parent(a, b) :− null. Variables that appear in the rule head are universally quantified (if x is a universally quantified variable for a rule, then the rule holds for every value assigned to the variable x); those that appear in the body but not in the head are existentially quantified (if y is an existentially quantified variable for a rule, then the rule holds for some value of y). For example, Rule (1), which has no variable appearing only in the body but not the head, says "for every X, for every Y, if X is a parent of Y, then X is an ancestor of Y". In other words,

Par	Child
a	b
b	c
c	d

FIGURE 7.1 Relation Parent

for any value of X and any value of Y, as long as the predicate parent(X, Y) is true, then the predicate ancestor(X, Y) is true. Suppose the database contains the *parent* relation given in Figure 7.1.

When X and Y take on the values a and b, respectively, then the predicate parent(a, b) is true. By the rule, the predicate ancestor(a, b) is true. Similarly, if X and Y take on the values c and d, respectively, the predicates parent(c, d) and ancestor(c, d) hold. Although the database contains information about parent-child relationships among people and not about ancestor-descendant relationships, the latter information can be deduced from the database and the rule. Thus, in a deductive relational database there are two types of relations. The first type is relations containing facts. For example, *parent* is a relation containing individual facts parent(a, b), parent(b, c), etc. The other type is relations that are derived or deduced from the stored relations and the rules in the system. For example, *ancestor* is a derived or deduced relation. A predicate in a rule takes on tuples as values from the corresponding relation, which may be a stored relation or a deduced relation. If a tuple exists or can be established in the relation, the value of the corresponding predicate is true; otherwise, the value is false.

A rule can be used to specify an integrity constraint, which is used to verify whether or not the data in a database satisfy certain constraints. For example, ancestor("Adam", X) and ancestor("Eve", Y) with null rule bodies denote that Adam and Eve are ancestors of all persons. The constraint that no two tuples in the same relation r can have the same key value can be written as the rule

$$\text{null} :- r(K_1, X), \quad r(K_2, Y), \quad K_1 = K_2, \quad X \neq Y$$

In this rule, if the variables K_1 and K_2 take on the same key value, and X and Y take on different values, then there is a contradiction (which is represented by the null in the rule head).

There may be multiple rules having the same rule head. For example, the following rule

$$\text{ancestor}(X, Y) :- \text{parent}(X, Z), \quad \text{ancestor}(Z, Y) \qquad \text{Rule (2)}$$

and Rule (1) have the same head predicate ancestor. This rule says that for every X and every Y, if there exists some Z such that X is a parent of Z and Z is an ancestor of Y, then X is an ancestor of Y. If there are multiple rules having the same head predicate, then the rule head predicate is true if the body of one of the rules is true. Thus, if either the body of Rule (1) is true or the body of Rule (2) is true, then the ancestor predicate is true. Another way of saying the same thing is that the ancestor relationships of the two rules are those produced by Rule (1) union those produced by Rule (2). To see this, consider the application of the rules to the *parent* relation given above. Rule (1) gives the ancestor relationships ancestor(a, b), ancestor(b, c), and ancestor(c, d). When Rule (2) is applied with X = a, Z = b, and Y = c, ancestor(a, c) is produced. Similarly, the application of Rule (2) with X = b, Z = c, and Y = d yields ancestor(b, d). Finally, by substituting X by a, Z by b, and Y by d (note that ancestor(b, d) has just been established), we obtain ancestor(a, d). Combining the results obtained by both rules, the set of ancestor relationships consists of ancestor(a, b), ancestor(b, c), ancestor(c, d), ancestor(a, c), ancestor(b, d), and ancestor(a, d).

Definition 7.1 *A rule is safe if the derived relation corresponding to the rule head predicate is finite.*

There are usually two sources of unsafeness. First, if a variable appears in the head but not in the body of the rule, then the variable may take on a potentially unbounded number of values. For example, in a rule such as g(X, Y) :− h(X), Y can take on essentially any value. This makes g(X, Y) potentially infinite. To prevent that from happening, we insist that any variable that appears in the head must appear in the body. This is assumed to be true for the remaining part of this chapter. Another source of unsafeness is the presence of system or negated predicates. An example of a system predicate (versus an ordinary predicate, which represents either a database relation or a derived relation) is greater-than(X, Y). This predicate is true, if X > Y. Clearly, there are infinitely many pairs of numbers satisfying this predicate. Therefore, the corresponding relation is infinite. A similar situation applies to negated predicates appearing in the body of a rule. For example, a rule p(X) :− NOT q(X) in which a negated predicate appears in the body of the rule may cause p to be infinite. In order to make a rule safe, we require that whenever a variable appears in a system predicate or a negated predicate in the body of a rule, it must appear in an ordinary nonnegated predicate in the body of the same rule. For example, in the rule h(X, Y) :− greater-than(X, Y), g(X), k(Y), the predicates g and k are ordinary and finite. As a result, although the greater-than predicate looks infinite, its first argument is bounded by g and its second argument is bounded by k, and thus h(X, Y) is finite.

In order to compute a derived relation systematically, it is usual to put the rules associated with a given rule head in a standard form. Specifically, the parameters associated with the rule head should be variables only, all of them should be distinct, and all rules having the same rule head should have the same vector of variables. In order to have a standard form, the following observations can be made.

1. Constants that appear in a rule head are constraints and can be moved to the body of the rule. For example, the rule

   h(X, Y, 3) :− g(X, Y),   k(Y)

can be rewritten to be

   h(X, Y, Z) :− g(X, Y),   k(Y),   = (Z, 3)

2. Variables that occur more than once in the rule head can be replaced by distinct variables, such that the duplicates are represented as constraints in the body. For example, the rule

   h(X, Y, X) :− g(X, Y), k(Y)

can be rewritten as

$$h(X, Y, Z) :- g(X, Y), \quad k(Y), \quad = (Z, X)$$

3. Consider a variable that appears in the head and in the body of a rule. Replace each occurrence of this variable by another variable, which does not occur in this rule. Such a replacement does not change the semantics of the rule because the variable is universally quantified. By making such changes, the head of a rule can have the same vector of variables in different rules. For example, in the two rules

$$h(X, Y, Z) = g(X, Y), \quad k(Y), \quad = (Z, 3)$$
$$h(A, B, C) = m(A), n(A, B), \quad p(B, C)$$

the vectors of variables are different, but they can be made the same, if in the second rule, A, B, and C are replaced by X, Y, and Z, respectively, in both the head and the body.

7.2 Computing Derived Relations

7.2.1 Computation of Nonrecursive Predicates

We first represent a rule by an equation in which the left-hand side is a derived relation corresponding to the rule head predicate and the right-hand side is a relational algebra expression corresponding to the rule body. Consider the body of the rule. Each predicate in the rule can be represented by a relation. If a variable appears in two or more predicates in the body of a rule, then the corresponding relations are equijoined. If a variable, say X, of a predicate is related by an inequality operator to another variable, say Y, in a different predicate, then the two corresponding relations are joined by a nonequal join. If a variable in a predicate is related to a constant or another variable in the same predicate, then this corresponds to a selection on the relation that is represented by the predicate. A Cartesian product of two or more relations is produced if there is no common variable between the corresponding predicates. Suppose a system predicate appears in the body. Recall that each variable in the system predicate must appear in an ordinary predicate. After the corresponding relations are joined together (or a Cartesian product of these relations is formed) to yield a relation, say Z, the system predicate corresponds to a selection on Z. For example, if the system predicate is ">(X, Y)", then the selection "X > Y" should be performed on the relation Z. The set of variables in the head of the rule is a subset of the set of the variables in the body. After the join (or Cartesian product) of the relations corresponding to the predicates in the body of the rule and possibly selections corresponding to the constraints imposed on the variables in those predicates are taken to produce a relation R, the relation corresponding to the head of the rule is obtained from R by taking a projection. In the following examples, the variables in the rules are replaced by attributes A_i in the corresponding relational algebra expression with the understanding that if a variable appears both in the rule head and the rule body, the corresponding attribute names are the same in the relational algebra equation.

Example 7.1 Let the *siblings* be defined by the following rule.

$$sib(X, Y) :- parent(Z, X), \quad parent(Z, Y), \quad Not\text{-}Equal(X, Y)$$

where Not-Equal is a predicate that is true if its two parameters are not equal. The rule says that X and Y are siblings if there is a Z such that Z is a parent of X, Z is a parent of Y, but X and Y are not the same.

The first occurrence of the parent predicate is represented by the relation $parent1(A_1, A_2)$ with attributes A_1 and A_2; the second occurrence is represented by $parent2(A_3, A_4)$. Both parent1 and parent2 are identical to the parent relation, containing the facts about who is a parent of whom. Since the first variable in both predicates are the same, there is an equijoin between these two relations. This is denoted by $parent1(A_1, A_2) \bowtie_{parent1.A_1=parent2.A_3} parent2(A_3, A_4)$. Suppose the resulting relation is $S(A_1, A_2, A_3, A_4)$. The Not-Equal predicate is represented by the selection on the relation S with the condition $S.A_2 \neq S.A_4$. Finally, the relation *sib* corresponding to the sibling predicate is obtained by taking the projection on the attributes A_2 and A_4. ∎

If negation appears in the body of a rule, it is represented by the complement operator. For the moment, we assume that negation does not exist. If there are multiple rules having the same rule head, then the right-hand side of each rule can be represented by a relational algebra expression given above. The union of these algebra expressions gives the relation corresponding to the head predicate.

Example 7.2 Suppose the following two rules are given.

$$f(A, B) :- g(A), \quad h(B)$$
$$f(A, B) :- k(A, C), \quad m(C, B), \quad \text{Greater-Than}(C, 3)$$

The body of the first rule gives $g(A_1) \times h(A_2)$. The body of the second rule gives the following expression: $\pi_{A_1, A_2}(\sigma_{A_3>3}(k(A_1, A_3) \bowtie_{k.A_3=m.A_4} m(A_4, A_2)))$. The union of the two expressions is an expression for the predicate in the rule head. ∎

7.2.2 Test for Recursions in Rules

Recursion within a rule can easily be recognized by the head predicate appearing also in the body. However, the absence of the head predicate in the body does not necessarily mean that there is no recursion. For example, a predicate p in the head of a rule can be defined in terms of another predicate p1 in the body of the rule. The predicate p1 is in turn defined in terms of p in another rule. This causes recursion indirectly. In order to test for recursion, a directed graph G(V, E), called the *dependency graph*, can be constructed such that each vertex in V represents an ordinary deduced relation (predicate) and a directed edge $e = (v_i, v_j)$ exists in E if there is a rule in which the head predicate, say p_i, is represented by v_i and a predicate, say p_j, represented by v_j appears in the body. This directed edge essentially denotes that the definition of the predicate p_i depends on that of predicate p_j. A recursion occurs if and only if there is a directed cycle in the graph G. In other words, if there is a directed cycle containing both v_i and v_j, then the definitions of p_i and p_j depend on each other, causing a recursion. A set of predicates or derived relations $\{p_1, p_2, \ldots, p_n\}$ are mutually recursive if they are in a directed cycle of the dependency graph.

Example 7.3 Consider the following set of rules. It is assumed that all the predicates given below represent derived relations. The variables are omitted, as they are not relevant for the recursion test.

$$p_1 :- p_2, p_7$$
$$p_2 :- p_3, p_4$$
$$p_3 :- p_1, p_5, p_6$$

The dependency graph G is given as follows where predicate p_i is represented by vertex v_i, $i = 1, 2, \ldots, 7$.

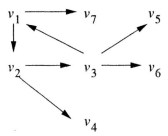

The directed cycle v_1 to v_2 to v_3 and back to v_1 can be detected. As a result, the set of rules is recursive. More specifically, the predicates p_1, p_2, and p_3, which appear in the directed cycle, are mutually recursive. ∎

7.2.3 Computation of Recursive Predicates

The method given above for computing nonrecursive predicates can be utilized to form a recursive equation involving recursive predicates. For example, in the *ancestor* predicate, given earlier, the rules defining the predicate are

ancestor(X, Y) :− parent(X, Y)

ancestor(X, Y) :− parent(X, Z), ancestor(Z, Y)

The expressions for the two rules are, respectively, parent(A_1, A_2) and π_{A_1,A_2}(parent(A_1, A_3) $\bowtie_{parent.A_3=ancestor.A_4}$ ancestor(A_4, A_2))

Thus, a recursive equation on the ancestor predicate is

ancestor(A_1, A_2) (7.1)

    = parent$(A_1, A_2) \cup \pi_{A_1,A_2}$(parent$(A_1, A_3) \bowtie_{parent.A_3=ancestor.A_4}$ ancestor(A_4, A_2))

If the ancestor relation is represented by X, which is a set of tuples, then the recursive equation can be rewritten as X = g(X), where g is the expression given on the right-hand side of Equation (7.1). A solution X satisfying the recursive equation is called a *fixed point*. In order to compute X, the following observations are made.

1. In the recursive equation, each operator, namely, join, selection, projection, Cartesian product, and union, is monotonic; i.e., if an operand O of an operator is replaced by a superset O', then the result of the operation using O is a subset of the result of the operation using O'. For example, selection(O) is contained in selection(O') if O is contained in O'. Similarly, join($R1$, $R2$) is contained in join($R1'$, $R2'$) if R1 is contained in $R1'$ and R2 is contained in $R2'$. As a result, the function g is monotonic.

2. We assume the domain of each attribute is finite and no function is applied to generate new values. Thus, the relation corresponding to each predicate is bounded.

The Naive Method to Compute a Fixed Point for X = g(X)

This method initializes X to be the null set. Then it applies g to X. If the result is null, then a fixed-point solution is obtained; otherwise, a new value of X given by g(old value of X) is obtained. The process of applying g to X and then testing whether the result is equal to X is repeated until the equality is reached. In other words, the sequence g(X), g(g(X)), g(g(g(X))), $\ldots$, etc., is generated with X initialized to null. The sequence is terminated as soon as two consecutive members of the sequence are equal. The termination of this process is guaranteed for the following reasons.

1. The sequence is monotonically nondecreasing due to the above observation (1); i.e., g(Y) is contained in g(g(Y)) for any set Y.

2. Each member of the sequence is bounded by the above observation (2).

Thus, for some integer i, $g^i(X) = g^{i+1}(X)$, where $g^i(X)$ represents that g is applied to X i times. Let X0 be such that $X0 = g^i(null) = g^{i+1}(null)$. Then, $X0 = g(X0)$, and X0 is a fixed point. In fact, X0 is the *least fixed point*, i.e., for any fixed point Y, X0 is contained in Y. To see this, consider any fixed point Y. Clearly, null is contained in Y. When g is applied to null and to Y i times, it yields X0 and Y, respectively, while retaining the containment relationship. Thus, X0 is contained in Y.

The computation of the least fixed point by a program is as follows. Let g be the relational algebra expression obtained from the rules whose rule head is the predicate corresponding to the derived relation, say R.

Naive-S(R, g)

/* The Naive method for a single derived relation. */

```
R = null;
NR = g(R); /* NR is the new value for R */
While (NR ≠ R)
    {R = NR;
    NR = g(R);}
```

When the program terminates, NR = R. These are the two consecutive values of R such that g(R) = R. Thus, R is the required fixed point.

The computational method given above applies to a single recursive relation. This method is readily generalizable to multiple mutually recursive derived relations. This is illustrated by the following example.

Example 7.4 Suppose we have the following set of rules.

1. R(X, Y) = S(X, C, A), T(A, B), U(B, Y)

2. R(X, Y) = W(X, Y)

3. S(Z, M, N) = R(Z, P), V(P, M, N)

The predicates R and S are recursive, but the predicates W, T, and U denote relations in the database. Rules (a) and (b) give the following relational algebra expression, which is denoted by g_1.

$$R(A_1, A_2)$$
$$= W(A_1, A_2) \cup \pi_{A_1, A_2}((S(A_1, A_3, A_4) \bowtie_{S.A_4=T.A_5} T(A_5, A_6)) \bowtie_{T.A_6=U.A_7} U(A_7, A_2))$$

Rule (c) gives the following relational algebra expression denoted by g_2.

$$S(A_1, A_2, A_3) = \pi_{A_1, A_2, A_3}(R(A_1, A_4) \bowtie_{R.A_4=V.A_5} V(A_5, A_2, A_3))$$

The following program computes the least fixed point for R and S.

```
R = null;
S = null;
NR = g₁(S);
NS = g₂(R);
While (NR ≠ R or NS ≠ S)
      {R = NR;
       S = NS;
       NR = g₁(S);
       NS = g₂(R);}
```

Termination occurs only when in an iteration the new R, NR, equals to R, and the new S, NS, equals to S. ∎

Based on the above example, the general Naive method for computing the least fixed point for a set of mutually recursive relations $R_1, R_2, \ldots, R_k$ is as follows. Let g_i be the relational algebra expression for the derived relation R_i, which is obtained from the rules whose rule head is R_i. In general, some subset of $R_1, \ldots, R_k$ may appear in g_i. To simplify the presentation of the algorithm, g_i is assumed to be a function of $R_1, \ldots, R_k$.

Naive($R_1, \ldots, R_k, g_1, \ldots, g_k$)

/* The Naive method for multiple mutually recursive relations.*/

```
For i = 1 to k
      Rᵢ = null;
For i = 1 to k
      NRᵢ = gᵢ(R₁, . . . , Rₖ);
While (there is some Rᵢ, Rᵢ ≠ NRᵢ, 1 ≤ i ≤ k)
      {For i = 1 to k
             Rᵢ = NRᵢ;
       For i = 1 to k
             NRᵢ = gᵢ(R₁, . . . , Rₖ);}
```

Semi-Naive Method

Although the Naive method computes the derived relations correctly, there are substantial inefficiencies, as certain tuples are computed repeatedly. This can be illustrated by the pair of rules for ancestor given in Figure 7.1.

ancestor(X, Y) :− parent(X, Y)

ancestor(X, Y) :− parent(X, Z), ancestor(Z, Y)

The relational algebra expression corresponding to the bodies of the two rules is $parent(A_1, A_2) \cup \pi_{A_1,A_2}(parent(A_1, A_3) \bowtie_{parent.A_3=ancestor.A_4} ancestor(A_4, A_2))$. Initially, the ancestor relation is null. At the end of the first iteration, the ancestor relation is equal to the parent relation because of the first rule. The second rule does not contribute any tuple, as initially the ancestor relation is null and the join of the parent relation with the null relation is null. At the end of the second iteration, the first rule does not contribute any new tuple and the second rule yields the set of tuples {(a, c), (b, d)}, each of which is new. The ancestor relation then becomes {(a, b), (b, c), (c, d), (a, c), (b, d)}. At the end of the third iteration, the first rule again does not generate any new tuple; the second rule generates the old tuples (a, c) and (b, d) in addition to the new tuple (a, d). Thus, the ancestor relation now becomes {(a, b), (b, c), (c, d), (a, c), (b, d), (a, d)}. No new tuple is generated in the next iteration and the algorithm terminates. It is obvious that the use of the first rule in the second and subsequent iterations is useless. Furthermore, the repeated generation of the tuples {(b, c), (c, d)} in the third iteration is redundant. The former inefficiency can be avoided if we utilize Rule 1 only in the first iteration, and in the later iterations we add in only the changes of the *parent* relation. Since the *parent* relation is constant, the changes are null. This essentially reduces to using Rule 1 only once. The latter inefficiency may be avoided if instead of using the entire ancestor relation at each iteration, we employ the newly generated tuples at iteration i to generate new tuples at iteration $(i + 1)$. Thus, at the end of the second iteration, the newly generated tuples denoted by Nancestor = {(a, c), (b, d)}. In the third iteration, Nancestor is utilized to generate the new tuple (a, d). The idea is that when a new tuple (such as (a, d)) is generated at the $(i + 1)$th iteration, some tuple (such as (a, c) or (b, d)) that is newly generated at the ith iteration must be utilized. This is formalized as follows.

For each relation R, Del(R) is the set of new tuples generated for R from one iteration to the next. If R is a database relation, Del(R) is null, as R is assumed not to change during the execution of the algorithm. If R is a derived but not a recursively defined relation, R is initially null, but after it gets its value from the relational algebra expression that is derived from the rules with R as the head predicate, it will be fixed. After that point, Del(R) is null. If R is a recursively defined relation, Del(R) may change from one iteration to the next. In the previous section, we obtain a relational algebra expression from the body of a rule r with head predicate R. Suppose the rule body contains relations $R_1, R_2, \ldots, R_m$. Let the relational algebra expression generated from rule r be Alg($r, R_1, R_2, \ldots, R_m$). Since only the new tuples are of interest, the relational algebra expression (due to rule r) to generate new tuples is $\bigcup_{i=1}^{m}$ Alg($r, R_1, \ldots, R_{i-1}$, Del(R_i), $R_{i+1}, \ldots, R_m$). This expression says that a newly generated tuple for R must come from some newly generated tuple of R_i, together with tuples of $R_1, \ldots, R_{i-1}$, $R_{i+1}, \ldots, R_m$, for some $1 \leq i \leq m$.

Example 7.5 Consider the pair of rules with ancestor as the head predicate, namely Rule (1) and Rule (2). Rule (1) is nonrecursive and Rule (2) is recursive. Since the *parent* relation is a database relation, Del(parent) is null and the relational algebra expression to generate new tuples for the first rule is null. The relational algebra expression for the second rule is

$$\pi_{A_1,A_2}(\text{parent}(A_1, A_3) \bowtie_{parent.A_3=\text{Del(ancestor)}.A_4} \text{Del(ancestor}(A_4, A_2))) \tag{7.2}$$

where Del(ancestor) refers to the newly generated tuples in the ith iteration to be used in the $(i+1)$th iteration. Suppose the recursive rule, Rule (2), for ancestor is replaced by the following rule.

$$\text{ancestor}(X, Y) = \text{ancestor}(X, Z), \text{ancestor}(Z, Y) \qquad \text{Rule (3)}$$

The body of this rule has two occurrences of ancestor that are recursive with respect to the head relation. As a result, the relational algebra expression for this rule is

$$\pi_{A_1,A_2}(\text{ancestor}(A_1, A_3) \bowtie_{ancestor.A_3=\text{Del(ancestor)}.A_4} \text{Del(ancestor}(A_4, A_2)))$$
$$\cup \, \pi_{A_1,A_2}(\text{Del(ancestor}(A_1, A_3)) \bowtie_{\text{Del(ancestor)}.A_3=ancestor.A_4} \text{ancestor}(A_4, A_2)) \tag{7.3}$$

■

Since a recursive relation S can be defined by a set of recursive rules, say $r_1, \ldots, r_p$, the relational algebra expression to generate new tuples for S using these recursive rules is $\bigcup_{i=1}^{p}$ Alg$(r_i, R_1, \ldots, R_m)$. In comparison with the Naive method, the above algebra expression has two differences. First, the nonrecursive rules are not included in the "while" part of the algorithm. Second, in the relational algebra expression Alg, Del(R_i), where R_i is a mutually recursive relation with respect to S, is used in addition to possibly other R_j's. The use of Del(R_i) instead of R_i reduces the amount of data to be processed by the algorithm. With these two modifications, we obtain the new relational algebra expressions.

Let $S_1, \ldots, S_k$ be the set of derived relations to be computed. In the first iteration, the original relational algebra expressions for the Naive method are still utilized. Let them be denoted by g_i, $1 \le i \le k$. In subsequent iterations, the new relational algebra expressions to generate new tuples are employed. Let them be denoted by f_i, $1 \le i \le k$. The Semi-Naive method is then given by the following algorithm.

Semi-Naive$(S_1, \ldots, S_k, g_1, \ldots, g_k, f_1, \ldots, f_k)$

```
For i = 1 to k
      S_i = null;
For i = 1 to k
      {Del(S_i) = g_i; /* each derived relation is set to null in g_i */
      S_i = Del(S_i);}
While (Del(S_i) ≠ null for some 1 ≤ i ≤ k)
      {For i = 1 to k
            TDel(S_i) = f_i(S_1, ..., S_k, Del(S_1), ..., Del(S_k))
      For i = 1 to k
            {Del(S_i) = TDel(S_i) − S_i;
            S_i = S_i ∪ Del(S_i);}
      }
```

The algorithm terminates when each $\text{Del}(S_i)$ is null. This means that no new tuple is generated for each recursive predicate.

Example 7.6 Consider the computation of the *ancestor* relation, which is defined by Rule (1) and Rule (2). There is only one recursive relation, namely *ancestor*.

When the Semi-Naive method is applied to this rule pair, $k = 1$, g_1 is given by the right-hand side of Equation (7.1) and f_1 is given by Expression (7.2). When the method is applied to Rules (1) and (3), g_1 is given by Expression (7.4) and f_1 is given by Expression (7.3).

$$\text{parent}(A_1, A_2) \cup \pi_{A_1,A_2} \text{ ancestor}(A_1, A_2) \bowtie_{\text{ancestor}.A_3=\text{ancestor}.A_4} \text{ ancestor}(A_4, A_2) \qquad (7.4)$$

■

Top-Down Method

A query is of the form $R(X_1, X_2, \ldots, X_n)$, where each X_i can be either a constant or a variable and R can be a database relation or a derived relation. If some of the X_i's are constants, then selections, which are applied to R and use the constants, are to be performed. If R is a derived relation, it may need to be computed before the selection is to be taken. Suppose the given query is placed at the top and the actual relations in the database are placed at the bottom. Then both the Naive method and the Semi-Naive method are bottom-up methods in the sense that each of these methods constructs the answer to the given query, starting from the bottom relations and building toward the requirements of the query. In contrast, a top-down method starts from the query and proceeds toward forming the answer. As an example, consider the query ancestor(b, Y), which seeks for the descendants of b, i.e., values of Y where (b, Y) is a tuple in the derived *ancestor* relation. A bottom-up method would construct the derived relation ancestor(A_1, A_2), consisting of all pairs of the form (r, s), where r is an ancestor of s. Then a selection, ancestor.$A_1 = 'b'$ is performed to form the answer to the query. It is clear that in constructing the answer to the query, tuples in which the first component is not b or is not a descendant of b are irrelevant and should not be formed. We now show a top-down method in which the constant(s) in the query are utilized to prevent unnecessary tuples from being constructed.

Consider the query ancestor(b, Y). If Rule (1) is utilized, then after replacing the variable X in both the head and the body by the constant b, the predicate ancestor(b, Y) is true if the predicate parent(b, Y) is true. The latter predicate yields $Y = \{c, f\}$ using the *parent* relation in Figure 7.2.

If Rule (2) is utilized instead of Rule (1), then after replacing the variable X by the constant b in both the head and the body, the head predicate is true, if parent(b, Z) and ancestor(Z, Y) are true. Since either Rule (1) or Rule (2) can be utilized, ancestor(b, Y) is true, if either parent(b, Y) is true or parent(b, Z) and ancestor(Z, Y) are true. This yields the top two levels in Figure 7.3. parent(b, Z) is true, if Z takes on one of the values in $\{c, f\}$. When Z = c, ancestor(Z, Y) becomes ancestor(c, Y). This is exactly the same form as the original query, and it causes a recursion. The recursion attempts to generate the next level of predicates. Specifically, ancestor(c, Y) is true, if parent(c, Y) is true or parent(c, Z_1) and ancestor(Z_1, Y) are true. parent(c, Y) is true, if Y = d. Similarly, parent(c, Z_1) is true for Z_1 = d. However, ancestor(d, Y) cannot be made true, because there is no tuple of the form (d,) in the *parent*

Par	Child
a	b
b	c
c	d
b	f

FIGURE 7.2 A New Parent Relation

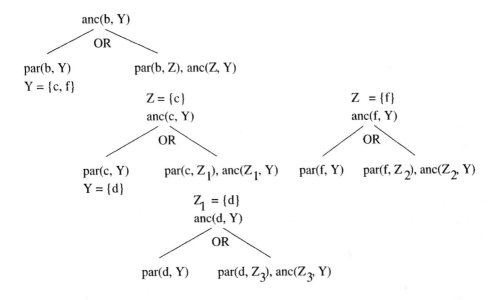

FIGURE 7.3 Illustrating the Top-Down Process

relation. Backtracking to the case Z = f, we find that ancestor(f, Y) cannot be made true, because no tuple of the form (f,) exists in relation *parent*. The entire process is shown in Figure 7.3. In this figure, par and anc denote the parent and the ancestor relations, respectively.

This example shows that the top-down method avoids computing tuples of form (m,), where m is not b nor a descendant of b. However, the method may produce quite a few small relations. For example, Y = {c, f} and Y = {d} are two such small relations. If the parent relations have descendants of b at different levels, then at least as many relations as the number of levels will be generated. It is also possible that a direct application of the top-down method may lead to an infinite recursion. For example, suppose the recursive rule for ancestor is rewritten as ancestor(X, Y) :− ancestor(X, Z), parent(Z, Y). Consider the query ancestor(b, Y). Ancestor(b, Y) is true, if ancestor(b, Z) and parent(Z, Y) are true. This causes infinite recursion, as ancestor(b, Z) is essentially the same as the original query. Even if the recursive rule is not modified, cyclic data may also cause an infinite recursion. For example, if the tuple (d, b) is also present in the parent relation, then with the original recursive rule and

Par	Child
d	b
d	e
b	a
b	c
e	f
a	g
c	h
f	i

FIGURE 7.4   A New Parent Relation

the query ancestor(b, Y), the top-down tree will eventually yield [parent(d, b), ancestor(b, Y)] (in Figure 7.3 replace Z_3 by b). This causes an infinite recursion. We would like a method that combines the advantages of both top-down and bottom-up methods.

Magic Set

The basic idea of the magic set method is to make use of the constants in the query to restrict the derived relations and then apply a bottom-up evaluation method, such as the Semi-Naive method, to compute the derived relations. This is illustrated by the following example.

Example 7.7 A set of rules to characterize persons of the same generation is given as follows.

sg(X, X) :– person(X)   Rule (4)

sg(X, Y) :– parent(PX, X), sg(PX, PY), parent(PY, Y)   Rule (5)

Rule (4) says that X is of the same generation as X, if X is a person. Rule (5) says that if X has parent PX, Y has parent PY, and PX and PY are of the same generation, then X and Y are of the same generation. Suppose the query is sg(a, Y) and the *parent* relation is given in Figure 7.4.

A tree representing the parent-child relationships and persons of the same generation is shown in Figure 7.5.

It is clear that the persons who are of the same generation as a are {c, f}. If we generate all tuples satisfying sg(X, Y), we will have (g, h), (g, i), etc., which are irrelevant to the answering of the query. In order to avoid generating unnecessary tuples, we proceed substituting X by 'a' in Rule (5). The body of the rule becomes: parent(PX, a), sg(PX, PY), parent(PY, Y). The constant 'a' places a restriction on PX through the *parent* relation, which in turn restricts the first argument of sg. By recursion, the rule is invoked again. When this set of values (which are the parents of 'a') are substituted into X in the rule head of sg, it will again restrict PX, which again bound the first argument of sg. In other words, the first argument of sg is bounded by certain constants (the ancestors of 'a' in this example), which are derived from the query

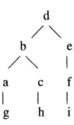

FIGURE 7.5 *Parent-Child Relationships*

constant 'a'. The bound on the first argument of sg is achieved by having a predicate called the *magic set* of sg, denoted by m-sg, with a single argument and by rewriting Rule (5) to be

$$sg(X, Y) :- parent(PX, X), m\text{-}sg(PX), sg(PX, PY), parent(PY, Y) \qquad \text{Rule (6)}$$

The magic set of sg, m-sg, is given by the following recursive rule.

$$m\text{-}sg(PX) :- m\text{-}sg(X), parent(PX, X) \qquad \text{Rule (7)}$$

Rule (7) is obtained from Rule (5). When the first argument of sg, X, is substituted by a set of values in the head of Rule (5), this set of values is propagated to X in parent(PX, X) in the body of the rule. This yields a set of values for PX, which is the first argument of sg in the body of the rule. Thus, PX is obtained from X through the relation parent(PX, X), as expressed in Rule (7). The initialization consists of

$$m\text{-}sg(a) :- null \qquad \text{Rule (8)}$$
$$sg(a, Y) :- \qquad \text{Rule (9)}$$

The solution to Rules (7) and (8) provide a bound to the first argument of sg. Specifically, Rules (7) and (8) yield m-sg(a), mg-sg(b), and mg-sg(d). With this bound incorporated as shown in Rule (6), the computation of the derived relation sg using Rules (6), (7), (8), and (9) would not have irrelevant elements, such as g, h, and i in the first argument of sg. ∎

In the above example, when recursive Rule (5) is invoked, a bound on the first argument of sg in the rule head causes a bound on the same argument of sg in the body. In general, a bound on a set of arguments of the rule head predicate may cause a bound on a different set of arguments of the predicate in the body. This can also be handled with some adjustments, since there are a finite number of such sets of arguments. However, the details are not given here.

Negation

Suppose we use the following rule to define potential friends.

$$pot\text{-}friend(X, Y) :- NOT\ enemy(X, Y)$$

This rule says that X and Y are potential friends if they are not enemies. If enemy is a relation, then the complement of the relation can represent potential friends. However, the complement of a finite relation can be infinite, if the variables X and Y are not restricted. In order to avoid an infinite relation, let X and Y be elements of the person relation. The rule is then modified to be

pot-friend(X, Y) :− NOT enemy(X, Y), person(X), person(Y)

A relational algebra expression representing potential friends is

pot-friend(A_1, A_2) = (person(A_1) × person(A_2)) − enemy(A_1, A_2)

In general, if a variable appears in a negated predicate in the body of a rule, it should also appear in a nonnegated relation (database or derived relation) of the same rule to ensure that an infinite relation will not be formed. The use of negations can cause multiple *minimal solutions* to recursive rules. Let $p_1, \ldots, p_k$ be a solution to a set of recursive rules. A solution is minimal if any solution to the set of recursive rules, say $p'_1, \ldots, p'_k$, has some p'_i properly contain p_i.

Example 7.8 Consider the following rules:

p(X) :− r(X)
p(X) :− s(X), NOT q(X)
q(X) :− t(X), NOT p(X)

where the database relations r, s, and t are given by r( ) = {1}, s( ) = {1, 3} and t( ) = {1, 2, 3, 4}. The following are two minimal solutions satisfying the above recursive rules: (1) p( ) = {1, 3}, q = {2, 4} and (2) p( ) = {1}, q( ) = {2, 3, 4}.   ∎

When there are multiple minimal solutions, it is not clear what the natural answer to a user query is. Thus, it is usual to impose additional constraints on a given set of recursive rules involving negations such that the "natural" answer can be provided.

Definition 7.2 *A set of rules is stratified, if in the dependency graph for the predicates of the rules, there is no directed path from a predicate q that occurs negated in the body of a rule r to the head predicate p of r.*

Example 7.9 The dependency graph for Example 7.8 is

q   p

In the second rule in Example 7.8, there is a directed path from the negated predicate q to the head predicate. Hence, the set of rules is not stratified.   ∎

The purpose of stratification is to partition predicates into different levels. Specifically, if the rule head predicate p has a negated predicate q in the body, then the level of p is strictly higher than the level of q; if the rule head predicate p has a nonnegated predicate q in the body, then the level of p is at least as high as that of q. It can be shown that if a set of rules can be stratified, then level numbers can be assigned to predicates to partition predicates into different levels satisfying the above two conditions. The starting level, level 1, is assigned to the relations that are either database relations or derived relations, each of whose definitions does not have a negated derived relation in its body.

Example 7.10 In Example 7.8, the rules cannot be stratified. If predicate q were assigned level 1, then predicate p would be at a higher level, since it is the head of a rule with an occurrence of the negated q in its body. However, the rule with q as rule head and with negated p in its body would require q to be at a higher level than that of p. This is clearly impossible. ∎

Example 7.11 Consider the following set of rules.

$$p(X) :- r(X)$$
$$p(X) :- s(X), t(Y), NOT\ q(X, Y)$$
$$q(X, Y) :- v(Y), q(X, Y)$$
$$q(X, Y) :- a(X, Y)$$
$$u(X) :- b(X), NOT\ p(X)$$

The dependency graph is as follows.

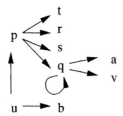

Since there is no directed path from q to p (the second rule) and no directed path from p to u (the fifth rule), the set of rules is stratified. Predicates a, b, r, s, t, v, and q can be assigned level 1. Predicate p can be assigned level 2, on account of the second rule. Predicate u can be assigned level 3, according to the last rule. ∎

When a set of rules is stratified, it is possible to construct a "natural" solution to the derived relations as follows. First, all derived relations at level 1 are obtained. This does not involve derived negated relations in the body of a rule. Thus, methods such as the Semi-Naive method can be applied. Then, all derived relations at level 2 can be computed, using complements. Recall that since all variables in a negated predicate must appear in ordinary predicates, finite complements are obtained. This is carried out at successively higher levels than 2. For the above example, the derived relation q at level 1 is computed. Then p is computed at level 2 and finally u is computed at level 3. The computation of a derived relation at level i depends on the computed relations at levels less than i. The set of derived relations, say S, computed by the method given above is called a *perfect fixed point* with the following property. (1) The derived relations S, when restricted to level 1, are the smallest among all possible solutions. (2) Let S_1 be any other solution. For any level higher than 1, if S_1 and S have the same solutions to the derived relations at levels less than i, then each derived relation of S at level i is contained in the corresponding derived relation of S_1.

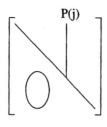

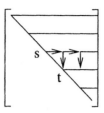

(a) Adjacency matrix A   **(b)** Matrix M and its partitioning

---

FIGURE 7.6   Matrices for Computing Transitive Closure

7.2.4 Transitive Closure

Computing the *transitive closure*, which is equivalent to computing the derived ancestor relationship, is a very common database operation. It arises in the part explosion problem where a part is made up of a set of subparts, each of which may be made up of other subparts, etc. The transitive closure problem can also be formulated as a *path problem* where there are directed edges from vertices to other vertices. Some common path problems are finding the shortest paths and the longest paths. Owing to the popularity of the transitive closure problem, we provide an algorithm here, although there are numerous algorithms on this problem. This algorithm has reasonable CPU and I/O costs.

Let G = (V,E) be a directed graph, where V are the vertices representing the persons in the ancestor problem and E are directed edges. (i, j) is a directed edge, if i is a parent of j. Let the number of vertices and the number of edges be n and e, respectively. We assume that the graph is acyclic; i.e., there is no directed cycle. In other words, no vertex can go through a sequence of directed edges and get back to itself. In the situation where directed cycles exist, the cyclic graph can be transformed into an acyclic graph as follows. Whenever a directed cycle exists, the vertices in the cycle can be merged into a single vertex and the resulting graph is acyclic. In an acyclic graph, vertices in the graph can be numbered such that whenever (i, j) is a directed edge, $i < j$. As a result, children are assigned numbers that are larger than those of their parents.

The directed graph G can be represented by an adjacency matrix A such that A(i,j) = 1 if (i,j) is a directed edge, 0 otherwise. Owing to acyclicity and the way numbers are associated with the vertices, the matrix A is upper triangular with nonzero entries only in the upper part of the matrix, as shown in Figure 7.6(a). Let P(j) denote the parents of j; it consists of the nonzero entries in the jth column of *A*.

Our aim is to compute a matrix M based on the given P(j)'s, $1 \leq j \leq n$, such that M(i,j) = 1 if and only if i is an ancestor of j. M is also upper triangular, since descendants are assigned larger numbers than ancestors. The upper triangular part of M is partitioned into horizontal blocks as shown in Figure 7.6(b) such that the main memory has enough space to store one block of M and the largest parent set, denoted by $\max_j |P(j)|$. Let the main memory size be S and the size of one block of M be *B*. Then from $S \leq B + \max_j |P(j)|$, we can determine $B \leq S - \max_j |P(j)|$. Each block can be computed independently from other blocks. For a given block, say with starting vertex s and ending vertex t (see Figure 7.6(b)), the parent sets

P(s+1), ... , P(*n*) are read into the main memory one at a time to compute the entries of M in that block.

The entries of a block of M are computed from top to bottom and from left to right as indicated in Figure 7.6(b). Initially, all entries in the block are set to zero. Then the following algorithm is invoked.

1. For j = s+1 to n /* column j */
2.   For i = s to min{j–1, t} /* row i */
3.   For each k in P(j)
4.   if (k = i or M(i,k) = 1)
5.   then M(i,j) = 1

Lines 3 through 5 say that M(i,j) = 1 if i is the parent of j (k = i and k is in P(j)) or i is an ancestor of k (M(i,k) = 1) and k is the parent of j, $i \leq k < j$. This is clearly true, if M(i,k) has been computed. This requires that the computation go from left to right, which is enforced by k < j (k in P(j)) and line 1. Line 2 permits a P(j) to be used for all rows within the block from s to t so that the P(j) is brought into the main memory only once for the block.

CPU cost. The computation of the entry M(i,j) requires time that is proportional to the size of P(j) (lines 3–5). This is the number of edges going into j. As j varies from s+1 to n (in the worst case s = 1, where all columns of M instead of those in the block are to be computed), all entries in the ith row of the upper triangular part of M are computed, requiring the sum of the sizes of the parent sets. This is e, the number of edges of the graph. When all rows are computed, the time required is $O(n \cdot e)$, where n is the number of vertices.

I/O cost. Clearly, we need to output the upper triangular matrix M. In addition, we need to input the P(j)'s for each block of M. The first block requires all P(j)'s to be read into the main memory; later blocks require fewer and fewer P(j)'s (line 1 with j goes from s+1 to n with later blocks having larger values of s). In the worst case, the total amount of data to be read into the main memory is b · e, where b is the number of blocks and e is the sum of the sizes of the P(j)'s. The number of blocks, b, is given by $|M|/B$, where $|M|$ is the size of the upper triangular matrix M and B is the size of a block given above.

Exercises

7.1 Suppose paths between vertices of a graph are defined as follows. There is an edge between vertices b and c, if there is an edge between vertices c and b. (In other words, the edges are undirected.) There is a path between two vertices, if there is an edge between them; there is a path between vertices b and c, if there is an edge between b and some vertex d and there is a path between d and c. Write a set of rules defining paths.

7.2 Consider the path definition given in Exercise (7.1). Given the following edges, find all valid paths. The edges are (a, b), (a, d), (b, e), (b, c), (d, c), (e, f), (c, g), (h, i), and (j, h).

7.3 Identify the critical difference between the definition of paths and that of ancestors.

7.4 Give a rule and a query on the rule such that the rule is not safe but the query has a finite answer. Explain why the rule is not safe.

7.5 Write a relational algebra expression for the following set of rules. Compute h(X, Y, b).

$$h(X, Y, Z) :- g(X, Y), f(Y, Z), e(X, Z), Equal(X, a)$$
$$h(X, Y, Z) :- d(X, Z), c(Z, Y)$$

7.6 Write a recursive equation for the following set of rules.

$$h(X, Y, Z) :- g(X, Y), f(Y, Z), h(X, Z, b), Equal(X, a)$$
$$h(X, Y, Z) :- d(X, Z), c(Z, Y)$$

Suppose the Naive method is used to compute the recursive equation. Populate the relations g, f, d, and c such that

(a) the recursion stops after one iteration;

(b) the recursion stops after two iterations;

(c) the recursion does not stop after one or two iterations.

7.7 Consider the following set of rules for ancestor.

$$ancestor(X, Y) :- ancestor(X, Z), ancestor(Z, Y)$$
$$ancestor(X, Y) :- parent(X, Y)$$

Suppose the Semi-Naive method is used, but the relational algebra expression to generate new tuples is given by

$$\pi_{A_1, A_2}(Del(ancestor(A_1, A_3)) \bowtie_{Del(ancestor).A_3=Del(ancestor).A_4} Del(ancestor(A_4, A_2)))$$

Explain why or why not the above algebra expression is adequate for getting all ancestors.

7.8 Apply the magic set method to the following set of rules, which is semantically equivalent to the same generation query. Note that in the modified rule, the parameters of sg are interchanged.

$$sg(X, X) :- person(X)$$
$$sg(X, Y) :- parent(PX, X), sg(PY, PX), parent(PY, Y)$$

7.9 Draw the dependency graph for the following set of rules.

$$f(A, B) :- g(A, C), h(C, D), k(D, B)$$
$$k(M, N) :- NOT\ g(E, M), f(E, N)$$

(a) Is the set of rules recursive?

(b) Is the set of rules stratified?

7.10 Modify, if necessary, the transitive closure given in this chapter so that it can be executed efficiently in parallel.

Bibliographic Notes

A significant portion of the materials of this chapter is extracted from [368, 369]. Other books on this subject include [1, 241]. Our intention is to provide some basic principles in answering queries in deductive databases. Sophisticated or advanced techniques are not presented here. For example, a more general way to handle negation can be found in [375]. Several deductive database systems have been built [277, 301]. A sample of contributors are [129, 130, 165] in basic results, [16] in giving an excellent survey of recursive query processing strategies, [374] in logic programming, [359] in the existence of least fixed points, [22, 16] in the Semi-Naive method, [300, 409] in safety of rules, and [61] in stratification of predicates involving negations. Numerous algorithms have been given to compute transitive closures; see, for example, [6, 5, 92, 187, 188]. Some parallel algorithms for transitive closures can be found in [372, 390]. SQL3 has adopted recursion as a built-in primitive. Thus, it is expected that basic principles of handling recursion are essential.

Multidimensional Search Structures

Multidimensional data such as points, line segments, and polygons can be encountered in many important applications. For example, a computer-aided VLSI design system may need to store tens of thousands of rectangles representing electronic gates and other elements. Fast identification of rectangles (i.e., electronic elements) that overlap with a given rectangle is important in such a system. Geographic information systems (GISs) store information about points (e.g., cities), line segments (e.g., roads and rivers), and polygons (e.g., regions). In GIS applications, we frequently need to respond to such queries as, "Find points of interest in a given region, where all points of interest have been prespecified in the multidimensional space," and "Find all regions that intersect with a given region." In image database systems, image features such as color, shape, and texture are usually represented as multidimensional vectors. For example, in such a vector for color, each dimension represents a range of colors. Even tuples in relational database systems can be perceived as points in a multidimensional space, with each attribute corresponding to one dimension. Usually, a query has conditions on only a subset of the attributes of a relation and only these attributes need to be considered. For example, a query finding all employees satisfying conditions "age between 25 and 30" and "salary between 50k and 75k" can be considered as a query for finding all points (age, salary) in a two-dimensional rectangle defined by $25 \leq age \leq 30$ and $50k \leq salary \leq 75k$, where each point corresponds to the age and salary values in one tuple. Although indexes on individual attributes can be used to process such a query, they may be inefficient if many employees satisfy either of the conditions but very few satisfy both conditions.

Over the past two decades, numerous data structures have been proposed for the efficient storage and manipulation of multidimensional data. Some of these structures include various types of quadtrees (point quadtree and region quadtree), different variations of R-trees (R-tree, R^+ tree, and R^*-tree), several grid structures (fixed grid file, grid file, and G-tree), k-d trees, and k-D-B trees. Most data structures are designed for point data. R-tree and its variations are primarily for rectangular data. The reason point data have received the most attention is that points are the most basic multidimensional objects. Often, other types of multidimensional objects can be represented in terms of points. For example, a line segment can be represented by two points. Rectangles whose sides are parallel with the axes can also be represented by two diagonal points. Rectangles are important because they are often used to approximate other types of spatial objects, such as polygons and irregularly shaped objects. Typically, a nonrectangular object is approximated by its *minimum bounding rectangle* (see Section 8.3).

In this chapter, we describe three representative multidimensional data structures. In Section 8.1, we describe G-tree (grid tree), which combines the advantages of grid file and B^+ tree. G-tree is designed to support the efficient storage and retrieval of points in any n-dimensional space. In Section 8.2, we describe both point quadtree and region quadtree. Whereas point quadtree is designed to support the efficient storage and retrieval of points, region quadtree is primarily developed for the efficient storage and manipulation of images. In Section 8.3, we describe R^*-tree, which is a variation of R-tree. R^*-tree is designed to support the efficient storage and retrieval of rectangles.

8.1 G-Tree

In this section, we describe G-tree (grid tree), which supports the efficient storage and retrieval of point data. An important application of G-tree is to use it as an index structure for composite keys (or any combination of attributes). Such an index can be useful for processing queries that have conditions on multiple attributes. We first describe the data structure of G-tree in Section 8.1.1. Then in Section 8.1.2, we discuss the operations on G-tree.

8.1.1 G-Tree Data Structure

For ease of presentation, it is assumed that the values of each attribute are normalized between 0 and 1. Thus, each tuple of a relation with n attributes can be considered as a point in an n-dimensional hypercube of size 1.

In this structure, the n-dimensional hypercube of size 1 is logically partitioned into many regions. Each region is an n-dimensional hyperrectangle, which is obtained by splitting some region (initially the n-dimensional hypercube) into halves repeatedly. Each region corresponds to one page in the secondary storage. That is, the page of a region is used to store all points or tuples in the region. If the storage requirement of the points in a region, say R, exceeds the capacity of a page, say due to insertion, then the region is partitioned into two equal-sized subregions, denoted by R1 and R2, by splitting one of the domains of the region R

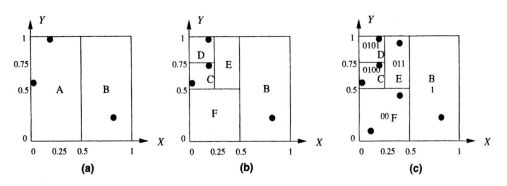

FIGURE 8.1 Partitioning a Two-Dimensional Square

into halves. Each such partition requires the allocation of a new page. If the page originally associated with R is now used to store the points in R1, then the new page will store the points in R2. In practice, no page will be allocated for regions that contain no points.

Partitions are carried out in certain order. The dimensions are ordered in advance. If a region is obtained by a partition that splits the *i*th dimension (or the *i*th attribute domain), then when the region itself needs to be partitioned, it will be split along the $(i + 1)$th dimension. If $i = n$, i.e., the *i*th dimension is the last dimension in the order, then the next partition will be along the first dimension.

Example 8.1 Consider the two-dimensional square in Figure 8.1(a). Suppose points are represented as black dots and each page can accommodate only two points. Suppose the domain along the X-axis is the first domain and the domain along the Y-axis is the second domain. Originally, the region has no points. After three points are inserted, the region is partitioned into two regions, A and B, along the X-axis (see Figure 8.1(a)). When another point is inserted into region A, it is partitioned into two smaller regions along the Y-axis. However, one of the new regions still has more than two points. Therefore, it is partitioned again, this time along the X-axis. Again, one of the new regions still has more than two points, and it is partitioned once more along the Y-axis. The resulting regions are shown in Figure 8.1(b). The subsequent insertion of three more points does not cause any new partition (see Figure 8.1(c); the binary string in each region will be explained in the next paragraph). ∎

Each region is represented as a binary string as follows. Initially, the entire region is represented by the null string. The first split results in the two regions denoted by 0 and 1. Those points whose first domain values lie between 0 and 0.5 (including 0.5) belong to region 0, and those whose first domain values lie between 0.5 (excluding 0.5) and 1 belong to region 1. In general, when a region R denoted by a binary string S is split into two subregions along the *i*th domain, the subregion whose *i*th domain has smaller values will be denoted by S"0" (i.e., add a bit "0" to the end of S) and the subregion whose *i*th domain has larger values will be denoted by S"1". Clearly, for a given region T with binary string P, the binary string of the region from which T is obtained by a single partition is P with the ending bit (i.e., the *least significant bit*) removed. It can also be observed that the number of bits in a binary string representing a region is also the number of consecutive partitions that are performed to obtain the region from the original region (i.e., the unit hypercube).

Example 8.2 Consider Figure 8.1(b). When the first partition is done, the left subregion will be denoted as 0 and the right subregion will be denoted as 1 because the domain values in the left subregion along the X-axis are smaller than those in the right subregion. When the left subregion is further partitioned, the two new subregions will be denoted as 00 and 01. The binary strings for all regions after all partitions are done are shown in Figure 8.1(c). ∎

An order can be defined for the binary strings as follows. For two strings S_1 and S_2, $S_1 < S_2$ if the first bit (i.e., the *most significant bit*) of S_1 is less than that of S_2 or they have the same first k bits, for some k, and the $(k + 1)$th bit of S_1 is less than the $(k + 1)$th bit of S_2. For the purpose of comparison, *null bits* can be added to the end of the shorter of the two binary strings. It is assumed that a null bit is less than any non-null bit. It can be observed that if S_2 is a binary string representing a region that is obtained by a partition of a region with binary string S_1, then $S_2 > S_1$. It can be shown that there is a *total order* among all binary strings generated by the above region partitions. In other words, for any two strings S_1 and S_2 generated, exactly one of $S_1 > S_2$ and $S_2 > S_1$ is true. This total order implies that all binary strings are unique and can serve as the keys for retrieving the regions. For convenience, a region and the binary string representing the region will be considered as the same.

Since there is a total order among all binary strings, they can be organized into a B+-tree-like structure, called the G-tree, for searching. Each leaf node in the G-tree consists of a number of cells of the form (S, P), where S is a binary string corresponding to a region that has no subregions and P is a pointer pointing to the disk page that contains all points in the region. All such cells in each node are arranged in ascending order of the binary strings. In addition, each leaf node N also has a pointer pointing to the next leaf node that contains cells whose binary strings are larger than those in N. Each internal node in the G-tree is of the form $(P_0; S_1, P_1; S_2, P_2; \ldots; S_m, P_m)$, where S_i is a binary string and P_i is a pointer pointing to a subtree containing all binary strings that are greater than or equal to S_i but less than S_{i+1}, $1 \le i < m, S_1 < S_2 < \cdots < S_m$. P_0 points to a subtree containing strings that are less than S_1, and P_m points to a subtree containing binary strings that are greater than or equal to S_m.

Example 8.3 Continue Example 8.2. The total order of the binary strings is $\{00, 0100, 0101, 011, 1\}$. Suppose each leaf node in the G-tree can accommodate only two cells. Figure 8.2 shows the G-tree for these binary strings. ∎

8.1.2 G-Tree Operations

The basic G-tree operations include the following: (1) the search for a point in the unit hypercube using the G-tree, (2) the search for all points in a hyperrectangle in the unit hypercube, (3) the insertion of a point into the G-tree (i.e., modify the G-tree after a new point is inserted into the unit hypercube), and (4) the deletion of a point from the G-tree.

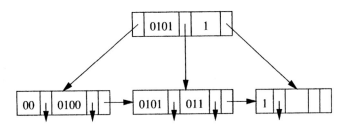

FIGURE 8.2 An Example G-Tree

Searching for a Point

Suppose the point under consideration is $P = (x_1, x_2, \ldots, x_n)$, where x_i is a constant in the ith domain, $1 \leq i \leq n$. Searching for such a point corresponds to a query for finding tuples with equality conditions on n of the attributes of the tuples. Let M be the number of bits in the longest binary string of all binary strings generated when the original hypercube is partitioned. The G-tree maintains this number M. As mentioned earlier, any subregion with such a binary string must be obtained through M consecutive partitions of the unit hypercube. Let G denote the pointer to the root of the G-tree. The point search algorithm is described as follows.

Point-Search(P, M, G)

1. Find the M-bit binary string S that represents a region R that contains P. This string is not necessarily one of the strings stored in the G-tree. The first bit of S is obtained by comparing x_1 with 0.5. If x_1 is greater than 0.5, then the first bit of S is 1; else it is 0. The second bit of S is obtained by comparing x_2 against 0.5 in a similar manner. If $n \geq M$, then this is repeated until x_M is compared with 0.5 to obtain the last bit of S. If $M > n$, then this is repeated for the first n bits of S. The $(n + 1)$th bit of S is obtained by comparing x_1 with either 0.25 in the case the first bit is 0 or with 0.75 in the case the first bit is 1. The $(n + 2)$th bit is obtained based on x_2. This is repeated until all M bits of S are obtained.

2. Search for S in the G-tree rooted at G. The purpose is to find an existing region, denoted as R_c, (i.e., the binary string of R_c, denoted as S_c, is in the G-tree) such that it contains P. Since S has M bits, the size of R is the same as the smallest existing region. Therefore, it is impossible for R to strictly contain any existing region. This implies that either R_c is the same as R or it contains R. Therefore, $S \geq S_c$.

    The search process is very much the same as the process of searching a value in a B$^+$ tree. The root node is searched first by a *binary search* until $S_{i-1} \leq S < S_i$, $1 \leq i \leq m$, or $S \geq S_m$ (S_0 is the null string, which is less than any non-null string). If $S_{i-1} \leq S < S_i$, then pointer P_{i-1} is followed to a node at the next level of the tree. If $S \geq S_m$, then pointer P_m is followed. If the new node is an internal node, then the above search process is repeated until a leaf node of the G-tree is encountered.

3. When a leaf node is encountered, a region whose binary string is the same as S or a prefix of S will be found. This region is R_c. The pointer associated with S_c points to a page containing all points in R_c. After the page is retrieved, P is compared against

each point in R_c for satisfaction. If P is found in the page, then the search succeeds; otherwise, it fails.

To guarantee the correctness of the algorithm, we need to show that when a pointer P_i, $0 \le i \le m$, is followed in the second step of the algorithm, S_c is also in the subtree pointed at by the same P_i. We consider only the case in which $S_{i-1} \le S < S_i$, $1 \le i \le m$. The other case (i.e., $S \ge S_m$) can be treated similarly. That is, we need to show $S_{i-1} \le S_c < S_i$. Since $S \ge S_c$ and $S < S_i$, $S_c < S_i$. Therefore, we only need to show that $S_{i-1} \le S_c$. This can be shown as follows: (a) If $S_{i-1} = S$, then there is an existing region whose binary string, namely S_{i-1}, is the same as S. Since no existing region strictly contains another existing region, $S_{i-1} = S_c$; (b) If $S_{i-1} < S$, compare the first t bits of S_{i-1} with those of S, where t is the number of bits of S_c. (Note: t does not need to be known.) Based on these t bits only, either $S_{i-1} < S$ or $S_{i-1} = S$. In the former case, $S_{i-1} < S_c$, since S_c and S have the same first t bits. In the latter case, S must have a bit beyond the tth bit that is greater than the corresponding bit in S_{i-1}, which is either a null bit or a non-null bit. That S_{i-1} has a non-null bit beyond the tth bit and $S_{i-1} = S$ (i.e., S and S_{i-1} have the same first t bits) would imply that S_c is a prefix of S_{i-1}, i.e., the region with string S_{i-1} would be a subregion of R_c. This is impossible because all regions whose binary strings are in the G-tree are disjoint. Thus, if S and S_{i-1} have the same first t bits, all bits of S_{i-1} beyond the tth bit must be null. Therefore, $S_c = S_{i-1}$.

Example 8.4 Consider the G-tree in Figure 8.2. Suppose the point to be searched for is P = (0.3, 0.6). Since the longest binary string in the G-tree has four bits, we first find the four-bit binary string S that represents a region that contains P. Since $0.3 \le 0.5$, the first bit of S is 0. From $0.6 > 0.5$, the second bit of S is 1. Next, since $0.3 > 0.25$, the third bit of S is 1. Finally, the fourth bit of S is 0 because $0.6 \le 0.75$. Thus, $S = 0110$. When S is used to search the G-tree in the root node, the pointer between 0101 and 1 is followed because $0101 \le 0110 < 1$. In the corresponding leaf node, we find that 011 is a prefix of S. Therefore, the page pointed at by the pointer of 011 should be fetched to see whether P is in the region.   ∎

Searching for All Points in a Region

Suppose the points to be searched for are in the region R = $\{(l_1, h_1), (l_2, h_2), \ldots, (l_n, h_n)\}$, where l_i and h_i are two constants indicating the lower and upper bounds of the ith domain of the region, $1 \le i \le n$. Note that R is not necessarily one of the existing regions in the G-tree. In fact, R could be contained in an existing region or across multiple existing regions. Searching for such a region corresponds to a *range query* for finding tuples with range conditions on n of the attributes of the tuples. Partial search in which there is no restriction on some attributes can be considered a special case. Again, let M be the number of bits in the longest binary string of all binary strings and let G denote the pointer to the root of the G-tree. The region search algorithm is as described below.

Region-Search(R, M, G)

1. Perform Point-Search(P1, M, G) to obtain a leaf node N1, where P1 = $(l_1, l_2, \ldots, l_n)$. P1 is the point that is contained in an existing region with the smallest binary string, among all points in the given region R.

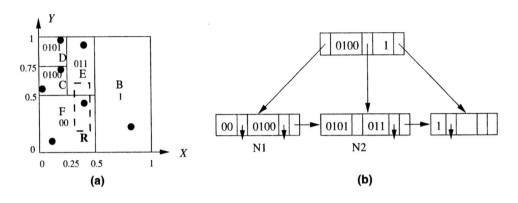

FIGURE 8.3 **Illustrating the Region-Search Algorithm**

2. Perform Point-Search(P2, M, G) to obtain a leaf node N2, where P2 = $(h_1, h_2, \ldots, h_n)$. P2 is the point that is contained in an existing region with the largest binary string, among all points in R.

3. The leaf nodes of the G-tree are linked together in ascending order of binary strings by a linked list. For each node from node N1 to node N2, check each binary string S to see if the corresponding region overlaps with the region R. To do this, we need to convert S representing a region R_S to the boundaries of the region along each domain. The conversion algorithm will be discussed shortly. For now, suppose S has been converted to $\{(x_1, y_1), (x_2, y_2), \ldots, (x_n, y_n)\}$. If $x_i \geq l_i$ and $y_i \leq h_i$ for all $1 \leq i \leq n$, then R_S is entirely contained in R; otherwise, if $x_i \leq h_i$ and $y_i \geq l_i$ for all $1 \leq i \leq n$, then R_S overlaps with R.

4. For each region that is entirely contained in R, the corresponding data page is fetched and all points in the region are qualified. For each region that overlaps with R but is not contained in R, the corresponding data page is fetched and each point in the page is checked for satisfaction with R.

We now describe the algorithm for converting any given binary string S representing a region R_S to the boundaries of the region along each domain. Let B be the number of bits in S and n be the number of domains (dimensions) of the unit hypercube. If the ith bit, $1 \leq i \leq n$, in S is 0, then $x_i = 0$ and $y_i = 0.5$; else, if it is 1, then $x_i = 0.5$ and $y_i = 1$; else, if it is a null bit (i.e., $B < i$), then $x_i = 0$ and $y_i = 1$. If $B > n$, then the next n bits of S are converted as follows. Consider the jth bit, $n < j \leq 2n$. If it is 0, then x_{j-n} remains unchanged and y_{j-n} is changed to $(x_{j-n} + y_{j-n})/2$; else, if it is 1, then y_{j-n} remains unchanged and x_{j-n} is changed to $(x_{j-n} + y_{j-n})/2$; else, if it is a null bit, both x_{j-n} and y_{j-n} remain unchanged. This process is repeated until all bits of S are considered.

Example 8.5 Consider the region partitions in Figure 8.3(a). Its corresponding G-tree is shown in Figure 8.3(b). Suppose we like to find all points in the region R = $\{(0.3, 0.4),$ $(0.2, 0.6)\}$ (see Figure 8.3(a)). By performing Point-Search(P1, 4, G), where P1 = (0.3, 0.2), the first leaf node is identified as N1. Similarly, by performing Point-Search(P2, 4, G), where P2 = (0.4, 0.6), the second leaf node is identified as N2. Next, each binary string in the leaf nodes between N1 and N2 is checked to see whether its corresponding region overlaps with R. Consider the first binary string 00 in N1. It is first converted to region $R_S = \{(0, 0.5), (0, 0.5)\}$. Since $x_1 = 0 \not\geq l_1 = 0.3$, R_S is not contained in R. Since $0 \leq 0.4$, $0 \leq 0.6$, $0.5 \geq 0.3$, and $0.5 \geq 0.2$, R_S overlaps with R. Thus, the corresponding disk page is fetched to find desired points. Next, consider binary string 0100. It is converted to the region $\{(0, 0.25), (0.5, 0.75)\}$. Since it neither is contained in nor overlaps with R, the corresponding page is not retrieved. Similarly, the page corresponding to the region with 0101 need not be retrieved, and the page corresponding to the region with 011 needs to be retrieved.   ■

Inserting a Point

Suppose the point under consideration is $P = (x_1, x_2, \ldots, x_n)$. Again, let M be the number of bits in the longest binary string and let G denote the pointer to the root of the G-tree. The algorithm for inserting the point P is described as follows.

Insert(P, M, G)

1. Apply algorithm Point-Search(P, M, G) to obtain the page PG corresponding to the region R that should contain P if P is in the unit hypercube. Let S be the binary string of R and LN be the leaf node in the G-tree that has the pointer to PG.

2. If point P is already in page PG and no duplicate points are allowed, report "The point is already there; insertion fails," and exit.

3. If point P is not already in page PG or if it is already in but duplicate points are allowed, insert P into PG.

   If the number of points in PG does not exceed the maximum allowed, then no further action is needed. Otherwise, split PG into two pages, PG1 and PG2, with binary strings $S_1 = S\text{"0"}$ and $S_2 = S\text{"1"}$, respectively. Each of S_1 and S_2 corresponds to a new region (see the above algorithm for converting a binary string to a region), and the new regions are subregions of R. If the new strings have more than M bits, then update M to $M + 1$. Points in PG are allocated to PG1 and PG2 depending on which subregion they belong to. More specifically, for each point P' in PG, a binary string S' with K bits (K denotes the number of bits in S_1) that represents a region containing P' can be constructed (see step 1 in algorithm Point-Search). Now if the last bit of S' is 0, then P' is allocated to PG1; else, it is allocated to PG2. If one of the new pages still contains too many points (i.e., the other page does not contain any point), then it is split again according to the above process. This is repeated until the number of points in each new page is within the maximum allowed. Without losing generality, we assume that PG1 and PG2 are the final new pages obtained (i.e., none of them is empty). Now replace the cell (S, T) in the leaf node LN by two cells $(S_1, T1)$ and $(S_2, T2)$, where T, T1, and T2 are the pointers to PG, PG1, and PG2, respectively. If there is no overflow in node LN, then no further action is needed. Otherwise, the overflow propagates to the parent of LN and possibly the higher-level ancestors of LN. This can be handled by standard B^+-tree techniques.

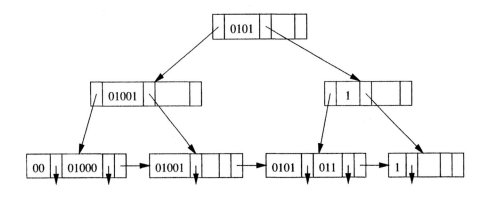

FIGURE 8.4 The G-Tree after P = (0.1, 0.7) Is Inserted

Example 8.6 Consider the region partitions in Figure 8.1(c). Its corresponding G-tree is shown in Figure 8.2. Suppose we would like to insert a point P = (0.1, 0.7) into the unit hypercube. Suppose when Point-Search(P, 4, G) is applied, the disk page PG corresponding to the region 0100 is found. Let LN be the leaf node in the G-tree that contains 0100. Suppose PG contains the two points P1 = (0.1, 0.6) and P2 = (0.2, 0.7) before P is inserted. After P is inserted, the number of points in PG exceeds the maximum (i.e., 2) allowed. Therefore, PG is split into two pages, PG1 and PG2, with binary strings 01000 and 01001. According to step 1 in algorithm Point-Search, the binary strings for P, P1, and P2 are 01000, 01000, and 01001, respectively. Therefore, P and P1 are allocated to PG1 and P2 is allocated to PG2. Next, the cell containing 0100 in LN is replaced by two new cells containing 01000 and 01001. This causes LN to overflow. As a result, LN needs to be split into two nodes. This in turn causes the root node to overflow. Figure 8.4 shows the modified G-tree after P is successfully inserted. ∎

Deleting a Point

We now provide an algorithm to delete a point P from the unit hypercube. We keep the notation used above.

Delete(P, M, G)

1. Apply algorithm Point-Search(P, M, G) to obtain the page PG corresponding to the region R that should contain P if P is in the unit hypercube. Let S be the binary string of R and LN be the leaf node in the G-tree that has the pointer to PG.

2. If P is not in page PG, then report, "The point to be deleted does not exist," and exit. If P is in PG, delete it from PG. Let R' be the *buddy region* of R (whose binary string, S', differs from S only in the last bit; i.e., S, and S' are obtained in the same partition). It is possible that S' is not in the G-tree because R' may have been further partitioned. We consider the following two cases.

(a) R' has been further partitioned. If PG becomes empty after P is deleted, then delete S fron LN; otherwise, no further action is needed.

(b) R' has not been further partitioned. If the total number of points in R and R' is greater than the maximum number of points allowed for a single region (this implies that both R and R' are non-empty and they cannot be merged), then no further action is needed; otherwise, combine the regions R and R' into a single region (the *parent region* of R and R'). This is achieved by (i) moving all points in the two pages corresponding to R and R' to one page, say PG, (ii) deleting S and S' from the G-tree, and (iii) inserting a new binary string, say S'', which is obtained by removing the last bit of S, into the G-tree.

For both cases, if the deletion of a binary string from a node causes the node to under-flow (i.e., has fewer than the minimum number of cells permitted), then it needs to be merged with one of its sibling nodes. This process is similar to that used for standard B^+ trees.

8.2 Quadtree

Quadtree represents a class of hierarchical data structures that are based on the recursive decomposition of space into four parts. There are large number of variations of quadtrees, and they are designed for different applications. Those that are primarily used to represent regions are known as *region quadtrees*, and those for points are called *point quadtrees*. We first discuss point quadtrees and then region quadtrees.

8.2.1 Point Quadtree Structure

A point quadtree is a nonbalanced search tree. Each node in the tree has exactly four child nodes. Each internal node represents a point in a two-dimensional space. All leaf nodes are empty, and they contain no real data. The root node divides the entire two-dimensional space into four quadrants, NE, NW, SW, and SE. Consider an internal node B. Suppose B is a child node of the root node A. This means that B is in one of the four quadrants divided by A (to resolve points on the boundaries of the four quadrants, quadrants NE and SW are supposed to be *closed*, while quadrants NW and SE are *open*). Node B divides the two-dimensional subspace corresponding to the quadrant containing B also into four quadrants. In general, each internal node divides the subspace it is in into four quadrants. Each internal node has the structure $(X, Y, P1, P2, P3, P4)$, where (X, Y) are the coordinates of the corresponding point, and P1, P2, P3, and P4 are pointers pointing to the four child nodes in quadrants NE, NW, SW, and SE, respectively. An example point quadtree and its corresponding point distribution in a two-dimensional space are shown in Figure 8.5.

Point quadtree can be used to build indexes on composite keys. For example, if a relation R has a composite key consisting of two attributes A_1 and A_2, then an index on A_1 and A_2 can be built using a point quadtree with A_1 as the X-axis and A_2 as the Y-axis to speed up the search based on the values of A_1 and A_2. For such an application, an additional pointer for the location of the corresponding tuple is added in each internal node.

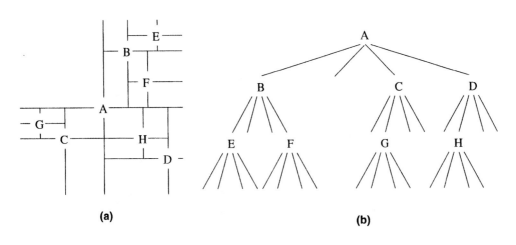

FIGURE 8.5 An Example Point Quadtree

Note that point quadtree can easily be extended to accommodate points in any general *n*-dimensional space. For example, in a three-dimensional space, each point divides the three-dimensional space into eight regions and the point quadtree becomes the point octree.

8.2.2 Point Quadtree Operations

The basic point quadtree operations include (1) the search for a point in a quadtree, (2) the search for all points in a rectangle, (3) the insertion of a new point into a quadtree, and (4) the deletion of a point from a quadtree. We now discuss these operations.

Searching for a Point

Suppose the point under consideration is P = (x, y). Let T denote the pointer to the root of the quadtree. The search algorithm is as follows.

Point-Search(P, T)

1. If T is a leaf node, return *not found* and exit.

2. If T is an internal node, the following two cases may occur:

 (a) If the point in T is the same as P, return *found* and exit.

 (b) If the point in T is different from P, check which quadrant of T may contain P. This can be determined as follows. Let (X, Y) be the coordinates of the point in T. If $x \geq X$ and $y \geq Y$, then P is in the NE quadrant. If $x > X$ and $y < Y$, then P is in the SE quadrant. If $x < X$ and $y > Y$, then P is in the NW quadrant. If $x \leq X$ and $y \leq Y$, then P is in the SW quadrant. Suppose S is the child pointer corresponding to the quadrant that may contain P. Recursively search the subtree by calling Point-Search(P, S).

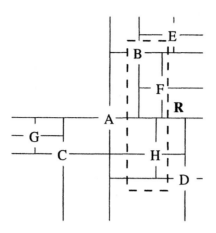

FIGURE 8.6 **Search for All Points in R**

Searching for All Points in a Rectangle

Suppose the rectangle R under consideration is represented by the point at the lower left corner (x_1, y_1) and the point at the upper right corner (x_2, y_2). Let T denote the pointer to the root of the quadtree and K be the set containing the result of the search. K is empty initially. The search algorithm is as follows.

Rectangle-Search(x_1, y_1, x_2, y_2, T)

1. If T is a leaf node, exit.

2. If T is an internal node, check whether the point in T, $P = (X, Y)$ is in R. This can be done by checking whether "$x_1 \leq X \leq x_2$ and $y_1 \leq Y \leq y_2$" is true. If P is in R, add P into K.

   For each quadrant of T, if the corresponding child pointer is not null, check whether it overlaps with R. Whether or not a quadrant overlaps with a rectangle can be determined by using the coordinate of the point at T and the coordinates of the rectangle. For example, the NE quadrant of T overlaps with R if $x_2 \geq X$ and $y_2 \geq Y$. For each quadrant that overlaps with R, replace R by R', the intersection of R and the quadrant. Let the lower left corner point and the upper right corner point of R' be (x_1', y_1') and (x_2', y_2'), respectively. These coordinates can be determined easily. For example, if the NE quadrant overlaps with R, then $x_1' = \max\{X, x_1\}$, $x_2' = x_2$, $y_1' = \max\{Y, y_1\}$, and $y_2' = y_2$. Suppose S is the child pointer corresponding to the quadrant that overlaps with R; recursively search the subtree by calling Rectangle-Search($x_1', y_1', x_2', y_2', S$).

   Note that several subtrees may be searched at each level of the tree.

Example 8.7 Consider the point quadtree in Figure 8.5. Suppose we want to find all points in the rectangle R shown in Figure 8.6. The search starts from the root node. Point A is not in R, and it is not returned. Among the quadrants of A, the NE and SE quadrants have non-null

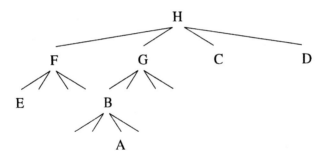

FIGURE 8.7 A Different Point Quadtree

pointers and overlap with R. The two quadrants partition R into R1 and R2, where R1 is the intersection rectangle of R and the NE quadrant, and R2 is the intersection rectangle of R and the SE quadrant. Thus the subtree rooted at B is searched against R1 and the subtree rooted at D is searched against R2. Consider the search of the subtree rooted at B against R1 first. B is in R1, and it is returned. R1 is then partitioned into R11 and R12, the intersection rectangles of R2 and the NE and SE quadrants of B, respectively. The search of the subtree rooted at E against R11 returns nothing, and the search of the subtree rooted at F against R12 returns F. Similarly, the search of the subtree rooted at D against R2 will eventually return H. Therefore, the result of the search is K = {B, F, H}. ∎

Inserting a New Point

Let P = (x, y) be the point to be inserted and T denote the pointer to the root node of the point quadtree. The insert algorithm is described below.

Insert(P, T)

1. If T is a leaf node, replace it with the internal node $(x, y, null, null, null, null)$ and exit.

2. If T is an internal node, determine the quadrant of T that contains P. Suppose S is the child pointer corresponding to the quadrant containing P. Insert P into the subtree rooted at S by calling Insert(P, S).

Point quadtree is a nonbalanced tree. The shape of a point quadtree is highly dependent on the order in which the points are inserted into the tree. In other words, the same set of points, when inserted in different orders, may result in very different quadtrees. As an example, the quadtree in Figure 8.5(b) could be obtained by inserting the points in the order {A, B, C, D, E, F, G, H}. If the insertion order is reversed, the quadtree shown in Figure 8.7 will be obtained. In the worst case, a point quadtree of n points could have a height of $n - 1$. Experiments indicate that when points are inserted in random order, the height of the tree is typically $O(\log n)$.

Deleting a Point

Point quadtree is not well suited for deletion. The main difficulty is determining where to place the points in the subtree rooted at the deleted node. For example, when point G in Figure 8.7 is deleted, we need to find places for points B and A. One possible solution is to reinsert those points into the tree as if they were new points.

8.2.3 Region Quadtree Structure

Region quadtrees are often used to represent black-and-white images on a two-dimensional space. As is not the case with a point quadtree, in which the space has no boundaries, the space used in a region quadtree is usually bounded and has a limited area. In fact, the space is usually a square. A black-and-white image in a square can be represented as a two-dimensional array $a[n, n]$, where n is the number of pixels in each dimension. For convenience, n is chosen to be 2^k for some integer k. Suppose $a[i, j] = 0$ represents a white pixel (i.e., a pixel not in the image) and $a[i, j] = 1$ represents a black pixel.

An image on an n-by-n square can be represented as a region quadtree as follows. The entire square is represented as the root node of the tree. If the square is not homogeneous— i.e., if it contains both 0s and 1s—then the square is divided into four equal-sized subsquares, or quadrants. The four subsquares are the four child nodes of the root. If any subsquare is not homogeneous, it is divided again into four smaller subsquares and they become the child nodes of the subsquare. This process of dividing a square into subsquares stops when the square becomes homogeneous.

Example 8.8 Consider the two-dimensional array in Figure 8.8(a). The corresponding image (the letter T) is shown in Figure 8.8(b). The eight-by-eight square, represented by the root node A of the region quadtree, is not homogeneous. Thus it is divided into four quadrants, NE, NW, SW, and SE. The four quadrants (subsquares) are represented by nodes B, C, D, and E, respectively. None of the four subsquares is homogeneous. Therefore, further division is needed. Consider the subsquare corresponding to the NE quadrant. When this subsquare is divided into four smaller subsquares, the ones corresponding to its NE and NW quadrants are homogeneous and the other two are not. Since the pixels in the NE and NW subsquares are all black, the two subsquares are represented by black squares. After the SW and SE subsquares are divided into four even smaller subsquares, these new subsquares are found to be homogeneous. As a result, no further division is needed. The division of other subsquares of the original square can be done similarly. The region quadtree in Figure 8.8(c) is the final representation of the image T. ∎

Color images can also be represented by region quadtrees. This can be achieved easily by defining homogeneous squares as those whose pixels all have the same color.

In summary, each internal node in a region quadtree has exactly four child nodes, representing the four quadrants of the square of the parent node, and each leaf node represents a homogeneous subsquare of the original square. A region quadtree is likely to be unbalanced. Shallower leaf nodes represent larger homogeneous subsquares. A deep subtree indicates more variations. Since each homogeneous square can be represented as a single leaf node, images with large homogeneous squares can be efficiently represented by a region quadtree.

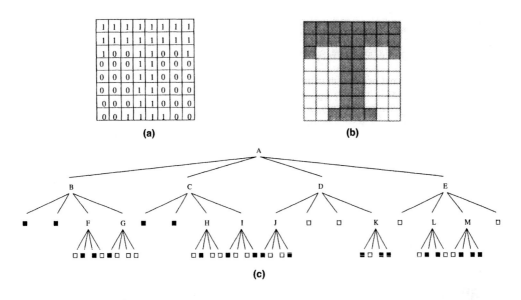

FIGURE 8.8 An Image and Its Region Quadtree

In fact, the main motivation for developing region quadtrees is to reduce the space needed to store image data.

8.2.4 Region Quadtree Operations

Unlike other tree structures discussed in this chapter, region quadtrees are not primarily used for searching. As a data structure for representing images, region quadtrees are often used to support operations on images, and such operations often become operations on region quadtrees. Some of the frequently used operations are point search, set operations (e.g., union and intersection), transformation (e.g., rotation), and clipping. In this subsection, we only describe point search and set intersection. Other operations on region quadtrees can be found in the references in the Bibliographic Notes.

Searching for a Point

Given a point $P = (x_1, y_1)$, to know whether P is in an image requires a search of the region quadtree representing the image for P. If the leaf subsquare containing P is white, then P is not in the image. Otherwise, P is in the image. A more general problem that requires the search of a point is to determine the color of a pixel. Without loss of generality, we assume that the square corresponding to the root node of the region quadtree is $l \le x \le r, b \le y \le t$. Let T be the pointer to the root of the quadtree. The search algorithm that returns the color of the given point is described as follows.

Search(x_1, y_1, l, r, b, t, T)

1. If T is a leaf node, return the color of the node and exit.

2. If T is an internal node, determine which quadrant of T contains P. This can be accomplished as follows. First, compute the center (x_c, y_c) of the square corresponding to T. It is easy to see that $x_c = (l + r)/2$ and $y_c = (b + t)/2$. Next, determine which quadrant contains P. This can be easily determined by comparing x_1 with x_c and y_1 with y_c. For example, if $x_1 > x_c$ and $y_1 > y_c$, then P is in the NE quadrant. In this case, the search can be continued in the subtree of the NE quadrant by invoking Search($x_1, y_1, x_c, r, y_c, t, S_{NE}$), where S_{NE} is the corresponding subtree pointer. Other cases can be handled similarly.

Intersection

The intersection of two images is a new image composed of the pixels in both of the original images. The new image can also be represented by a region quadtree. The intersection algorithm described below takes the region quadtrees of the original images as the input and produces the region quadtree of the new image. It is assumed that the two original images are placed on squares of the same size. Only black-and-white images are considered. The algorithm starts from the root nodes of the two region quadtrees and moves down the trees in a synchronized manner. Let T, S, and N be the pointers to the root nodes of the two input region quadtrees and the new region quadtree, respectively. Initially, N is null.

Intersect(T, S, N)

1. If at least one of T and S is a leaf node, then consider the following two cases.

    (a) Both T and S are leaf nodes. If one of the nodes is white, create a white node for N, because the intersection of a white and anything else produces a white. If one of the nodes is black, copy the other node into N, because when any image intersects with a black, the image remains unchanged.

    (b) Exactly one of T and S is a leaf node. Suppose T is a leaf node. If T is white, create a white node for N. This is because the intersection between any image and a white square is the white square. If T is black, copy S into N. This is because the intersection between any image and a black square is the image itself.

2. Both T and S are internal nodes. First, make N an internal node with four null child pointers. Next, recursively call the algorithm to perform intersection between corresponding subtrees. For example, let T_{NE}, S_{NE}, and N_{NE} denote the pointers to the subtrees corresponding to their respective NE quadrants. Then the intersection of T_{NE} and S_{NE} into N_{NE} can be performed by Intersect(T_{NE}, S_{NE}, N_{NE}).

    If all child nodes of N are leaf nodes and have the same color (white or black), they will be removed and N will become a leaf node with the color. This step is to merge homogeneous subsquares into a single square.

Example 8.9 Consider the two images that are in the NE and SW quadrants of the square in Figure 8.8(b). Their region quadtrees are the subtrees rooted at B and D, respectively, in

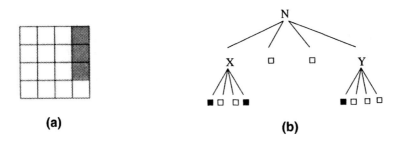

(a)   (b)

FIGURE 8.9 Illustrating Region Quadtree Intersection

Figure 8.8(c). To find the region quadtree of the new image resulting from the intersection of the given images, the root nodes are first examined. Since both B and D are internal nodes, the root node N of the new quadtree is created. Next, we try to intersect the leftmost subtrees of B and D. Since the leftmost child node of B is a black leaf node and node J is an internal node, the subtree rooted at J will become the leftmost subtree of N (J is renamed X in the resulting quadtree). It can be easily seen that the intersection of the second leftmost subtrees of B and D will result in a white node as the second leftmost child of N, and the intersection of the second rightmost subtrees of B and D will also result in a white node as the second rightmost child of N. The rightmost child of N will be an internal node, denoted Y, since both G and K are internal nodes. The intersections of the child nodes of G and K will result in four child leaf nodes for Y, one black (the leftmost one) and three white. The image from the intersection of the two given images and its corresponding region quadtree representation are shown in Figure 8.9(a) and (b), respectively.   ∎

8.3 R*-Tree

Given a spatial object O in a two-dimensional space (i.e., the plane), the smallest rectangle containing O whose sides are parallel to the axes can be easily determined. Let the rectangle be represented by the two points at the lower left corner, say (x_1, y_1), and at the upper right corner, say (x_2, y_2). Then x_1 is the smallest possible x-coordinate of all points on O and y_1 is the smallest possible y-coordinate of all points on O. Similarly, x_2 is the largest possible x-coordinate of all points on O and y_2 is the largest possible y-coordinate of all points on O. This rectangle is called the *minimum bounding rectangle*. Figure 8.10(a) illustrates the minimum bounding rectangle of an irregular object. Note that it is possible for the minimum bounding rectangle of one object to be contained in or to overlap with the minimum bounding rectangle of another object even when the two objects themselves do not overlap (see Figure 8.10(b)). The concept of the minimum bounding rectangle of one object can easily be extended to that of multiple objects (see Figure 8.10(c)). Finally, this concept can be extended to the *minimum bounding hypercube* for objects in any n-dimensional space, $n \geq 2$.

R*-tree is designed to speed up the search for multidimensional objects based on their locations in a multidimensional space.

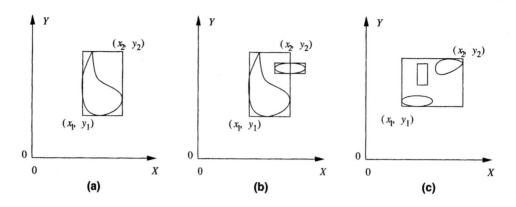

FIGURE 8.10   Minimum Bounding Rectangle of One or More Objects

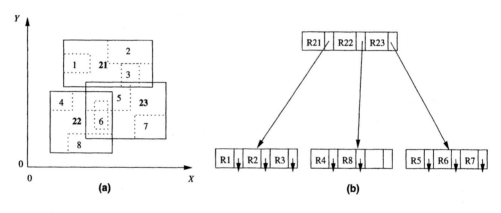

FIGURE 8.11   An Example R*-Tree

8.3.1   R*-Tree Structure

R-tree is a class of multidimensional structures designed for fast access of multidimensional objects based on their locations. R*-tree is a particularly useful variation of R-tree. R-tree (as well as R*-tree) has a B+-tree-like structure. An internal node N of an R*-tree consists of cells of the form (R, P), where P is a pointer to a child node of N and R is the minimum bounding rectangle of the set of minimum bounding rectangles in the child node pointed to by P (i.e., R is the minimum bounding rectangle of the set of rectangle objects in the node pointed to by P). Rectangle R1 is called a child rectangle of rectangle R if R1 is in the child node pointed to by the pointer associated with R. Note that a rectangle, say S, being contained in another rectangle, say R, does not always imply that S is a child rectangle of R. In other words, it is possible for S to be contained in several higher-level rectangles while it is the child of only one of them. As an example, in Figure 8.11, rectangles 22 and 23 both contain rectangle 6. However, only rectangle 23 is the parent of rectangle 6 (see Example 8.10 for more detail). A leaf node of an R*-tree also consists of cells of the form (R, P), except that P here is the pointer to a spatial object and R is the minimum bounding rectangle of the object. We call such a rectangle an *object rectangle*. Nonobject rectangles will be called *directory rectangles*. Each node (internal or leaf) is stored as a physical page in the secondary storage.

There are two important differences between an R*-tree and a B^+ tree. The first difference is that cells in each node in a B^+ tree are ordered whereas there is no order among the cells in any node in an R*-tree. The second difference is that rectangles corresponding to sibling cells in an R*-tree may overlap whereas there is no overlap between the ranges covered by sibling cells in a B^+ tree. These differences have significant impacts on the way in which an R*-tree is searched and maintained.

Let M be the maximum number of cells that can be held in one node. Let m be the minimum number of cells required to be in a node. Usually, m is chosen to be between 2 and $M/2$. Extensive experiments suggest that choosing $m = 0.4M$ can yield excellent performance. An R*-tree satisfies the following properties:

1. The root node has at least two child nodes unless it is the only node of the tree.

2. Every node has between m and M cells unless it is the root node. This implies that each nonroot internal node has m to M child nodes.

3. All leaf nodes appear at the same level. That is, R*-tree is a balanced tree.

Example 8.10 Consider the rectangles in Figure 8.11(a). Suppose the rectangles with dotted edges are the object rectangles, i.e., they are the basic minimum bounding rectangles of two-dimensional spatial objects in the database. Figure 8.11(b) shows an R*-tree with $M = 3$ and $m = 2$ based on Figure 8.11(a) (R_i is used to denote rectangle i). Each rectangle with solid edges in Figure 8.11(a) represents a directory rectangle. Directory rectangles are numbered in boldfaced numbers. Note that rectangles 22 and 23 both contain rectangle 6. However, only rectangle 23 is the parent of rectangle 6 (see Figure 8.11(b)). How to choose a parent rectangle will be discussed in the next subsection.   ∎

8.3.2   R*-Tree Operations

The basic R*-tree operations include the following: (1) Given a rectangle S, find all object rectangles in the R*-tree that overlap with S. A special case is to find all object rectangles that contain a given point. (2) Insert a new object rectangle into the R*-tree. (3) Delete an object rectangle from the R*-tree. We now discuss these operations below.

Searching for Overlapping Rectangles

Let S be the rectangle under consideration. That is, we want to find all object rectangles in the R*-tree that overlap with S. Let (R, P) be a cell in an internal node N of the R*-tree. If S overlaps with R, then there is the possibility that an object rectangle contained in R will overlap with S. This means that pointer P should be followed so that the child rectangles of R can be examined against S. Clearly, this should be repeated for every cell in N whose rectangle overlaps with S. Since there is no order among the cells in N, we have to compare S with the rectangle of every cell in N in order to avoid missing any qualified object rectangle.

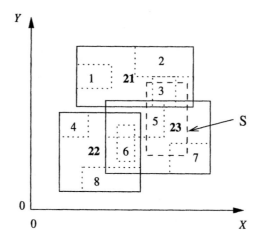

FIGURE 8.12 *Search for Overlapping Object Rectangles with S*

In summary, if a node in the R*-tree is reached during the search process, then all cells in the node must be examined. Let T denote the pointer to the root of the R*-tree. The search algorithm is as follows.

Search(S, T)

1. If T is not a leaf node, check each cell (R, P) in T to determine whether R overlaps with S. The two rectangles $R = \{(x_1, y_1), (x_2, y_2)\}$, where (x_1, y_1) is the point at the lower left corner and (x_2, y_2) is the point at the upper right corner, and $S = \{(x_3, y_3), (x_4, y_4)\}$ overlap if $x_3 \leq x_2$, $y_3 \leq y_2$, $x_4 \geq x_1$, and $y_4 \geq y_1$. If R overlaps with S, recursively check the cells in the child node by calling Search(S, P).

2. If T is a leaf node, check each cell (R, P) in T to determine whether R overlaps with S. If R overlaps with S, return R.

Example 8.11 Continue Example 8.10. Suppose the broken-edged rectangle in Figure 8.12 is the rectangle S under consideration. When the root node of the R*-tree is searched (see Figure 8.11(b)), rectangles 21 and 23 are found to overlap with S. Among the child rectangles of rectangle 21, rectangle 3 overlaps with S. Among the child rectangles of rectangle 23, rectangles 5 and 7 overlap with S. Therefore, the object rectangles that overlap with S are those numbered 3, 5, and 7. ∎

Inserting a New Object Rectangle

Let S be the object rectangle to be inserted. Inserting a new object rectangle into an R*-tree is similar to inserting a record into a secondary index B$^+$ tree in that the cell corresponding to the new object rectangle will be inserted into a leaf node, and if the insertion causes an overflow, the node will be split into two nodes. In the worst case, the split may result in a split of the parent node, and the grandparent node, and so on, all the way to the root node. However, there is also a fundamental difference between inserting into an R*-tree and inserting into a B$^+$ tree. For the latter, there is a unique node into which the new cell can be inserted. This is because the ranges corresponding to different nodes at the same level in a B$^+$ tree form a partition of the domain of the indexing attribute. However, because the directory rectangles corresponding to different nodes at the same level in an R*-tree may overlap and the new object rectangle S may overlap with multiple existing directory rectangles, S may be inserted into one of several possible nodes. In other words, at each nonleaf level of the R*-tree, we may need to choose one directory rectangle among a number of directory rectangles to be the parent rectangle of S. The chosen rectangle may need to be enlarged in order to contain S. In fact, one difference between the original R-tree (see Reference [156]) and R*-tree is in the way the parent rectangle is chosen. A number of optimization criteria could be used to guide the choice. For example, least area enlargement to the parent rectangle is the criterion used by R-tree. Different criteria are used by R*-tree depending on whether the directory rectangles are the parents of object rectangles (see the algorithm below). After a leaf node N into which S is to be inserted is determined, an attempt is made to insert S into N. If N has available space to accommodate S, the insertion will be carried out and the algorithm will terminate. However, if the insertion causes an overflow, then the following two cases will be considered.

1. If this is the first overflow at the leaf level caused by the insertion of S, then several of the $M + 1$ cells (the M cells in N plus the new cell to be inserted) will be selected for reinsertion (i.e., the selected cells will first be removed from N and then reinserted into the R*-tree as if they were new cells) and the remaining ones will be kept in N. There are two reasons for employing reinsertion. First, it may reduce the number of splits needed (see case 2 below). Second, it is an important technique for dynamically reorganizing the tree.

2. If this is not the first overflow, the $M + 1$ cells will be split into two nodes. How to split the $M + 1$ cells is the major difference between different variations of R-tree.

    If a split occurs, two cells will be generated for the parent node to replace the original cell. This means that a new cell needs to be inserted into the parent node. Such an insertion may result in an overflow for the parent node. In general, the overflow may be propagated all the way to the root node. When an overflow occurs for a node N1 at any particular level for the first time, the aforementioned reinsertion technique can be applied to reinsert several cells of N1. Note that cells selected for reinsertion must be reinserted into some nodes at the same level with N1. Thus, to support reinsertion, the insertion algorithm must allow the insertion of cells at any specified level, not just at the leaf level. Note that one reinsertion may cause one or more new reinsertions and an infinite loop may occur as a result. To prevent this from happening, new reinsertions at any level are allowed only for the first overflow at this level for each original insertion. For any additional overflow, split is applied.

The following definition is needed for presenting the insertion algorithm.

Definition 8.1 *Let* T *be a node in an R*-tree. The* overlap *of a rectangle* R *in* T *is the sum of the overlapping areas of other rectangles in* T *with* R.

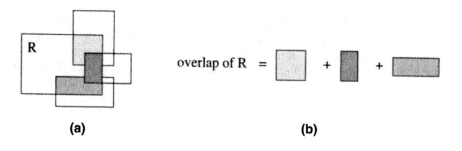

FIGURE 8.13   Overlap of R in T

Example 8.12 Let the rectangles in a node T be as shown in Figure 8.13(a). Figure 8.13(b) illustrates the overlap of R in T. ∎

When inserting a rectangle, say S, into a child node of T, some rectangle, say R, in T needs to be chosen as the parent rectangle of S. R may need to be enlarged in order to contain S. One optimization technique is to choose such an R in T that needs the least *overlap* enlargement to contain S. Clearly, when R is enlarged, the overlap of R in T is likely to increase. It is also clear that if R contains S already, then zero enlargement to R is needed. Minimizing the overlap tends to reduce the number of subtrees to follow for search operations.

We now present the insertion algorithm more rigorously. Let T denote the pointer to the root of the R*-tree and let (S, P_S) be the cell to be inserted, where P_S is the address pointer of rectangle S. Let L be the level at which (S, P_S) is to be inserted. Initially, L is the leaf level. Each level has an overflow flag indicating whether an overflow has occurred at this level. At the beginning, overflow flags at all levels are set to off.

Insert(S, P_S, L, T)

1. Select a node N at level L to insert S. This is carried out recursively from the root node to a node at level L. If T is a node at level L, return T. Otherwise, select a subtree to go down. This is done by choosing a proper cell in T. Two cases are considered.

    (a) If T is a parent of leaf nodes, choose the cell in T whose corresponding rectangle needs the least overlap enlargement to contain S. If several rectangles in T need the same least overlap enlargement to contain S, choose the rectangle whose *area* needs the least enlargement. (Note that the *area* of a rectangle and the *overlap* of a rectangle in T are different concepts.) If again several rectangles in T have the same least area enlargement, choose the rectangle with the smallest area.

    (b) If T is not a leaf node nor a parent of leaf nodes, choose the rectangle in T whose area needs the least enlargement. If several rectangles in T need the same least area enlargement, then choose the rectangle with the smallest area.

Let (R, P) be the cell chosen. Replace T by P and continue the process of selecting a node at level L to insert S.

2. Let N be the node at level L returned from step 1. If N has available space to hold (S, P_S), insert it into N and exit. Otherwise, an overflow occurs. Execute step 3 to handle the overflow.

3. Check the overflow flag at level L to see whether this is the first overflow at this level. If the answer is yes (i.e., the overflow flag is still off) and N is not the root, set the overflow flag on and execute step 4a; else go to step 4b. Since the root level will always have one node, reinsertion at this level is useless. Therefore, if N is the root, go to step 4b directly to split the node.

4a. Select w cells from the $M + 1$ cells in node N for reinsertion. This is carried out as follows. First, compute the distances between the centers of the $M + 1$ rectangles and the center of the directory rectangle for node N. Next, order the $M + 1$ cells in descending order of the distances. The first w cells in this order will be used for reinsertion, and the directory rectangle will be adjusted (i.e., reduced in size) accordingly. (The selection tends to keep the remaining rectangles as close as possible. Experiments suggest that $w = 0.3M$ is a good choice.)

Let (S_i, P_{S_i}), $i = 1, \ldots, w$, be the w cells selected. Reinsert them in ascending order of the distances by calling Insert(S_i, P_{S_i}, L, T), $i = w, w-1, \ldots, 1$. (Experiments indicate that reinserting the w cells in ascending order of the distances outperforms reinserting the w cells in descending order of the distances.)

4b. Split the $M + 1$ cells into two sets for distribution into two nodes. The constraint is that each node needs to have at least m cells. The split algorithm is described below.

(i) For the ith axis in the n-dimensional space, sort the $M + 1$ cells first by the lower values and then by the higher values of their rectangles. For each sort, the following $M - 2m + 2$ different ways to partition the $M + 1$ cells into two sets are considered. The jth way, $1 \leq j \leq M - 2m + 2$, is to let the first set have the first $m - 1 + j$ cells and the second set have the remaining cells. Note that the $M - 2m + 2$ different partitions enumerate all possible ways to split the $M + 1$ cells in such a way that each set has at least m cells and no cell in the first set appears before any cell in the second set according to the sort. For the jth partition, let b_{j1} and b_{j2} be the minimum bounding rectangles of the rectangles in the first set and the second set, respectively. Let p_{j1} and p_{j2} be the perimeters of b_{j1} and b_{j2}, respectively. Let $X_i = \sum_{j=1}^{M-2m+2}(p_{j1} + p_{j2})$ denote the sum of the perimeters of all the minimum bounding rectangles for the ith axis, $i = 1, \ldots, n$.

The axis with the smallest X_i is called the *split axis*. Only the partitions based on the sort for the split axis will be considered for identifying the best split. By making an effort to minimize the perimeters, directory rectangles have the tendency to converge to squares. Since squares can be grouped more easily, smaller directory rectangles at the next level can be expected.

(ii) Among the $M - 2m + 2$ partitions along the split axis, find the partition with the smallest area overlap between b_{j1} and b_{j2}. If two or more partitions have the same smallest area overlap, choose the one with the least area sum.

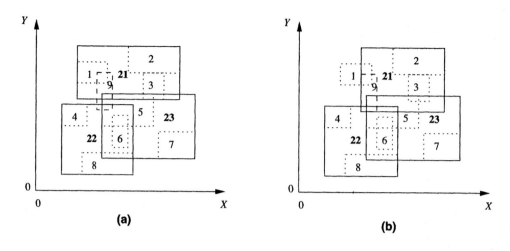

FIGURE 8.14 Inserting Rectangle 9

(iii) Split the $M + 1$ cells based on the partition chosen in (ii) and use the two new nodes to replace node N.

Two cells corresponding to the two new nodes will be generated for the parent node N_P of N to replace the old cell. The rectangle in each new cell is the minimum bounding rectangle of the rectangles in the corresponding child node. If there is available room in N_P for the additional cell, replace the old cell by the two new cells in N_P and exit. Otherwise, with N replaced by N_P and the current level replaced by its parent level, go to step 3 to determine whether reinsertion or a split should be applied to handle the overflow. A split may be propagated all the way up to the root node. If the root node needs to be split, then a new root node will be created and the height of the R*-tree will be increased by 1.

Example 8.13 Consider Figure 8.11. Suppose we have inserted an object rectangle in the database (see the broken-edged rectangle—rectangle 9—in Figure 8.14(a)) and we would like to insert the corresponding new cell into the R*-tree. We start from the root node of the R*-tree in Figure 8.11(b). Since it is the parent of leaf nodes, we find the directory rectangle in the root node that needs the least overlap enlargement to contain rectangle 9. Suppose rectangle 21 is the directory rectangle found. By following the pointer associated with rectangle 21, the leftmost leaf node is reached. Since this node does not have enough room (recall that each node is assumed to accommodate at most three cells) to accommodate the new cell, an overflow occurs. Since this is the first overflow at the leaf level, a reinsertion is invoked. Suppose one cell is to be reinserted. Suppose further that object rectangle 1 is selected for reinsertion. Directory rectangle 21 needs to be adjusted as a result (see Figure 8.14(b)). For this example, the reinsertion effort brings us back to the same leaf node and causes another overflow. This time, we need to apply the split process to partition the four cells (three originally in the node plus the new cell) into two nodes.

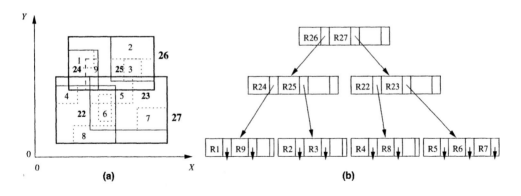

FIGURE 8.15 **After Rectangle 9 Is Inserted**

A sort of the four cells along the X-axis produces {R1, R9, R2, R3}, and a sort along the Y-axis produces {R9, R3, R1, R2}. For each axis, there is only one way to partition the four cells into two sets since $m = 2$ for our example. For the sort along the X-axis, the partition is {(R1, R9), (R2, R3)}. For the sort along the Y-axis, the partition is {(R9, R3), (R1, R2)}. Clearly, the sum of the perimeters of the minimum bounding rectangles for (R1, R9) and (R2, R3) is smaller than that for (R9, R3) and (R1, R2). Thus the X-axis is chosen as the split axis. Consequently, two new nodes containing {R1, R9} and {R2, R3} will be created to replace the original node.

Let the minimum bounding rectangle for (R1, R9) be denoted as R24 and that for (R2, R3) as R25. Then two new cells will be created for the current root node (see Figure 8.11(b)) to replace R21. Since there is not enough space in the root node to hold the four cells, an overflow occurs at the root level. Since this is the root level, the reinsertion process is not invoked. Instead, a split is performed. By using the same method, a split along the Y-axis will be performed. As a result, the original root node is replaced by the two new nodes, one containing (R24, R25) and the other containing (R22, R23). Let the minimum bounding rectangle for (R24, R25) be denoted as R26 and that for (R22, R23) as R27. A new root node with two cells corresponding to R26 and R27 will be generated as a result. The final result is shown in Figure 8.15. ∎

Deleting an Object Rectangle

To delete a rectangle from an R*-tree, we first locate the node that should contain the cell corresponding to the rectangle and then remove it if it is indeed in the node. Deleting a cell from a node may cause an underflow to occur (i.e., the number of cells in the node is less than m). Rather than merging an underflowed node with its sibling node as in a B$^+$ tree, such a node is removed from the R*-tree and the remaining cells in the node are reinserted into the R*-tree. The removal of the node causes the deletion of a cell in the parent node. To accommodate such a deletion, the delete algorithm is designed for deleting a rectangle from any specified level in an R*-tree. Note that the deletion of a cell in a parent node may result in an underflow at the parent node. The underflow may be propagated to the root node and result in a decrease of the height of the tree.

In the following delete algorithm, T denotes the pointer to the root of the R*-tree, S denotes the rectangle to be deleted, and L denotes the level at which S is to be deleted. Initially, L is the leaf level and S is an object rectangle.

Delete(S, L, T)

1. Find the node at level L that should contain S. This can be carried out as follows. If T is not a node at level L, check each cell (R, P) in T to determine if R contains S. If R contains S, recursively check the cells in the child node pointed to by P.

2. Search each node at level L returned in step 1 for the presence of S. If S is not found in all of these nodes, report "not found" and exit. If S is found in a node N, remove the corresponding cell from N. If N still has m or more cells after the deletion, adjust the directory rectangle for N in the parent node of N and exit. The adjusted directory rectangle is the minimum bounding rectangle of the remaining rectangles in N. If N has only $m - 1$ cells after the deletion, process the underflow in the next step.

3. First, remove node N from the R*-tree. This is carried out by calling Delete(S_P, L_P, T), where S_P is the directory rectangle for N and L_P is the parent level of level L. If the original parent node of N is the root node and it has only one child node left after the removal of N, make the child node to be the new root. Second, call Insert(S_i, P_{S_i}, L, T) to insert each of the remaining $m - 1$ cells in N, where each (S_i, P_{S_i}) represents a remaining cell in N.

Extensive experimental results with various distributions of rectangles indicate that R*-tree substantially outperforms other variations of R-trees in almost every category (point search, rectangle search, insertion, and storage utilization).

Exercises

8.1 Show that there is a *total order* among all binary strings representing the regions in a G-tree.

8.2 Consider a two-dimensional space. Convert the following binary strings to the boundaries of the regions they represent:

   (a) 100101

   (b) 0101000

8.3 Continue Example 8.6 and show the G-tree after each of the following points is inserted into the G-tree in Figure 8.4 in the given order:

   (a) (0.6, 0.4)

   (b) (0.4, 0.3)

   (c) (0.9, 0.2)

8.4 Show the G-tree after each of the following points is deleted from the final G-tree obtained in Exercise 8.3 in the given order:

(a) (0.1, 0.7)

(b) (0.4, 0.3)

(c) (0.9, 0.2)

8.5 Both the G-tree and the point quadtree can be used to search for a point or all points in a rectangle. Discuss the major differences between the two types of trees.

8.6 Consider the problem of creating a point quadtree for a set of points in a plane. The shape of the point quadtree depends on the order in which the points are inserted into the tree. Outline a method to order the points such that when the points are inserted in the order, the tree is more likely to be balanced (i.e., the height of the tree is likely to be small).

8.7 Create a region quadtree for the following image (it is the letter T placed upside down).

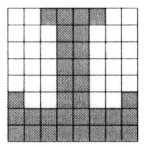

8.8 Design an algorithm for unioning two images into a new image based on region quadtree. Apply your algorithm to the image in Figure 8.8 and the image in Exercise 8.7.

8.9 An image may be represented by a *bintree* (a binary tree) as follows. The entire space (a square) is represented as the root node of the tree. If the square is not homogeneous, then the square is divided into two equal-sized regions. The two regions are the two child nodes of the root. If any of the regions is not homogeneous, it is divided again into two smaller regions. The divisions are carried out along the axes in an alternate fashion. The first division is along the X-axis. If a region is obtained by a division along the X-axis (Y-axis), then when it needs to be divided, it will be divided along the Y-axis (X-axis). This process of dividing a region into two smaller regions stops when every region becomes homogeneous.

Draw the bintree that represents the image in Figure 8.8(b).

8.10 In a bintree representing an image, each leaf node corresponds to a homogeneous region (see Exercise 8.9). Suppose the image is in a unit square. Propose a method for placing a 0 or 1 on each edge of a bintree such that the binary string formed by concatenating the 0s and 1s on the edges from the root node to a leaf node is the same as that representing the region corresponding to the leaf node as in a G-tree.

8.11 In an R*-tree, the cells in each node are not ordered. As a result, when a node is reached by the search algorithm, every cell in the node must be examined. Propose a method to order the cells in each node such that with a modified search algorithm it becomes possible to avoid examining every cell when a node is reached by the search algorithm. Discuss also how to modify the search algorithm.

8.12 Suppose we have an R*-tree for n-dimensional rectangles. Suppose further that the height of the tree is H (i.e., the tree has $H + 1$ levels of nodes) and m and M are the minimum and maximum numbers of cells in a node. Analyze the worst-case time complexity of the insertion algorithm.

8.13 Show the new R*-tree after object rectangle R4 is deleted from the R*-tree in Figure 8.15(b) ($m = 2$ and $M = 3$ are assumed).

Bibliographic Notes

Data structures for multidimensional data have been studied extensively in the past two decades. Numerous structures have been proposed. The structures presented in this chapter are only a few representatives.

Fixed grid file is presented in [210]. This is later extended in [167, 279] to allow a region to be divided into subregions of different sizes. G-tree [213] also allows a region to be divided into subregions of different sizes. However, the division is done in a nested manner and each division always divides a region or a subregion into halves. The regions are organized into a B^+ tree for efficient search. G-tree can also be used to represent a bintree efficiently with nodes stored as pages on disk. S^+ tree [99] is another efficient representation of a bintree.

Point quadtree was proposed in [120]. Region quadtree has received a tremendous amount of attention in the literature [256, 318, 319] due to its various applications to imagery and geographic data. The representations of the quadtrees discussed in this chapter are only suitable for in-memory storage. To store quadtrees on secondary storage, certain encoding methods are usually used (see, for example, [99, 357]). Another advantage of these encoding methods is that the storage of child pointers of each node in the quadtree can often be avoided.

R-tree was invented by Guttman [156]. R*-tree was proposed in [25]. It is a variation of R-tree. Other variations of R-tree also exist [148, 325]. The basic material about the R*-tree in Section 8.3 is from [25]. The deletion algorithm is adapted from [156] since no deletion algorithm is discussed in [25].

Text Retrieval

$\mathbf{T}$ext is the usual form of communication among humans. We read text in newspapers, magazines, memos, etc. Text is clearly a medium where a very significant amount of information is stored. Its retrieval and classification have many applications. Some of these applications are identified as follows: searching for papers and books in libraries; searching for related patents in filing inventions; searching for financial information embedded in texts; searching for relevant information in newspapers or in the Information Superhighway; searching for appropriate legal cases; automatic classification of information to determine consumer opinion; classification to permit word sense disambiguation; organizing mail into different categories; etc. In this chapter, an overview of text retrieval and classification is given in Section 9.1. Details are provided for text retrieval in this chapter, whereas text classification is deferred to the next chapter.

In the overview, each document is represented by an n-dimensional vector, where n is the number of distinct keywords or terms in the collection of documents. Similarly, a query is also represented by an n-dimensional vector. Most entries in a document or a query vector are zero, as most keywords are absent in the document or the query. The closeness or similarity between a query and a document is measured by the closeness of the corresponding vectors in the n-dimensional space. (Closeness may involve the nonzero entries of the two vectors only or it can be an inverse of Euclidean distance or angular distance or some other distance measure.) Documents that are sufficiently close to the user query are retrieved. Since the similarity of a document with respect to a query is not necessarily related to its relevance or usefulness to the user, a relevance feedback process is introduced to assist the user to reformulate his or her query. In this process, the user needs to identify the relevant documents among the initially retrieved documents. Based on the relevance information supplied by the user, the system will attempt to form a new query, which hopefully will retrieve more relevant documents. Retrieval effectiveness, which is a measure for evaluating the quality of documents retrieved by the system, is also introduced in Section 9.1. In Sections 9.2 and 9.3, several probabilistic models that attempt to achieve high retrieval effectiveness are provided. The simplest one assumes that terms are distributed independently. Under this assumption, a simple formula to retrieve documents optimally is derived. Since the assumption may not hold, term dependencies are incorporated to yield more realistic probabilistic retrieval models. All such probabilistic models require certain parameters to be known. The relevance feedback process permits some of these parameters to be estimated. Instead of modeling dependencies of terms directly, an alternative approach is to transform the dependent terms into terms that are more or less independent. One such transformation may reduce the number of terms significantly. This potentially improves both retrieval effectiveness and efficiency. As text retrieval gains popularity, the number of users and the sizes of collections increase. Thus, in Section 9.4, several types of hardware to speed up retrieval are introduced. Section 9.5 provides two other retrieval methods.

9.1 An Overview of Text Retrieval and Classification

A text document is a unit of text. It can be a technical paper or a book in a library. It can be a patent in a patent-searching application. The purpose of a text retrieval system is to retrieve documents that are similar in contents to a given query. This may be approximated by finding documents that have many content words in common with the query. Various weights that are usually automatically determined by the retrieval system may be assigned to different content words to reflect their degrees of significance. In other words, two documents having the same number of content words (but different sets of content words) in common with the query may have different degrees of similarity with respect to the query.

9.1.1 Representation of a Text Document

The contents of a text document can be characterized by the *content words* that appear in the document. Thus, if we eliminate all *noncontent words* from a document, the remaining words can be used to indicate the contents of the document. Words like "a," "the," and "of," which do not convey any semantics, are *noncontent words*. They can be identified as NC, the set of noncontent words. Then, any word from a document that is not in NC can be used to characterize the document. A *term* is a content word. Let C be the set of terms in the document collection. Each term in C can be uniquely identified by a number. The set of all terms can thus be represented by the set of integers from 1 to n, where n is the total number of terms. A document D can then be represented by an n-dimensional vector of the form $(d_1, \ldots, d_i, \ldots, d_n)$, where d_i is a nonnegative number; $d_i = 0$ indicates that the ith term does not appear in the document and $d_i > 0$ indicates that the ith term appears in the document;

the value of a positive d_i is used to represent the significance of the ith term in the document. As will be explained later, the significance of a term in a document is usually a combination of two factors, one involving the number of occurrences of the term in the document and the other involving the number of documents having the term. The higher the significance value, the more important the term is in describing the document. The *vector space model* is the representation of documents by n-dimensional vectors.

There are a number of improvements that can be made to improve this representation. Different variations of a word may have the same meaning and should be represented by the same term. For example, the words "beautiful" and "beautify" come from the same stem, "beauty." Thus, they are often identified by one term only. *Stemming* is a process that transforms variations of a word into a stem. It is usually obtained by possibly eliminating the suffix of the given word and possibly replacing some ending characters by other ending characters. For example, after removing the suffix "ful" from the word "beautiful," the ending character "i" is replaced by "y." This is done according to rules consistent with general usage in the English language. However, no stemming algorithm is perfect. That is, some variations of the same word may not be stemmed to the same stem, and words that do not have the same semantics may be stemmed to the same stem. For example, some stemmers may stem "genealogic" and "genealogical" to different stems, while stemming "tasty" and "tasteless" to the same stem.

Another improvement is that certain word combinations should be represented by a single term instead of multiple terms. As an example, the phrase "operating system" denotes a meaning different from that conveyed by the individual words *system* and *operating*. There are programs that recognize phrases automatically. However, they are again by no means perfect. Valid phrases may be missed, and word combinations that are not phrases may be erroneously taken as phrases.

It should be pointed out that the representation given above is not a perfect characterization of the contents of a document. For example, it does not distinguish "a cat chases a mouse" from "a mouse chases a cat," since the ordering of the terms in a document is not recorded and no distinction is made between the subject and the object. It is clear that the distinction is important if the text is very short. Natural language–processing techniques employing grammars may be utilized for making the distinction. However, in a paper that contains several thousand words, it is not clear whether fine distinction is essential for accurate retrieval.

9.1.2 Term Significance

The significance of a term may be indicated by two quantities, *document frequency* and *term occurrence frequency*. The document frequency of a term is the number of documents having the term. Usually, the more documents having the term, the less useful the term is in discriminating those documents having it from those not having it. The *inverse document frequency* (idf) method assigns a weight, called the *inverse document frequency weight*, to a term that is equal to $\log \frac{m}{d}$, where m is the total number of documents in the entire collection of documents and d is the document frequency of the term. Consider two extreme cases. First, when $d = m$, then the weight is zero. This is reasonable, because if a term occurs in every document, it has essentially no discrimination power for any document. Second, when $d = 1$, then the weight will be high, as m is usually large. This large weight causes the document having it to be distinguished strongly from other documents.

The term occurrence frequency (tf) is the number of times the term occurs in the document. If a term occurs many times, then it is likely that the term is significant in representing the contents of the document because the author keeps on using it. Conversely, if it occurs only once in a long document having many terms, then the term is not likely to be critical for representing the document.

Combining the effects of the two factors discussed above, the significance of a term in a document can be reflected by the product of its frequency of occurrence in the document and its inverse document frequency weight, often referred to as the *tf-idf* weight. A formula for the tf-idf weight of a term in a document D is $f \cdot \log \frac{m}{d}$, where f is the number of times the term occurs in D, m is the total number of documents in the collection, and d is the number of documents having the term. In practice, a complicated but effective formula giving the significance of the kth term in the document with term frequency f a value between 0 and 1 is

$$\frac{\left(a_1 + a_2 \cdot \frac{f}{\max_k \{f_k\}}\right) \log \frac{m}{d}}{\sqrt{\sum_{i=1} \left(a_1 + a_2 \cdot \frac{f_i}{\max_k \{f_k\}}\right)^2 \left(\log \frac{m}{d_i}\right)^2}}$$

where a_1 and a_2 are small constants, typically 0.5, f_k is the number of occurrences of term k that is present in the document, d_i is the document frequency of the ith term in the document and both the maximum and the sum are over all terms in the document. Consider the numerator. Suppose a term has the highest term frequency in the document. Then the numerator becomes $(a_1 + a_2) \cdot \log \frac{m}{d}$. In comparison, a term that has the same document frequency d but a lower term frequency has the numerator equal to $(a_1 + a_2 \cdot e) \cdot \log \frac{m}{d}$, where $0 < e < 1$. Thus, the term with the highest term frequency has a larger numerator. The constant a_1 ensures that any term present in the document has at least the value of a_1 in the numerator. The constant a_2 is very often $(1 - a_1)$. The denominator is a normalization factor, ensuring that the final weight is between 0 and 1.

9.1.3 Query Representation

A query in the form of natural language text can be represented in a manner similar to the way a document is represented. That is, all noncontent words are first eliminated; then after possibly executing a stemming process, a phrase recognition process, and possibly adding synonymous or related words, the query is represented as an n-dimensional vector. For example, a query "get documents that refer to software sales and distribution in the Internet", may be represented by an n-dimensional vector with positive entries under the terms "document," "software," "sale," "distribution," and "Internet." The noncontent words "to," "in," etc., are eliminated. It is possible to replace the terms "software," "sale," and "distribution" by the term phrases "software sale" and "software distribution." Related terms such as "information superhighway" may also be added to the query. Weights may be assigned to the various terms by the retrieval system. For example, if the inverse document frequency weighting method is applied, terms with different document frequencies will be assigned different weights. This is done automatically by the system without the user's knowledge. Clearly, users can designate that certain terms get higher weights. However, most users are incapable of assigning weights to terms appropriately.

There is also another common query representation. It is a *Boolean query*. Each such query has a number of terms, and these terms are connected by Boolean operators AND, OR, and NOT. A document D satisfies the query "t_1 AND t_2 AND ... AND t_k," where t_i's are terms, if document D has all the k terms. Document D satisfies the query "t_1 OR t_2 OR ... OR t_k" if it has one or more of the k terms. It satisfies "NOT t" if it does not have term t. A *Boolean expression* in conjunctive normal form is the AND of several *factors*, where each factor is the OR of *literals* and each literal is either a term or the NOT of the term. For example, one such expression is (t_1 OR t_2) AND (t_3 OR NOT t_4 OR t_5). Document D satisfies the query if it has one or more of the terms t_1 or t_2, and it has one or more of the terms t_3 or t_5 or does not have t_4. A document that satisfies the query will be retrieved. There are several problems with the use of Boolean queries. First, since only satisfied documents are retrieved, it happens quite often that either too many or too few documents are retrieved. A restrictive query such as "t_1 AND t_2 ... AND t_k" for a reasonably large k may not have enough documents satisfying the query. On the other hand, a loosely formed query such as "t_1 OR t_2 ... OR t_k" may retrieve too many documents. Second, the retrieved documents are not ranked; i.e., there is no preference ordering among the documents. As a result, if there are too many satisfied documents, it will be too time consuming for a user to look up all those documents and identify the ones of interest. Third, the use of the Boolean operators AND and OR can be confusing to the end users. As a result, a user may formulate a Boolean query that is not intended. Although some of these problems can be remedied and the use of Boolean queries can be combined with queries in vector form, we will restrict ourselves mostly to queries in vector form in later sections of this chapter and the next.

9.1.4 Retrieval

Retrieval with respect to a query Q in the form of a vector consists of all those document vectors $\{D_i\}$ that are sufficiently *close* to the vector Q. In order to accomplish this, a *similarity function f* is defined to measure the *closeness* between any two vectors. As for example, assume that all vectors are binary, in that each component of a vector is either 0 or 1 (where 0 and 1 represent the absence and the presence, respectively, of a term in the document/query). Let the two vectors be $X = (x_1, \ldots, x_i, \ldots, x_n)$ and $Y = (y_1, \ldots, y_i, \ldots, y_n)$. One possible similarity function is the dot product $\sum_{i=1}^{n} x_i \cdot y_i$. For binary vectors, the similarity value gives the number of terms in common between the two vectors. Instead of using binary information, a quantitative measure of the significance of a term in a document can be used. As mentioned earlier, this measure of significance can be the product of the inverse document frequency weight and the occurrence frequency of the term in the document. It is easy to see that a document having many terms has a higher chance of having more terms in common with a query than a document having few terms. As a result, a long document is likely to have a larger similarity value than a short document. In other words, the dot product similarity function favors long documents. Another function, the *Cosine function* given below, is a possible remedy for this situation.

If the number of documents is large, which is usually the case for many applications of document retrieval, it is natural for the user to specify a number, k, and the text retrieval system will retrieve the k closest documents. Closeness is measured by the similarity function f; i.e., if $f(Q, D_i) < f(Q, D_j)$, then D_j is closer to Q than D_i.

A similarity function that is used frequently in information retrieval is the *Cosine* function, given as follows.

$$Cosine(X, Y) = \frac{X \cdot Y}{\sqrt{(X \cdot X) \bullet (Y \cdot Y)}}$$

where $X \cdot Y$ is the dot product given before, and the big dot ($\bullet$) denotes the familiar scalar multiplication. Usually, each component of the vectors X and Y is greater than or equal to zero. It is easy to verify for such vectors that $Cosine(X, Y) \geq 0$. The $\sqrt{X \cdot X}$ is the norm, or length, of X. The similarity function can be rewritten as $X_n \cdot Y_n$, where $X_n = \frac{X}{\sqrt{X \cdot X}}$ is the normalized vector of X. Thus, $Cosine(X, Y) = Cosine(cX, Y) = Cosine(X, cY)$ for any positive constant c, as the normalized vector X_n or Y_n remains unchanged. It is easy to see that $X_n \cdot X_n = 1$. As the numerator can be shown to be no larger than the denominator, $Cosine(X, Y) \leq 1$. $Cosine(X, Y) = 0$ is attained when the vectors have no term in common, in which case they are said to be orthogonal to each other. $Cosine(X, Y) = 1$ is attained when $X = kY$, for some positive constant k. When this happens, the angle between the two vectors is zero. In general, the *Cosine* function can be visualized as measuring the angular distance between the two vectors. As the angle between the two vectors X and Y increases, $Cosine(X, Y)$ decreases.

It has recently been observed that the *Cosine* function overcompensates the short documents. More precisely, the probability that a short document is retrieved by the *Cosine* function is higher than the probability that it is relevant, whereas the probability that a long document is retrieved is lower than the probability that it is relevant. Thus, it may be worthwhile to modify the *Cosine* function such that the modified function retrieves fewer short documents and more long documents in comparison to the regular *Cosine* function.

9.1.5   Quality of Terms

It was mentioned that rare terms get higher weights than frequent terms. It may be of interest to characterize the quality of a term in a more systematic manner. Broadly speaking, "good" terms get high weights, and "poor" terms get low weights. This should permit more relevant documents to be retrieved than if all terms were assigned the same weight, when the number of documents to be retrieved is fixed.

Definition 9.1 *The compactness of a set of document vectors is defined to be $\sum_{i \neq j} Cosine(D_i, D_j)$, where the summation is over all pairs of documents that are different.*

If all documents are close together, then the compactness is high and it is difficult to differentiate the documents of interest from the other documents with respect to a given query. Thus, it is desirable to have a low compactness. Suppose that a new term is added to the existing terms. Note that when a term is added, although the numerator of the *Cosine* of two vectors may increase, the denominator will also increase. Thus, the *Cosine* function may or may not increase. If the compactness decreases as a result of the addition of a new term, then the new term is a good term; the larger the decrease, the better the term. Conversely, if the compactness increases, then the term is a poor one. In practice, it is of interest to evaluate the quality of existing terms. Thus, instead of adding a term, we study the effect of potentially eliminating a term. If the compactness increases as a result of the deletion of an existing term,

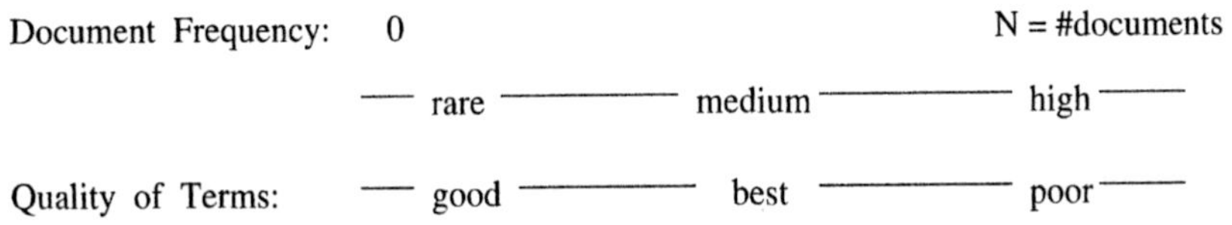

Document Frequency: 0   N = #documents

—— rare ————— medium ————— high ——

Quality of Terms: —— good ————— best ————— poor ——

FIGURE 9.1 Relationship between Quality of Term and Document Frequency

then the term is a good term; the larger the increase, the better the term. Poor terms are those whose deletions lead to a decrease of compactness. (It should be noted that no poor term is actually deleted. We are simply comparing the effect of having a term in the compactness measure versus not having the term.) Experiments with several document collections indicate the following results. Poor terms are usually those with high document frequencies; i.e., terms that occur in many documents. Good terms tend to occur in few documents. Yet the best terms are found to be those with medium document frequencies; i.e., they do not occur in too many or too few documents. Even though the rare terms are very good terms, there are reasons why they are not the best terms. First, there may not be too many queries containing them. As a result, their effects on overall retrieval performance may be insignificant. Second, there may be quite a few synonyms to these rare terms. If a user uses a rare term but a document contains a synonym of the rare term, the rare term may not be useful in retrieving the document. The effect of document frequency on quality of terms is illustrated in Figure 9.1.

If two terms occur in the same number of documents, then the one whose actual numbers of occurrences in the documents has a higher variance than those of the other is a better term for the following reason. Take for example a term, t_1, which occurs exactly twice in each of the documents containing it. Consider another term, t_2, occurring in exactly the same set of documents, say S, as that of t_1. However, some documents in S contain t_2 once, some contain twice, and others contain t_2 more than twice. It is clear that t_1 cannot differentiate documents in S, whereas these documents may be differentiated by their occurrences of term t_2. Thus, the best terms are those with medium document frequencies and with high variation of occurrences in the documents.

Transformation into Better Terms

Based on the discussion of how the quality of terms is related to document frequencies, it is desirable to transform both low document frequency terms and high document frequency terms into medium document frequency terms. Consider first the transformation of low document frequency terms into medium. As an example, suppose the two terms "beautiful" and "pretty" are low frequency terms and are synonyms. We can replace each by a single term t_0 such that t_0 will occur in a document whenever "beautiful" or "pretty" occurs in the document. In general, a term t can be used to represent a set of synonymous terms $\{t_i\}$ such that whenever one or more component terms t_i occur in a document D, t is considered to have occurred in D. In this sense, t can be considered as the *union* of the component terms. Clearly, the document frequency of t is at least as high as that of each of its component terms t_i. In the above example, the document frequency of t_0 is at least as high as that of "beautiful" and that of "pretty." The actual number of occurrences of t in document D is the sum of the numbers of occurrences of the component terms in D.

There have been several attempts to automate the recognition of synonyms. One way is to make use of co-occurrences of terms in documents. In other words, if two terms co-occur much more often than they are expected to co-occur (i.e., the expected frequency of co-occurrence if the terms are distributed independently), then these two terms are very much related and may be used as synonyms. Unfortunately, experiments testing this approach yield mixed results, because some of the discovered "synonyms" are really not semantically related. Recently, it has been suggested that frequently co-occurring terms that appear in the same sections (or sufficiently close together) in documents be used as "synonyms." Such terms are more likely to be related than if they are in different sections. Combining co-occurrence and proximity information yields better results than that using only co-occurrence information. Experiments have also been carried out where the "discovered" synonyms are filtered by a dictionary. If the dictionary indicates that a pair of terms are semantically related, then they are treated as synonyms. There has been some limited success using this approach; the number of pairs of terms satisfying the co-occurrence condition and the semantic condition imposed by the dictionary are limited, reducing the overall effect on performance. Furthermore, words have different senses. It is possible that two words are semantically related in some situations but are unrelated in others.

Now consider transforming high document frequency terms into medium document frequency terms. As an example, suppose there are two terms "program" and "language," which occur in two sets of documents S1 and S2, respectively. Furthermore, suppose both S1 and S2 have large cardinalities; i.e., the terms are high document frequency terms. It is possible that quite a few documents in the intersection of S1 and S2 are better represented by the phrase "programming language." The phrase, if applicable to those documents, is a more precise description than the combination of the individual terms. Documents that are not represented by the phrase will still contain the individual terms, depending on which terms they originally have. Clearly, the document frequency of the phrase is no higher (and usually much lower) than those of the individual terms. In addition, the number of documents that now have either the term "program" or the term "language" is decreased, because some of the these documents are now indexed by the phrase "programming language" instead. In general, a phrase t can be used to index some of the documents in the intersection of the documents containing the individual terms, if the individual terms form a phrase representing t. Those documents having one or more component terms but not the phrase will continue to be indexed by the individual terms. It is also possible that some documents having the phrase may also have isolated instances of some of the individual terms as well.

There have been attempts to automate the construction of phrases using grammars as well as by statistical (nonsyntactic) methods. Although grammars can be utilized to recognize phrases in many sentences, there are significant numbers of unrecognizable phrases as well as sequences of terms that are not phrases but are incorrectly categorized as phrases by the grammar. A typical nonsyntactic method to recognize phrases is to find sequences of high document frequency terms that are separated by no more than three words. Experimental results indicate that the words that form phrases are rarely more than three words apart. There are clearly exceptions to this observation. For example, there could be many adjectives qualifying a noun such that each adjective with the noun forms a phrase, but the first few adjectives are separated from the noun by more than three words. On the other hand, two adjacent words may look like a phrase, but not be a phrase. For example, in the sentence such as "there is a system that operates very well," we may mistakenly recognize the phrase "operating system": the words *system* and *operates* are close together and when these words are stemmed, *operating* becomes indistinguishable from *operates*.

Automatic methods to recognize phrases have been used in information retrieval with some success.

9.1.6 Performance Evaluation

Unlike standard database systems, such as relational or object-oriented systems, documents retrieved by an information retrieval system are not necessarily of use to the user. This is due mainly to the inaccuracies in the representations of the documents and the users' queries and the inability for users to express their retrieval needs precisely. A *relevant document* is a document of use to the user in response to his or her query, whereas an *irrelevant document* is one of little or of no use. The effectiveness of retrieval is usually measured by the following two quantities, *recall* and *precision*:

$$\text{Recall} = \frac{\text{the number of relevant documents that are retrieved}}{\text{the number of relevant documents}}$$

$$\text{Precision} = \frac{\text{the number of relevant documents that are retrieved}}{\text{the number of retrieved documents}}$$

In terms of the above Venn diagram, where Rel represents the set of relevant documents and Ret represents the set of retrieved documents, the above measures can be redefined as

$$\text{Recall} = \frac{|\text{Rel} \cap \text{Ret}|}{|\text{Rel}|}$$

$$\text{Precision} = \frac{|\text{Rel} \cap \text{Ret}|}{|\text{Ret}|}$$

As an example, if 10 documents are retrieved, of which 7 are relevant, and the total number of relevant documents is 20, then recall = 7/20 and precision is 7/10. In order to evaluate the retrieval effectiveness of an algorithm, the number of retrieved documents is varied. This causes changes in recall and precision. After the retrieval results are averaged over many queries, a graph of precision versus recall can be plotted. A common phenomenon is that as recall increases, precision decreases. This means that when more relevant documents need to be retrieved, a higher percentage of irrelevant documents will also be retrieved.

In Figure 9.2, three example recall and precision curves are shown. They are labeled A, B, and C. It can be seen that curves A and B have higher precision values than curve C at every

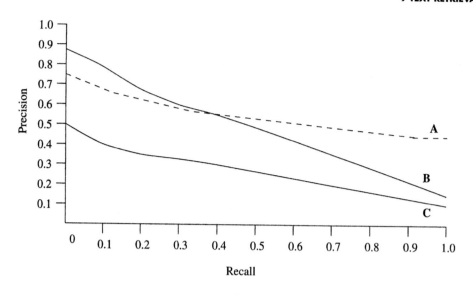

FIGURE 9.2 *Performance Using Recall-Precision Curves*

recall level. This means that if a user requires that a certain number of relevant documents be retrieved, then the systems producing curves A and B can retrieve fewer documents than the system producing curve C, which retrieves the same number of desired relevant documents. This implies that the systems yielding A and B are better than the one described by C. In comparing the curves A and B, we observe that although curve B dominates curve A for recall between 0.0 and 0.4, curve A outperforms B for other recall values. Thus, if a user wants to retrieve a small percentage of relevant documents, up to 40 percent, then the system producing curve B is more desirable. If a higher percentage of relevant documents must be retrieved, then the system producing curve A is better. It should be noted that even though precision can easily be computed after a number of documents are retrieved and the user has indicated his or her preference, recall can be computed only if each document in the entire collection has been determined by the user to be either relevant or irrelevant. For some experimental systems, this has been carried out for small collections. For larger collections, several retrieval algorithms are used to retrieve documents, and the evaluation is done by a judge on the union of the retrieved documents instead of all documents. For example, the TREC (Text REtrieval Conference) collections of documents and queries were collected by the National Institute of Standards and Technology, and the relevance of each document with respect to each query was manually evaluated using sets of documents retrieved by different algorithms. This is an approximation of the actual recall.

9.1.7 Relevance Feedback

If both recall and precision are 100%, then retrieval effectiveness is perfect. This is unlikely to occur in practice. In a realistic environment, it is essential to provide additional mechanisms

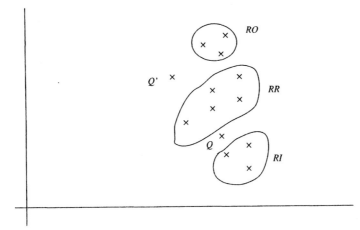

Q = original query; RR = retrieved relevant documents; RI = retrieved irrelevant documents.
Q' = modified query; RO = relevant documents that may be retrieved by Q'.

FIGURE 9.3   Relevance Feedback in an n-dimensional Space

that help users to retrieve relevant documents. The relevance feedback mechanism operates as follows. After a set, R, of documents is retrieved by the information retrieval system for a user query Q and is shown to the user, the user is asked to identify among R which documents are relevant. From the response of the user, R is partitioned into two sets, RR, containing the retrieved relevant documents, and RI, containing the retrieved irrelevant documents. The initial query Q is then modified, taking into consideration the additional feedback from the user. One such modification is

$$Q' = Q + C_1 \cdot \sum_{D_i \in RR} D_i - C_2 \cdot \sum_{D_j \in RI} D_j$$

where C_1 and C_2 are constants and Q' is the modified user query. The addition and the subtraction in the above formula are in vector form. Addition of the documents in RR is to move the query toward the retrieved and relevant documents, whereas the subtraction is to shift the query away from the retrieved and irrelevant documents. By combining the additions and the subtractions, the terms responsible for retrieving the relevant documents in RR but not the irrelevant documents in RI will be emphasized. At the same time, those terms responsible for retrieving the irrelevant documents in RI but not the relevant documents in RR will be deemphasized. If the documents that are relevant but not retrieved by Q are close to the documents in RR, the modified query Q' is likely to retrieve them. In Figure 9.3, the modified query Q' is closer to the retrieved relevant documents in RR than the retrieved irrelevant documents in RI. If all relevant documents are clustered together, then Q' will be able to retrieve relevant documents that are not retrievable by Q. If the user is satisfied with the retrieved result, then the feedback process is terminated; otherwise, another modified query Q'' is generated to retrieve more documents. More details about this form of relevance feedback will be given in Section 9.3, which also describes two other forms of relevance feedback.

	t_1	t_2	t_3	t_4
D_1	0	3	2	1
D_2	1	0	0	0
D_3	4	3	0	0
D_4	0	0	0	5
D_5	0	1	0	0

FIGURE 9.4 **A Document-Term Matrix**

9.1.8 Clustering

Clustering, or *classification*, places similar documents into the same class. Usually, this means that the average similarity of two documents in the same class is larger than that of two documents in different classes. A number of important applications arise from classification. If a relevant document is found in a class, it is desirable for a user to browse other documents in the same class, as these documents have a higher chance of being relevant to the user than documents in other classes. In addition to this browsing capability, automatic classification has many business applications. For example, if business cards are scanned and then classified into different types, it facilitates business contacts. As another example, e-mail may be classified by type and priority so that the urgent ones can be answered quickly. Details of clustering will be given in Chapter 10.

9.1.9 Searching

Searching can be performed using indexes, employing signature files (see Section 9.4.1), making use of clusters, or utilizing specialized hardware that permits parallel execution. The use of indexes and a sketch of clustered search are given here, but a detailed description of clustered search will be given in Chapter 10. A brief description of searching by signatures is provided in the subsection on Connection Machine (Section 9.4.1).

Searching Using Indexes

Associated with each term, an *inverted list* can be created. As an example, suppose that there are five documents and four terms and the occurrences of the terms in the documents are represented by a matrix, M; this is called a *document-term matrix*. The entries along a row give the number of occurrences of the terms in the document corresponding to the row. The entries along a column identify the number of occurrences of the term in different documents. An example of document-term matrix is shown in Figure 9.4.

An *inverted list* consists of a header identifying the term number, say term j, followed by pairs of the form (D_i, M_{ij}), where M_{ij} is the number of occurrences of term j in document D_i. The pairs are usually sorted in ascending document numbers. For example, the inverted list for term t_2 is $\langle t_2, (D_1, 3), (D_3, 3), (D_5, 1) \rangle$. If saving space (which also has an impact on the I/O time to read the inverted list from the disk) is important, then each frequency of occurrences that is common to several documents can be factored out. For example, the list can also be represented by $\langle t_2, \{1, (D_5)\}, \{3, (D_1, D_3)\}\rangle$, where all documents having the same frequency of the term are grouped together. The key aspect of an inverted list is that all zero entries in the matrix M are not stored. This not only saves space but also improves search performance as shown below.

Suppose a query $Q = (0, 1, 0, 1) = (q_1, q_2, q_3, q_4)$ is submitted and the similarities $\{f(Q, D_i),$ $1 \leq i \leq 5\}$ need to be computed. Assume further that the similarity function is the standard dot product. Since the nonzero entries in the query belong to terms t_2 and t_4, the inverted lists of t_2 and t_4 will be searched. Suppose there is an array S such that $S(i)$ will eventually contain the similarity $f(Q, D_i)$, $1 \leq i \leq 5$. Initialize $S(i)$ to be zero for each i. When the inverted list of term j is traversed, for every entry (D_i, M_{ij}) encountered in the list, the similarity of document D_i with respect to Q, $S(i)$, is updated to $S(i) + q_j \cdot M_{ij}$. The contribution is due to the occurrences of term j in the query with significance q_j and in the document D_i with significance M_{ij}. This is repeated for every nonzero entry in the query. When this is completed, the similarities of all documents with respect to the query are computed. In our example, the similarities are as follows.

$S(1) = 1 \cdot 3 + 1 \cdot 1$, due to the terms t_2 and t_4;

$S(2) = 0$, since D_2 does not have term t_2 or term t_4, the entry is not updated;

$S(3) = 1 \cdot 3$, due to term t_2;

$S(4) = 1 \cdot 5$, due to term t_4;

$S(5) = 1 \cdot 1$, due to term t_2.

The algorithm is essentially traversing those columns of the matrix M corresponding to the terms specified in the user's query. Since each inverted list stores only the nonzero entries, only those entries in the chosen columns are processed. Each such entry contributes to the computation of the similarities. To see the advantage of using the inverted lists, consider the following alternative algorithm in which the similarities of documents with respect to each query are computed one document at a time. An efficient way of doing this consists of storing only the nonzero entries in ascending term number for each document. Similarly, the nonzero entries of a query are also sorted in ascending order of term numbers. The similarity between a document and a query is then obtained by merging the nonzero entries in the document with those in the query. Since both sets are in ascending order of term number, the merging can be completed in time proportional to the sum of the number of nonzero entries in the two lists. This process is repeated for each document. Thus, all nonzero entries in the document-term matrix contribute to the processing cost; also, each query term is accessed once for each document. In contrast, the indexed search method processes all nonzero entries only in the columns of the document-term matrix corresponding to the nonzero query terms. Thus, the indexed search method is clearly faster. To examine the difference in efficiency between the two algorithms, we observe that terms that occur in documents but do not appear in the query are not processed by the indexed search algorithm, but are processed by the latter algorithm during the merge process. As a result, all those documents that have similarities of zero with the query are processed by the latter algorithm but not by the former. The savings in cost is substantial, because we expect that most documents in a large collection have no terms in common with a typical query.

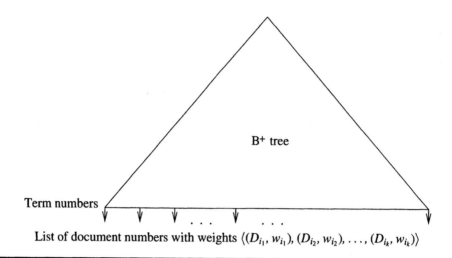

FIGURE 9.5   An Organization of an Inverted List in a B+ Tree

In an actual implementation of the inverted lists, all term numbers can be stored in a B$^+$ tree. At the bottom level of the tree are the term numbers, each of which points to its inverted list. In Figure 9.5, at the bottom level of a B$^+$ tree, the pointer associated with the term number i points to the list $\langle (D_{i1}, w_{i1}), \ldots, (D_{ij}, w_{ij}), \ldots, (D_{ik}, w_{ik}) \rangle$, where D_{ij} denotes a document containing term i with weight w_{ij}. For each query term, the B$^+$ tree is searched and the inverted list is returned to update similarities of documents. Instead of storing the similarities in the array S, a hash table can be employed. If term t_j has an entry (D_i, M_{ij}), then i is hashed into the hash table. If D_i has an entry already in the hash table, it will be in the same bucket and the similarity will be updated as before; otherwise a new entry will be created to contain the similarity of D_i with Q due to term t_j. The use of the hash table is to save the storage for those documents that have no term in common with the query Q. *Collisions*, i.e., different documents hashed to the same address in the hash table can be handled by standard techniques, such as chaining or by employing a dynamic hashing function.

Suppose the $Cosine(Q, D_i)$ is required. First, we observe that the actual similarities are not critical for retrieval. What we need are their relative values. That is, it is sufficient for us to compute $C \cdot Cosine(Q, D_i)$ for some positive constant C, which is independent of the documents, as $Cosine(Q, D_i) > Cosine(Q, D_j)$ if and only if $C \cdot Cosine(Q, D_i) > C \cdot Cosine(Q, D_j)$. Thus, we will compute the function $Cosine(Q, D_i) \cdot \sqrt{Q \cdot Q}$ instead. This is the same as $Q \cdot D_i / \sqrt{D_i \cdot D_i}$. In order to take into consideration the norm of each document, D_i, $N_i = \sqrt{D_i \cdot D_i}$ is precomputed for each document D_i and stored in an array. Before the computation of the similarities is finalized, the array element $S(i)$ is multiplied by $\frac{1}{N_i}$. The remaining computation proceeds as described before.

It is also possible to replace the B$^+$ tree by a hash table, where the entries of the table are the terms (with their term identifiers), each of which is associated with a pointer pointing to a list of the form (d, w), where the term occurs in document d with weight w.

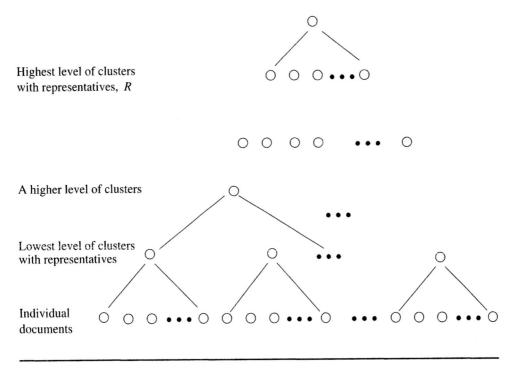

Highest level of clusters
with representatives, *R*

A higher level of clusters

Lowest level of clusters
with representatives

Individual
documents

FIGURE 9.6   A Hierarchy of Clusters

Clustered Search

An important application of clustered search is to determine the sources (databases) on the Internet to be searched for a given query. Since the number of Internet sources can be extremely large, it is critical that thorough searching for the query is performed for just a few sources. In this application, each source can be considered as a cluster of documents, and the problem is to choose which clusters require elaborate computation of similarities. It is assumed that similar documents are placed into the same class (cluster), and dissimilar documents are placed into different classes. The clusters may be obtained by a clustering algorithm (see Chapter 10), or each cluster is simply all documents in a database. For each class C_i, there is a representative R_i, which indicates approximately the contents of the documents in the class. Classes may be placed in a hierarchy; i.e., similar classes may be merged into a larger class and the process of merging may continue until all documents are in one class. Another view is that similar representatives that are vectors themselves are placed into the same higher-level class. Figure 9.6 shows a hierarchy of classes.

Consider a query Q. In order to determine which documents are similar to Q, it is compared to all the representatives at the highest level. Based on how similar representative R_i is to Q relative to other representatives, a decision is made whether class C_i needs to be examined. For example, if R_i is most similar to Q, then certain documents in C_i will likely be of interest. Recall that C_i may contain a few subclasses, as there is a hierarchy of classes. Thus, Q will be compared to the representatives that represent the subclasses in C_i. Based on these comparisons, the most similar subclass in C_i can be selected for further examination. This process is continued until a class that has no subclass is reached. At that point, Q is compared to all documents in that class. If the number of documents to be retrieved, k, is less than or equal to the number of documents in the class that are sufficiently similar to Q, then the process stops; otherwise, the search backs up to a higher-level class to identify another subclass with sufficiently high similarity so as to obtain the remaining most similar documents.

The above search process is essentially a depth-first search in which the class with the closest representative is selected to be examined further. Backup is sometimes required, if not enough similar documents are retrieved along a single path. A breadth-first search can sometimes be desirable if the required documents are not within a single cluster. Suppose that when Q is compared to representative R_i, an estimate of the number of documents in C_i that have high similarities with Q can be obtained. When this information is obtained for each class, it is then possible to eliminate classes that have estimates of small numbers of documents having high similarities with Q. Each of the remaining classes are then examined in exactly the same fashion, resulting in several subclasses in a lower level. This process terminates when the lowest level of classes is reached when the query Q is compared to the individual documents in these classes. Breadth-first search does not require backup. If different classes are placed into different disks, then parallel searching can be achieved.

9.2 Retrieval Effectiveness

9.2.1 Optimal Retrieval of Documents

Whether a document is relevant to a user is highly subjective. For two users who submit the same query, one can find a document relevant and another can find it irrelevant. A reason for this inconsistency is that users are usually unable to express precisely what they want and they may have certain assumptions that are not explicitly included in their queries. Even the same person who submits the same query at different times may find a document relevant at one time and irrelevant at the next. One possible reason is that once a user retrieves a relevant document and reads its contents, then the document may become irrelevant in a subsequent retrieval. That is, the user is interested in obtaining a completely different document on the same subject. Due to these and other reasons, it may be desirable to assign a probability of relevance to each document, after a user submits a query. This probability will be used to determine which documents should be retrieved. The following principle can be used to retrieve documents optimally.

Optimal Document Retrieval Principle *Arrange documents in descending order of probability of relevance. Let the resulting list be denoted by OP-List. If k documents are required, then take the first k documents from the OP-List.*

To see that this yields an optimal retrieval, let $p_{i1} > p_{i2} > p_{i3} > \cdots > p_{in}$ be the probabilities of relevance of the n documents in descending order. Then, the expected number of relevant documents to be retrieved for retrieving the first k documents from the OP-List is $ER = \sum_{j=1}^{k} p_{ij}$. Suppose one of these k documents, say D_{is} with $1 \leq s \leq k$, is replaced by another document, say D_{it} with $k < t \leq n$, then the expected number of relevant documents to be retrieved will be lower, as $p_{is} > p_{it}$, due to the descending order of probability of relevance. This argument can be repeated if several of the first k documents are replaced by other documents. As an example, consider the probabilities of relevance of the documents in the OP-List to be $[0.8, 0.75, 0.7, 0.64, 0.6, 0.5, 0.4]$. If three documents are retrieved, then $ER = 0.8 + 0.75 + 0.7$. If the second document in the list is replaced by the document with probability 0.5, then it is obvious that ER decreases.

Recall that it is usually the case that when recall is increased, precision decreases. Retrieval using the optimal document retrieval principle exhibits exactly the same behavior. As noted in the last paragraph, the expected number of relevant documents to be retrieved for retrieving the first k documents from the OP-List is $ER = \sum_{j=1}^{k} p_{ij}$. When the $(k + 1)$th document is also retrieved, the expected number of relevant documents increases by $p_{i,k+1}$. Since $p_{i,k+1}$ is smaller than p_{ij}, $1 \leq j \leq k$, it is easy to verify that the precision of retrieving the first k documents (which is ER/k) is greater than $(ER + p_{i,k+1})/(k+1)$, which is the precision when the additional document is retrieved.

The optimal document retrieval principle requires that the probability of relevance of each document be known. In practice, the actual probabilities may not be easily obtained. The following approach shows that the actual probabilities are not needed. Recall that when documents are to be retrieved, we compute $f(Q, D_{ij})$, where f is a similarity function, Q is the query submitted by the user, and the similarities are obtained for each document D_{ij}. It is sufficient to ensure that the OP-List obtained by the optimal document retrieval principle is identical to the list obtained by arranging the documents in descending order of similarity values. More precisely, let p_{ij} and p_{ik} be the probabilities of relevance of two documents in the list and $f(Q, D_{ij})$ and $f(Q, D_{ik})$ be their similarities. Then the two lists are identical if the following condition is satisfied: $p_{ij} > p_{ik}$ if and only if $f(Q, D_{ij}) > f(Q, D_{ik})$, for every pair of documents D_{ij} and D_{ik}. The inequality on the left-hand side says that D_{ij} is ahead of D_{ik} according to the probability of relevance. The inequality on the right-hand side says that D_{ij} is retrieved before D_{ik} according to their similarities. If this is true for every pair of documents, then the two lists are identical. We now proceed to make this idea more precise so that an appropriate similarity function can be constructed to permit optimal retrieval.

Let Q be the user's query. Let R denote the event that a document is relevant to the user and $P(A \mid B)$ denote the conditional probability of event A given the event B. Then $P(R \mid D_i)$ denotes the probability that D_i is relevant to the user, given the terms and their weights appearing in document D_i. Then the two lists being identical can be reexpressed as

$$P(R \mid D_i) > P(R \mid D_j) \quad \text{iff} \quad f(Q, D_i) > f(Q, D_j) \tag{9.1}$$

Bayes's theorem states that for events A and B and with A' denoting the complement of A,

$$P(A \mid B) = \frac{P(B \mid A)P(A)}{P(B \mid A)P(A) + P(B \mid A')P(A')}$$

Using Bayes's theorem and with A replaced by R and B replaced by D_i and then by D_j, the left-hand side of (9.1) can be rewritten as

$$\frac{P(D_i \mid R)}{P(D_i \mid R)P(R) + P(D_i \mid I)P(I)} > \frac{P(D_j \mid R)}{P(D_j \mid R)P(R) + P(D_j \mid I)P(I)} \tag{9.2}$$

where I denotes the complement of R, i.e., a document being irrelevant. After cross multiplication, canceling of the common expression from both sides, and placing information of each document on one side only, (9.2) can be written as

$$\frac{P(D_i \mid R)}{P(D_i \mid I)} > \frac{P(D_j \mid R)}{P(D_j \mid I)} \tag{9.3}$$

Inequality (9.3) will be expressed in terms of the similarities of the query Q with the documents D_i and D_j (i.e., relating (9.3) with (9.1)) in several ways, depending on the distributions of the terms in the set of all documents. In the next three subsections, different ways to compute $P(D \mid R)$ and $P(D \mid I)$ in (9.3) will be presented. The simplest case is to assume the independence of terms. That situation is covered in the next subsection. A limited dependence model, incorporating some dependencies between terms, is then introduced. A general dependence model is given in Section 9.2.4. Although capturing more dependencies among terms implies more accurate modeling of reality, it also leads to some disadvantages. Specifically, the retrieval formulas become more complicated and parameters that appear in the formulas may be difficult to estimate.

9.2.2 Independence Model

The set of all documents is partitioned with respect to the query Q (and the user) into two subsets, the set of relevant documents R and the set of irrelevant documents I; the set of all terms are distributed independently in R and they are also distributed independently in I. The two subsets of relevant and irrelevant documents will change from one query (or user) to another query. It is unlikely that the distributions will remain independent when the subsets change. In spite of the somewhat unrealistic assumption, the following derivation sheds some light on how terms should be weighted, based on their frequencies of occurrence in the set of relevant documents and in the set of irrelevant documents.

Let the occurrences of the terms in document D_i be $(d_{i1}, \ldots, d_{ik}, \ldots, d_{im})$, where m is the number of terms and d_{ik} is the number of occurrences of term k in the document. Let "$t_k = d_{ik}$" be the event that a document has d_{ik} occurrences of term k. Using the term independence assumption, we have

$$P(D_i \mid R) = \prod_{k=1}^{m} P(t_k = d_{ik} \mid R)$$

and

$$P(D_i \mid I) = \prod_{k=1}^{m} P(t_k = d_{ik} \mid I)$$

By denoting $p_{ik} = P(t_k = d_{ik} \mid R)$, $q_{ik} = P(t_k = d_{ik} \mid I)$, $r_{ik} = p_{ik}/q_{ik}$ and substituting the above products into Inequality (9.3), we obtain

$$\prod_{k=1}^{m} r_{ik} > \prod_{k=1}^{m} r_{jk}$$

Since the log function is monotonically increasing, by taking log to both sides and letting $w_{ik} = \log r_{ik}$, the inequality becomes

$$\sum_{k=1}^{m} w_{ik} > \sum_{k=1}^{m} w_{jk} \qquad (9.4)$$

For each document $D_i = (d_{i1}, \ldots, d_{ik}, \ldots, d_{im})$, a vector D_i'' with w_{ik} reflecting the weight or the significance of the kth term in the document can be defined by

$$D_i'' = (w_{i1}, \ldots, w_{ik}, \ldots, w_{in})$$

Note that in the above vector, the significance or weight of the kth term in the ith document, w_{ik}, depends on d_{ik}, the frequency of occurrence of the term in the document and how that frequency of occurrence is distributed in the set of relevant documents and in the set of irrelevant documents. This is an important relationship between the weight of a term with a certain frequency of occurrence and its distribution in the set of relevant documents and in the set of irrelevant documents.

Inequality (9.4) holds if and only if the inequality on the left-hand side of (9.1) holds, because (9.4) is derived based on that inequality. Assuming that the query $Q = (1, 1, \ldots, 1)$, and the similarity function f is the dot product, then $f(Q, D_i'') = \sum_{k=1}^{m} w_{ik}$. Thus, (9.4) represents the relative magnitudes of similarity values of two different documents. As a result, if the terms are independently distributed in each of the set of relevant documents and the set of irrelevant documents, then by using the dot product as the similarity function and designating the significance of each term k, $1 \le k \le m$, in each document D_i to be w_{ik}, then the optimal OP-List and the retrieval list are identical. Note that r_{ik} is the ratio of the percentage of relevant documents having d_{ik} occurrences of term k to the percentage of irrelevant documents having the same number of occurrences of the term. If the set of relevant and the set of irrelevant documents are known, then clearly the quantity can be computed. Later, we will see how this quantity can be estimated after some documents are retrieved and the user identifies the relevant documents among the retrieved set of documents.

We first observe that the computation of similarities of all documents and comparing them using (9.4) is not efficient, even if there is an inverted list for each term. Recall that an inverted list does not store the "0" entries and as a result, all those entries are not encountered during the computation of similarities. This gives substantial savings, as the number of "0" entries is usually much larger than the number of nonzero entries. In (9.4), when $d_{ik} = 0$, it is usually the case that w_{ik} is not zero, by definition of w_{ik}. Thus, the use of inverted lists to skip over the zero entries (in significance or weight) is not likely to be effective, as there will be too few "0" entries. To remedy this, we define the weight of term k when it is absent from a document, w_{0k}, to be $\log(p_{0k}/q_{0k})$, where p_{0k} and q_{0k} are, respectively, the percentages of relevant documents and irrelevant documents that do not have term k (i.e., $p_{0k} = P(t_k = O/R)$ and $q_{0k} = P(t_k = O/I)$). Let

$$w_{ik}' = w_{ik} - w_{0k} \qquad (9.5)$$

i.e., for each document, the significance of term k is redefined such that w_{0k} is subtracted from its original weight w_{ik}. If the ith document does not have term k, then $w_{ik}' = 0$, as w_{ik} is the same as w_{0k}. In other words, a document that does not have term k will now have significance

= 0, due to term k. (The document has similarity that is equal to the sum of significances of the terms present in the document.) Thus, all those "0" entries can be skipped over during the computation of similarities. An observation is that when w_{0k} is subtracted from both sides of (9.4) for each term k, Inequality (9.4) is preserved. Thus, using w'_{ik} as the significance of term k will not affect optimality of retrieval and at the same time, it improves retrieval efficiency. w'_{ik} is the significance of the kth term with a certain number of occurrences relative to the significance of the same term with zero occurrence. (Note, however, when the query changes, the sets of relevant and irrelevant documents change. As a result, w_{0k} and w_{ik} vary. Thus, it is usually not possible to fix the weights in the documents for different queries.)

An ideal good term has the following characteristics: For those documents having t occurrences of the term, when t is large, then a high percentage of relevant documents but a low percentage of irrelevant documents will have the term with t occurrences; as t decreases, the percentage of relevant documents to that of irrelevant documents also decreases; when t becomes one, the ratio of the number of relevant documents to the number of irrelevant documents is sufficiently smaller than that when t is larger. This will give a very high weight to the term when it occurs many times in a document. The weight will decrease as the number of occurrences decreases. Conversely, a bad term has different characteristics. For those documents having t occurrences of the term, when t is high, it appears in a low percentage of relevant documents and a high percentage of irrelevant documents. When t decreases, the percentage of relevant documents to the percentage of irrelevant documents may fluctuate or even increase. As a result, its weight will be low when t is nonzero.

We now consider the special case when t is allowed to be 1 or 0 only. In other words, only the presence or the absence of each term in each document is recorded and multiple occurrences of a term in a document are treated as a single occurrence. This assumption yields the *binary independence model*. Under this model, the significance of term k in a document having the term r_k is given by

$$\log \frac{p_k/(1-p_k)}{q_k/(1-q_k)} \tag{9.6}$$

where p_k and q_k are, respectively, the probabilities that a relevant document and an irrelevant document have term k. This follows from (9.5) directly. To see this, $w_{ik} - w_{0k}$ in (9.5) is $\log(p_{ik}/q_{ik}) - \log(p_{0k}/q_{0k})$. As there is no distinction between multiple occurrences of a term in a document from a single occurrence in the binary independence model, when the number of occurrences $d_{ik} > 0$, p_{ik} is the same as p_k, q_{ik} is the same as q_k, p_{0k} is $(1 - p_k)$, and q_{0k} is $(1 - q_k)$. The derivation given above is obtained by giving a significance of 1 to each query term specified by the user and a significance specified by (9.6) for the same term appearing in a document. In the binary independence model, the reverse is usually done, i.e., whenever a term appears in a document, it is given the significance of 1 (as required by the binary independence model); its significance in the user's query is given by (9.6). Since the dot product is symmetrical with respect to its argument, the two different ways of assigning significances yield identical results. Note that this model is relatively easy to implement, as the significance of each term that occurs in a document is fixed to be 1, whereas the significance of each term in a query is dynamically determined based on the query.

Example 9.1 This example is used to illustrate the computation of the term weights. Since the terms are independent, it is sufficient to consider a single term. Let the distribution of the term in the relevant documents be $(2, 2, 2, 1, 1, 0)$; i.e., there are 6 relevant documents of which 3 documents have two occurrences of the term, 2 documents have one occurrence of the term, and 1 document does not have the term. Let the distribution of the term in the 8 irrelevant documents be $(2, 1, 0, 0, 0, 0, 0, 0)$. Let p_2, p_1, and p_0 denote the probabilities that a relevant document has two occurrences, one occurrence, and zero occurrences of the term, respectively. Let q_2, q_1, and q_0 be the corresponding probabilities for the irrelevant documents. Let the significance of the term with two occurrences, one occurrence, and zero occurrences be, respectively, w_2, w_1, and w_0. Then, $p_2 = \frac{3}{6}$; $p_1 = \frac{2}{6}$; $p_0 = \frac{1}{6}$; $q_2 = \frac{1}{8}$; $q_1 = \frac{1}{8}$; and $q_0 = \frac{6}{8}$. This implies that $w_2 = \log \frac{3/6}{1/8}$; $w_1 = \log \frac{8}{3}$; and $w_0 = \log \frac{2}{9}$. By setting the significance of a term with 0 occurrences to be zero, the redefined significances of the term with different numbers of occurrences are, by equation (9.5), $w_0' = 0$, $w_1' = w_1 - w_0 = \log 12$, and $w_2' = w_2 - w_0 = \log 18$. Using the binary independence model, the distribution of the term in the set of relevant documents becomes $(1, 1, 1, 1, 1, 0)$; its distribution in the set of irrelevant documents becomes $(1, 1, 0, 0, 0, 0, 0, 0)$. Let p and q be the probability that a relevant document and an irrelevant document has the term, respectively. Then, since there are 5 out of 6 relevant documents having the term and 2 out of 8 irrelevant documents having the term, $p = \frac{5}{6}$ and $q = \frac{2}{8}$. Thus, the weight of the term is $\log 15$. ∎

9.2.3 Tree Dependence Model

In practice, some terms are likely to be dependent on other terms. For example, the term *snow* and the term *cold* are correlated to some extent because when one occurs in a document it is likely that the other occurs there. In order to retrieve documents accurately, it is important to capture the dependencies of terms in the retrieval process. In other words, when the similarity of a document is computed, not only must the significances of individual terms be included in the similarities but the co-occurrences of the terms must also be taken into consideration. Term dependencies can be very complex. We now consider a special type of term dependency, modeled by the tree dependence model. This type of dependency is relatively easy to manage. We now sketch the tree dependence model and its application in document retrieval.

1. A function, I, is defined to measure the degree in which an actual probability distribution, say $P1$, of n variables in the form of a vector X is approximated by another probability distribution, say $P2$.

$$I(P1, P2) = \sum_X P1(X) \log \frac{P1(X)}{P2(X)}$$

Let $X = (x_1, \ldots, x_i, \ldots, x_n)$, where each x_i is binary. Then there are altogether 2^n possible vectors. The summation in the above equation is over these 2^n vectors. It is known in information theory that $I \geq 0$. It is 0 if and only if $P1 = P2$ for each vector X. The larger I is, the bigger the divergence between the two distributions becomes. This function is applied to the following two distributions. One of them is the joint distribution of any two given terms, say t_i and t_j, in the set of documents, i.e., the distribution of having both terms, having t_i but not t_j, having t_j but not t_i, and not having any of the two terms. Let this distribution be denoted by $P(t_i, t_j)$. This is $P1$ in the above I function. The other distribution, namely $P2$, is the distribution obtained by assuming that t_i and

t_j are independent. More precisely, if $P(t_i)$ and $P(t_j)$ are the distributions of terms t_i and t_j in the set of documents, respectively, then $P(t_i) \cdot P(t_j)$ is the resulting distribution by the independence assumption. $I(P(t_i, t_j), P(t_i) \cdot P(t_j))$ allows us to compute the degree of dependence of the two terms. If the value of I is 0, then $P1$ and $P2$ are identical. Since $P2$ assumes that the two terms are independent, then by the equivalence of $P1$ and $P2$, the two terms are actually distributed independently. The higher the value of I is, the more dependent the two terms.

Example 9.2 Suppose the distribution of terms t_i and t_j on four documents is $D_1 = (1, 1)$ (i.e., D_1 has both terms), $D_2 = (0, 0)$, $D_3 = (1, 1)$, and $D_4 = (0, 1)$ (i.e., D_4 does not have term t_i but has term t_j). Then the distribution $P(t_i, t_j)$ is as follows. The probability $P(t_i = 1, t_j = 1) = \frac{2}{4}$, as two out of the four documents have both terms; the probability $P(t_i = 0, t_j = 1) = \frac{1}{4}$; the probability $P(t_i = 1, t_j = 0) = 0$, as no document has term t_i but not t_j; the probability $P(t_i = 0, t_j = 0) = \frac{1}{4}$. The probability distribution $P(t_i)$ is given by $P(t_i = 1) = \frac{2}{4}$ and $P(t_i = 0) = \frac{2}{4}$. The probability distribution $P(t_j)$ is given by $P(t_j = 1) = \frac{3}{4}$ and $P(t_j = 0) = \frac{1}{4}$. Thus, the distribution $P(t_i) \cdot P(t_j)$, which is obtained by assuming that the terms are independently distributed, is given by $P'(t_i = 1, t_j = 1) = \frac{2}{4} \cdot \frac{3}{4} = \frac{3}{8}$; $P'(t_i = 0, t_j = 1) = \frac{2}{4} \cdot \frac{3}{4} = \frac{3}{8}$; $P'(t_i = 1, t_j = 0) = \frac{1}{2} \cdot \frac{1}{4} = \frac{1}{8}$; $P'(t_i = 0, t_j = 0) = \frac{2}{4} \cdot \frac{1}{4} = \frac{1}{8}$. The degree of dependence of the two terms is given by

$$I(P(t_i, t_j), P'(t_i, t_j)) = \frac{2}{4} \log \frac{2/4}{3/8} + \frac{1}{4} \log \frac{1/4}{3/8} + 0 + \frac{1}{4} \log \frac{1/4}{1/8} = \frac{3}{4} \log \frac{4}{3}$$

As the value is larger than 0, this indicates that the terms are dependent. In fact, when t_i occurs in a document, t_j also occurs. ∎

2. A graph $G_d = (V, E)$ can be drawn in which the vertex set V consists of all terms with each vertex v_i corresponding to term t_i. Each edge $e = (v_i, v_j)$ measures the degree of dependence between terms t_i and t_j. The degree of dependence associated with the edge is given by $I(P(t_i, t_j), P(t_i) \cdot P(t_j))$, which is simply denoted by $I(t_i, t_j)$. If $I(t_i, t_j)$ is 0 (or close to zero), then t_i and t_j are independent and the edge is not present. The intention is to include a subset of the edges that denotes the significant dependencies among the terms. The tree dependence model is to pick $(m - 1)$ edges from the possible $O(m^2)$ edges such that the following two properties are satisfied, where m is the number of terms.

    (a) The vertices and the chosen edges have to form a tree; i.e., the graph containing the m vertices and the $(m - 1)$ edges does not contain any cycle (i.e., there are no multiple paths from one vertex to another). From graph theory, it follows that the graph is a connected component. (Each vertex in a connected component can reach every other vertex in the same connected component via edges in the graph. A precise definition will be given in Chapter 10.) In the situation where there are "clusters" of terms with no significant dependencies between terms across clusters, then a number of connected components, each corresponding to a cluster, may be formed. In that case, each connected component is required to be a tree. In the remaining part of this section, we assume that there is a single connected component; otherwise, the process is repeated for each connected component.

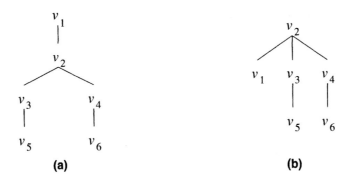

(a)   (b)

FIGURE 9.7   The Tree Dependence Model

(b) For each tree t there is an associated distribution of the terms in the documents. This associated distribution is given as follows. Arbitrarily pick a term and call it the "root" of the tree. Let it be vertex v_1. Let the probability distribution $P(t)$ be defined as follows. It is initialized to be the probability distribution of term t_1, $P(t_1)$. For every vertex v_j adjacent to v_1, v_j is placed at the next level below v_1 and $P(t)$ is modified to $P(t) \cdot P(t_j \mid t_1)$, where $P(t_j = a \mid t_1 = b)$ is the conditional probability of $t_j = a$, given that $t_1 = b$. This is repeated for every vertex below the vertices that have not appeared before. For example, if v_k is below v_j, then $P(t)$ is modified to become $P(t) \cdot P(t_k \mid t_j)$. For the tree given in Figure 9.7(a), the probability distribution $P(t)$ is $P(t_1) \cdot P(t_2 \mid t_1) \cdot P(t_3 \mid t_2) \cdot P(t_4 \mid t_2) \cdot P(t_5 \mid t_3) \cdot P(t_6 \mid t_4)$. When the terms take on specific values, the corresponding conditional probabilities can be computed. For example, in $P(t_1 = 0, t_2 = 1, t_3 = 1, t_4 = 0, t_5 = 1, t_6 = 0)$, $t_1 = 0$ and $t_2 = 1$ can be used to compute the conditional probability $P(t_2 = 1 \mid t_1 = 0)$ in the above expression.

It is essential that the distribution given above is well defined; i.e., the same tree but with a different vertex as the root gives the same expression. To see that, assume that v_2 instead of v_1 is the root. Then, the tree in Figure 9.7(a) becomes the tree in Figure 9.7(b). The corresponding expression becomes $P(t_2) \cdot P(t_1 \mid t_2) \cdot Y$, where Y involves the terms t_3, t_4, t_5, and t_6 and is identical to that in the previous expression derived when v_1 is the root. The two expressions are identical as $P(t_1) \cdot P(t_2 \mid t_1) = P(t_1, t_2) = P(t_2) \cdot P(t_1 \mid t_2)$. This shows that the tree dependence expression with root $= v_1$, denoted by $E(v_1)$, is equivalent to that with root $= v_2$, denoted by $E(v_2)$, when v_1 and v_2 are adjacent. That is, $E(v_1) = E(v_2)$. The above process is repeated by selecting a vertex, say v_3, that is adjacent to v_2 or to v_1, as the root. Based on the argument given above, $E(v_3) = E(v_2) = E(v_1)$. Since all vertices in a connected component are connected, the expression with any vertex as the root is the same as that with any other vertex as the root, by repeated application of the argument given above. In fact, it can be shown that the probability distribution $P(t)$ can be rewritten as

$$\frac{\prod_{(v_i, v_j)} P(t_i, t_j)}{\prod_{v_k} P(t_k)^{d_k - 1}} \tag{9.7}$$

where the product in the numerator is over each edge (v_i, v_j); the product in the denominator is over each vertex v_k; and d_k is the degree of the vertex v_k, which is the number of edges incident on v_k. Clearly, the above expression is not dependent on whatever vertex is chosen as the root. If (9.7) is applied to the trees in Figure 9.7, we obtain

$$\frac{P(t_1, t_2) \cdot P(t_2, t_4) \cdot P(t_4, t_6) \cdot P(t_2, t_3) \cdot P(t_3, t_5)}{P(t_2)^2 \cdot P(t_4) \cdot P(t_3)}$$

as there are three edges incident on v_2, two edges incident on each of v_3 and v_4, and one edge incident on each of v_1, v_5, and v_6.

The tree dependence model chooses a tree t_0, which approximates the actual distribution of the n terms on the documents, $P(t_1, t_2, \ldots, t_n)$, the best, among all possible trees. More precisely, let $P(t_0)$ be the probability distribution of the terms on the documents associated with the tree t_0 and let $P(t)$ be that due to any other tree t. Then, t_0 satisfies $I(P(t_1, t_2, \ldots, t_n), P(t_0)) \leq I(P(t_1, t_2, \ldots, t_n), P(t))$. Recall that the I-function measures the closeness between its two arguments. Thus, the above inequality implies that the probability distribution $P(t_0)$ approximates $P(t_1, t_2, \ldots, t_n)$ at least as well as $P(t)$, for any tree t.

At first glance, it seems that it is very time consuming to find the tree t_0, as there is an exponential number of trees. Fortunately, the tree can be obtained by the following procedure rather efficiently.

From the graph G_d, obtain a *maximum spanning tree* as follows. Recall that the label on the edge between the terms t_i and t_j is the degree of dependence between the two terms. A maximum spanning tree is a tree such that the sum of the labels on the edges is the largest among all trees in G_d. (It is essentially the same as a *minimum spanning tree*, except the maximum instead of the minimum is sought. The minimum spanning tree is given by well-known algorithms in standard graph-theory textbooks.) It can be obtained as follows:

Let E_d be the edges of a maximum spanning tree (the tree is not necessarily unique, as multiple edges may have the same label).

1. Initialize E_d = null.
2. While (a tree involving all vertices has not been formed)
     if (an edge e having the next highest label does not form a cycle with the edges in E_d)
          then $E_d := E_d \cup \{e\}$

In the above algorithm, if all the edges have been sorted in descending order of label, then the first edge is the one with the largest label. It will be chosen and added to E_d. The second edge will also be selected and added to E_d, as no cycle can be formed. If the next edge forms a cycle with E_d, then it will be discarded, otherwise it is added to E_d. This process continues until a tree involving all vertices is formed. The dominating operation is the sorting of the edges in descending order of label, which incurs time $O(f \log f)$, where f is the number of

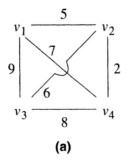

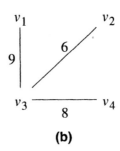

(a) **(b)**

FIGURE 9.8 Constructing a Maximum Spanning Tree

edges. It can be shown that after all the edges have been sorted in descending order of label, then a maximum spanning tree can be obtained in time $O(f \log n)$, where n is the number of vertices in the graph. Detection of a cycle can be carried out as follows. Whenever an edge (v_i, v_j) is added, it places the vertices v_i and v_j in the same connected component. If the connected component containing v_i and that containing v_j before the edge (v_i, v_j) is added are different, then the newly added edge does not create a cycle; otherwise, a cycle is created. This detection can be done in time $O(n \log n)$.

Example 9.3 This example illustrates the process of obtaining a maximum spanning tree. Suppose that the graph G_d has four vertices. Let the labels be given as: $l(v_1, v_2) = 5$; $l(v_1, v_3) = 9$; $l(v_1, v_4) = 7$; $l(v_2, v_3) = 6$; $l(v_2, v_4) = 2$; $l(v_3, v_4) = 8$ (see Figure 9.8(a)).

Initially, E_d = null. The edge with the highest label is (v_1, v_3). It is added to E_d. The edge with the next highest label is (v_3, v_4). Since it does not form a cycle with the edge in E_d, it is added to E_d. The edge with the next highest label is (v_1, v_4). If it is added to E_d, a cycle involving the vertices v_1, v_3, and v_4 will be formed. As a result, it is not added to E_d. The edge with the next highest label is (v_2, v_3). As no cycle will be formed when it is added to E_d, it is included. Now a maximum spanning tree containing the edges (v_1, v_3), (v_3, v_4), and (v_2, v_3) is obtained (see Figure 9.8(b)). ∎

It has been shown that the probability distribution of the terms in the documents associated with a maximum spanning tree indeed approximates the actual distribution the best, among all distributions in the form of a tree.

Utilizing the Tree Dependence Model in Retrieval

Recall that the optimal document retrieval principle is to retrieve document D_i ahead of document D_j if

$$\frac{P(D_i \mid R)}{P(D_i \mid I)} > \frac{P(D_j \mid R)}{P(D_j \mid I)}$$

where R and I denote the set of relevant documents and the set of irrelevant documents, respectively. This is the same as computing, for each document D, the ratio

$$\frac{P(D \mid R)}{P(D \mid I)}$$

and then retrieving the documents in descending order of the ratio. If the terms are distributed independently in the set of relevant documents and also independently in the set of irrelevant documents, then Formulas (9.5) and (9.6) can be applied to assign weights to individual terms. If the terms are dependent, the tree dependence model may be utilized. We assume that in the set of relevant documents R, $P(D \mid R)$ can be approximated by the probability distribution of a maximum spanning tree; similarly, in the set of irrelevant documents I, $P(D \mid I)$ can also be approximated by the probability distribution of some maximum spanning tree. The maximum spanning tree for the set of relevant documents may be different from that for the set of irrelevant documents. Since the two sets of documents vary from one query to another and the set of relevant documents are usually not known in advance, it is difficult to determine the two maximum dependence trees. In practice, without the consideration of any query, one may use the entire collection of documents to determine a single maximum dependence tree. Since the distributions of terms in the entire collection that are not dependent on any query are known, the determination is possible. After a query is submitted and some relevance information is obtained from the user about the set of retrieved relevant documents and the set of retrieved irrelevant documents, this maximum dependence tree is then used for both the set of relevant documents and the set of irrelevant documents for the query as an approximation. Note that even though the trees and the expressions for both sets of documents can be the same, the actual probability values can be very different. For example, with the tree in Figure 9.7, the value $P(t_1 = 0)$ in the set of relevant documents that may be estimated from the set of retrieved relevant documents can be different from the value $P(t_1 = 0)$ in the set of irrelevant documents that may be estimated from the set of retrieved irrelevant documents.

9.2.4 Generalized Dependence Model

The tree dependence model is a restricted dependence model in the sense that only certain dependencies between pairs of terms are utilized. The *Bahadur-Lazarsfeld expansion* (BLE)—which incorporates dependencies of all pairs of terms, all triplets of terms, etc., and which will be described in the next chapter—is exact in representing arbitrary probability distributions. However, it requires all possible subsets of terms and therefore is computationally expensive. A truncated version of BLE is an approximation of a given actual distribution. Usually but not always, the fewer the terms that are left out, the more accurate the approximation. Unfortunately, it is possible that a truncated expansion yields a negative value. Since probability should not be negative, it means that the truncated BLE can be rather poor. We would like to combine the tree dependence model and the truncated BLE model in such a way that the new model always produces a (probability) value between 0 and 1, is guaranteed to be more accurate than the tree dependence model, and whenever an additional dependence of terms is incorporated, a higher accuracy is guaranteed.

The expression for the tree dependence model is now rewritten in such a way that the generalization can be carried out easily. Let G be the graph (which is a tree) representing the

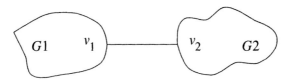

FIGURE 9.9 Illustrating Expression (9.8)

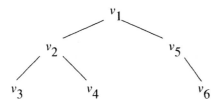

FIGURE 9.10 Illustrating the Use of Expressions (9.8) and (9.9)

dependencies of the terms. Let $Ptree(G)$ be the expression for the tree dependence model with graph G. If an edge $e = (v_1, v_2)$ in which neither v_1 nor v_2 is a leaf node is taken from the tree G, the tree is decomposed into two subtrees, $G1$ and $G2$. This decomposition allows a recursive expression for $Ptree(G)$.

$$Ptree(G) = \frac{P(v_1, v_2)}{P(v_1) \cdot P(v_2)} \cdot Ptree(G1) \cdot Ptree(G2) \qquad (9.8)$$

Expression (9.8) is illustrated by Figure 9.9. If v_1 or v_2 is a leaf node, then $G1$ or $G2$ is the isolated node v_1 or v_2. In that case, $Ptree$ (an isolated vertex v) is defined to be

$$Ptree(v) = P(v) \qquad (9.9)$$

Example 9.4 Consider the graph in Figure 9.10. If the edge (v_1, v_2) is chosen, then

$$Ptree(G) = \frac{P(v_1, v_2)}{P(v_1) \cdot P(v_2)} \cdot Ptree(G1) \cdot Ptree(G2)$$

where $G1$ is the subgraph containing vertices v_2, v_3, and v_4 and $G2$ contains v_1, v_5, and v_6. If instead (v_2, v_3) is chosen, then

$$Ptree(G) = \frac{P(v_2, v_3)}{P(v_2) \cdot P(v_3)} \cdot Ptree(G4) \cdot Ptree(G5)$$

where $G4$ contains the isolated vertex v_3 and $G5$ contains the vertices v_2, v_4, v_1, v_5, and v_6. $Ptree(G4)$ is given by $P(v_3)$, according to Expression (9.9); Expression (9.8) can be applied recursively to $Ptree(G5)$ or $Ptree(G1)$ or $Ptree(G2)$. ∎

Expression (9.8) can be generalized to permit the inclusion of dependencies of triplets of terms. Each triplet is geometrically a triangle. Edges can be added to a tree in such a way that

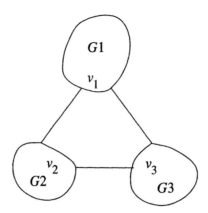

FIGURE 9.11   The Generalized Dependence Model

triangles are formed but there are no cycles of length 4 or more. By not allowing those cycles, each deletion of the three edges of a triangle decomposes the graph G into three subgraphs $G1$, $G2$, and $G3$ as shown in Figure 9.11.

The expression for the generalized dependence model, $Pgd(G)$, analogous to Expression (9.8), is as follows. Let the vertices of the triangle be v_1, v_2, and v_3.

$$Pgd(G) = \frac{P(v_1, v_2, v_3)}{P(v_1) \cdot P(v_2) \cdot P(v_3)} \cdot Pgd(G1) \cdot Pgd(G2) \cdot Pgd(G3) \tag{9.10}$$

If a subgraph, say $G1$, has no triangle, then $Pgd(G1)$ can be computed using Expression (9.8) or (9.9), depending on whether it is an ordinary tree or an isolated vertex; otherwise, the recursive expression, (9.10), can be applied.

Example 9.5 Continue as in Example 9.4, assume that in Figure 9.10 there is a triangle with vertices v_1, v_2, and v_5. In this case, we have

$$Pgd(G) = \frac{P(v_1, v_2, v_5)}{P(v_1) \cdot P(v_2) \cdot P(v_5)} \cdot Pgd(G6) \cdot Pgd(G7) \cdot Pgd(G8)$$

where $G6$ contains the isolated vertex v_1; $G7$ is a tree containing the vertices v_2, v_3, and v_4; and $G8$ is a tree containing the vertices v_5 and v_6. Expression (9.9) can be applied to $G6$, whereas Expression (9.8) can be applied to $G7$ and $G8$.   ∎

It can be shown that whenever an additional triplet (triangle) is included (but no cycle of four or more edges is formed), then a better approximation of the actual probability distribution results. More precisely, let $Pgd(G, (i + 1))$ be the generalized dependence distribution with $(i + 1)$ triplets and $Pgd(G, i)$ be the generalized dependence distribution with one of the $(i + 1)$ triplets eliminated. Let $P(G)$ be the actual probability distribution. Then, the following result holds.

$$I(P(G), Pgd(G, (i + 1))) \leq I(P(G), Pgd(G, i))$$

Recall that the *I*-function measures the divergence of two distributions; the smaller the value, the closer the two distributions are. Thus, $Pgd(G, (i+1))$ is closer to $P(G)$ than $Pgd(G, i)$. When $i = 0$, $Pgd(G, i)$ is the standard tree dependence model. Thus, the generalized dependence model approximates the actual distribution better than the standard tree dependence model. Although the approach given above can be generalized further to incorporate quadruples (dependencies among four terms) and higher-order dependencies, the complexity is too high to be of practical use.

9.2.5 Transforming a Set of Dependent Terms into a Set of "Independent" Terms

In the binary independence model and the nonbinary independence model, the formulas to achieve optimal results are simple and the parameters in these formulas can be estimated. Unfortunately, term independence does not occur in practice. On the other hand, although dependence models such as the tree dependence model and the Bahadur-Lazarsfeld expansion can model the behavior of terms in documents reasonably well, accurate estimation of the necessary parameters is difficult. It is therefore desirable to transform the original set of dependent terms into a set of new terms that are more or less independent. This subsection introduces several such transformations.

Singular Value Decomposition

Consider the term-document matrix T, in which the rows are the m terms and the columns are the n documents. The entries in the ith row give the occurrences (significances) of the ith term in the n documents; the entries in the jth column give the occurrences (significances) of the m terms in the jth document. Let $Y_1 = T * T_t$, where $*$ is matrix multiplication and T_t stands for the *transpose* of the matrix T. The (i, j) entry of Y_1 is given by the dot product of the ith row of T and the jth column of T_t. The latter is the same as the jth row of T. Thus, $Y_1(i, j)$ is a measure of the co-occurrences of the ith and jth terms in the documents; the higher the value, the more documents contain both terms. Let $Y_2 = T_t * T$. The ith row of T_t gives the document vector of the ith document. The (i, j)th entry of Y_2 is the dot product of the ith row of T_t and the jth column of T. Since the latter is the same as the jth row of T_t, the (i, j)th entry of Y_2 is a measure of the similarity of the ith and the jth documents, if the dot product is used as the similarity function. By the *singular value decomposition* method, matrix T can be written as a product of three matrices.

$$T = T' * E' * D' \tag{9.11}$$

where T' is an m-by-m matrix, E' is an m-by-n matrix with zero entries off the diagonal, and D' is an n-by-n matrix. T' has the property that $T_t'T'$ is the identity matrix I of dimension m by m. In order words, each column of T' is a unit orthogonal vector such that the dot product of two different columns of T' is zero, and the dot product of any column by itself is 1. D' satisfies $D'D_t' = I$, and E' is a diagonal matrix of the form as shown below.

$$\begin{pmatrix} e_1 & & & & & \\ & \ddots & & & & 0 \\ & & \cdot e_i & & & \\ & & & \ddots & & \\ & & & & e_p & 0 \\ & 0 & & & & \ddots \\ & & & & & & \cdot 0 \end{pmatrix}$$

where each e is the square root of an *eigenvalue* of Y_2 (recall that $Y_2 = T_t*T$); i.e., $Y_2*v = e^2*v$ with v being an *eigenvector*. The e's are arranged in descending value, i.e., $e_1 \geq e_2 \geq \cdots \geq e_p > 0$, where p is the *rank* of the matrix T. Clearly, $p \leq \min\{n, m\}$.

Equation (9.11) can be rewritten as

$$T = \begin{pmatrix} T_p & T'' \end{pmatrix} \begin{pmatrix} E_p & 0 \\ 0 & 0 \end{pmatrix} \begin{pmatrix} D_p \\ D'' \end{pmatrix} \tag{9.12}$$

where T_p is an m-by-p matrix, T'' is an m-by-$(m-p)$ matrix, E_p is p-by-p, D_p and D'' are p-by-n and $(n-p)$-by-n, respectively. In other words, T' is decomposed into T_p and T'', where T_p consists of the first p columns of T', E_p retains the positive entries of E', and D' is decomposed into D_p and D'' with D_p consisting of the first p rows of D'.

By direct matrix multiplication in (9.12), we have

$$T = T_p * E_p * D_p \tag{9.13}$$

because T'' and D'' will not contribute anything due to zero entries in E'.

Note that T_p, E_p, and D_p retain the properties of T', E', and D', respectively. That is, the columns of T_p are unit orthogonal vectors, E_p has positive entries along the diagonal only and they are in descending order, and the rows of D_p are unit orthogonal vectors. Since the columns of T_p are orthogonal, they are *linearly independent*. Although linear independence is not the same as *statistical independence*, they can be treated the same for most practical purposes. The entries of T_p can also be seen as providing relationships between the original set of terms and the set of p new terms. D_p is a p-by-n matrix. Each column of the matrix can be interpreted as a document vector in the space of the p new terms.

Suppose that instead of taking p terms, a much smaller number of terms, say k, is used. By the above interpretation, the most significant k new terms should be retained. This means that the first k columns of T_p, the submatrix of size k by k containing the largest e_i values, and the first k rows of D_p are retained. The result is that

$$T \approx T_k * E_k * D_k \tag{9.14}$$

where the less-significant columns, submatrices, and rows of the matrices in (9.13) are discarded. Note that T_k is an m-by-k matrix, E_k is a k-by-k matrix, and D_k is a k-by-n matrix. The choice of k depends on the values of the e's. The e's that are significantly greater than 0 should be retained. There are two potential advantages of reducing p to k. First, the vector space given by the k terms is much smaller, permitting efficiency. Second, it is hoped that if there are minor errors (noises) in representing the contents of the documents by the matrix T, these errors can be removed by this truncation process.

We now consider the transformation of a given user query using the original set of terms into the same query expressed using the new set of terms. By (9.14), the columns of T, which are the document vectors of the original set of terms, are transformed to the columns of D_k, which are the document vectors of the new set of terms. Since a query can be visualized as a document vector, we can make use of (9.14) to write

$$Q_t = T_k * E_k * (Q')_t$$

where Q_t represents the original query as a column in T and $(Q')_t$ represents the new query as a column in D_k. Since the columns of T_k are unit orthogonal vectors, $(T_k)_t * T_k = I$, the unit matrix. Thus,

$$(T_k)_t * Q_t = E_k * (Q')_t \qquad (9.15)$$

The inverse of E_k, denoted by E_k^{-1}, is simply another diagonal matrix, where the diagonal entries are $1/e_i$, $1 \le i \le k$. Thus, if it is multiplied to both the left and the right sides of (9.15), the result is

$$E_k^{-1} * (T_k)_t * Q_t = (Q')_t$$

Finally, $Q' = Q * T_k * E_k^{-1}$, as the transpose of a diagonal matrix is itself. It has been reported that when using k new terms, with k significantly less than m, for both the queries and the documents, retrieval performance can be improved. However, the singular value decomposition method is a very time consuming process (it takes time $O(m^2 n)$), and it is not clear whether this approach is practical for reasonably large document collections. If the singular value decomposition method for a document collection is feasible, it may be worthwhile to apply the nonbinary independence model to the collection, as the new set of terms are linearly independent. The method of applying singular value decomposition to text retrieval is known as *latent semantic indexing*.

Transforming into Known "Concepts"

The set of new terms obtained above are not prespecified and cannot be interpreted meaningfully. The singular value decomposition method given by Equation (9.11) can be utilized to find connections between a set of terms and a prespecified set of concepts. The set of terms are simply the words or phrases found in the description of the text documents. The set of concepts are categories that are manually assigned to the documents. For example, in MEDLINE, a large medical collection, subject categories are assigned to each document by indexers at the National Library of Medicine.

We first describe how the singular value decomposition method is used to solve the *linear least squares* problem and how the least squares problem is related to finding the connections between a given set of terms and a given set of concepts.

$$\left(T_{\substack{m \times n}} \right) \left(X_{\substack{n \times 1}} \right) \approx \left(C_{\substack{m \times 1}} \right)$$

FIGURE 9.12   Illustrating the Least Squares Problem

Solving the Least Squares Problem

Given an m-by-n matrix T and an m-by-1 matrix C, find a vector $X = (x_1, x_2, \ldots, x_n)_t$ of dimension n by 1 such that TX approximates C in the sum of squares; i.e., if $(TX - C)_t = (f_1, f_2, \ldots, f_m)$, then $\sum_{i=1}^{m} f_i^2$ is the smallest, among all matrices X of dimension n by 1. This is illustrated by Figure 9.12.

A typical application is the interpolation problem in which the coefficients of a polynomial of degree $(n - 1)$ need to be determined such that the polynomial fits approximately a given set of m points. Specifically, we want to determine the coefficients $\{a_0, a_1, \ldots, a_{n-1}\}$ of the polynomial $a_0 + a_1 x + \cdots + a_{n-1} x^{n-1}$ that fit the set of points $\{(x_i, y_i) \mid 1 \leq i \leq m\}$ best in the least squares sense. This is expressed as

$$a_0 + a_1 x_i + \cdots + a_{n-1} x_i^{n-1} \approx y_i, \quad 1 \leq i \leq m$$

The matrix representation of these equations is

$$\begin{pmatrix} 1 & x_1 & x_1^2 & \cdots & x_1^{n-1} \\ & & \vdots & & \\ 1 & x_i & x_i^2 & \cdots & x_i^{n-1} \\ & & \vdots & & \\ 1 & x_m & x_m^2 & \cdots & x_m^{n-1} \end{pmatrix} \begin{pmatrix} a_0 \\ a_1 \\ \vdots \\ a_{n-1} \end{pmatrix} = \begin{pmatrix} y_1 \\ y_2 \\ \vdots \\ y_m \end{pmatrix}$$

Thus, in the interpolation problem,

$$T = \begin{pmatrix} 1 & x_1 & x_1^2 & \cdots & x_1^{n-1} \\ & & \vdots & & \\ 1 & x_i & x_i^2 & \cdots & x_i^{n-1} \\ & & \vdots & & \\ 1 & x_m & x_m^2 & \cdots & x_m^{n-1} \end{pmatrix}, \quad X = \begin{pmatrix} a_0 \\ a_1 \\ \vdots \\ a_{n-1} \end{pmatrix}, \quad \text{and} \quad C = \begin{pmatrix} y_1 \\ y_2 \\ \vdots \\ y_m \end{pmatrix}$$

We now seek X such that the approximation in the least squares sense is achieved.

By Equation (9.11), $TX - C = T'E'D'X - C$. Recall that T' (and therefore T_t') is an m-by-m orthogonal matrix. It is easy to see that for any vector V of dimension m by 1 and any orthogonal matrix O of dimension m by m, the norm of the vector $\|V\| = \|OV\|$, because $\|OV\|^2 = (OV)_t(OV) = V_t O_t OV = V_t V$, due to the orthogonality of O. Thus, $\|OV\| = \|V\|$. Consequently, by orthogonality of T_t', $\|TX - C\| = \|T_t'(T'E'D'X - C)\|$, which is equal to

$\|E'D'X - T'_t C\|$, since $T'_t T' = I$. Let $T'_t C = (g_1, g_2, \ldots, g_m)_t$ and $D'X = (z_1, z_2, \ldots, z_n)_t$. Then

$$E'D'X = \begin{pmatrix} e_1 z_1 \\ \vdots \\ e_p z_p \\ 0 \\ \vdots \\ 0 \end{pmatrix}$$

where p is the rank of matrix T, and

$$E'D'X - T'_t C = \begin{pmatrix} e_1 z_1 - g_1 \\ \vdots \\ e_p z_p - g_p \\ -g_{p+1} \\ \vdots \\ -g_m \end{pmatrix}$$

If $p = n$, i.e., the rank of matrix T is n, then the x's in X can be chosen such that $e_i z_i - g_i = 0$, $1 \leq i \leq n$ and $\|E'D'X - T'_t C\|^2 = g_{n+1}^2 + \cdots + g_m^2$. Since z_i can be determined to be g_i/e_i, $1 \leq i \leq n$, $D'X = (z_1, z_2, \ldots, z_n)_t$ has a unique solution with n unknowns $(x_1, x_2, \ldots, x_n)$ and n equations.

If $p < n$, then set $z_{p+1} = \cdots = z_n = 0$. In this case, the x's in X can be chosen such that $e_i z_i - g_i = 0$, $1 \leq i \leq p$ and $\|E'D'X - T'_t C\|^2 = g_{p+1}^2 + \cdots + g_m^2$. The x's can be determined by $D_p X = (z_1, z_2, \ldots, z_p)$, where D_p consists of the first p rows of D'. They are not unique, as there are n unknowns $(x_1, \ldots, x_n)$ with p equations, $p < n$.

The above method is readily generalizable to the case where the matrix C is of dimension m by q and the matrix X of dimension n by q such that TX approximates C best in the sum of least squares. Basically, this generalized problem reduces to the last problem when the ith column of X is considered against the ith column of C, $1 \leq i \leq q$.

Finding Connections between Terms and Concepts

Consider the generalized problem $TX \approx C$ given as follows.

$$[T_{m \times n}] [X_{n \times q}] \approx [C_{m \times q}]$$

Here, T can be visualized as a set of documents represented as vectors of terms. The rows of T are the documents in vector form; the columns of T are the terms; the (i, j)th entry of T is the weight (significance) of term j in document i. C is the same set of documents represented as vectors of concepts. The rows of C are the documents; there are q concepts corresponding to the q columns of C. As mentioned previously, certain collections have the concepts manually assigned. Clearly, the sets of terms for the documents can be obtained automatically, using the techniques described in Section 9.1.1. Thus, both T and C are known.

The solution matrix X of dimension n by q is interpreted as the connection between the terms and the concepts. Specifically, the rows of X are the terms; the columns are the concepts and the (i, j)th entry, x_{ij}, indicates the significance of the relationship between the ith term and the jth concept. If x_{ij} is large, then the ith term is heavily related to the jth concept.

Consider the dot product of the ith row of T denoted by $D_i = (t_{i1}, \ldots, t_{ik}, \ldots, t_{in})$ and the jth column of X denoted by $(x_{1j}, \ldots, x_{kj}, \ldots, x_{nj})$, where t_{ik} is the weight of term k in document i; x_{kj} is the significance of the relationship between the kth term and the jth concept. Thus, $t_{ik} \cdot x_{kj}$ can be interpreted as the weight of concept j in document i due to term k and $\sum_{k=1}^{n} t_{ik} \cdot x_{kj}$ is the weight of concept j in document i due to all terms k from 1 to n. To represent document D_i as a vector of the q concepts, we simply take $D_i * X$. This yields a vector of concepts D_i'. This should be close to the ith row of C, as required by the least squares approximation. A query Q represented by a vector of terms can similarly be written as Q', a vector of concepts, by $Q' = Q * X$. Then, the similarity of Q' and D_i' (or the ith row of C) can be computed, say using the *Cosine* similarity function. It should be noted that two different terms, one occurring in Q but not in D_i and another occurring in D_i but not in Q, may be mapped to one or more common concepts. As a result, matchings that are not possible using the original set of terms may become feasible with the concepts.

A Less Costly Term Transformation

We now provide another method to transform dependent terms to independent terms. The new method is computationally more efficient than the singular value decomposition method. A set of independent terms can be constructed from all possible combinations of the original set of terms. For example, if $\{t_1, t_2\}$ is the original set of terms, then the $2^2 = 4$ combinations are identified by $f_1 = t_1 t_2, f_2 = t_1 t_2^*, f_3 = t_1^* t_2$, and $f_4 = t_1^* t_2^*$, where t_i^* stands for the *complement* of term t_i. (When a document does not have term t_i, it has the complemented term t_i^*.) In Boolean algebra, these combinations are the fundamental products (called *minterms*) in which every Boolean expression can be expressed. For example, the term t_1 can be expressed as f_1 OR f_2. Thus, if there are m original terms, 2^m possible fundamental products can be produced from which each original term can be expressed. As a result, we may view these fundamental products as the axis of a 2^m dimensional space. In this space, the ith fundamental product is of the form $(0, \ldots, 0, 1, 0, \ldots, 0)$, where the ith position is occupied by "1", $1 \le i \le 2^m$. These are orthogonal and therefore independent vectors in this space.

In order to reduce the total number of new independent terms, the following observation is made. A document has a certain combination of terms while some combination of terms may have no document corresponding to it. Thus, instead of having 2^m new independent terms, those combinations of terms with no corresponding documents are discarded. For example, consider the following document-term matrix:

	t_1	t_2	t_3
D_1	1	0	1
D_2	0	1	1
D_3	1	0	0

In this example, each new term is a combination of the original terms, which correspond to some document. Thus, there are three new terms t_1', t_2', and t_3' corresponding to the three documents. For example, the new term t_1' corresponding to document D_1 represents the combination $t_1 t_2^* t_3$. Each original term is then expressed as a linear combination of the new terms by utilizing the nonzero entries in the column of the matrix corresponding to the term as

$$t_1 = t_1' + t_3'$$
$$t_2 = t_2'$$
$$t_3 = t_1' + t_2'$$

In general, if the column of t_i is $(d_1, \ldots, d_j, \ldots, d_m)$, where d_j is the number of occurrences of term t_i in document D_j, then t_i can be expressed in terms of the new independent terms as follows.

$$t_i = \sum_{j=1}^{m} d_j t_j' \qquad (9.16)$$

In this manner, both binary and nonbinary occurrences of terms in documents can be taken care of. If two or more documents have exactly the same weighted combinations of terms, then they can be merged together as one document in the formation of the document–term matrix before the transformation takes place. This is reasonable, as these documents are indistinguishable from the set of terms. This seldom occurs in practice, as each document usually has many terms. Each term can also be normalized. For example, we may write

$$t_i = \sum_{j=1}^{m} (d_j / |T_j|) t_j', \qquad \text{where } |T_j| = \sqrt{\sum_{j=1}^{m} d_j^2}$$

From the relationships between the original terms and the new terms by Equation (9.16) or its normalized version, each document that is a combination of old terms can be immediately expressed as a combination of the new terms. The same applies to a query. Thus, it is possible to compute the similarities between the query and all documents using the new set of independent terms as the basis of the vector space. It is clear that the transformation process discussed in this section is less time consuming than the singular value decomposition approach given earlier, as expressing all terms as combinations of new terms by Equation (9.16) takes time proportional to the number of nonzero entries in the document-term matrix. Thus, the time complexity is bounded by $O(m \cdot n)$. Experimental results on small collections indicate that both approaches give better retrieval performance than when term transformation is not performed. However, a comparison between the two approaches has not been carried out.

9.3 Relevance Feedback

There are three forms of relevance feedback. The first uses relevance information from a given query and applies it to retrieve more relevant documents for the same query. The second uses the relevance information from many previously submitted queries and applies it to future queries; this is sometimes called *permanent learning*. The third form does not actually make use of relevance information from the users. These three forms will be discussed in the next three subsections.

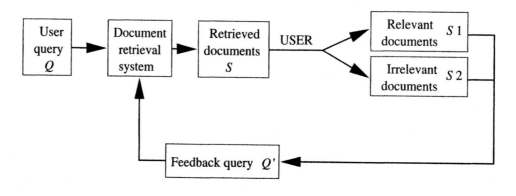

FIGURE 9.13 The Relevance Feedback Process

9.3.1 Applying Relevance Information to the Same Query

The relevance feedback process for a single query is as follows. A user submits a query Q and the system retrieves a set of documents, say S. When the system presents documents in S to the user, the user identifies the relevant documents in S. Based on the relevance information supplied by the user, the system modifies Q to a new query Q' in hopes that the new query will yield more relevant documents to the user. This process of retrieving documents and identifying the relevant ones among the retrieved documents continues until the user is satisfied with the retrieved results or no sufficient progress is made to convince the user to continue. This process is illustrated in Figure 9.13.

Parameter Estimation

In the binary independence model, optimal retrieval of documents can be achieved by assigning the weight of the ith term in the user query to be

$$\sum \log \frac{p_i/(1 - p_i)}{q_i/(1 - q_i)}$$

where p_i is the probability that a relevant document has the ith term and q_i is the probability that an irrelevant document has the ith term and the sum is over all terms. In practice, only those terms appearing in the original query Q or in a retrieved document will be assigned weights. We want to estimate the values of p_i and q_i. The process of estimating q_i is similar to that of estimating p_i. Thus, we concentrate on the latter process. In order to simplify our notation, we estimate p_1, the probability that a relevant document has the first term, as all other p's can be estimated in a similar manner.

Case 1. The term whose probability is to be estimated is a query term; i.e., the query Q contains the first term t_1.

    Recall that in the binary independence model, a document $D = (d_1, d_2, \ldots, d_m)$ satisfies each $d_i = 0$ or 1 and the similarity function is the dot product function. Suppose the

TABLE 9.1 **Contingency Table**

	$t_1 = 1$	$t_1 = 0$
$S_1 \leq T$	a	0
$S_1 > T$	b	c

document is retrieved by the query $Q = (w_1, w_2, \ldots, w_m)$; i.e., its similarity S is sufficiently high. More precisely, $S = \sum_{i=1}^{m} w_i \cdot d_i > T$ for some threshold T. The similarity S can be rewritten as $w_1 \cdot d_1 + S_1$, where $S_1 = \sum_{j=2}^{m} w_j \cdot d_j$. Suppose document D is relevant to the user query Q. Although S is greater than T, S_1 can be either greater than T or less than or equal to T. Also, term t_1 may or may not be present in D. Altogether there are four possible combinations based on whether $S_1 > T$ or not and term t_1 is present or not. The set of retrieved relevant documents can be partitioned into four classes and they are placed into a 2-by-2 contingency table as shown in Table 9.1. Let $t_1 = 1$ and $t_1 = 0$ denote the presence and absence of term t_1, respectively.

In Table 9.1, each entry is the number of retrieved relevant documents that satisfy the conditions imposed on its column and its row. For example, a is the number of retrieved relevant documents having the first term but with $S_1 \leq T$. There is no retrieved relevant document that satisfies $S_1 \leq T$ and does not have the first term (i.e., $t = 0$), because any document that satisfies the latter condition has similarity $S = S_1 \leq T$, which implies that it will not be retrieved. Similarly, b and c are the numbers of retrieved relevant documents satisfying $S_1 > T$ and having term t_1 and not having term t_1, respectively. Restrict ourselves to the set of relevant documents. Let the probability that a relevant document has t_1 be expressed as $\text{Prob}\{t_1 = 1\}$. Since the terms involved in the computation of S_1 are different from t_1 and by the term independence assumption, $p_1 = \text{Prob}\{t_1 = 1\} = \text{Prob}\{t_1 = 1 \mid S_1 > T\}$. (Recall from probability theory that $\text{Prob}\{A\} = \text{Prob}\{A \mid B\}$, if A and B are independent.) Note that terms in the computation of S_1 are different from t_1. By the definition of conditional probability, the probability can be reexpressed as

$$\frac{\text{Prob}\{t_1 = 1, S_1 > T\}}{\text{Prob}\{S_1 > T\}} = \frac{b}{b + c} \qquad (9.17)$$

The numerator is the entry satisfying the conditions imposed by the first column and the bottom row, and the denominator is the sum of the two entries in the bottom row. The following two observations can be made.

Observation 1. It should be noted that any document D with $S_1 > T$ has its similarity $S > T$. Thus, it is retrieved and its relevance is known. As a result, it is placed into Table 9.1. On the other hand, a document with similarity $S \leq T$ is not retrieved and has unknown relevance. It cannot be used for the estimation of p_1.

Observation 2. If we assume that the probability that t_1 appears in the set of relevant documents is the same as that it occurs in the set of retrieved relevant documents, then the probability can be estimated to be

$$\frac{a + b}{a + b + c} \qquad (9.18)$$

TABLE 9.2   **Contingency Table for Nonbinary Independence Model**

	$t_1 = 0$	$t_1 = 1$	$t_1 = 2$
$S_1 \leq T$	0	a_1	a_2
$S_1 > T$	c	b_1	b_2

It can be easily seen that Expression (9.18) is greater than Expression (9.17). This is not surprising, as a query term has a higher chance of appearing in a retrieved (relevant) document than a random (relevant) document.

Case 2. The term whose probability is to be estimated is not a query term.

Intuitively, such a term has the same probability of appearing in the set of retrieved relevant documents as that of appearing in the set of relevant documents, as it is not used in the retrieval process (see below). Thus, it can be estimated by

$$\frac{\text{the number of retrieved relevant documents having the term}}{\text{the number of retrieved relevant documents}}$$

Since t_1 is not among the terms in the computation of S and all terms are independent, we have $\mathrm{Prob}\{t_1 = 1\} = \mathrm{Prob}\{t_1 = 1 \mid S > T\}$.

The above approach can be extended to the nonbinary independence model, where each term may take on values other than 0 and 1. Suppose that a term may take on three values 0, 1, and 2. Then, the above 2-by-2 contingency table is extended to a 2-by-3 table, where the three columns represent $t_1 = 0$, $t_1 = 1$, and $t_1 = 2$, respectively. In other words, each of the two entries a and b in Table 9.1 is split into two entries: a into a_1 and a_2 and b into b_1 and b_2. Table 9.2 is the new table.

Then, the desired probability can be estimated in a similar manner. For example, if term t_1 is in the query, the probability that a relevant document has $t_1 = 2$ is $b_2/(b_1 + b_2 + c)$, where b_i is the number of retrieved relevant documents satisfying $t_1 = i, i = 1, 2$, and $S_1 > T$. When a term has many possible values, its set of values can be partitioned into a set of ranges. Although the estimation process is reasonable, the estimated probabilities on the relevant documents are usually inaccurate, because the term independence assumption does not hold and there are too few retrieved and relevant documents.

Traditional (A, B) Approach

In this approach, the underlying assumption is that the relevant documents of a query are close together (i.e., they share quite a few common terms), whereas the irrelevant documents are dispersed.

Consider the set of all relevant documents, R, and the set of all irrelevant documents, I, of the query Q. An ideal query should separate the relevant documents from the irrelevant documents. Thus, the following function is to be maximized.

$$\sum f(Q, D_r) - \sum f(Q, D_i) \tag{9.19}$$

where D_r is a relevant document and the first summation is over the set of all relevant documents R, D_i is an irrelevant document and the second summation is over the set of all irrelevant documents I, and f is the similarity function.

To be more specific, let the similarity function f be the *Cosine* function. Then, $f(Q, D)$, for any document D, can be written as (Q^n, D^n), where $(,)$ denotes the dot product and Q^n and D^n are the normalized query and the normalized document, respectively. (Recall that for a normalized vector X, $(X, X) = 1$). Thus, (9.19) can be rewritten as

$$\sum (Q^n, D_r^n) - \sum (Q^n, D_i^n) \tag{9.20}$$

It is easy to verify that the dot product is *bilinear*, i.e., $(X, Y_1 + Y_2) = (X, Y_1) + (X, Y_2)$, for any vectors X, Y_1, and Y_2. Thus, we rewrite (9.20) into

$$\left(Q^n, \sum D_r^n \right) - \left(Q^n, \sum D_i^n \right) = \left(Q^n, \sum D_r^n - \sum D_i^n \right)$$

Let P denote the vector $\sum D_r^n - \sum D_i^n$. In order to find a query Q, which maximizes the above dot product, (Q^n, P), two observations are made. First, the length of Q (which is the square root of the dot product of Q with itself) is unimportant, because Q is normalized in the product. Second, the dot product achieves the maximum when the angular distance between Q and P is zero. In other words, Q should be $c \cdot P$ for some positive constant c. In a relevance feedback environment, since only the set of retrieved and relevant documents, RR, and the set of retrieved and irrelevant documents, RI, are known, Q is set to be $c \cdot (\sum_r D_r^n - \sum_i D_i^n)$, where the first summation is over RR and the second summation is over RI. A slight generalization yields

$$Q(i + 1) = A \cdot \sum D_r^n - B \cdot \sum D_i^n + Q(i) \tag{9.21}$$

where A and B are positive constants, and $Q(i)$ is the query in the ith iteration. Initially, $i = 0$ and $Q(0)$ is the original user-submitted query and $Q(1)$ is the first feedback query. If the user is satisfied with the newly retrieved documents, then the feedback process terminates; otherwise, i is increased by 1 and $Q(2)$ is obtained by Formula (9.21) from the first feedback query $Q(1)$ and its retrieved documents whose relevances are known. This process continues, until either the user is satisfied or runs out of patience. The parameters A and B denote the significance of the retrieved relevant documents relative to the retrieved irrelevant documents. If A is greater than B, then a higher significance is placed on the former documents than on the latter documents. Preliminary experimental results indicate that $A = 1/|RR|$ and $B = 1/|RI|$ give reasonable retrieval results. However, the optimal values for A and B are unknown. The underlying assumption in (9.21) is that the retrieved relevant documents are close to the unretrieved relevant documents. By adding the weights to terms in the retrieved relevant documents and subtracting weights from terms in the retrieved irrelevant documents, it is hoped that the unretrieved relevant documents can be found by the feedback query.

Feedback Using the Perceptron Criterion from Pattern Recognition

The basic idea is to define the next feedback query $Q(i + 1)$ in terms of the present feedback query $Q(i)$, the retrieved relevant documents, and the retrieved irrelevant documents, similar to that given in Formula (9.21). However, the new method also takes into consideration the rankings of the retrieved relevant documents relative to those of the retrieved irrelevant documents. As in the (A, B) *feedback* method, the derivation will be based on all relevant documents and all irrelevant documents. But when the method is applied, only the retrieved relevant documents and the retrieved irrelevant documents are employed.

Definition 9.2 *Let R and I be the set of relevant documents and the set of irrelevant documents, respectively. The set of* difference vectors *is defined to be* $\{b \mid b = D_r - D_i, D_r \in R, D_i \in I, (Q, D_r) < (Q, D_i)\}$.

Ideally, a relevant document D_r should have its similarity with the query, (Q, D_r), greater than that of any irrelevant document with the query, (Q, D_i). Each *difference vector* represents an instance in which the ideal situation does not occur. The following example illustrates this concept.

Example 9.6 Suppose there are four documents D_1, D_2, D_3, and D_4 in descending order of similarity with the query Q. Suppose that D_2 and D_4 are relevant and the other two documents are irrelevant. Then, the following pairs of documents will be used to form the *difference vectors*: $[D_2, D_1], [D_4, D_3], [D_4, D_1]$. In each pair, the relevant document has a smaller similarity than the corresponding irrelevant document. ∎

The feedback algorithm is as follows.

Initialization:
    k = 0;
    Q(k) = Q; /* Q = the original user-submitted query.*/

Iteration:
    If $(Q(k), D_r) > (Q(k), D_i)$ for each pair of relevant document D_r and irrelevant
        document D_i, then the algorithm terminates;
    /* this is obvious, as the new query ranks all relevant documents ahead of any irrelevant
        document. */
    Else $Q(k+1) = Q(k) + \sum b_j$; /* b_j is a *difference vector* and the summation
        is over all difference vectors. */

This iteration continues until the feedback query ranks all relevant documents ahead of all irrelevant documents or the user terminates the process.

The key difference between this algorithm and the (A, B) *feedback* method can be illustrated by the following example.

Example 9.7 Using the four documents in Example 9.6, we have $\sum b_j = D_2 - D_1 + D_4 - D_3 + D_4 - D_1$. If the (A, B) feedback formula is used, $A = B = 1$ and all documents are of the same length, the corresponding vector to be added to the previous query is $D_2 - D_1 + D_4 - D_3$. Each relevant document and each irrelevant document occur once in the (A, B) method. Using the new method, D_4 occurs twice, because there are two irrelevant documents that are ranked higher than it; D_1 occurs twice, because there are two relevant documents with lower ranks. ∎

Thus, the new method incorporates the rankings of the relevant and the irrelevant documents into the feedback process. If a relevant document has a lower rank than t irrelevant documents, then it will appear t times in the *difference vectors*; the same applies to an irrelevant document that has a higher rank than a set of relevant documents. A justification that the new feedback scheme is reasonable is that if an ideal query Q^* exists, then the feedback queries converge to it, where Q^* ranks all relevant documents ahead of all irrelevant ones. Q^* satisfies

$$(Q^*, D_r) > (Q^*, D_i) \tag{9.22}$$

for any relevant document D_r and any irrelevant document D_i. Convergence essentially means that the separation between $Q(k)$ and Q^* decreases, as k increases. This is translated to $|Q(k+1) - Q^*| < |Q(k) - Q^*|$, where $|X|$, the norm or the length of the vector X, is given by the square root of the dot product of X with itself, i.e., $\sqrt{(X, X)}$. Unfortunately, the above inequality cannot be proved. However, a slightly weaker condition can be established. It is $|Q(k+1) - cQ^*|^2 < |Q(k) - cQ^*|^2$, for a sufficiently large constant c. We now proceed to show this result. Due to bilinearity,

$$\begin{aligned}|Q(k+1) - cQ^*|^2 &= (Q(k+1) - cQ^*, Q(k+1) - cQ^*) \\ &= (Q(k) - cQ^* + \sum b_j, Q(k) - cQ^* + \sum b_j) \\ &= (Q(k) - cQ^*, Q(k) - cQ^*) + 2(Q(k) - cQ^*, \sum b_j) + (\sum b_j, \sum b_j)\end{aligned} \tag{9.23}$$

It is sufficient to show that the summation of the last two terms is less than zero. Consider the second term, but ignore the constant factor 2. Again using bilinearity,

$$(Q(k) - cQ^*, \sum b_j) = (Q(k), \sum b_j) - c(Q^*, \sum b_j) \tag{9.24}$$

Note that each b_j is of the form $(D_r - D_i)$ for a relevant document D_r and an irrelevant document D_i. Since this is a difference vector for feedback query $Q(k)$ satisfying $(Q, D_r) < (Q, D_i)$, the following inequality is satisfied.

$$(Q(k), b_j) < 0 \tag{9.25}$$

Now, consider the second part on the right-hand side of (9.24). By (9.22), $(Q^*, b_j) > 0$. Thus, the second part of (9.24) is arbitrarily negative, as c can be arbitrarily large. Combining with (9.25), (9.24) is arbitrarily negative. Since the last term of (9.23), $(\sum b_j, \sum b_j)$, has bounded magnitude, and the second-to-last term of (9.23) is arbitrarily negative, the desired inequality, $|Q(k+1) - cQ^*| < |Q(k) - cQ^*|$, follows.

Feedback with Restricted Information

Both the (A, B) method and the perceptron method have reasonable but not spectacular retrieval success. It has recently been reported that retrieval by the initial query via a two-stage process yields better retrieval results than the standard one-stage process. The standard one-stage process computes the similarities of the documents, ranks them in descending order, and then takes the top k documents, for any user-specified k. The two-stage process computes the similarities of the documents, ranks them in descending order, takes the top k' documents with $k' > k$ and performs more thorough similarity computations for these k' documents before outputting the k documents selected from the k' documents. Thus, the first stage serves as a screening process. In the second stage, for each logical unit of a document, a similarity computation of that logical unit with the query is computed. A logical unit can be a chapter in a book or a section in a paper. The similarity of a document with the query in the second stage is the maximum over all the similarities of the logical units of the document with the query. The underlying assumption is that the semantics of a document is better represented by terms that are physically close together than the set of all terms dispersed over the entire document. Furthermore, a user may be interested in a certain part of a document rather than the entire document. Thus, in the second stage, the new similarities are used to rank the k' documents and the top k documents are retrieved. In feedback, we may adopt a similar process. Instead of adding all terms of each relevant document and subtracting all terms of each irrelevant document, we may want to restrict the terms to be those appearing in the logical unit yielding the largest similarity of a retrieved document. This is appealing, because intuitively the feedback query is oriented more toward the semantic space of the retrieved relevant documents and away from that of the retrieved irrelevant ones. Furthermore, efficiency is gained, as fewer terms are employed in the process.

9.3.2 Permanent Learning

In order to extract important parameter values and utilize them to improve retrieval effectiveness for future queries, it is assumed that the information retrieval system has obtained relevance information from many previously submitted queries. More precisely, let $QS = \{Q_1, Q_2, \ldots, Q_s\}$ be a set of previously submitted queries and $DS = \{D_1, D_2, \ldots, D_t\}$ be a collection of documents where relevance assessment information is obtained; i.e., for many pairs of (Q_i, D_j), it is known that D_j is relevant or not relevant to Q_i. In practice, if the collection is reasonably large, documents that have not been retrieved with respect to the queries have unknown relevance assessment. Based on the query document pairs with known relevance assessment, we now extract useful information, which can then be used to estimate the probability of relevance of a document to a new query.

Consider a specific query document pair, (Q_i, D_j), whose relevance assessment is known. Parameters that have a significant impact on determining the relevance of D_j with respect to Q_i may consist of the number of terms in D_j, the inverse document frequency of a term occurring in both D_j and Q_i, the maximum number of occurrences of a term in D_j, etc. Let these parameters be denoted by $(x_1, x_2, \ldots, x_m)$, where m is the total number of such parameters. We seek the coefficients of a polynomial $p(x_1, x_2, \ldots, x_m) = a_0 + a_2 x_1 + a_2 x_2 + \cdots + a_m x_m + a_{m+1} x_1 x_2 + \cdots$ such that for each term in common between the document and the query in a query document pair, $p(x_1, x_2, \ldots, x_m)$ approximates 1, if the document is relevant to the query and it approximates 0, if the document is irrelevant. For a query document pair that has c terms in common between the document and the query, there are c such approximate equations. This is carried out for every query document pair, resulting in a large number of approximate equations. The raw parameters given above may be transformed before they are actually used in the polynomial. For example, instead of using the inverse document frequency of a term, the logarithm of the quantity can be employed. These parameters can be combined in the polynomial. For example, a factor in the polynomial can be $x_1x_2x_3$, where x_1 is the number of occurrences of the term in a document, x_2 is the logarithm of the inverse document frequency of the term, and x_3 is 1/(the maximum number of occurrences of any term in the document). The choice of such a product is subjective, but is clearly in line with the intuition that the significance of a term is reflected by its frequency of occurrence relative to the largest frequency of some term in the document and its inverse document frequency weight. The aim is to find the coefficients $\{a_0, a_1, \ldots, \}$ such that the equations are satisfied in the sense of having the least square error. This is an instance of the interpolation problem whose solution is given in Section 9.2.5. *Logistic regression* can also be employed to determine the coefficients of the polynomial.

The polynomial essentially estimates the probability that a document D is relevant to a query Q, given that a term that occurs in both D and Q has the frequency statistics $x_1, x_2, \ldots,$ x_m. Since D and Q may have multiple terms in common, these estimates of relevance can be combined to obtain an overall probability of relevance of the document D as follows.

Let E be an event. The odds $ODDS(E)$ are defined to be $\frac{P(E)}{P(E')}$, where E' is the complement of E. The *logodd* of $ODDS(R \mid T_i)$ is defined to be log $\frac{P(R|T_i)}{P(I|T_i)}$, where in our application, R and I stand for relevance and irrelevance, respectively, and T_i denotes a term in common between the document D and the query Q. In the context of this problem, $ODDS(R \mid T_i)$ is given by the polynomial p, where the coefficients of p are estimated by the process given above. When there are k terms in common between D and Q, log $ODDS(R \mid T_1, T_2, \ldots, T_k)$ can be estimated as follows, based on some simplifying assumptions.

$$\log ODDS(R \mid T_1, T_2, \ldots, T_k) = \log ODDS(R) + \sum_{i=1}^{k}(\log ODDS(R \mid T_i) - \log ODDS(R))$$

If a document is longer, i.e., having more terms, the number of terms in common with the query, namely k, is larger. This usually causes the above equation to overestimate the overall (logodd) probability of relevance. This may be compensated by subtracting a parameter such as log L from the right-hand side of the equation, where L is the number of occurrences of terms in the document. The parameter value $ODDS(R)$ needs to be estimated.

9.3.3 Feedback without User's Information

In this last form of relevance feedback, users are not involved in the feedback process. The basic idea is to modify the initial query Q submitted by the user as follows. (1) The information retrieval system uses Q to retrieve an initial set of documents. (2) From this set of documents, the i most highly ranked (most similar to Q) documents are retained, where i is a parameter to be determined. The intuition is that the i documents, for small values of i, are likely to be relevant. Let S be this set of i documents. (3) From S, select j terms to be added to Q, where j is another parameter to be determined. These j terms may have different weights in the modified query Q'. This modified query Q' is then used to retrieve documents to be presented to the user.

There are several ways to implement the steps (1), (2), and (3). For example, in step (1), instead of retrieving whole documents, sections of documents that have high similarities with Q can be the initial set obtained in this step. The main reason for using sections is that terms within a section are likely to be semantically related, whereas a document may have different sections addressing different topics. Terms appearing in different sections may be totally unrelated. If sections are used in step (1), then in step (2), the i most similar sections to Q are selected. One way to select the terms in step (3) is to make use of the tf-idf weighting method. Specifically, terms that occur in the i most similar sections are ranked according to their tf-idf weights, and the j most highly ranked terms are added to the query Q. Experiments indicate that the use of sections yields better retrieval effectiveness than the original query Q, as proximity of terms tends to imply their relatedness. The j most highly weighted terms may be given different weights in the modified query depending on their tf-idf weights—the higher the tf-idf weight, the higher weight it receives in the modified query. The j selected terms may also be chosen in a different manner. For example, the added terms may be restricted to terms that co-occur frequently in sections (or paragraphs or within a few sentences) in the entire corpus with terms in the original query. Thus, if t appears in the original query and t_1 co-occurs with t in many sections in numerous documents, then t_1 is a good candidate to be added to the query. In order to implement this policy, all documents in the collection have to be processed in order to identify pairs of terms that co-occur frequently in sections or paragraphs. Clearly, this is a time-consuming process. However, such term pairs can be precomputed, as they are independent of any given query. The choice of the methods to implement steps (1), (2), and (3) as well as the parameters i and j are research issues.

9.4 Specialized Hardware

There have been suggestions for having specialized hardware to speed up query processing for textual data. We present here a review of three specific types of proposed hardwares. They are (1) the Connection Machine: CM-2; (2) associative memory (or logic in memory); and (3) pattern matching by finite state machine. The first two machines are essentially main memory based, whereas the last one is disk based. With main memory cost dropping rapidly and its capacity increasing at a fast pace, small-to-medium-size collections can be placed completely in main memory. If they are accessed frequently, then the specialized hardware (1) and (2) can provide significant advantages over conventional hardware. The disk-based specialized hardware (3) may be coupled with the specialized hardware (1) or (2) to support query processing with good response time for both large and small collections.

As pointed out earlier, there are various types of queries in information retrieval systems, as described below.

Boolean queries. A Boolean query can be placed in conjunctive normal form, where clauses are "AND"ed together and each clause is the "OR" of a number of terms or their negation. For example, Q = "$(A$ OR B OR $C)$ AND (NOT D OR $E)$ AND $(F$ OR $G)$" is in conjunctive normal form with three clauses and NOT D is the negation of term D. In order to satisfy Q, all three clauses need to be satisfied. The first clause can be satisfied by having term A or term B or term C; the second clause is satisfied by having term E or not having term D; and the last one is satisfied by having either term F or term G. Given a Boolean query, it is always possible to transform it into conjunctive normal form by applications of distributive laws. For example, $(A$ AND $B)$ OR

$C = (A$ OR $C)$ AND $(B$ OR $C)$. Another standard form is the disjunctive normal form, which is the "OR" of several clauses, each clause being the "AND" of several literals, where each literal involves either a term or its complement (i.e., NOT the term). Any Boolean query can also be transformed into this normal form. We will use either one of these normal forms, depending on the ease of presentation.

Proximity queries. In order to detect possible semantic relationships among terms, a restriction is usually imposed on their occurrences with a separation of no more than a given number of words apart. For example, a query $Q' = (A$ AND B with proximity $\leq$ 3) requires a satisfied document to have both terms A and B and their occurrences are separated by no more than three words. Such a specification can simulate recognition of phrases whose component terms are A and B, as it has been observed empirically that most phrases satisfy the above property.

Other proximity conditions include a certain term preceding another term or several terms appearing in the same paragraph. The latter condition can be checked if the paragraph number is recorded or the occurrences of the terms are separated by, say, no more than 500 words.

Inner product queries. This is the type of query involving the dot product or the *Cosine* function.

It should be noted that the three types of queries can be used in combination. For example, $Q'' = A$ AND $(B1, (B2$ AND $B3$ with proximity $\leq 3), B4, B5)$ requires a satisfied document to have term A and have high similarity with the vector $(B1, B2, B3, B4, B5)$. In addition, when terms $B2$ and $B3$ are considered, their proximity or the lack of it is of significance.

9.4.1 Connection Machine

The Connection Machine (CM-2 is described here; CM-5 is a later version, but it seems that the newer version is intended for other applications) has up to four modules, with each module having 16,384 *processing elements*. Thus, up to 65,536 processing elements are possible in a single Connection Machine. Each processing element has 4,096 bits and 1 arithmetic and logical unit. Processing elements within the same module execute the same instruction at the same time, but processing elements in different modules may execute different instructions at the same time. The processing elements are connected by three independent communication networks: one for global communications (such as obtaining global maximum and global-OR), one for communications among neighboring elements, and one for communications between arbitrary elements.

Consider the storage of information within each processing element. Due to the limited 4,096 bits, the documents are not explicitly stored within the processing elements. Instead, conceptually, each processing element contains a number of one-dimensional bit vectors, each of which is used to represent the contents (terms) of a document, which logically resides in a processing element (or across several processing elements). Some area is reserved for auxiliary data and for computation. A "signature file" is created as follows, which allows the presence or absence of terms to be detected. Consider a bit vector having n bits. Initially, all bits are set to zero. A distinct set of bits is assigned to each term. The assignment of bits to a term can be performed by a hashing function on the term. For each term of a document that logically belongs to a processing element, the bits associated with the term are set to 1 in the bit vector of the processing element. For example, if the term "hunger" is assigned the bits {2, 5, 10, 19}, then the 2nd, 5th, 10th, and 19th bits in the bit vector are set to 1. Multiple terms may have common bits. For example, the term "angry" may have the bits {3, 5, 10, 21}.

Suppose we want to determine whether a given term is in a processing element. First, the bits associated with the term are obtained. Then these bits in the bit vector are checked. If all these bits are 1, then the term is assumed to be present. Clearly, if the term is present in the processing element, this method is guaranteed to find it. However, some false positives may occur. In other words, it is possible that the desired term is absent from the bit vector, but the bits associated with the term are all set to 1 in the bit vector. As an example, suppose only the above two terms (i.e., "hunger" and "angry") are present in the bit vector and the term "happy" with the set of bits {2, 3, 19, 21} is to be searched. Although the term is absent from the bit vector, all the bits {2, 3, 19, 21} have been set to 1 due to the terms "hunger" and "angry." It is clear that as the number of words logically residing in a bit vector of a processing element increases, the false positive rate increases; i.e., the probability that a term is absent but all its bits are set to 1 becomes higher. With a given bit-vector length n, the number of bits associated with each term (4 in the above example) and w, the number of words assigned to a bit vector, it is not difficult to derive a formula for the false positive rate. Thus, w should be adjusted such that the false positive rate is acceptable and a reasonable number of words can be logically assigned to each bit vector. Suppose each processing element contains 6 one-dimensional bit vectors, each is capable of holding 20 terms with a low false positive rate, and a document has 100 terms. Then the first 20 terms of the document will be used to set the 1 bits of a bit vector of a processing element, the next 20 terms will be used to set the 1 bits of a bit vector of another processing unit, and so on. Thus, 5 bit vectors of 5 processing elements are utilized to represent the terms of this document and these bit vectors are chained together. The terms of another document will be used to set the 1 bits of different bit vectors. In other words, different documents use different bit vectors to indicate their terms, and a document may span several bit vectors.

The processing of Boolean and inner product queries can be performed as follows.

Boolean queries.   Suppose the query is (t1 OR t2), where t1 and t2 are two terms. First, the bit vectors of different processing units are checked independently for the presence of t1 and the presence of t2. Then, the results obtained in the chained vectors corresponding to a document are "OR"ed together. If the final result is 1, then the Boolean query is satisfied by the document (recall that false positives may occur); otherwise, the document will definitely not satisfy the Boolean query. As an example, suppose the terms of a document are used to set the 1 bits of the 5 bit vectors that are chained together. After these 5 bit vectors are probed for t1 and t2, each bit vector returns 1 or 0, depending on whether it contains at least one of the terms or not. The results from these 5 bit vectors are then "OR"ed together to yield a final result. If the final result is 1, then the document is retrieved and has to be verified to satisfy the query, as a false positive due to the bit vectors is possible. If the final result is 0, then there is no need to retrieve any document associated with the bit vectors, as such a document is guaranteed not to satisfy the query.

Now consider query (t1 AND t2). As before, the bit vectors are probed independently to check for the presence of the terms. However, each bit vector is required to count the number of terms in the query it satisfies. Then, the counts of the chained bit vectors are added. If the total count associated with the chained bit vectors of a document is equal to the number of terms in the AND query, then the document satisfies the query (again subject to false positives); otherwise, the document fails to satisfy the query. It is assumed that only distinct terms of a document are used to set the bit vectors. If a term, say t1, were allowed to occur multiple number of times in different bit vectors that are chained together, then the term by itself would generate a count > 1 and would falsely indicate that the query is satisfied.

Inner product queries. Suppose the query is $(t_1, t_2, \ldots, t_k)$. The weight, say the inverse document frequency weight, of each term is looked up before the bit vectors are probed for each term. Whenever a term, say t_i, is *found* in a bit vector, its weight, say w_i, is added to the accumulated weight associated with the bit vector. Finally, the accumulated weights associated with the chained bit vectors are added to give the overall similarity. It seems that the initial version of CM-2 does not store the actual frequencies of terms in the document, due to the fact that the bit vectors indicate only the presence or absence of terms. As a result, recall and precision may suffer. To retrieve the k most similar documents, one of the communication networks is used to find a processing element containing a document having the largest similarity. After masking out this document with the largest similarity, the process is repeated to find a document having the second largest similarity. This process is repeated to yield a prespecified number of documents.

No algorithm is specified for processing proximity queries.

If a document collection is very large, then some of the documents are logically stored in the processing elements and the remaining documents are stored on disks. After searching the documents in the processing elements, other documents on disks will be loaded into the processing elements to be searched. This is repeated until all documents in the collection are searched.

9.4.2 Associative Memory

A Dynamic Associative Access Memory (DAAM) chip is a *dynamic random access memory* chip that has been modified so that it can perform certain basic logical and arithmetical functions. A 4-megabit chip can be visualized as an array with 1,024 rows and 4,096 columns, with each entry corresponding to 1 bit.

Each row can be considered as a processor, executing in parallel with other rows (processors). The columns, for the sake of processing queries, can be considered as being partitioned into two sets. The first set contains $80 \cdot 6 \cdot 8$ bits, and the second set contains the remaining 256 bits. The first set with all the rows form a region that is used to store the data associated with the documents. This is called the *data area*. The second region formed from the second set with all the rows is reserved to contain certain auxiliary data and working space to permit efficient answering of queries. This is called the *working area*. The two areas are illustrated in Figure 9.14.

The data in each document are placed into the data area as follows. Each *content word* in a document is represented by an *atom*, which has four components: (mark_bit, term#, weight,

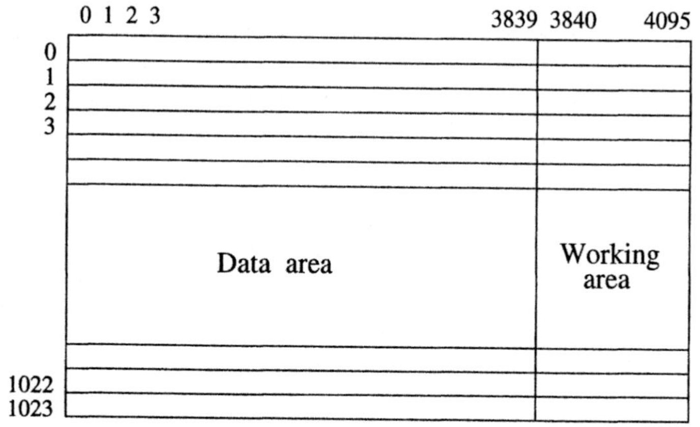

FIGURE 9.14   Areas of a DAAM Chip

location). The mark_bit is used for processing queries and will be discussed later. The frequency of a term is the number of times the term occurs in the document. The weight of a term can be its frequency, or it can be derived from the frequency of the term in the document and other factors, such as the inverse document frequency. If a term appears multiple times in a document, then the term will have the same number of atoms, each having the same weight but with a different location. The location is the position of the term in the row. Although the noncontent words are not stored in the DAAM chip, the position of a term takes into consideration the positions occupied by the noncontent stop words. The first atom in a row has location 1. The location of the ith atom in the same row is the number of words, including noncontent words that occur in the row, starting from the first word and ending with the word contained in the atom. Thus, two consecutive atoms in a row may have locations differing by more than one, if there are noncontent words in between. This location information will be used to answer proximity queries. Each atom occupies 6 bytes, with mark_bit occupying 1 bit, the term number occupying 4 bytes, the weight occupying 7 bits, and the location field occupying 1 byte. Given the size of the data area, each row, when restricted to the data area, contains exactly 80 atoms. Some typical auxiliary data in the working area are a bit, indicating the end of a document, and for each row a count of the exact number of words, including noncontent words logically stored in that row. The latter information, denoted by *word-count*, will be used to answer proximity queries.

Some basic operations with the chip are described below:

Comparison.   For example, compare a given term number against the set of term numbers stored in all rows under a given set of columns. Recall that each term number occupies 4 bytes and requires a set of 32 columns for storage.

Shift.   The set of numbers stored in all rows under a given set of columns are shifted to another set of columns. Numbers from one row can also be shifted up or down to the next row, with all rows executing in parallel.

Arithmetical and logical operations. Add, subtract, multiply, or divide a number to or from a set of numbers stored in all rows under a given set of columns. The arithmetic operations can also be applied on two sets of numbers that are stored under two specified sets of columns. Logical operations using AND, OR, and NOT are permitted.

Answering Queries with DAAM

First, we discuss the detection of a term. After indicating the set of columns to be compared, a given term number is compared against all the term numbers stored in the atoms under the specified columns. The comparisons are carried out in parallel with all rows participating in the equality comparison. If the ith row under the specified columns satisfies the comparison, then the mark_bit in the corresponding atom will be set to 1. The actions to be taken next depend on the type of the query to be answered.

Boolean queries. In each row, three columns corresponding to 3 bits in the working area will be reserved for processing Boolean queries. The last row of each document is pre-marked to prevent information from one document being shifted to areas of another document. Let the 3 bits corresponding to the three reserved columns in the last row of each document be denoted as b1, b2, and b3.

After a term is compared, the processing of Boolean queries is as follows. The mark_bit, which indicates whether the term is present in the specified columns in each row, is shifted to the first reserved column in the working area. This bit in each row is then shifted downward to the next row and is "OR"ed with the corresponding bit in the latter row. This operation is repeated until the last row in each document *receives* the propagated information. This *compare-shift* operation is repeated 80 times, once for each set of columns denoting an atom. At the end of these executions, a document has a term if and only if the bit b1 in the last row of the document is 1. The bit b2 in the last row of the document is used to indicate the satisfaction or nonsatisfaction of the document of the current clause up to and including the term just processed. It is initially set to 0, indicating initial nonsatisfaction for the document. The bit b3 in the last row of the document is used to indicate the same, except it is for all processed clauses. Initially, b3 is set to 1, indicating satisfaction. In summary, 3 bits at b1, b2, and b3 in the last row of each document are used to monitor the processing of the document. Bit b1 is for recording the satisfaction or nonsatisfaction of the document with respect to the current term; b2 is for the current clause up to and including the current term; b3 is for all processed clauses.

Example 9.8 Consider the Boolean query (t1 OR t2) AND (t3 OR t4). After processing term t1 in the first clause, a document will have b1 = 1, if term t1 is present. This bit is "OR"ed with b2. After term t2 is processed, the first bit indicating whether the document has term t2 is "OR"ed with the second bit. Now, b2 yields the value of 1 if and only if the document has term t1 or term t2 (i.e., the currently processed clause is satisfied). Bit b2 is then "AND"ed with bit b3, when a clause has been processed. Since b3 is initialized to 1, it will be 1 if and only if all processed clauses (in this case, the first clause) are satisfied. After the completion of a clause, bit b2 is reset to 0 before the next clause is processed. In general, whenever a term is processed, the information stored in b1 is "OR"ed with bit b2. Whenever a clause has been processed, the satisfaction information stored in b2 is "AND"ed into b3, and b2 is reset to 0.   ∎

Proximity queries.   If a term is found in a row, then the term's location is transferred to some byte in the working area. Suppose a proximity query is (t1, t2 with proximity of words $\leq$ 3). Then, transfer the locations of the two terms to location1 and location2 in the working area, respectively. If the two terms are in the same row and (location2 − location1) is less than or equal to 3, then the proximity condition will be satisfied. A complication occurs if t1 is at the end of one row and t2 is at the beginning of the next row. As an example, suppose the row having t1 has 86 words, t1 is at location 85 and t2 is at location 1 in the next row. Then, the proximity condition can be verified by (word count of the row containing t1 + location2 − location1) = (86 + 1 − 85), which is less than or equal to 3.

Inner product queries.   If a term is found in the row, then the weight of the term is transferred to some byte in the working area at the same row. This is propagated to the last row of the document. Suppose the inner product query is $((t_{i_1}, w_{i_1}), (t_{i_2}, w_{i_2}))$, where t's are terms and w's are weights. Suppose a document has both terms with weights w_{j_1} and w_{j_2}, respectively. After the detection of term t_{i_1}, the weight w_{j_1} is transferred to some location in the working area of the document. After it is transferred to the last row of the document, it is then multiplied by weight w_{i_1} and then added to another location, say the *accumulator*, in the document. After the detection of term i_2, the process of multiplying by the weight of the term in the query and then adding to the accumulator is executed.

9.4.3   Finite State Automata

The documents are placed in disks. The key aspect of this approach is to have specialized processors connected to each disk drive, head, or groups of drives such that terms can be recognized at a speed that is the same as the delivery rate of the disks. In other words, the "intelligent" disks serve as filters, outputting character strings satisfying certain given conditions. The term recognition process is based on the concept of the *finite state automata*, described as follows. Suppose we want to recognize the term *CAT* or a string having CAT as a substring. Then the state diagram as shown in Figure 9.15 can be utilized.

In Figure 9.15, S_0 is the initial state. If character C is encountered, then state S_1 is entered; if any other character is encountered, then state S_0 is unchanged. When the state is S_1 and the next character encountered is A, then state S_2 is reached; if character C is encountered, then the state S_1 is unchanged. The reason is that state S_1 indicates that the last encountered character is C. When the state is S_1 and the character encountered is neither A nor C, then the initial state S_0 is reached. When the state is S_2 and the character T is encountered, then the final or output state S_3 is reached. The output state indicates that the required term is detected. When the state is S_2 and the character encountered is C, then state S_1 is reached; if the encountered character is neither T nor C, then the initial state S_0 is reached.

Finite state automata can be utilized to match one of the terms from a set of terms. For example, suppose the terms *HUNGER* and *HUNGRY* are to be recognized. From the above

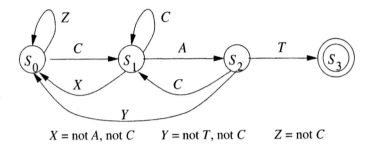

$X = $ not A, not C $Y = $ not T, not C $Z = $ not C

FIGURE 9.15   Finite State Machine for CAT or a String Containing CAT as a Substring

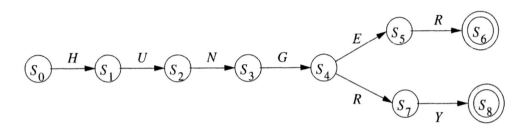

FIGURE 9.16   Finite State Machine for HUNGER or HUNGRY

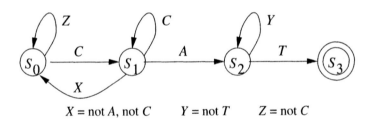

$X = $ not A, not C $Y = $ not T $Z = $ not C

FIGURE 9.17   Finite State Machine for CA*T

discussion, it is easy to draw a finite state machine for HUNGER and another one for HUN-GRY. It is clear that these two finite state diagrams can be combined, as the terms to be recognized have the substring *HUNG* in common. The finite state machine for the two terms is shown in Figure 9.16. Fine details are not included. For example, at state S_1 when H is encountered, the state remains S_1.

Finite state automata can be used to recognize "don't care strings". Suppose we are interested in recognizing $CA*T$, where * is a "don't care" string that can be of an arbitrary length including an empty string. Consider Figure 9.17. At state S_2, if a character other than T is encountered, state S_2 is unchanged, waiting for the character T to be encountered. This can go on for a string of arbitrary length.

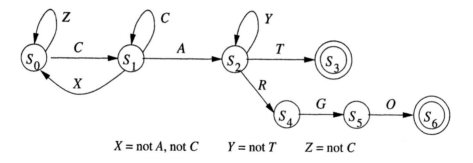

$X = \text{not } A, \text{not } C$ $Y = \text{not } T$ $Z = \text{not } C$

FIGURE 9.18 Nondeterministic Finite State Machine for CA*T or CARGO

Suppose the strings $CA*T$ or $CARGO$ are to be recognized. Then, at state S_2 in Figure 9.18, if the character R is encountered, then either state S_2 is unchanged or the state S_4 is reached to register the occurrence of the character R, which is essential for recognizing the string CARGO. Since there are two possibilities, one staying at state S_2 and one changing to state S_4, the finite machine is nondeterministic. In automata theory, it is well known that nondeterministic finite automata can be converted to deterministic finite state automata.

Using finite state automata to process different types of queries is described below.

Proximity queries. After the recognition of certain terms in a user query, it is relatively easy to add some simple logic to answer proximity conditions. For example, if the query is "t1 AND t2 with term t2 no more than 3 words after term t1", then after recognizing t1, a counter is set. For each word after t1, if the word is not t2, then the count is increased by 1. If the word encountered is t2, then the count is checked. If it is less than or equal to 3, then the query condition is satisfied. If t1 is detected but t2 is not detected within 3 words, then the process restarts for the detection of t1.

Boolean queries. Boolean combinations of terms can also be answered. For example, suppose the query is "t1 AND t2". After one of the two terms is detected, the other is to be detected. When both terms are detected, the query condition is satisfied. Similarly, if the query is "t1 OR t2," then as soon as one of the terms is detected, the query condition is satisfied. In general, a Boolean query can be placed in conjunctive normal form; i.e., it is of the form $(t_{11} \text{ OR } t_{12} \text{ OR } \ldots \text{ OR } t_{1k}) \text{ AND } (t_{21} \text{ OR } t_{22} \text{ OR } \ldots \text{ OR } t_{2j}) \text{ AND } \ldots \text{ AND } (t_{s1} \text{ OR } \ldots \text{ OR } t_{sp})$. In this expression, there are s clauses, each consisting of several terms which are OR-ed together. As soon as a term in a clause is detected, that subexpression is satisfied. If a count with initial value 0 is increased by 1 for each satisfied subexpression, then the query is satisfied when the count reaches s.

Inner product queries. For each query term, whenever the term in a document is detected, the weight of the term in the query is multiplied by its weight in the document and the product is added to the accumulated weight with initialized value = 0. After a document is processed, the accumulated weight is the similarity of the document with the query.

9.5 Other Retrieval Methods

In this section, two methods that are very different from those given in the earlier sections are presented. A thorough comparison in retrieval effectiveness between these methods and the earlier methods is lacking.

9.5.1 Inference Network

Consider a knowledge space of terms. A query or a document is a subset of terms. A *proposition* can also be considered as a subset of terms. Thus, a query or a document is a proposition. A document D implies a query Q if the set of terms in D contains the set of terms in Q. When D implies Q, we consider D as evidence in support of Q. Although this type of logical inference is theoretically interesting, it is unlikely to be of practical use, because most relevant documents of a query do not contain all terms of the query. In practice, uncertain or plausible inference is desirable. We define the *belief of Q given D*, which is an estimate that D is relevant to Q, to be $P(Q \mid D) = P(Q, D)/P(D)$. Here, $P(D)$ can be interpreted as the degree to which the entire knowledge space is *covered* by the knowledge represented by the terms in D, whereas $P(Q, D)$ is the degree to which the entire space is covered by the knowledge that is in common between the query Q and the document D. The expression can be written as $\sum_t P(Q, D, t)/P(D)$, where t is a term in the knowledge space and the sum is over all terms in the space. Consider the use of a term t in the query Q and the document D. The term t is used in Q when the user believes that the term is useful in representing the contents of the query. It is used in D if the indexer believes that the term that has been chosen in content representation of the collection of documents is appropriate for the document D. Since the process of formulating the query Q and the process of indexing documents are independent, the tree dependence model may be applied to the tree with the root being t and its children Q and D. Using the tree dependence formula, we have $P(Q, D, t) = P(t) \cdot P(Q \mid t) \cdot P(D \mid t)$. Thus,

$$P(Q \mid D) = P(Q, D)/P(D) = \sum_t P(Q, D, t)/P(D) = \sum_t P(t \mid D) \cdot P(Q \mid t) \qquad (9.26)$$

Note that the above equation is an approximation, since the tree dependence model is an approximation.

$P(t \mid D)$ can be considered an estimate that D is relevant to the term t (i.e., during the indexing process, the user examines each term t and estimates the degree to which a document D is relevant to it), whereas $P(Q \mid t)$ is an estimate of the significance of term t in representing the query Q (i.e., during the query formulation process, the user estimates the degree to which the term t is relevant to the representation of the query). These parameters may be estimated as follows. Let $o(D, t)$ be the number of occurrences of the term t in document D. Then $P(t \mid D)$ is estimated by $o(D, t)/\sum_s o(D, s)$, where the sum is over all terms in D. Thus, if term t occurs many times in D, but the total number of occurrences of other terms in D is not high, then $P(t \mid D)$ is expected to be relatively large (in comparison to other terms in D). This estimate makes use of frequencies within D. $P(Q \mid t)$ can be estimated by $o(Q, t)/\sum_D o(D, t)$, where the sum is over all documents having term t. If term t occurs in the query multiple times, but

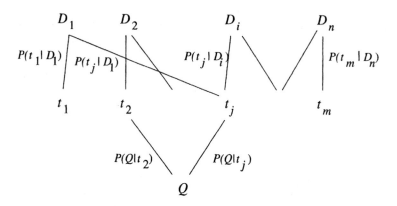

FIGURE 9.19 An Inference Network

occurs with low frequency in the documents, then $P(Q \mid t)$ will get a high value. The estimate depends on frequencies within Q as well as the inverse frequency of t across the documents.

Example 9.9 Suppose there are three documents D_1, D_2, and D_3 and four terms t_1, t_2, t_3, and t_4 and their frequencies of occurrence in the documents are given as follows:

$$D_1 = (3, 4, 0, 2);$$
$$D_2 = (0, 1, 2, 0);$$
$$D_3 = (1, 0, 4, 3).$$

Then, we have $P(t_1 \mid D_1) = \frac{3}{9}$; $P(t_2 \mid D_1) = \frac{4}{9}$; $P(t_3 \mid D_1) = 0$; $P(t_4 \mid D_1) = \frac{2}{9}$. Suppose the query Q is $(3, 0, 1, 3)$. Then $P(Q \mid t_1) = \frac{3}{4}$; $P(Q \mid t_2) = 0$; $P(Q \mid t_3) = \frac{1}{6}$; $P(Q \mid t_4) = \frac{3}{5}$. Therefore, $P(Q \mid D_1) = \frac{3}{9} \cdot \frac{3}{4} + 0 + 0 + \frac{2}{9} \cdot \frac{3}{5}$. ∎

Equation (9.26) may be represented by a network as follows. There are three layers in the network. The first layer consists of document nodes $D_1, D_2, \ldots, D_n$. The second layer consists of term nodes $t_1, t_2, \ldots, t_m$. The third layer contains the single query Q (see Figure 9.19). There are connections from the documents to the terms and from the terms to the query Q. If a document D_i has terms $t_{i1}, t_{i2}, \ldots, t_{ik}$, then there are edges from document D_i to the terms t_{ij}, $1 \leq j \leq k$. The connection from D_i to term t_{ij} is labeled $P(t_{ij} \mid D_i)$. An estimate of $P(t_{ij} \mid D_i)$ can be given by the method discussed above. Similarly, there are connections from terms to the query Q. If Q has terms $t_{s1}, t_{s2}, \ldots, t_{sp}$, then there are edges from t_{sj}, $1 \leq j \leq p$ to Q. The edge from t_{sj} to Q is initially labeled $P(Q \mid t_{ij})$ (see Figure 9.19).

The probabilities given above may be modified as follows when relevance information is available. Let R be the set of relevant documents of the query Q. One way to quantify the degree of relevance (usefulness) of term t for the query, given its sets of relevant and irrelevant documents, is based on its frequencies of occurrence in the two sets. More precisely, let $f(R, t)$ be the number of occurrences of term t in the set of relevant documents R; i.e., $f(R, t) = \sum_D o(D, t)$, where the sum is over all documents D in R (if not all relevant documents are known, then the set of retrieved relevant documents should be used). The probability that an occurrence of a term in R is term t, denoted by R_t, is $f(R, t)/\sum_j f(R, j)$, where the sum is over all terms. Similarly, let $f(I, t)$ be the number of occurrences of term t in the set of irrelevant documents I. The probability that an occurrence of a term in the set of irrelevant documents I is term t, denoted by I_t, is $f(I, t)/\sum_j f(I, j)$, where the sum is over all terms. Then, the degree of usefulness of the term t for the query Q, denoted by U_t, is

$$\log \frac{R_t/(1 - R_t)}{I_t/(1 - I_t)}$$

Clearly, other estimates, such as those given by the nonbinary independence model as well as models involving term dependencies, are possible. The similarity of D with respect to Q is the sum of the products of the labels, where each product involves the label on an edge from D to a term t and the label on the edge from t to Q, and the sum is over all terms contained in D.

Example 9.10 In Example 9.9, suppose document D_1 is relevant to query Q, but documents D_2 and D_3 are irrelevant to Q. Then, $R_{t_1} = \frac{3}{9}$; $R_{t_2} = \frac{4}{9}$; $R_{t_3} = \frac{0}{9}$; $R_{t_4} = \frac{2}{9}$; $I_{t_1} = \frac{1}{11}$; $I_{t_2} = \frac{1}{11}$; $I_{t_3} = \frac{6}{11}$; $I_{t_4} = \frac{3}{11}$. Thus, the usefulness of the term t_1 to the query, U_1, may be measured by

$$\log \frac{(3/9)/(6/9)}{(1/11)/(10/11)} \qquad \blacksquare$$

9.5.2 Parsimonious Covering Theory

In this subsection, another method of retrieving documents with high effectiveness is presented. This method is couched as providing a diagnosis of a person given his or her symptoms. The correspondence between this problem and the standard retrieval problem will be established.

The diagnostic problem in parsimonious theory consists of the following four components:

1. a set of *disorders* $D = \{D_1, D_2, \ldots, D_n\}$, which corresponds to the set of documents in information retrieval.

2. a set of *manifestations* $M = \{m_1, m_2, \ldots, m_q\}$, which corresponds to the set of terms.

3. a set of *causation probabilities* $\{c_{ij} \mid c_{ij}$ is the probability in which disorder D_i causes manifestation $m_j\}$. If c_{ij} is greater than 0, then disorder D_i causes manifestation m_j. Causation probability c_{ij} corresponds to the strength or significance of term t_j on document D_i.

4. a subset of manifestations $M+$. This corresponds to the set of terms in a given query.

Suppose D_p is a subset of disorders. The set of manifestations caused by D_p is the union of the sets of manifestations, each of which is caused by some disorder in D_p. The problem is to find a minimal subset of disorders, D_s, which causes a given set of manifestations $M+$ with the largest probability, where a subset is minimal if the removal of any disorder from D_s results in the inability to contain $M+$. Our aim is to find D_s such that D_s is a minimal set of disorders causing the set of manifestations $M+$ and $P(D_s \mid M+)$ is the largest. This corresponds to computing a minimal set of documents, D_s, having the highest probability of relevance to a query containing a set of terms, $M+$. The documents in D_s will eventually be ranked among themselves.

Example 9.11 Suppose there are four disorders D_1, D_2, D_3, and D_4, and three manifestations m_1, m_2, and m_3. Suppose D_1 causes m_1 and m_2, D_2 causes m_2, D_3 causes m_2 and m_3, and D_4 causes m_1. Let $M+$ be $\{m_1, m_3\}$. Then, $\{D_1, D_3, D_4\}$ is not a minimal set causing $M+$ because removal of D_1 from the set still causes $M+$. $\{D_3, D_4\}$ is a minimal set because removal of either disorder will not be able to cause $M+$.   ∎

We now discuss the computation of the probability that a subset of disorders, D_s, causes a given set of manifestations $M+$. The following assumptions are made to simplify the computation:

1. Disorder independence: the probability that a subset of disorders occurs is the product of the probabilities that a disorder in the subset occurs. As an example, $P(D_1, D_2, D_3) = \prod_{i=1}^{3} P(D_i)$, where $P(D_i)$ stands for the probability of occurrence of a disorder D_i.

2. The probability of having exactly the set of manifestations $M+$ given a subset of disorders D_s is defined to be $P(M+ \mid D_s) = (\prod P(m_j \mid D_s))(\prod P(m'_k \mid D_s))$, where the first product is over all manifestations in $M+$, m'_k denotes the absence of manifestation m_k, and the second product is over the set of manifestations $M'+ = M - M+$. Thus, manifestations in a given set of disorders are assumed to be independent.

We now proceed to compute $P(D_s \mid M+)$. By Bayes's theorem,

$$P(D_s \mid M+) = \frac{P(M+ \mid D_s) \cdot P(D_s)}{P(M+)} \tag{9.27}$$

By the first assumption above and the minimality of D_s, $P(D_s) = (\prod p_i) \cdot (\prod (1 - p_k))$, where the first product is over all disorders in D_s, the second product is over all disorders in $D - D_s$, and p_j is the prior probability of having disorder D_j. (In information retrieval, each document can be assumed to have the same prior probability.) The expression can be rewritten as

$$P(D_s) = \left(\prod p_i / (1 - p_i) \right) \cdot \left(\prod (1 - p_k) \right) \tag{9.28}$$

where the second product is over all disorders D and is independent of D_s. For a given $M+$, $P(M+)$ is a constant. Thus, if two subsets of disorders D_{s_1} and D_{s_2} are compared in Equation (9.27), $P(M+)$ can be ignored.

By the second assumption above, to compute $P(M+ \mid D_s)$, it is sufficient to compute $P(m_j \mid D_s)$ and $P(m'_k \mid D_s)$. Consider the former. For each disorder D_i in D_s, the probability that m_j occurs given disorder D_i is c_{ij} and the probability that manifestation m_j is absent given D_i is $(1 - c_{ij})$. Thus, the probability that manifestation m_j is present due to one or more disorders in the given set of disorders D_s is

$$P(m_j \mid D_s) = 1 - \prod (1 - c_{ij}) \tag{9.29}$$

where the product is over each disorder D_i in D_s. Now consider $P(m'_k \mid D_s)$. The probability that m_k is absent given a disorder D_i is $(1 - c_{ik})$. Thus, the probability that m_k is absent given all disorders in D_s is

$$P(m'_k \mid D_s) = \prod (1 - c_{ik}) \tag{9.30}$$

where the product is over each D_i in D_s.

In comparing the probability $P(D_s \mid M+)$ with that due to another disorder set, it is sufficient to compute the relative likelihood measure $L(D_s, M+)$ defined below, due to (9.27), (9.28), (9.29), and (9.30).

$$L(D_s, M+) = \prod_{M+} \left(1 - \prod_{D_s}(1 - c_{ij}) \right) \cdot \prod_{M'+} \prod_{D_s}(1 - c_{ik}) \cdot \prod_{D_s}(p_i/(1 - p_i)) \tag{9.31}$$

In the second term of (9.31), since whenever c_{ik} is zero, i.e., when D_i does not cause manifestation m_k, then $c_{ik} = 0$ and therefore $(1 - c_{ik})$ can be ignored in the product. Thus, the second term can be rewritten as

$$\prod_{D_s} \prod_{DM'}(1 - c_{ik})$$

where DM' is the set of manifestations in $M'+$ having positive c_{ik} with D_i in D_s and m_k in $M - M+$. Since the set of manifestations caused by disorders in D_s, for D_s not too large, is usually much smaller than $M'+$, the latter expression is more efficient in computation.

Example 9.12 Continue Example 9.11 with the additional data: $c_{11} = 0.3$, $c_{12} = 0.2$, $c_{22} = 0.1$, $c_{32} = 0.4$, $c_{33} = 0.5$, $c_{41} = 0.6$, and each $p_i = 1/4$. Then the relative likelihood of $D_s = \{D_3, D_4\}$ with respect to $M+ = \{m_1, m_3\}$ is

$$L(D_s, M+) = [1 - (1 - c_{41})] \cdot [1 - (1 - c_{33})] \cdot [1 - c_{32}] \cdot p_3/(1 - p_3) \cdot p_4/(1 - p_4)$$
$$= [1 - (1 - 0.6)][1 - (1 - 0.5)] \cdot [1 - 0.4] \cdot ((1/4)/(3/4))^2 \tag{9.32}$$

DM' in this example is $\{m_2\}$. If c_{31} were positive, then $L(D_s, M+)$ would be $[1 - (1 - c_{41})(1 - c_{31})] \cdot [1 - (1 - c_{33})] \cdot [1 - c_{32}] \cdot p_3/(1 - p_3) \cdot p_4/(1 - p_4)$. ∎

Our aim is to find a subset of disorders D_s that maximizes $L(D_s, M+)$. One way to achieve this is to rewrite (9.31) by introducing a vector of variables $X = (x_1, x_2, \ldots, x_n)$ such that $x_i = 1$ if the ith disorder is in D_s, otherwise 0. The equation is restated as

$$F(X) = \prod_{m_j \in M+} \left(1 - \prod_{k=1}^{n}(1 - c_{kj} \cdot x_k) \right) \cdot \prod_{m_j \in M'+} \prod_{k=1}^{n}(1 - c_{kj} \cdot x_k) \cdot \prod_{k=1}^{n} \frac{1 - x_k \cdot (1 - p_k)}{1 - p_k \cdot x_k} \tag{9.33}$$

In the numerator of the last product, we have $(1 - x_k \cdot (1 - p_k))$. When x_k is 1, then the expression is p_k, which is the original expression. When x_k is 0, the expression is 1. This ensures that zero is not involved in the product.

Example 9.13 Continue Example 9.12. Recall $M+ = \{m_1, m_3\}$ and $M'+ = \{m_2\}$.

$$F(X) = [1 - (1 - c_{11}x_1)(1 - c_{41}x_4)][1 - (1 - c_{33}x_3)](1 - c_{12}x_1)(1 - c_{22}x_2)(1 - c_{32}x_3)$$
$$\cdot \frac{1 - x_1(1 - p_1)}{1 - p_1 x_1} \cdot \frac{1 - x_2(1 - p_2)}{1 - p_2 x_2} \cdot \frac{1 - x_3(1 - p_3)}{1 - x_3 p_3} \cdot \frac{1 - x_4(1 - p_4)}{1 - p_4 x_4}$$

With $x_1 = 0$, $x_2 = 0$, $x_3 = 1$, and $x_4 = 1$, $F(X)$ is identical to that given in Equation (9.32). ∎

We want to maximize $F(X)$. The discrete values of X make the optimization computationally expensive, as there are 2^n all possible values. Instead, we assume that the values are continuous in [0, 1]. A strategy to carry out the optimization for the continuous situation is that each disorder is "activated" to cause changes in values for the manifestations, which in turn cause changes in values for the disorders. An activated value may take on any value in [0, 1]. The activated values of disorder D_i and manifestation m_j at time t are denoted by $D_i(t)$ and $m_j(t)$, respectively. These iterations of changes continue until all disorders converge to values of either 0 or 1. When a value is 1, the corresponding disorder is in the solution set; when a value is 0, the disorder is not in the solution set. Details are provided as follows:

1. Initialization: Each disorder is assigned its prior probability. (For information retrieval, the probability that a document is retrieved in response to a query is initially set to be $1/n$, where n is the number of documents.)

2. Activation for each manifestation: Let $C(j)$ be the set of disorders that cause manifestation m_j; i.e., if disorder D_i is in $C(j)$, then $c_{ij} > 0$. The probability that $D_i(t)$ does not cause $m_j(t)$ is $(1 - c_{ij} \cdot D_i(t))$. Thus, $m_j(t)$, the manifestation at time t, is $1 - \prod_{C(j)}(1 - c_{ij} \cdot D_i(t))$. This is performed for each manifestation. The changes of the manifestations cause the values of the disorders to be modified as follows.

3. Activation of each disorder D_i: Our aim is to optimize $F(X)$ in (9.33) by deciding the value of $X = (x_1, \ldots, x_i, \ldots, x_n)$. F depends on the vector of variables $X = (x_1, \ldots, x_i, \ldots, x_n)$, which decides the set of disorders. A global optimal value for $F(X)$ is difficult to obtain. Instead, we first produce a local version of $F(X)$, $F_i(D_i(t))$, which indicates the influence of disorder D_i on F. Let $m(D_i)$ be the set of manifestations caused by D_i; i.e., c_{ij} is positive for each j in $m(D_i)$. Let M_i+ denote $M+ \cap m(D_i)$ and M'_i+ denote $(M - M+) \cap m(D_i)$. Then $F_i(D_i(t))$ is written as

$$F_i(D_i(t)) = \prod_{m_j \in M_i+} \left(1 - \prod_{k=1}^{n}(1 - c_{kj} \cdot D_k(t))\right)$$
$$\cdot \prod_{m_j \in M'_i+} \prod_{k=1}^{n}(1 - c_{kj} \cdot D_k(t)) \prod_{k=1}^{n} \frac{1 - (1 - p_k) \cdot D_k(t)}{1 - D_k(t) \cdot p_k}$$

Example 9.14 Continue Example 9.13. Consider $F_3(X)$. $M_3+ = \{m_1, m_3\}$ $\cap \{m_2, m_3\} = \{m_3\}$. $M'_3+ = \{m_2\} \cap \{m_2, m_3\} = \{m_2\}$.

$$F_3(D_3(t)) = [1 - (1 - c_{33} \cdot D_3(t))] \cdot (1 - c_{12} \cdot D_1(t)) \cdot (1 - c_{22} \cdot D_2(t)) \cdot (1 - c_{32} \cdot D_3(t))$$
$$\cdot \frac{1 - D_1(t)(1 - p_1)}{1 - p_1 D_1(t)} \cdot \frac{1 - D_2(t)(1 - p_2)}{1 - p_2 D_2(t)} \cdot \frac{1 - D_3(t)(1 - p_3)}{1 - p_3 D_3(t)}$$
$$\cdot \frac{1 - D_4(t)(1 - p_4)}{1 - p_4 D_4(t)}$$

∎

Optimization of $F_i(D_i(t))$ is attempted by assuming that all other $D_j(t)$'s, $j \neq i$, are fixed. This is accomplished by computing the ratio $r_i(D_i(t)) = (F_i(D_i(t))$ with $D_i(t) = 1)/(F_i(D_i(t))$ with $D_i(t) = 0)$. If the ratio is greater than 1, then $D_i(t)$ will be increased; otherwise $D_i(t)$ should be decreased. Note that although the manifestations $m_j(t)$ are not explicitly stated in the above expression, the first part of the expression is exactly the product of $m_j(t)$ for m_j in M_i+. It has been shown in [291] that

$$r_i(t) = \prod_{M'_i+} \frac{1 + c_{ij} \cdot (1 - m_j(t))}{m_j(t) - c_{ij} \cdot D_i(t - \delta)} \cdot K_i$$

where K_i is given by

$$K_i = \prod_{M'_i+} (1 - c_{ik}) \cdot \frac{p_i}{1 - p_i}$$

After $r_i(t)$ is computed, $D_i(t)$ is computed as follows.

$$D_i(t) = D_i(t - \delta) + f(r_i(t) - 1) \cdot (1 - D_i(t - \delta)) \cdot \delta$$

where $f(\ )$ ensures that the activated value of D_i changes slowly by assigning a value between -1 and 1; if its argument has a value between -1 and 1, it leaves it unchanged; otherwise, it sets the value to 1 if the values exceeds 1, or to -1 if the value is below -1. δ is a small value to be adjusted. It can be shown that if D_i and D_k share some manifestations in $M+$, then if one increases, the r of the other decreases. In this sense, they compete against each other.

Step 2 and step 3 are repeated until all disorder nodes reach equilibrium. It is reached when $|D_i(t) - D_i(t - \delta)|$ is very small. At equilibrium, if $D_i(t)$ exceeds 0.95, then it is within the solution D_s; if it is less than 0.05, it is outside D_s; otherwise a convergence is not reached for $D_i(t)$.

The above process attempts to find a set of disorders that cause a given set of manifestations M with largest probabilities. In text retrieval, each document corresponds to a disorder; documents need to be ranked in descending order of being relevant to the query. The relative degree of relevance of document D_i, $R(D_i)$, can be estimated by modifying the relative likelihood measure $L(D_i, M+)$ as follows.

$$R(D_i) = \prod_{m_j \in M_i+} \left[1 - \prod_{D_k \in D_s} (1 - c_{kj}) \right] \cdot \prod_{m_h \in M'_i} \prod_{D_k \in D_s} (1 - c_{kh})$$

where M_i+ is the set of manifestations in $M+$ that are caused by D_i, M'_i is the set of manifestations in $M - M+$ caused by D_i, and D_s is the set of disorders obtained at the termination of the above algorithm. In comparison with Equation (9.31), the last term of (9.31) is left out, because it is a constant with respect to different documents in D_s. The critical differences are that $M+$ is replaced by M_i+, and $M'+$ is replaced by M'_i. These replacements guarantee that c_{kj} and c_{kh} are positive. As a result, $R(D_i)$ will not be zero. As an example, using Example 9.14 with $D_s = \{D_3, D_4\}$, $M+ = \{m_1, m_3\}$, the document under consideration is D_3, $M_3+ = \{m_3\}$, and $M'_3 = \{m_2\}$, $R(D_3) = [1 - (1 - c_{33})] \cdot (1 - c_{32})$, where the first subexpression is due to term m_3 with respect to document D_3 and the second subexpression is due to term m_2 with respect to document D_3.

Exercises

9.1 Find the inverse document frequency weights of terms having document frequency **(a)** 1; **(b)** 2; **(c)** 100 in a collection having 100,000 documents. Compare the results of (a) and (b) and comment whether the weights assigned according to the inverse document frequency method are reasonable.

9.2 Describe a technique in which words such as *tasty* and *tasteless* will not be stemmed to the same stem.

9.3 A nonsyntactic technique to recognize phrases relies on the fact that words in a phrase are within three words apart. Give a sentence in which the words within a phrase are separated by more than three words. Provide a technique for remedying the situation.

9.4 Give a similarity function other than the *Cosine* function but the similarity value is guaranteed to lie between 0 and 1 for any two vectors that do not have negative components.

9.5 Consider the following distributions of the two terms t_i and t_j in the set of documents $\{D_i, 1 \le i \le 6\}$.

	D_1	D_2	D_3	D_4	D_5	D_6
t_i	1	0	3	0	0	5
t_j	2	1	2	0	0	0

Which term is a better term? Why?

9.6 Suppose that there are 10 relevant documents of a given query. Compute the first few recall and precision values for the following situations.

(a) The 5 most similar documents in descending order of similarity are D_5, D_9, D_1, D_7, and D_{13} and they have distinct similarities. The relevant documents among these five documents are D_9 and D_7.

(b) Same situation as (a), except D_1 and D_7 have the same similarity with the query.

9.7 Consider the binary independence model if the relevant documents to a given query are (1, 0, 0, 1), (1, 1, 0, 1), (1, 0, 0, 0), and (0, 1, 1, 0), and the irrelevant documents of the query are (0, 1, 0, 1) and (1, 1, 0, 0):

(a) Find the probability that a relevant document has the first term.

(b) Find the probability that an irrelevant document has the first term.

(c) Find the weight of the first term assigned to the query.

9.8 Consider the nonbinary independence model if the relevant documents to a given query are (2, 0, 0, 1), (2, 1, 0, 1), (1, 0, 0, 0), and (0, 1, 0, 0), and the irrelevant documents of the query are (0, 1, 0, 1) and (1, 1, 0, 0):

(a) Find the probability that a relevant document has two occurrences of the first term.

(b) Find the probability that an irrelevant document has two occurrences of the first term.

(c) Find the weight of the first term having two occurrences in a document.

(Note: It is possible that an entry is zero. Thus, very often a probability that a document having k occurrences of a term is estimated by (the number of documents having k occurrences of the term + c)/(the number of documents + c), where c is a small positive constant.)

9.9 Consider the tree dependency model. Suppose the dependence tree is

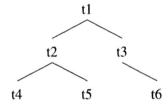

Compute the probability $P(1, 0, 0, 1, 0, 1)$ in terms of the probabilities of individual terms or term pairs.

9.10 Suppose the five documents in Exercise 9.6 are initially retrieved by the query. Let the documents be $D_5 = (2, 0, 3)$; $D_9 = (0, 1, 3)$; $D_1 = (0, 2, 0)$; $D_7 = (2, 1, 0)$; $D_{13} = (1, 1, 0)$. Compute the relevance feedback query using

(a) the traditional (A, B) method, and

(b) the perceptron technique from pattern recognition.

(c) Estimate the parameter P(a relevant document has two occurrences of the first term).

9.11 Consider a document-query pair (D, Q) where the document is (2, 3, 0, 1) and the query is (1, 0, 0, 2), and a similarity function is given by the polynomial $p(x_1, x_2, x_3)$ $= a_0 + a_1 \cdot x_1 + a_2 \cdot x_2 + a_3 \cdot x_3$, where x_1 is the number of terms in common between a document and a query, x_2 is the number of occurrences of a matching term, and x_3 is the inverse of the norm of the document. If the document D is relevant to the query, write the approximate equations for the terms in common between D and Q.

9.12 Suppose in the Connection Machine a one-dimensional bit vector of n bits is used to store terms and each term sets t bits to 1. Find the probability that a term is falsely assumed to be present but actually it is absent when the number of terms stored in the bit vector is k.

9.13 Sketch an algorithm to answer proximity queries where the terms specified in such a query are within k words apart, but k can be more than the number of words that can be stored in a row of a DAAM chip.

9.14 One time-consuming step in answering proximity queries, inner product queries, or boolean queries is to determine whether a document has a given term. A straight-forward algorithm compares the given term with all terms in a given set of columns and repeats this process as many times as the number of terms that can be stored in a row. Design an algorithm that can speed up this step.

(Hint: If the terms are stored in the documents in a particular way, then it may not be necessary to compare a given term with terms stored under all columns.)

9.15 Design a finite state machine to answer the Boolean query STRONG or STRENGTH.

9.16 Describe how a text retrieval system can be implemented using a relational database management system.

9.17 Let a query be $(2, 0, 1, 4)$. Let $D_1 = (1, 0, 2, 0)$, $D_2 = (3, 1, 0, 1)$, $D_3 = (1, 1, 0, 2)$, and $D_4 = (0, 0, 1, 1)$. Draw a network with documents in the first layer, terms in the second layer, and the query in the third layer. Label each edge. If D_1 is the only relevant document, show the new labels associated with the edges.

Bibliographic Notes

Most materials on the overview of text retrieval can be found in the two texts [312, 315]. The vector space model, which is most commonly used in text retrieval, is due to G. Salton (see, for example, [311]). The inverse document frequency weighting method is due to [341]. The use of document and term frequency in indicating the quality of terms is due to [316]. Other approaches in identifying content words can be found in [39]. An approach of combining Boolean queries and the vector space model can be found in [314]. Descriptions of reasonable size collections and the performances of different information retrieval systems on these collections can be found in [163]. (Note that the references of different information retrieval systems change as modifications have been made to these systems.) Description of B$^+$ tree can be found in Chapter 1 as well as in most database textbooks with a chapter on physical access. Thorough discussion on signature files is available in [77, 118, 226]. A hashing method that preserves the order of the keys, requires minimal hashing space, and avoids collision can be found in [123]. This type of hash function is suitable for collections that are relatively static and require direct and sequential access. One such application domain is with CD-ROMs.

The approach of using probability for indexing and retrieval is from [255]. Arranging documents in descending order of relevance is due to [86, 304]. The binary independence model is due to [405], although the term is coined by [305]. It is shown in [405] that by suitably assigning weights to terms of a query in ascending order of their significances, retrieval performance will be improved. Optimality of retrieval of documents using the binary independence model is due to [305]. A thorough discussion of independence assumptions and whether data can satisfy these assumptions can be found in [87]. Approximating distribution by the tree dependence model is by [73]; its use in information retrieval is by [376]. The Bahadur-Lazarsfeld expansion can be found in [113]. Incorporating triplets and higher-order dependencies is by [395]. The nonbinary independence model is by [399, 402]. Another nonbinary independence model is the two-Poisson model, where each term is distributed in the set of relevant documents according to the Poisson model with a certain parameter and it is distributed in the set of irrelevant documents with a different parameter [41]. This can be generalized to the *linked-two-Poisson model* [40]. The transformation of dependent terms into "independent" terms using the singular value decomposition method is due to [98, 126]. This approach is known as *latent semantic indexing*. Establishing connections between the original terms and the "known" concepts and its application to improve retrieval effectiveness are due to [391, 392]. A less time-consuming method for transformation into independent terms is given in [385].

The first relevance feedback method in information retrieval, the traditional (A, B), is by [307]. A thorough analysis of this method, assuming that the similarities of the relevant documents and the irrelevant documents with the query follow two normal distributions, can be found in [400]. The parameter estimation method and a slight generalization are due to [74, 386]. The perceptron approach is due to [382]. The material on permanent learning is extracted from [88, 125]. It has recently been demonstrated that feedback without user's assessment can be effective [50]. Similar ideas can be found in [13, 388].

The contents of the Connection Machine is from [345]. It is possible that the deficiency of having only the presence and absence of terms in documents is removed in a later version. The material on DAAM is from [231, 232, 233]. Its use in answering proximity queries is given in [239]. The material on finite state automata is taken from [164, 169], although inner product queries are not mentioned. Actually, more elaborate finite automata called *partitioned finite state automata* are utilized in [164] to ensure efficient recognition of terms.

Logical inference has been used in [85]. Plausible inference, which is preferable, is introduced by [377]. The equation that relates the belief of the query Q for a given document D with the indexing process and the query formulation process for each term is due to [383]. The estimates of the parameters are from [214, 383]. The use of network is from [366]. The network given in [366] is much more involved, having more layers containing concepts and their connections to terms as well as different representations of an information need. It is shown that by having both the vector space probabilistic representation of queries and documents and the structure of Boolean queries, better retrieval results are obtainable than with a single representation of an information need. The parsimonious covering theory is due to [290, 291]. Its application to text retrieval is from [356].

10

Text Clustering and Clustered Search

The problem of *text clustering* is to assign each text document to a class (cluster) or a number of classes. It is a very general problem. The problem of *text retrieval*, discussed in Chapter 9, can be considered a subproblem in which there are two classes (clusters)—the class of relevant documents and the class of irrelevant documents—and each text document has to be assigned to one of the two classes with respect to any given query. Most of the algorithms to be introduced in this chapter, with the exception of the learning automaton algorithm and the exponentiated gradient algorithm, do not have a prespecified number of classes. Text clustering has numerous applications, and some of them are mentioned in Chapter 9. After text documents are clustered into classes, it is easier or more efficient to search for documents within a class than to search in all classes, assuming that the class where the desired documents are located is known. If each class has a representative (a representative of a class is sometimes called a *centroid*) to indicate its contents, browsing can be supported. If a relevant document is found to exist in a class, it is likely that other relevant documents can be found within the class. *Selective information dissemination* is another application. There are numerous users, each having a profile of interests. The problem is to send each new document to only those users who are likely to find the document useful. Here, each user is a class, and it is required to determine whether a new document belongs to each class. In this problem, classes may have overlapping documents because multiple users may have documents of mutual interests. Another application is to automatically assign categories (for example, disease and procedure codes) to patient records for reimbursements and research purposes.

There are numerous text clustering algorithms. Only a few such algorithms are covered in Section 10.1. They are roughly classified into three types, those based on graph theory, those requiring a single pass of the data, and those with learning capabilities. They are given in Sections 10.1.1, 10.1.2, and 10.1.3, respectively. These algorithms are not necessarily restricted to textual data. They have been utilized in classification of texts but may be useful for all types of data. The problem of finding the correct class to search, i.e., *clustered search*, is given in Section 10.2.

10.1 Text Clustering

10.1.1 Graph-Theoretical Methods

In this approach, a graph $G(V, E)$ is formed to capture the similarity relationships between documents, where V is a set of vertices and each vertex in V represents a document, and E is a set of edges and each edge in E represents a pair of documents that are sufficiently similar. One way of determining the edges is to set a threshold T such that an edge (v_i, v_j) exists in E if and only if the similarity of the corresponding documents is greater than the threshold T. The threshold can be in terms of the highest percentage h of the similarity values, for some chosen h. After the formation of the graph, its characteristics can be used to identify clusters. In the following, we use two common characteristics to define clusters. Their relative advantages and disadvantages will also be discussed.

Connected Components

Definition 10.1 *Two vertices are* adjacent *if there is an edge between them. Two vertices v and w are* connected *if there is a sequence of vertices $v_1, v_2, \ldots, v_k$ such that v and v_1 are adjacent, v_i and v_{i+1} are adjacent, $1 \leq i \leq k - 1$, and v_k and w are adjacent.*

Example 10.1 Consider the following graph.

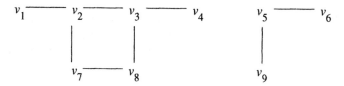

In the above graph, v_1 and v_8 are connected, because v_1 and v_2 are adjacent, v_2 and v_3 are adjacent, and v_3 and v_8 are adjacent. The vertices v_1 and v_8 are not adjacent.   ■

Definition 10.2 *Let V′ be a subset of vertices of V. A subgraph G′ = (V′, E′) is obtained from G = (V, E) by making E′ be a subset of E and making each edge in E′ have both endpoints in V′. The subgraph is connected if any two vertices in V′ are connected using edges in E′. The subgraph forms a connected component if it is connected and any subgraph of G properly containing G′ is not connected.*

Example 10.2 In the above graph, the subgraph G′ containing vertices V′ = $\{v_1, v_2, v_3, v_8\}$ is connected. However, it is not a connected component, because the subgraph containing G′ with an additional vertex v_7 (and the corresponding edges) is connected. A connected component in the graph contains the vertices V″ = $\{v_1, v_2, v_3, v_4, v_7, v_8\}$. Any vertex, say v_5, added to this subgraph will make the resulting graph not connected. We do not want just connected subgraphs to be clusters, because there would be too many small connected subgraphs that overlap each other. For example, the subgraph containing $\{v_1, v_2, v_7\}$ and the subgraph containing $\{v_2, v_7, v_3\}$ are connected subgraphs having substantial overlap.   ∎

One way to identify clusters is to define a cluster to be a connected component. In order to identify all connected components, the following process can be invoked on the graph G(V, E).

Initially, all vertices are not marked.
1. Pick an arbitrary unmarked vertex v. Let W = $\{v\}$.
2. For each unmarked vertex v in W
    { mark v;
      For each vertex x adjacent to v
         if x is not in W, then place it in W;
    }
/* After steps 1 and 2 are executed, the vertices contained in W are those in one connected
    component. */
3. Repeat steps 1 and 2 for each connected component until all vertices in V have been marked.

The complexity of the algorithm is $O(|V| + |E|)$. To see this, observe that each unmarked vertex is considered exactly once in step 1 and in step 2, resulting in complexity $O(|V|)$. Consider an edge $e = (v, w)$. Initially, neither v nor w is marked. When step 2 is executed on vertex v, edge e is traversed once to bring in w, which will be examined to determine whether it belongs to W. At some later stage, when step 2 is executed on vertex w, edge e is traversed again, but this time in the reverse direction to bring in v. Since v is already in W, no further action is taken, implying that the edge e will not be traversed anymore. Since each edge is traversed twice, the complexity is $O(|E|)$. Note that checking whether a vertex x belongs to W can be performed by having a bit vector such that whenever the ith vertex is placed in W, the ith bit is set to 1. Each check takes constant time. It is carried out when an edge (v, x) is traversed. Thus, all such checks require a time complexity bounded by $O(|E|)$.

Example 10.3 Consider the graph given above and suppose vertex v_2 is picked initially. Thus W = $\{v_2\}$. This vertex brings in vertices $\{v_1, v_7, v_3\}$, because they are adjacent to v_2. Therefore, W is updated to $\{v_1, v_7, v_3, v_2\}$. Each of these vertices except v_2 will be examined and they may bring in new vertices. When v_1 is examined, no new vertex will be brought in since its only adjacent vertex v_2 is already in W. Thus, W is not modified. When vertex v_7 is examined, v_8 is added to W. When v_3 is examined, v_4 is added to W. The examination of v_8 and v_4 does not increase W any further. Since all vertices in W have been examined and no further increase in W is possible, the loop in step 2 of the algorithm terminates. The connected component containing $\{v_1, v_2, v_3, v_4, v_7, v_8\}$ is found as a result.   ∎

An important advantage of having connected components as clusters is its relatively low time complexity. However, it has a serious disadvantage: the clusters so formed may not conform to our intuition. For example, consider the following graph.

$$v_1 \text{——} v_2 \text{——} v_3 \text{——} \cdots v_k \text{——} v_{k+1}$$

In this graph, each vertex is adjacent to its left neighbor, if it exists, and its right neighbor, if it exists. By the definition of a connected component, the entire set of vertices forms a single cluster. However, according to our intuition, the vertices v_1 and v_{k+1} are not necessarily similar, since the relation *similar* is not transitive. As an example, consider the case in which each document has a set, T_1, of terms in common with its left neighbor and a set, T_2, of terms in common with its right neighbor, but T_1 and T_2 are disjoint. Furthermore, the left and right neighbors may have no terms in common. Thus, when a connected component is used as a cluster, documents that are not at all similar may end up in the same cluster, violating our intuition.

Maximal Complete Subgraphs

Definition 10.3 *A subgraph* $G' = (V', E')$ *of the graph* $G = (V, E)$ *is a* complete subgraph *if every two vertices in* V' *are adjacent.* G' *is a* maximal complete subgraph *if it is a complete subgraph and any subgraph of* G *properly containing* G' *is not a complete subgraph.*

Example 10.4 In the graph in Example 10.1, there are many maximal complete subgraphs in the connected component containing the vertices $\{v_1, v_2, v_7, v_3, v_8, v_4\}$. Two such maximal complete subgraphs, G_1 and G_2, contain $\{v_1, v_2\}$ and $\{v_2, v_7\}$, respectively. It can easily be verified that v_1 and v_2 are adjacent and v_2 and v_7 are adjacent, and therefore the subgraphs are complete. If v_7 is added to the subgraph G_1, then the resulting subgraph is not complete, because v_1 and v_7 are not adjacent. If v_1 and v_7 were adjacent, then the subgraph containing the vertices $\{v_1, v_2, v_7\}$ would form a maximal complete subgraph. ∎

A maximal complete subgraph can be used to define a cluster. As in the connected component situation, we want to avoid having clusters that are properly contained in other clusters. This is enforced by the maximal property.

This definition of a cluster seems to agree with our intuition that only similar documents are within the same cluster. Unlike the connected components, maximal complete subgraphs may overlap, as shown in the above example. The overlaps among this type of cluster may be excessive to the extent that an exponential number of clusters can result, as shown in the following example.

Suppose there are n vertices that can be arranged in two rows and $n/2$ columns such that each row has $n/2$ vertices and each column has two vertices. A graph can be constructed from these vertices by letting each vertex be adjacent to all vertices, except for the vertex in its own column. In this graph, any subgraph containing exactly one vertex from each column is a maximal complete subgraph. To see that, observe that any two vertices in this subgraph are adjacent, by construction. If an additional vertex, say v, is added to this subgraph, then v is not adjacent to the vertex in the same column as v, by construction. This implies maximality. The total number of maximal complete subgraphs in this graph is $2^{n/2}$, as two choices can be made from each column, and the choices from the columns are independent. The following figure gives the situation in which $n = 4$.

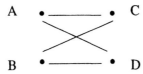

It is not difficult to enumerate all maximal complete subgraphs, but as the example shows, any algorithm is bound to be exponential. One way to generate a complete subgraph, say S, having k vertices is to first obtain a subgraph of S having $k - 1$ vertices and then verify that the remaining vertex, say r, is adjacent to the other $k - 1$ vertices. There are many ways to generate S. In order to avoid generating S a number of times, we can impose the restriction that r be higher in some numbering system than the other $k - 1$ vertices, assuming that each vertex is assigned a unique number. Initially, $k = 2$ and this process of *growing* clusters continues until no cluster can increase in size. Any such cluster is a maximal complete subgraph, as any two vertices in it are adjacent and no additional vertex when added to the cluster is adjacent to all vertices in it. The following algorithm, Grow(C, C′), forms the set, C′, of complete subgraphs, each having no more than $k + 1$ vertices from the set, C, of complete subgraphs, each having no more than k vertices. It is assumed that all complete subgraphs, each having two vertices, have been identified. By repeatedly calling Grow until no new complete subgraph is formed or n, the number of vertices in the entire graph, is reached, all maximal complete subgraphs will be formed. The following algorithm assumes that vertices in a complete subgraph are arranged in ascending order of vertex number, and that for each vertex V, there is a linked list of vertices that are adjacent to V.

Grow(C, C′)

/* Each complete subgraph in C has at least two vertices but no more than k. */

```
for each complete subgraph CS in C
    {Get the first vertex V in CS;
     for each vertex V′ that is not in CS but is adjacent to V
        {condition = true; /* Condition remains true if each vertex in CS is adjacent to V′. */
         for any other vertex V″ (V″ ≠ V, V″ ≠ V′) in CS
            if (V′ and V″ are not adjacent)
                then condition = false;
         if (condition = true) /* CS ∪{V′} is a complete subgraph of (k+1) vertices. */
            then if (V′ > last vertex in CS) /* indicates CS ∪ {V′} will not be constructed
                                                from a different complete subgraph in C. */
                then {CS′ = CS ∪ {V′};
                      V′ is arranged as the last vertex in CS′;
                      delete CS;
                      } /* It is contained in CS′. */
            else delete CS; /* CS′ can be formed in a different way. */
        }
    }
```

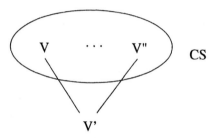

V′ is added to CS if V′ is adjacent to every vertex in CS and
is larger (in index number) than the last vertex V″ in CS.

FIGURE 10.1   Illustrating Algorithm Grow

Figure 10.1 illustrates the algorithm.

The complexity of the algorithm Grow is determined as follows. It is possible to check whether two vertices are adjacent in constant time on average, if some hashing scheme is utilized. Thus, checking whether each vertex in CS is adjacent to a vertex V′ takes time $O(k)$, since CS has no more than k vertices. This is repeated for each vertex adjacent to a vertex in CS. The number of such adjacent vertices is bounded by $O(n)$. Thus, the amount of work for each cluster CS is $O(nk)$. If #nc is the number of clusters in C, then the time complexity is $O(nk \cdot \text{#nc})$. Since #nc can be $O(n^k)$, the time complexity of Grow can be $O(kn^{k+1})$. When k reaches n, the time complexity is clearly exponential.

Connected components and maximal complete subgraphs represent two extremes of a spectrum of graph-theoretical algorithms. Clusters defined by connected components are disjoint and can be obtained in relatively low time complexity. Clusters defined by maximal complete subgraphs may have large overlaps, and the time complexity is exponential. It is possible to define clusters in such a way that the number of vertices in common between any two clusters is bounded by a given constant, say k. When $k = 0$, the connected components are obtained. When k is the number of vertices in the entire graph, i.e., there is no restriction on the amount of overlap between any two clusters, the maximal complete subgraphs are obtained. As k increases, the time complexity also increases.

The clusters defined as connected components or as maximal complete subgraphs given above are of one level only. It is possible to make a hierarchy of clusters by modifying the threshold T that determines whether two vertices are adjacent. When the threshold T is high, there are few edges and each cluster contains just a few vertices. When the threshold is lowered, then there will be more edges and previously distinct clusters may be merged together. For instance, in the graph in Example 10.1, if there is an edge between v_4 and v_5, then the two connected components will be merged into one connected component. In this case, a hierarchy of two levels will be formed, with the lowest level containing the two original clusters.

10.1.2 Single-Pass Method

As the title suggests, the method is to scan each document once in the formation of the clusters. The aim is to have low time complexity. A more detailed description is given as follows.

The first document is scanned. It forms a cluster by itself, with itself also being the representative of the cluster. For each of the remaining documents, the following process is executed. A document D is compared with the representatives of the existing clusters. Either the document D is sufficiently close to some representative R as measured by some threshold, i.e., $f(D, R) \geq T$, where f is a similarity function and T is the threshold, or it is not close to any representative. In the latter case, it forms a new cluster, with itself being the representative. In the former case, it is inserted into the cluster whose representative is closest to D, if clusters are not allowed to have documents in common. In the unlikely event that there are multiple representatives that are all closest to D, one such cluster is randomly picked to contain D. If clusters are allowed to overlap, then the document D is inserted into all those clusters whose representatives are close to D, as determined by the threshold T. At first glance, it appears that each document is processed once and therefore the algorithm has linear time complexity. However, the following worst-case scenario shows that a quadratic time complexity is possible. To see that, consider the situation that each document is far away from the remaining documents and therefore forms a cluster by itself. Now, consider the ith processed document. It has to be compared to the $i - 1$ representatives of the previously processed documents, each having its own cluster. This takes time $O(i - 1)$. As this is done for i ranging from 1 to n, where n is the number of documents, the total time is $O(\sum_{i=1}^{n}(i - 1)) = O(n^2)$. A more precise description of the algorithm is as follows.

Single-Pass(C)

/* C is the collection of documents. */

$R_1 = D_1$; /* The first representative is the first document. */
#nc = 1; /* #nc is the number of clusters. */
for $k = 2$ to n /* n is the total number of documents. */
    {condition = true /* Condition is true if D_k is not in an existing cluster. */
    for $j = 1$ to #nc
        if $(f(D_k, R_j) \geq T)$
            then {insert D_k into cluster C_j; /* assuming overlap of clusters is allowed */
                update representative R_j by including D_k;
                condition = false; }
        if (condition = true)
            then {#nc = #nc + 1;
                $R_{\#nc} = D_k$;}
    }

Balanced Tree

When used in conjunction with the concept of balanced trees, the single-pass method can reduce the time complexity to $O(n \log n)$ time. We illustrate this idea with a 2-3 tree, for the sake of simplicity. For implementation, a B^+ tree is more appropriate. A 2-3 tree is a tree such that (1) each nonleaf node has two or three child nodes, and (2) each leaf node is at the same distance away from the root of the tree. For the purpose of clustering, each leaf node is a document and each nonleaf node is the representative of the cluster containing the documents

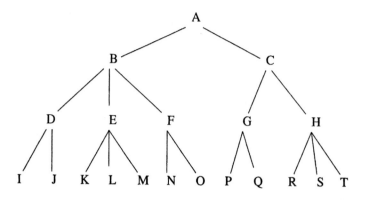

FIGURE 10.2   An Example 2-3 Tree

represented by the leaf nodes. In Figure 10.2, A is the root. It has two child nodes B and C, which have children D, E, and F and children G and H, respectively. Each of these nodes has children as shown in the figure. The leaf nodes that are the documents are I, J, K, ... , S, and T. The node D, which is a nonleaf node, is the representative of the cluster containing I and J. The node B, which is the representative of a higher-level cluster, contains I, J, ... , O.

Suppose a new document Z is inserted into the 2-3 tree. It is first compared to the representatives B and C. It is inserted into the cluster whose representative is closest to it. In our example, it is inserted into the cluster with representative B, if $f(Z, B) > f(Z, C)$; otherwise, it is inserted into the cluster with representative C. This process of inserting the new document into a subcluster whose representative is closest to the document is repeated until a cluster at the lowest level is reached. In our example, Z is inserted into one of the clusters with representatives D, E, F, G, and H. If the document is inserted into a cluster having two documents, say the cluster containing I and J, then the processing of this document is completed, as the cluster now has three documents and both conditions 1 and 2 of a 2-3 tree are preserved. However, if it is inserted into a cluster that initially has three documents, then the representative of the expanded cluster will have four child nodes, in violation of condition 1 of a 2-3 tree. For example, if Z is inserted into the cluster with representative H, then the cluster will have R, S, T, and Z. To preserve the 2-3 tree structure, the cluster is split into two subclusters, each having two documents. The splitting is done in such a way that the sum of the similarities of the pairs of documents within the two subclusters is the largest among all possible splittings. That is, we want to choose documents in the two subclusters to maximize $\sum \sum f(D_i, D_j)$, where the inner sum is over all pairs of documents of the form (D_i, D_j) within a subcluster and the outer sum is for the two subclusters. For example, if $f(Z, R) + f(S, T)$ is the largest value among the different ways of splitting the four documents into two subclusters, each having two documents, then $\{Z, R\}$ and $\{S, T\}$ will form two subclusters with representatives, say H_1 and H_2, respectively. A representative of a subcluster could be the average vector of the documents within the subcluster. The newly formed representatives are then linked to the parent of the old representative. If the parent now has three child nodes, then condition 1 of a 2-3 tree is preserved and the processing of the newly inserted document is completed. In our example, C now has child nodes G, H_1, and H_2 and no further action is required. However, in general it is

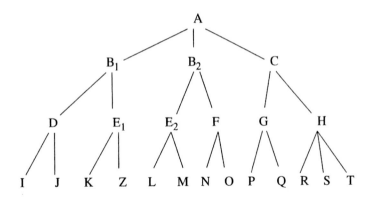

FIGURE 10.3   Illustrating the Insertion of Z

possible that the parent may now have four child nodes, after one of its former child nodes is split into two. In that case, the higher-level cluster having four children needs to be split into two high-level subclusters. For example, if Z is inserted into the cluster containing K, L, and M, then the cluster is first split into two subclusters with new representatives E_1 and E_2. This causes the cluster with representative B to have four child nodes D, E_1, E_2, and F. In order to preserve condition 1 of a 2-3 tree, this cluster is split into two high-level subclusters, say with representatives B_1 and B_2, one containing two children and the other containing the remaining two children. The splitting is done based on the maximum sum of similarities. Suppose B_1 contains the subclusters D and E_1, and B_2 contains the subclusters E_2 and F. The resulting tree is shown in Figure 10.3.

In the most complicated case, the splitting would be carried out all the way to the root of the tree, which may need to be split into two nodes, with a new root created to be their parent. In that case, the height of the tree is increased by 1.

The complexity of the algorithm is determined as follows. Let h be the height of the tree. Since each nonleaf node has either two or three children, $2^h \leq n \leq 3^h$, where n is the number of documents. Thus $h = O(\log n)$. As explained above, the processing of a document consists of two phases. In the first phase, the document is inserted into an appropriate cluster. In the second phase, the 2-3 tree is rebalanced, if necessary. Consider the first phase. When a new document is processed, it is compared to two or three representatives at the second-highest level (one level below the root of the tree). Then it is inserted into the cluster CL whose representative is closest to it. The inserted document is again compared to two or three children of the cluster CL that are the representatives at the next lower level. This process is repeated until the leaf nodes are reached. Since each level requires the computations of two or three similarities and choosing the largest similarity, a constant amount of work is carried out per level. The amount of work is constant in the number of similarity computations, but each computation takes time proportional to the number of terms in the corresponding documents. The number of levels is the height of the tree. Thus, determining the lowest-level cluster in which the new document is to be inserted takes $O(\log n)$ time. As discussed before, in the second phase, after the new document is inserted into a cluster, the cluster may need to be split into two. A splitting involves computing the similarities of the six pairs of documents (note that there are four documents in the cluster) and some comparisons. Therefore, each splitting takes constant time. This type of splitting may be repeated from the lowest level of clusters all the way to the root, with constant work per level. Thus, as much as $O(\log n)$ time may be required, so the total time to process a document in the two phases is $O(\log n)$. With n documents, the time complexity is $O(n \log n)$. A more precise description of the algorithm to insert a document D into a cluster having at least two documents is as follows. The set of all clusters can be obtained by invoking this algorithm $n - 1$ times, assuming that an initial cluster having two documents has been formed.

Insert(D, R)

/* Document D is to be inserted into the tree with root R. */

if (R is a cluster at the lowest level) /* Only documents but not subclusters are below R. */
    then {insert document D into cluster R;
        if the number of documents in R < 4
            then {update the representative of R;
                exit from the algorithm;}
            else {decompose R into two subclusters R_1 and R_2 such that the sum of
                similarities within clusters is the highest;
                apply B^+ tree technique to rebalance the tree;} /* See Chapter 1. */
        else {find the subcluster R' whose representative T' is closest to D;
            /* R' is a child of R. */
            Insert(D, R');} /* Assume that clusters are disjoint and only one
                representative is closest to D. */
        }

Although the complexity of the algorithm is very reasonable, there is a key disadvantage to this method: the algorithm is *order dependent*. A clustering method is *order independent* if the clusters formed by the method are independent of the order in which the documents are processed. In other words, the clusters formed by processing documents in the order $D_1, D_2, \ldots, D_n$ should be the same as those formed by processing the documents in any other order. The graph-theoretical methods in which clusters are defined as connected components or as maximal complete subgraphs are order independent, because connected components and maximal complete subgraphs are well defined when the vertices and the edges of the graph are specified. In the one-pass balanced tree method, it is possible that documents that are not close together when all documents are taken into consideration are relatively close together when they are processed together in the beginning portion of the algorithm and end up in the same cluster. In other words, if the method is applied to two different sequences of the same n documents, it is possible that two different sets of clusters are obtained. In that case, it is not clear whether proper clustering has been carried out. To remedy this situation, we can perform cluster quality enhancements as follows.

Let the quality of the clusters be defined as $Q = \sum \sum f(D_i, R_j)$, where the first summation is over all clusters and the second summation is for each document D_i in the jth cluster with representative R_j. The inner sum gives the *closeness* of the documents with respect to their representative, and the outer sum gives the overall closeness, taking into consideration all clusters. Clearly, if clusters are well formed, we expect that Q has a high value. In other words, if Q can be increased, the quality of the clusters can be improved. One way to improve the quality of a set of clusters is to interchange two documents in two different clusters: if the interchange gives a higher value of Q, then the quality of the clusters can be assumed to have been improved. The two documents to be interchanged can be chosen from the documents that have least similarity with their representatives. The interchange continues until Q cannot be increased further. The disadvantages of this enhancement method are that the time complexity of $O(n \log n)$ is no longer guaranteed, and also that a local maximum, instead of the global maximum, of Q is likely to be reached.

10.1.3 On-Line Learning Clustering Methods

A clustering method is a *learning algorithm* if it makes use of training data to classify documents. The training data can be in the form of the knowledge that certain documents are known to belong to certain classes. Another possibility is that for some previously submitted queries, the set of documents relevant to each of these queries is known. In either of these cases, the information about the documents in the classes is utilized to classify new or existing documents. The methods described in the last two subsections do not make use of training data. Learning algorithms can be roughly classified as follows. An algorithm is *parametric* if a particular distribution of data is assumed; otherwise, it is *nonparametric*. The parameter estimation algorithm given in Section 9.3.1 of Chapter 9 on relevance feedback is parametric, whereas the algorithms given in this section are nonparametric. An algorithm is *on-line* if the algorithm acts on each training datum one at a time and discards it after each action, whereas a *batch algorithm* acts on a set of data. The permanent learning algorithm in Section 9.3.2 is a batch algorithm, whereas the algorithms given here are on-line algorithms. Since an on-line algorithm discards each training datum as soon as it is acted upon, such an algorithm usually requires less space than a batch algorithm. It is also more responsive to changes: when changes occur frequently, on-line algorithms can adapt quickly.

We first define a very simple clustering problem and provide a learning algorithm to solve it. Then we generalize the problem to the common *record-to-page assignment problem*, which arises in database systems.

A Simple Clustering Problem

We assume that each user query accesses two documents, the number of clusters is predetermined, and each cluster has the same number of documents. The problem is to determine the clusters such that documents within a cluster are frequently jointly accessed, but documents across different clusters are less frequently jointly accessed. The restrictions imposed on the method are somewhat severe. If the assumption that each user query accesses exactly two documents is removed, then the standard record-to-page assignment problem given below satisfies the remaining assumptions.

The Record-to-Page Assignment Problem *Each page in the secondary storage has a fixed size. Records are not duplicated, and they are of the same size. If a query retrieves records that reside in P pages, then P page accesses are required. The problem is to assign*

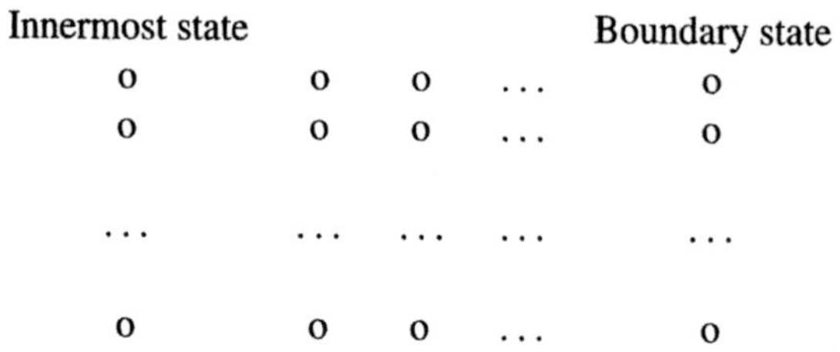

Innermost state   Boundary state

o   o   o   . . .   o

o   o   o   . . .   o

. . .   .

o   o   o   . . .   o

FIGURE 1 0 . 4   Illustrating the Learning Automaton

*the set of all records to pages in such a way that the number of pages that need to be accessed
for a set of queries is minimized.*

It is easy to see that if the number of pages needed to answer a query is minimized by
assigning the records satisfying the query to as few pages as possible, that assignment may
cause some other queries to access more pages than is necessary, because of the restriction
that records are not duplicated. Thus the minimization problem is not trivial. In fact, it can
be shown that this record-to-page assignment problem is an NP-complete problem, i.e., it is
computationally equivalent to other well-known hard problems, such as the knapsack problem and the traveling salesman problem. Existing optimal algorithms for these problems take
exponential time.

We employ a learning automaton for the simple clustering problem in which each query
accesses exactly two records. Let the number of clusters be m and let each cluster have r
records. The learning automaton has m rows, each representing a cluster and having s states.
The leftmost state of each row is the innermost state; the understanding is that a record in
the innermost state is very likely to belong to the cluster. The rightmost state of each row is a
boundary state. Records in the boundary state are likely to leave the cluster. A record in a state
between the boundary state and the innermost state is more likely to remain in the cluster than
a record in the boundary state, but it is less likely to remain than a record in the innermost state.
The number of states in a row is the depth of memory that permits the system to remember the
past history. A state may contain 0, 1, or multiple records. Figure 10.4 illustrates the learning
automaton. Initially, r records are arbitrarily assigned to the states of each row.

For each query accessing records r_i and r_j, the following cases may occur.

Case 1. Both r_i and r_j are in states of the same row. In this situation, the records belong to
the same cluster and the query reinforces what is recorded in the system. The actions
to be taken are that both r_i and r_j move one state to the left toward the innermost state.
The intuition is that r_i and r_j are more likely to remain in this cluster than before. In the
situation that r_i is in the innermost state before the execution of this query, it stays in
the same state. The same applies to r_j. In that situation, there is a loss of information, as
the depth of memory is bounded by s, the number of states in a row.

Case 2. The two records r_i and r_j are in states of different rows.

   Subcase 1. Both of them are in the boundary states of two different rows; say r_i is in
   row k and r_j is in row t. The query suggests that the two records should belong to the

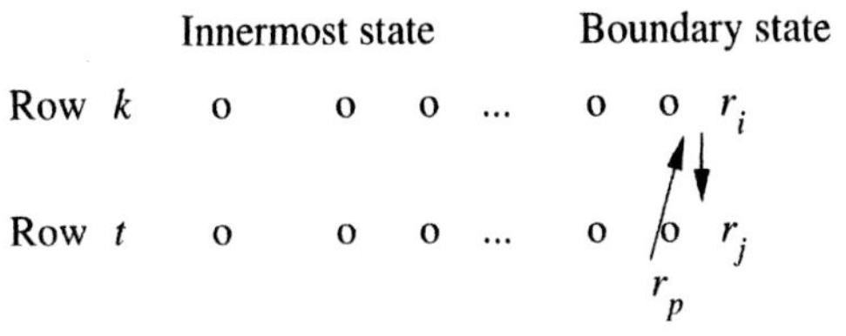

r_p is either at the boundary state of row t, if such a record
exists, or it is at a state closest to the boundary state.

FIGURE 10.5 *Illustrating Subcase 1*

same cluster. To accomplish this, one of them, say r_i, is moved to the boundary state
of row t. (We could just as well move r_j to the boundary state of row k instead.) If this
query appears over and over again, both r_i and r_j will move closer and closer to the
innermost state, as governed by Case 1. This will satisfy our intuition. Since each row
should have the same number of records but row t has an additional record after r_i is
moved to it, we need to take a record from row t and move it to the boundary state of
row k. If there is another record other than r_j at the boundary state of row t, it should
be chosen for the move, as it is likely to leave row t; otherwise, pick a record in a state
closest to the boundary state, as this record is most likely to leave row t. This subcase is
illustrated in Figure 10.5.

In the foregoing description, r_i is moved to row t. Alternatively, r_j can be moved to
row k. The choice of row t or row k depends on whether the chosen row has a record,
other than records r_i and r_j, at or closest to the boundary state.

Subcase 2. Both of them are not in the boundary states of their rows. In that situation,
both r_i and r_j are moved one state to the right, closer to their boundary states. If this
query occurs over and over again, then either one of the records will reach the boundary
state while the other record reaches a nonboundary state (subcase 3) or both of these
records will eventually reach their boundary states at the same time (subcase 1) and the
next such query will move them to the same row.

Subcase 3. One of the records, say r_i, is in the boundary state of row k and the other
record, r_j, is not in the boundary state of row t. There are two cases.

(a) If there is a record, say r_p, in the boundary state of row t, then interchange r_i and
r_p. This is reasonable, as both r_i and r_p are likely to leave their rows and, after the
interchange, r_i and r_j are in the same row, consistent with the current query.

(b) If there is no record in the boundary state of row t, then record r_j is moved one
state to the right, toward its boundary state. In contrast to case (a), no record in
row t is to be interchanged with r_i, as no record is extremely likely to leave row t
at the present time.

The number of states in a row, s (or the depth of memory), need not be fixed. In an actual
implementation, a record in a state is associated with a number, starting with 0, which stands
for the boundary state. Whenever a record is moved one state away from the boundary state,

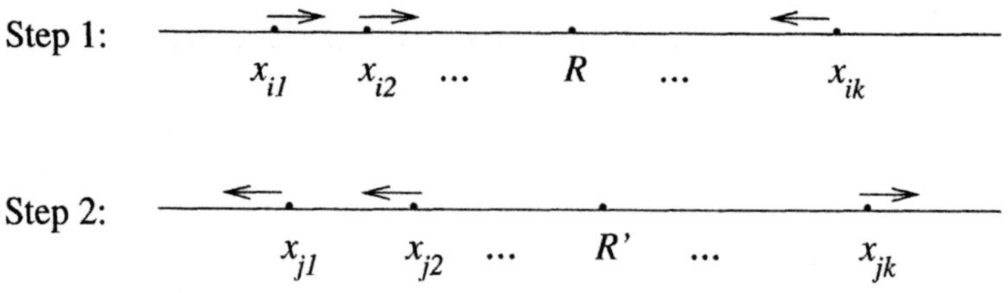

Step 1:

$$x_{i1} \quad x_{i2} \quad \ldots \quad R \quad \ldots \quad x_{ik}$$

Step 2:

$$x_{j1} \quad x_{j2} \quad \ldots \quad R' \quad \ldots \quad x_{jk}$$

FIGURE 10.6   Illustrating Algorithm Adapt

the number associated with the record is increased by 1. The higher the number, the farther the state is from the boundary state. Clearly, there is no need to have a bound for these numbers. Whenever a record is moved one state toward the boundary state, the number is decreased by 1. When the number reaches zero, the boundary state is reached.

One way to speed up the convergence of the algorithm is to initially assign all records to the boundary states of different rows. This permits records that should belong to the same clusters to migrate to the same rows quickly.

Adaptive Record Clustering

We now consider the case in which the number of clusters is unknown and the number of documents in a cluster may vary from one cluster to another.

Initially, each document is arbitrarily assigned a point on the real line. Whenever a query is executed, the points associated with certain documents will be modified. At the termination of the algorithm, documents whose points are sufficiently close will be members of a cluster. The modifications of the points per query are given in the following algorithm. Let the points associated with the document D_i be x_i, $1 \le i \le n$.

Adapt

For each query that accesses a set of documents, say, $D_{i1}, D_{i2}, \ldots, D_{ik}$, do

Step 1. Move each document D_{ij}, $1 \le j \le k$, closer to the representative of the accessed documents, which is located at $R = \sum_{t=1}^{k} x_{it}/k$, by a distance $A \cdot |x_{ij} - R|$, where A is a constant slightly greater than 0 but much less than 1.

Step 2. Randomly pick k documents, say $D_{j1}, D_{j2}, \ldots, D_{jk}$, and move each of them, D_{js}, away from its representative, which is located at $R' = \sum_{t=1}^{k} x_{jt}/k$ by a distance $A \cdot |x_{js} - R'|$.

This algorithm is illustrated in Figure 10.6.

If the same query is executed over and over again, then the documents accessed by the query will become closer and closer together by the repeated executions of Step 1. However, it is also possible that all documents become very close together. To see that, consider the leftmost point associated with a document D_s and the rightmost point associated with another document D_t. Whenever a query accesses several documents of which one of them is either D_s or D_t, either the leftmost point will move right or the rightmost point will move left, by Step 1. This shows that the range containing all the points associated with the documents will keep on shrinking, leading possibly to the situation that all points are very close together. If this happens, we may not be able to differentiate members of a cluster from members of another cluster. In order that not all documents be close together, Step 2 pulls randomly chosen documents apart. The combination of the two steps has the following effects. Documents that are frequently jointly accessed are pushed together frequently by Step 1 but are randomly chosen to be pulled apart by Step 2. Since the former action is much more frequent than the latter action, the frequently jointly accessed documents will stay together. Conversely, documents that are rarely jointly accessed are rarely pushed together and are randomly chosen to be pulled apart. If the probability associated with the rarely jointly accessed documents is less than or equal to the probability that documents are randomly chosen, then the rarely jointly accessed documents will stay apart. This allows clusters to be recognized. A more rigorous analysis is given as follows. Consider the special case in which there are two clusters. Let the points associated with elements of one cluster be denoted $y_1, y_2, \ldots, y_k$ and those associated with elements of another cluster be denoted by $z_1, z_2, \ldots, z_t$. Define the *within distance*, W, to be $\sum_{i,j=1}^{k}(y_i - y_j)^2 + \sum_{i,j=1}^{t}(z_i - z_j)^2$ and the *between distance*, B, to be $\sum_{i=1,\ldots,k,j=1,\ldots,t}(y_i - z_j)^2$. When W is 0, then all the elements of the same cluster are at the same location. However, this may not be sufficient to identify the two clusters, because all documents may be at the same location. To prevent the latter situation from happening, we need $B > 0$. In general, it is desirable to have W close to 0 and B significantly different from 0 so that the clusters can be easily identified. Ideally, if each execution of a query causes $E(W)$ to decrease and $E(B)$ to increase, where E stands for the expected value, then the desirable situation can be attained. Unfortunately, the ideal situation cannot be proved. Nevertheless, it can be shown that $E(W)/E(B)$ is decreasing, for proper choices of the constant A. In other words, the expected value of W is decreasing at a faster rate than the expected value of B for each execution of a query. When the ratio is sufficiently small, it is relatively easy to identify elements of individual clusters, as a small value of W implies that elements of the same cluster are close together and a large value of B implies that the elements of one cluster are separated from those of another cluster.

Initially, since the documents are arbitrarily assigned points, the ratio $E(W)/E(B)$ is likely to be large. After repeated executions of the algorithm Adapt, the ratio will keep on dropping. After a while, the ratio will oscillate, as the constant A used in Step 1 is not small enough to guarantee the continual decrease of the ratio. To detect the oscillation, we proceed as follows. Initially, as the documents are arbitrarily assigned points, even points associated with documents within the same cluster can be far apart. As a result, the average distance moved by each document in Step 1, denoted by d, is relatively large. As documents within individual clusters become closer, d decreases. In other words, when cluster formation, which is defined by the ratio $E(W)/E(B)$, improves, d is expected to decrease. When d oscillates, there is no improvement in cluster formation and the ratio will also oscillate. When that happens, the constant A is replaced by a smaller constant, say, $\frac{1}{2}A$, and the algorithm Adapt will be executed to yield better cluster formation. This process of executing the algorithm and occasionally decreasing A is repeated until the clusters are easily recognizable. One way to recognize the elements of the clusters is to first determine the average distance between two points, say f; if the distance between two adjacent points is significantly less than f, then the corresponding documents are within a cluster.

In the presentation given above, the within distance W and the between distance B are defined for two clusters only. They are readily generalizable to an arbitrary number of clusters. Step 2 in the algorithm Adapt requires some overhead, because points associated with documents that are not accessed by the query have to be selected and modified. To avoid this overhead and at the same time prevent the points of documents that are not within a cluster from becoming closer, Step 2 can be modified as follows. The location of the representative of all documents, AR, is computed. (It is given by the sum of the points divided by the number of documents. It is computed once at the beginning of the algorithm and is updated whenever the points of the accessed documents of a query are modified. It is easy to observe that the update takes a time proportional to the number of accessed documents.) The location of the representative of the accessed documents of the query Q, QR, is also computed. A comparison is made between AR and QR. If QR is on the left of AR, then in Step 2 the point of each accessed document is shifted to the left by a distance g given as follows; otherwise each of them is shifted to the right by a distance g. The intention is to ensure that the two representatives are not getting closer together. If QR and AR are separated by a distance t before Step 1 is executed, then g is chosen in such a way that the distance between the two representatives is at least as large as t. Since all points of the accessed documents are shifted in the same direction in the new Step 2, the accessed documents are becoming closer together because of the effects of Step 1. Furthermore, the set of all documents are not becoming closer together as a result of the new Step 2. It is easy to see that since all points that are affected by Step 1 and those in the new Step 2 are the same, the two steps can be combined into one step. Thus, this modification achieves the desirable effects, while reducing the overhead.

Exponentiated Gradient Algorithm

For this algorithm, the number of clusters is assumed to be prespecified. For each cluster, a representative vector $cr = (cr_1, cr_2, \ldots, cr_n)$ is maintained, where n is the number of terms in the entire collection of documents. Initially, cr is set to be $(1/n, 1/n, \ldots, 1/n)$; i.e., each term has the same weight and the sum of the weights is 1. During the training phase each document $D = (d_1, d_2, \ldots, d_n)$ is known to belong to or not to belong to the cluster with representative cr. With the known cluster information, the cluster representative vector is updated for each document D as follows.

For each jth component of the representative,

$$cr_j = \frac{cr_j e^{-2v((cr,D)-y)d_j}}{\sum_{k=1}^{n} cr_k e^{-2v((cr,D)-y)d_k}}$$

where $y = 1$ if document D belongs to the cluster with representative cr and 0 otherwise, (cr, D) stands for the dot product of the two vectors, and $v > 0$ regulates the rate of learning. Consider the exponent portion of the numerator. Suppose the document D does not belong to the cluster; then $y = 0$. Thus, $(cr, D) - y > 0$. If d_j is positive, then the exponent will be negative, causing a decrease in cr_j. The denominator is for normalization; i.e., the sum of the n components of the representative is 1. Similarly, if the document is judged to belong to the cluster; then with $(cr, D) - y < 0$ and $d_j \geq 0$, the exponent will be positive, causing cr_j to increase. If d_j is 0, then the exponent in the numerator is 0. This implies that the numerator is not changed. However, the denominator may be modified.

It has been shown that with some assumptions about the random presentation of the training data and with $v = 2/3M^2$, where M satisfies $\max_j\{d_j\} - \min_j\{d_j\} \leq M$, the expected error bound is given by

$$E[((cr, D) - y)^2] \leq \frac{3}{2}\left(E\left[((u, D) - y)^2\right] + \frac{M^2 \ln n}{m + 1}\right)$$

where m is the number of documents in the training data and u is a vector with nonnegative components summing to 1 that best fits the data. For normalized document vectors, $0 \leq \min_j\{d_j\} \leq \max_j\{d_j\} \leq 1$. Thus, $M \leq 1$. The error bound depends on the logarithm of the number of dimensions, $\log n$, instead of the number of dimensions. This is favorable, because the number of dimensions in representing documents for information retrieval is usually very large.

10.1.4 Reduction of Time by Sampling

Suppose the desired complexity of clustering is $O(kn)$, where n is the number of documents and k is the number of clusters (k may be estimated by the method given in the next subsection). One way to achieve the desired complexity is by sampling and applying a clustering algorithm to the selected sample of documents. A sketch of this method is as follows. Suppose a clustering algorithm with quadratic time complexity, such as one defining clusters as connected components, is used. Then a sample of $\sqrt{kn}$ documents is selected. When the clustering algorithm with quadratic time complexity is applied to the sample, the time spent is $O(kn)$. For each cluster in the sample, a representative is formed. Each document that is not in the sample is compared to the representatives and is assigned to the cluster whose representative is closest to it. Since there are k representatives and each document is compared against k representatives, the assignment of these documents takes $O(kn)$ time. It can be shown that for reasonable values of n and k (more specifically, n should be much larger than $k \ln k$), a sample of $\sqrt{kn}$ documents will have a probability close to 1 of having at least one document from each of the k clusters. If the clusters are disjoint and the smallest similarity between any two documents within a cluster is larger than the largest similarity between any two documents in different clusters, then k clusters will be formed. Usually, the clusters formed from the samples are not perfect and some refinement process is applied to improve the clusters. As discussed in Section 10.1.2, a measure, Q, can be given to indicate the quality of the clusters. It was given by a sum over all clusters, such that for each cluster we have the sum of the similarities of the documents of the cluster with their representative. For each cluster, those documents that are not very close to their representative, i.e., those documents having relatively small similarities, are identified. For each such document, if it is reassigned to another cluster and yields a higher value for Q, then it is carried out. Although each such iteration takes no more than $O(kn)$ time, it is not clear whether termination is achieved in a constant number of iterations. In practice, the number of iterations is predetermined so as to have a reasonable time complexity. Another heuristic to improve the quality of a set of clusters is to examine whether two clusters should be merged. Two clusters may be merged if their representatives have a similarity greater than some preset constant. This heuristic can be used in conjunction with the document reassignment heuristic. Again, the number of iterations to reach termination is usually predetermined.

10.1.5 Determination of the Number of Clusters and Their Representatives

In the learning automaton method given in Section 10.1.3, the number of clusters is assumed to be known. In the sampling method given above, the number of clusters is determined by the sample. There is a nonzero probability that the sample is not good enough to give the appropriate number of clusters. Thus it is worthwhile to have a method that can give an estimate of the number of clusters and also their representatives. For a given document-term matrix with n documents and m terms, the quantity c_{ij}, referred to as the *covering* of document i by document j, $1 \le i, j \le n$, can be computed; it is given by the formula $\sum p_k \cdot p(k, j)$, where p_k is the probability that a term randomly chosen from document i is term k and $p(k, j)$ is the probability that a document taken randomly from the set of documents having term k is document j; the summation is over each term k in the set of all terms. Let n_i be the number of terms in document i. It is clear that if document i does not have term k, then p_k is 0; otherwise, p_k is $1/n_i$. Let n_{dk} be the number of documents having term k. If document j is not within the set of documents having term k, then $p(k, j)$ is zero; otherwise, it is $1/n_{dk}$. If term k occurs in very few documents, then $p(k, j)$ will be relatively large. Among all the terms of document i, some terms appear in many documents, and some appear in very few documents. Let b and s be the largest number and the smallest number, respectively, of documents containing a term of document i. When document j contains all terms of document i, $1/b \le c_{ij} \le 1/s$, because for each term k of document i, the contribution is between $1/b \cdot 1/n_i$ and $1/s \cdot 1/n_i$. Clearly, document i has all its own terms and therefore c_{ii} satisfies the above inequality. If no term of document i is possessed by any other document, then $c_{ii} = 1$, because each term of document i contributes $1/n_i$. Suppose there is a set of documents, say S, of cardinality t, each having exactly the same set of terms but having none of its terms shared by documents outside S. Consider a term in document i having n_i terms within the set S. The contribution of this term is $1/t \cdot 1/n_i$, as the term occurs in precisely t documents. When this is summed over all n_i terms in document i and then summed over t documents in S, we obtain $\sum c_{ii} = 1$ for the documents in S. This set of documents clearly defines a cluster. If there are p such clusters in the entire collection of documents, then $\sum c_{ii} = p$ for the collection of documents. Therefore, an estimate of the number of clusters is $\sum c_{ii}$, where the sum is over all documents.

Example 10.5 Consider the following documents.

$$
\begin{array}{c c c c c c c c}
 & t_1 & t_2 & t_3 & t_4 & t_5 & t_6 & t_7 \\
D_1 \ (& 1, & 1, & 1, & 1, & 0, & 0, & 0 \ ) \\
D_2 \ (& 1, & 1, & 1, & 1, & 0, & 0, & 0 \ ) \\
D_3 \ (& 0, & 0, & 0, & 1, & 1, & 1, & 1 \ ) \\
D_4 \ (& 0, & 0, & 0, & 1, & 1, & 1, & 1 \ ) \\
\end{array}
$$

Consider c_{11} for document D_1. For term t_1, the contribution is $1/4 \cdot 1/2$, since there are four terms in D_1 and t_1 occurs in two documents. The same is true for terms t_2 and t_3. For terms t_4, the contribution is $1/4 \cdot 1/4$, since there are four terms in D_1 and t_4 occurs in four documents. Thus, $c_{11} = (1/4 \cdot 1/2) \cdot 3 + 1/4 \cdot 1/4 = 7/16$. Since all documents in the collection have the same characteristics, $\sum c_{ii} = 7/4$. However, the number of clusters should be 2, one containing D_1 and D_2 and the other containing D_3 and D_4. If the documents have many more terms and the number of terms in common between the documents across the two clusters remains small, $\sum c_{ii}$ will approach 2. The extreme case in which there is no term in common between documents in different clusters is given in the above paragraph. It should be noted that the estimate of the number of clusters by $\sum c_{ii}$ is a rough one. ∎

To determine the suitability of document i to be the representative of a cluster, compute the quantity $T = c_{ii} \cdot (1 - c_{ii}) \cdot n_i$. As explained before, c_{ii} is usually much smaller than 1; it is large if it contains quite a few rare terms. A document, say D, has a large value for T if it has many terms and quite a few of them are rare ones. This suggests that D has much potential to serve as a cluster representative. In fact, the $\sum c_{ii}$ documents having the largest T values are chosen to be the representatives of the clusters.

It is easy to observe that when all nonzero terms of the document-term matrix are scanned once, n_i (the number of terms in document i) for each document i and n_{dk} (the number of documents containing term k) for each term k can be computed. This allows the computation of c_{ii} in time proportional to the number of terms in document i. Thus, $\sum c_{ii}$ can be computed in time proportional to the number of nonzero terms in the matrix.

10.2 Clustered Search

In this section, we discuss how to determine the clusters to search. Each cluster has a representative. A given query is compared against the representatives of the clusters. Based on these comparisons, a small subset of clusters is selected, each of which is likely to contain documents of interest to the user. Let the subset of clusters be S. Clusters outside S are not considered any further, yielding efficiency. If clusters in S have subclusters, then this process will be repeated to select smaller subclusters. Finally, a set of subclusters that have no subclusters of their own is identified. Each document in each of these identified subclusters will be compared against the query to determine the documents to be retrieved. One potential application of this scheme is the determination of databases to search in the Internet, where each database is considered to be a cluster.

Four cases can be identified depending on whether terms are *binary* (i.e., only 0 and 1 are used to represent the weight of each term) and whether terms are *independently* distributed (i.e., the distribution of the occurrences of one term in the documents of the cluster is independent of the distribution of the occurrences of other terms in the documents of the cluster). These four cases will be discussed in the following four subsections.

10.2.1 Terms Are Binary and Independent in the Documents of Each Cluster

It is assumed that the terms that appear in each cluster are ordered. For notational simplicity, we also assume that the query Q under consideration contains the first k terms of a cluster and each term has a weight of 1 in the query. Since only 0 and 1 are used to represent the weight of each term, each document is a binary vector. The documents are organized into clusters, each having a representative. It is assumed that the clusters are disjoint. The objective is to find the s documents, for a given integer s supplied by a user, that are closest to the query Q among all clusters. The idea is to compare the query Q with the representative of each cluster C_i and, based on the comparison, estimate the number of documents in C_i, denoted by N_i, that have t or more terms in common with Q (this estimate is denoted by N_i); t is chosen in such a way that the sum of N_i over all clusters is just greater than or equal to s; i.e., if t is replaced by $t + 1$, then the sum is less than s. The estimation process is described in detail as follows.

Let the representative $R = (r_1, r_2, \ldots, r_k, \ldots, r_n)$ of a cluster C of documents be defined as follows.

$$R = \frac{\sum_{D_i \in C} D_i}{m}$$

where m is the number of documents in C. Since the documents are binary vectors, r_i is the number of documents in C having the ith term divided by m, i.e., it is the probability that a document in C has the ith term. Since the query Q has the first k terms, it is sufficient to consider these k terms only. With the assumption that terms are distributed independently in the cluster, the probability that a document in C has the vector representation $\vec{x} = (x_1, x_2, \ldots, x_k)$ is

$$I(\vec{x}) = \prod_{i=1}^{k} r_i^{x_i} \cdot (1 - r_i)^{1-x_i} \tag{10.1}$$

When x_i is 1, $r_i^{x_i} = r_i$ and $(1 - r_i)^{1-x_i} = 1$. Their product is r_i, which is the probability that a document in C has the ith term. Similarly, when $x_i = 0$, the corresponding product is $1 - r_i$, which is the probability that a document in C does not have the ith term. By the independence assumption, $I(\vec{x})$ represents the probability that a document in C has the combination of terms indicated in $\vec{x}$.

The probability that a document in C has precisely u terms in common with Q is given by the sum of $I(\vec{x})$ over all those vectors $\vec{x}$ having exactly u x's equal to 1. It is given by the following expression:

$$\sum I(\vec{x}) \tag{10.2}$$

where the summation is over all possible ways of choosing u terms from the k terms.

Example 10.6 Consider the case in which $k = 4$ and $u = 3$. Then the sets of three terms in common with Q are $\{1, 2, 3\}$, $\{1, 2, 4\}$, $\{1, 3, 4\}$, and $\{2, 3, 4\}$. The required expression representing the probability that a document in the cluster C has exactly three terms in common with the query is denoted by

$$P(3) = r_1 \cdot r_2 \cdot r_3 \cdot (1 - r_4) + r_1 \cdot r_2 \cdot r_4 \cdot (1 - r_3)$$
$$+ r_1 \cdot r_3 \cdot r_4 \cdot (1 - r_2) + r_2 \cdot r_3 \cdot r_4 \cdot (1 - r_1)$$

In this expression, $r_1 r_2 r_3 (1 - r_4)$ represents the probability that a document in C has the set of terms t_1, t_2, and t_3 in common with Q but t_4 is not in common. The probabilities of the other combinations of three terms in common with Q are given by the remaining part of the expression.   ■

We now proceed to compute Expression (10.2). Since this expression involves an exponential number of combinations of products, we need to seek an efficient method for the computation. For the ith term, we construct the linear polynomial $r_iX + (1 - r_i)$, where X is simply a dummy variable. Then we consider the product of k linear polynomials, one for each term of the query:

$$\prod_{i=1}^{k}(r_iX + (1 - r_i)) \qquad (10.3)$$

The coefficient of X raised to the power of u is precisely Expression (10.2). To see this, observe that in order to obtain X to the power u, we have to pick, among the k linear polynomials, u terms that involve X and $k - u$ terms that do not involve X. Whenever an X term is picked, an r_i is chosen; whenever a term not involving X is picked, a $(1 - r_j)$ term is chosen. Thus, we obtain a product of u r's and $(k - u)$ $(1 - r)$'s. Since there are $\binom{k}{u}$ ways to choose u out of k X's, the result is exactly the one given by Expression (10.2). As an example, the coefficient of X raised to the power 3 in $(r_1X + (1 - r_1)) \cdot (r_2X + (1 - r_2)) \cdot (r_3X + (1 - r_3)) \cdot (r_4X + (1 - r_4))$ is $P(3)$ given in Example 10.6.

It is relatively easy to compute the polynomial in Expression (10.3). To simplify the analysis, assume that k is 2 raised to some integer. The product in (10.3) can then be computed by taking the product of the first half of the linear polynomials, denoted by $\text{Pr}(k/2)$, the product of the remaining half, denoted by $\text{Pr}(k)$, and then the product of $\text{Pr}(k/2)$ and $\text{Pr}(k)$. $\text{Pr}(k/2)$ and $\text{Pr}(k)$ are both polynomials of degree $k/2$. When $\text{Pr}(k/2)$ and $\text{Pr}(k)$ are multiplied, each coefficient of $\text{Pr}(k/2)$ is multiplied with $k/2+1$ coefficients in $\text{Pr}(k)$. Thus, the number of multiplications involved in computing the product of $\text{Pr}(k/2)$ and $\text{Pr}(k)$ is $O((k/2)^2)$. It can be seen that the number of additions is also $O((k/2)^2)$. The complexity of the product of $\text{Pr}(k/2)$ and $\text{Pr}(k)$ is therefore $O((k/2)^2)$. Let $T(k)$ be the time complexity for computing Expression (10.3) by the above approach. Then the time complexity to compute $\text{Pr}(k/2)$ is $T(k/2)$, as the number of linear polynomials in $\text{Pr}(k/2)$ is $k/2$. For the same reason, the time complexity to compute $\text{Pr}(k)$ is $T(k/2)$. Since the product in (10.3) is obtained by computing $\text{Pr}(k/2)$, then $\text{Pr}(k)$, and then their product, the following inequality is obtained.

$$T(k) \le T(k/2) + T(k/2) + O((k/2)^2) = 2T(k/2) + O((k/2)^2) = 2T(k/2) + C_1 \cdot (k/2)^2$$

where C_1 is some constant. Since the above inequality holds for any value of k as long as it is divisible by 2, it can be used to give a bound for $T(k/2)$. We then obtain $T(k/2) \le 2T(k/4) + C_1 \cdot (k/4)^2$. Substituting the latter inequality into the former and simplifying, we can obtain $T(k) \le 4T(k/4) + C_1 \cdot (k/2)^2 + 2C_1 \cdot (k/4)^2$. If this process is repeated, then a geometric series $C_1 \cdot (k/2)^2 + 1/2C_1 \cdot (k/2)^2 + \cdots$ is obtained in which the next term is always one-half of the term before it. Thus, the sum of the series is $O(k^2)$.

It should be noted that (10.3) can be computed by the fast Fourier transform with a lower time complexity, but the number of terms, k, in a query is usually not large enough for the actual computing time using the fast Fourier transform to be lower.

10.2.2 Terms Are Binary and Arbitrarily Dependent in the Documents of Each Cluster

In this subsection, as in the previous subsection, only the presence or absence of terms in documents is recorded. However, dependencies between terms that are very common among terms are incorporated into the estimation process. As a result, a more accurate estimation is expected. We will follow an approach that is very similar to that used in Section 10.2.1. However, the representative will need to contain the significant dependencies (i.e., *covariances* that are significantly different from 0; see below for a definition of covariance) between terms in addition to the probabilities of occurrences (r's) of the terms. The probability that a document in the cluster C has the vector representation $\vec{x} = (x_1, x_2, \ldots, x_k, \ldots, x_n)$ is given by the *Bahadur-Lazarsfeld expansion*:

$$D(\vec{x}) = I(\vec{x}) \left[1 + \sum_{i<j} \text{corr}(i, j) \frac{(x_i - r_i)(x_j - r_j)}{r_i \cdot r_j \cdot (1 - r_i) \cdot (1 - r_j)} \right.$$

$$+ \sum_{i<j<t} \text{corr}(i, j, t) \frac{(x_i - r_i)(x_j - r_j)(x_k - r_t)}{r_i \cdot r_j \cdot r_t \cdot (1 - r_i) \cdot (1 - r_j) \cdot (1 - r_t)}$$

$$\left. + \cdots + \text{corr}(1, 2, \ldots, k) \frac{(x_1 - r_1) \cdots (x_k - r_k)}{r_1 \cdot r_2 \cdot \ldots \cdot r_k \cdot (1 - r_1) \cdot \ldots \cdot (1 - r_k)} \right] \quad (10.4)$$

In the above expansion, the first summation is for all (i, j) pairs; the second and subsequent summations are for all (i, j, t) triplets and for all quadruplets, etc. The function $\text{corr}(i, j)$ is the *correlation coefficient* between the ith and the jth terms and is defined as $E[(Y_i - r_i)(Y_j - r_j)]/(r_i \cdot r_j \cdot (1 - r_i) \cdot (1 - r_j))$, where E stands for the expected value, Y_i is the random variable associated with the ith term taking on values of 0 and 1, and $E(Y_i) = r_i$. The function $\text{corr}(i, j, t)$ is similarly defined. If terms i and j are independent, then $\text{corr}(i, j)$ is 0; $\text{corr}(i, j)$ is a measure of the degree of dependency between the ith and the jth terms. Similarly, $\text{corr}(i, j, t) = 0$ implies the independence of the three terms. It is therefore sufficient to take into consideration only correlations that are significantly larger than 0. Expression (10.4) can be interpreted as follows. If the terms are distributed independently in the documents of the cluster, then $I(\vec{x})$ is the required expression. Since the distributions are not necessarily independent, corrections are made by incorporating dependencies of terms in pairs involving $\text{corr}(i, j)$, dependencies of terms in triplets involving $\text{corr}(i, j, t)$, etc. If all possible combinations of term dependencies between terms are taken into consideration, then the expansion is exact.

The probability that a document in C has exactly u terms in common with Q is $\sum D(\vec{x})$, where the summation is over all vectors $\vec{x}$ having exactly u x's equal to 1. Applying the summation to Expression (10.4) and simplifying, the probability is

$$\sum I(\vec{x}) + \sum_{i<j} \text{var}(i, j) \left(\sum \text{Dep}(i, j)(\vec{x}) \right) + \sum_{i<j<t} \text{var}(i, j, t) \left(\sum \text{Dep}(i, j, t)(\vec{x}) \right)$$

$$+ \cdots + \text{var}(1, 2, \ldots, k) \, \text{Dep}(1, 2, \ldots, k) \quad (10.5)$$

where $\text{var}(i, j)$, the *covariance* of the ith and jth terms, is $\text{corr}(i, j) \cdot (r_i \cdot r_j \cdot (1 - r_i) \cdot (1 - r_j))$, and $\text{var}(i, j, t)$, the covariance of the three terms, is $\text{corr}(i, j, t) \cdot (r_i \cdot r_j \cdot r_t \cdot (1 - r_i) \cdot (1 - r_j) \cdot (1 - r_t))$. Other covariances are similarly defined. $\text{Dep}(i, j)(\vec{x})$ is given by

$$\frac{r_i^{x_i} \cdot (1 - r_i)^{1-x_i} \cdot (x_i - r_i) \cdot [r_j^{x_j} \cdot (1 - r_j)^{1-x_j} \cdot (x_j - r_j)] \cdot \prod_{t \neq i, t \neq j} r_t^{x_t} \cdot (1 - r_t)^{1-x_t}}{[r_i \cdot r_j \cdot (1 - r_i) \cdot (1 - r_j)]}$$

$\text{Dep}(i, j, t)(\vec{x})$ is similarly defined. If terms i and j are independent, then both $\text{corr}(i, j)$ and $\text{var}(i, j)$ are zero and therefore there is no need to compute $\text{Dep}(i, j)(\vec{x})$. The cluster representative contains the r's and those var(i, j)'s and var(i, j, t)'s that are significantly different from zero.

In Expression (10.5), recall that $\sum I(\vec{x})$ is computed by means of the coefficients of the product of the linear polynomial (10.3). It turns out that the other terms in (10.5) can be computed in a similar manner. Consider the pair of terms i and j. $\sum \text{Dep}(i, j)(\vec{x})$, where the summation is over all vectors $\vec{x}$ with exactly u 1s in each such vector, is given by the coefficients of the following product of linear polynomials.

$$(X-1)^2 \prod_{t\neq i, t\neq j} (r_t X + (1 - r_t)) \tag{10.6}$$

When Expression (10.6) is compared with Expression (10.3), we observe that $r_i X + (1 - r_i)$ in (10.3) is replaced by $X - 1$ in (10.6); similarly, $r_j X + (1 - r_j)$ in (10.3) is replaced by $X - 1$. Thus, if terms i and j are dependent, their linear polynomials are replaced by $(X - 1)^2$. After the coefficient is obtained, it is multiplied by var(i, j) and then added to those obtained by employing Expression (10.3). It is clear that Expression (10.6) can be obtained by Expression (10.3) in $O(k)$ time. This is repeated for every pair of dependent terms. Therefore, if $O(k)$ pairs of terms are highly dependent, their effects can be computed in time $O(k^2)$. When term dependencies in triplets need to be incorporated, each of the three terms, say term p, would have its linear polynomial $r_p X + (1 - r_p)$ in (10.3) replaced by $X - 1$, as in (10.6). The resulting expression for the dependent triplet $\{i, j, t\}$ is $(X - 1)^3 \prod_{s\neq i, s\neq j, s\neq t}(r_s X + (1 - r_s))$. Again, after the coefficient of the product of the polynomials is obtained, it is multiplied by var(i, j, t), if terms i, j, and t form the triplet. This is repeated for every triplet of terms that are dependent.

It has been verified experimentally that as more and more term dependencies are incorporated, it is usually the case that the approximation to the actual distribution is closer than the approximation using the assumption of term independence. However, it is not always true, because a truncated Bahadur-Lazarsfeld expansion may even give a negative value, which is not a probability.

10.2.3 Terms Are Nonbinary and Independent

In this case, terms in queries as well as in documents can have weights other than 0 and 1. The representative of a cluster is now defined to be $([r_1, w_1], [r_2, w_2], \dots, [r_n, w_n])$, where r_i is the probability that a document in the cluster has the ith term, as defined before, and w_i is the average weight of the ith term in those documents having it in the cluster. Suppose in a cluster of five documents, the occurrences of the ith term are 2, 0, 3, 0, and 1. Then r_i is 3/5 and w_i is $2 = (2 + 3 + 1)/3$.

Suppose the user query has the first k terms and is represented by $(q_1, q_2, \dots, q_k)$. When a document in the cluster matches the ith term in the query, the expected increase in similarity due to this term is $w_i \cdot q_i$. This occurs with probability r_i. This event can be represented by the function $r_i \cdot X^{w_i \cdot q_i} + (1 - r_i)$. It can then be shown that if each occurence of the ith term has weight w_i in those documents containing it, the coefficient of X^s in the following generating function is the probability that a document in the cluster has similarity s with the query.

$$\prod_{i=1}^{k} (r_i \cdot X^{w_i \cdot q_i} + (1 - r_i)) \tag{10.7}$$

Example 10.7 Suppose the query is (1, 1, 1), there are five documents in a cluster, and their representations with respect to the query are (2, 0, 2), (0, 1, 1), (2, 0, 0), (0, 0, 3), and (0, 0, 0). Then ($[r_1, w_1], [r_2, w_2], [r_3, w_3]$) are ([0.4, 2], [0.2, 1], [0.6, 2]). The generating function is

$$(0.4 \cdot X^2 + 0.6)(0.2 \cdot X + 0.8)(0.6 \cdot X^2 + 0.4)$$

Consider the coefficient of X^3 in the generating function. It is the sum of $r_1 \cdot r_2 \cdot (1 - r_3)$ and $(1 - r_1) \cdot r_2 \cdot r_3$. The former is the probability that a document has exactly the first and second query terms with average weights 2 and 1, respectively. The average similarity of such a document is 3. (Note that the weights of the first and the second terms of such a document may not be exactly 2 and 1, respectively.) The latter is the probability that a document has exactly the last two query terms, and the corresponding average similarity is also 3. The coefficient of X^3 in the above polynomial is 0.104. This is the estimated probability that a document in the cluster has similarity 3 with the query. Note that the actual probability is $\frac{1}{5} = 0.2$ because of the document with representation (0, 0, 3). This document has term 3 in common with the query. In the estimation, we judge that documents having similarity 3 with the query have the characteristics that the set of terms in common with the query is either the set {term 1, term 2} or the set {term 2, term 3}.   ∎

10.2.4 Terms Are Nonbinary and Arbitrarily Dependent

In this case, term dependencies are captured by the Bahadur-Lazarsfeld expansion and each component of a representative has a weight as well as a probability, as in the last subsection. Specifically, the representative R of a cluster contains the significant covariances among the terms, as in Section 10.2.2, and contains the probabilities of occurrences of the terms and their average weights, i.e., ($[r_1, w_1], [r_2, w_2], \ldots, [r_n, w_n]$), as in Section 10.2.3. Following the same line of reasoning as given in the preceding cases, the coefficient of X^s in the following generating function is the probability that a document in the cluster has similarity s with the query. In the generating functions, dependencies among terms are taken into consideration by the Bahadur-Lazarsfeld expansion.

$$\prod_{t=1}^{k} [r_t \cdot X^{w_t \cdot q_t} + (1 - r_t)] + \sum_{i<j} \text{var}(i, j) \prod_{t \neq i, t \neq j} [r_t \cdot X^{w_t \cdot q_t} + (1 - r_t)](X^{w_i \cdot q_i} - 1)(X^{w_j \cdot q_j} - 1)$$

$$+ \cdots + \text{var}(1, 2, \ldots, k) \prod_{t=1}^{k} (X^{w_t \cdot q_t} - 1)$$

Similar to Equation (10.6), the above expressions incorporates the dependency between term i and term j by means of the polynomial $(X^{w_i \cdot q_i} - 1)(X^{w_j \cdot q_j} - 1) \prod_{t \neq i, t \neq j} (r_t X^{w_t \cdot q_t} + (1 - r_t))$. Essentially, $(r_i X^{w_i \cdot q_i} + (1 - r_i))(r_j X^{w_j \cdot q_j} + (1 - r_j))$, which is the polynomial that would be obtained if term i and term j were independent, is replaced by $(X^{w_i \cdot q_i} - 1)(X^{w_j \cdot q_j} - 1)$. After the coefficients are obtained, they are multiplied by var(i, j) and then added to those obtained in Equation (10.7). The same approach applies to dependent triplets, quadruplets, etc.

Example 10.8 Consider the documents and the query in Example 10.7. The covariances between pairs of terms are $\text{var}(1, 2) = -0.08$, $\text{var}(2, 3) = 0.08$, and $\text{var}(1, 3) = -0.04$. Ignoring the dependency of the three terms—i.e., assuming that $\text{var}(1, 2, 3) = 0$—the following generating function is obtained.

$$(0.4 \cdot X^2 + 0.6)(0.2 \cdot X + 0.8)(0.6 \cdot X^2 + 0.4) - 0.08(0.6 \cdot X^2 + 0.4)(X^2 - 1)(X - 1)$$
$$+ 0.08(0.4 \cdot X^2 + 0.6)(X - 1)(X^2 - 1) - 0.04(0.2 \cdot X + 0.8)(X^2 - 1)(X^2 - 1)$$

The coefficient of X^3 in the above function is 0.152. As the actual probability that a document has similarity 3 is 0.2, the estimation using the above generating function is more accurate than that using the independence assumption. ■

If a cluster is treated as a database, then the cluster search problem becomes the problem of locating the databases (for example, in the Internet) that are potentially useful to a given query. This is known as the *resource discovery problem*.

Exercises

10.1 Identify all maximal complete subgraphs in the given graph.

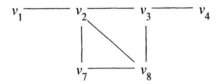

10.2 Draw a graph in which the number of connected components is larger than the number of maximal complete subgraphs. Explain your answer.

10.3 What is the smallest time complexity for any graph-theoretical algorithm? (Hint: What is the time complexity for defining the vertices and edges of a graph?)

10.4 Provide a procedure that decomposes a node having too many children (documents) into two nodes such that each of the two new nodes has approximately the same number of children and the sum of the similarities of D_i with D_j, where D_i and D_j are within each node, is more or less maximized.

10.5 Suppose the access patterns are (A_1, A_2), (A_1, A_3), (A_2, A_3), (B_1, B_2), (B_1, B_3), and (B_2, B_3). Specifically, assume that records identified by the same character are accessed very frequently and records identified by different characters are not accessed at all. Use examples to show the following situations.

(a) The learning automaton algorithm converges to the correct configuration.

(b) If case (a) of Subcase 3 is absent (i.e., when the condition for Subcase 3 is satisfied, always execute according to case (b)), then the desired configuration is not reached.

10.6 Identify conditions that can be handled by algorithm Adapt but are not explicitly handled by the learning automaton.

10.7 Identify situations in which adaptive algorithms such as algorithm Adapt and the learning automaton may not work well.

10.8 Suppose the representative of a cluster is initialized to be $(\frac{1}{4}, \frac{1}{4}, \frac{1}{4}, \frac{1}{4})$, where there are four terms for each document. Compute the representative for the exponentiated gradient algorithm for the document $D_1 = (\frac{1}{4}, 0, \frac{1}{2}, \frac{1}{4})$ and then the document $D_2 = (\frac{1}{2}, 0, \frac{1}{2}, 0)$, assuming that both documents belong to the cluster. What is the time complexity of the exponentiated gradient algorithm? Let the rate of learning parameter v be 0.1.

10.9 In Example 10.5, the documents D_1 and D_2 overlap with the documents D_3 and D_4 in two terms. Suppose there are six terms (instead of seven terms in the example) in the set of all terms, each of the documents has exactly four terms (the same as in the example), and the documents D_1 and D_2 overlap with the documents D_3 and D_4 in two terms (more precisely, D_1 and D_2 remain unchanged, but documents D_3 and D_4 are both $(0, 0, 1, 1, 1, 1)$). Compute $\sum_{i=1}^{n} c_{ii}$. Comment on the use of this quantity on the estimation of the number of clusters.

10.10 The documents in a cluster are $D_1 = (1, 0, 1, 0), D_2 = (1, 1, 0, 1)$, and $D_3 = (0, 1, 0, 0)$. The query $Q = (0, 1, 1, 1)$ is submitted. Use the Binary Independence Model.

  (a) Compute the probability that a document has exactly two terms in common with Q, assuming that terms are independently distributed in the cluster.

  (b) Write down the polynomial with respect to each term. Then multiply the polynomials together to obtain the probability that a document has exactly two terms in common with Q.

10.11 The documents in a cluster are $D_1 = (2, 0, 3, 0), D_2 = (1, 1, 0, 1)$, and $D_3 = (0, 2, 0, 0)$. The query $Q = (0, 2, 1, 1)$ is submitted. Use the Non-binary Independence Model. Write down the polynomial with respect to each term. Then multiply the polynomials together to obtain the probability that documents have similarity s with the query, for various values of s.

Bibliographic Notes

Many people have contributed to the clustering method using connected components, including having the clusters in hierarchies; see, for example, [90, 334, 378]. As pointed out, the use of maximal connected components in clustering is not as practical as connected compounds, because of its potentially high complexity.

The one-pass method can be found in [315]. The use of a balanced tree is due to Robert Dattola, whose algorithm can be found in [313].

The learning automaton approach is due to [283]. However, in [283], there are no cases (a) and (b) for Subcase 3; case (b) is always executed. As a result, the algorithm may not converge even if the access pattern is stable. The introduction of case (a) to permit convergence and the initial assignment of all records to the boundary states to speed up convergence are due to [128]. The adaptive record clustering approach is due to [406]. The exponentiated gradient method is from [208]. Its use in information retrieval is due to [228]. The sampling approach is due to [91].

The estimation of the number of clusters is due to [53].

This version of estimating the number of documents having many terms in common with the query under the term independence assumption is from [401]. The Bahadur-Lazarsfeld expansion can be found in [113]. The estimation using the expansion and the generating functions is by [217]. The approach in which both nonbinary term weights and dependencies between terms are incorporated into the estimation process is given in [261]. Other approaches to determining which clusters to search can be found in [54, 146].

11

Image and Video Retrieval

People understand the contents of pictures and videos much faster than they understand text. This is expressed by the old saying that "a picture is worth a thousand words." People also enjoy seeing pictures and videos. Thus, the use of pictures and videos is exploding. (Throughout this chapter, the words *picture* and *image* will be used interchangeably.) With storage cost decreasing rather rapidly, it is feasible to have databases containing numerous images or videos. There are many applications involving their use. Some typical applications are photograph retrieval in which there is a database of photographs and a user is interested in finding some photographs fitting certain descriptions; image retrieval in which images of the Earth or other planets are taken by satellites and images with certain known features are desired (this is rather common for NASA applications); and retrieval of images for medical use, in which case the images might have been taken by X ray, MRI, or other techniques. Image/video retrieval can be used for security applications. For example, cameras constantly take pictures of customers in a bank, and it is desired to find images in which some people are holding guns.

It is possible to build a customized image/video database system for each application. However, that would be too costly, as each new application requires the development of substantial software. Clearly, it would be ideal to have an image database system that works for most applications. If this can be achieved, then the success of relational database systems can be carried over to image database systems. Since query processing is our main concern, the aim of this chapter is to define components that are essential for most image retrieval

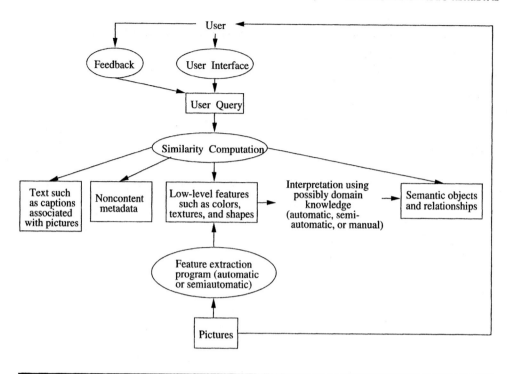

FIGURE 11.1   The Components of a Picture Retrieval System

applications. The components for image retrieval include the representation of the contents of images in the database as well as for formulating user queries. In either case, the representation can be in the form of text, high-level semantics that are easily understood by end users, and/or in the form of low-level image features, such as colors and textures, which may be extracted automatically by image analysis programs. In the case of text representation, enough information has been provided in Chapter 9 and further elaboration is unnecessary. It would be ideal if low-level image features could be converted automatically into high-level semantics using some domain information. So far, there is no general reliable technique for such a conversion unless the domain is rather narrow. The skin cancer detection application described in this chapter permits automatic feature extraction and interpretation of the features in terms of properties that can be understood by humans. In the absence of automatic conversion, either these low-level image features are directly utilized for retrieval or manual or semiautomatic conversion is carried out.

In Figure 11.1 the various components of an image retrieval system are circled. The user interface component facilitates a user in formulating a user query. Metadata, which are data describing the contents of the pictures, can be in one of the following forms:

1. Text associated with the pictures

2. Low-level features, such as colors and textures, that are extracted by feature extraction programs

3. Objects, their properties, and their relationships that are interpreted from the low-level features automatically, semiautomatically, or manually

4. A combination of the above

Metadata not involving the visual contents of pictures, such as dates on which the pictures are taken and the mediums, may also be associated with the pictures.

The similarity computation component of the system uses the metadata and the user query to compute the similarities of the pictures with respect to the query. Pictures that are sufficiently similar to the user query are retrieved and presented to the user. As in text retrieval, there can be a user feedback component to reformulate the user's query, based on relevance information from the user. This component will not be elaborated in this chapter.

The first section of this chapter discusses the representation of contents, common image features, and the similarity computation mechanism. Video retrieval is discussed in the second section.

11.1 Picture Retrieval

11.1.1 Picture Representation

We first sketch the description of the contents of pictures at the user's semantic level. The *entity-relationship model* or the *semantic net model* may be used to represent the contents of a picture.

The entities in a picture are the objects. For example, if a man, a woman, and a car are in a picture, then the entities are the man, the woman, and the car. Each entity usually has a number of properties. For example, the properties associated with the man can be *young*, *wearing glasses*, and *wearing a suit*. There may be relationships between entities in a picture. Relationships between entities may be roughly classified into two types: *spatial* or *action*. A spatial relationship between two entities indicates the relative locations of the two objects. For example, the man is to the left of the woman. Typical spatial relationships are *left of*, *right of*, *in front of*, *behind*, *above*, *below*, *inside*, and *overlaps*. It is possible to incorporate the concept of distance into spatial relationships. For example, a man can be to the left of another man within a certain distance. Sometimes distance need not be captured precisely. For example, a picture can be partitioned into regions such that objects within the same region do not have any *left of*, *above*, or *in front of* relationships with respect to each other and the distance between two objects is assumed to be the number of regions separating the regions that contain the objects. An action relationship between a set of entities is an action that can be visualized from the picture. For example, the man is driving the car. A relationship, whether spatial or nonspatial, can be *symmetric* or *asymmetric*. An asymmetric relationship, such as driving, has a subject-entity, such as the man, and an object-entity, such as the car. The spatial relationship *overlaps* is symmetric, because there is no difference between *A overlaps B* (*A overlaps B* here means that there is a common area or volume between A and B) and *B overlaps A*. The spatial relationships identified above are binary relationships, as only two entities are involved. An action relationship may involve two or more entities. For example, if two teams are playing basketball against each other, the number of players is usually more than two. To facilitate this representation, the concept of a *group* is introduced. In this case, all members of one team are placed within one group, say group1, while all members of another team are placed into another group, say group2, and the action relationship is (group1, plays basketball, group2). This group concept can also be applied to the simplification of the specification of spatial relationships. For example, if A is to the left of B and A is to the left of C, then instead of stating the two spatial relationships, A is placed into group1 and B and C are placed into group2 and the spatial relationships are represented by (group1, left-of, group2). It is possible that there are multiple relationships between two groups of entities. For example, a man (as the only member of one group) is inside a car (as the only member of another group). At the same time, he is driving the car. Clearly, these are two different relationships. A common problem in using the entity-relationship model is the classical type mismatch problem. In other words, the three types *entity*, *property* (*attribute*), and *relationship* may be used interchangeably by different users. A property of a person such as *wearing a suit* can also be visualized as a relationship *wearing* between the two entities *person* and *suit*. We will address this issue in Section 11.1.2.

In addition to the spatial and action relationships, *composition* relationships can also be of use. For example, a complicated object such as a car can be composed of several smaller objects such as a car body and several tires. In many pictures, there is a foreground and a background. It may be desirable to make a distinction between the two, as it is easier for the user to specify his or her intention and for the system to retrieve what is intended. In addition to the visual information that can be observed from the pictures, other information obtained elsewhere, such as from the captions of pictures, may be included. For example, the name of a person in a picture is usually not observable from the picture, unless the person is well known. The relationship of two persons—for example, one person is the father of another—is also not immediately known from observing a picture but could be stated in an accompanying text. Thus, there are two types of metadata: visual and nonvisual, the visual metadata being observable from the pictures.

The description given above is suitable for people to understand, but may be difficult for computers to generate automatically. Furthermore, different users may have different interpretations of the same picture. Thus it is desirable to have different representations of a picture. At the lowest level, the *raw data level*, the pixels are stored. At a higher level, the *image feature level*, lines, contours, shapes, color distributions, etc., will be recognized. In order to associate semantics with objects perceived by humans, domain knowledge is utilized to convert features in the image feature level to objects and relationships in the *user semantic level*. For example, if the shape of an object is circular and the domain of interest is basketball, then the object may be recognized to be a basketball. However, automatic recognition of the type of an object in a general setting is a very challenging task. For example, since objects may overlap in a picture, the shapes of objects in a picture may differ from their original shapes. Even determining the boundaries of individual objects that overlap is by no means trivial. Thus, recognizing a human or differentiating a man from a woman is not easy. Because of the uncertainties of recognizing object types, systems have been built utilizing the image features instead of objects and relationships at the users' semantic level. The common features employed in these systems are shapes, textures, and colors.

Characterization by color can be performed by using the *red*, *green*, and *blue* components (RGB), as each color pixel is a linear combination of the three components. An equivalent characterization is by using *hue*, *saturation*, and *intensity* (HSI), defined as follows.

$$H = \cos^{-1} \frac{2R - G - B}{2\sqrt{(R - G)^2 + (R - B) \cdot (G - B)}}$$

$$S = 1 - 3 \cdot \frac{\min\{R, G, B\}}{R + G + B}$$

$$I = \frac{R + G + B}{3}$$

It has been observed that the latter characterization could be better for recognizing real-life objects, because hue is not much affected by the amount of light. Very often, a histogram is obtained to characterize an image, an object, or a concept; the horizontal axis of the histogram represents the different distinct colors, and the vertical axis represents, for each distinct color, the number or percentage of pixels having that color. Clearly, this can be represented as an n-dimensional vector, where the ith component is the percentage or number of pixels in the ith color.

The shape of an object can be characterized by a set of features such as *area, circularity, eccentricity*, and *major axis orientation*. The area of an object is simply the number of pixels within the boundary of the object. Circularity is the ratio of the square of the perimeter to the area. This has a fixed value for circles, as the radius of the circle will cancel out from the numerator and the denominator of the ratio. Eccentricity is essentially the ratio of the smaller axis to the bigger axis, if the object is an ellipse. It can be obtained by taking the ratio of the smallest eigenvalue to the largest eigenvalue of the covariance matrix from the pixels in the boundary of the object. The major axis orientation is the direction of the eigenvector corresponding to the largest eigenvalue. Clearly, other features characterizing shapes are possible. For example, after the boundary and the center of gravity of an object have been determined, rays at constant angle can be drawn from the center of gravity to the boundary. The lengths of these rays can be used to characterize the shape of the object. For example, a circle will have rays all of the same length, and an ellipse will have rays varying in length from the length of the major axis to that of the minor axis.

Texture is a visual pattern in which a large number of visible elements are densely and evenly arranged (see Figure 11.2 for an example). A visual element (sometimes called a *texel* or a *texon*) is a set of pixels that has a certain gray level or color characteristic and is repeated. In essence, an image region can be regarded as having a texture as long as the complete region can be regenerated from a subwindow of the region with repetitions.[1] Some properties associated with texture are *contrast, coarseness*, and *directionality*. Contrast is a measure of local variations, based on the intensity histogram.[2] A texture with greater variation in the intensity is said to have higher contrast (see Figure 11.3) than one with lower variation (see Figure 11.4). Coarseness measures the scale of the texture. For a fixed window size, a texture with a smaller number of texture elements is said to be more coarse than one with a larger number of elements (see Figures 11.5 and 11.6). Directionality describes whether an image has a favored direction. It therefore describes how the visual elements are arranged in the

---

[1] The regeneration may possibly involve simple transformations such as scaling and rotating.

[2] Intensity means the brightness in the case of a gray-level image and any measure of color perception, such as hue, in the case of a color image.

FIGURE 11.2   A Sample Texture

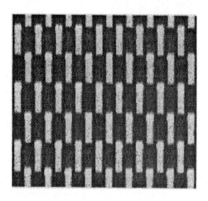

FIGURE 11.3   High-Contrast Texture   **FIGURE 11.4   Low-Contrast Texture**

pattern. Texture can be utilized for detecting areas of nature, such as crops and trees, as well as objects such as human faces and tumors.

Each of these features in a picture (color, shape, or texture) can be quantified. Thus, an image or a portion of an image can be represented by a high-dimensional vector. For example, if there are n possible colors and a picture has $x_i\%$ of pixels of color i, $1 \leq i \leq n$, then the vector $(x_1, x_2, \ldots, x_n)$ represents the color of the image. (This vector is called the *color histogram* of the image. Although this is a reasonable characterization of an image, there may be multiple images having the same histogram.) Similarly, another vector can be utilized to represent the same image for a different type of feature, such as texture. In principle, these vectors can be concatenated to form a long vector representing the different characteristics of the image.

In the usual operation of these image-feature-oriented systems, the user supplies a given picture and the system retrieves pictures with similar features. For example, the user may provide the picture of a fish, which may be hand-drawn by the user or already stored in the system, and indicate that the criterion of retrieval is the shape. The system will retrieve and

FIGURE 11.5 Dense Texture

FIGURE 11.6 Coarse Texture

display fish of similar shapes. Surprisingly, certain abstract concepts can also be expressed by image features. For example, the concept *sunset* can be defined to be a picture having certain percentages of red, orange, and yellow. A combination of different characteristics instead of a single characteristic can be utilized. For example, a user may specify that pictures are to be retrieved on the basis of a combination of the color, texture, and shape of a given picture. The significance of each component in the combination can also be specified. It should be noted that characterization by low-level features may be inaccurate, causing some irrelevant pictures to be retrieved. For example, a picture having the desired percentages of red, orange, and yellow may have nothing to do with a sunset. Furthermore, systems utilizing image features alone may have difficulty accurately retrieving pictures having multiple objects. On the other hand, because image features are extracted automatically, they are less dependent on users, who may have different interpretations of the contents of a picture. When humans are involved in manual extraction of metadata, errors are likely to occur. Automatic methods are less error-prone and are more efficient.

It is possible that pictures have some metadata that have been manually or semiautomatically generated, some low-level features that have been generated automatically, and some text describing the pictures. The text may come together with the pictures. For example, in magazines, each picture usually has an accompanying text. Thus a picture may be characterized by a combination of low-level features, some objects and relationships at the users' semantic level, and some text.

Representation of User Queries and User Interface

The representation of a user query is the same as the representation of a picture. If the user is allowed to specify his or her intention at the semantic level, he or she will specify the entities, their properties, and the relationships among the entities in the desired pictures. On the other hand, if image features are available for the specification, the user can indicate the features of interest and their relative weights. For example, a user can specify a relative weighting of 70% color and 30% texture. This indicates that color plays a more important role in the computation of similarities (or distances). In specifying a low-level feature characteristic such as color,

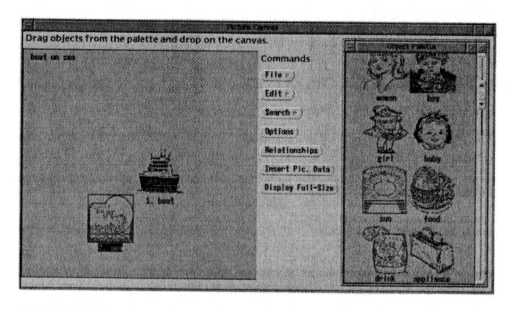

FIGURE 11.7 A Sample Query Canvas

a color palette may be provided, enabling a user to choose a set of colors with a certain percentage for each chosen color. Several features may be jointly specified. For example, a user can choose the shape to be circular and the colors in this circle to be 50% red and 50% orange. Alternatively, a picture stored by the system or supplied by the user may be used as the user query. Tools are usually provided with which the user can draw a picture, if needed. In such situations, feature extraction programs have to be invoked to compute a vector representing the feature characteristics of the user query. Sometimes, a user is allowed to specify certain keywords or a paragraph. With keywords or texts, text retrieval techniques can be employed. Irrespective of the way the query is specified, it is desirable to allow a user to indicate the number of pictures to be retrieved.

We now concentrate on the specification of users' queries at the semantic level. In many situations, it is desirable to assume that the user is not trained in the use of query languages. In other words, a graphical interface with icons and a drag-and-drop facility is likely to be acceptable. Figure 11.7 shows such an interface.

The following scenario may arise. The user is provided with a representation area where a sketch of the desired picture in the form of icons representing entities will be displayed. First, the user specifies objects of interest from several prespecified types in the icon window. The prespecified types are those that are commonly encountered in the application. After the type of an entity is specified, the system displays several attributes of the chosen type. For example, if the user specifies a man, the attributes that are displayed may consist of age, height, clothing, position in picture, state of motion, etc. (see Figure 11.8). Since the exact values of the attributes are unlikely to be specified by the user, a prespecified range of values or *fuzzy labels* (see Chapter 6) or both can be employed (see Figure 11.9). For example, under the attribute age, the fuzzy labels *young, middle-aged, old,* etc., together with a range of values for each fuzzy label (for example, a range associated with young can be between

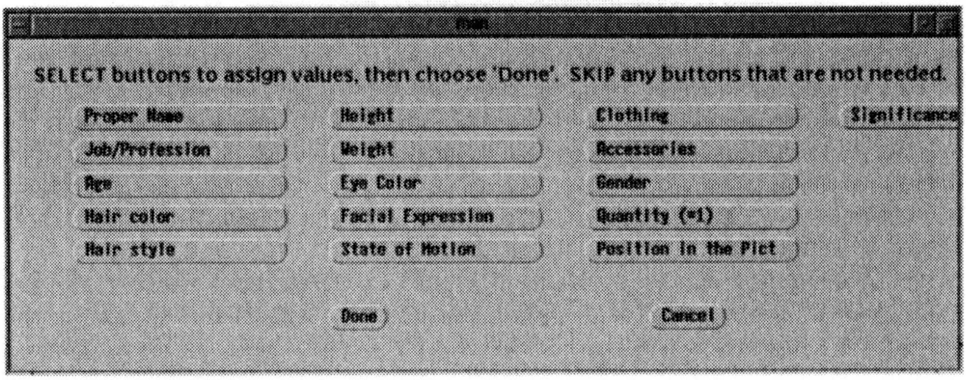

FIGURE 11.8   A Sample Attribute Set for Object Type Man

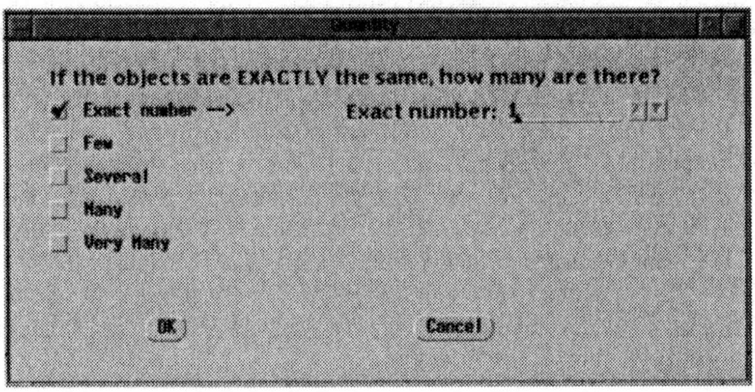

FIGURE 11.9   Fuzzy Attribute Values

20 and 35) can be prespecified, and the user is asked to click on one of these values. Precise specification of the clothes worn by a person is not easy. It may be approximated by a set of prespecified clothes, such as suit, tie, shirt, shorts, etc., and the user is to check off a subset from this set. Some attribute values, such as the positions of objects in the picture, may be automatically obtained. In the user representation area, the screen is divided into a grid of $m \times n$ regions, where m and n are the number of divisions along the horizontal and the vertical axes, respectively. When a user specifies an entity from several entity types, the user also drags the entity into the user representation area. This automatically registers the position of the entity in the picture. If a user's entity is not within one of the prespecified entity types, the user can specify its type using his or her own words. A prestored thesaurus will match the user's entity with those in the dictionary. Each of the matched words in the dictionary is shown to the user, who picks the desired one. The set of attributes for that chosen entity are the attributes used to describe the entity specified by the user.

This process of specifying an entity and its attribute values is repeated until all the entities in the picture are identified in the user representation area. For each relationship, the user first specifies whether it is a spatial or an action relationship. All spatial relationships are prespecified, and the user picks the desired one. On the other hand, the user can use his or her own words to specify an action. After indicating whether the relationship should be symmetric or asymmetric, the user identifies the elements in each of the two groups participating in the relationship. Each relationship together with the group elements will be displayed in textual form in one corner of the user representation area. After all relationships are specified, the user will examine whether the information is accurate or whether changes need to be made. If no change is needed, then the retrieve button is pressed.

The above description assumes that the user prefers a graphical user interface. Alternatively, a formal query language interface that is an extension of SQL to retrieve pictures can be utilized. The extended SQL language has additional types of predicates described as follows:

Object type. This compares a variable in the query with an object type. For example, X is man compares the variable X with the object type *man*. The variable is associated with an object in the picture and the predicate X is man is evaluated. Clearly, in order that the predicate can be evaluated, the types of the objects in the picture have to be recognized automatically, semiautomatically, or manually. If the recognition is done automatically, it is likely that the object type is not determined with 100% accuracy. Since the predicate may not be satisfied completely (possibly because of the inability to recognize the object with 100% accuracy), the evaluation of the predicate may yield a value between 0 and 1, which represent "definitely not true" and "definitely true," respectively.

Other comparison operators are possible. For example, a predicate such as the is-a predicate can be utilized. The predicate X is-a human is true if the object associated with X is a man, because *man is-a human* is true. After a variable, say X, is associated with an object, a predicate involving an attribute of the object type can be evaluated. For example, if X is associated with person, then $X.age$ = "young" can be evaluated according to fuzzy logic (see Chapter 6).

Spatial relationship type. A predicate of this type evaluates the relative positions of two objects. The evaluation result is either true or false—no fuzziness or degree of satisfaction other than 0 or 1 will be obtained. As an example, the evaluation of X left of Y against a picture yields true or false depending on whether the object associated with X in the picture is to the left of the object associated with Y in the picture.

Action relationship type. An action predicate is of the form $(\{X_1, X_2, \ldots, X_n\}$, ac, $\{Y_1, \ldots, Y_m\})$, where each X_i and each Y_i denote object variables and ac is an action. For example, when the action predicate (X, handshake, Y) is evaluated against the picture, X and Y may be assigned certain objects and a similarity between 0 and 1 is assigned to the predicate with respect to the picture, depending to the extent "X handshakes Y" is satisfied. A more detailed description of how action relationships are matched will be given in Section 11.1.2.

Image feature type. A user can provide an image I and request that a desired picture should contain an object similar to the object contained in I. For example, X similar to Picture-ID when evaluated against a picture yields a similarity value if an object in the picture that is associated with X is found to be similar to the object in the picture with the given Picture-ID. It is assumed that the given picture has a single object. The feature to be compared to yield the similarity value can be a single characteristic, such as color, shape, or texture, or a weighted combination of characteristics.

There may be multiple predicates in a query. Each predicate against a picture yields a degree of satisfaction or a similarity value. It should be noted that true and false are special cases of similarity values and an evaluation of a predicate involving fuzzy labels and numbers yields a degree of satisfaction between 0 and 1, which can be considered as a similarity value. These degrees or similarity values need to be combined together to form a similarity for the entire picture. One way of doing it is by making use of a similarity function such as the one to be given in the next subsection. The following is an example of an extended SQL query:

```
select picture P
from collection C
where X is "man" and Y is "fish" and X left-of Y and X.age = "young"
     and Y similar-to Picture-ID 10 (shape)
```

In this query, it is assumed that the variables X and Y refer to objects within a picture referenced by P, the last predicate is a feature comparison predicate in which shape is the only feature to be compared, and the picture supplied by the user has ID = 10.

11.1.2 Picture Retrieval

As mentioned in the preceding subsection, representations of the contents of pictures and queries can be at the semantic level, at the feature level, by text, or by a combination of these. Common to these representations is that similarity-based retrieval is likely to be most suitable. As pointed out in Chapter 9, it is likely that the contents of the documents and those of the queries are not precisely represented or the users may not have a clear idea of what precisely they want to retrieve. As a result, exact retrieval is not appropriate. The same situation applies to picture retrieval. If the query specification is a mixture of different representations, then the similarity of a picture with respect to the query is a weighted average of the similarities due to the different representations. We have covered the situation of text retrieval in Chapter 9. We now consider situations in which image features and semantic information are utilized for retrieval as follows.

Retrieval Based on Image Features

If image features are used, then a distance function (an inverse of a similarity function) can be specified. For example, if a color histogram is utilized, then the distance between two images can be given by the sum of the absolute differences between the numbers of pixels having the same color in the two histograms. Alternatively, the square root of the sum of the squares of the differences (i.e., the Euclidean distance) can be utilized. In either case, each histogram is represented as an n-dimensional vector, where n is the number of colors in the histogram. If the number of dimensions is very high, dimension reduction techniques should be used as indicated below.

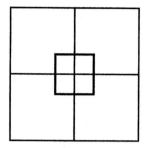

FIGURE 11.10   Five Rectangles

When image features involving color, shape, and texture are used to characterize the contents of pictures, the representation is usually in the form of an n-dimensional vector, where each entry of the vector is the magnitude of a subfeature in the picture or an object in the picture. The number of dimensions depends on the type of features. In the case of texture, a three-dimensional space with the dimensions representing coarseness, contrast, and directionality could be sufficient. Thus, there may not be a need to reduce the number of dimensions for texture representation. However, the number of dimensions associated with color and shape features is usually very large. In the case of color, the QBIC (Query By Image Content) system uses 256 or 64 dimensions, with each dimension representing a range of colors. In the case of shape, QBIC uses approximately 20 dimensions. Multidimensional structures such as R*-trees, quadtrees, and grid files are often employed to speed up the retrieval process. Unfortunately, it is known that when the number of dimensions, n, increases, the retrieval time increases rapidly. As an example, consider four neighboring rectangles in a two-dimensional space as shown in Figure 11.10. A query, which is represented by the small rectangle, intersects all of the four large rectangles. Thus, all four large rectangles need to be retrieved. When the number of dimensions is increased by 1, there are eight neighboring hyperrectangles in the three-dimensional space and a query represented by a small hyperrectangle in the middle needs to retrieve the eight hyperrectangles. For high-dimensional space, retrieval can be even more time consuming. One way to gain efficiency is to reduce the dimensionality by suitable transformations. Let D be a distance function such as the Euclidean distance; if $(x_1, x_2, \ldots, x_n)$ and $(y_1, y_2, \ldots, y_n)$ are two points in the n-dimensional space, the Euclidean distance between the points is $\sqrt{\sum_{i=1}^{n}(x_i - y_i)^2}$. The similarity of the two points can be taken to be the inverse of their distance.

Let T be a transformation that reduces the n-dimensional space to an m-dimensional space, with m much smaller than n. Let v_1 and v_2 be two vectors in the n-dimensional space. Their transformed vectors are $T(v_1)$ and $T(v_2)$. The property desired for the transformation is that the distance between the transformed vectors be no larger than that between the original vectors. This can be stated precisely as

$$D(T(v_1), T(v_2)) \leq D(v_1, v_2) \tag{11.1}$$

The reason why this property is essential is as follows. Suppose in the original n-dimensional space, vectors that are within distance d of a given image v are to be retrieved.

This corresponds to obtaining all images that are sufficiently close (having similarity $\geq 1/d$) to v. By using a multidimensional data structure such as R*-tree, all those desired images in $S = \{s \mid s$ is an image and $D(s, v) \leq d\}$ can be retrieved. Suppose the space has been transformed using transformation T and the multidimensional structure is applied to the transformed vectors. Let the threshold for retrieval in the transformed space be the same as that in the original space, i.e., d. Then, by Inequality (11.1), any desired image s in S satisfies $D(T(s), T(v)) \leq d$ and therefore will be retrieved by the multidimensional structure on the transformed vectors with threshold d. It should be noted that some vector, say s', that is retrieved using the transformed space, i.e., $D(T(s'), T(v)) \leq d$, may not satisfy $D(s', v) \leq d$, since (11.1) is an inequality instead of an equality. In order to eliminate the undesired retrieved images, each image retrieved by the multidimensional structure in the reduced space is compared against the image v, and any image having distance larger than d is discarded.

One transformation, known as the discrete Fourier transform, which guarantees the satisfaction of Inequality (11.1), is given as follows. Let $(x_1, x_2, \ldots, x_n)$ be a vector in the original space. The discrete Fourier transform of the vector is $(y_1, y_2, \ldots, y_n)$, where each component y_i satisfies

$$y_i = \frac{1}{\sqrt{n}} \sum_{k=1}^{n} x_k e^{-2\pi j(k-1)(i-1)/n}$$

where j is the unit imaginary number. The original vector can be recovered by the following formula:

$$x_i = \frac{1}{\sqrt{n}} \sum_{k=1}^{n} y_k e^{2\pi j(k-1)(i-1)/n}$$

It can be shown that $\sum_{i=1}^{n} |x_i|^2 = \sum_{i=1}^{n} |y_i|^2$. In other words, in the transformed space, if all n dimensions are utilized, the distances are preserved and Inequality (11.1) becomes an equality. In practice, only the first few dimensions are utilized in the transformed space. That is, pick an m that is much smaller than n and ignore all $y_j, j > m$. This results in an m-dimensional space. The reason is that realistic data usually follow a skewed distribution of the magnitude of the components, with heavy concentration in the few first ones. As a result, discarding the less significant ones would cause very little inaccuracy.

Many other transformations are possible. The SVD (singular value decomposition method), discussed in Chapter 9, which is also known as the KL (Karhunen-Loeve) transform, is a potentially good choice for the following reason. The properties associated with the dimensions are not necessarily unrelated. For example, in the case of color, two ranges of colors are associated with two dimensions and it is possible that these two ranges are closely related. Thus, using the Euclidean distance, which implicitly assumes that the dimensions are independent, to measure the distance of two given vectors of color (or using the dot product to measure their similarity) may not be accurate. An n-by-n matrix, where the (i, j)th entry measures the correlation between the ith range and the jth range of colors in the n-dimensional space, can be incorporated to give a better measure of similarity/distance. However, multidimensional data structures are incapable of handling the additional matrix. By using the SVD or KL transform, the transformed space has little or no relationship between the different dimensions. Thus, there is no need to make use of the matrix in the new space. Furthermore, after an m

that is much smaller than n is picked, the m-dimensional space can be handled efficiently by multidimensional structures.

Retrieval Based on Semantic Information

We now concentrate on retrieval based on information at the semantic level. The following environment is assumed. A user has an imprecise idea of what he or she wants to retrieve. For example, the user might have seen some pictures a while ago and, based on his or her vague recollection, want to retrieve those pictures. Clearly, in such a situation, exact match using the user specification would be inappropriate, because the user's recollection could be imprecise. In addition, the metadata generated by image analysis algorithms or by humans can be too incomplete or imprecise to permit exact match. As in text retrieval, a similarity approach is taken, in which a degree of closeness is assigned to each picture relative to the user's specification. Then the k closest pictures are shown to the user, for any user-specified constant k. The similarity of a picture with respect to a query Q is the sum of two components: similarity due to the matching of entities and that due to the matching of relationships.

We first discuss the matching of entities. The matching has two steps. In the first step, entity types are matched. In the second step, attributes of entities are matched. More detailed descriptions are provided below.

Type match. Each entity, say E, specified by the user, is first matched against the type (e.g., a man) of some entity in the picture. If the types match—i.e., they are identical or one is related to the other via a stored dictionary—then some positive similarity is assigned. Synonyms and is-a relationships (e.g., a man *is-a* person) are included in the stored dictionary. An exact match has a higher similarity than matching via the dictionary.

Attribute match. After the type match, each attribute value of the entity specified by the user is matched against the corresponding value of the matched entity in the picture. A fuzzy match means that two attribute values are not identical but can be the same due to different subjective judgments. For example, person X may judge person Z to be old, while person Y may describe person Z to be very old. Matching of fuzzy labels and numbers against exact numbers or fuzzy labels or fuzzy numbers has been discussed in Chapter 6. An exact match of attribute values will give a higher similarity than a fuzzy match. If two attribute values differ by a large extent (for example, with respect to the age attribute, the values *old* and *young* are very different), then two options are available. One is to assign a zero similarity due to the matching of these attribute values. This is simply to ignore the information on this attribute value as applied to the matched entity in the picture. Another option is to assign a negative infinity to the similarity of the two entities due to the significant difference between their attribute values. This effectively eliminates this entity in the picture from being related to E, although another entity in the picture may be matched against E. The underlying assumption is that the user can be imprecise but not totally inaccurate in his or her specification. It is possible to determine which option is appropriate if the user is willing to indicate whether he or she is confident in his or her specification. If the use is confident, then the *negative infinity* option should be applied; otherwise, the *zero* option is more appropriate. Note, however, that this requires more interactions with the user, who may be impatient. (It should be noted that there is still another option, which is to assign a number between 0 and negative infinity. The choice of which option to take is a research issue.)

The matching of an entity in Q with an entity in the picture is complete after all attributes of the entity have been considered. When an entity type or an attribute value specified by the user matches the corresponding part in a picture, a significance value or weight is usually assigned to the match. This is in addition to fuzzy match or matching via an is-a hierarchy, but is analogous to term matching in text retrieval. Recall that in text matching, the significance of a term in a piece of text is given by its *inverse frequency weighting* in the collection of texts and the number of occurrences of the term in the text. The inverse frequency weighting can be directly employed; i.e., the weight associated with an entity type or an attribute value is proportional to $\log N/m$, where N is the total number of pictures in the entire database and m is the number of pictures having the desired entity type or attribute value. The concept of multiple occurrences of a term in a text is used to reflect its significance. In picture retrieval, the number of occurrences of an entity type is also captured. For example, Figure 11.9 shows how the number of occurrences of an entity type can be specified in a user query. In picture retrieval, there is an additional indicator of importance of an entity as reflected by its size. If an entity is much larger than another entity, it is likely that the former entity draws more attention to viewers than the latter. However, a particular user may have more interest in the smaller entity. In text retrieval, it is known that users usually have difficulty in assigning relative degrees of importance to different terms. Thus, it is likely that ordinary users will have difficulty in assigning relative degrees of importance to entities. As a consequence, in the absence of the user's preference, it is more desirable to assign the degree of importance on the basis of size than to assign equal importance to different entities. Yet another way to reflect the significance of an entity is by its distance from the center of the picture. The shorter the distance, the higher the significance the entity has. Photographers usually place the central entities close to the center of the picture. A measure combining both indicators can be given by the ratio (size of object)/(distance of object from the center of the picture).

We now discuss the matching of relationships. Such matches yield the second component of the similarity between a user query and a picture in the database. The matching of action relationships and the matching of spatial relationships are described separately below.

Matching action relationships. For an action relationship (group1, action, group2), an inexact matching approach is also taken. In other words, if an action relationship (gp1, action', gp2) exists in the picture, then as long as action and action' are the same term after stemming or are related by a prestored dictionary and the corresponding groups have at least two members in common, then a positive similarity will be applied. The reason for the leniency in matching is that perceptions of an action relationship differ from one person to another. For example, if a man together with a child are playing basketball against a woman with another child, there are the following two representations as well as others: ({man, one child}, play basketball, {woman, another child}); ({man, woman, one child, another child}, play, {basketball}). The restriction of the specification of an action relationship to only two groups is likely to help in the matching process. Again, an exact matching will yield a higher similarity than an inexact matching. A common problem in using the entity-relationship model to model the contents of a picture is the classical type mismatch problem. In other words, the three types—entity, property (attribute), and relationship—are used interchangeably by different users. A user or an image analysis system may represent something of significance as an entity while another user may represent the same thing as an attribute value. To remedy this situation, matching across types is permitted in restricted situations. For example, a picture retrieval system may record an entity *dancer*, while a user may represent the entity as a person with attribute value *dancing* under the attribute *state of motion*. A match between *dancer* and *dancing* is possible if certain entities are allowed to match against certain attributes and the words (in this case, *dancer* and *dancing*) are stemmed before they are compared against each other.

Matching spatial relationships. This is somewhat more complicated. For example, a user may specify that an entity A is to the left of some entity B, which is to the left of an entity C. In the user's mind, the entities A and C are important but B is of no consequence, and after the user identifies A, he or she recalls C via the entity B. If a picture has the entities A and C and the spatial relationship that A is to the left of C, then the spatial relationship in the picture would not match any spatial relationship directly in the user's specification. However, it can be observed from the given spatial relationships that the relationship *A to the left of C* can in fact be deduced. Rules involving the spatial relationships identified earlier can be constructed. For example, in the rule

$$(A, above, D) :- (A, above, B),(B, overlaps, C),(C, above, D)$$

the spatial relationship (A, above, D) can be deduced from the other three given relationships on the right-hand side of the rule. It can be shown that the rules given in the next subsection are *sound* and *complete* for three-dimensional objects; i.e., the relationships deduced using the rules are logically implied and what is logically implied can in fact be deduced by using the rules.

As an example to show that the deduced relationship *A above D* can be logically implied, a sketch is provided as follows. *A above B* means that every point in A is greater than every point in B along the Z-axis, which represents height. *B overlaps C* implies that there is a point common to both B and C. Let such a common point be *x*. Then every point in A is greater than *x* along the Z-axis. *C above D* implies that *x* is greater than any point in D along the Z-axis. Since *greater than* is transitive, every point in A is greater than every point in D along the Z-axis. This verifies that the deduced relationship *A above D* is logically implied.

Algorithms can be devised to compute the deduced spatial relationships. Usually, deductions using general-purpose deductive database systems, which take rules as input and produce deduced relationships, may not be as efficient as direct algorithms, but they permit more flexibility. When additional spatial operators are included, it is sufficient to add the rules relating the additional spatial operators and their interactions with the existing spatial operators. This concept will be explained further in the next subsection. In contrast, when additional spatial operators are added, direct algorithms that compute the deduced relationships may need to be rewritten.

In order to compute the similarity between a query and a picture due to spatial relationships, another process is required. Let S be a given set of spatial relationships. Let (A, overlaps, B) and (B, overlaps, A), be represented by (overlaps, {A, B}), as the relationship is symmetric whenever two entities A and B overlap. Suppose further that *A inside B* and *B inside A* are not possible for any two distinct entities A and B. Then it can be shown that the minimal set of relationships that can deduce S, denoted by R, is unique. For example, if S = {(A, above, B), (overlaps, {B, C}), (C, above, D), (A, above, D)}, then R consists of the first three relationships. When a query Q is matched against a picture P, the set of relationships satisfied by P with respect to Q is computed. This is obtained by taking the intersection of Ded(P) and Ded(Q), where Ded(X) is the set of the spatial relationships that can be deduced by X. Let S be this set of satisfied relationships; i.e., S is the intersection of Ded(P) and Ded(Q). It is important to distinguish two sets, *MinR* and *Redund*, of spatial relationships in S. MinR is the minimal set of reduced spatial relationships in S, i.e., MinR is contained in S, but among all subsets in S that can deduce S, MinR is the minimal. Redund is a subset in S containing spatial relationships outside MinR. It is clear that any spatial relationship in Redund is unlikely to contribute additional similarity to the picture P with respect to the query Q because it can be deduced from the satisfied spatial relationships in MinR. Our aim is to find MinR and discard any relationship in Redund. A reduction algorithm can be constructed such that given a set S of spatial relationships, the minimal set of relationships that can deduce S (i.e., MinR) can be obtained in the same time complexity as the deduction algorithm.

Another complication with matching spatial relationships arises because one entity in the query Q may match to some extent with multiple entities in a picture. For example, a user specifies that there is a strong man and a tall woman, and in a picture there are three men, one strong, one medium-built, and one weak, and two women, one tall and one very tall. Let the man in Q match the ith man in the picture with similarity b_i, and the woman in Q match the jth woman in the picture with similarity c_j. Suppose in Q the man has a spatial relationship with the woman. Let the similarity between the specified spatial relationship in Q and that of the ith man and the jth woman in the picture be d_{ij}, $1 \leq i \leq 3$, $1 \leq j \leq 2$. Then the similarity of the picture is defined to be $\max\{b_i + c_j + d_{ij}\}$. In general, it is likely that an exponential algorithm is needed to compute the similarity between a query Q and a picture P, as the problem can be shown to be NP-hard (see Figure 11.11). In order to minimize the time complexity, a simplification can be made. This is carried out by matching each entity in Q with the most similar entity in the picture P. In this example, the strong man and the tall woman in P will be selected and there is no need to enumerate the six possible combinations. In theory, this may not give the correct match, because the strong man and the very tall woman in P may have the specified spatial relationship, whereas the strong man and the tall woman may not have that specified spatial relationship. In practice, each entity is likely to have quite a few attribute values and a picture is unlikely to have many similar entities to cause the mismatch.

Let items denote both entities and relationships. Suppose matchings between individual items in the user's query Q and those in a picture P have been computed. The matched values can be utilized to produce a similarity value, sim(Q, P), which indicates the extent to which the picture P is close to the query Q. One such similarity function is as follows.

Let C(Q, P) be the set of items in Q that can be matched with those in the picture P. Here, the corresponding items in P and Q need not be identical due to is-a hierarchy matching, fuzzy attribute value matching, or inexact relationship matching. Suppose the matching of the

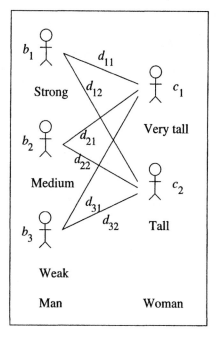

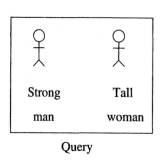

Query

Matches

FIGURE 11.11 **Combinatorial Explosion of Entity and Spatial Relationship Matching**

ith item in Q with itself and the matching of the ith item in Q with the corresponding item in P yield the values w_i and w_i', respectively. It is clear that $0 \leq w_i' \leq w_i$, since an exact match yields a higher weight than an inexact or fuzzy match. Let $M(Q, P)$ denote the total matching value between the items in Q and those in P; i.e., it is the sum of the w_i'. A similarity value, $\text{sim}(Q, P)$, between P and Q can be defined to be

$$\text{sim}(Q, P) = \frac{M(Q, P)}{M(Q, Q)} \cdot \frac{1}{1 + \dfrac{M(P - Q, P) \cdot \text{minmatch}}{M(P, P) \cdot M(P, Q)}}$$

where $P - Q$ denotes the set of items that are in P but do not have corresponding matching items in Q and minmatch is the smallest matching value due to the items in $C(P, Q)$, i.e., the smallest w_i'. The usage of the various symbols in the formula is as follows.

$M(Q, Q)$ is used for normalization purposes; i.e., the similarity value, $\text{sim}(Q, P)$, is between 0 and 1, and has the value 1 when the picture P is identical to the query Q. This can be observed in the fact that $P - Q$ is null (i.e., empty) and therefore $M(\text{null}, P)$ is 0. When there are items in P but not in Q, the denominator is increased by $M(P - Q, P)/M(P, P)$, which is the weighted proportion of unmatched items, multiplied by $\text{minmatch}/M(P, Q)$, which is a proportion of the total matching value. Two properties of this similarity function are as follows. Let P1, P2, and P3 be three pictures with the following characteristics with the query Q containing items $i_1, i_2, \ldots, i_k, \ldots, i_s$.

1. If the set of items in P1 that match items in Q is contained in the set of items in P2, then the similarity between Q and P2 is higher than that between Q and P1. More precisely, if P1 and P2 have the set of items $\{i'_1, i'_2, \ldots, i'_k\} \cup NC1$ and $\{i'_1, i'_2, \ldots, i'_k, i'_{k+1}\} \cup NC2$, where i_j matches with i'_j in pictures P1 or P2, $1 \leq j \leq k+1$, and NC1 and NC2 are two sets of items that do not have any corresponding matching items with Q, then $sim(Q, P2) > sim(Q, P1)$.

2. If P3 and P1 have the same set of matched items with Q, but P3 has additional unmatched items, then the similarity between Q and P1 is higher than that between Q and P3. More precisely, with P1 as given in (1) and P3 given as P1 $\cup$ NC3, where NC1 is properly contained in NC3 and no item in NC3 has a corresponding matching item in Q, then $sim(Q, P3) < sim(Q, P1)$.

Essentially, these two properties imply that matches of items are much more important than mismatches of items to the extent that any additional match yields a higher similarity (property 1). Mismatches can be used to differentiate two pictures that have identical matches but different mismatches (property 2). To what extent this similarity function reflects user's relevance remains to be seen. It should be noted that recall and precision, which are defined in Chapter 9 with regard to effective text retrieval, are also the criteria for the effectiveness of the retrieval of pictures.

11.1.3 Deduction and Reduction of Spatial Relationships

A set of rules can be given for the deduction of spatial relationships (Sistla, Yu, and Haddock, 1994 [335]). That is, when a set of spatial relationships for a set of entities holds in a picture, the set of rules will be able to infer other spatial relationships among the given entities that must hold for the picture. This inference is especially important when a user specifies a query that states some but not all spatial relationships. For example, if the user specifies that *A is to the left of B* and *B is to the left of C*, then *A is to the left of C* can be inferred but may not be explicitly stated in the user's query. This is not surprising, as we expect most users may not want or be able to perform all possible deductions. A picture may have the spatial relationship *A is to the left of C*, without the other spatial relationships. If the deduction is not performed, then the picture may not be retrieved, as pointed out in the last subsection. The use of rules to deduce spatial relationships permits flexibility. More precisely, when additional spatial relationships are added, then it is sufficient to produce rules for the new spatial relationships and rules that take into consideration the interactions between the new spatial relationships and the existing ones. For example, suppose *A strictly left of B* means that every point in A along the X-axis is less than every point in B along the same axis and this is an existing spatial relationship. Suppose a new spatial relationship *left of* is added and *A left of B* means that every point in A along the X-axis is less than or equal to every point in B along the same axis. Then we can derive a rule for the new spatial relationship as follows.

A left of C :− A left of B, B left of C

We can also derive rules representing the interactions between *strictly left of* and *left of* as follows.

> A strictly left of C :– A left of B, B strictly left of C
>
> A strictly left of C :– A strictly left of B, B left of C

The following is a set of rules for deducing spatial relationships:

I. This rule regards the transitivity of *left of*, *above*, *behind*, and *inside*. Let *x* denote any relationship symbol in {*left of*, *above*, *behind*, *inside*}. We have the following rule for each such *x*:

> A *x* C :– A *x* B, B *x* C

II. This rule captures the interaction between relationships involving *overlaps* and relationships involving *left of*, *above*, and *behind*. Let *x* denote any of the relationship symbols in {*left of*, *above*, *behind*}. We have the following rule for each such *x*:

> A *x* D :– A *x* B, B overlaps C, C *x* D

III. These rules capture the interaction between relationships involving *inside* and relationships involving *left of*, *above*, *behind*, and *outside*. Let *x* denote any relationship symbol in {*left of*, *above*, *behind*, *outside*}. We have the following rules for each such *x*:

> **(a)** A *x* C :– A inside B, B *x* C
>
> **(b)** A *x* C :– A *x* B, C inside B

Rule (b) is redundant for the case in which *x* is the relationship symbol *outside*; for other cases, (a) and (b) are independent.

IV. This rule captures the symmetry of *overlaps* and *outside*. Let *x* denote either of *overlaps* or *outside*. We have the following rule for each such *x*:

> A *x* B :– B *x* A

V. This rule enables one to deduce that two entities are outside each other if one of them is to the *left of*, *above*, or *behind* the other entity. Let *x* denote any of the relationship symbols in {*left of*, *above*, *behind*}. We have the following rule for each such *x*:

> A outside B :– A *x* B

VI. This rule enables one to deduce that if an entity is inside another entity, then the two entities overlap.

> A overlaps B :– A inside B

VII. This rule enables one to deduce that A overlaps with B if B overlaps with an entity inside A.

> A overlaps B :– C inside A, C overlaps B

VIII. This rule says that every entity is inside itself. Note that this rule has no body.

> A inside A :−

It is clear that relationships involving *right of* can be reexpressed using the corresponding *left of* relationships. For example, *A right of B* can be rewritten as *B left of A*. Similarly, the spatial operators *below* and *in front of* can be reexpressed using the spatial operators *above* and *behind*, respectively. After all these rules are derived, it is sufficient to apply a general deductive database system to perform deductions. In spite of this advantage of being flexible, it may be inefficient. The reason is that a general deductive system works for all valid rules and may not be optimized for a given set of rules. As a result, the following algorithms are suggested for the deductions.

It is clear that *inside* relationships can be deduced using the standard transitive closure algorithm. The reason is that the rule

> A inside C :− A inside B, B inside C

is essentially the same as that for the ancestor relationships discussed in Chapter 7. After all *inside* relationships are obtained, all *overlaps* relationships can be obtained as follows. First, for every *A inside B*, then *A overlaps B* is obtained, due to rule VI. Second, for every *A overlaps B*, *B overlaps A* is obtained, by rule IV. Third, by rule VII, the *overlaps* relationships can be obtained by a join between the relation representing all the *inside* relationships and the relation representing the *overlaps* relationships that are obtained in the last two steps. The *outside* relationships are exactly those due to the *left of* relationships, the *above* relationships, and the *behind* relationships and their duals (i.e., *right of*, *below*, and *in front of*), by rule V. We now concentrate on the derivation of the *above* relationships. The *left of* relationships and the *behind* relationships can be obtained by the same procedure and will not be discussed further.

Observe that the *above* relationships are deduced using rules I, II, and III. Rules I, II, and III(a) satisfy the chain property; i.e., each rule is of the form

$$x_1 \text{ above } x_{i+1} :− (x_1, r_1, x_2), (x_2, r_2, x_3), \ldots, (x_i, r_i, x_{i+1})$$

where the x's denote the entities, the r's denote the relationships, and the second entity of each triplet on the right-hand side of the rule is the same as the first entity of the next triplet. Rule III(b) can be rewritten to satisfy the same property as follows. Define *B contains C* as *C inside B*. Then the rule becomes *A above C :− A above B, B contains C*. Because of this chain property, an automaton can be constructed such that if the right-hand side of each rule is scanned from left to right starting from an initial state S0, for each relationship encountered, a transition of state occurs, and finally when the last relationship on the right-hand side is encountered, an output state in the automaton is reached. The automaton with two states S0 and S1 is given in Figure 11.12.

As an example, consider rule II with x as *above*. The first relationship, *above*, takes the state from S0 to S1; the second relationship, *overlaps*, takes the state back to S0; finally, the last relationship, *above*, takes the state to S1, which is the only output state in the automaton. It can be verified that this automaton performs as described for each of the rules involving the *above* relationship, namely, I, II, III(a), and III(b). This automaton will be used to generate all the *above* relationships from a given set F of spatial relationships as follows.

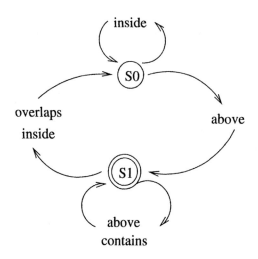

FIGURE 11.12   An Automaton for Deduction Rules

Consider a graph G = (V, E), where each vertex v in V represents an entity among the entities in a picture F and each edge e = (v_1, r, v_2) in E represents the relationship (v_1, r, v_2) in F, with r being one of {*inside, above, overlaps*}. Also, for each relationship (A, inside, B), there is an edge (B, contains, A) in G. If n and m are the number of entities and relationships in F, respectively, then the number of vertices and the number of edges in G are n and $O(m)$, respectively.

From the automaton and the graph G, a new graph GG = (VV, EE) can be constructed. Each vertex v' in VV is of the form (A, S_i), where A is an entity v in V in the graph G and S_i is a state in the automaton. Since there are two states in the automaton, there are $2 \cdot |V|$ vertices in VV. There is an edge e' in EE from (A, S_i) to (B, S_j) with label r if there is an edge in G from A to B with label r and there is a transition from S_i to S_j with label r. Thus, if A *above B* is in F, then the edge from (A, S_0) to (B, S_1) with label *above* is in the graph GG. It can be shown that there exists a path from the vertex (A, S_0) to the vertex (B, S_1) if and only if the relationship *A above B* can be deduced from the given set F of relationships. If the transitive closure of GG is computed, then all *above* relationships of the form (A, above, B) can be obtained by outputting edges from (A, S_0) to (B, S_1) in the closure. The graph GG can be shown to be acyclic. As a result, the transitive closure can be obtained in time $O(mn)$.

Example 11.1 The spatial relationships in F are given in Figure 11.13(a). The graph GG for deducing the *above* relationships is given in Figure 11.13(b). From the graph GG, there is a directed path from (A, S_0) to (D, S_1) and another path from (A, S_0) to (E, S_1). Thus, A is above D and A is above E. The first spatial relationship can be deduced using rule II, while the second one is obtained by deducing the first spatial relationship and then applying rule I.
∎

Suppose deductions of spatial relationships are performed on the user's query Q and on a picture P. Then the intersection of the two sets of deduced spatial relationships, I, is the

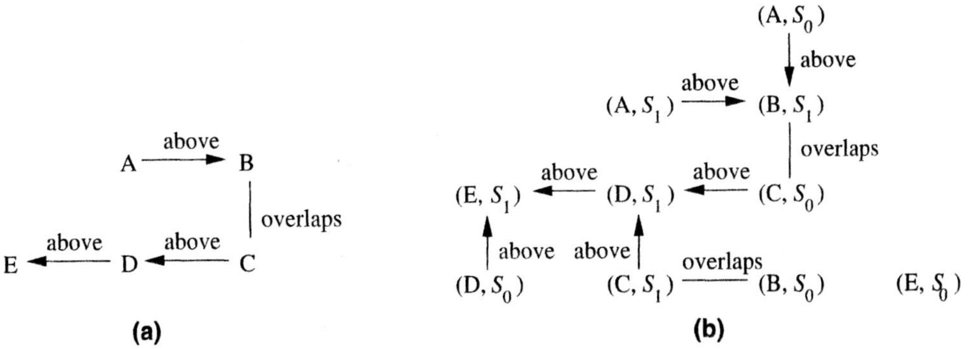

$$(A, S_0)$$

$$\downarrow \text{above}$$

$$(A, S_1) \xrightarrow{\text{above}} (B, S_1)$$

$$\text{above} \qquad \downarrow \text{overlaps}$$

$$A \xrightarrow{\text{above}} B \qquad (E, S_1) \xleftarrow{\text{above}} (D, S_1) \xleftarrow{\text{above}} (C, S_0)$$

$$\downarrow \text{overlaps} \qquad \uparrow \text{above} \quad \text{above} \uparrow$$

$$E \xleftarrow{\text{above}} D \xleftarrow{\text{above}} C \qquad (D, S_0) \qquad (C, S_1) \xrightarrow{\text{overlaps}} (B, S_0) \qquad (E, S_0)$$

(a) (b)

FIGURE 11.13 Illustrating Deduction/Reduction of Spatial Relationships

---

set of spatial relationships satisfied by the picture P with respect to the query Q. However, some of the relationships in I are redundant. For example, if *A above B* and *B above C* are in both P and Q, then I will contain these relationships as well as *A above C*. Clearly, the last relationship is redundant, as it can be deduced from the first two relationships in I. We are interested in finding all nonredundant relationships in I, i.e., the smallest subset in I that can deduce I. This is the *reduction problem*, which is to find the smallest subset S that can deduce a given set F of spatial relationships. In general, the reduction is not unique, because when both *A overlaps B* and *B overlaps A* hold, one of them but not both is in the reduction. This problem can be avoided by taking *overlaps* as an unordered relationship, i.e., by making no distinction between *A overlaps B* and *B overlaps A*. The same applies to the *outside* relationships. With these modifications, it can be shown that the minimal reduction of a given set of relationships is unique and can be obtained by a process similar to that of deduction. Consider the computation of the *above* relationships in the reduction of F. Exactly the same graph GG as described above is constructed. Then it can be shown that *A above B* is in the reduction if and only if the longest path from (A, S_0) to (B, S_1) is of length 1, where each edge in GG is of length 1. (Recall that the graph GG is used to deduce the *above* relationships. If there is a path of length more than 1 from (A, S_0) to (B, S_1), then the relationship *A above B* can be deduced from the rules and therefore should not appear in the reduction.) The computation of the longest lengths of paths between all pairs of vertices in GG takes time of $O(mn)$, as the number of vertices and the number of edges in GG are $O(n)$ and $O(m)$, respectively.

All the *inside* relationships can be deduced by using transitive closure. As a result, all the *inside* relationships in the reduction of F can be obtained by the standard transitive reduction process given in graph theory books. Alternatively, a modified automaton can be constructed to capture the chain property of the rule for the deduction of the *inside* relationships. This automaton has two states, S_0 and S_1; S_0 goes to S_1 when the *inside* relationship is encountered, and it stays in state S_1 when the *inside* relationship is repeated. This automaton can be combined with the graph G to form a graph GG', similar to GG. Then *A inside B* is in the reduction of F if and only if the longest path from (A, S_0) to (B, S_1) is of length 1. The same reasoning but with minor modifications applies to the computation of *overlaps* and *outside* relationships in the reduction of F. Specifically, after the above process is applied, the obtained *overlaps* relationships and the obtained *outside* relationships have to undergo further elimination. Each *overlaps* relationship of the form *A overlaps B* is eliminated whenever *A inside B* is in the deduction. Each *outside* relationship of the form *A outside B* is eliminated whenever *A above B, A left of B, A behind B*, or any of its duals are in the deduction.

11.1.4 Indexes for Similarity Computation

We have mentioned that among the spatial relationships satisfied by picture P with respect to a user query Q, some of them are redundant and should not be given positive weights in computing the similarity $f(Q, P)$. Thus, it is of interest to differentiate the reduction of the satisfied spatial relationships from that of the redundant ones. Clearly, the distinction can easily be made by applying the reduction process as given in the previous section. However, if there are numerous pictures and the process is applied to each picture, it could be very time consuming.

We now discuss the use of indexes for efficient computation. We consider the spatial relationship *above*. Other spatial relationships can be handled in a similar fashion. Each object has a type. For example, object A can be of type *man*. The relationship *above* is a binary relationship with a left operand and a right operand. Thus, the types of the *above* relationships are of the form {type(L)·type(R)}, where L and R are the entities satisfying *L above R*. There are t^2 such types, where *t* is the number of types of entities. In the *index tree* of the *above* relationships, pictures are classified by these t^2 types. For example, under the type *man above tower*, each picture having a man above a tower will have a tuple in the index tree. Clearly, this structure facilitates answering a query satisfying the spatial relationship between a man and a tower, as only those pictures need to be examined. A tuple in the index tree is of the form (pic, obid1, obid2, r/d), where pic is the ID of the picture having an entity with ID = obid1 above an entity with ID = obid2. If this spatial relationship is in the reduction of the set of spatial relationships in the picture, then r/d is set to r, indicating reduction; otherwise, it is set to d, indicating that it is obtained by deduction. When a query Q is submitted, both the reduction and the deduction processes are applied to the spatial relationships in Q. Let the spatial relationships in the reduction and the deduction of a set of spatial relationships F be denoted by red(F) and ded(F), respectively. Each relationship in ded(Q) is identified to be either in red(Q) or not. Our aim is to identify those relationships in T = red(ded(Q) ∩ ded(P)) for each picture P, as only those spatial relationships have positive contributions to the similarity sim(Q, P). The following results identify some situations in which certain satisfied relationships are or are not in the reduction T.

1. Let r be a spatial relationship in ded(Q) ∩ ded(P). If r is in red(P) or in red(Q), where P and Q are a picture and a query, respectively, then r is in red(ded(P) ∩ ded(Q)). (With a slight abuse of terminology, we do not distinguish between the picture P and the set of spatial relationships in P.) Whether r is in red(P) or not is given in the "r/d" bit of a tuple of the picture P in the index tree. When the query is processed, whether r is in red(Q) or not can be determined. Thus, if the hypothesis of the observation is satisfied, then r is in the reduction of the satisfied relationships.

Some situations in which certain satisfied *overlaps* relationships are not in the reduction can also be identified by the following observation.

2. If r = *A inside B* is in ded(P) ∩ ded(Q), then r′ = *A overlaps B* is not in red(ded(P) ∩ ded(Q)).

The former relationship r implies the latter relationship r′. Thus, r′ is not in the reduction.

There are satisfied spatial relationships that do not satisfy observation 1 or observation 2. Whether these spatial relationships belong to the reduction T cannot be easily determined from the indexes and the query. We apply a heuristic to assign a probability that such a spatial relationship is in the reduction. Suppose the number of relationships in red(P) for each picture P, $n(P)$, is also kept in the index tree. During the processing of a query, whenever a relationship in red(P) is satisfied, $n(P)$ is decreased by 1. When $n(P)$ is zero, all relationships in red(P) have been satisfied. Any additional satisfied relationship in P must be outside the reduction of P. Thus, it may be argued that the probability that a satisfied spatial relationship is in the reduction is an inverse function of the percentage of satisfied relationships in the reduction— i.e., the higher the percentage, the lower the probability. The two extreme points are 100% and 0%: when the percentage is 100%, the probability that the next satisfied spatial relationship is in the reduction is definitely zero; when the percentage is zero, the probability that some satisfied spatial relationship is in the reduction is guaranteed to be one. Interpolation can be applied to yield a probability based on the percentage when a spatial relationship known not to be covered under observations 1 or 2 is satisfied. Experimental results indicate that the cardinality of red(ded(P) ∩ ded(Q)) can be estimated reasonably accurately by the use of the observations and the heuristic.

11.1.5 An Application

In this section, we will describe a medical application of image retrieval. Although this application has a single object in each image and therefore no spatial relationship is involved, the use of spatial relationships in medical applications is rather common. (Refer to the Bibliographic Notes for a reference.) The medical application is for the detection of skin cancer and in particular melanoma. This kind of skin disease occurs at an increasing frequency. It has been reported that during the past decade the number of melanoma cases has doubled. A projection is that 1% of people will develop this disease during their lifetime. It is also known that if the disease is discovered at an early stage, it is very curable; if it is discovered at an advanced stage, it could be fatal. Thus, the problem of determining the disease is of high significance. A special property of this application is that there is only one entity in the picture, namely, the lesion. The boundary of the lesion can be identified without too much difficulty, and the different attribute values of the lesion can be extracted automatically. In other words, in this application, the low-level features can be extracted automatically and the entity (lesion) and its properties can be derived from the extracted features.

The problem can be defined as follows. Given the medical history of a patient, including information about the patient's age and sex, previous skin disease, whether family members had melanoma, etc., and information about the lesion (an image of the lesion and the location of the lesion), determine the lesion's category. Roughly speaking, lesions can be classified into three categories: *malignant*, *premalignant*, and *benign*. In addition to the information given above, there is also a database containing information about lesions of previous patients, their medical histories, and the characteristics of the lesions. In this database, the categories of the lesions are known. The problem is in essence to extract statistics from the database containing characteristics of different lesions with known diagnoses (categories) so that the probabilities that the given lesion is in the three categories, i.e., malignant, premalignant, and benign, can be determined.

We now illustrate the process with a simple database. Suppose the database contains a relation *Lesion* with attributes (color, asymmetry, diameter, border, sex, type). For a given lesion L, *color* is the distribution of colors in L, *asymmetry* indicates the degree of deviation of L from being symmetric, *diameter* is the longest distance between two points in the boundary of L, *border* is a measure of the smoothness of its boundary, *sex* is the sex of the patient having the lesion, and *type* of L is benign, premalignant, or malignant. Very often, values of certain attributes such as diameter and border are grouped into nonoverlapping ranges. As a result, another relation *Lesion-Aggregate* with attributes (color-r, asymmetry-r, diameter-r, border-r, sex, type, number) is formed, where each attribute A whose values are grouped into ranges is denoted by A-r. A tuple (c, a, d, b, s, t, n) in the relation *Lesion-Aggregate* means that there are n lesions of type t belonging to patients having sex s and the image characteristics of these n lesions are that they have colors within a range c, asymmetries within a range a, diameters within a range d, and borders within a range b. Let the attributes color, asymmetry, diameter, and border be denoted by A_1, A_2, A_3, and A_4, respectively. Let the lesion L to be diagnosed belong to a male patient and have values v_1, v_2, v_3, and v_4 under attributes A_1, A_2, A_3, and A_4, respectively. Let the ranges containing the attribute values v_1, v_2, v_3, and v_4 be r_1, r_2, r_3, and r_4, respectively. Then, the probability of interest is $P(C_j \mid (r_1 \text{ in } A_1, r_2 \text{ in } A_2, r_3 \text{ in } A_3, r_4 \text{ in } A_4)$, male), where r_i in A_i means that the value of the lesion in attribute A_i is within the range of r_i, *male* stands for a male patient, and C_j stands for one of the three categories {malignant, premalignant, benign}. By Bayes's theorem, the desired probability can be reexpressed as

$$P(C_j \mid B) = \frac{P(B \mid C_j) \cdot P(C_j)}{\sum_{k=1}^{3} P(B \mid C_k) \cdot P(C_k)}$$

where B stands for the condition $(r_t \text{ in } A_t, 1 \leq t \leq 4$, male). $P(C_j)$ can be estimated by (the number of lesions in class C_j in the database)/(the total number of lesions in the database). $P(B \mid C_j)$ can be estimated by (the number of lesions in class C_j and satisfying the condition B in the database)/(the number of lesions in class C_j in the database). If the database is sufficiently large, then these quantities can be estimated accurately. However, it is very possible that within a database that is not too large and has many attributes and B consists of conditions on these attributes, there is no lesion satisfying the specification B in class C_j. If the attributes A_i, $1 \leq i \leq 4$, are independent within class C_j, then we can rewrite $P(B \mid C_j)$ to be $\prod_{i=1}^{4} P(r_i \text{ in } A_i, \text{male} \mid C_j)$.

It is likely that the probabilities $P(r_i \text{ in } A_i, \text{male} \mid C_j)$ can be estimated without difficulty based on the statistics in the database. However, the independence assumption is unlikely to be satisfied. To improve the accuracy of the estimate, some dependency model, such as the tree dependency model discussed in Section 9.2.3 of Chapter 9, can be employed. In order to apply this model, the I-function, which measures the dependencies of attributes, is applied. Specifically,

$$I(A_i, A_j) = \sum_{x,y} P(x \text{ in } A_i, y \text{ in } A_j) \cdot \log \frac{P(x \text{ in } A_i, y \text{ in } A_j)}{P(x \text{ in } A_i) \cdot P(y \text{ in } A_j)}$$

is computed, where (x, y) is a pair with x being a range in A_i and y a range in A_j, and the sum is over all such pairs. After all pairwise dependencies between attributes are computed, the *maximum spanning tree* algorithm is invoked to find a tree having the largest sum of dependencies. As an example, consider the following maximum dependency tree:

The probability $P(B \mid C_j)$ can be estimated as follows:

$$\frac{P(r_1 \text{ in } A_1, r_2 \text{ in } A_2, \text{ male } \mid C_j) \cdot P(r_2 \text{ in } A_2, r_3 \text{ in } A_3, \text{ male } \mid C_j) \cdot P(r_3 \text{ in } A_3, r_4 \text{ in } A_4, \text{ male } \mid C_j)}{P(r_2 \text{ in } A_2, \text{ male } \mid C_j) \cdot P(r_3 \text{ in } A_3, \text{ male } \mid C_j)}$$

Although a dependence model is likely to yield better results than the independence model, it is not clear whether high accuracy is achievable. It is probable that for a database containing numerous lesions, the required probabilities can be estimated accurately. However, this may involve gathering information from multiple sources, which may introduce noise into the collected data. For example, the color of a lesion in an image made in one environment may differ from its color in an image made in a different environment. In other words, the colors of lesions whose images are made in different environments are not exactly what they would be if the images were made in the same environment. For this reason, standardization of colors in different environments is essential.

Another situation that affects accuracy of diagnosis is that although many characteristics of lesions that differentiate cancerous ones from noncancerous ones are known, the science of diagnosis is incomplete. Thus, it is worthwhile to provide tools enabling physicians or medical researchers to make more thorough analyses or to perform explorations easily. The following feedback approach is suggested for this purpose. In addition to providing the probabilities that a given lesion L is malignant, premalignant, or benign, the system can also produce the five most similar malignant lesions, the five most similar premalignant lesions, and the five most similar benign lesions and their associated similarities. By comparing the lesion L with these 15 lesions and their similarities, a physician or medical researcher may be able to make a better diagnosis. Furthermore, he or she can make small changes to the characteristics of L or alter the relative significances of the attributes to make another retrieval. (Recall that images of lesions may be made under different lighting conditions. Even if standardization of colors is performed, small variations of colors of the same image are possible.) For example, the color of L may be adjusted to be *more brownish* or the attribute *diameter* can be given higher significance. With the adjustment, another 15 most similar lesions and their similarities will again be retrieved. It is possible that by comparing the two sets of 15 images and their similarities, important information affecting the outcome of malignancy can be found. For example, by making the lesion L *more brownish*, the color of L belongs to a different range. This could affect the probabilities that a lesion belongs to the three lesion types significantly. It is hoped that the visual effect of seeing the images and the capability of the system to interact with the users will bring about better diagnosis.

One way to compute the similarity between a given lesion L and another lesion L1 in one of the three categories C_1, C_2, and C_3 is as follows. For each category C_i, compute its centroid vector $CC_i = (\sum_{v \text{ in } C_i} v)/n_i$, where v is a four-dimensional vector representing (the attributes A_1, A_2, A_3, and A_4 of) a lesion in category C_i and n_i is the number of lesions in C_i. The covariance matrix M_i for the class C_i is defined to be $\sum_{v \text{ in } C_i}((v - CC_i) * (v - CC_i)_t)$, where $(v - CC_i)$ is a column vector, t stands for the transpose of the vector, and $*$ is matrix multiplication. The (i, j)th entry of this matrix gives the covariance of the ith and the jth attributes. The Mahalanobis distance between a lesion L with vector v and a lesion with vector v_j in class C_i is given by

$$M_d = (v - v_j)_t * M_i^{-1} * (v - v_j)$$

where -1 stands for the inverse of a matrix. Since the covariance matrix is incorporated, the distance function takes into consideration the interactions between different attributes. The normalized Mahalanobis distance between the two vectors is

$$NM_d = \frac{1}{2}(k \ln(2\pi) + \ln |M_i| + M_d)$$

where k is the number of dimensions of the vectors and $|X|$ is the determinant of the matrix X. Finally, the similarity between the two lesions is defined to be e^{-NM_d}, which has a value between 0 and 1.

11.2 Video Retrieval

11.2.1 Introduction

Video retrieval differs from image retrieval in at least two aspects. One is the temporal aspect: certain images follow others in the time domain. This is critical in video retrieval. The other aspect is that a logical hierarchy of video images can be formed. A common hierarchy is as follows. At the lowest level are individual *images*. An unbroken sequence of images from one camera can be called a *shot*. For example, a shot can be a sequence of images showing John Wayne drawing a gun. A sequence of shots focusing on the same point of interest can form a *scene*. For example, consider a scene in which John Wayne shoots some bandits. This scene can be a sequence of two shots. In the first shot John Wayne draws a gun, and in the second shot some bandits are hit and fall to the ground. A sequence of scenes can be organized into a *subplot*. For example, a subplot in which John Wayne rescues some villagers is a sequence of three scenes. In the first scene, John Wayne rides a horse to the village; in the second scene, he shoots some bandits; and this is followed by a scene in which the villagers celebrate their rescue. At the highest level, a video is classified according to its type. For example, it is a western movie.

This image hierarchy may be represented by a forest. Each node at the highest level represents a video. Let this level be called the *video level*. The children of a node at the video level, say node X_1, are different subplots of the video X_1. The children are denoted by $X_{11}, X_{12}, \ldots, X_{1s}$, in which node X_{1i} is followed by node $X_{1(i+1)}$ (see Figure 11.14). This lower level is called the *subplot level*. The children of a subplot, say X_{11}, are the various scenes associated with this subplot. They are denoted by $X_{111}, X_{112}, \ldots, X_{11p}$ in the figure. This is the *scene level*. The children of a scene, say X_{111}, are the shots of that scene. They are denoted

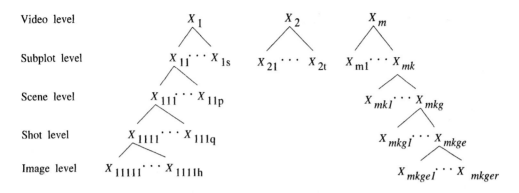

Video level

Subplot level

Scene level

Shot level

Image level

FIGURE 11.14 A Hierarchy of Images Modeling Video Data

by $X_{1111}, X_{1112}, \ldots, X_{111n}$. This is the *shot level*, and the images, as the children of this level, compose the lowest level. Figure 11.14 illustrates the hierarchy. Although the use of a hierarchy is reasonable for video retrieval, the number of levels and the names of the levels depend on the application. For example, the names associated with the levels for news broadcasts are different from those for movies. It should be noted that the hierarchy described above is not sufficiently general, as there could be sequences of images that span the same time interval. A directed acyclic graph can be employed to model sequences of images with overlapping time intervals, which are not allowed in a strict hierarchy. In the remaining part of this section, we shall limit ourselves to strict hierarchies.

Associated with each node in the hierarchy is some metadata describing the contents of the node. For example, the metadata associated with an image describe the contents of the image. Metadata of a shot can be considered a summary of the contents of the associated images. The contents of a shot can also be modeled by the entity-relationship model in image retrieval, because an action usually involves multiple images. Similarly, the metadata of a scene provide a summary of the associated shots, and the metadata of a subplot provide a summary of the associated scenes. Finally, the metadata at the video level may provide information about the type of the video, its title, its main characters, etc. If there are too many metadata to be generated or stored for videos, it may be desirable to have metadata associated with only shots and higher levels; i.e., metadata would not be stored at the image level. Currently, most metadata that are at a sufficiently high semantic level are manually generated. The recognition of objects that may overlap with other objects in still images is a very difficult problem in vision research. The recognition problem is easier in video, as certain objects, for example humans, may move in consecutive frames and it is possible to track moving objects. In addition, a video may have an audio component, which may provide some clues for detecting certain objects.

A *cut* separates two consecutive shots. By detecting cuts, images can be organized into shots automatically. Cuts may be detected by comparing the gray level/intensity/color of consecutive images either globally for the entire images or locally. If the difference between consecutive images exceeds a certain threshold, then a cut is assumed to be present. Automatic methods may generate some false cuts or may miss some real cuts.

11.2.2 A Language for Video Retrieval

As mentioned above, videos have temporal and hierarchical aspects. The temporal aspect will be described first. Temporal logic comes in different forms. The following description is based on modifications of *future temporal logic* (FTL). The key operators of this logic are FOLLOWED BY, UNTIL, and NEXT. Traditionally, formulas based on these operators are either satisfied or not satisfied. Since the image retrieval techniques presented earlier are similarity based, the semantics of these operators will be adjusted to permit similarity-based video retrieval. These will be defined as follows. A *segment* is an image at the image level, a shot at the shot level, a scene at the scene level, and a subplot at the subplot level. Consider a video v and a subsequence of v at some level denoted s. Let u be a segment in s. For a formula f that does not involve any temporal operator, the similarity of u with f is the same as that given by the image similarity formula given previously. With the use of temporal operators, the following cases are possible.

- $f = g_1$ FOLLOWED BY g_2: The similarity of f at u is the sum of the similarity of g_1 at u and $maxg2$, where $maxg2$ is the maximum of the similarities of segments with g_2 that occur after u. Specifically, if segments occurring after u have similarities $a_1, a_2, \ldots, a_k$ with g_2, then the $maxg2$ is the maximum of these a's.

- $f = g_1$ I-FOLLOWED g_2: This is the same as the FOLLOWED BY operator except that the segment satisfying g_2 should immediately follow the segment satisfying g_1.

- $f = g$ UNTIL h: Intuitively, this formula measures the extent that h is satisfied for a segment p that appears after u, assuming that all segments from u to p satisfy g to a reasonable extent. We assume that there is a threshold value t that determines whether g is satisfied to a reasonable extent. If the similarity of u with g is less than or equal to t, then g is assumed to be not satisfied at u and the similarity of f is zero; otherwise, let $ufar$ be the segment occurring after u and farthest away from u such that the similarity of g with any segment from u to $ufar$, including both end segments, exceeds threshold t. Let the maximum similarity of h with any of the segments in $[u + 1, ufar]$ and the one immediately following $ufar$ (if segment $ufar$ is not the last segment) be $hmax$; then the similarity of f is $hmax$.

- $f = [var \leftarrow h] g(var)$: The value of an attribute of an object may differ in different segments. For example, a moving object changes its location from one image to another. In order to relate the positions of the same object in different images, the assignment operator ($\leftarrow$) can be employed to capture the position of the object in one image, which is then compared to its position in a subsequent image. Clearly, the assignment operator and the comparison can be utilized for different objects instead of the same object. The similarity of f at u is the same as that of g at u with the following modification: when g is evaluated at u, the value of var is replaced by h.

Example 11.2 Suppose we require a portion of a video in which there is an image with two lions and the image is followed by an image with a tiger. This may be specified by the following formula:

$\exists X_1 \exists X_2 (\text{type}(X_1) = \text{"lion"}, \text{type}(X_2) = \text{"lion"})$

FOLLOWED BY

$\exists Y_1 (\text{type}(Y_1) = \text{"tiger"})$

In this example, the temporal operator FOLLOWED BY is outside the scope of the existential quantifiers. Let the specification referring to the lions be denoted L and that referring to a tiger be denoted T. ∎

Example 11.3 Suppose the required portion of the video satisfies the specification that there is an image containing two lions that are sleeping and this image is followed by one in which the two lions are fighting. The specification of the video portion could be

$\exists X_1 \exists X_2 (\text{type}(X_1) = \text{"lion"}, \text{type}(X_2) = \text{"lion"},$

$\quad (\text{state-of-motion}(X_1) = \text{"sleeping"}, \text{state-of-motion}(X_2) = \text{"sleeping"})$

$\quad \text{FOLLOWED BY } (X_1 \text{ fights } X_2))$

As was not the case in Example 11.2, the temporal operator is within the scope of the existential quantifiers for this example. ∎

Example 11.4 Suppose the required portion of the video satisfies the specification that there is an image containing two lions that are sleeping and this image is followed by one in which the two lions are jumping in the air. Suppose a sleeping lion has a height of zero relative to the ground. Then a jumping lion has a height greater than zero. The specification of the required video portion can be given by

$\exists X_1 \exists X_2 (\text{type}(X_1) = \text{"lion"}, \text{type}(X_2) = \text{"lion"},$

$\quad [h_1 \leftarrow \text{height}(X_1), h_2 \leftarrow \text{height}(X_2)],$

$\quad (\text{state-of-motion}(X_1) = \text{"sleeping"}, \text{state-of-motion}(X_2) = \text{"sleeping"})$

$\quad \text{FOLLOWED BY } (\text{height}(X_1) > h_1, \text{height}(X_2) > h_2))$ ∎

Many other temporal operators can be defined to facilitate the formulation of video retrieval. For example, g_1 FOLLOWED BY (n) g_2 can be utilized to retrieve video segments in which a segment satisfying g_1 to a certain extent is followed by a segment satisfying g_2 to some extent and the two segments are separated by no more than n segments. Another formula, g_1 UNORDERED g_2, can be used to specify segments in which a segment satisfies g_1 to some extent and a segment that may be the same segment satisfies g_2 to a certain extent, but these two segments, if different, may be in any order. For the remaining part of this section, we will concentrate on FOLLOWED BY, UNTIL, and the assignment operators. The algorithms for processing other temporal operators will be similar.

We now specify more complicated queries by making use of the hierarchy given previously (see Figure 11.14) by introducing level operators. It is sometimes useful to specify certain portions of a query at one level and other portions of the query at other levels. For example, a user may be interested in the movie *Born Free* and have the sequence of shots of the lions as given in Example 11.4. Then a reasonable specification might be as follows:

video level: title = "Born Free"
shot level: $\exists X_1 \exists X_2 (type(X_1) = $ "lion", $type(X_2) = $ "lion",
      $[h_1 \leftarrow height(X_1), h_2 \leftarrow height(X_2)]$,
      $(state\text{-}of\text{-}motion(X_1) = $ "sleeping", $state\text{-}of\text{-}motion(X_2) = $ "sleeping")
      FOLLOWED BY $(height(X_1) > h_1, height(X_2) > h_2))$

In general, a user may specify an explicit level by name, such as the video level or the shot level, and after indicating the contents to be satisfied at one level, specify what needs to be satisfied at the next level. The latter situation is provided by the keywords NEXT LEVEL. The similarity of a video segment with respect to a multilevel query can be given by a weighted sum of the similarities of the segments at different levels, with higher weights associated with higher levels. For example, if the conditions specified at the video level are not satisfied, it is unlikely that a video segment will be of interest to the user.

Although the query language specified above is formal, ordinary users will use a graphical interface. This can be obtained by adding three features to the graphical interface for image retrieval. The first feature is the specification of the level. This can be accomplished by showing the different levels that are possible and allowing the user to click on the levels that are appropriate for the current query. At the video level, information such as the title, the names of key actors, etc., need to be filled in by the users. The second feature to be added is the use of the temporal operators such as FOLLOWED BY and UNTIL. Consider Example 11.2. Suppose spec1 is the graphical specification for the segment having two lions and spec2 is that for the segment containing the tigers. Then a graphical specification for the video query is simply "spec1 FOLLOWED BY spec2". In Example 11.3, there is some complication, as the lions in the first segment are the same as those in the second segment. In order to achieve that, a condition box specifying conditions that need to be satisfied across different segments can be utilized. In this case, assume that the first segment and the second segment are identified by 1 and 2, respectively, and the lions in segment 1 and those in segment 2 are identified by IDs a, b, c, and d, respectively. Then the conditions that should appear in the condition box to ensure that the lions are the same in the two segments are "1.a = 2.c , 1.b = 2.d". In Example 11.4, the lions have different heights. This can be specified by adding the following conditions to the condition box: "1.a.height < 2.c.height, 1.b.height < 2.d.height". The third feature to be added is to simulate actions that are permitted by a VCR. These include play, stop, pause, fast forward, and fast rewind. Buttons for these actions should be provided.

Consider the display of segments satisfying "g_1 FOLLOWED BY g_2". Pairs of segments $\{(s_1, s_2)\}$ should be displayed to the user in descending order of similarity, where s_1 is a segment satisfying g_1 to a certain extent and s_2 is a segment occurring after s_1 and satisfying g_2 to a certain extent. As mentioned before, the sum of the two similarities is computed to obtain a similarity for each pair of segments and these similarities should be arranged in descending order to permit the display of pairs of segments with sufficiently high similarities. In the display of "g UNTIL h," a set of segments $\{[g_s, h_s]\}$ will be shown to the user in descending order of similarity, where the similarity of each segment in $[g_s, h_s - 1]$ satisfying g exceeds the required threshold and h_s is the segment after g_s having the maximum similarity. (The computation of the maximum similarity is detailed in the definition of the UNTIL operator.) Since all segments from g_s to h_s are shown to the user, the sequence of segments in $[g_s, h_s]$ can be considered as a single segment.

11.2.3 Processing Video Queries

Video queries can be classified as follows. Video queries without assignment operators and whose temporal operators are not within the scopes of existential quantifiers (which are the only quantifiers considered here) are relatively easy to process. They are typified by the query in Example 11.2. Queries of this type are denoted by NON-ASSIGN-SCOPE. Queries of the second type have temporal operators within the scopes of the existential operators, but no assignment operator is allowed. They are typified by the query in Example 11.3 and are denoted by NON-ASSIGN. The third type allows the assignment operator and is denoted by ASSIGN. These query types are considered below.

Processing of NON-ASSIGN-SCOPE Video Queries

If a query does not involve temporal operators or level operators, then it is processed as an image query. We assume that all images of a video are sequenced by IDs ranging from 1 to n, where 1 is the first image and n is the last image. For each image, a similarity value with such a query can be computed. Most images will have a similarity of 0 with the query and will not be utilized for later computations. The remaining images are grouped into intervals such that a sequence of segments (images, shots, etc.) having the same similarity are in the same interval. This can be represented by $([i, j], s)$, where each image within the interval $[i, j]$ has similarity s. We now consider the processing of temporal operators on intervals that were obtained previously. Only a sketch of the key ideas will be provided below.

Case 1. $f = g_1$ FOLLOWED BY g_2: If each g_k, $k = 1$ or 2, does not contain the FOL-LOWED BY operator, then it will produce a set of intervals of the form $([a, b], s)$, where the similarity of any image in $[a, b]$ has similarity s with g_k. (Note that b can be equal to a.) If g_k contains a single FOLLOWED BY operator, i.e., g_k is h_1 FOLLOWED BY h_2, then the processing of g_k will produce a set of the form $([a, b], [c, d], s)$, where $[a, b]$ strictly precedes $[c, d]$; segments in $[a, b]$ satisfy h_1 to a certain extent, say with similarity s_1, whereas segments in $[c, d]$ satisfy h_2 to a certain extent, say with similarity s_2; and the similarity of the combined two segments in the two intervals with g_k is $s = s_1 + s_2$. As mentioned before, the user will be shown the pairs of intervals in descending order of similarity. This is illustrated by Figure 11.15.

To facilitate the discussion of handling multiple occurrences of the FOLLOWED BY operator, we define an i-interval to be a sequence of i intervals in the form of $([a_1, b_1], [a_2, b_2], \dots, [a_i, b_i], s)$, where $b_{i-1} < a_i$, and s is the similarity of the combined segments in these intervals with the formula under consideration. Clearly, if g_k contains multiple occurrences of the FOLLOWED BY operator, it yields a set of i-intervals for some integer i. Suppose g_1 yields a set of i-intervals and g_2 yields a set of j-intervals. Let the set of i-intervals be denoted $\{([a_1, b_1], \dots, [a_i, b_i], s_1)\}$ and the set of j-intervals be denoted $\{([c_1, d_1], \dots, [c_j, d_j], s_2)\}$. We consider the merging of an i-interval $([a_1, b_1], \dots, [a_i, b_i], s_1)$ with a j-interval $([c_1, d_1], \dots, [c_j, d_j], s_2)$. The following subcases arise:

1. If $[c_1, d_1]$ precedes $[a_i, b_i]$, i.e., $d_1 < a_i$, then the similarity of the segments in the intervals with respect to f is zero. This is because the FOLLOWED BY operator requires the intervals associated with g_1 to precede those associated with g_2.

Interval	Similarity
[1, 2]	0.2
[4, 7]	0.3

h_1

Interval	Similarity
[9, 10]	0.1
[12, 13]	0.4

h_2

Pairs of intervals	Similarity
[1, 2] [9, 10]	0.3
[1, 2] [12, 13]	0.6
[4, 7] [9, 10]	0.4
[4, 7] [12, 13]	0.7

h_1 FOLLOWED BY h_2

FIGURE 11.15   Illustrating the FOLLOWED BY Operator

ii. If $[c_1, d_1]$ occurs after $[a_i, b_i]$, i.e., $c_1 > b_i$, then the result is the concatenation of the i-interval with the j-interval, and the similarity is $s_1 + s_2$.

iii. If $[c_1, d_1]$ overlaps with $[a_i, b_i]$, then either $d_1 = a_i$ or $d_1 > a_i$. In the former case, it is not possible to have an interval within $[a_i, b_i]$ followed by an interval within $[c_1, d_1]$. Thus, the similarity of the i-interval and the j-interval with respect to f is zero. In the latter situation, there exist t's satisfying $\max\{a_i, c_1 - 1\} \leq t \leq \min\{b_i, d_1 - 1\}$. Choose a t to form the intervals $[a_i, t]$ and $[t + 1, d_1]$. Note that $[a_i, t]$ is contained in $[a_i, b_i]$ and $[t + 1, d_1]$ is contained in $[c_1, d_1]$. Thus, segments in $([a_1, b_1], \ldots, [a_{i-1}, b_{i-1}], [a_i, t])$ have similarity s_1 with g_1 and segments in $([t + 1, d_1], \ldots, [c_j, d_j])$ have similarity s_2 with g_2. As a result, segments in the $(i + j)$-interval $([a_1, b_1], \ldots, [a_{i-1}, b_{i-1}], [a_i, t], [t+1, d_1], \ldots, [a_j, b_j])$ have similarity $s_1 + s_2$ with f.

Case 2. $f = g$ UNTIL h: Consider the case in which g and h do not contain the FOLLOWED BY operator. By definition of UNTIL, a threshold t is assumed such that if the similarity of a segment obtained for g is below t, then it is discarded. After the threshold process is carried out, we obtain a set of intervals such that segments in an interval have similarities beyond threshold t. Let I be a typical interval for g. Similarly, there is a set of intervals for h such that segments within an interval have the same similarity with h. Suppose the intervals associated with h that overlap with I are $J_1, J_2, \ldots, J_k$, where the beginning point of J_1 may be smaller than the beginning point of I, $J_2, \ldots, J_{k-1}$ are contained within I, the ending point of J_k may be larger than the ending point of I, and J_{k-1} precedes J_k. Let the beginning point and the ending point of an interval P be denoted by b_P and e_P, respectively. Let the similarities of the segments in interval J_d with h be s_d, $1 \leq d \leq k$. This is shown in Figure 11.16.

Let s_t be the maximum of $\{s_1, s_2, \ldots, s_k\}$ and J_t be the interval where the maximum occurs. If $t = k$, then a single interval is formed. This interval is $[b_I, e_I + 1]$ if $e_I < e_k$, and $[b_I, e_{J_k}]$ otherwise, where b_I is the beginning point of I and e_I is the ending point of I. Segments in this interval satisfy f with similarity s_t, and the process terminates.

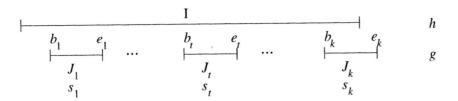

FIGURE 11.16   Illustrating the UNTIL Operator

Otherwise (i.e., $t < k$), segments in the interval $[b_1, e_{J_t}]$ have similarity s_t because segments in the first part of the interval (i.e., those before b_{J_t}) satisfy g and segments in the remaining part $[b_{J_t}, e_{J_t}]$ have similarity s_t with h. Other intervals from $\{I, J_1, J_2, \ldots, J_k\}$ also satisfy f to a certain extent. These intervals can be constructed by invoking the same process but with I replaced by $[e_{J_t} + 1, e_1]$ and $\{J_1, J_2, \ldots, J_k\}$ replaced by $\{J_{t+1}, \ldots, J_k\}$.

Consider the case in which h or g contain the FOLLOWED BY or the UNTIL operator. In order to apply the technique iteratively, we note that the processing of UNTIL yields a set of intervals. Although the processing of FOLLOWED BY may yield a set of i-intervals, each i-interval may be visualized as a single interval containing the i subintervals. In this way, a temporal formula may be processed iteratively.

Example 11.5 Consider the temporal query in Example 11.2 in which the segment containing the lions (specified by formula L) is followed by a segment containing a tiger (specified by formula T). Suppose the processing of formulas L and T yields the following results.

Result for L	Result for T
([10, 20], 0.4)	([30, 40], 0.3)
([15, 35], 0.5)	

The processing of the FOLLOWED BY operator yields

Result for L FOLLOWED BY T
([10, 20], [30, 40], 0.7)
([15, t], [t + 1, 40], 0.8), $29 \leq t \leq 35$

The interpretation is that it is likely that the segments in $[15, t]$ contain the lions and the segments in $[t + 1, 40]$ contain the tiger, $29 \leq t \leq 34$. ∎

Example 11.6 Suppose a portion of a video is required in which two lions are fighting in a sequence of images and this sequence is immediately followed by an image in which there are two tigers. This query can be expressed as

$\exists X_1 \exists X_2 (\text{type}(X_1) = \text{"lion"}, \text{type}(X_2) = \text{"lion"}, X_1 \text{ fights } X_2)$
UNTIL $\exists X_3 \exists X_4 (\text{type}(X_3) = \text{"tiger"}, \text{type}(X_4) = \text{"tiger"})$

Suppose the evaluation of the subformula before UNTIL yields the following table T_1. Let the threshold be 0.3, implying that all entries below 0.3 are left out.

$$([10, 40], 0.4)$$
$$([50, 70], 0.5)$$
Table T_1

Suppose the evaluation of the formula after UNTIL yields the following table T_2.

$$([15, 20], 0.3)$$
$$([25, 30], 0.5)$$
$$([35, 45], 0.4)$$
Table T_2

Then the final result of evaluating the query is given by the following table T_3.

$$([10, 30], 0.5)$$
$$([31, 41], 0.4)$$
Table T_3

Let $I = [10, 40]$, $J_1 = [15, 20]$, $J_2 = [25, 30]$, and $J_3 = [35, 45]$. Note that I, J_1, J_2, and J_3 satisfy the situation given before Example 11.5. Note that J_2 has the maximum similarity. When the first entry in table T_1, say E_{11}, is evaluated against the first entry in T_2, say E_{21}, the result is $R_0 = ([10, 20], 0.3)$. When E_{11} is evaluated against the second entry of T_2, say E_{22}, the result is $R_1 = ([10, 30], 0.5)$. Since R_1 has a higher similarity than R_0 and the interval of images in R_0 is contained in that of R_1, i.e., $[10, 20]$ is contained in $[10, 30]$, R_0 is eliminated. This corresponds to $[b_1, e_{J_2}]$, where the beginning point of I, b_1, is 10 and the ending point of J_2, e_{J_2}, is 30. When E_{11} is evaluated against the third entry of T_2, the result is $([10, 41], 0.4)$. This is equivalent to $([10, 30], 0.4)$ together with $([31, 41], 0.4)$. The former entry is dominated by R_1 and is eliminated, yielding the entry $([31, 41], 0.4)$. The evaluation of the second entry of table T_1 with any entry of table T_2 yields null. ■

Processing NON-ASSIGN Video Queries

Consider the formula

$$f = \exists X_1 \exists X_2 \ldots \exists X_k(g_1 \, T_1 \, g_2 \, T_2 \ldots g_s)$$

where each g_i is a subformula with possibly some *free* variables, the T_j's are temporal operators, and $\exists$ is the existential quantifier. For example, if

$$f = \exists X_1 \exists X_2(g_1(X_1, X_2) \text{ UNTIL } g_2(X_1)),$$

then X_1 and X_2 are free in g_1 and X_1 is free in g_2. Although the assignment operator is not considered, the variables that are free in a g_i subformula corresponding to objects need to be set equal to the same free variables that appear in other g_j subformulas. This can be effectively achieved by the relational *natural join* operator. More precisely, consider g_1 with f_1 free variables and g_2 with f_2 free variables, and suppose they are combined using a temporal operator T to form h, i.e., $h = g_1 \, T \, g_2$. When g_1 is processed, an object-oriented table with $f_1 + 1$ columns will be obtained. The first f_1 columns are for the f_1 free variables, and the next column contains sets of i-intervals and their similarities. A row $(c_1, c_2, \ldots, c_{f_1}, \{(I_1, s_1), \ldots, (I_p, s_p)\})$

in the table has the following interpretation. When the free variables in g_1 take on the values $c_1, c_2, \ldots, c_{f_1}$, the segments in the i-intervals (which can be simple intervals) $I_1, I_2, \ldots, I_p$ have similarities $s_1, s_2, \ldots, s_p$, respectively, with respect to g_1. Similarly, there is another table with $f_2 + 1$ columns for g_2. When certain variables in g_1 are the same as certain variables in g_2, the natural join of the two tables is taken to ensure that the corresponding variables take on the same values. The column for the intervals for h in the natural join is obtained from the corresponding columns for g_1 and g_2 using the the the algorithm for the temporal operator T. If T is UNTIL or FOLLOWED BY, the process given in the previous subsection is invoked to combine the intervals. After the entire formula has been computed, the rows should be sorted in descending order of similarity and the segments corresponding to these rows should be presented to the user in the same order.

Example 11.7 Let g_1 denote the subformula representing the two sleeping lions and g_2 denote the subformula representing the fighting lions. The free variables in g_1 are X_1 and X_2, denoting the lions; the free variables in g_2 are also X_1 and X_2, because they denote the same lions. Let the tables for g_1 and g_2 be

X_1	X_2	I
1	2	([10, 20], 0.5)
3	4	([10, 20], 0.4)

Table for g_1

X_1	X_2	J
1	2	([30, 40], 0.4)
3	4	([50, 60], 0.2)

Table for g_2

The interpretation of the tables is that there are four lions in the interval [10, 20]. The similarity for the segments containing the lions with IDs 1 and 2, which are sleeping, is 0.5; that for the other lions, with IDs 3 and 4, is 0.4; the similarity for the segments in the interval [30, 40] containing lions with IDs 1 and 2 that are fighting is 0.4; and the similarity for the segments in the interval [50, 60] containing lions with IDs 3 and 4 is 0.2. The formula h is

$$\exists X_1 \exists X_2 (g_1(X_1, X_2) \text{ FOLLOWED BY } g_2(X_1, X_2)).$$

By performing the FOLLOWED BY operation, the following table is obtained. In this table, the first interval in each pair comes from the table for g_1, and the second interval is obtained from the table for g_2.

X_1	X_2	K
1	2	([10, 20], [30, 40], 0.9)
3	4	([10, 20], [50, 60], 0.6)

The segments given in the first row of the table will be shown to the user before the segments in the second row, because the segments in the first row have a higher similarity value. ∎

11 IMAGE AND VIDEO RETRIEVAL

Processing ASSIGN Queries

We first motivate the processing of such queries by examining Example 11.4. In that example, we have the following specification:

$\exists X_1 \exists X_2 (\text{type}(X_1) = \text{"lion"}, \text{type}(X_2) = \text{"lion"},$

$[h_1 \leftarrow \text{height}(X_1), h_2 \leftarrow \text{height}(X_2)],$

$(\text{state-of-motion}(X_1) = \text{"sleeping"}, \text{state-of-motion}(X_2) = \text{"sleeping"})$

FOLLOWED BY $(\text{height}(X_1) > h_1, \text{height}(X_2) > h_2)).$

In this example, there are two subformulas g_1 and g_2, where g_1 refers to the lions; there are two occurrences of the assignment operator in g_1; and g_2 refers to the lions with comparisons of their heights with those in earlier segments. As in the section on processing NON-ASSIGN queries, we will obtain a table for each formula. The columns of a table correspond to free object variables appearing in the corresponding subformula. In order to evaluate the assignment operator and the comparison predicates, the attribute variables and the attribute values in these operators and predicates need to be included in the table. For example, the columns of table T_1 for g_1 correspond to the object variables X_1 and X_2, the variables h_1 and h_2, and the intervals of similarities. Similarly, the columns of table T_2 for g_2 will contain the object variables X_1 and X_2, the attributes height(X_1) and height(X_2), and the intervals of similarities. In table T_1, for each row $(c_1, c_2, a_1, a_2, (I, s_1))$, the interpretation is that when object variables X_1 and X_2 take on values c_1 and c_2 and $h_1 = a_1$, $h_2 = a_2$, the segments in I satisfy g_1 with similarity s_1. The interpretation of table T_2 is slightly different, because the results of evaluating the predicates height$(X_1) > h_1$ and height$(X_2) > h_2$ are not included in this table. In other words, each row $(d_1, d_2, e_1, e_2, (J, s_2))$ means that when X_1 and X_2 take on the values d_1 and d_2, and when height$(X_1) = e_1$ and height$(X_2) = e_2$, the similarity of the segments in J with respect to g_2, with the exception that the predicates (height$(X_1) > h_1$, height$(X_2) > h_2$) are not evaluated, is s_2. In order to evaluate these predicates and to ensure that the object variables take on the same values, equijoins on the object variables and inequality joins on the two pairs of heights are taken together with the evaluation of the temporal operator FOLLOWED BY. This is illustrated by the following example, which uses the query in Example 11.4.

Example 11.8 Suppose the evaluation of g_1 yields table T_1.

X_1	X_2	h_1	h_2	interval$_1$	similarity
1	2	0	0	[10, 20]	0.4
3	4	50	100	[10, 20]	0.6

Table T_1 for subformula g_1

Suppose the evaluation of g_2, with the exception of the inequality predicates, yields the table T_2.

X_1	X_2	height(X_1)	height(X_2)	interval$_2$	similarity
1	2	20	30	[30, 40]	0.3
3	4	10	20	[40, 50]	0.5

Table for subformula g_2 without evaluating the inequality predicates

When the equality joins ($T_1.X_1 = T_2.X_1, T_1.X_2 = T_2.X_2$), inequality joins (height(X_1) > h_1, height(X_2) > h_2), and the temporal operator FOLLOWED BY are evaluated, the second tuple from each of the two tables is eliminated, because the inequality joins cannot be satisfied. The final result is the following table for the entire formula.

X_1	X_2	2-interval	similarity
1	2	([10, 20], [30, 40])	0.7

Table for combining the two subformulas

It should be noted that the heights of objects in video segments may not be determined precisely. In that situation, a fuzzy comparison instead of a precise comparison is made, resulting in a similarity. This similarity should be combined with the similarities associated with the intervals. ∎

In general, a table is created for each subformula and this table includes the free object variables (X_1 and X_2 in the above example), the attribute variables (h_1 and h_2), and the attribute values (height(X_1) and height(X_2)) that appear in the subformula. When the same object variable appears in different tables, an equijoin is constructed. When an attribute variable is related to another attribute variable or attribute value, a join, which can be an equijoin or an inequality join, is constructed. Then, for each row, the temporal operators are evaluated to form the similarities for various intervals.

Exercises

11.1 Suppose we are given a two-dimensional grid, with objects located in the grid as follows:

A B	C	
	D	E

Within a region, there is no ordering among the objects. Suppose X | Y means that X is to the left of Y and X > Y means that X is above Y. Give a minimal description of the spatial relationships among the objects in a grid so that all spatial relationships can be deduced from the minimal description. Use the above example to illustrate your answer.

11.2 Suppose the similarity between a query Q and a picture P is determined by enumerating all possible matchings between objects in Q and objects in P and all possible matchings between relationships in Q and relationships in P and choosing the largest value among all possible matchings. Give a systematic way to compute the similarity. Show by an example that the way given in the book, in which each object in Q is matched against the most similar object in P, may not yield the largest similarity.

11.3 Two images may have the same or similar histograms even though the images are very different in contents. A more elaborate scheme to eliminate most false positives is as follows. A histogram is constructed for each object, and two images are considered similar only if the histograms associated with the objects in one image are very similar to the histograms associated with the corresponding objects in the other image.

(a) Give an important disadvantage of the elaborate scheme.

(b) Give a scheme that is more sophisticated than the one-histogram-per-image scheme but is simpler than the elaborate scheme.

11.4 Transformation from one space to another space is very often used in computer vision, because certain objects can be recognized more easily in the transformed space than in the original space. Give an example of such a case.

11.5 Give two reasons why similarity match is more appropriate than exact match for image retrieval.

11.6 Given the spatial relationships (A, above, B), (B, overlaps, C), (D, inside, B), (D, inside, C), and (B, above, E), find a deduced spatial relationship between A and E.

11.7 Given the spatial relationships (B, overlaps, C), (B, inside, A), (A, overlaps, D), (C, inside, D), and (B, overlaps, A), find the minimum reduction of the spatial relationships.

11.8 Identify several situations in which the extended entity-relationship model may fail to match a query against desired pictures.

11.9 The video query language given in this chapter does not allow multiple video sequences to be shown in different windows at the same time. Suppose the parallel display capability is to be desired. Provide an operator that permits parallel display, and explain its semantics. Incorporate it into an SQL-like query language and show an example illustrating its use.

11.10 The language given in this chapter for image retrieval does not handle disjunction or negation. Describe how the processing of these operators can be handled.

Bibliographic Notes

The discussion of the representations of pictures and their retrieval at the semantic levels was extracted from [10, 335, 336]. Materials on characterization of color, texture, and shape features can be found in [136, 152, 151, 142, 225, 361]. Texture characterization using fractal codes is given in [162]. Retrieval using image features is provided in [121, 154, 151, 142, 189, 257, 278]. The QBIC system, now commercially available, is described in several papers, including [117, 121, 278]. Virage is another commercial system [154]. The extended SQL is based on [230]. The key idea in the reduction of dimensions is extracted from [4, 117, 119].

Retrieval using keywords, textual description, or captions is given in [78, 142, 249, 343]. A system using both keywords and image features for retrieval is described in [281]. A hierarchy of image representations from raw image data to objects and relations at the user semantic level is given in [63, 155]. Representation of spatial relations with some measure of distance is available in [64]. Spatial relationships involving angles are handled in [153]. The use of rules in representing spatial relationships, the concept of the completeness of rules, and reduction of spatial relationships can be found in [335, 336]. An important application in image retrieval is face recognition. Sample papers in face recognition are [14, 227]. A medical application involving spatial relationships among multiple objects can be found in [175].

The temporal language, the hierarchical structure of videos, and the processing of video queries are derived from [337], although the semantics of the temporal operators there are slightly different from the semantics of the temporal operators given here. Specification of temporal conditions can be done in many ways. Another common way is to employ regular expressions. For example, "P FOLLOWED BY Q" can be expressed by the regular expression $P(X)^*Q$, where X stands for any formula and $*$ means zero or more occurrences, and "P UNTIL Q" can be expressed by the regular expression P^+Q, where $+$ means one or more occurrences. Refer to [60, 138, 139] for specification of temporal conditions. Cut detection methods can be found in [134, 160, 209, 274, 362]. Detection of common camera operations, such as pans, tilts, and zooms can be found in [57]. Many other video querying systems exist. For example, [412, 413] uses low-level features and keywords for retrieval, [57] uses camera operations in addition to low-level features and keywords, and [181] employs an SQL-like language for video retrieval. It seems that their retrieval is exact, instead of similarity based. A classification of metadata and their use appears in [190]. Web-based image and video retrieval systems can be found in [339, 355].

References

[1] S. Abiteboul, R. Hull, and V. Vianu. *Foundations of Databases.* Reading, MA: Addison-Wesley, 1995.

[2] S. Abiteboul, P. Kanellakis, and G. Grahne. On the Representation and Querying of Sets of Possible Worlds. *Theoretical Computer Science*, 78:1, 1991, pp. 158–187.

[3] R. Agrawal. A Super Scalar Sort Algorithm for RISC Processors. ACM SIGMOD International Conference on Management of Data, Montreal, June 1996, pp. 240–246.

[4] R. Agrawal, C. Faloutsos, and A. Swami. Efficient Similarity Search in Sequence Databases. International Conference on Foundations of Data Organization and Algorithms, Evanston, IL, October 1993, pp. 69–84.

[5] R. Agrawal, and H. V. Jagadish. Hybrid Transitive Closure Algorithms. International Conference on Very Large Data Bases, Brisbane, Australia, August 1990, pp. 326–334.

[6] R. Agrawal, and H. V. Jagadish. Direct Transitive Closure Algorithms: Design and Performance Evaluations. *ACM Transactions on Database Systems,* 15:3, September 1990, pp. 427–438.

[7] R. Ahmed, P. DeSmedt, W. Du, W. Kent, M. Ketabchi, W. Litwin, A. Raffi, and M. Shan. The Pegasus Heterogeneous Multidatabase System. *IEEE Computer,* 33:1, 1991, pp. 19–27.

[8] A. Aho, M. Garey, and J. Ullman. The Transitive Reduction of a Directed Graph. *SIAM Journal of Computing,* 1:2, June 1972, pp. 131–137.

[9] A. Arpaci-Dusseau, R. Arpaci-Dusseau, A. Culler, J. Hellerstein, and D. Patterson. High-Performance Sorting on Networks of Workstations. ACM SIGMOD International Conference on Management of Data, Tucson, AZ, May 1997.

[10] A. Aslandogan, C. Thier, C. Yu, C. Liu, and K. Nair. Design, Implementation and Evaluation of SCORE (A System for COntent based REtrieval of Pictures). International Conference on Data Engineering, Taipei, Taiwan, March 1995, pp. 280–287.

[11] A. Aslandogan, C. Thier, C. Yu, J. Zou, and N. Rishe. Using Semantic Contents and WordNet in Image Retrieval. International ACM SIGIR Conference, Philadelphia, July 1997, pp. 286–295.

[12] M. Astrahan, et al. System R, A Relational Approach to Data Base Management. *ACM Transactions on Database Systems,* 1:2, June 1976, pp. 97–137.

[13] R. Attar, and A. Fraenkel. Local Feedback in Full-Text Retrieval Systems. *Journal of the ACM,* 24:3, July 1977, pp. 397–417.

[14] J. Bach, S. Paul, and R. Jain. A Visual Information Management System for Interactive Retrieval of Faces. *IEEE Transactions on Knowledge and Data Engineering,* 5:4, August 1993, pp. 619–628.

[15] F. Bancilhon, C. Delobel, and P. Kanellakis (editors). *Building an Object-Oriented Database System: The Story of O2.* San Francisco: Morgan Kaufmann, 1992.

[16] F. Bancilhon, and R. Ramakrishnan. An Amateur's Introduction to Recursive Query-Processing Strategies. ACM SIGMOD International Conference on Management of Data, Washington, DC, May 1986, pp. 16–52.

[17] C. Baru, and G. Fecteau. An Overview of DB2 Parallel Edition. ACM SIGMOD International Conference on Management of Data, San Jose, CA, May 1995, pp. 460–462.

[18] C. Baru, and O. Frieder. Database Operations in a Cube-Connected Multicomputer System. *IEEE Transactions on Computers,* 38:6, June 1989, pp. 920–927.

[19] K. Batcher. Sorting Networks and Their Applications. 1968 Spring Joint Computer Conference, Atlantic City, NJ, April 1968, pp. 307–314.

[20] G. Baudet, and D. Stevenson. Optimal Sorting Algorithms for Parallel Computers. *IEEE Transactions on Computers,* 27:1, January 1978.

[21] B. Baugsto, and J. Greipsland. Parallel Sorting Methods for Large Data Volumes on a Hypercube Database Computer. Sixth International Workshop on Database Machines, Deauville, France, June 1989, pp. 127–141.

[22] R. Bayer. Query Evaluation and Recursion in Deductive Database Systems. Unpublished memorandum, Technical U. of Munich, 1985.

[23] R. Bayer, and K. Unterauer. Prefix B-Trees. *ACM Transactions on Database Systems,* 2:1, March 1977, pp. 11–26.

[24] M. Beck, D. Bitton, and W. K. Wilkinson. Sorting Large Files on a Backend Multiprocessor. *IEEE Transactions on Computers,* 37:7, July 1988, pp. 769–778.

[25] N. Beckmann, H-P. Kriegel, R. Schneider, and B. Seeger, The R*-Tree: An Efficient and Robust Access Method for Points and Rectangles. ACM SIGMOD International Conference on Management of Data, Atlantic City, NJ, May 1990, pp. 322–331.

[26] C. Beeri, and Y. Kornatzky. Algebraic Optimization of Object-Oriented Query Languages. International Conference on Database Theory, Paris, December 1990, pp. 72–88.

[27] J. Bentley. Multi-dimensional Binary Search Trees Used for Associative Searching. *Communications of the ACM,* 18:9, September 1975, pp. 509–517.

[28] V. Benzaken, and C. Delobel. Enhancing Performance in a Persistent Object Store: Clustering Strategies in O_2. Technical Report 50-90, Altair, 1990.

[29] P. Bernstein, and D. Chiu. Using Semi-joins to Solve Relational Queries. *Journal of the ACM,* 28:1, January 1981, pp. 25–40.

[30] P. Bernstein, N. Goodman, E. Wong, C. Reeve, and J. Rothnie. Query Processing in a System for Distributed Databases (SDD-1). *ACM Transactions on Data Base Systems,* 6:4, December 1981, pp. 602–625.

[31] E. Bertino, and P. Fosoli. Index Organizations for Object-Oriented Database Systems. *IEEE Transactions on Knowledge and Data Engineering,* 7:2, April 1995, pp. 193–209.

[32] E. Bertino, and W. Kim. Indexing Techniques for Queries on Nested Objects. *IEEE Transactions on Knowledge and Data Engineering,* 1:2, 1989, pp. 196–214.

[33] A. Bhide. An Analysis of Three Transaction Processing Architectures. International Conference on Very Large Data Bases, Los Angeles, August 1988, pp. 339–350.

[34] D. Bitton, H. Boral, D. DeWitt, and W. K. Wilkinson. Parallel Algorithms for the Execution of Relational Database Operations. *ACM Transactions on Database Systems,* 8:3, September 1983, pp. 324–353.

[35] D. Bitton, D. DeWitt, D. Hsiao, and J. Menon. A Taxonomy of Parallel Sorting. *ACM Computing Surveys,* 16:3, September 1984, pp. 287–318.

[36] J. Blakeley, W. J. McKenna, and G. Graefe. Experiences Building the Open OODB Query Optimizer. ACM SIGMOD International Conference on Management of Data, Washington, DC, May 1993, pp. 287–296.

[37] M. Blasgen, and K. Eswaran. On the Evaluation of Queries in a Relational Database System. *IBM Systems Journal,* 16:1, 1977, pp. 363–377.

[38] M. Blasgen, and K. Eswaran. Storage and Access in Relational Databases. *IBM Systems Journal,* 16:4, 1977, pp. 362–377.

[39] A. Bookstein, S. Klein, and T. Raita. Detecting Content-Bearing Words by Serial Clustering (Extended Abstract). International ACM SIGIR Conference, Seattle, July 1995, pp. 319–327.

[40] A. Bookstein, and D. Kraft. Operation Research Applied to Document Indexing and Retrieval Decisions. *Journal of the ACM*, 24:3, July 1977, pp. 418–427.

[41] A. Bookstein, and D. Swanson. Decision Theoretic Formulation for Indexing. *Journal of the American Society for Information Science*, 26, 1975, pp. 45–50.

[42] H. Boral. Parallelism in Bubba. International Symposium on Databases in Parallel and Distributed Systems, Austin, TX, December 1988, pp. 68–71.

[43] H. Boral, W. Alexander, L. Clay, G. Copeland, S. Danforth, M. Franklin, B. Hart, M. Smith, and P. Valduriez. Prototyping Bubba, A Highly Parallel Database System. *IEEE Transactions on Knowledge and Data Engineering*, 2:1, March 1990, pp. 4–24.

[44] P. Bosc, M. Galibourg, and G. Hamon. Fuzzy Querying with SQL: Extensions and Implementation Aspects. *Fuzzy Sets and Systems*, 28, 1988, pp. 333–349.

[45] K. Bratbergsengen. Hashing Methods and Relational Algebra Operations. International Conference on Very Large Data Bases, Singapore, August 1984, pp. 323–333.

[46] K. Bratbergsengen. Algebra Operations on a Parallel Computer—Performance Evaluation. In *Database Machines and Knowledge Base Machines*, edited by M. Mitsuregawa and H. Tanaka. Norwell, MA: Kluwer Academic, 1987.

[47] M. Bright, and A. Hurson. A Taxonomy and Current Issues in Multidatabase Systems. *IEEE Computer*, 25:3, March 1992, pp. 50–60.

[48] B. Buckles, and F. Petry. A Fuzzy Model for Relational Databases. *Fuzzy Sets and Systems*, 7:3, May 1982, pp. 213–226.

[49] B. Buckles, F. Petry, and H. Sachar. Design of Similarity-Based Relational Databases. In *Fuzzy Logic in Knowledge Engineering*, edited by H. Prade and C. Negoita. Cologne, Germany: Verlag Tüv Rheinland, 1986.

[50] C. Buckley, A. Singhal, M. Mitra, and G. Salton. New Retrieval Approaches Using SMART: TREC 4. In *Proceedings of the TREC 4 Conference*, edited by D. Harman. NIST Special Publication, Gaithersburg, MD, 1996.

[51] O. Bukhres, and A. Elmagarmid (editors). *Object-Oriented Multidatabase Systems*. Englewood Cliffs, NJ: Prentice Hall, 1996.

[52] G. Bultzingslowen. Optimizing SQL Queries for Parallel Processing. *SIGMOD Record*, December 1989, pp. 17–22.

[53] F. Can, and E. Ozkarahan. Concepts and Effectiveness of the Cover-Coefficient-Based Clustering Methodology for Text Databases. ACM Transactions on Database Systems, 15:4, December 1990, pp. 483–517.

[54] J. Callan, Z. Lu, and W. Croft. Searching Distributed Collections with Inference Networks. International ACM SIGIR Conference, Seattle, July 1995, pp. 21–28.

[55] A. Cardenas. Heterogeneous Distributed Database Management: The HD-DBMS. *Proceedings of the IEEE,* 75:5, May 1987, pp. 588–600.

[56] A. Cardenas, and G. Wang. Translation of SQL/DS Data Access/Update into Entity/Relationship Data Access/Update. Fourth International Conference on the E-R Approach, Chicago, October 1985, pp. 256–267.

[57] M. Cascia, and E. Ardizzone. JACOB: Just a Content-Based Query System for Video Databases. IEEE International Conference on Acoustics, Speech and Signal Processing, Atlanta, GA, May 1996.

[58] R. Cattell (editor). *The Object Database Standard: ODMG-93, Release 1.2.* San Francisco: Morgan Kaufmann, 1996.

[59] S. Ceri, and G. Pelagatti. *Distributed Databases: Principles and Systems.* New York: McGraw-Hill, 1984.

[60] S. Chakravarthy, and P. Mishra. An Event Specification Language (Snoop) for Active Databases and its Detection. Technical Report, U. of Florida, 1991.

[61] A. Chandra, and D. Harel. Structure and Complexity of Relational Queries. IEEE Symposium on Foundations of Computer Science, Syracuse, New York, October 1980, pp. 333–347.

[62] A. Chandra, and P. Merlin. Optimal Implementation of Conjunctive Queries in Relational Databases. Ninth ACM Symposium on the Theory of Computing, Boulder, CO, May 1977, pp. 77–90.

[63] S. K. Chang, and A. Hsu. Image Information Systems: Where Do We Go from Here? *IEEE Transactions on Data and Knowledge Engineering,* 4:5, October 1992, pp. 431–442.

[64] S. K. Chang, Q. Shi, and C. Yan. Iconic Indexing by 2-D Strings. *IEEE Transactions on Pattern Analysis and Machine Intelligence*, 9:3, May 1987, pp. 413–428.

[65] A. Chen. Outerjoin Optimization in Multidatabase Systems. Second International Symposium on Distributed and Parallel Database Systems, Dublin, Ireland, July 1990, pp. 211–218.

[66] A. Chen, D. Brill, M. Templeton, and C. Yu. Distributed Query Processing in a Multiple Database System. *IEEE Journal on Selected Areas in Communications,* 7:3, 1989, pp. 390–398.

[67] M. Chen, M. Lo, P. Yu, and H. Young. Using Segmented Right-Deep Trees for the Execution of Pipelined Hash Joins. International Conference on Very Large Data Bases, Vancouver, August 1992, pp. 15–26.

[68] M. Chen, M. Lo, P. Yu, and H. Young. Applying Segmented Right-Deep Trees for Pipelining Multiple Hash Joins. *IEEE Transactions on Knowledge and Data Engineering,* 7:3, August 1995, pp. 656–668.

[69] M. Chen, and P. Yu. Interleaving a Join Sequence with Semi-joins in Distributed Query Processing. *IEEE Transactions of Parallel and Distributed Systems,* 3:5, September 1992, pp. 611–621.

[70] M. Chen, P. Yu, and K. Wu. Optimization of Parallel Execution for Multi-join Queries. *IEEE Transactions on Knowledge and Data Engineering,* 8:3, June 1996, pp. 416–428.

[71] J. Cheng, and A. Hurson. Effective Clustering of Complex Objects in Object-Oriented Databases. ACM SIGMOD International Conference on Management of Data, Denver, May 1991, pp. 22–31.

[72] D. Chiu, and Y. Ho. A Method for Interpreting Tree Queries into Optimal Semi-join Expressions. ACM SIGMOD International Conference on Management of Data, Santa Monica, CA, May 1980, pp. 169–178.

[73] C. Chow, and C. Liu. Approximating Discrete Probability Distributions with Dependence Trees. *IEEE Transactions on Information Theory,* 14:3, May 1968, pp. 462–468.

[74] D. Chow, and C. Yu. On the Construction of Feedback Queries. *Journal of the ACM,* 29:1, January 1982, pp. 127–151.

[75] S. Christodoulakis. Estimating Record Selectivities. *Information Systems,* 8:2, 1983, pp. 105–115.

[76] S. Christodoulakis. Estimating Block Transfers and Join Sizes. ACM SIGMOD International Conference on Management of Data, San Jose, CA, May 1983, pp. 40–54.

[77] S. Christodoulakis, and C. Faloutsos. Signature Files: An Access Method for Documents and Its Analytical Performance Evaluation. *ACM Transactions on Office Information Systems,* 2:4, October 1984, pp. 267–288.

[78] T. Chua, H. Pung, G. Lu, and H. Jong. A Concept Based Image Retrieval System. IEEE International Conference on System Science, 1994, pp. 590–598.

[79] C-W. Chung. DATAPLEX: An Access to Heterogeneous Distributed Databases. *Communications of the ACM,* 33:1, January 1990, pp. 70–80.

[80] S. Cluet, and C. Delobel. A General Framework for the Optimization of Object-Oriented Queries. ACM SIGMOD International Conference on Management of Data, San Diego, CA, June 1992, pp. 383–392.

[81] S. Cluet, and C. Delobel. Towards a Unification of Rewrite-Based Optimization Techniques for Object-Oriented Queries. In *Query Processing for Advanced Database Systems,* edited by J. C. Freytag, D. Maier, and G. Vossen. San Francisco: Morgan Kaufmann, 1994, pp. 245–272.

[82] E. Codd. A Relational Model for Shared Large Data Banks. *Communications of the ACM,* 13:6, June 1970, pp. 377–387.

[83] E. Codd. Extending the Database Relational Model to Capture More Meaning. *ACM Transactions on Database Systems,* 4:4, 1979, pp. 397–434.

[84] D. Comer. The Ubiquitous B-Tree. *ACM Computing Surveys,* 11:2, June 1979, pp. 121–137.

[85] W. Cooper. A Definition of Relevance for Information Retrieval. *Information Storage and Retrieval,* 1971, pp. 19–37.

[86] W. Cooper. The Inadequacy of Probability of Usefulness as a Ranking Criterion for Retrieval System Output. School of Library and Information Studies, Technical Report, U. of California at Berkeley, 1971.

[87] W. Cooper. Some Inconsistencies and Misidentified Modeling Assumptions in Probabilistic Information Retrieval. *ACM Transactions on Information Systems,* 13:1, January 1995, pp. 100–111.

[88] W. Cooper, F. Gey, and A. Chen. Probabilistic Retrieval in the TIPSTER Collection: An Application of Staged Logistic Regression. In *The First Text Retrieval Conference,* edited by D. Harman. NIST Special Publication, Gaithersburg, MD, 1993.

[89] G. Copeland, W. Alexander, E. Boughter, and T. Keller. Data Placement in Bubba. ACM SIGMOD International Conference on Management of Data, Chicago, May 1988, pp. 99–108.

[90] W. Croft. Clustering Large Files of Documents Using the Single-Linked Method. *Journal of the American Society for Information Science,* 28, 1977, pp. 341–344.

[91] D. Cutting, D. Karger, J. Pedersen, and J. Tukey. Scatter/Gather: A Cluster-Based Approach to Browsing Large Document Collections. International ACM SIGIR Conference, Copenhagen, Denmark, June 1992, pp. 318–329.

[92] S. Dar, and R. Ramakrishnan. A Performance Study of Transitive Closure Algorithms. ACM SIGMOD International Conference on Management of Data, Minneapolis, MN, May 1994, pp. 454–465.

[93] C. J. Date. *An Introduction to Database Systems.* Reading, MA: Addison-Wesley, 1995.

[94] U. Dayal. Processing Queries over Generalization Hierarchies in a Multidatabase System. International Conference on Very Large Data Bases, Florence, Italy, November 1983, pp. 342–353.

[95] U. Dayal, and H-Y. Hwang. View Definition and Generalization for Database Integration in a Multidatabase System. *IEEE Transactions on Software Engineering,* 10:6, 1984, pp. 628–644.

[96] *DBC/1012, Data Base Computer Concepts and Facilities.* Document C02-0001-00, Teradata Corporation, El Segundo, CA, 1983.

[97] *DBC/1012, Data Base Computer Concepts and Facilities.* Release 3.1, Document C02-0001-05, Teradata Corporation, El Segundo, CA, 1988.

[98] S. Deerwester, S. Dumais, G. Furnas, T. Landauer, and R. Harshman. Indexing by Latent Semantic Analysis. *Journal of the American Society for Information Science,* 41:6, 1990, pp. 391–407.

[99] W. De Jonge, P. Scheuermann, and A. Schiff. S$^+$-Trees: An Efficient Structure for the Representation of Large Pictures. *Journal of Computer Vision, Graphics, Image Processing: Image Understanding,* 59: 3, May 1994, pp. 265–280.

[100] B. Demuth, A. Geppert, and T. Gorchs. Algebraic Query Optimization in the CoOMS Structurally Object-Oriented Database System. In *Query Processing for Advanced Database Systems,* edited by J. C. Freytag, D. Maier, and G. Vossen. San Francisco: Morgan Kaufmann, 1994, pp. 122–142.

[101] D. DeWitt, and R. Gerber. Multiprocessor Hash-Based Join Algorithms. International Conference on Very Large Data Bases, Stockholm, August 1985, pp. 151–164.

[102] D. DeWitt, S. Ghandeharizadeh, and D. Schneider. A Performance Analysis of the Gamma Database Machine. ACM SIGMOD International Conference on Management of Data, Chicago, June 1988, pp. 350–360.

[103] D. DeWitt, S. Ghandeharizadeh, D. Schneider, A. Bricker, H. Hsiao, and R. Rasmussen. The Gamma Database Machine Project. *IEEE Transactions on Knowledge and Data Engineering,* 2:1, 1990, pp. 44–62.

[104] D. DeWitt, and J. Gray. Parallel Database Systems: The Future of High Performance Database Systems. *Communications of the ACM,* 35:6, June 1992, pp. 85–98.

[105] D. DeWitt, R. Katz, F. Olken, L. Shapiro, M. Stonebraker, and D. Wood. Implementation Techniques for Main Memory Database Systems. ACM SIGMOD International Conference on Management of Data, Boston, June 1984, pp. 1–8.

[106] D. DeWitt, J. Naughton, and J. Burger. Nested Loop Revisited. Second Parallel and Distributed Database Systems Conference, Los Alamitos, CA, January 1993, pp. 230–242.

[107] D. DeWitt, J. Naughton, and D. Schneider. Parallel Sorting on a Shared-Nothing Architecture Using Probabilistic Splitting. Parallel and Distributed Information Systems, Miami, December 1991, pp. 280–291.

[108] D. DeWitt, J. Naughton, D. Schneider, and S. Seshadri. Practical Skew Handling in Parallel Joins. International Conference on Very Large Data Bases, Vancouver, August 1992, pp. 27–40.

[109] W. Du, R. Krishnamurthy, and M-C. Shan. Query Optimization in Heterogeneous DBMS. International Conference on Very Large Data Bases, Vancouver, August 1992, pp. 277–291.

[110] W. Du, and M-C. Shan. Query Processing in Pegasus. In *Object-Oriented Multidatabase Systems*, edited by O. Bukhres and A. Elmagarmid. Englewood Cliffs, NJ: Prentice Hall, 1996, pp. 449–471.

[111] W. Du, M-C. Shan, and U. Dayal. Reducing Multidatabase Query Response Time by Tree Balancing. ACM SIGMOD International Conference on Management of Data, San Jose, CA, May 1995, pp. 293–303.

[112] D. Dubois, and H. Prade. Fuzzy Sets—A Survey of Engineering Applications. *Computers and Chemical Engineering,* 17, 1993, pp. 373–380.

[113] R. Duda, and P. Hart. *Pattern Classification and Scene Analysis.* New York: John Wiley & Sons, 1973.

[114] R. Elmasri, and S. Navathe. Fundamentals of Database Systems. Redwood City, CA: Benjamin/Cummings, 1994.

[115] R. Epstein, M. Stonebraker, and E. Wong. Distributed Query Processing in a Relational Database System. ACM SIGMOD International Conference on Management of Data, Austin, TX, May 1978, pp. 169–180.

[116] R. Fagin, J. Nievergelt, N. Pippenger, and H. R. Strong. Extendible Hashing—A Fast Access Method for Dynamic Files. *ACM Transactions on Database Systems,* 4:3, September 1979, pp. 314–344.

[117] C. Faloutsos, R. Barber, M. Flickner, J. Hafner, W. Niblack, D. Petkovic, and W. Equitz. Efficient and Effective Querying by Image Content. *Journal of Intelligent Information Systems,* 3:3/4, July 1994, pp. 231–262.

[118] C. Faloutsos, and S. Christodoulakis. Design of a Signature File Method That Accounts for Non-uniform Occurrence and Query Frequencies. International Conference on Very Large Data Bases, Stockholm, August 1985, pp. 165–170.

[119] C. Faloutsos, M. Ranganathan, and Y. Manolopoulos. Fast Subsequence Matching in Time-Series Databases. ACM SIGMOD International Conference on Management of Data, Minneapolis, MN, May 1994, pp. 419–429.

[120] R. Finkel, and J. Bentley. Quad Trees: A Data Structure for Retrieval on Composite Keys. *ACTA Informatica,* 4, 1974, pp. 1–9.

[121] M. Flickner, H. Sawhney, W. Niblack, J. Ashley, Q. Huang, B. Dom, M. Gorkani, J. Hafner, D. Lee, D. Petkovic, D. Steele, and P. Yanker. Query by Image and Video Content: The QBIC System. *IEEE Computer,* 28:9, September 1995, pp. 23–32.

[122] G. Forsythe, M. Malcolm, and C. Moler. Least Squares and Singular Value Decomposition. Chapter 9 in *Computer Mathematical Computations.* Englewood Cliffs, NJ: Prentice Hall, 1977.

[123] E. Fox, Q. Chen, A. Daoud, and L. Heath. Order-Preserving Minimal Perfect Hash Functions and Information Retrieval. *ACM Transactions on Information Systems,* 9:3, 1991, pp. 281–308.

[124] J. C. Freytag, D. Maier, and G. Vossen (editors). *Query Processing for Advanced Database Systems.* San Francisco: Morgan Kaufmann, 1994.

[125] N. Fuhr, and C. Buckley. Optimizing Document Indexing and Search Term Weighting Based on Probabilistic Models. In *The First Text Retrieval Conference,* edited by D. Harman. NIST Special Publication, Gaithersburg, MD, 1993, pp. 89–99.

[126] G. Furnas, S. Deerwester, S. Dumais, T. Landauer, R. Harshman, L. Streeter, and K. Lochbaum. Information Retrieval Using a Singular Value Decomposition Model of Latent Semantic Structure. International ACM SIGIR Conference, Grenoble, France, 1988, pp. 465–480.

[127] *Fuzzy LUNA—Fuzzy Database Systems Library User's Manual.* Omron Corporation, Japan, 1992.

[128] W. Gale, D. Sumit, and C. Yu. Improvements to an Algorithm for Equi-partitioning. *IEEE Transactions on Computers,* 39:5, May 1990, pp. 706–710.

[129] H. Gallaire, and J. Minker. *Logic and Databases.* New York: Plenum, 1978.

[130] H. Gallaire, J. Minker, and J. Nicolas. Logic and Databases: A Deductive Approach. *ACM Computing Surveys,* 16:2, 1984, pp. 153–185.

[131] S. Ganguly, P. Gibbons, Y. Matias, and A. Silberschatz. Bifocal Sampling for Skew-Resistant Join Size Estimation. ACM SIGMOD International Conference on Management of Data, Montreal, June 1996, pp. 271–281.

[132] S. Ganguly, W. Hasan, and R. Krishnamurthy. Query Optimization for Parallel Execution. ACM SIGMOD International Conference on Management of Data, San Diego, CA, June 1992, pp. 9–18.

[133] R. Ganski, and H. Wong. Optimization of Nested SQL Queries Revisited. ACM SIGMOD International Conference on Management of Data, San Francisco, May 1987, pp. 23–33.

[134] U. Gargi, S. Oswald, D. Kosiba, S. Devadiga, and R. Kasturi. Evaluation of Video Sequence Indexing and Hierarchical Video Indexing. SPIE Conference on Storage and Retrieval for Image and Video Databases III, Vol. 2420, 1995.

[135] M. Garofalakis, and Y. Ioannidis. Multi-dimensional Resource Scheduling for Parallel Queries. ACM SIGMOD International Conference on Management of Data, Montreal, June 1996, pp. 365–376.

[136] J. Gary, and R. Mehrotra. Shape Similarity Based Retrieval in Image Database Systems. *SPIE Vol. 1662, Image Storage and Retrieval Systems,* 1992.

[137] B. Gavish, and A. Segev. Set Query Optimization in Distributed Database Systems, *ACM Transactions on Database Systems,* 11:3, 1986, pp. 265–293.

[138] N. Gehani, H. Jagadish, and O. Shmueli. Event Specification in an Active Object-Oriented Database. ACM SIGMOD International Conference on Management of Data, San Diego, CA, June 1992, pp. 81–90.

[139] N. Gehani, H. Jagadish, and O. Shmueli. Composite Event Specification in Active Databases: Model and Implementation. International Conference on Very Large Data Bases, Vancouver, August 1992, pp. 327–733.

[140] S. Ghandeharizadeh, and D. DeWitt. Hybrid-Range Partitioning Strategy: A New Declustering Strategy for Multiprocessor Database Machines. International Conference on Very Large Data Bases, Brisbane, Australia, August 1990, pp. 481–492.

[141] J. Gibbs. Massively Parallel Systems: Rethinking Computing for Business and Science. *Oracle,* 6:1, December 1991.

[142] Y. Gong, H. Zhang, H. Chuan, and M. Sakauchi. An Image Database System with Content Capturing and Fast Image Indexing Abilities. International Conference on Multimedia Computing and Systems, May 1994, pp. 121–128.

[143] L. Gotlieb. Computing Joins of Relations. ACM SIGMOD International Conference on Management of Data, San Jose, CA, May 1975, pp. 55–63.

[144] G. Graefe. Query Evaluation Techniques for Large Databases. *ACM Computing Surveys,* 25:2, June 1993, pp. 73–170.

[145] G. Graefe, and D. DeWitt. The EXODUS Optimizer Generator. ACM SIGMOD International Conference on Management of Data, San Francisco, May 1987, pp. 160–172.

[146] L. Gravano, and H. Garcia-Molina. Generalizing GLOSS to Vector-Space Databases and Broker Hierarchies. International Conference on Very Large Data Bases, Zurich, Switzerland, September 1995, pp. 78–89.

[147] P. Gray. *Logic, Algebra and Databases.* New York: John Wiley & Sons, 1984.

[148] D. Greene. An Implementation and Performance Analysis of Spatial Data Access Methods. International Conference on Data Engineering, Los Angeles, February 1989, pp. 606–615.

[149] N. Griffeth. Nonprocedural Query Processing for Databases with Access Paths. ACM SIGMOD International Conference on Management of Data, Austin, TX, May 1978, pp. 160–168.

[150] W. Grosky. Multimedia Information Systems. *IEEE Computer,* 1994, pp. 12–24.

[151] W. Grosky, and R. Mehrotra. Indexed Based Object Recognition in Pictorial Data Management. *Computer Vision, Graphics and Image Processing,* 52, 1990, pp. 416–436.

[152] W. Grosky, P. Neo, and R. Mehrotra. A Pictoral Index Mechanism for Model Based Matching. Fifth International Conference on Data Engineering, Los Angeles, February 1989, pp. 180–187.

[153] V. Gudivada, and V. Raghavan. Design and Evaluation of Algorithms for Image Retrieval by Spatial Similarity. *ACM Transactions on Information Systems*, 13:2, April 1995, pp. 115–144.

[154] A. Gupta. *Vision Information Retrieval Technology: A Virage Perspective*. Virage Inc., San Mateo, CA, 1995.

[155] A. Gupta, T. Weymouth, and R. Jain. Semantic Queries with Pictures: The VIM-SYS Model. International Conference on Very Large Data Bases, Barcelona, Spain, September 1991, pp. 69–79.

[156] A. Guttman. R-Tree: A Dynamic Index Structure for Spatial Searching. ACM SIGMOD International Conference on Management of Data, Boston, June 1984, pp. 47–57.

[157] P. Haas, and A. Swami. Sequential Sampling Procedures for Query Size Estimation. ACM SIGMOD International Conference on Management of Data, San Diego, CA, June 1992, pp. 341–350.

[158] R. Hagmann. An Observation on Database Buffering Performance Metrics. International Conference on Very Large Data Bases, Kyoto, August 1986, pp. 289–293.

[159] P. Hall. Optimization of a Single Relational Expression in a Relational Database. *IBM Journal of Research and Development*, 20:3, 1976, pp. 244–257.

[160] A. Hampapur, R. Jain, and T. Weymouth. Production Model Based Digital Video Segmentation. *Multimedia Tools*, 1, 1995, pp. 1–38.

[161] J. Han. Constraint-Based Query Evaluation in Deductive Databases. *IEEE Transactions on Knowledge and Data Engineering*, 6:1, 1994, pp. 96–107.

[162] D. Hang, B. Cheng, and R. Acharya. Texture-Based Image Retrieval Using Fractal Codes. Dept. of Computer Science, State U. of New York at Buffalo, Buffalo, NY, 1995.

[163] D. Harman. *Overview of the First Text REtrieval Conference (TREC-1)*. NIST Special Publication 500-207, Gaithersburg, MD, 1993.

[164] R. Haskin, and L. Hollar. Operational Characteristics of a Hardware-Based Pattern Matcher. *ACM Transactions on Database Systems*, 8:1, March 1983, pp. 15–40.

[165] L. Henschen, and S. Naqvi. On Compiling Queries in Recursive First-Order Databases, *Journal of the Association of Computing Machinery*, 31:1, 1984, pp. 47–85.

[166] A. Hevner, and S. B. Yao. Query Processing in Distributed Database Systems. *IEEE Transactions on Software Engineering*, 5:3, March 1979, pp. 177–182.

[167] K. Hinrichs. Implementation of the Grid File: Design Concepts and Experiences. *BIT,* 25:4, 1985, pp. 569–592.

[168] U. Hohenstein. Automatic Transformation of an Entity-Relationship Query Language into SQL. Eighth International Conference on E-R Approach, Toronto, October 1989, pp. 303–321.

[169] L. Hollar. Hardware Systems for Text Information Retrieval. International ACM SIGIR Conference, Washington, DC, 1983, pp. 3–9.

[170] W. Hong. Exploiting Inter-operation Parallelism in XPRS. ACM SIGMOD International Conference on Management of Data, San Diego, CA, June 1992, pp. 19–28.

[171] W. Hou, G. Ozsoyoglu, and E. Dogdu. Error-Constrained COUNT Query Evaluation in Relational Databases. ACM SIGMOD International Conference on Management of Data, Denver, May 1991, pp. 278–287.

[172] W. Hou, G. Ozsoyoglu, and B. Taneja. Statistical Estimators for Relational Algebra Expressions. ACM Symposium on Principles of Database Systems, Austin, TX, March 1988, pp. 276–287.

[173] D. Hsiao, and M. Kamel. Heterogeneous Databases: Proliferations, Issues and Solutions. *IEEE Transactions on Knowledge and Data Engineering,* 1:1, March 1989, pp. 45–62.

[174] H. Hsiao, M. Chen, and P. Yu. On Parallel Execution of Multiple Pipelined Hash Joins. ACM SIGMOD International Conference on Management of Data, Minneapolis, MN, May 1994, pp. 185–196.

[175] C. Hsu, W. Chu, and R. Taira. A Knowledge-Based Approach for Retrieving Images by Contents. *IEEE Transactions on Knowledge and Data Engineering,* 8:4, August 1996, pp. 522–532.

[176] K. Hua, and C. Lee. An Adaptive Data Placement Scheme for Parallel Database Computer Systems. International Conference on Very Large Data Bases, Brisbane, Australia, August 1990, pp. 493–506.

[177] K. Hua, and C. Lee. Handling Data Skew in Multiprocessor Database Computers Using Partitioning Tuning. International Conference on Very Large Data Bases, Barcelona, Spain, September 1991, pp. 525–535.

[178] K. Hua, W. Tavanapong, and H. Young. A Performance Evaluation of Load Balancing Techniques for Join Operations on Multicomputer Database Systems. International Conference on Data Engineering, March 1995, Taipei, Taiwan, pp. 44–51.

[179] G. Hunter, and K. Steiglitz. Operations on Images Using Quad Trees. *IEEE Transactions on Pattern Analysis and Machine Intelligence,* 1:2, April 1979, pp. 145–153.

[180] G. Hunter, and K. Steiglitz. Linear Transformation of Pictures Represented by Quad Trees. *Computer Graphics and Image Processing,* 10:9, July 1979, pp. 289–296.

[181] E. Hwang, and V. Subrahmanian. Querying Video Databases. Technical Report, Dept. of Computer Science, Institute for Systems Research, U. of Maryland, 1995.

[182] H-Y. Hwang, and U. Dayal. Using the Entity-Relationship Model for Implementing Multi-model Database Systems. In *The Second International Conference on the E-R Approach*. Amsterdam: North-Holland, 1981, pp. 237–258.

[183] T. Ichikawa. ARES: A Relational Database with the Capability of Performing Flexible Interpretation of Queries. *IEEE Transactions on Software Engineering*, 12:5, 1986, pp. 624–634.

[184] T. Imielinski, and W. Lipski. Incomplete Information in Relational Databases. *Journal of the ACM*, 31:4, 1984, pp. 761–791.

[185] Y. Ioannidis, and S. Christodoulakis. Optimal Histograms for Limiting Worst-Case Error Propagation in the Size of Join Results. *ACM Transactions on Database Systems*, 18:4, December 1993, pp. 709–748.

[186] Y. Ioannidis, and V. Poosala. Balancing Histogram Optimality and Practicality for Query Result Size Estimation. ACM SIGMOD International Conference on Management of Data, San Jose, CA, May 1995, pp. 233–244.

[187] Y. Ioannidis, and R. Ramakrishnan. Efficient Transitive Closure Algorithms. International Conference on Very Large Data Bases, Los Angeles, August 1988, pp. 382–394.

[188] Y. Ioannidis, R. Ramakrishnan, and L. Winger. Transitive Closure Algorithms Based on Graph Traversal. *ACM Transactions on Database Systems*, 18:3, 1993, pp. 512–576.

[189] H. Jagadish. A Retrieval Technique for Similar Shapes. ACM SIGMOD International Conference on Management of Data, Denver, CO, May 1991, pp. 208–217.

[190] R. Jain, and A. Hampapur. Metadata in Video Databases. *SIGMOD Record*, 23:4, December 1994, pp. 27–33.

[191] R. Jain, R. Kasturi, and B. Schunck. *Machine Vision*. New York: McGraw-Hill, 1995.

[192] J. Jang, C. Sun, and E. Mizutani. *Neuro-Fuzzy and Soft Computing: A Computational Approach to Learning and Machine Intelligence*, Englewood Cliffs, NJ: Prentice Hall, 1997.

[193] M. Jarke, and J. Koch. Query Optimization in Database Systems. *ACM Computing Surveys*, 16:2, June 1984, pp. 111–152.

[194] B. P. Jenq, D. Woelk, W. Kim, and W-L. Lee. Query Processing in Distributed ORION. International Conference on Extending Database Technology, Venice, March 1990, pp. 169–187.

[195] Y. Kambayashi, M. Yoshikawa, and S. Yajima. Query Processing for Distributed Databases Using Generalized Semi-join. ACM SIGMOD International Conference on Management of Data, San Jose, CA, May 1983, pp. 151–160.

[196] D. Keim, H. Kriegel, and A. Miethsam. Object-Oriented Querying of Existing Relational Databases. Fourth International Conference on Database and Expert Systems Applications, Prague, Czech Republic, September 1993, pp. 325–336.

[197] A. Kemper, C. Kilger, and G. Moerkotte. Function Materialization in Object Bases: Design, Realization, and Evaluation. *IEEE Transactions on Knowledge and Data Engineering,* 6:4, August 1994, pp. 587–608.

[198] A. Kemper, and G. Moerkotte. Advanced Query Processing in Object Bases Using Access Support Relations. International Conference on Very Large Data Bases, Brisbane, Australia, August 1990, pp. 290–301.

[199] A. Kemper, and G. Moerkotte. Object-Oriented Database Management. Englewood Cliffs, NJ: Prentice Hall, 1994.

[200] W. Kim. A New Way to Compute the Product and Join. ACM SIGMOD International Conference on Management of Data, Santa Monica, CA, May 1980, pp. 179–187.

[201] W. Kim. On Optimizing an SQL-Like Nested Query. *ACM Transactions on Database Systems,* 7:3, September 1982, pp. 443–469.

[202] W. Kim. *Introduction to Object-Oriented Databases.* Cambridge, MA: MIT Press, 1990.

[203] W. Kim (editor). *Modern Database Systems: The Object Model, Interoperability, and Beyond.* Reading, MA: Addison-Wesley/ACM Press, 1995.

[204] W. Kim, K. C. Kim, and A. Dale. Indexing Techniques for Object-Oriented Databases. In *Object-Oriented Concepts, Databases, and Applications,* edited by W. Kim and F. Lochovsky, Reading, MA: Addison-Wesley, 1989, pp. 371–394.

[205] M. Kitsuregawa, and Y. Ogawa. Bucket Spreading Parallel Hashing: A New, Robust, Parallel Hash Join Method for Data Skew in the Super Database Computer (SDC). International Conference on Very Large Data Bases, Brisbane, Australia, August 1990, pp. 210–221.

[206] M. Kitsuregawa, M. Tanaka, and T. Moto-Oka. Application of Hash to Data Base Machine and Its Architecture. *New Generation Computing,* 1:1, 1983, pp. 66–77.

[207] M. Kitsuregawa, W. Yang, and S. Fushimi. Evaluation of 18-Stage Pipeline Hardware Sorter. Sixth International Workshop on Database Machines, Deauville, France, June 1989, pp. 142–155.

[208] J. Kivinen, and M. Warmuth. Exponentiated Gradient versus Gradient Descent for Linear Predictors. Technical Report, Basking Center for Computer Engineering and Information Sciences, U. of California, Santa Cruz, 1994.

[209] O. Kiyotaka, and T. Yoshinobu. Projection Detection Filter for Video Cut Detection. *Multimedia Systems,* 1, 1995, pp. 205–210.

[210] D. Knuth. *Sorting and Searching.* Volume 3 of *The Art of Computer Programming.* Reading, MA: Addison-Wesley, 1973.

[211] H. Korth, and A. Silberschatz. *Database System Concepts.* New York: McGraw-Hill, 1991.

[212] N. Kronenberg, H. Levy, and W. Strecker. VAXclusters: A Closely-Coupled Distributed System. *ACM Transactions on Computer Systems,* 4:2, May 1986, pp. 130–146.

[213] A. Kumar. G-Tree: A New Data Structure for Organizing Multidimensional Data. *IEEE Transactions on Knowledge and Data Engineering,* 6:2, April 1994, pp. 341–347.

[214] K. Kwok. A Network Approach to Probabilistic Information Retrieval. *ACM Transactions on Information Systems,* 13:3, July 1995, pp. 325–354.

[215] S. Lafortune, and E. Wong. A State Transition Model for Distributed Query Processing. *ACM Transactions on Database Systems,* 11:3, 1986, pp. 294–322.

[216] M. Lakshmi, and P. Yu. Effectiveness of Parallel Join. *IEEE Transactions on Knowledge and Data Engineering,* 2:4, December 1990, pp. 410–424.

[217] K. Lam, and C. Yu. A Clustered Search Algorithm Incorporating Arbitrary Term Dependencies. *ACM Transactions on Database Systems,* 7:3, September 1982, pp. 500–508.

[218] T. Landers, and R. Rosenberg. An Overview of MULTIBASE. In *Distributed Data Bases,* edited by H. J. Schneider. Amsterdam: North-Holland, 1982.

[219] R. Lanzelotte, and P. Valduriez. Extending the Search Strategy in a Query Optimizer. International Conference on Very Large Data Bases, Barcelona, Spain, September 1991, pp. 363–373.

[220] R. Lanzelotte, P. Valduriez, and M. Zait. Optimization of Object-Oriented Recursive Queries Using Cost-Controlled Strategies. ACM SIGMOD International Conference on Management of Data, San Diego, CA, June 1992, pp. 256–265.

[221] R. Lanzelotte, P. Valduriez, and M. Zait. On the Effectiveness of Optimization Search Strategies for Parallel Execution Spaces. International Conference on Very Large Data Bases, Dublin, Ireland, August 1993, pp. 493–504.

[222] R. Lanzelotte, P. Valduriez, M. Ziane, and J. Cheiney. Optimization of Nonrecursive Queries in OODBs. International Conference on Deductive and Object-Oriented Databases, Munich, December 1991, pp. 1–21.

[223] P. Larson. Dynamic Hashing. *BIT,* 18, 1978, pp. 184–201.

[224] P. Larson. SQL-GATE: Providing SQL Access to Network and Hierarchical Databases. Demonstration at ACM SIGMOD International Conference on Management of Data, Atlantic City, NJ, May 1990.

[225] R. Ledley, M. Buas, and T. Golab. Fundamentals of True Color Image Processing. *IEEE IAPR,* 1990, pp. 791–795.

[226] D. Lee, and C. Leng. Partitioned Signature Files: Design Issues and Performance Evaluation. *ACM Transactions on Information Systems,* 7:2, April 1989, pp. 158–180.

[227] E. Lee, and T. Whalen. Computer Image Retrieval by Features: Suspect Identification. INTERCHI '93 Conference on Human Factors in Computing Systems. Amsterdam, April 1993, pp. 494–499.

[228] D. Lewis, R. Schapire, J. Callan, and R. Papka. Training Algorithms for Linear Text Classifiers. International ACM SIGIR Conference, Zurich, Switzerland, August 1996, pp. 298–306.

[229] D. Li, and D. Liu. *A Fuzzy Prolog Database System.* New York: John Wiley & Sons, Research Studies Press, 1990.

[230] W. Li, and K. Candan. SEMCOG: An Integration of SEMantics and COGnition-Based Approaches for Image Retrieval. Technical Report, NEC, 1996.

[231] G. Lipovski. Dynamic Systolic Associative Memory Chips. Proceedings of Application Specific Array Processors, Princeton, NJ, 1990, pp. 481–492.

[232] G. Lipovski. Dynamic Memory with Logic-In Refresh. Patent number 4,989,180, January 1991.

[233] G. Lipovski. A Four Megabit Dynamic Systolic Associative Memory Chip. *Journal of VLSI Signal Processing,* 1992, pp. 37–51.

[234] R. Lipton, and J. Naughton. Query Size Estimation by Adaptive Sampling. ACM Symposium on Principles of Database Systems, Nashville, TN, April 1990, pp. 40–46.

[235] R. Lipton, J. Naughton, and D. Schneider. Practical Selectivity Estimation through Adaptive Sampling. ACM SIGMOD International Conference on Management of Data, Atlantic City, NJ, May 1990, pp. 1–11.

[236] W. Litwin. Trie Hashing. ACM SIGMOD International Conference on Management of Data, Ann Arbor, MI, April 1981, pp. 19–29.

[237] W. Litwin. O*SQL: A Language for Object-Oriented Multidatabase Interoperability. IFIP WG 2.6 Database Semantics Conference on Interoperable Database Systems (DS-5). Lorne, Australia, November 1992, pp. 119–137.

[238] W. Litwin, L. Mark, and N. Roussopoulos. Interoperability of Multiple Autonomous Databases. *ACM Computing Surveys,* 22:3, September 1990, pp. 267–293.

[239] K. Liu, G. Lipovski, C. Yu, and N. Rishe. Efficient Processing of One and Two Dimensional Proximity Queries in Associative Memory. International ACM SIGIR Conference, Zurich, Switzerland, August 1996, pp. 138–146.

[240] M. Lo, M. Chen, C. Ravishankar, and P. Yu. On Optimal Processor Allocation to Support Pipelined Hash Joins. ACM SIGMOD International Conference on Management of Data, Washington, DC, May 1993, pp. 69–78.

[241] J. Lobo, J. Minker, and A. Rajasekar. *Foundations of Disjunctive Logic Programming.* Cambridge, MA: MIT Press, 1992.

[242] G. Lohman, C. Mohan, L. Haas, D. Daniels, B. Lindsay, P. Selinger, and P. Wilms. Query Processing in R*. In *Query Processing in Database Systems,* edited by W. Kim, D. Reiner, and D. Batory. New York: Springer-Verlag, 1985.

[243] R. Lorie, and H. Young. A Low Communication Sort Algorithm for a Parallel Database Machine. International Conference on Very Large Data Bases, Amsterdam, August 1989, pp. 125–134.

[244] C. C. Low, B. C. Ooi, and H. Lu. H-Trees: A Dynamic Associative Search Index for OODB. ACM SIGMOD International Conference on Management of Data, San Diego, CA, June 1992, pp. 134–143.

[245] H. Lu, B. Ooi, and C. Goh. Multidatabase Query Optimization: Issues and Solutions. Third International Workshop on Research Issues in Data Engineering: Interoperability in Multidatabase Systems, Vienna, Austria, April 1993, pp. 137–143.

[246] H. Lu, B-C. Ooi, and K-L. Tan. *Query Processing in Parallel Relational Database Systems.* Los Alamitos, CA: IEEE Computer Society Press, 1994.

[247] H. Lu, M. Shan, and K. Tan. Optimization of Multi-way Join Queries for Parallel Execution. International Conference on Very Large Data Bases, Barcelona, Spain, September 1991, pp. 549–560.

[248] H. Lu, K. Tan, and M. Shan. Hash Based Join Algorithms for Multiprocessor Computers with Shared Memory. International Conference on Very Large Data Bases, Brisbane, Australia, August 1990, pp. 198–209.

[249] V. Lum, and K. Wong. A Model and Technique for Approximate Matching of Natural Language Queries. Technical Report, Chinese University of Hong Kong, Hong Kong, 1993.

[250] C. Lynch. Selectivity Estimation and Query Optimization in Large Databases with Highly Skewed Distributions of Column Values. International Conference on Very Large Data Bases, Los Angeles, August 1988, pp. 240–251.

[251] L. Mackert, and G. Lohman. R* Optimizer: Validation and Performance Evaluation for Distributed Queries. International Conference on Very Large Data Bases, Kyoto, August 1986, pp. 149–159.

[252] S. Madnick. From VLDB to VMLDB (Very Many Large Data Bases): Dealing with Large-Scale Semantic Heterogeneity. International Conference on Very Large Data Bases, Zurich, September 1995, pp. 11–16.

[253] D. Maier, S. Deniels, T. Keller, D. Vance, G. Graefe, and W. McKenna. Challenges for Query Processing in Object-Oriented Databases. In *Query Processing for Advanced Database Systems*, edited by J. C. Freytag, D. Maier, and G. Vossen. San Francisco: Morgan Kaufmann, 1994, pp. 337–380.

[254] D. Maier, and J. Stein. Indexing in an Object-Oriented DBMS. International Workshop for Object-Oriented Database Systems, Pacific Grove, CA, September 1986, pp. 171–182.

[255] M. Maron, and J. Kuhn. On Relevance, Probabilistic Indexing and Information Retrieval. *Journal of the ACM,* 7:3, July 1960, pp. 216–244.

[256] J. Martin. Organization of Geographic Data with Quadtrees and Least Square Approximation. Conference on Pattern Recognition and Image Processing, Las Vegas, 1982, pp. 458–463.

[257] R. Mehrotra, and J. Gary. Similar-Shape Retrieval in Shape Data Management. *IEEE Computer,* 28:9, September 1995, pp. 57–62.

[258] M. Mehta, and D. DeWitt. Managing Intra-operator Parallelism in Parallel Database Systems. International Conference on Very Large Data Bases, Zurich, Switzerland, September 1995, pp. 382–394.

[259] W. Meng, A. Kamada, and Y. Chang. Transformation of Relational Schemas to Object-Oriented Schemas. Annual International Computer Software and Applications Conference, Dallas, TX, August 1995, pp. 356–361.

[260] W. Meng, K-L. Liu, and C. Yu. Query Decomposition in Multidatabase Systems. Technical Report CS-TR-93-9, Department of Computer Science, State University of New York at Binghamton, 1993.

[261] W. Meng, K. Liu, C. Yu, Y. Chang, X. Wang, and N. Rishe. Determine Text Databases to Search in the Internet. Technical Report, Department of Computer Science, State University of New York at Binghamton, 1997.

[262] W. Meng, and C. Yu. Query Processing in Multidatabase Systems. In *Modern Database Systems: The Object Model, Interoperability, and Beyond,* edited by W. Kim. Reading, MA: Addison-Wesley/ACM Press, 1995, pp. 551–572.

[263] W. Meng, C. Yu, R. Chen, K-C. Guh, and N. Rishe. Efficient Materialization of Global Relations in a Multidatabase System. Technical Report CS-TR-95-06, Department of Computer Science, State University of New York at Binghamton, 1995.

[264] W. Meng, C. Yu, and W. Kim. A Theory of Translation from Relational Queries to Hierarchical Queries. *IEEE Transactions on Knowledge and Data Engineering,* 7:2, April 1995, pp. 228–245.

[265] W. Meng, C. Yu, W. Kim, G. Wang, T. Pham, and S. Dao. Construction of Relational Front-End for Object-Oriented Database Systems. Ninth International Conference on Data Engineering, Vienna, Austria, April 1993, pp. 476–483.

[266] J. Menon. A Study of Sort Algorithms for Multiprocessor Database Machines. International Conference on Very Large Data Bases, Kyoto, August 1986, pp. 197–206.

[267] J. Minker. Search Strategy and Selection Function for an Inferential Relational System. *ACM Transactions on Database Systems,* 3:1, March 1978, pp. 1–31.

[268] P. Mishra, and M. Eich. Join Processing in Relational Databases. *ACM Computing Surveys,* 24:1, March 1992, pp. 63–113.

[269] T. Mostardi. Estimating the Size of Relational SPJ Operation Results: An Analytic Approach. *Information Systems,* 15:5, 1990, pp. 591–601.

[270] A. Motro. Superview: Virtual Integration of Multiple Databases. *IEEE Transactions on Software Engineering,* 13:7, July 1987, pp. 785–798.

[271] A. Motro. VAGUE: A User Interface to Relational Databases That Permit Vague Queries. *ACM Transactions on Office Information Systems,* 6:3, 1988, pp. 187–214.

[272] M. Muralikrishna. Improved Unnesting Algorithms for Join Aggregate SQL Queries. International Conference on Very Large Data Bases, Vancouver, August 1992, pp. 91–102.

[273] M. Muralikrishna, and D. DeWitt. Equi-depth Histograms for Estimating Selectivity Factors for Multi-dimensional Queries. ACM SIGMOD International Conference on Management of Data, Chicago, June 1988, pp. 28–36.

[274] A. Nagasaka, and K. Tanaka. Automatic Video Indexing and Full Video Search for Object Appearances. Second Working Conference on Visual Database Systems, Budapest, Hungary, October 1991, pp. 113–127.

[275] H. Nakajima. Development of an Efficient Fuzzy SQL for Large Scale Fuzzy Relational Database. Fifth International Fuzzy Systems Association World Congress, 1993, pp. 517–520.

[276] M. Nakayama, M. Kitsuregawa, and M. Takagi. Hash-Partitioned Join Method Using Dynamic Destaging Strategy. International Conference on Very Large Data Bases, Los Angeles, August 1988, pp. 468–478.

[277] S. Naqvi, and S. Tsur. *A Logical Language for Data and Knowledge Base.* New York: Computer Science Press, 1989.

[278] W. Niblack, R. Barber, W. Equitz, M. Flickner, E. Glasman, D. Petkovic, P. Yanker, C. Faloutsos, and G. Taubin. The QBIC Project: Querying Images by Contents Using Color, Texture and Shape. SPIE 1993 Symposium, Storage and Retrieval for Image and Video Databases, Vol. 1908, February 1993, pp. 173–187.

[279] J. Nievergelt, H. Hinterberger, and K. Sevcik. The Grid File: An Adaptable, Symmetric Multikey File Structure. *ACM Transactions on Database Systems,* 9:1, March 1984, pp. 38–71.

[280] C. Nyberg, T. Barclay, Z. Cvetanovic, J. Gray, and D. Lomet. AlphaSort: A RISC Machine Sort. ACM SIGMOD International Conference on Management of Data, Minneapolis, MN, May 1994, pp. 233–242.

[281] V. Ogle, and M. Stonebraker. Chabot: Retrieval from a Relational Database of Images. *IEEE Computer,* 28:9, September 1995, pp. 40–48.

[282] P. O'Neil. *Data Base: Principles, Programming, Performance.* San Francisco: Morgan Kaufmann, 1994.

[283] B. Oommen, and D. Ma. Deterministic Learning Automata Solutions to the Equipartitioning Problem. *IEEE Transactions on Computers,* 37:1, January 1988, pp. 2–13.

[284] J. Orenstein, S. Haradhvala, B. Margulies, and D. Sakahara. Query Processing in the ObjectStore Database System. ACM SIGMOD International Conference on Management of Data, San Diego, CA, June 1992, pp. 403–412.

[285] M. Ozsu, and J. Blakeley. Query Processing in Object-Oriented Database Systems. In *Modern Database Systems: The Object Model, Interoperability, and Beyond,* edited by W. Kim, Reading, MA: Addison-Wesley/ACM Press, 1995, pp. 146–174.

[286] M. Ozsu, and P. Valduriez. *Principles of Distributed Database Systems.* Englewood Cliffs, NJ: Prentice Hall, 1991.

[287] M. Papazoglou, Z. Tari, and N. Russell. Object-Oriented Technology for Interschema and Language Mappings. In *Object-Oriented Multidatabase Systems,* edited by O. Bukhres, and A. Elmagarmid. Englewood Cliffs, NJ: Prentice Hall, 1996, pp. 203–250.

[288] R. Pecherer. Efficient Evaluation of Expressions in a Relational Algebra. ACM Pacific 75 Conference, 1975, pp. 44–49.

[289] R. Pecherer. Efficient Exploration of Product Spaces. ACM SIGMOD International Conference on Management of Data, Washington, DC, June 1976, pp. 169–177.

[290] Y. Peng, and J. Reggia. A Probabilistic Causal Model for Diagnostic Problem Solving Part 1: Integrating Symbolic Causal Inference with Numeric Probabilistic Inferencer. *IEEE Transactions on Systems, Man and Cybernetics,* 17:2, March/April 1987, pp. 146–162.

[291] Y. Peng, and J. Reggia. A Connectionist Model for Diagnostic Problem Solving. *IEEE Transactions on Systems, Man and Cybernetics,* 19:2, March/April 1989, pp. 285–298.

[292] G. Piatetsky-Shapiro, and C. Connell. Accurate Estimation of the Number of Tuples Satisfying a Condition. ACM SIGMOD International Conference on Management of Data, Boston, June 1984, pp. 256–276.

[293] E. Pitoura, O. Bukhres, and A. Elmagarmid. Object Orientation in Multidatabase Systems. *ACM Computing Surveys,* 27:2, June 1995, pp. 141–195.

[294] V. Poosala, and Y. Ioannidis. Estimation of Query-Result Distribution and Its Application in Parallel-Join Load Balancing. International Conference on Very Large Data Bases, Bombay, India, 1996, pp. 448–459.

[295] V. Poosala, Y. Ioannidis, P. Haas, and E. Shekita. Improved Histograms for Selectivity Estimation of Range Predicates. ACM SIGMOD International Conference on Management of Data, Montreal, June 1996, pp. 294–305.

[296] H. Prade, and C. Testemale. Generalizing Database Relational Algebra for the Treatment of Incomplete or Uncertain Information and Vague Queries. *Information Science,* 34:2, 1984, pp. 115–143.

[297] H. Prade, and C. Testemale. Representation of Software Constraints and Fuzzy Attribute Values by Means of Possibility Distribution in Databases. In *Artificial Intelligence and Decision Systems.* Vol. 2 of *Analysis of Fuzzy Information,* edited by J. Bezdek. Baca Raton, FL: CRC Press, 1987.

[298] X. Qian, and L. Raschid. Query Interoperation among Object-Oriented and Relational Databases. Eleventh International Conference on Data Engineering, Taipei, Taiwan, March 1995, pp. 271–278.

[299] E. Rahm, and R. Marek. Dynamic Multi-resource Load Balancing in Parallel Database Systems. International Conference on Very Large Data Bases, Zurich, Switzerland, September 1995, pp. 395–406.

[300] R. Ramakrishnan, F. Bancilhon, and A. Silberschatz. Safety of Recursive Horn Clauses with Infinite Relations. Sixth ACM Symposium on Principles of Database Systems, San Diego, CA, March 1987, pp. 328–339.

[301] R. Ramakrishnan, D. Srivasta, and S. Sudarshan. CORAL—Control, Relations and Logic. International Conference on Very Large Data Bases, Vancouver, August 1992, pp. 238–250.

[302] R. Ramakrishnan, and J. Ullman. A Survey of Research on Deductive Systems. *Journal of Logic Programming,* 23:2, 1995, pp. 125–149.

[303] S. Ramaswamy, and P. Kanellakis. OODB Indexing by Class-Division. ACM SIGMOD International Conference on Management of Data, San Jose, CA, May 1995, pp. 139–150.

[304] S. Robertson. The Probability Ranking Principle in IR. *Journal of Documentation,* 1977, pp. 294–304.

[305] S. Robertson, and K. Sparck Jones. Relevance Weighting of Search Terms. *Journal of the American Society for Information Science,* 1976, pp. 129–146.

[306] J. Robinson. The k-D-B-Tree: A Search Structure for Large Multi-dimensional Dynamic Indexes. ACM SIGMOD International Conference on Management of Data, Ann Arbor, MI, May 1981, pp. 10–18.

[307] J. Rocchio. Relevance Feedback in Information Retrieval. In *The SMART System: Experiments in Automatic Document Processing,* edited by J. Salton. Englewood Cliffs, NJ: Prentice Hall, 1971, pp. 313–323.

[308] A. Rosenthal, and D. Reiner. Querying Relational Views of Networks. In *Query Processing in Database Systems,* edited by W. Kim, D. S. Reiner, and D. S. Batory. New York: Springer-Verlag, 1985, pp. 109–124.

[309] N. Roussopoulos, and H. Kang. A Pipeline N-Way Join Algorithm Based on the 2-Way Semi-join Program. *IEEE Transactions on Knowledge and Data Engineering,* 3:4, 1991, pp. 486–495.

[310] E. Rundensteiner, and L. Bic. Aggregates in Possibilistic Databases. International Conference on Very Large Data Bases, Amsterdam, August 1989, pp. 287–295.

[311] G. Salton. *Automatic Information Organization and Retrieval.* New York: McGraw-Hill, 1968.

[312] G. Salton. *Automatic Text Processing.* Reading, MA: Addison-Wesley, 1989.

[313] G. Salton (editor). *The SMART Retrieval System: Experiments in Automatic Document Processing.* Englewood Cliffs, NJ: Prentice Hall, 1971.

[314] G. Salton, E. Fox, and H. Wu. Extended Boolean Information Retrieval. *Communications of the ACM,* 26, 1983, pp. 1022–1036.

[315] G. Salton, and M. McGill. *Introduction to Modern Information Retrieval.* New York: McGraw-Hill, 1983.

[316] G. Salton, C. Yang, and C. Yu. A Theory of Term Importance in Automatic Text Analysis. *Journal of the American Society for Information Science,* 1975, pp. 33–44. (Reprinted in *Key Papers in Information Science.* Knowledge Industry Publication, 1980.)

[317] B. Salzberg, A. Tsukerman, J. Gray, M. Steward, S. Uren, and B. Vaughan. FastSort: A Distributed Single-Input Single-Output External Sort. ACM SIGMOD International Conference on Management of Data, Atlantic City, NJ, May 1990, pp. 94–101.

[318] H. Samet. The Quadtree and Related Hierarchical Data Structures. *ACM Computing Surveys,* 16:2, June 1984, pp. 187–260.

[319] H. Samet. Applications of Spatial Data Structures: Computer Graphics, Image Processing, and GIS. Reading, MA: Addison-Wesley, 1990.

[320] P. Scheuermann, and E. Chong. Distributed Join Processing Using Bipartite Graphs. IEEE International Conference on Distributed Computing Systems, Vancouver, May 1995, pp. 387–394.

[321] D. Schneider, and D. DeWitt. A Performance Evaluation of Four Parallel Join Algorithms in a Shared-Nothing Multiprocessor Environment. ACM SIGMOD International Conference on Management of Data, Portland, May 1989, pp. 110–121.

[322] D. Schneider, and D. DeWitt. Tradeoffs in Processing Complex Join Queries via Hashing in Multiprocessor Database Machines. International Conference on Very Large Data Bases, Brisbane, Australia, August 1990, pp. 469–480.

[323] P. Selinger, and M. Adiba. Access Path Selection in Distributed Data Base Management Systems. First International Conference on Data Bases, Aberdeen, Scotland, 1980, pp. 204–215.

[324] P. Selinger, et al. Access Path Selection in a Relational Database Management System. ACM SIGMOD International Conference on Management of Data, Boston, May 1979, pp. 23–34.

[325] T. Sellis, N. Roussopoulos, and C. Faloutsos. The R+-Tree: A Dynamic Index for Multi-dimensional Objects. International Conference on Very Large Data Bases, Brighton, UK, September 1987, pp. 507–518.

[326] P. Seshadri, H. Pirahesh, and T. Leung. Complex Query Decorrelation. International Conference on Data Engineering, New Orleans, February 1996, pp. 450–458.

[327] L. Shapiro. Join Processing in Database Systems with Large Main Memories. *ACM Transactions on Database Systems,* 11:3, September 1986, pp. 239–264.

[328] D. Shasha, and T. Wang. Optimizing Equi-join Queries in Distributed Databases Where Relations Are Hashed Partitioned, *ACM Transactions on Database Systems,* 16:2, 1991, pp. 279–308.

[329] G. Shaw, and S. Zdonik. An Object-Oriented Query Algebra. International Workshop on Database Programming Languages, Portland, June 1989, pp. 103–112.

[330] E. Shekita, H. Young, and K. Tan. Multi-join Optimization for Symmetric Multiprocessors. International Conference on Very Large Data Bases, Dublin, Ireland, August 1993, pp. 479–492.

[331] S. Shenoi, and A. Melton. An Extended Version of the Fuzzy Relational Database Model. *Information Science,* 52:1, 1990, pp. 35–52.

[332] A. Sheth, and L. Larson. Federated Database Systems for Managing Distributed, Heterogeneous, and Autonomous Databases. *ACM Computing Surveys,* 22:3, September 1990, pp. 183–236.

[333] D. Shipman. The Functional Data Model and the Data Language DAPLEX. *ACM Transactions on Database Systems,* 6:1, 1981, pp. 140–173.

[334] R. Sibson. Slink: An Optimally Efficient Algorithm for the Single Link Cluster Method. *Computer Journal,* 1973, pp. 30–34.

[335] A. P. Sistla, C. Yu, and R. Haddock. Reasoning about Spatial Relationships in Picture Retrieval Systems. International Conference on Very Large Data Bases, Santiago, Chile, September 1994, pp. 570–581.

[336] A. P. Sistla, C. Yu, C. Liu, and K. Liu. Deduction and Reduction of Spatial Relationships in Picture Retrieval Systems. International Conference on Very Large Data Bases, Zurich, Switzerland, September 1995, pp. 619–629.

[337] A. P. Sistla, C. Yu, and R. Venkatasubrahmanian. Similarity Based Retrieval of Videos. International Conference on Data Engineering, Birmingham, UK, April 1997.

[338] J. Smith, and P. Chang. Optimizing the Performance of a Relational Algebra Interface. Communications of the ACM, 18:10, October 1975, pp. 568–579.

[339] J. Smith, and S. Chang. VisualSeek: A fully Automated Content-Based Image Query System. ACM Multimedia Conference, Boston, November 1996, pp. 87–98.

[340] M. Soo, R. Snograss, and C. Jensen. Efficient Evaluation of the Valid Time Natural Join. International Conference on Data Engineering, Houston, February 1994, pp. 282–292.

[341] K. Sparck Jones. Statistical Interpretation of Term Specificity and Its Application in Retrieval. Journal of Documentation, 28:1, 1972, pp. 11–20.

[342] B. Sreenath, and S. Seshadri. The hcC-Tree: An Efficient Index Structure for Object-Oriented Databases. International Conference on Very Large Data Bases, Santiago, Chile, September 1994, pp. 203–213.

[343] R. Srihari. Automatic Indexing and Content-Based Retrieval of Captioned Images. IEEE Computer, 28:9, September 1995, pp. 49–56.

[344] J. Stamos. Static Grouping of Small Objects to Enhance Performance of a Paged Virtual Memory. ACM Transactions on Computer Systems, 2:2, May 1984, pp. 155–180.

[345] C. Stanfill, and B. Kahle. Parallel Free-Text Search on the Connection Machine. Communications of the ACM, 29:12, December 1986, pp. 1229–1239.

[346] M. Stonebraker. The Case for Shared Nothing. IEEE Database Engineering, 9:1, March 1986, pp. 4–9.

[347] M. Stonebraker. Managing Persistent Objects in a Multi-level Store. ACM SIGMOD International Conference on Management of Data, Denver, May 1991, pp. 2–11.

[348] M. Stonebraker, J. Frew, K. Gardels, and J. Meredith. The SEQUOIA 2000 Storage Benchmark. ACM SIGMOD International Conference on Management of Data, Washington, DC, May 1993, pp. 2–11.

[349] M. Stonebraker, R. Katz, D. Patterson, and J. Ousterhout. The Design of XPRS. International Conference on Very Large Data Bases, Los Angeles, August 1988, pp. 318–330.

[350] D. D. Straube, and M. T. Ozsu. Queries and Query Processing in Object-Oriented Database Systems. ACM Transactions on Information Systems, 8:4, 1990, pp. 387–430.

[351] D. D. Straube, and M. T. Ozsu. Query Optimization and Execution Plan Generation in Object-Oriented Database Systems. *IEEE Transactions on Knowledge and Data Engineering,* 7:2, April 1995, pp. 210–227.

[352] S. Su, M. Guo, and H. Lam. Association Algebra: A Mathematical Foundation for Object-Oriented Databases. *IEEE Transactions on Knowledge and Data Engineering,* 5:4, October 1993, pp. 775–798.

[353] W. Sun, Y. Ling, N. Rishe, and Y. Deng. An Instant and Accurate Size Estimation Method for Joins and Selection in a Retrieval-Intensive Environment. ACM SIG-MOD International Conference on Management of Data, Washington, DC, May 1993, pp. 79–88.

[354] W. Sun, W. Meng, and C. Yu. Query Optimization in Distributed Object-Oriented Database Systems. *The Computer Journal,* 35:2, April 1992, pp. 98–107.

[355] M. Swain, C. Frankel, and V. Athitsos. Webseer: An Image Search Engine for the World Wide Web. Technical Report, Department of Computer Science, U. of Chicago, July 1996.

[356] I. Syu, S. Lang, and K. Hua. A Heuristic Information Retrieval Model on a Massively Parallel Processor. International Conference on Data Engineering, Taipei, Taiwan, March 1995, pp. 365–372.

[357] M. Tamminen. Encoding Pixel Trees. *Journal of Computer Vision, Graphics, Image Processing: Image Understanding,* 28, 1984, pp. 44–57.

[358] Tandem Performance Group. A Benchmark of Non-stop SQL on the Debit Credit Transaction. ACM SIGMOD International Conference on Management of Data, Chicago, May 1988, pp. 337–341.

[359] A. Tarski. A Lattice Theoretical Fixpoint Theorem and Its Application. *Pacific Journal of Mathematics,* 1955, pp. 285–309.

[360] M. Templeton, D. Brill, S. Dao, E. Lunk, P. Ward, A. Chen, and R. MacGregor. Mermaid—A Front-End to Distributed Heterogeneous Databases. *Proceedings of IEEE,* 75:5, May 1987, pp. 695–708.

[361] F. Tomita, and S. Tssuji. *Computer Analysis of Visual Textures.* Norwell, MA: Kluwer Academic, 1990.

[362] Y. Tonomura, A. Akutsu, Y. Taniguchi, and G. Suzuki. Structured Video Computing. *IEEE Multimedia,* 1:3, 1994, pp. 34–43.

[363] M. Tsangaris, and J. Naughton. A Stochastic Approach for Clustering in Object Stores. ACM SIGMOD International Conference on Management of Data, Denver, May 1991, pp. 12–21.

[364] M. Tsangaris, and J. Naughton. On the Performance of Object Clustering Techniques. ACM SIGMOD International Conference on Management of Data, San Diego, CA, June 1992, pp. 144–153.

[365] S. G. Tucker. The IBM 3090 System: An Overview. *IBM System Journal,* 25:1, 1986, pp. 4–19.

[366] H. Turtle, and W. Croft. Evaluation of an Inference Network-Based Retrieval Model. *ACM Transactions on Information Systems,* 9:3, July 1991, pp. 187–222.

[367] J. Ullman. *Principles of Database Systems.* London: Pitman, 1982.

[368] J. Ullman. *Principles of Database and Knowledge-Base Systems,* vol. 1. New York: Computer Science Press, 1988.

[369] J. Ullman. *Principles of Database and Knowledge-Base Systems,* vol. 2. New York: Computer Science Press, 1989.

[370] P. Valduriez. Parallel Database Systems: Open Problems and New Issues. *Distributed and Parallel Databases,* 1:2, April 1993, pp. 137–165.

[371] P. Valduriez, and G. Gardarin. Join and Semi-join Algorithms for a Multiprocessor Database Machine. *ACM Transactions on Database Systems,* 9:1, March 1984, pp. 133–161.

[372] P. Valduriez, and S. Khoshafian. Parallel Evaluation of the Transitive Closure of a Database Relation. *International Journal of Parallel Programming,* 17:1, 1988, pp. 19–42.

[373] S. L. Vanderberg, and D. J. DeWitt. Algebraic Support for Complex Objects with Arrays, Identity, and Inheritance. ACM SIGMOD International Conference on Management of Data, Denver, May 1991, pp. 158–167.

[374] M. Van Emden, and R. Kowalski. The Semantics of Predicate Logic as a Programming Language. *Journal of the ACM,* 23:4, October 1976, pp. 733–742.

[375] A. Van Gelder, K. Ross, and S. Schlipf. The Well-Founded Semantics for General Logic Programs. *Journal of the ACM,* 38:3, July 1991, pp. 620–650.

[376] C. Van Rijsbergen. A Theoretical Basis for the Use of Co-occurrence Data in Information Retrieval. *Journal of Documentation,* 33:2, June 1977, pp. 106–119.

[377] C. Van Rijsbergen. A Non-classical Logic for Information Retrieval. *The Computer Journal,* 29:6, December 1986, pp. 481–485.

[378] P. Willett. Recent Trends in Hierarchical Document Clustering: A Critical Review. *Information Processing and Management,* 24:5, 1988, pp. 577–597.

[379] A. Wilschut, J. Flokstra, and P. Apers. Parallel Evaluation of Multi-join Queries. ACM SIGMOD International Conference on Management of Data, San Jose, CA, May 1995, pp. 115–126.

[380] E. Wong, and R. Katz. Distributing a Database for Parallelism. ACM SIGMOD International Conference on Management of Data, San Jose, CA, May 1983, pp. 23–29.

[381] E. Wong, and K. Youssefi. Decomposition—A Strategy for Query Processing. *ACM Transactions on Database Systems*, 1:3, September 1976, pp. 223–241.

[382] S. Wong, and Y. Yao. Query Formulation in Linear Retrieval Models. *Journal of the American Society for Information Science*, 1990, pp. 334–341.

[383] S. Wong, and Y. Yao. On Modeling of Probabilistic Inference. *ACM Transactions on Information Systems*, 13:1, January 1995, pp. 38–68.

[384] S. Wong, and W. Ziarko. A Machine Learning Approach to Information Retrieval. International ACM SIGIR Conference, Pisa, Italy, 1986, pp. 228–233.

[385] S. Wong, W. Ziarko, and P. Wong. Generalized Vector Space Model in Information Retrieval. International ACM SIGIR Conference, Montreal, 1985, pp. 18–25.

[386] H. Wu, and G. Salton. The Estimation of Term Relevance Weights Using Relevance Feedback. *Journal of Documentation*, 37:4, December 1981, pp. 194–214.

[387] Z. Xie, and J. Han. Join Index Hierarchies for Supporting Efficient Navigations in Object-Oriented Databases. International Conference on Very Large Data Bases, Santiago, Chile, September 1994, pp. 522–533.

[388] J. Xu, and W. Croft. Query Expansion Using Local and Global Document Analysis. International ACM SIGIR Conference, Zurich, Switzerland, August 1996, pp. 4–11.

[389] Q. Yang, C. Liu, J. Wu, C. Yu, S. Dao, H. Nakajima, and N. Rishe. Efficient Processing of Nested Fuzzy SQL Queries in Fuzzy Databases. International Conference on Data Engineering, Taipei, Taiwan, March 1995, pp. 131–138.

[390] Q. Yang, C. Yu, C. Liu, S. Dao, G. Wang, and T. Pham. A Hybrid Transitive Closure Algorithm for Sequential and Parallel Processing. International Conference on Data Engineering, Houston, February 1994, pp. 498–505.

[391] Y. Yang, and C. Chute. An Application to Least Squares Fit Mapping to Text Information Retrieval. International ACM SIGIR Conference, Pittsburgh, June 1993, pp. 281–290.

[392] Y. Yang, and C. Chute. An Example-Based Mapping Method for Text Categorization and Retrieval. *ACM Transactions on Information Systems*, 12:3, July 1994, pp. 252–277.

[393] S. Yao. Approximating Block Accesses in Database Organization. *Communications of the ACM*, 20:4, April 1977, pp. 260–261.

[394] S. Yao. Optimization of Query Evaluation Algorithms. *ACM Transactions on Database Systems*, 4:2, June 1979, pp. 133–155.

[395] C. Yu, C. Buckley, K. Lam, and G. Salton. A Generalized Term Dependence Model in Information Retrieval. *Information Technology,* 2:4, October 1983, pp. 129–154.

[396] C. Yu, and C. Chang. Distributed Query Processing. *ACM Computing Surveys,* 16:4, December 1984, pp. 399–433.

[397] C. Yu, C. Chang, M. Templeton, D. Brill, and E. Lund. Query Processing in a Fragmented Relational Distributed System: Mermaid. *IEEE Transactions on Software Engineering,* 11:8, August 1985, pp. 795–810.

[398] C. Yu, K. Guh, W. Zhang, M. Templeton, D. Brill, and A. Chen. Algorithms to Process Distributed Queries in Fast Local Networks. *IEEE Transactions on Computers,* 36:10, October 1987, pp. 1153–1164.

[399] C. Yu, and T. Lee. Non-binary Independence Model. International ACM SIGIR Conference, Pisa, Italy, 1986, pp. 1021–1028.

[400] C. Yu, W. Luk, and T. Cheung. A Statistical Model for Relevance Feedback in Information Retrieval. *Journal of the ACM,* 23:2, April 1976, pp. 273–286.

[401] C. Yu, W. Luk, and M. Siu. On the Estimation of the Number of Desired Records with Respect to a Given Query. *ACM Transactions on Database Systems,* 3:1, March 1978, pp. 41–56.

[402] C. Yu, W. Meng, and S. Park. A Framework for Effective Information Retrieval. *ACM Transactions on Database Systems,* 14:2, June 1989, pp. 147–167.

[403] C. Yu, and M. Ozsoyoglu. An Algorithm for Tree Query Membership of a Distributed Query. Annual International Computer Software and Applications Conference, Chicago, November 1979, pp. 409–445.

[404] C. Yu, M. Ozsoyoglu, and K. Lam. Optimization of Distributed Tree Queries. *Journal of Computer and System Sciences,* 29:3, December 1984, pp. 409–445.

[405] C. Yu, and G. Salton. Precision Weighting: An Effective Automatic Indexing Method. *Journal of the ACM,* 23:1, June 1976, pp. 76–89.

[406] C. Yu, C. Suen, K. Lam, and M. Siu. Adaptive Record Clustering. *ACM Transactions on Database Systems,* 10:2, June 1985, pp. 280–290.

[407] C. Yu, Y. Zhang, W. Meng, W. Kim, G. Wang, T. Pham, and S. Dao. Translation of Object-Oriented Queries to Relational Queries. Eleventh International Conference on Data Engineering, Taipei, Taiwan, March 1995, pp. 90–97.

[408] L. Zadeh. Fuzzy Sets. *Information and Control,* 8, 1965, pp. 338–353.

[409] C. Zaniolo. Safety and Compilation of Nonrecursive Horn Clauses. First International Conference on Expert Database Systems, Menlo Park, CA, 1986, pp. 167–178.

[410] H. Zeller, and J. Gray. An Adaptive Hash Join Algorithm for Multiuser Environments. International Conference on Very Large Data Bases, Brisbane, Australia, August 1990, pp. 186–197.

[411] M. Zemankova, and A. Kandel. Implementing Imprecision in Information Systems. *Information Science,* 37:1, 1985, pp. 107–141.

[412] H. Zhang, C. Low, S. Smoliar, and J. Wu. Video Parsing, Retrieval and Browsing: An Integrated and Content-Based Solution. ACM Multimedia Conference, San Francisco, November 1995.

[413] H. Zhang, J. Wu, C. Low, and S. Smoliar. A Video Parsing, Indexing and Retrieval System. ACM Multimedia Conference, San Francisco, November 1995.

[414] W. Zhang, C. Yu, B. Reagan, and H. Nakajima. Context Dependent Interpretation of Linguistic Terms in Fuzzy Relational Queries. International Conference on Data Engineering, Taipei, Taiwan, March 1995, pp. 139–146.

[415] W. Zhang, C. Yu, G. Wang, T. Pham, and H. Nakajima. A Relational Model for Imprecise Queries. International Symposium on Methodologies in Intelligent Systems, Trondheim, Norway, 1993.

[416] Q. Zhu, and P-A. Larson. A Query Sampling Method for Estimating Local Cost Parameters in a Multidatabase System. Tenth International Conference on Data Engineering, Houston, February 1994, pp. 144–153.

Index

Printed in the United States
49554LVS00003B/3-10